Classical Indian Metaphysics

Classical Indian Metaphysics

Refutations of Realism and the Emergence of "New Logic"

Stephen H. Phillips

Open Court
Chicago and La Salle, Illinois

OPEN COURT and the above logo are registered in the U. S. Patent and Trademark Office.

First printing 1995

Printed and bound in the United States of America.

Library of Congress Cataloging-in-Publication-Data

Phillips, Stephen H.
Classical Indian metaphysics : refutations of realism and the emergence of "new logic" / Stephen H. Phillips.
p. cm.
Includes bibliographical references and index.
ISBN 0-8126-9298-5 (pbk. : alk. paper)
1. Knowledge, Theory of (Hinduism). 2. Nyāya. 3. Śrīharṣa, 12th cent. 4. Navya Nyāya. I. Title.
B132.K6P48 1995
181′.4—dc20 95-37563
CIP

To Arabinda Basu and Robert Nozick

CONTENTS

ACKNOWLEDGMENTS

Of the many who have contributed to this publication, Sibajiban Bhattacharyya—primarily by his own books and papers but also through gracious criticisms of my work—most deserves acknowledgment. I have enormous admiration for Sibajiban, and my gratitude is heartfelt. Other heroes of mine (and of our field) have also contributed, especially Karl Potter, J. N. Mohanty, and Ashok Aklujkar. Their insightful comments have made this a better book. The book has been improved too by telephone conversations I had with Arindam Chakrabarti during a year-long sojourn of his in the States. A couple of difficult knots in Gaṅgeśa's text, and another in that of Śaṅkara Miśra, were untied by Arindam, and he has helped me think through the Logic system on almost every issue and topic. Others who helped informally are P. K. Mukhopadhyay, who directed me to Śaṅkara Miśra's *Bhedaratna*, and Kisor Chakrabarti, who at a meeting of the American Philosophical Association (Chicago, April 1993) commented on a paper I read on Gaṅgeśa's ontology.

In 1991, I spent six months in India on a grant from the American Institute of Indian Studies supplemented by an award from the University of Texas Research Institute. This funding was crucial. In India, I got help from numerous scholars. In particular, concerning Gaṅgeśa and New Logic, I worked with Dr. N. S. Ramanuja Tatacharya, Vice Chancellor, Kendriya Sanskrit Vidyapeetha, Tirupati, who edited most of Gaṅgeśa's philosophic masterpiece, the *Tattvacintāmaṇi*. In Tirupati, I made a tape recording of a reading and interpretation of sections from Gaṅgeśa by Dr. Tatacharya, who, in Sanskrit, patiently explained the text. Several passages in my translations here in chapter 5 might well have remained incomprehensible did I not have what is in effect a Sanskrit commentary by Dr. Tatacharya on tape. Dr. Tatacharya has received the Padmabhusana, the highest civilian award given by the Government of India. Sibajiban Bhattacharyya has called Dr. Tatacharya the greatest living Indian philosopher. I feel most privileged to have had his personal direction and help.

Sri Jagannatha Vedalankara, of the Sri Aurobindo International Centre for Education, Pondicherry, with whom I have studied Sanskrit off and on dating back to 1972, and to whom I owe my limited ability to converse in the language, helped especially with some difficult passages in Śrīharṣa, also in Śaṅkara Miśra, Udayana, and Vācaspati II.

Daniel Ingalls introduced the Logic system to me while I was a graduate student at Harvard. The depth of his scholarship has remained an inspiration to me ever since.

At the University of Texas at Austin, I have given four graduate philosophy seminars on the classical Indian realist-idealist debate, the first in 1983 on Buddhist idealism, then on Śrīharṣa and Logic in 1988, 1990, and 1993. Of the many students who have contributed to my understanding of one or another classical philosopher or school, Eric Loomis (especially), Bryan Hopkins, Mary Beth Mader, Alan Cates, Kent Appleberry, and William Burns wrote papers with original insights or made particularly helpful remarks. Roger Wasson read carefully a late draft and suggested edits, many of which have been incorporated. To these and other students of the past twelve years—undergraduates as well as graduates—I owe a debt.

Colleagues of mine at Texas—Herbert Hochberg (especially), Daniel Bonevac, Thomas Seung, Edwin Allaire, and Richard Lariviere—have advanced my understanding of issues involved here, or of classical views.

At Open Court, thanks go to Kerri Mommer, general editor, who expertly negotiated all stages of the publication process, and to Kathleen League, copy editor, who has made this a much better written book.

Part of the translation of Gaṅgeśa on dialectical reasoning appeared in *Understanding Non-Western Philosophy*, edited by Daniel Bonevac and Stephen Phillips (1993), pp. 188–89. An earlier draft of the translation of Gaṅgeśa on characterizing veridical awareness appeared in the *Journal of Indian Philosophy* 21, no. 2 (June 1993), pp. 107–68.

Finally, I wish to thank my wife Hope for twenty years of love and encouragement.

INTRODUCTION

The Realist-Idealist Debate: Śrīharṣa and the New Logicians

In different periods of philosophic reflection—and in distinct cultures and traditions of critical inquiry—idealists and realists have squared off on issues many of which are unresolved today. Both camps are diverse, and significant infighting has gone on: the long and varied history of philosophy does not present two neatly definable camps. But an idealist tends to presume that all we know and understand depends on mind or consciousness, whereas a realist would presume that facts or realities independent of mind and consciousness ground our understandings and knowledge. For example, concerning the relation "north of," a realist would hold that if a cosmic neutron bomb were to destroy all life and consciousness, the earth's equator would still be *north of* Antarctica. An idealist (of most stripes) would argue, in contrast, that "north of" has to be understood in the context of larger theories, or of the usefulness of the concept to conscious agents. We understand what it means to say that the equator is north of Antarctica, because, in effect, we have set up our maps that way (in order to mark correlations of experience). To the idealist, the realist seems to assume too much, to make proposals that are otiose or impossible, and that—according to some—prevent a sounding of depths (religious or otherwise). To the realist, the idealist seems to be merely skeptical in disposition, as well as to lack common sense.

Within ancient and classical Indian civilization, schools of realism and of idealism flourished and engaged one another for more than two millennia. Many of the motivations for realism or idealism that are found in this context are peculiar to the Indian scene. Some of the issues and positions are similarly unique. Other motivations, issues, and views that emerge reverberate with much Western philosophy.

This book focuses on the controversy between, on the one hand, a renowned twelfth-century dialectician named Śrīharṣa (pronounced shreeharsha[1])—who inherits long-standing traditions of idealist metaphysics from Buddhists and others who promote a mystical *summum bonum*—and, on the other, a school of realism in India known most commonly as Nyāya, "Logic." Almost the whole of classical Indian philosophy informs this debate, and I devote the first two chapters here to presenting about a thousand years of metaphysical speculation and argument, that which precedes Śrīharṣa. The school of New Logic, Navya Nyāya, which extends from approximately 1300 to the contemporary period, is treated in the last two chapters. Our focus in these chapters is the school's emergence along with the first two centuries of its realist response to the dialectical attacks of Śrīharṣa.

Śrīharṣa is motivated by religious considerations—and perhaps by personal experience as well—to uphold the reality of Brahman, the Absolute and Unity beyond all appearance of differentiation. Brahman is the sole reality and the single self. Only Brahman may authentically be said *to be*. Śrīharṣa, in keeping with the primacy of his religious or mystical concerns, bases his Brahman-centered philosophy on scriptures called Upanishads and Vedānta, which were composed over centuries beginning as early as 800 BCE. An interpretation of Upanishadic teachings known as Advaita Vedānta is embraced by Śrīharṣa. Advaita Vedānta is a monistic interpretation of the mystical experience believed taught by the Upanishads. It is foremost a religious philosophy in that it is founded in these texts, which its advocates take to be (non-theistically) revealed. However, in certain impossibilities that Śrīharṣa says are entailed by central Logic theses, he purports to find further supports for his Brahman-centered world view.

The Logic positions that Śrīharṣa attacks he sees as presupposing divisions in Brahman, divisions in the indivisible One. Thus by refuting them, by revealing the paradoxes to which they lead, he would strengthen the Advaita position: appearances of division are appearances only and not realities. Worldly appearances are not caused by "facts," nor do they stand in any discernible relation whatsoever to the truly real—except that, the Advaitin argues, when we try to systematize appearances on an assumption of fundamental distinctness, paradoxes ensue. The reality of Brahman entails the impossibility of coherently conceiving a diverse world.

Indian realists have their own motives and some distinct axes to grind. Though Nyāya is little known in the West, there are a thousand years of Nyāya literature before Śrīharṣa, with positions in metaphysics, epistemology, logic, and theory of meaning that become increasingly refined. After Śrīharṣa, New Logic emerges with further advances. But progress occurs incrementally, and not even with post-Śrīharṣa Logicians is there overthrowing of inherited positions wholesale. Innovations are usually a matter of a new distinction or a new analytic technique and not of a new position. Nyāya's realism is conservative.

Are then the difficulties raised by Śrīharṣa ignored? No, innovations prompted by the Advaitin can be discerned. Furthermore, over the centuries,

Naiyāyikas (''philosophers of the Nyāya school'') develop a comprehensive rebuttal. The scholarly question is just when and how much reaction to the Advaitin there is within the realist camp. That question is answered here. But the scope of this book is much broader.

It is tempting to read Śrīharṣa as a free-wheeling deconstructionist of the Indian classical age, with no agenda except to reveal a mess of presuppositions in Nyāya claims. But his attacks, as well as the responses provoked, are usually grounded in the long history of critical inquiry preserved in the common intellectual language of Sanskrit. In other words, both Śrīharṣa and the Logicians are enormously learned, well-read in centuries of earlier philosophic debate, and skilled in employing particular arguments and counterarguments. It must be stressed—for too much Western ethnocentrism has reigned, even of late—that a wide-ranging philosophic literature—concerning ontology, puzzles of metaphysics, means of knowledge (the nature of perception and of inference, in particular), veridical versus illusory awareness, grammar and linguistic philosophy, the ''supreme personal good'' (*parama-puruṣārtha*) and a good life—had emerged by the early centuries of the Common Era. Philosophy in India built on itself, with later reasoners profiting from the earlier. Philosophy continued in unbroken traditions until modern times (and continues to this day uninfluenced by the West among a few traditionally learned). The focus of this book is the realist-idealist debate as found in Śrīharṣa and later Nyāya. But we will provide an overview of much early classical thought before turning to the specific arguments and responses Śrīharṣa and the Naiyāyikas make. Understanding early strands of Indian metaphysics is crucial to appreciating the realist-idealist debate in its more sophisticated stage.

This book is written both for specialists in Advaita and Nyāya and for those unfamiliar with Indian thought. No knowledge of classical Indian philosophy has been presupposed: the first two chapters have been written in the spirit of a textbook for those not acquainted with the relevant history of ideas. Specialists and students who know the early classics of Indian speculation may want to begin with chapter 3—concerning Śrīharṣa—although all but the very learned should also read section 3 of chapter 2. There major positions of Old Nyāya are spelled out; they are the positions of the Nyāya—through Udayana (c. 1000)—that Śrīharṣa attacks.

Nyāya enjoys enormous proliferation in the late classical age (1200–1800+), and there is such refinement that, post-Śrīharṣa, the school assumes a new name: Navya Nyāya, ''New Logic.'' Scholars commonly suppose that the Advaitin plays a key role in the emergence of the New school. That Śrīharṣa sparks the development of New Nyāya is an oft-repeated thesis.[2] It has become almost common indological lore.[3] But, as this book shows, if there is a revolution in Logic sparked by the dialectical Advaitin, it is a revolution in precision and analytic tools, not in fundamental outlook. Gaṅgeśa

(c. 1325), the commonly credited founder of New Logic, defends inherited positions in all but a few instances; his followers are similarly conservative. There are, nevertheless, innovations in argument and argumentative apparatus whereby the pressure of the attacks of Śrīharṣa can indeed be discerned.

Yet even in this less sweeping sense of change, Śrīharṣa can hardly be counted as alone sparking the revisions that New Logic represents. Every position is recast, reclothed in the more precise terms of a cognitive or epistemic logic that is Navya Nyāya's outstanding achievement. Furthermore, there are hot internecine disputes, and challengers from non-Vedāntic schools are rebutted by Gaṅgeśa and other Naiyāyikas. To say that the debate with the Advaita idealist was solely responsible for the emergence of the new realist philosophy would be a crude exaggeration.

The importance of Śrīharṣa's criticism of Old Nyāya nevertheless remains. It can be seen in Gaṅgeśa's reflections, and within a few generations of the appearance of Navya methods a detailed response to Śrīharṣa is forged. Commentaries by Naiyāyikas are written on Śrīharṣa's text, and there are New Logicians who dispute the Advaitin's arguments point by point. The work of Śaṅkara Miśra (c. 1430) and Vācaspati Miśra II (c. 1450) at once make clear the influence of Śrīharṣa and carry the realist-idealist debate to a higher stage.

Gaṅgeśa, however, mentions Śrīharṣa only once in his entire masterwork, the *Tattvacintāmaṇi* (*Jewel of Reflection on the Real*). Thus the extent of *his* debt to the Advaitin requires some digging and reconstruction. Now, although Gaṅgeśa has left us only the monumental *Tattvacintāmaṇi* (only!), his son Vardhamāna (c. 1350) was prolific, with several commentaries on earlier Nyāya works written incorporating his father's innovations. Vardhamāna was the great popularizer of New Logic. And Vardhamāna wrote a commentary on Śrīharṣa's masterpiece, the *Khaṇḍanakhaṇḍakhādya* (*Sweetmeats of Refutation*)—an unusual phenomenon in that commentaries were normally composed by advocates, not adversaries. Several other Naiyāyika commentaries on the Advaitin's work followed in the next few centuries. One has to suspect that Vardhamāna was encouraged to take up Śrīharṣa's text by his father. I show here that despite the single mention, Gaṅgeśa often had Śrīharṣa in mind. The extent of his dependence is decidedly less, however, than has been suggested by some. Let me repeat: the context of the emergence of Navya Nyāya was philosophically rich; there was much more on Gaṅgeśa's agenda than Śrīharṣa's objections. To show the extent of the Advaitin's influence is also to show the limits of that influence.

Because an appreciation of the earlier stages of the debate helps one understand Śrīharṣa vis-à-vis Gaṅgeśa et al., my exposition of Śrīharṣa's relation to what is really early Navya Nyāya should, I hope, help future research on the latest period of classical Indian philosophy. As mentioned, the work of the Navya Nyāya thinkers Śaṅkara Miśra (c. 1430) and Vācaspati Miśra II

(c. 1450) are utilized here. But there are several even later players on both sides who advance the debate and make further innovations in response to the rival side's arguments. Madhusūdhana Sarasvatī (c. 1570), Bālabhadra (c. 1610), Gauḍa Brahmānanda (c. 1680), and others are Advaitins who learn the terminology of Navya Nyāya, but they maintain that the master dialectician's objections have not been met, and they find new realist difficulties. In the other camp, there are equally late advocates and defenders of Nyāya (as well as of a Vedāntic theism that borrows from Nyāya). Some of this later development will be sketched here, especially as it concerns realist reactions and counterarguments. But most will have to be left for future research.

While little in chapters 1 or 2 advances basic scholarship of classical Indian philosophies—the intent instead is to encapsulate the literature to set the stage for the investigation to follow—in chapter 3 an original reading of the great Advaitin Śrīharṣa is presented. The extent to which Śrīharṣa has a positive program of philosophy has not been appreciated—indeed has been misunderstood by several experts—and the corresponding intent and scope of his attempted refutations has been missed. My reading of Śrīharṣa would not have been possible without the pioneering work of, first, Sir Ganganatha Jha (1871–1941), scholar, Principal of the Government Sanskrit College, Benares (Varanasi), and prolific translator of philosophic texts, including the entirety of Śrīharṣa's only extant philosophic work; and, second, Professor Phyllis Granoff, who published a detailed study and a new, much more readable translation of approximately the first sixth of Śrīharṣa's text (1978). But both Jha and Granoff misunderstand key facets of Śrīharṣa's argumentation, and others seem to have been led by them to misrepresentation of the Advaitin's stance.[4] Such misrepresentation is especially unfortunate since Śrīharṣa is central to almost all later classical Advaita Vedānta, and to much modern thought. Advaita remains a prominent philosophy in modern India: its proponents include several well-known professional academics, as well as famous yogins and spiritual figures such as Ramakrishna and Vivekananda. But reading Śrīharṣa correctly is also important because of his role in the overall development of Indian metaphysics.

Let me hasten to add that despite my quarrels with earlier interpreters, chapter 3 is not devoted to academic squabbling. The point is to establish Śrīharṣa as not only a skeptic and a gadfly to Logicians, but as a mystically monist Advaitin who summons us (and not just Logicians) to plumb the depths of the self.

Chapter 4 lays forth positions of New Nyāya especially as they relate to the refutations advanced by the Vedāntin idealist. There I present the analytic apparatus of the New school, and reconstruct the realist response. The chapter is not intended to be much of a scholarly advance; most of what I say about

Navya Nyāya claims and techniques has appeared before. On the other hand, scholarship of the system is still in a beginning stage. Even Gaṅgeśa's *Tattvacintāmaṇi* has been translated only in part (the translations here in chapter 5 from Gaṅgeśa contribute significantly to the task). The enormous achievement of classical Indian New Logic is even now barely appreciated in the global community of modern philosophy. Probably the chief virtue of this book is its introduction of Navya Nyāya, an introduction that stresses the context of the realist-idealist debate in which it emerges. (On the other hand, *the* chief virtue of this book may be my effort to keep the needs of the indological novice, the lover of philosophy unfamiliar with Indian metaphysics, always in sight.)

Chapter 5 is comprised of nine sections of annotated translation. These translations make much previously unavailable material available to the English-reading, non-sanskritist world. I have tried to choose passages that reveal the heart of the realist-idealist controversy that exercised some of the greatest of the classical minds.

A final note. Sanskrit terms have been avoided wherever possible. The single greatest block to a wider appreciation of the philosophies of India seems to be inordinate use of Sanskrit terminology by scholars writing for a general audience. Whenever it has seemed that a Sanskrit word is called for, I have provided English equivalents—in parentheses or in expressions set off by quotation marks. But there are some cases, such as "Vedānta," that either defy easy translation or are sufficiently anglicized that I have not given an English equivalent. Nevertheless, all Sanskrit names and terms used here, even the most anglicized, are defined in an appended glossary (see Appendix B, divided into two parts by proper names and terms); please consult this whenever a Sanskrit borrowing is unclear.

CHAPTER ONE

Early Indian Idealism and Mysticism

1. Early Mysticism

All Indian idealism, even that of the latest classical philosophers, is tied to a tradition or traditions of mysticism as old as three thousand years. Distinct traditions maintain in common that to understand mystical experiences, one must have a view of things' dependence on awareness. After some remarks about the language Sanskrit, we will review early Indian mysticism with an eye to the philosophic idealism that it engenders.

First we must know something about Sanskrit, an Indo-European language that is highly inflected, like Greek and Latin. Sanskrit is the language of almost all classical Indian literature (which consists of thousands upon thousands of texts), and of pre-classical texts as well (which are found in somewhat less abundance);[1] composition in Sanskrit extends for more than three thousand years. The language of most of classical India's major and minor epics, (long) religious didactic verse, jurisprudence, court poetry, crafts, and the sciences (including philosophy, *darśana* and *tarka-śāstra*), among other genre, is Sanskrit. Though it ceased to be anyone's mother tongue probably before 200 CE, it was by that date, and perhaps earlier, being learned by priests and intellectuals all over the Indian subcontinent. Sanskrit continued to be the dominant intellectual language until the rule of the Moghuls, when it was partially supplanted by Persian. Sanskrit lost currency only in the contemporary age, when it was supplanted by English and modern regional languages. A comprehensive Sanskrit grammar that standardized usage was written at an early date (c. 450 BCE). This established the earliest grammarian tradition in the world, earlier than the Graeco-Roman. Vocabulary continued to develop, but structurally the language ceased to change.

1.1. The Upanishads

Sanskrit-speaking tribes began invading the Indian subcontinent from the northwest as early as 1500 BCE; Sanskrit verses known as the Veda—"Revealed Knowledge"—composed over centuries, came to be regarded by them as sacred. The four Vedas are the oldest documents in Sanskrit (theirs is an archaic, pre-classical Sanskrit).

Vedic poems and hymns express various themes, some of which are philosophic and important to the speculation of later periods. But the Upanishads, the "secret doctrines" of the ancient culture, are what decisively launched Indian philosophy—especially Indian idealism. Early Upanishads (from 800 to 300 BCE) represent a break with previous literature in the freeing of an abstract intellect from myth and ritual. Prose appears, and the poetry is usually discursive, didactic, and less imagistic than that of the Veda. Though argument and elaborations of positions are not nearly as pronounced and professionalized as in later periods, even the earliest Upanishads employ self-conscious argumentation. They contain several reports of debates on metaphysical topics held in the courts of kings. In particular, with the depictions of the sage Yājñavalkya and King Janaka in the *Bṛhadāraṇyaka*, important idealist arguments about an Absolute—called Brahman—find articulation at an early date (c. 800 BCE).

However, early Upanishads are above all mystical texts: they report mystical experiences. They are also commonly regarded—in later times—as revelation. Views about their nature as revelation vary, but their champions, known as Vedāntins (Śrīharṣa is a Vedāntin), concur that a mystical awareness of Brahman, *brahma-vidyā*, is the core teaching concerning human destiny and a "supreme personal good," *parama-puruṣārtha*. The monistic idealism at the bottom of Śrīharṣa's perspective grows out of this notion, as will become clear.

While we will focus on Upanishadic themes most evident in the philosophy of Śrīharṣa, it should be kept in mind that early Upanishads present variations on central views; there are elaborations in one direction or another, as well as contradictory claims. Some passages are indeed idealist, but some are not; some are theistic, some not; some ritualist, some anti-ritualist, et cetera. There is at best a unity of tone, which is decidedly sonorous and authoritative (a voice of thunder). Despite what later exegetes claim, no unity of theory obtains in the twelve or thirteen most commonly recognized early Upanishadic texts. Classical Vedāntins look for an overall unity because they view the texts as revealed truth. Nevertheless, there are recurrent themes: most importantly, each early Upanishad attempts to specify a mystical reality of consciousness or "self" (*ātman*), and these efforts are key to the views of Śrīharṣa, who, I repeat, like all classical Vedāntins, takes his basic positions to derive from Upanishadic authority.

There are nine Upanishadic themes that are important for an appreciation of Śrīharṣa's Vedānta. All concern Brahman, the Absolute, the Real.

1. Brahman is self (*ātman*) and consciousness.[2]
2. Brahman is world ground.[3]
3. Brahman is transcendent of "names and forms" (*nāma-rūpa*), i.e., is transcendent of finite individuality.[4]
4. Brahman is unitary, the coincidence of opposites, and omnipresent.[5]
5. Brahman has "non-dual" (*advaita*) self-awareness.[6]
6. Brahman is the essence or finest part of everything.[7]
7. Brahman is the locus of value, and awareness of Brahman is the "supreme personal good" (*parama-puruṣārtha*) and "liberation" (*mukti*) from fear and evil.[8]
8. Brahman is mystically discoverable.[9]
9. Brahman is beyond the power of thought uninformed by mystical awareness.[10]

These themes are present in Śrīharṣa, who inherits them through a more than millennium-long commentarial and philosophic tradition, Vedānta.

The great intra-camp debate among classical Vedāntins concerns the question of the theism of the early Upanishads, or, more broadly, how the Absolute relates to the world. The theistic interpretation—of Brahman as God creating a world of real particulars—had, by Śrīharṣa's time, become eschewed by his Advaita (Non-Dualist) school. Theistic Vedāntins cite Upanishadic passages stating that Brahman is determinant of individual names and forms, *nāma-rūpa*. In their view, Brahman is a primordial Will and Controller—"God," *īśvara*.[11] Advaitins apparently saw the theistic statements as incompatible with their theory of Brahman's transcendence and unitary consciousness, and they developed exegetical strategies to reinterpret the troublesome texts.

Now a brief digression concerning the theism of Śrīharṣa's realist opponents. Except in the earliest realist texts,[12] philosophers of the sister schools of Logic (Nyāya) and Atomism (Vaiśeṣika) uphold a view of God that, even though it finds God's creative activity limited, circumscribed by a variety of factors, has much in common with theistic Vedānta. Over time—particularly in the New Logic period—these theisms come closer together, generally speaking. However, not only does the Logicians' "God" seem diminished from the Vedāntic perspective, Logicians favor rational considerations in support of their theism, not proclamations of the Upanishads: Naiyāyikas are the great rational theologians in the Indian context. They are not usually considered Vedāntins, then, because it is not the Upanishads, i.e., not scripture, but certain arguments that they take to ground their theistic views. On the other hand, Śaṅkara Miśra (c. 1430), a New Logician who writes a book answering Śrīharṣa (portions of which are translated in chapter 5), considers himself an Upanishadic theist, citing even controversial Upanishadic texts in support of his non-Advaitic views.[13]

This book is not the place to air exegetical disputes. For our purposes, it is sufficient to review a few Upanishadic passages that support the Advaita reading. This is a reading emphasizing the nine themes presented above, in particular themes 4 and 5, of the unity and self-awareness of Brahman. These Upanishadic ideas are developed into Advaita monism. Brahman's unity comes to be taken to mean that appearances of individualities ("names and forms") are illusory, unreal.

An incipient Advaita monism is indeed evident in what is probably the earliest Upanishad, the *Bṛhadāraṇyaka*:

> They do not see him, for [then he would be] not whole. Breath is just this one breathing; sight [this one] seeing; hearing [his] hearing; thinking [his] thinking. All these things here are just names of his acts. Thus one who worships [or meditates on—*upāste*] one or the other of these knows not, for as he is not whole he comes to be one or the other of these. With only the idea "*ātman*," "self," should one meditate, for here [in the self] all these things become one.[14]

The prominence of the monistic idea here—a "spiritual" monism in accordance with the idea (theme 1) that Brahman is self or consciousness—provides ground for interpreting individuality (the Upanishadic expression for individuality is *nāma-rūpa*, "names and forms") as *mere* names and forms, as the Advaita school would do. The logic of the reasoning is not complex: if there is just one thing, then how can there also be many?[15]

There is no Upanishadic passage where such illusionism (*māyā-vāda*) is more pronounced than in a portion of the Yājñavalkya-Janaka discourse that constitutes the third and fourth *brāhmaṇa*s of the fourth chapter of the *Bṛhadāraṇyaka Upaniṣad*. At the core of this extremely important passage is an elaborate discussion of dream.[16] The text includes several monistic proclamations boldly applied to world appearance, for example, "*na iha nānā asti kiṃcana*," "There is here no diversity whatsoever."[17] Here also is the proclamation probably most often quoted by Advaitins, "*neti neti*" ("[Brahman is] not thus, not thus").[18] This statement underscores themes 3 and 9, the transcendence and inconceivability of Brahman. The Yājñavalkya-Janaka passage also contains summary statements of core psychological doctrines. Finally, crucial to the alternative, theistic interpretation of the Upanishads is an emanationist/creationist view: God manifests, or spins out, finite material forms out of God's own self, like a spider its web. But in this passage the Advaitins find a tool for subordinating the emanationist story to their idea of the One.

Yājñavalkya, in the Upanishad, is described as *brahmavid*, a "Brahman-knower." Speaking to King Janaka in a public contest of wisdom (where he vanquishes all comers), Yājñavalkya puts forth the Brahman conception with reference to states of the self: "[Sleeping,] one takes along the stuff of this all-embracing universe [and] tears it apart himself [and] shapes it himself . . . He is the all-maker, for he is the maker of everything."[19] "He" is the self, *ātman*, who enjoys various states of himself, characterized specifically as waking, dreaming, and a state transcending both, where the self is "aware only of its own light" (*svayaṃ jyotiḥ*).

> "An ocean, a single seer without duality becomes he whose world is *brahman*, O King," Yājñavalkya instructed. "This is his supreme way. This is his supreme achievement. This is his supreme world. This is his supreme bliss. Other beings live on just a small portion of this bliss."[20]

Thus a state of self-illumination is exalted over the waking and dream states. The dream state is where theistic emanationism and creationism have their validity. The waking state is like that of dream. Crucially, these two states involving awareness of objects other than the self are said to be less valuable than the state of self-illumination. Thus a subordination of the theist emanationist/creationist cosmology to a view of diversity as illusion seems to be called for, too: this is the Advaita reading. The idea that Brahman is one is given special psychological and axiological meaning: the state where the self knows only itself is the state that is most valuable.

Classical Advaitins draw an analogy to perceptual illusion to explain Brahman's relation to the world. But that analogy is not found in the early Upanishads; rather, a dream analogy is presented.[21] For classical Advaita, the point of the dream analogy is, first, idealism—the reality of the dream is dependent on the dreamer—and, second, illusionism—the dream misrepresents reality.

1.2. Yoga

All Indian mysticism—from the very early to the very late—incorporates practices of yoga, specifically, meditation and ascetic practices of self-discipline. Śrīharṣa makes key references to yoga and yoga textbooks.[22] Yoga is tied to the mysticism of the Upanishads; several passages say that yoga is the means to a mystical awareness of Brahman.[23] The relation between Vedāntic philosophy, on the one hand, and yogic practices and psychology, on the other, is complex, the subject of several classics of scholarship and current research.[24] Our treatment is limited to a broad overview.

The task at hand is complicated by an ambiguity: the term *yoga* is regularly used in philosophic contexts both (a) as a generic term for physical and meditational practices considered conducive to mystical awareness, and (b) as the name of a philosophic system, Yoga. For Advaita idealism, the former usage, concerning the practices, is more important. But we need to know something about the Yoga system, too.

Cults of yogic practice may have flourished in India among indigenous non-Sanskrit-speaking populations before the coming of Indo-Europeans and the composition of the Veda and the Upanishads, as some archeological discoveries suggest.[25] The evidence is inconclusive, however, and scholars are divided on the point. Nevertheless, early in the first millennium BCE, at the time when the oldest Upanishads were being composed, yogic practice must have found a place within the Sanskrit culture, for there are, as indicated, explicit mentions of it. In the Upanishads, the value of the meditational techniques and psycho-physical self-discipline is not said to lie in health or penance, as some have represented, but in mysticism: the practices are thought to lead to special experiences—mystical experiences—taken to reveal the reality of things or of self. Apparently for this reason, the experiences are considered supremely valuable, the goal of life. (They are also characterized as blissful.)

Now, Advaitins in general hold, as does Śrīharṣa, that what is most valuable is in fact a certain mystical experience. This is thought of popularly as *mukti*, "liberation," a liberation of consciousness from all world determination, and, in the technical terms preferred by Advaitin professionals, as *brahma-vidyā*, "mystical knowledge of Brahman." According to some Advaitins, the supreme experience is to be gained by study of the Upanishads: if one may speak of *means* to the supreme good, the Upanishads are those means. It is, however, the *reality* of Brahman that accounts for the possibility of liberation, it is said. Thus, ontologically Brahman underpins the mystical *summum bonum*, while epistemologically we learn of Brahman from the Upanishads. But an intellectual understanding is not the mystical *brahma-vidyā*, and most Advaitins are clear on the point. Thus there is room for yoga; in fact, there is advocacy. Advaitins typically hold that one becomes "fit" (*adhikārin*) for the experience through yogic practices. We may say, then, that yogic practices are considered indirectly instrumental; the understanding of the reality of Brahman conveyed by the Upanishads is what is most directly instrumental to the supreme experience, according to the Advaita view inherited by Śrīharṣa. But both reading the Upanishads and yogic practices are enjoined by Advaitins for those seeking the supreme good.

Others—theistic Vedāntins, Buddhists, Jainas—view yogic practices and mystical experience differently. The classical school of Yoga itself stands in sharp disagreement with Advaita. World diversity is not in the supreme experience revealed to be *māyā*, "illusion." The everyday world is real.

Furthermore, Yoga disputes the monism of Advaita. The self discovered in the supreme experience is not a single self of all persons, a universal *ātman*. According to the Yoga school, there are many selves, each an individual, each discovering only himself (or itself: the conscious being, *puruṣa*, is not sexed). However, the Yoga school does hold in common with Advaita that a supremely valuable experience reveals a person's true consciousness to be aloof from nature, transcendent (*kūṭastha*) to world appearance, and "liberated" from the course of birth and rebirth.

In summary, we may say, then, that though yogic practices are incorporated within philosophies that compete, there are several ideas about them held in common across schools.

The Logicians, too, subscribe to the efficacy of yogic practices. However, these realists may be thought of as pundits not much concerned with mystical experience. When Logicians take up the topic of mystical experience, they tend to look upon it within a theistic frame. Or they talk in a fashion that jibes with their realism about external objects: yogins have special abilities of perception regarding worldly facts. The power to maintain a mystic trance, *yoga-samādhi*, is commonly held, in agreement with Vedānta and Yoga, to be the "supreme good,"[26] but, especially with many later Naiyāyikas, this appears to be lip-service endorsement of an item of popular faith.

1.3. The Buddha

Another teaching of a mystical supreme good that has enormous importance not only for Śrīharṣa but for the entire history of Indian philosophy belongs to the Buddha (c. 500 BCE). The Buddha taught the supreme goal of life to be *nirvāṇa*, an "extinction" or "blowing out" of suffering and desire, and an awakening to what is most real. In Sanskrit, the word *buddha* literally means "awakened."

The Buddha, Siddhārtha Gautama, was a historical person. But he himself did not write anything, and we are left to reconstruct his teachings from disciples' writings. Over the centuries, disputes about the original views become pronounced. Nevertheless, that a mystical enlightenment or awakening is possible, and is the one possibility in life that should be sought, is a thesis on which all Buddhists agree. Other core doctrines include "no soul" (*anātman*)—in which false identification with the body and the mind is considered an impediment to enlightenment—and "interdependent origination" (*pratītya-samutpāda*), a causal doctrine, variously interpreted, that apparently would underpin teachings about the way to enlightenment. The way to enlightenment is the greatest pre-occupation of the literature that seems the most directly influenced by the Buddha, much of which is ethical in tone and concerned with requirements of the mystic path.

Early in the history of Buddhism, there was a split concerning how the goal of Buddhist practice should precisely be conceived. According to the schools that came to be associated with a Southern Canon (recognized in Sri Lanka, Burma, Thailand, etc.), the "saint," *arhat*, loses all individual personality in a universal, impersonal, unconceptualizable bliss and awareness that somehow underlie all appearance. According to Mahāyāna Buddhism, in contrast—that is, Northern Buddhism (Nepal, Tibet, China, Korea, Japan, etc.)—the truest aim is to become a Bodhisattva, who, unlike the Arhat, turns back from the final Bliss and extinction of personality in *nirvāṇa* to help every conscious being attain it. From the perspective of a Mahāyānist, the Southern Canon presents, by and large, a course of spiritual discipline and a goal that are not the best and highest since they are personally oriented. If one strives for one's own personal salvation alone, if one has no career (*yāna*) of helping others to the supreme good, one would belong to the Hīnayāna, and would be "one with no career," a term used by Mahāyānists in deprecation of such a path. Mahāyānists, "those with wide and great careers," in contrast, seek not only their own personal salvation but "deliverance of every sentient being from suffering and ignorance." A follower of this, the wide path, attempts to acquire six moral, intellectual, and spiritual perfections (*pāramitā*) considered to have been possessed by the Buddha. He or she endeavors to become a Bodhisattva, a person who has one foot in the bliss of *nirvāṇa*, so to say, but who is naturally turned through compassion toward the welfare of all beings.

Beyond the division of Bodhisattva vs. Arhat, the issue of just how the supreme state of enlightenment is to be conceived in itself—as well as with regard to life and a psychology of the everyday—is an issue to which tomes were addressed in the long history of Buddhist philosophy in India. Such Buddhist issues have some influence on Śrīharṣa, but many points of internecine Buddhist debate are remote to the concerns of the Advaitin. Śrīharṣa stands at a greater remove from Buddhist philosophy in doctrine than in method of argument, however, albeit no hard and fast distinction between the doctrinal and argumentational sides of his thought is defensible, nor, in the case of some Buddhist philosophers, is there so very great a difference in the content of his and their views. In any case, among Buddhists, it is an anti-intellectual and skeptic, Nāgārjuna, and an idealist, systematic Buddhist philosophy, Yogācāra, that hold by far the most interest for later classical metaphysics. In this context, several Buddhist arguments against realist conceptions presage Śrīharṣa's refutations of Nyāya. We turn now to Nāgārjuna and the great seventh-century Yogācāra idealist, Dharmakīrti—key precursors of Advaita dialectical idealism.

2. Nāgārjuna: Conundra of Thought

The Buddhist Nāgārjuna (c. 150 CE) is to be credited with having been the first to identify several of the basic problems that Śrīharṣa throws in the face of the Logician realists. Nāgārjuna and Śrīharṣa also seem similar in their soteriological purpose in proferring refutations. Although Śrīharṣa does not mention Nāgārjuna by name, he does mention the Mādhyamika school that Nāgārjuna founded (the school of the "Middle" or "in balance"),[27] and the Advaitin often echoes the great Buddhist anti-intellectual. This same Nāgārjuna also seems to have provoked a professionalization within all Indian schools: there is after him a sharp upturn in sophistication of argument. If Śrīharṣa may be said to have sparked a second revolution resulting in the fine-honed tools of the Navyas, then the history of thought broadly repeats itself in the Indian subcontinent: Nāgārjuna forces a rethinking and tighter argumentation within distinct Indian schools. We will review his thought fairly thoroughly.

The records we have of early Buddhist writings indicate that there were, prior to Nāgārjuna, disputes about how to understand the aggregate of "elements" or "qualities" (*dharma*) taught by the Buddha to make up an apparent person. This aggregate has to be transcended to achieve the supreme good. As mentioned, a doctrine of "no real self" (*anātman*) is very early, and some Buddhist thinkers believed that the components of the false appearance of self could be identified and analyzed. Thus they attempted to provide comprehensive lists of the components, i.e., "qualities" (*dharma*) and their groupings (*skanda*), sometimes with considerable sophistication.[28]

But there are also scriptural passages suggesting that the Buddha himself had considered similar intellectual activity counterproductive. In famous fables he asks, "When your house is on fire, is it wise to discourse on the nature of fire? No, it is wise to put the fire out. When shot with an arrow, would you discourse on the nature of arrows, or pull the arrow out?"[29] The implication is that we are ablaze with suffering, and we need not discourse on its nature but rather should do something, principally meditate and act with compassion, in order to put the suffering out.

Nāgārjuna was a reformer. He found the intellectualizing tendencies of those purveying lists of qualities to stray from the practical end that he saw as the true message of the Buddha. Nāgārjuna identified paradoxes, contradictions, and impossibilities in the positions of the quarreling Buddhist schools, apparently out of a sense that the practical end is something to which thought and mind have no direct access.

Nāgārjuna was also a Mahāyāna Buddhist, as opposed to a Hīnayānist. As noted, Mahāyānists eschew personal salvation and embrace the ideal of an enlightenment for all: one aims to become a Bodhisattva. A Bodhisattva is thought to embody six "perfections," *pāramitā*. It seems that Nāgārjuna saw the ability to knock down others' views as a manifestation of *prajñā*, "wisdom," the sixth and most important of the perfections that are the mark of a Bodhisattva.

In this way, Nāgārjuna's identification of impossibilities may be seen as part of a soteriological strategy: by discerning absurdities that arise in viewing anything as having an independent existence, one realizes that everything is *niḥsvabhāva*, "without a reality of its own." Applying this to oneself, one comes to see the truth of the Buddha's teaching of *anātman*, "no-self," which is viewed as a decisive step toward the *summum bonum* of enlightenment and perfection (*prajñā-pāramitā*: see the glossary).

The doctrine of "no-self" (*anātman*) is a central theme of the Buddha's Sermons,[30] and the view that everything is "without a reality of its own" (*niḥsvabhāva*) is apparently Nāgārjuna's interpretation of the "wheel of dependent origination" (*bhāva-cakra*) that also figures prominently in the earliest stratum of Buddhist literature.[31] These doctrines emerge as important for the Mahāyāna understanding of the supreme good. Perhaps we should look upon them with Nāgārjuna as meta-theses, as experientially heuristic, or as impossible to appreciate except non-intellectually, experientially, and mystically.[32] It is difficult to say how Nāgārjuna himself saw logical problems of his position (especially, problems of self-reference: are his own views to be included in the rejection of *all* philosophic positions?). The most important point, then, for an overall understanding of Nāgārjuna is, apparently, the mystical motivation.

However, Nāgārjuna's fame as a philosopher rests with the difficult questions he raised—and not only for Buddhist theorists but for others as well, especially Logicians. Nāgārjuna presents, in particular, three lines of argument whose importance looms large in later debates. Two are directed by him against positions that are Naiyāyika. The third is to be induced from Nāgārjuna's texts. The three are as follows:

a. a justification regress,

b. a problem of the meaning of terms that refer to non-existents,

c. conundra concerning relations, predication, and the fundamental ontological tie.

We will look at each of these. But first a short word about the historical connection between Nāgārjuna and Logic.

The final redaction of the *Nyāya-sūtra* (c. 400) shows an awareness of the Buddhist dialectician. (The *Nyāya-sūtra* is the oldest Logic text and the school's root text until Gaṅgeśa and the New school: see the glossary under "Nyāya.") The *Nyāya-sūtra* contains in fact quite an extended response to much that Nāgārjuna alleges. Thus one might conclude that there was no *Nyāya-sūtra* prior to Nāgārjuna. On the other hand, there must have been an early form of Nyāya extant before Nāgārjuna, because although Nāgārjuna does not mention Nyāya by name, he uses several Nyāya technical terms and discusses tenets central to the *Nyāya-sūtra* and its early commentaries.[33] Moreover, Nyāya's sister school, Vaiśeṣika (Atomism), clearly predates the Buddhist philosopher. Nāgārjuna explicitly refers to Vaiśeṣika (specifically, by way of its legendary founder, Kaṇāda, known as "the owl," *ulūka*) as one of several non-Buddhist schools. A younger contemporary disciple explicitly refutes Vaiśeṣika notions.[34]

Nāgārjuna's onslaught (*prasaṅga*) on the Logician notion of a "justifier" or "source of knowledge" (*pramāṇa*) launches one of the greatest of all controversies in classical Indian philosophy, that of epistemology, or, we might say, meta-epistemology. This line of critique is present in the responses of the *Nyāya-sūtra* itself.

Nāgārjuna's attack is, textually, less of a frontal assault than a counterattack: it occurs in his *Vigrahavyāvartanī* (*Vv*: *Averting Strife* or *Averting Opponents' Arguments*) in the context of a defense of his own contention that everything is *niḥsvabhāva*, "devoid of independent reality." An objector asks what is his *pramāṇa*, "reason" or "source of knowledge," for this position. Nāgārjuna's defense—that is, counterattack—is to say, in effect, "If I subscribed to your view that any position has to be 'justified'—i.e., has to arise out of a reliable source—then you might well fault me in this way. But I don't. I have no 'thesis' (in your *pramāṇa*-grounded sense)."

I have paraphrased Nāgārjuna's statement in *Vv*, verse 29. Let me translate more literally the dramatic turning of the tables that follows:

> And if you hold that establishment of these and those objects must be through *pramāṇa*, tell me just how those your *pramāṇa* are established. If you say the *pramāṇa* are proved through other *pramāṇa*, then you must have an unending stream of them.[35]

Thus Nāgārjuna identifies the meta-epistemological problem of an infinite regress concerning justification: What is your *pramāṇa* for your *pramāṇa*? If my sense experience justifies my belief that I am now typing on a computer keyboard, what justifies my taking my sense experience to play this role? Any answer would seem to invite a further question, *ad infinitum*.

Nāgārjuna goes on to anticipate two lines of possible response: (1) that a justifier (*pramāṇa*) justifies itself as well as objects it reveals or the claims it substantiates, and (2) that what the justifiers justify, namely the "justified" (*prameya*), can be viewed in turn as justifying the justifiers. (This seems to presage the modern epistemological position that claims and principles are ideally brought into a "reflective equilibrium."[36]) However, the great dialectician finds further problems with each of these.

Nāgārjuna, in his *Vv*, also impugns reference, the linchpin of the Naiyāyika theory of meaning. What about, he asks, the meaning of terms that fail to refer? (This is currently called the problem of negative existentials, or Plato's beard.[37])

Again, Nāgārjuna's attack (*prasaṅga*) is framed in the textual context as a counterattack, a response to a realist objection to his claim that all things are without an independent reality (*niḥsvabhāva*). The realist objects that Nāgārjuna's view of "no independent reality" must match a reality of its own, otherwise the claim would be meaningless. Nāgārjuna counters by denying the key presupposition, that meaningful terms must refer. He asks, "To what does 'the non-existent' refer?" The realists owe us an answer. Then, further, he wonders how his realist and referentialist opponent might analyze the statement "Devadatta is not at home."[38] As we will see, the set of problems involved here taxes the best Naiyāyika minds, long past Śrīharṣa well into Navya Nyāya.

Finally, in the *Mūlamadhyamakakārikā* (*MMK*)—Nāgārjuna's *chef d'oeuvre* and the touchstone whereby the authenticity of other works is determined[39]—various paradoxes of relation are presented.[40] These problems are not spelled out using terms like "predication" or "fundamental tie" (between "substance" and "attribute"). The Sanskrit technical terms used by later logicians to frame the problems, Buddhist and Naiyāyika, are not Nāgārjuna's. He uses locutions of everyday speech. For this reason, modern interpreters have had difficulty determining just what issues are being raised.[41] But an attack on relations is evident in Nāgārjuna's use of the nominative and genitive cases in Sanskrit to express what the Naiyāyika realists take to be the relation of property (e.g., blue) and property-bearer (e.g., something blue). Still, it bears repeating, Nāgārjuna has no meta-language of logical terms, and the hermeneutical difficulties are many. In the next section, we will see the problem of a relation regress made explicit by the Buddhist Yogācārin, Dharmakīrti.

Verse 3 of chapter 2 of the *MMK* translates,

> How indeed could it occur that there be a moving [nominative case] belonging to something that is currently being moved [genitive case]? And that something that is currently being moved is not moving is never possible.[42]

This, again, like many of the conundra, is vague. Still, Nāgārjuna may be interpreted as having hit upon a true problem. If only something not currently being moved can be meaningfully be said to be being moved, then the *moving*, of the pair *moving* and *not moving*, is excluded as a candidate for meaningful predication of "what is being moved." But for something currently being moved it is impossible that it be not moving. Other than the moving and the not moving, there is no alternative. Thus the relation of property and property-bearer (as expressed by the nominative and genitive cases in the Sanskrit) is impossible. And since this predicative relation is presupposed in all intellectualization, intellectualization is not to be trusted: it betrays itself in incoherence as shown by this (*prasaṅga*) analysis.

To be honest, I do not feel that Nāgārjuna intended quite so specific an interpretation as mine above. He does, however, point toward the dilemma that is involved in talk about properties, property-bearers, and the relations between them. It is a mother dilemma that spawns many baby dilemmas. If an individual *a* is essentially an M, then it is pointless to use both names. But then if *a* is not-M, how could it be M? This would be a contradiction. The dilemma is between something like contradiction in essence on the one hand and pointless predication on the other.

Epistemologically, the problem would be that of identification of an M as an M; linguistically, the problem is that we would break a pragmatic rule in saying the unnecessary. Without being able to identify "bare particulars," that is to say, to identify individuals apart from their properties, it would seem meaningless to predicate anything of them. And how can we identify *bare* particulars! But if the particulars of which we predicate are clothed in properties, then when we predicate we do nothing but reiterate a property that the particular is already assumed to have. In this light, there can be no synthetic statements. In the Nyāya context, the problem would be that an awareness of a pot presupposes the thing's, so to say, pothood. But then how can it be meaningful to say of the pot that it is a pot? and so on with any other attribution?[43]

Later, we will draw out ramifications of the conundra concerning relations, conundra that were arguably originally discovered by Nāgārjuna. The full discussion has to be put off until we have reviewed several later contributions to the debate.[44]

3. Systematic Buddhist Idealism (Yogācāra)

Despite Nāgārjuna's efforts to ban speculation among Buddhists and to encourage a skeptical attitude toward intellectualization, Buddhist metaphysics did not cease. Mahāyāna scriptures seem to propose a cosmological understanding of enlightenment such that everything would be in essence the Buddha Mind.[45] Within Mahāyāna, the most noteworthy example of renewed positive philosophic effort occurs in the school of Buddhist Idealism, called Yogācāra. Yogācārins try to explain phenomena on idealist premises.

The motivation for Yogācāra seems suggested in part by the following (religious) response to Nāgārjuna (evident in several figures within a few centuries of the great reformer, such as Asaṅga and Vasubandhu).[46] Not every element of our ordinary life should be considered illusory or intellectually problematic, because, if it were, there would be no possibility of a living experience of *nirvāṇa*. We have the reliable testimony of the Buddha (as preserved in Buddhist scripture) that there is such a possibility. Therefore, there must be some element of our ordinary existence that serves as the means of transition to *nirvāṇa* experience. Yogācārins claim that this element is pure, immediate awareness, *vijñapti*. Thus Yogācārins accepted the dialectic of Nāgārjuna only to an extent: an imputation of reality and externality to objects apart from experience is considered problematic, but not awareness itself. This move clearly anticipates the view of consciousness embraced by Śrīharṣa and his Advaita tradition in general: consciousness itself is real and "self-illumining" (*svayamprakāśamāna*).[47]

Early Buddhist Idealists try to show that on an assumption of the sole reality of a stream of awareness that is aware in itself, our ordinary experience can still be explained. (In this they are opposed by Śrīharṣa, who lines up with Nāgārjuna's school on the score: the relation of ordinary experience to the mystical *summum bonum* "cannot be explained," *anirvacanīya*.) In other words, the Yogācārins take up the Buddhist equivalent of Christian theodicy, to explain why we do not ordinarily experience *nirvāṇa* (just as Christians try to explain why evil occurs, even though God is omnipotent and omnibenevolent). These Buddhists apparently feel that we should experience *nirvāṇa* (*nirvāṇa* is seen as the natural state), and propound a doctrine of *vijñaptimātra*, "Awareness alone." This doctrine is taken to mean that awareness is by nature nothing but the purity of the *nirvāṇa* type of meditation. The task is not to explain that original state but deviation from it. To this end, early Yogācārins posit a beginningless *ālayavijñāna*, "storehouse consciousness," consisting of numberless generalized subliminal urges and memory-impressions (*vāsanā* and *saṃskāra*) whose arisings deform awareness yet account for our ordinary experience.

Taking a slightly different angle on the motivations that give rise to the school, we see that the Buddhists face a difficulty in the apparent intersubjectivity of diverse objects in the external world. We seem to see the same trees, flowers, birds, and so on, but our individual moments of experience are different. Objects cannot be independent of our perceivings because a religious thesis would be contradicted: everyone and everything is interconnected, and someday we shall all pass together into the final Bliss. The storehouse accounts for intersubjectivity and diverse experiencings in the meantime.

Dharmakīrti (c. 600), known as both a late Yogācārin and as the preëminent Buddhist logician, and his forerunner, Dignāga (c. 450), become uninterested in the notion of a storehouse consciousness. Although the two are to be counted as Yogācārins, Dharmakīrti in particular makes such revolutionary innovations that it is necessary to distinguish his views from those of earlier Buddhist Idealists. Both Dignāga and Dharmakīrti are well-known to Śrīharṣa and his Advaita school, as well as to the Naiyāyikas; they exert a complex influence on each side of the later Advaita-Nyāya debate.

Dignāga turns his attention almost exclusively to questions of epistemology, that is, to questions about how we know anything and the means whereby we know it or are justified in our beliefs.[48] He argues that there are only two "sources of knowledge" or "justifiers" (*pramāṇa*), namely, (1) sensation and (2) inference (Naiyāyikas add two more; see the glossary under *pramāṇa*), and then defines and elaborates at length the nature of these.

Dignāga's greatest claim to fame rests with his formalization of rules of inference; his scheme of syllogism was studied closely by all succeeding philosophers, whatever the school. Concerning sensation, he remains closely allied to the earlier Buddhist Idealist camp—particularly in comparison with his successor Dharmakīrti—although both pressure the Indian realists to admit an "indeterminate perception" (*nirvikalpaka pratyakṣa*) into their system.[49] For the Buddhists, sensation is concept-free; conceptualization is imaginative construction. So far, the two Buddhists agree. But Dignāga's is also a *phenomenalist* view, as is evident in his understanding of illusion: false perceptual beliefs (such as, "This is a snake," when in fact the object is a rope) result from error only on the level of judgment or ideation. They are not perceptual errors but rather misinterpretations.[50]

Dharmakīrti takes a different view: sensation is not always reliable. In some circumstances, such as when a person has hepatitis (and sees white objects as yellow) or travels on a ship (and sees stationary objects as moving), sense presentations are not to be trusted. The judgments that would express them (e.g., "That is yellow") are false, not because of misinterpretation but because of something having gone wrong in the *causal nexus* that results in sensation (e.g., having hepatitis).[51] Dharmakīrti, like Dignāga, is concerned chiefly with issues of epistemology and logic. However, he takes a metaphysical overview concerning what an object is, and makes causal relations central. In this way, the great Buddhist advances in some respects the Naiyāyika cause.

But then true to his Buddhist Idealist upbringing, Dharmakīrti argues that all this is valid only so long as we are conditioned by desire, untransformed and unadept in the Buddhist Way. Indeed, there is not only the teaching of the Buddha, preserved in scripture, to this effect, but by looking closely with disinterested intellect, we (in the manner of Nāgārjuna) find paradoxes in the naïve causal view of the world. Dharmakīrti's brilliance lies in his ability to maintain a dual perspective: he both proposes a view of causal interaction that accounts for the everyday world (conditioned by our desires), and identifies paradoxes in that very view. The paradoxes indicate that the everyday world is only appearance and not reality. Let me fill out the rest of the everyday picture, before turning to the higher-order Idealist critique.

Anything existent (in the realm conditioned by desire) has causal efficacy, while something non-existent, say, the horn of a hare, has none.[52] The purpose of philosophy, according to Dharmakīrti, is to investigate human cognition, because successful action (of course, motivated by desire) is invariably preceded by right cognition. If we successfully milk Bessie and make butter, we have rightly cognized that Bessie is a milkcow, that from milk we make butter, and so on. Right cognition, or knowledge, arises within a causal nexus that includes both an object's effect on us (e.g., our sight of Bessie) and our action in the world (e.g., milking her).

Dharmakīrti views certain types of inference as having causal underpinnings. When, for example, we reason from the sight of smoke rising from a hill that there is fire there, the inference is based on the causal relation of smoke and fire. (This is also the earliest Naiyāyika view.) Similarly, when we do not see an elephant in the room and infer that none is present, we are reasoning based on a causal relation that would obtain were an elephant nearby: we would necessarily perceive it, so long as we were not blind, etc. Dharmakīrti also recognizes inferences based on natural classifications, such as "Bessie is a cow and therefore an animal." But much meaningful inferential knowledge—"meaningful" because it helps us get what we want—is based on relations of effect and cause. Here he sounds like a Naiyāyika.[53] Of course, Dharmakīrti was well aware of Naiyāyika positions, which, by his time, had become rather advanced—partly under the pressure of the critiques of Nāgārjuna, but also of Dignāga, Dharmakīrti's teacher a few generations removed.

There are several other positions of Dharmakīrti's—and several arguments—that are interesting philosophically, though they do not have the highest relevance here. Dharmakīrti is one of the great minds of Indian philosophy, and of all philosophy, for that matter. Let us turn now to the "higher" perspective of the Idealism and look at the Yogācārin's use of Nāgārjuna's *prasaṅga* method in exposing the illusion of relations, including, to be sure, the causal relations that are the stock in trade of his philosophy of everyday life.

Dharmakīrti identifies some of the difficulties later asserted by Śrīharṣa against Naiyāyika views. For example, he states in plain terms—using technical terms of the Naiyāyikas themselves—the Bradley problem, or *the* paradox of relations, that Śrīharṣa, we will see, parlays into not only demolition of the Naiyāyika attribution theory, but also other key refutations:

Since of two relata there is a connection through one, this one is a relation—

> well, then, if that is proposed, what is the relation of the two, the relation and the relata? There is an infinite regress, and therefore the idea of a relation does not hold.[54]

Dharmakīrti states the problem lucidly, and I will make only a few remarks. The regress is set up by treating the relation as a term, as the same sort of thing, logically, as its relata. Without an argument that a relation is a different sort of critter, it seems that if a third thing is required to relate two things, then the third thing requires equally a fourth and fifth to tie it up with the first two, *ad infinitum*. The regress is vicious: unlike an infinite series of causes that does not undermine the notion that a present x has y as its cause, the relation regress does undermine the work proposed for the relator. The relator, the third thing, cannot relate the two terms without help from the fourth and fifth things (*ad infinitum*) needed to tie it up with the first two. We can accept, on the other hand, a causal infinite series without threatening the notion that y has caused x: our ability to trace the series will simply flag at some point. Of course, when causality is framed as a matter of causal *relation*, the relation regress can wreak its destruction, as Dharmakīrti is well aware.

That Dharmakīrti includes causal relations within his general critique is most significant.[55] Dharmakīrti declares that what we ordinarily take to be causal relations are no more than "conventional signs" (*saṃketa*), dependent upon an *imaginary* construction of a world, just as we take a dewlap to be in general a sign of a cow (or of "cowness").[56] Indeed, that all relations are furnished by imagination is Dharmakīrti's general conclusion from his *prasaṅga* on relations: "Thus in themselves existents are unrelated; it is imagination that relates them."[57] Dharmakīrti does not, therefore, in the final analysis diverge radically from Dignāga: the verbalized world of concepts is a world of imaginary constructs, not, contra Nyāya, of cognitions and terms reflecting and referring to extra-mental realities.

However, Dharmakīrti should not be said to be merely skeptical of intellectualization in the fashion of Nāgārjuna. His philosophy is much more complex; it engages the Naiyāyikas along several dimensions.[58] Two further parts of his philosophy that we need to review are, first, an idealist theory of "universals" (this is crucial for our later consideration of Nyāya, because it stands for centuries as the chief competitor to Nyāya), and second, a masterful, religious, and pragmatic integration by Dharmakīrti of the two levels of his philosophy.

Dharmakīrti is a nominalist. In his view, sensation presents particulars; generalities and all relations, including causality, are contributed by our minds or imagination—our "desire-infected" imagination, to be sure. Furthermore, particulars are (to use Nyāya terms) qualities such as colors and tastes, not substances; they are fleeting qualities, moreover.

That these sensory objects are *unconceptualizably* particular does not mean, however, that concepts are, in the broadest sense, unrelated to them. Concepts are in fact thought to be *constrained* by sensation, but not to capture the exact particularity of the object, because that is the outer limit of conceptualization in general.

The central idea in Dharmakīrti's theory of concept-formation is *apoha*, "exclusion," exclusion of the other. In the case of a cow, the other would be mountains, oceans, stars, horses, and so on, all of which are, given the appropriate context, significantly other to the cows with which Bessie is most appropriately grouped. Through concepts we exclude other concepts, precisely those which would mislead us in action. The character of sensation, however, is what first indicates that the concept "non-cow" is inadequate when we are in the presence of a cow, and thus that the contrary concept, "cow," is adequate, given the realm of desire. Sensation has a transcendental negational character with regard to concepts: *not* a non-cow (this is the stock analysis of cowness, of being a cow). On the other hand, the presentations of sensation themselves are purely positive; the fact that the concept "cow" excludes the "non-cow"—i.e., is negational—is another indication of concepts' imaginary and mental character. (Idealist arguments concerning negation prove particularly troublesome for our empiricist and realist Logicians, as we will see.)

Concepts combined into verbalizable judgments serve as guides for action. A sensory cognition arouses certain expectations about an object of desire or aversion. Judgments are hypothetical in that they could be contradicted through action and ensuing judgments. In this way, Dharmakīrti mitigates his critique of relations and finds through his anthropology of desire a way to view both causal relations and generalities as, though illusory, still meaningful from a desire-ridden point of view—all without admitting reality to "universals" even from the worldly perspective. Points of this pragmatism are relied upon by Śrīharṣa.

Furthermore, on this model, concepts have their own nature and obey certain laws. All concepts make clean sortings according to a basic principle of the logic of concepts, namely, the law of contradiction.[59] There is no grey area or fuzzy middle ground.[60] This is, by the way, an understanding of contradiction opposed to the naturalist orientations of the Nyāya realists, but one serving well Śrīharṣa's polemics.

Now, finally, let us consider the religious dimension of the great Buddhist's philosophy, though it is of questionable relevance (Śrīharṣa does present a religious dimension, but very differently). Does Dharmakīrti at all manage to integrate these moves into a philosophy that is Buddhist? Does he uphold an experiential *summum bonum* and the Mahāyāna "way?" Or is his religious faith a separate matter from his philosophic reflection? The answer lies in Dharmakīrti's view of the possibility, within the Buddhist way, of transforming desire back into a pristine state of compassion. The realization of this possibility would, in his view, eliminate the essential precondition of worldly activity, namely, desire for results of action. Thus Dharmakīrti's upholding of a possible suspension of desire-provoked activity gives his philosophy two tiers, one world-oriented and one not. What they have in common is pragmatic justification: Buddhist soteriology, too, is useful—for attaining what *should* be a person's number-one desire, namely, the experience of *nirvāṇa*, the supreme good.[61]

4. Śaṅkara and Vedāntic Mystical Monism

Vedānta, specifically Advaita Vedānta, is the school to which Śrīharṣa openly expresses allegiance. We come now to the most pertinent background for our study of idealism. Śrīharṣa (c. 1150) inherits an Advaita version of Vedānta that had long been given a definitive formulation—principally by the great Śaṅkara (c. 700) but also by some of Śaṅkara's disciples prior to Śrīharṣa. Younger contemporaries of Śaṅkara's and later disciples pushed forward an Upanishadic exegetical program and developed epistemological and metaphysical positions they took to be implicit in Śaṅkara's stated views. But disagreements on details soon emerged, especially on the question of the Absolute's relation to the cosmos, and distinct Advaita cosmologies were worked out by the time of Śrīharṣa.[62]

However, the cosmological developments and much else in Advaita have only marginal relevance to our focus. Śrīharṣa is a different sort of Advaitin. He might be called a minimalist. Although, as I will show, he presents positive considerations in favor of a core Advaita view, he is little concerned with exegetical issues or with the substantive psychological and cosmological theories that emerged in post-Śaṅkara Advaita philosophy. Though he embraces much previous Advaita epistemology, he ignores the details of most prior Advaita reflection, even the great Śaṅkara's. Śrīharṣa takes over themes and endorses positions, but his philosophic masterpiece, the *Khaṇḍanakhaṇḍakhādya*, falls within a genre different from the works of earlier Advaitins. His is a dialectics in which issues of interpretation suffer diminution, and engagement with other viewpoints looms large.

We will look briefly now at Vedānta's cultural affiliations and store up some general ideative background. Next, our focus will be the development of two lines of Śaṅkara's argumentation that have premier importance with the later dialectician, first, a sublatability argument, and second, an attack on relations. Finally, we will review some important themes best developed, pre-Śrīharṣa, by Advaitins other than Śaṅkara.

4.1. Cultural and Textual Background

Culturally, Advaita—and all Vedānta—has its closest affinity with Mīmāṃsā, "Exegesis," a very old and conservative school bent upon defending Brahminism, the religion and social order of ritual and caste. Brahmins set themselves up as priests, with their offices hereditary. Within the umbrella religion of Hinduism, Brahminism may be considered the traditionalist camp. Texts older than the Upanishads, namely, the Vedas, have central importance. However, the Upanishads, though probably not all composed by Brahmins, came to be preserved in Brahminical lineages (called *śākhā*s, "branches"). Thus Vedāntic philosophy came to be known as *Uttara* Mīmāṃsā, the "later" Mīmāṃsā, with the school of Exegesis proper known as *Pūrva* Mīmāṃsā, "former" Mīmāṃsā. According to Vedāntins, Pūrva Mīmāṃsā is concerned with the right interpretation of the first portions of Vedic literature, while Vedānta is concerned with the later portions, namely, Upanishads. One important task the Advaitin Śaṅkara sets for himself as a Vedāntin is to show that the teachings of the Upanishads are not to be interpreted as mere adjuncts to the Vedic injunctions that Mīmāṃsā proper focuses on. That he feels called to do this—and takes great pains in his arguments—reveals the close affinity of Vedānta with Brahminism, an affinity that is underscored by Śaṅkara's and other Vedāntins' maintaining distinctions of social class.[63]

Culturally and historically speaking, there is still another school of classical philosophy that is important to the development of Advaita—and to Vedānta in all its branches—and that is Sāṃkhya, "Analysis." Sāṃkhya is a philosophy similar to classical Yoga in that both hold to a dualism of Nature (*prakṛti*) and conscious beings (*puruṣa*s).[64] The declared ground for all Vedāntic views—despite injunctions to yoga practice and philosophical dialectics—is the revelations of the Upanishads (as well as, according to some, of the *Bhagavad-Gītā*, c. 200 CE, the *Song of God*, a portion of the *Mahābhārata*, the *Great Indian Epic*). "Analysis" is a world view that often seems endorsed in these texts, as early commentators were well aware. Sāṃkhya finds several early formulations both in the Upanishads and in the *Gītā*. Thus Śaṅkara and other Vedāntic commentators feel called upon to argue that Analysis is not the teaching of the Upanishads; and in so arguing they find, or some of them find, room for several Sāṃkhya-like claims.[65]

However, considering the ideative affinities of Śrīharṣa—who stands roughly in the middle of the history of the Advaita school (c. 1150)—neither Mīmāṃsā nor Sāṃkhya is as important as the Buddhist thought we have already reviewed. Certain doctrines that emerge in the Mīmāṃsaka tradition—for example, "self-certification of cognition," *svataḥ pramāṇa*—are embraced by Śrīharṣa. But Mīmāṃsaka philosophers are realists, and line up on most metaphysical issues in opposition to Śrīharṣa's camp, the common scriptural tradition notwithstanding. Mīmāṃsā in fact is extremely important for New Logic; Gaṅgeśa on some topics goes to great lengths, as we will see, to show that his realist positions are superior to those of Mīmāṃsakas. Analysis, on the other hand, is a philosophy that has spent its influence by Śrīharṣa's time.

The enigmatic figure of Bhartṛhari (450 ?) must also be mentioned. Writing as a grammarian within the tradition of commentary on Pāṇini (c. 400 BCE), he weaves an idealist metaphysics within reflection on syntax and semiotics. He is, we may say, an idealist of the word (Brahman is fundamentally word or speech). In some instances, however, it is unclear to which positions he is himself committed. He discusses an impressive array—Buddhist, Sāṃkhya, Nyāya, Vaiśeṣika, others—and he clearly attacks reference, the linchpin of Naiyāyika theory of meaning, by formulating a "paradox of signification": if "cow" refers to cows, then we need some other term to refer to "cow," *ad infinitum*.[66] Bhartṛhari apparently thinks his discovery undercuts further notions crucial to the realist enterprise, such as inherence, and it may well be that in the overall problem space framed by idealist attacks, his reasoning, though largely unacknowledged, is as important as Nāgārjuna's.[67] But Bhartṛhari does not seem to have a major role in the Advaita tradition most directly leading to Śrīharṣa.

Moreover, the "regress" that Bhartṛhari touts seems as harmless as a so-called truth regress: This is a book. It is true that this is a book. It is true that it is true that this is a book. And so on. In contrast, a vicious regress undercuts a problematic notion's use initially, or intrinsically. (Again, the relation regress is vicious if in order to have a term *a* related to a term *b* by a relation R (*a*R*b*), a further relation is required to relate R to *a*, and another to *b*, *ad infinitum*.)

Finally, while the celebrated Śaṅkara (c. 710) is generally viewed as the greatest Advaitin and, according to many, the very founder of the Advaita school, Śaṅkara sees himself as belonging to a tradition of Advaita philosophy. Although it is disputed whether the earliest Upanishads express exclusively an Advaita philosophy, there are middle and late Upanishads that do seem to interpret the earliest Upanishads according to the central precepts of Śaṅkara's school.[68] Two other major precursors of Śaṅkara's Advaita are the *Brahma-sūtra* (c. 200, maybe as early as Nāgārjuna?) attributed to Bādarāyaṇa, and certain *kārikā*s (verses) on the *Māṇḍūkya Upaniṣad* attributed to Gauḍapāda (c. 525 ?). The *Brahma-sūtra* and Gauḍapāda's *kārikā*s do express a Vedāntic philosophy. But the latter, although clearly Advaitic, are mainly yogic and psychological; they do not much polemically engage other views; and though they are not exactly brief, they are, taken together, a short work, and for that reason insignificant compared to the lengthy treatises of Śaṅkara. The former, the *Brahma-sūtra*, though sufficiently comprehensive, is ambiguous on the question of endorsing an Advaita reading of early Upanishads.[69] Śaṅkara is rightly viewed as the definitive Advaitin, if only because this is the judgment of the Advaita tradition, including Śrīharṣa, who at the very beginning of his dialectical dissertation mentions Śaṅkara's *Brahmasūtra-bhāṣya* (henceforth *BSB*).[70]

Much folklore has grown up around the great Śaṅkara. There are stories that he vanquished Buddhists and others in debates all over India. Modern Advaitins have suggested that because of Śaṅkara, Buddhist Sanskrit philosophy came to an end. Now Buddhism, and Buddhist philosophy, did disappear in India, but not until three or four centuries after Śaṅkara, though a case could be made for an earlier decline. Probably the demise of Buddhism in the land of its birth had more to do with Muslim conquests in the western and northern portions of the subcontinent than with any intellectual development: Buddhist centers of learning lost necessary sponsorship from princes and kings. Nevertheless, it may be said that Śaṅkara tries to steal the Buddhists' thunder: his soteriology, or enlightenment theory, is not far different from theirs.

4.2. The Sublatability Argument

We saw above that in the Upanishads a comparison of everyday experience to dream lends itself, in connection with distinctly monistic proclamations, to a philosophy of illusionism (*māyā-vāda*). Advaita is above all, doctrinally, a philosophy of self; the world has a problematic status, like the object of an illusion. And argumentationally, the great Śaṅkara does not rely solely on Upanishadic exegesis to establish this Advaita outlook. He presents—apparently taking his cue from the Upanishadic dream analogies (or from Gauḍapāda)—a sublatability argument. In this way, he tries to make polemical hay out of familiar instances of perceptual illusion.[71] Could not the world be like the object of an illusion? In contrast, he points out, no one says, or can say, "I am not."[72] The self, in contrast with the world, cannot possibly not be. Self cannot be sublated. Perceptual illusion shows that anything else can be sublated.

The appearances of a rope as a snake, of mother-of-pearl as silver, and so on, show that the worldly content of experiences is not to be trusted. Only self-experience is sure. Śrīharṣa rehearses exactly these moves. He also follows the mystical twist Śaṅkara gives to the argument: veridical or non-illusory experience, true self-experience and experience of what is real, is *brahma-vidyā*, "mystical realization of Brahman." Neither Śaṅkara nor Śrīharṣa means to defend in this way a Transcendental Ego or a phenomenology of a *cogito*—comparable to moves found in the Western tradition stretching from Descartes through Edmund Husserl (and recent followers). It is, it must be stressed, a mystical self-experience that the Advaitins have in mind, a radical change of consciousness, not an intellectual view. Śaṅkara believes that in the enlightenment experience called *brahma-vidyā*, ordinary perceptions of the world are in fact sublated, revealed to be illusory. There is nothing real but Brahman, and insofar as one perceives things as distinct or separate from Brahman, one perceives illusorily. One must transcend ordinary perceptions and live in the true consciousness that reveals Brahman in order to perceive veridically.

Or, to be precise, we should say that, according to Śaṅkara, perceptual illusion shows the possibility of world sublation, and the Upanishads, not the actual mystical experience, teach the fact of illusion. The mystical experience does not teach; it liberates. The illusion is a "cosmic illusion," *māyā*, governing even the most sublime thought. The Upanishads themselves are part of *māyā*. There can be no teaching of any sort that does not presuppose *māyā*, or "spiritual ignorance," *avidyā*,[73] which is the psychological mainstay of the cosmological fact, or non-fact. In other words, the precise view is that Upanishadic declarations about Brahman as the Real, the "One without a second," form the core of Advaita in that they inspire the personal immediate experience. This, in turn, sublates world appearance such that one becomes "immediately Brahman-aware" (*brahma-sākṣātkāra*), and thus realizes the Upanishadic teaching of a supreme personal good, *parama-puruṣārtha*.

Cosmologically, objects, or appearances, are said to rest on Brahman in a relation of *adhyāsa*, normally translated "superimposition."[74] Brahman is thus the locus of the world, somewhat in the fashion that a real rope is the locus of a snake illusion. Of course, Brahman is understood as identical with the self, and some stress that only as self is Brahman a locus. With Śaṅkara, Brahman would thus seem to be only psychologically a locus, a position developed by Padmapāda (c. 725), a junior contemporary of Śaṅkara's. A diversity of view emerges among later Advaitins. But despite the differences of opinion on the issue of Brahman's precise relation to the world, an identity thesis, self = Brahman, takes premier place with all Advaita. Self-Brahman identity is absolutely central. This thesis, above all, secures the idealism of Advaita and of Śrīharṣa.[75]

We will scrutinize the sublatability argument, complete with the mystical twist, in chapter 3, in connection with Śrīharṣa's polemics.

Another argument of Śaṅkara's looms large with Śrīharṣa. Śaṅkara views awareness as intrinsic to the self, and uses a regress argument to attack competing views. The attack is directed first against Buddhists, who hold that cognitions are momentary, and then against Vaiśeṣikas (Atomists), who hold that they are qualities inherent in the self. Logicians generally defend the latter position, and are opposed to Śaṅkara's thesis, namely, that awareness is essential to the self (who does not change). Śaṅkara argues that awareness is not adventitious or dependent on any extrinsic factors whatsoever,[76] whereas the psychological position embraced by Nyāya is that any given awareness is adventitious, dependent on factors outside of the self. The heart of Śaṅkara's argument is that if awareness were knowable only by another awareness, then an infinite regress would result. Śrīharṣa elaborates the point at great length in upholding the view that awareness is both "self-illumining" (*svaprakāśamāna*) and—more importantly in the context of his onslaught on Nyāya—"self-justifying" or "self-certifying" (*svataḥ pramāṇa*). In chapter 3, we will scrutinize the putative regress concerning awareness of awareness as well as the self-certification claim.

4.3. Śaṅkara's Attack on Relations

Śaṅkara's illusion analogy is probably his most studied piece of philosophy. However, attacks of his on opposed views—including, to be sure, realist views of Nyāya—count as fine pieces of reasoning. Naiyāyika positions are not, as with Śrīharṣa, the main focus of his complaints: Śaṅkara is much more concerned with criticizing Buddhists—in part with a mind to distance his views from theirs—and with supporting his reading of the Upanishads through faulting Mīmāṃsaka and Sāṃkhya tenets especially.

Nevertheless, Śaṅkara presents a polished attack on relations, an onslaught specifically on the Nyāya and Vaiśeṣika notion of inherence, *samavāya*, developing an argument adumbrated in the *Brahma-sūtra* itself. (Inherence is the key relation in the Logician realist philosophy: see below, chapter 2, pp. 48–9; a translation of Gaṅgeśa on inherence appears in chapter 5.) From the second chapter (of four) of Śaṅkara's *BSB* comes this passage:

> Since neither (an inherent) cause and effect (a whole in its parts) nor a substance and its qualities invoke notions of distinct realities, unlike a horse and a buffalo, their identity must be accepted. (Opponent: the relation of inherence, *samavāya*, guarantees the distinctness.) But even on the supposition that there is such inherence relating two relata, if you accept that there is a relation with the inherent, another relation for each relatum must be imagined. Thus you face the difficulty of an infinite series. If you do not accept that there is a relation with the inherent, then the difficulty is that the (original) connection is broken.[77]

Thus Śaṅkara makes pellucid the vicious dilemma that a theory of a real relator presents: (a) infinite regress or (b) dissolution of the connection. His ultimate conclusion is, however, distinct from that of Śrīharṣa, who widens the polemic.

As is evident from the surrounding text, Śaṅkara takes his dialectical criticism to show that the right view of inherent causality is *satkāryavāda*: "the effect is present in the cause."[78] The Upanishads teach that the reality of an individual thing is not its individual form but rather its "essence" or material cause, namely Brahman. A gold bracelet is similarly nothing but gold (recall Upanishadic theme 6 above, p. 9). Śrīharṣa, in contrast, takes the relation regress to show the incoherence of the entire Naiyāyika project, and to serve as an eliminative argument for Brahman, as we will see in chapter 3. Nevertheless, Śaṅkara does clearly present the Bradley problem. It is probable that Śaṅkara is the immediate or proximate influence on Śrīharṣa on this score. In fact, the difference in conclusion is not so terribly wide. Śaṅkara's view of causality does challenge the Logician ontology arguably almost as thoroughly as any of Śrīharṣa's refutations: a thing exists *indistinctly* in its material cause according to the Advaita analogy (a gold bracelet is essentially gold), whereas distinctness, *bheda*, is fundamental to the Nyāya realism—whether that distinctness holds between entities related by inherence or otherwise. A substance particular, such as a pot, for example, is considered an entity distinct from its color and other qualities, as well as from the parts that make it up. Śrīharṣa brings out a full range of untoward consequences from the relation regress for Nyāya. Śaṅkara shows only one, concerning the part-whole relation. But the earlier Advaitin makes plain the underlying logic of the problem.

This logic is, again, a logic that regards the relator as a term. We will see that the Naiyāyika solution is, in part, to resist this view of inherence.

4.4. Advaita Philosophers through Vācaspati Miśra I

There are other themes and positions in Śaṅkara's writings that are important for Śrīharṣa, some explicit with Śaṅkara himself, others more to be credited to intervening Advaitins. We will briefly review the former, then complete this chapter by surveying Advaita views important to Śrīharṣa developed by Śaṅkara's followers. I also have a few words to say about the overall development of Advaita.

Logicians sometimes evoke pragmatic criteria to defeat Advaita's view of awareness: awareness provokes activity with regard to real things desired, and it is the success of activity that proves awareness veridical. However, both Śaṅkara and Śrīharṣa argue that something unreal can be a cause of activity and can provoke a sense of satisfaction as well (for example, imaginary sweets).[79] Then, concerning scripture (*śruti*) as teaching experiential *brahma-vidyā*, "knowledge of Brahman," both argue that such knowledge is outside the scope or sphere of everyday knowledge sources (*pramāṇa*), and thus that scripture alone is the appropriate source, "like vision concerning color."[80] Moreover, Śaṅkara says reasoning and argument are to be distrusted, and gives at least one reason why, namely, that disputes among philosophers are notoriously inconclusive, and that someday someone might well come up with a better argument.[81] This point connects not only with the endorsement of scripture but with the Upanishadic theme (9 above) that Brahman is not the object of a mental activity of knowing. Advaita suspicion of world-oriented argument and epistemology also connects with the idealist thesis—filled out in several ways (and at numerous places in Śaṅkara's corpus)—that Brahman as consciousness is the only reality; only it may authentically be said *to be*. This entire nexus of theses and themes weighs heavily with Śrīharṣa. Finally, note that Śaṅkara embraces the "self-illumining" thesis already mentioned, that consciousness is essential to itself and requires no extrinsic factor to be self-aware. These are instances of direct influence on Śrīharṣa, and there are a few others as well. However, Śrīharṣa's indebtedness to the great earlier Advaitin is most importantly a matter of overall outlook, less of individual positions or arguments.

Maṇḍana Miśra, whom scholars believe was roughly contemporary with Śaṅkara, possibly slightly his elder (that is, c. 700), anticipates if not the arguments of Śrīharṣa, at least much of his concern in his refutations. For example, in Maṇḍana's *Brahmasiddhi*, there is an attack on the notion of *bheda*, "difference" or "distinctness," that is remarkable both for its focus and for its contrast with what Śaṅkara has to say. The *Brahmasiddhi* is Maṇḍana's only work written from an Advaita perspective. He wrote several works as a Mīmāṃsaka.

Śaṅkara, although he attacks Atomism, Logic, and other world views, sometimes appears to make room for a hierarchy of metaphysical positions with statements about the compatibility of Brahman as the One with worldly phenomena exhibiting divisions and distinctness, *bheda*. In a particularly noteworthy passage, *BSB* 2.1.13, he tells us,

> although foam, waves, bubbles, and other modifications of the sea really are not other than the sea, in the phenomenal world (*vyavahāra*) they are experienced as mutually divided, and could be characterized as coming into contact with one another, et cetera. But it is not the case that these modifications—foam, waves, etc.—in not being other than the sea or sea-water come to be mutually inclusive; nor is it the case that in not coming to be mutually inclusive they are not other than the sea (that is, their oneness with the sea is of a different order). Thus here too—with enjoyers and the objects of enjoyment—these do not come to be mutually inclusive, and they do not come to be other than the highest Brahman. And although the enjoyer is not really a modification of Brahman . . . still there is (phenomenal) division based on limiting conditions (*upādhi*), as with ether delimited by the likes of a pot. Thus is it possible that although they (enjoyers and the enjoyed) are not other than the highest cause, Brahman, there is division of this kind—enjoyers and the enjoyed—on analogy to the sea and its waves and so on.[82]

Such statements militate against an exclusivistic reading of Śaṅkara's Advaita, and may be taken to have encouraged symbiosis and mutuality as found, arguably, with Vācaspati Miśra I (c. 960), who, as will be discussed, writes both as an Advaitin and a Naiyāyika. Inclusivism on a model of philosophic hierarchy is clearly found with later Advaitins, such as Mādhava (c. 1515) in his famous doxography, the *Sarvadarśanasaṃgraha*,[83] and is crucial to the religious and philosophic stances of the influential modern Indian intellectuals Ram Mohan Roy, Vivekananda, and Sarvepalli Radhakrishnan.

But Maṇḍana, like Śrīharṣa after him, holds that the truth of "non-distinctness" entails that the notion of distinctness is suspect, even in every-day terms. Whereas Śrīharṣa tries to show its incoherence, Maṇḍana is intent on proving that things are not in themselves distinct; they are instead Brahman. Thus he launches an onslaught against *bheda* as objectively real. Let us look at one or two lines of this criticism.[84]

Maṇḍana, as Madeleine Biardeau stresses,[85] feels that the reality of non-distinctness (Brahman admits no distinctness) entails that the thesis that things are in themselves distinct must be unwarranted. To show this, he attacks the justificational power of perception, in particular in the context of a contrast with the authoritativeness of scripture. But, as Allen Thrasher argues,[86] Maṇḍana's deep view, emergent in the course of his defense of scripture, is that perception is "concept-free" (*nirvikalpa*) and indeed as such is *of* Brahman, the universal being-ness present everywhere. Maṇḍana thinks of Brahman not only as subject, but as object, the one true object of all perception. Non-distinctness is directly experienced; distinctness, *bheda*, is a mental construct, as is shown by argument. Unlike Śrīharṣa, Maṇḍana's point is not to prove the incoherence of distinctness—and of all relational notions—but their dependence on human purposes. Distinctness is not a matter of what something is in itself. Distinctness cannot be the intrinsic nature of a thing because it is a relational notion. Relational notions, such as "father/son" and "long/short," are contributed by human thought; therefore, distinctness is, too.[87]

Some scholars have claimed that Maṇḍana is identical with the immediate disciple of Śaṅkara known as Sureśvara (c. 750), who wrote a long subcommentary on Śaṅkara's *Bṛhadāraṇyaka-bhāṣya*, among other works.[88] Sureśvara repeats, and perhaps develops somewhat, Maṇḍana's attack on distinctness.[89]

Padmapāda (c. 725) develops the subjectivism of Śaṅkara; he refuses to consider Brahman as object. His most notable work concerns analysis of perceptual illusion, particularly a defense of the "indeterminability" view of it (*anirvacanīyatva*): in principle no story can be told about how perceptual illusions occur.[90] This position stands in stark contrast with the assiduous efforts of Logicians to provide an explanation of perceptual illusion. Padmapāda also refuses to speculate cosmologically on Brahman's relation to the world, other than to insist that only Brahman is real. In this way, he stands close to our dialectical Advaitin who also refuses to consider any cosmological thesis seriously, although Padmapāda's followers, in particular Prakāśātman (c. 975), develop a barrage of arguments as to why Brahman does not change but only undergoes "transmogrification" (*vivarta*) in being identical with the world. Such development is apparently provoked not only by Padmapāda's statements that Brahman as consciousness is the locus of the world, but also by intra-school squabbles. But the important point is that both Padmapāda and Śrīharṣa hold that the relation between Brahman and the world is not explainable (*anirvacanīya*): how Brahman comes to appear as distinct individualities cannot be said. Similarly, the relation of an illusory snake to a real rope—*mutatis mutandi* with other illusions—cannot be explained.

Vācaspati Miśra I (c. 960) develops a line of Advaita absolutism quite distinct from that of Śrīharṣa. In fact, Vācaspati's Advaita may be seen as diverging from our dialectician's in two crucial ways. First, and indisputably, Vācaspati presents a cosmological version of Advaita, where spiritual ignorance, *avidyā* (or *māyā*, the cosmic illusion) becomes rather substantial, much like Analysis's "Nature" or *prakṛti*. Vācaspati tries to explain Brahman's relation to the world, and is not shy about speculation. Thus the first contrast with Śrīharṣa is that between Vācaspati's cosmological projects and Śrīharṣa's anti-cosmological stance.

Second, it is tempting to say that with Vācaspati, Nyāya and Advaita are able to rest in relative peace: he views Nyāya as generally authoritative for the everyday world, and Advaita as authoritative about the Supreme Reality, Brahman. The analyses of Logic would be confined to the structure of appearance; Advaita would tell us instead about reality. Vācaspati's cosmological speculations, in particular the position that *avidyā* is objective (with nature emitted by and re-absorbed into Brahman), seem to make room for what Nyāya has to say. Then, given that Vācaspati is highly regarded by Logicians for his (long!) subcommentary on the *Nyāya-sūtra*, one would not be surprised to find him endorsing a two-tiered philosophy in the manner of Dharmakīrti. A similar compatibility between Sāṃkhya and Advaita is hinted at by Śaṅkara himself, and there are such compatibilist metaphors used by him as that, quoted above, about the waves and the sea.[91] If this reading is right, then Śrīharṣa decidely breaks the peace with his refutations.

However, Vācaspati should probably not be read as an outright compatibilist. Vācaspati has indeed written major works both from an Advaita perspective and from that of Nyāya. But he has written a treatise on Sāṃkhya, another on Yoga, and a couple as a Mīmāṃsaka as well. His most vehement attacks are reserved for Buddhists. Is he then a pan-Brahminical genius of philosophical synthesis and accommodation? No, the anti-Nyāya passages in the *Brahma-sūtra* and Śaṅkara's *BSB* are interpreted as truly anti-Nyāya by Vācaspati, and are endorsed by him. Similarly, the anti-Advaita passages in his Nyāya work remain anti-Advaita.[92] My own view is that there was no peace between Advaita and Nyāya. Vācaspati mastered different philosophies without attempting to reconcile them (as do many academics today). Doubtless, his understanding of one influenced his understanding of another. But on certain key issues I doubt that he believed that both philosophies could somehow be right. Perspectivalism is associated in the Indian context principally with the Jainas (see the glossary entry). I have something to say about it in the next chapter in the context of discussing Udayana, the Logician whose theories Śrīharṣa most closely follows in dismantling the realist world view. Vācaspati simply changed his mind, or changed hats, without directly addressing the change.

In sum, Vācaspati was a virtuoso, setting a precedent, we might add, for the New Logicians, Vardhamāna, Śaṅkara Miśra, and others, who write commentaries on Śrīharṣa's Advaita text. Note that Vardhamāna and Śaṅkara Miśra do not confess their Logician allegiance within the context of their formal commentaries on Śrīharṣa's *Khaṇḍanakhaṇḍakhādya*. Likewise, Vācaspati invariably assumes the persona of an advocate. My sense is that advocacy of even a cosmological version of Advaita makes grumpy company with Naiyāyikas—modern universalism (such as that of Radhakrishnan, et al.) notwithstanding—and the same goes in the other direction. Śrīharṣa's dialectical Advaita may well sharpen the disagreements, but Śrīharṣa does not break the peace: there was no peace to be broken. Śaṅkara and all the early disciples mention Nyāya only infrequently, and until Udayana (c. 1000), Logicians, as Karl Potter points out, also rarely mention Advaita.[93] But there are serious differences nonetheless, with no explicit attempt to mediate them by Vācaspati.

Finally, Śrīharṣa is not, let me repeat, much influenced by Vācaspati. Śrīharṣa's version of Advaita derives much more directly from Śaṅkara, perhaps also from Maṇḍana and Padmapāda (though they are not mentioned by him), and, as discussed, the Buddhists Dharmakīrti and Nāgārjuna. (The possible influence of the philosophic skeptic Jayarāśi is discussed at the end of the next chapter.)

There are a few other Advaita authors, whose texts are extant, between Śaṅkara and Śrīharṣa: we might mention Jñānaghana (c. 900), Vimuktātman (c. 950), Sarvajñātman (c. 1027), whose work is commented on by a follower of Śrīharṣa's (namely, by Madhusūdana Sarasvatī), and Śaṅkhapāṇi (c. 1070 ?), who wrote a commentary on Maṇḍana's *Brahmasiddhi*. Some of these writers may have influenced Śrīharṣa, but I am personally capable of no judgment. For summaries of their views, one may consult Surendranath Dasgupta's work on the history of Indian philosophy.[94]

Advaita Vedānta is not a monolithic movement. It develops lines of cosmological argument and anti-cosmological argument, epistemology (where there is less intra-camp disagreement), exegetical strategies, and ethical theories and views about the way to liberation or *brahma-vidyā*, along with arguments against other philosophies on any point of concern. Śrīharṣa directs many of these currents into his version of Advaita, which combines, in particular, previous epistemological thinking with dialectical arguments—some innovative, others inherited from Nāgārjuna, et al.—against what he sees as views incompatible with Upanishadic teachings about Brahman and the self.

CHAPTER TWO

Early Systematic Realism

There is less need to review historical background with classical Indian realism than there is with the idealism of Advaita Vedānta: contextualization is less called for with philosophers purporting to systemize common sense. Nevertheless, important precursors of the positions of the realist philosophies occur in early traditions of grammar and debate. We will look briefly at these precursors before proceeding to the realist literature and then to the substance of realist metaphysics pre-Śrīharṣa.

The two classical schools, Vaiśeṣika (Atomism) and Nyāya (Logic), both take a realist attitude toward objects of experience. Each for centuries was considered distinct by Indian philosophers; each has a distinct, early literature that is self-defining. But as will be further explained, the two may be said to be unified by Udayana (c. 1000) as Nyāya. Even before Udayana, Logicians accepted, at least implicitly, key Atomist positions, and Atomists accepted key claims developed by Logicians. The two are sister schools in the early period.

1. The Grammarians and Early Manuals of Debate

Centuries before Nāgārjuna, grammarians—such as the renowned Pāṇini (c. 400 BCE), the originator of the Sanskrit grammatical system used through all periods, and Patañjali (150 BCE)—articulated what were to become key elements of Nyāya and Vaiśeṣika.[1] In particular, they forged realist positions on meaning and reference. On the other hand, the specialists in *vyākaraṇa-śāstra*—the science of grammar—do not speak with a single voice philosophically. As we have seen, the grammarian Bhartṛhari (450 CE ?) is an idealist of the word (Brahman is fundamentally word or speech), who attacks the view that discrete individuals existing independently of words or speech form the referents of what realists see as referring expressions. Bhartṛhari's variety of idealism remains a distinct though minor voice even in late stages of classical metaphysics.[2]

Probably the most important positive contribution to realist perspectives made by early grammarians concerns the notion of *padārtha*, "category." The nature and number of categories becomes an organizing motif both with the early Naiyāyikas and Vaiśeṣikas.[3] Both the *Nyāya-sūtra* (c. 200 CE) and the *Vaiśeṣika-sūtra* (c. 150 CE) present lists of *padārtha*. With the former, the word means little more than "topic," but in the latter it designates the basic unit of ontic commitment or "type of thing to which words refer," a meaning that is carried on through Navya Nyāya. The early grammarians tend to take primary meaning (*abhidhā*, as opposed to suggestive or connotative meaning, *lakṣaṇā*) as a matter of reference to external objects, although whether these objects are particulars or universals is much debated.[4] Some types of words pick out types of thing (thus *kriyā*, for example, means both verb and motion). Apparently, therefore, different grammatical categories underlie the Vaiśeṣika *padārtha* that are understood to be the basic types of things there are. However, there are other motivations (epistemological and systemic) for the notion as well.[5]

Furthermore, grammarian discussions presage Nyāya-Vaiśeṣika realism about universals. As suggested, some considered primary meaning to consist of universals as designated by common nouns. But also, less contentiously, the meanings of abstract terms—i.e., terms generated (in various ways but paradigmatically) by the suffixes, *-tva* and *-tā* (roughly equivalent to "-ness" and "-hood" in English)—were considered to be universals. It is easy to understand how this feature of Sanskrit, coupled with the assumption that meaning is reference, would generate at least the outlines of a realist view of universals. This is a topic that will engage us later in this and following chapters. Speculation on the topic occurs as early as Patañjali's *Mahābhāṣya*, and continues in the work of his followers.[6]

The point is worth stressing: grammarians introduce the concept of the universal (*jāti* = *sāmānya*) to explain the meaning of certain terms, especially those felt to capture the recurrent features of things that are all of the same type. Cowhood is what is common to cows; every cow has cowhood, though Bessie and Flossie have individual differences. Other than by supposing a semantic tie to a universal, how could the same word, "cow," for instance, be used for any and every cow, past, present, and future? The early philosophers of Nyāya and Vaiśeṣika address other dimensions of the notion, the epistemic and the ontological, respectively. But they also do not lose sight of the semantic motivation first recognized by grammarians. We need not suppose that early Logicians or Atomists lifted the notion of a universal directly from grammatical texts. This may or may not have been the case. But the notion was pioneered by grammarians, and probably they made it familiar within scholarly circles in very early classical times.

As with many works of early Indian science and philosophy, rules of grammar are formulated in *sūtra*s, literally, "threads." The *sūtra*s of Pāṇini come to be called *lakṣaṇa*, "definitions," and the proper usages formed in accordance with them, *lakṣya*, "that which is to be defined." The formulating of definitions by Naiyāyikas is a central philosophic procedure, and theory of definition an important concern. In accordance with the grammarians' practice, many Naiyāyikas use definitions in philosophy as "explanation through characterization."[7] Indeed, "characterization" is probably a better rendering of *lakṣaṇa* than "definition"; both the grammarian and Naiyāyika efforts are directed to determining what a thing or law is, identifying properties that differentiate something from other things, or specifying the ontological ground for the meaning of a term. Providing synonyms or equivalent verbal meaning is not the aim.

There are other lines of likely grammarian influence on our realists and indeed on all the classical schools. But the most important point about the (again, strikingly early—fifth century BCE—as well as rich and long-lived) grammatical tradition in Sanskrit is simply that every philosopher knew the Pāṇinian grammatical system. Probably before Nāgārjuna and even the earliest Naiyāyika or Vaiśeṣika texts (c. 200 CE), Sanskrit had ceased to be anyone's mother tongue. Thus to learn it was to learn its grammar as systemized by grammarians. Proper Sanskrit conforms to invariable grammatical rules, and philosophers could not help but be influenced by them in broad ways, somewhat in the fashion that modern logicians' talk of (logical) subjects and predicates derives from grammatical findings. Sometimes appeals are explicitly made to grammatical principles to resolve a dispute.[8]

Considering early Vaiśeṣika to represent more the ontological dimensions of the later philosophy and early Nyāya the epistemic and logical, we may say, speaking roughly, that pre-classical grammarians tend more decisively to presage Vaiśeṣika positions. Early Nyāya, in contrast, may be imagined to be rooted more firmly in early manuals of debate, now lost, but discernible in the *Nyāya-sūtra* itself, c. 200 CE, the founding text of the Nyāya school and the oldest extant Nyāya text. Given the large numbers of this type of book for various trades and practices of Indian society (e.g., textbooks on dramatic dance, sexual love, courtly advice, yoga, etc.), the compiler of the *sūtra*s of the *Nyāya-sūtra* probably drew on earlier "how-to books" concerning staged disputation. The *Nyāya-sūtra* spells out both rhetorical strategies and veritable (proto-)scientific methodologies to be used in contexts ranging from legal and medical controversies to debates about metaphysics and religion.

We know that philosophical debates were staged in courts of kings from very early on: witness the exchanges in the court of King Janaka reported in the *Bṛhadāraṇyaka Upaniṣad*.[9] The evidence abounds that organized philosophical debate was a common practice long before Nāgārjuna and the final redaction of the *Nyāya-sūtra*. A textbook of debate seems a subset of the *Nyāya-sūtra* as a whole, most evident in the fifth of its five chapters. In the

Buddhist Canon, Jaina *Āgamas*, early grammatical literature, early works on law and social conduct, and, surprisingly, early medical literature, there are numerous references to debate, with types of debate differentiated and rules specified.[10] Brahmin pundits—the keepers of Sanskrit grammar as well as the priests of Brahminism, and perhaps also professional debate coaches or even professional Naiyāyikas—can be imagined as contributors to the science of debate. Consequently, the *Nyāya-sūtra* should be regarded as the product of centuries of development. (Gautama, Nyāya's legendary founder, may have been an ingenious and original metaphysician, but he was also, most probably, a compiler and editor.)

In the *Great Indian Epic*, the *Mahābhārata*—a poem of more than 100,000 verses probably itself composed over several centuries, from approximately 400 BCE—courtly debates are reported. In a few instances, details of rhetoric and informal logic are spelled out explicitly, including enumeration and elaboration of various fallacies. (The *Nyāya-sūtra* analyzes fallacies in its fifth chapter.) For example, scholar Ester Solomon draws our attention to the *Mahābhārata* story of a beautiful young woman named Sulabhā, who approaches King Janaka and inquires about the means to *mukti*, "liberation of the soul." Janaka upbraids her for asking the question, assuming that no such vibrant young woman could really be serious about this, and uses rather indecorous language in his reply. Sulabhā counters with a serious statement, and in the course of her response specifies a broad range of criteria for judging what should count as a good speech (*vācana*). She identifies various fallacies, such as irrelevance, that are listed in the *Nyāya-sūtra* as "grounds for rebuke" (*nigrahasthāna*) in its more comprehensive theory.[11]

It is safe to assume, therefore, that long before the final redaction of the *Nyāya-sūtra*, attention and reflection had been devoted to matters of proper reasoning and successful debate strategies. In sum, the *Nyāya-sūtra* appears in significant part to be the result of a long tradition of working these matters out and, especially, of framing them succinctly (in "definitions," *lakṣaṇa*) so that they might be easily appreciated by students. The more speculative and systematically philosophic portions of the work may be viewed as overlays on the textbook of debate and logic. On the other hand, the overlays are in themselves so important that it would be wrong to say that the *Nyāya-sūtra* is somehow basically or principally a textbook of critical reasoning. The *Nyāya-sūtra* also expresses not only much epistemology but a wide-ranging metaphysics: the text formulates a veritable world view. It is as though a philosopher stuffed a logic textbook with so many positions ranging over a great breadth of philosophic interest that the textbook almost disappears. In fact, the textbook is recognizable, but its concerns are not predominant in the *Nyāya-sūtra* as a whole.

Finally, without impugning the motives of those reflecting on debate in the early periods, we may imagine that funding for monasteries and schools as well as the attracting of pupils depended in many instances—and were recognized as depending—upon success in debates held in the courts of kings and princes. In some instances, patronage may have been won because of a reputation for logical professionalism; later the pundits would have had the leisure to develop more wide-ranging views. But here we begin to indulge a taste for historical fiction. Materially, Nyāya—and Vaiśeṣika, too—begin with their respective *sūtra* texts.

2. Vaiśeṣika and Nyāya Literature through Udayana

The *Vaiśeṣika-sūtra*, traditionally ascribed to Kaṇāda, is the earliest work of either the Nyāya or the Vaiśeṣika tradition, pre-dating Nāgārjuna in its final redaction (150 CE ?). However, this *sūtra* text is not nearly as focal for the approximately one-thousand-year span of early Vaiśeṣika philosophy, i.e., pre-Udayana, as the *Nyāya-sūtra* is for early Nyāya. The earliest extant *Vaiśeṣika-sūtra* commentary, that of Praśastapāda (c. 530), is less a commentary than a wholesale rearrangement of topics; it also adds much that is original. This, Praśastapāda's "*bhāṣya*," or *Padārthadharmasaṃgraha* (*Compendium on the Nature of the Fundamental Categories*), became the focus of the later tradition (with a few exceptions), buttressed by a commentary by the pivotal Udayana.[12]

Praśastapāda shows marked influence from the Nyāya tradition. Moreover, the extant commentaries on the *Padārthadharmasaṃgraha* written by Vyomaśiva (c. 950), Śrīdhara (c. 990), and Udayana, further draw upon Naiyāyika works. Thus, by the last of these, Udayana's *Kiraṇāvalī*, it is pointless to talk of two separate schools—with one exception (discussed below). Again, much the same can be said for Naiyāyika authors' relation to Vaiśeṣika: that relation becomes tighter over time, culminating in the complete merger with Udayana.[13]

Statements in the works of Buddhists, Jainas, and others indicate that several further commentaries on the *Vaiśeṣika-sūtra*, as well as a few independent Vaiśeṣika treatises, were popular in the centuries before Udayana.[14] Yet except for one work, recently discovered, by Candrānanda, no others have come down to our time.[15]

More precisely, no others—except Candrānanda's commentary—have come down to us in Sanskrit. In Chinese translation, a short non-commentarial text, entitled *Daśapadārthaśāstra* (*The Science of the Ten Categories*), attributed to Candramati (or Maticandra, c. 550) has been preserved.[16] Unlike Candrānanda's *Vaiśeṣika-sūtra* commentary, this work appears to have had some influence—though, according to scholar Erich

Frauwallner, it was too innovative too early and for this reason supplanted by the more conservative *Padārthadharmasaṃgraha* of the roughly contemporary Praśastapāda.[17] Candramati shows originality in proposing ten fundamental categories as opposed to Praśastapāda's six. The category of absence, *abhāva*—which Udayana endorses and Śrīharṣa vehemently attacks, and which is enormously important with the New Logicians—is one of four that Candramati adds.

There is one Vaiśeṣika work post-Udayana but before the period of Navya Nyāya (1300+), indeed before Śrīharṣa (1150): the *Nyāyalīlāvatī* by Śrīvallabha (c. 1100). Though the work is a lucid exposition of Vaiśeṣika tenets, with some original argumentation, Śrīharṣa seems unaware of it and we will largely ignore it. Śrīharṣa is well aware of Udayana's work and of the earlier tradition as well, though much of that apparently *through* his study of Udayana: it is unclear whether Śrīharṣa had a direct knowledge of Śrīdhara's work, for example, but Udayana read Śrīdhara, disputing in some instances his interpretation of Praśastapāda.[18]

Gaṅgeśa and the New Logicians explicitly embrace as their own the tradition of early Vaiśeṣika as well as that of Nyāya. For example, Gaṅgeśa's son Vardhamāna wrote a commentary on Praśastapāda's *Padārthadharmasaṃgraha* (including Udayana's commentary), as did other post-Gaṅgeśa Logicians. And there is one Navya commentary on the *Vaiśeṣika-sūtra* itself, by Śaṅkara Miśra (c. 1430).

The extant literature of early Nyāya is more extensive than that of early Vaiśeṣika, although much, too, has been lost here (texts known only by Buddhist and Jaina references, etc.). As noted, Nāgārjuna is aware of the *pramāṇa* theory—the theory of justification—of early Nyāya. Gautama, the (legendary?) *Nyāya-sūtra* author, seems also to be aware of Nāgārjuna, as we noted: the *Nyāya-sūtra* attempts to meet the Buddhist's "meta-epistemological" objection of what justifies the justifiers.[19]

The *Nyāya-sūtra* commentary of Vātsyāyana (c. 400) is the oldest extant. There were some before his, scholars believe, partly because Vātsyāyana mentions other interpretations of particular *sūtra*s. All *sūtra* texts seem to have been composed to help students remember the subject being taught. Most *sūtra* texts are unintelligible without a commentary, and we may imagine that an oral commentary was provided by an instructor in the earlier periods. Written commentaries were doubtless a later phenomenon, and were probably used in large part, and for centuries, as supplements to a living teacher's explanations.

Vātsyāyana knows Vaiśeṣika views, declaring that the Vaiśeṣika categories (*padārtha*s) can be included in the list of knowables (*prameya*s) provided by Gautama.[20] Vātsyāyana is also well aware of Buddhist criticisms, and indeed of Advaita Vedānta long before Śaṅkara: under *Nyāya-sūtra* 1.1.22, the

Upanishadic notion of Brahman is discussed along with the supreme good, and under 4.1.21 what we recognize as the Advaitic view of Brahman seems rejected in favor of a variety of theism. Many if not most of the characteristic pre-Śrīharṣa Naiyāyika patterns of defense and of attack on rival views are present in Vātsyāyana's work, which is referred to simply as the commentary, or *bhāṣya*, among later proponents. No doubt the great early Naiyāyika himself pioneered some of these. But probably others he inherited from a flourishing early Nyāya, whose works are now lost except in this single instance.

Uddyotakara (c. 600) is the next Naiyāyika author whose work has come down to us. Uddyotakara wrote an "elucidation," or *vārttika*, on Vātsyāyana's *Nyāya-sūtra* commentary. Others before Uddyotakara (whose name means "the enlightener") wrote commentaries on Vātsyāyana and the *Nyāya-sūtra*, but their work is lost. Uddyotakara is concerned to defend Naiyāyika views against Dignāga (c. 450), the Buddhist Idealist (see above, p. 21), who, though eventually eclipsed by the great Dharmakīrti (c. 625), originated both a theory of inference that rivalled Nyāya's and the *apoha* or "exclusion" theory of meaning and generality. The *apoha* theory of universals, which we reviewed following Dharmakīrti's thought, is present in Dignāga, and first resisted among Naiyāyikas by Uddyotakara.[21]

These three, then, Gautama with the *Nyāya-sūtra*, Vātsyāyana with his *Bhāṣya*, and Uddyotakara with his *Vārttika*, form the core of early Nyāya. No *Nyāya-sūtra* commentary after Uddyotakara is extant until that of Vācaspati Miśra I who flourished in the latter part of the tenth century. Vācaspati, we noted in the previous chapter, writes as an Advaita Vedāntin as well as a Naiyāyika—he wrote under still other philosophic banners also. Vācaspati does not mark by his Nyāya contribution, I argued, a compatibilist branch of Advaita that contrasts with that of Śrīharṣa, despite the fact that his objectivist and cosmological Advaita appears to make room for Nyāya world-oriented analysis. He wears more than one hat. Still, it is not from Vācaspati but from his near contemporaries of the Nyāya side, that there is expressed much belligerent opposition to Advaita. On the Nyāya side, outspoken opposition seems to commence with Bhāsarvajña, Śrīdhara, and, most notably, Udayana (more about whom below).

There are also two non-commentarial, independent treatises composed before Vācaspati that are extant, namely, the *Nyāya-mañjari* (*Compendium of Nyāya*), of Jayanta Bhaṭṭa (c. 875) and the *Nyāya-bhūṣaṇa* (*Ornament of Nyāya*), which is a commentary and elaboration of the author's own *Nyāya-sāra* (*The Essence of Nyāya*), by Bhāsarvajña (c. 950). Both works were widely read by later Naiyāyikas and became classics alongside the core material, with Jayanta's treatise perhaps slightly less important than Bhāsarvajña's. Both texts advance criticism of Buddhism and defenses against Buddhist attacks, focusing on Dharmakīrti, although there is also, particularly with Bhāsarvajña, criticism of Advaita. Both philosophers apparently lived in Kashmir.[22]

Vācaspati I and Udayana are the last two major Naiyāyika authors before Śrīharṣa. Their two *Nyāya-sūtra* commentaries close the Prācīna or Old Nyāya, though both, particularly Udayana, are responsible for innovations that are endorsed by Gaṅgeśa and the New school. Udayana, we noted, wrote a commentary on Praśastapāda's *Padārthadharmasaṃgraha*; he also wrote four independent treatises, two of which are long and enormously influential throughout the Navya movement.[23] He makes several advances in Naiyāyika theory, but is best known for his refutations of Buddhist positions and for his rational theology. However, he also clearly attacks Advaita (the reading that Udayana is a compatibilist is thus undermined[24]). Śrīharṣa knows Udayana's works well, and it often seems it is this particular Naiyāyika whom he has in mind when he attacks Nyāya views. Udayana could have provoked the barrage from Śrīharṣa: the Logician expressly defends the Nyāya view of distinctness, and launches a corresponding attack on the Advaita non-distinctness stance. A large portion of the passage (from Udayana's *Ātmatattvaviveka*) is quoted by Śrīharṣa verbatim and deconstructed and denounced.[25]

Udayana has been counted the founder of Navya Nyāya. But that judgment is misleading. As will be elaborated at the beginning of chapter 4, Gaṅgeśa, though following Udayana more closely than any other philosopher, establishes the traditional division between the Old and the New, with Udayana not on Gaṅgeśa's own side of the line. Furthermore, there is the matter of the Navya response to Śrīharṣa, not an inconsiderable factor, as will be shown. However, this study can hardly be the last word on who deserves credit for which thesis and innovative Navya technique. Nyāya literature proliferates enormously with Vācaspati I and Udayana through Gaṅgeśa and the host of Navya authors. Much must remain for future scholarship.[26]

3. Nyāya-Vaiśeṣika through Udayana

We turn now to the content of the philosophy as it had evolved (roughly) through Udayana. We begin with the more distinctively Vaiśeṣika, or ontological, side of the combined school: the theory of categories or types of things to which words refer (*padārtha*). The theory becomes increasingly sophisticated (particularly with respect to universals), and some of the earliest considerations weighed come to be taken for granted. Here I will try to be faithful to the earlier literature, and in later sections focus on refinements achieved by Udayana and other intermediate authors.

3.1. *What is Real: Theory of "Primitive Types" (padārtha)*

When we talk about the things we experience and interact with, and indicate and describe them, what in general are we talking about? The Vaiśeṣika answer[27] is that most generally there are three types of existent (*sat*). These are: (1) substances (*dravya*), including non-composite substances such as the atoms of the four atomic elements (earth, water, fire, and air); non-atomic substances such as space and time; and composite substances such as trees, houses, and people we know such as Devadatta; (2) qualities (*guṇa*), such as color, magnitude, weight, shape, et cetera, which, although they always appear *in* or as *qualifying* individual substances, are a radically different kind of thing (Buddhist Idealists vehemently dispute this position); and (3) motions (*karma*), such as moving straight ahead, upwards, and so on. (See figure 2.1.) An individual substance, such as a pot, can be the bearer of diverse qualities and motions. This is a fundamental plank of the earliest Nyāya as well as of Vaiśeṣika, and our realist philosophers never abandon it. That we can touch what we see is an early Nyāya argument used against Buddhist Idealists.[28] That the pot as property-bearer is distinct from its multiple properties is also said to account for its intersubjectivity—i.e., one and the same thing's perceptibility by different perceivers and by the same perceiver at different times.

Figure 2.1.

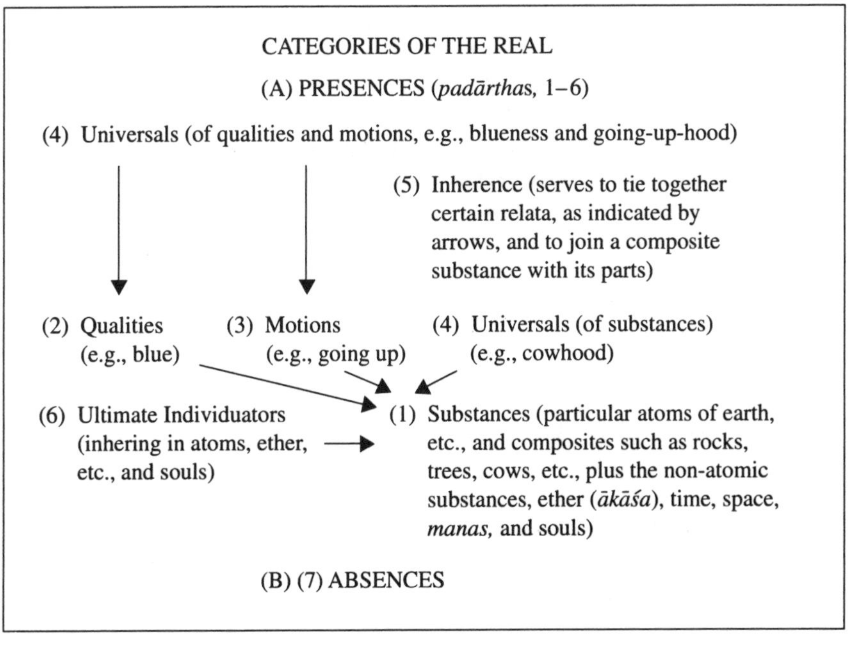

Qualities and motions are both thought of as properties (*dharmas*). Both appear in individual substances. But motions have causal effects that qualities by themselves do not have, in that they bring about conjunctions and disjunctions, for example.[29] Conjunctions, by the way, are relational qualities, pertaining to two particulars, as opposed to non-relational qualities, such as colors and shapes, that qualify single particulars.

Now while these three may be the most general types of existent that we talk about and experience, there must be other categories as well, things that do not "exist" in the way substances, etc., do, but which are present (*bhāva*) in the way the world is structured—as reflected by our modes of speech and revealed in our experience. One of these categories consists of (4) universals (*sāmānya* or *jāti*, "natural kinds"; see figure 2.1). Without now reviewing the full range of arguments used to defend universals, we can appreciate that the categories identified so far are universals, universals that, with the sole exception of "being-ness" (*sattā*), have the widest extension: "being a substance," "being a quality," and "being a motion" mark the first fundamental divisions of what is. Less extensive universals are the species of substance, etc., including such kinds as cowhood and humanity. Except for being-ness, the *summum genus*, the extension of every universal is included in that of a wider universal: all earthen things are substances, for example, and all substances exist; some universals, the *infimae species*, however, have extensions that include no sub-groups except for single-membered sub-groups, namely, the individuals that exhibit these universals, such as cowhood, for instance, whose extension is each and every cow. Moreover, every universal differentiates as well as groups together. Thus, no horse has cowhood. Universals differentiate the broad kinds recognized in everyday discourse.

Universals inhere inseparably in substance, quality, and motion particulars, but not in universals; universals are related to one another only by way of their extensions, i.e., the particulars in which they inhere. Thus potness, earthhood, substanceness, and being-ness are all present in a particular pot, and in all particular pots, though earthhood, etc., also appear elsewhere. A pot thus necessarily has potness, earthhood, etc.

The *Nyāya-sūtra* also contributes, in the *sūtras* themselves, to the theory of universals: when we say "Bessie is a cow," we imply that Bessie exhibits cowhood, the class character or the meaning of the general term.[30] Thus is recognized the semantic motivation for the theory, that we mentioned in discussing the grammarians. Moreover, as Uddyotakara argues, in identifying Bessie as a cow, we recognize a common or consecutive character (*anuvṛtti* or *anugata*) running through all individuals of that type, namely cowhood, what it is to be a cow.[31] Our experience of a common character (*anuvṛtti-pratyaya*) is evidence for a universal as the experience's ontological ground.

Nature exhibits repeatable features and recurrent kinds that are, on this view, *directly cognized* (not abstracted, as in Aristotle's view, whose thought in other respects resonates with the theory here). Now in the *Vaiśeṣika-sūtra*, universals seem to be any recurrent feature. But later, with Praśastapāda and others, universals come to be understood as natural kinds, the joints of nature, and thus differentiated from repeatable features that do not line up with nature's basic divisions. By the time of Udayana, a variety of considerations were understood to impinge on the theory of generality. Udayana brings them together in presenting restrictions on what counts as a true natural kind, restrictions that are, then, criteria for culling out abstract, surplus properties (*upādhi*). We will look closely at the arguments for universals, and in particular Udayana's reflection, two sections below.

A fifth basic category is (5) the "individualizer," *viśeṣa*. In a loose sense, individualizers and universals are correlate categories in that, except for "being-ness," universals exclude or particularize as well as include or group together: cowhood, for example, excludes horses, as well as groups together cows. This is recognized by the *Vaiśeṣika-sūtra*.[32] But the sense in which, according to Praśastapāda, individualizer is a basic category is as an *ultimate* particularizer (*atyanta viśeṣa*) inherent in non-composite individual substances, i.e., single atoms as well as non-atomic substances.[33] One reason the category is needed is that otherwise, individual atoms all of the same type (water, for example) would be identical: maybe a better translation of *viśeṣa* would be "numeralizer."[34] Since this category does not command much attention in the debate between Śrīharṣa and the Logicians, we will largely ignore it.[35]

However, individuation—beyond that accomplished by the special primitive, the individualizer—is an important topic. All substances, qualities, and motions exist as particulars, and only as particulars are they thought to be effects or causes. Not until the New Logic period is the particular discussed as (in effect) a distinct primitive, but even the earliest Logicians treat particulars as basic to the system. This is most evident in the discussions of the whole as (in many cases) something over and above its parts.[36] But Uddyotakara also makes several arguments against the Buddhist Idealist position that there is no meaningful distinction between the particular as property-bearer (*dharmin*) and its properties (*dharma*).[37] Not only (a) can we touch what we see—with the existence of the bare particular as property-bearer necessary to this possibility—and (b) perceive that something remains constant through the change of its properties, but also (c) all notion of similarity presupposes distinct individuals. Whether the similarity between two things is to be accounted for by a universal or not, whenever we experience or talk about two things as resembling one another, we presuppose two distinct individuals, two distinct property-bearers. A fourth argument (d) concerns counting. Two cows exhibit sameness, i.e., exhibit the universal cowhood, but as individuals they remain distinct. Otherwise, counting would be impossible.

The various ways Buddhists would explain such phenomena—by proposing, for example, that "configuration" performs the individuating work—are frauds, Uddyotakara and other early Logicians argue: "configuration" becomes a stand-in for what we Naiyāyikas mean by the existence of the individual property-bearer as distinct from its properties. Such arguments are voiced again by Udayana—and by New Logicians in responding to Śrīharṣa.

The penultimate category (6) is relational; it is inherence, or inseparable inherence, *samavāya*. Recall that this is the target of Śaṅkara's attack on relations, where he invokes the logic of the "Bradley problem." Chapter 5 includes a translation of Gaṅgeśa's reflection on *samavāya*, as well as portions of Śrīharṣa's sharp critique of the notion of relationality.

Now the term *samavāya* is artificially translated, whatever English word is used: the category is motivated by systematic needs. English perhaps best conveys an intuitive sense of the relating accomplished by *samavāya* in the meaning of the predicative copula.[38] Thus, when we say "This pot is blue," the pot is a substance and blue is a quality, and the "is" means inherence, *samavāya*. From an ontological perspective, in response to the question, "What relates the blue to the pot?" the answer is inherence. Inherence is a special ontic glue that binds qualities to substances, likewise motions, universals, and individualizers to substances, and universals to qualities and motions as well as to substances. It also has a mereological role, as I will explain.[39]

Except in the case of universals, any necessity in the connection occurs only in one direction. Qualities and motions, like universals, cannot exist disembodied; that is to say, they necessarily appear in substance particulars. But individual substances themselves are not red, e.g., necessarily, but persist, on this view, through qualitative change. Universals, in contrast, while necessarily *in re*—there are no universals apart from their instances—are also necessarily exhibited by their instances. A cow necessarily has cowness. Nevertheless, the inseparability of inherence is considered to be only a matter of the universal's dependence on its instances.[40] Inherence itself is invariably asymmetrical: a cow's necessarily having cowness is not attributed to the relator but to the nature of the relata.

Inherence performs still further work for the system: substances inhere in other substances. Thus we may understand the relation as that of a "nesting in."[41] A piece of cloth is nested in its threads, and the threads in what make them up, all the way down to atoms. Similarly, qualities, etc., are nested in individuals exhibiting them. A single grain of rice could be removed from a pile; each individual grain is related to others by conjunction, *saṃyoga*, or contact. Any conjunction, a quality, is by nature destructible; any two atoms could be disjoined.[42] Yet, a pile of rice would exist inseparably in the totality of the grains. Thus a whole X inheres in its parts. X and its parts are not the types of things that could be disjoined. Similarly, qualities, motions, and universals are thought to depend on their substrata; as noted, they do not exist independently, nor while they exist could they be disjoined, although motions and qualities can cease to occur while the substrata endure. I repeat, although a pot can be red at one time and then later black, the color is nested in the pot and is inseparably dependent on the substratum so long as the color remains.

There is difference of opinion concerning how inherence is known. The Nyāya view is generally that it is perceptible insofar as its relata are perceptible. But Praśastapāda says inherence is inferred. And he ties the epistemological question to the Bradley problem, or at least to one of the horns of the relation dilemma. It is worth looking at this bit of his text. The passage occurs, by the way, at the very end of the *Padārthadharmasaṃgraha*; in other words, this is Praśastapāda's way of closing his *Vaiśeṣika-sūtra* "commentary" that rearranges the topics of Vaiśeṣika philosophy. I translate:

> Question: By what kind of occurrence or relation (*vṛtti*) does inherence nest in [or occur in, *vartate*: a verbal form of the same root from which *vṛtti* is a derivative] substances and so on? Conjunction is ruled out, since as a quality it can reside in substances only. Nor can it be inherence, because that is unitary (not being able to perform two functions at once). Nor is there another type of relation or occurrence (in the system).
>
> Answer: This is mistaken. (The relating occurs) by identity. Similarly, there is no further connection with "being-ness" on the part of the kind of presence (*bhāva*, contrasting with absence, *abhāva*), that is of the nature of the existent pertaining to (the first three categories) substances, qualities, and motions (in which the universal, being-ness, inheres). In this way, we conclude: from the fact that there is no further relation (occurrence) of inherence, which is itself of the nature of a relation (occurrence, *vṛtti*) not separate (from its relata), (inherence is) self-relating (or self-occurrent, *svātma-vṛtti*). Therefore, (inherence is) beyond the range of the senses (and known only by inference). It does not occur in perceptible things in the same way as being-ness (and other universals) etc. do. Moreover, it is not known in and of itself (as some claim, e.g., consciousness is). Therefore, inherence is to be inferred from the cognition "(Something is) here (in this thing)."[43]

In this passage, Praśastapāda provides the germ of the Navya response to Śrīharṣa. Gaṅgeśa does alter and fill out the position. But it is much to Praśastapāda's credit that he sees that inherence has to self-tie, to relate to its relata by what it is.

Udayana makes much mention of inherence in his philosophic definitions, but he does not address the problem of what relates inherence to its terms, nor the question of how it is known.[44] It remains for him the fundamental relation, a relation that is, in sum, two-termed (except in its mereological role), irreflexive, non-transitive, and asymmetrical.

Finally, a radically different category is needed, a negative category as opposed to the previous six which are positive, the category (7) of absence, or negative fact. Udayana begins his *Lakṣaṇāvalī* (*Garland of Definitions*), by defining *padārtha* as that which can be named, and immediately proceeds to divide *padārtha*s into those that are positive (namely, the first six)—or that are presences, *bhāva*—as opposed to absences, *abhāva*, or negative facts.[45] Thus are delineated circles of reality: at the center are substances, qualities, and motions, things that exist; next come universals, individuators, and inherence, things that do not "exist" in that the universal "being-ness" (*sattā*) does not inhere in them, but that are present (*bhāva*) as revealed by our experience and everyday speech; next, absences, which neither exist nor are positive presences but are nevertheless real, or at least objective, as knowable (*jñeya*) and nameable (*abhidheya*); and last, beyond the pale of the real, the unreal, for example, a hare's horn on the table (there is an absence of horns on a hare but "absence of a hare's horn on the table" is nonsense) or the son of a barren woman. See figure 2.2.

Figure 2.2.

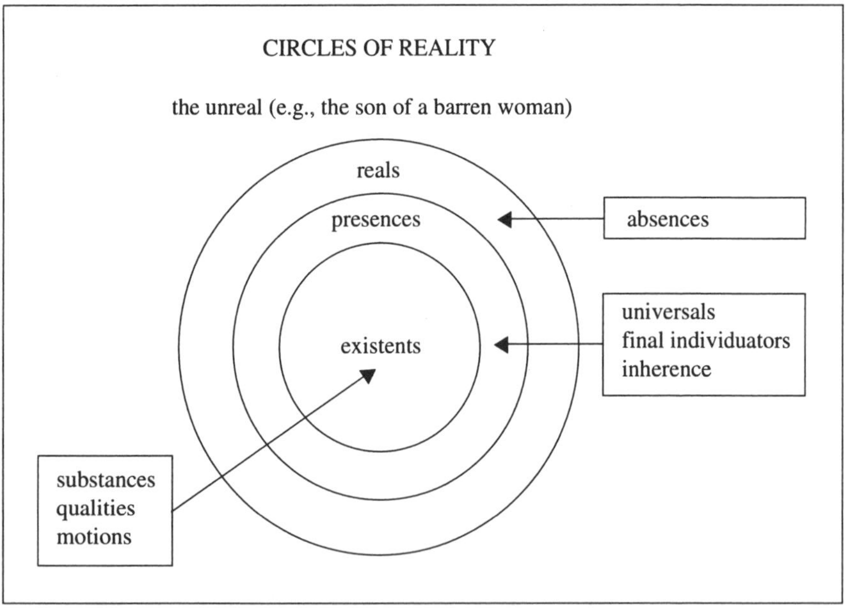

The posit of absence as an ontological primitive is motivated both semantically and epistemologically. The semantic consideration is that without absences it would be impossible meaningfully to deny anything—given an assumption of primary meaning as reference. When we deny that there is an elephant in the room, we mean that there is an absence, or lack, of an elephant there. Absences are the truth-makers of true denials. In the language of modern logic, negation is understood exclusively as of terms, not of sentences, quantifiers, etc. A second line of argument insists that we experience absences. If I am looking for my glasses, I see directly their *lack* on the table (i.e., the negative fact that they are not there). We experience lacks and do make denials, and this category accounts ontologically for these phenomena, Nyāya-Vaiśeṣika claims.

Types of absence are (1) prior absence, e.g., of a pot, before it is produced, (2) destructional absence, e.g., of a pot after it has been destroyed, (3) absolute absence, e.g., of color in air, and (4) mutual absence, or mutual exclusion, e.g., between a pot and a cloth (a cloth is not a pot and conversely a pot is not a cloth). Later, the division becomes that between relational absences on the one hand (1 through 3) and mutual exclusion (4) on the other.[46] The logic of these absences differ, particularly with mutual exclusion in contrast with the other three; nevertheless, all absences have an absentee, what the absence is *of*. (The absentee is termed in Sanskrit the *pratiyogin*, usually translated "counterpositive.")[47] Thus an absence of a pot on the floor has a pot as the absentee.[48] The logic of absences also involves location: absences invariably occur somewhere. Absences qualify a qualificandum, but do not inhere. Like inherence, they tie up with what they qualify just by the nature of what they are.

Almost every realist philosopher worries about precisely how absences are cognized; most seem to think they are directly perceived.[49] Cognition of a real absentee (previously experienced and remembered) plays a decisive role, however. So the cognizer furnishes, so to say, the absentee. Thus subjectivity has a more constitutive role here than in many other types of direct perception. (Is this a dangerous concession to idealism?)

There is no absence whose absentee is unreal: one speaks nonsense to say that there is no hare's horn on the floor. One can deny that hares have horns: an absence of horns obtains with hares. But no absence of a hare's horn obtains anywhere. A causal relation between the absentee and the locus of the absence runs through the cognizer and his or her memory.

Absence is a principal target of Śrīharṣa's attacks. Indeed, distinctness, or difference, *bheda*, is commonly understood by Naiyāyikas as equivalent to the species of absence called mutual absence, or mutual exclusion, *anyonyābhāva*. It is above all this that Śrīharṣa believes is incompatible with Brahman. Śaṅkara Miśra (c. 1430) entitles his counter-refutation of the Advaitin, *Jewel of Distinctness*, *Bhedaratna* (a portion of which is translated in chapter 5). As with inherence, we will carefully review the notion in later chapters.

3.2. Theory of Cognition and Justification

The foregoing ontology, or theory of categories, is matched by an equally important *pramāṇa* theory, or epistemology (*pramāṇa* = justifier or source of knowledge), coupled with a theory of cognition, *jñāna*.

The nature and number of *pramāṇa*s is a prime topic of intra-school debate from very early on, with the *Vaiśeṣika-sūtra* as well as the *Nyāya-sūtra* staking out explicit positions. Other early classical philosophies, such as Sāṃkhya, Yoga, Mīmāṃsā, and the Yogācāra Buddhist, specify two or more *pramāṇa*s. Indeed, Nyāya views emerged within such lively controversy that, long before Udayana, they had become highly refined.[50]

Some portions of the theory seem even Śrīharṣa-proof. The answer to an alleged justification regress appears so. To be sure, Śrīharṣa does claim, in an important passage, that the Nyāya view of justification succumbs to this fault, and he criticizes the Nyāya response to the regress charge as well. But his most extended assaults are mounted against definitions of individual *pramāṇa*—and this within the context of whether distinctness is proved. Perhaps because an answer to the alleged justification regress had become well known, Śrīharṣa occupies himself principally with the Nyāya views of "veridical awareness" (*pramā*), and of individual *pramāṇa* (especially perception and inference).

We saw in chapter 1 that the Buddhist Nāgārjuna challenges the *pramāṇa* project by asking, "What justifies the justifiers?" The first line of Nyāya reply: that depends on what you are worried about. Consider what you would do were you worried about the correctness of a scale used to weigh gold, Vātsyāyana says in commenting on *Nyāya-sūtra* 2.1.16, "As a scale can be an object of knowledge as well."[51] According to this earliest *Nyāya-sūtra* commentator, you would take a piece of gold to another scale—maybe two or three other scales—determine its precise weight, and bring it back to calibrate the scale in question. What was formerly an instrument in determining the weight of gold—thus a justifier in the sense that the scale is what is consulted for the weight of the gold—becomes what is justified, *prameya*, in this special instance. Similarly, the piece of gold, which was the object of knowledge, becomes an instrument of knowledge. There is no rule that a specific instance of a source of knowledge—whether perception, inference, analogical vocabulary acquisition, or testimony (the four *pramāṇa* recognized by Naiyāyikas)—may not itself become the object of inquiry. In that case, some other instrument or justifier would be employed.

"Then you are faced with an infinite regress, since the question would arise of what would justify that new instrument, *ad infinitum*." The Nyāya response to this criticism is fourfold: (a) to draw upon a theory of doubt, (b) to embrace a fallibilism, (c) to reveal a confusion about the charge of an infinite regress, and (d) to point to an invariable concomitance (*vyāpti*, "pervasion") between success in action and the cognition guiding action having a reliable source.

Doubt is meaningful only in certain circumstances.[52] Doubt provokes inquiry and attention to the sources of knowledge, but the cognitive default is "doubt-free." Normally, we do not need to wonder about justification. Meaningful doubt itself has grounds; all-encompassing doubt is self-defeating.[53]

Moreover, the process of questioning and providing justification normally ends somewhere. We make our best determination, that best supported by the evidence available. The determination may turn out to be wrong; there seems to be nothing in principle about which we might not be in error. Naiyāyikas are fallibilists. The central position is that cognition guides action. When circumstances lead to doubt, we find out enough to guide our behavior—which might involve our giving up some of our former opinions (nothing is held infallibly)—and go on with our lives.[54]

We will look for answers, say the Naiyāyikas, so long as you, or we, have meaningful questions. If you present an infinite series of meaningful questions, then so be it (though we doubt that you would have the time or energy for such a pursuit). But there is nothing *per se* wrong with an infinite series. Consider causal infinite series, as with a seed, a sprout, a seed, and so on. If you want us to answer what stands at the end of the series, we say that your question is framed in confused terms, that it could have no possible answer: infinite series have no ends. We will consider issues of justification as far back as you wish. But again, in our view, say the Naiyāyikas, we do not doubt every cognition just for the sake of doubting; we doubt and try to resolve doubt under circumstances that call for it, in other words, under circumstances where the doubt is meaningful.

If the question is, however, what justifies the entire *pramāṇa* program, the answer is inference, an inductive generalization from the success of action based on awareness arising out of *pramāṇa*. This is implied by Vātsyāyana's opening statements in his *NyS-Bh.* The answer invites the further question of the justification for inductive generalization, a question that Śrīharṣa insists upon, thereby prompting an explicit response from Gaṅgeśa, the founder of New Nyāya. This exchange is translated at the beginning of chapter 5. In brief, the answer is that it is presupposed in all acts of communication, such that no doubt about the general permissibility of inductive generalization could be meaningful (although particular inductive generalizations may be dubious and indeed proved wrong). We will look into this response later.

In general, Naiyāyika reflections on doubt, fallibility, and causal series arise out of a philosophy with a consistently hard-headed, commonsense, and pragmatic view of the world and how we know it. A complex of pragmatism, reliabilism, and a causal theory of knowing may indeed—as is recognized by teachers of the system, prior to Navya Nyāya—be said to be one side of the Nyāya realism, the epistemological half of the philosophy, with the other the

Vaiśeṣika ontology.[55] To point to the natural, causal process whereby a veridical awareness arises is to justify the proposition; the process is reliable, i.e., cognitively hooks one up with the world such that action can be successful. Indeed, one can assess the accuracy of one's awareness in light of the success or failure of actions that are guided by it. We will return to this picture in each of the chapters to come.

Pragmatism, reliabilism, and a causal theory of knowing are a complex of positions articulated by Vātsyāyana and the *Nyāya-sūtra* itself, although the positions are, to be sure, much elaborated and developed by Uddyotakara, Vācaspati, and Udayana, i.e., by each of the Prācīna *Nyāya-sūtra* commentators, and in the extra-commentarial literature as well.[56] We rely on our awareness to get what we want, and both our getting it and knowing it are natural, causal processes. The pragmatism, reliabilism, and causal theory are further refined by Gaṅgeśa. In chapter 4, we will see several instances of theoretic advance.

As mentioned, Śrīharṣa focuses, in an extended discussion, on definitions of individual *pramāṇa*, perception and inference in particular. Let us look briefly at these in the *Nyāya-sūtra* and other early works.

Naiyāyikas of all periods, including Gaṅgeśa and the New school, identify four *pramāṇa*s, all related to perception. The Logicians are empiricists in the precise sense of viewing perception as our principal cognitive link with the world. The three additional knowledge sources—inference, expert testimony, and analogical acquisition of vocabulary—are all related to perception in specific ways.

Perception is characterized at *Nyāya-sūtra* 1.1.4 as (1) a cognition (*jñāna*) (2) that arises out of the operative relation between an object and a sense faculty, (3) that is not intrinsically conceptual or verbal (although it is verbalizable), (4) that accurately presents the world (the term *pratyakṣa*, "perception"—like the English word "knowledge," whose meaning normally implies truth of belief—is used by Naiyāyikas only for veridical sensory cognitions[57]), and (5) that is sufficiently specific not to give rise to doubts (excluding, therefore, indistinct awarenesses, such as that prompting the doubt, "Is that in the distance smoke or dust?").

Every term in the definition (and sometimes the statement's syntax as well) receives oceans of attention in the *Nyāya-sūtra* commentaries and other early literature. We will return to portions of the discussion in chapters 3 and 4 in the context of Śrīharṣa's attacks. In chapter 4, we will review the fully elaborated theory of perception and awareness as we focus on the New school. Gaṅgeśa's treatment of perception is a significant advance. Śrīharṣa directs numerous objections against the Nyāya understanding of perception, as he sees, rightly, that it is crucial to the realists' upholding of *bheda*, fundamental distinctness among things.

Naiyāyika thought on the nature and scope of inference has gotten much modern attention, but it has often been misunderstood. Scholars projecting Aristotelian logic on Nyāya theory have misrepresented it.[58] A prime difficulty is that in this area, sustained progress occurs, particularly with Gaṅgeśa and the New school. Pronouncements generalizing over many centuries of logic are at extreme risk. In this chapter, I hazard only a rudimentary overview of early Nyāya, drawing principally on the *Nyāya-sūtra*, Vātsyāyana, and Uddyotakara.[59]

A good inference must have premises that are themselves justified. Naiyāyikas are concerned with what the world is like, and with inference just insofar as it reveals it. Thus Logicians do not distinguish between a formally "valid" deductive argument (which may or may not contain premises known to be false) and deductive arguments that are "cogent" (with no unjustified premises and no errors in the logic).[60] Though the Nyāya theory abstracts from all actual employment, it holds that any good inference must have a conclusion about the real world, a conclusion, that is, that should be believed because the premises should be believed and because a rule of inference has been correctly used.[61] The stock example:

1. There is fire on yonder hill. (This is the conclusion to be proved. How? By means of the following observations and connections:)
2. There is smoke rising from it. (We are justified in believing this because we *see* the smoke there—alternatively, because we are told smoke is there by someone who sees it. Further:)
3. Wherever there's smoke, there's fire. (We are justified in believing this because of wide experience of positive correlations, such as smoke and fire in kitchens, and negative correlations, such as the absence of smoke on a lake where there is absence of fire. In addition:)
4. This smoke-possessing hill is an example of the "wherever" of the general rule, "Wherever . . . " (Therefore:)
5. There is fire on yonder hill.

The logic is deductive, although premises are arrived at inductively. The reasoning is, then, defeasible or non-monotonic. That is to say, new information can affect the warrant of the general premise—i.e., the premise expressing invariable concomitance, or (literally) "pervasion," *vyāpti*, between two things *x* and *y*—in the example above, premise 3. Reasoning based on an assumption of *vyāpti* can in principle be defeated. The Naiyāyikas here as elsewhere are fallibilists;[62] pervasions are only fallibly known.[63]

Inference-grounding pervasions, *vyāpti*, are of different sorts, but they all obtain in nature, such as that between smoke and fire. The question of how these natural connections and relations that ground inferences are themselves known comes more and more to occupy great Naiyāyika minds. For Udayana, causal relations—which, as a kind of *vyāpti*, underpin inferences—are relations among universals. We can know that a particular x is invariably present where any particular y is present by knowing that x-ness and y-ness are suitably connected, Udayana says. Gaṅgeśa—indeed all Navya Nyāya—is also much occupied with pervasions, their nature, and how they are known. Issues surrounding inference-grounding *vyāpti* are on our agenda in all succeeding chapters.

The remaining two knowledge sources on the Naiyāyikas' list—specifically, analogy as a means of vocabulary acquisition and expert testimony—are not admitted by the early Vaiśeṣikas as distinct *pramāṇa*s. Vaiśeṣika agrees with Nyāya about the *pramāṇa* status of perception and inference, but analogy and testimony are viewed as types of inference.[64] The dispute is not severe in that it is only whether these two are reducible to the others. The same may be said for "presumption" (*arthāpatti*), which is a very important pattern of reasoning in philosophical debates and which is admitted by Mīmāṃsakas and others as a separate, irreducible *pramāṇa*. (A standard case: that Devadatta is fat and does not eat during the day entails that he eats at night. The debate is over the epistemological status of a hidden assumption.) The Naiyāyikas admit the validity of the pattern of reasoning, but say it is simply a type of inference.[65]

Expert testimony, in contrast, is defended by the Naiyāyikas as irreducible to perception and inference. An example would be that when I tell you something you did not know before, e.g., that I have a dog named Malone, you know it through my testimony insofar as I am an *āpta*, an "authority" on the subject. The question is then what in general makes a person an expert, and the answer is first, knowing and second, having no reason to lie or mislead.[66] (Śrīharṣa attacks this as circular and begging the question.)

There are also examples given—from Vātsyāyana on—of new vocabulary acquired through "analogical references," *upamāna*. Told that a water buffalo is *like* a cow except in certain respects, one, previously ignorant, acquires the term "water buffalo." This is proved by the ability to use the term correctly in identifying a water buffalo even for the first time.[67] According to most Naiyāyikas (though not all), knowledge of the term's meaning has as its source a *pramāṇa* irreducible to the other three.[68]

Finally, a few words about "cognition," *jñāna* (see the glossary entry), a term covering both awarenesses and rememberings. Cognition is the most central focus of Gaṅgeśa and the entire New school. Indeed, it is just in clarifying what cognition is—and in particular the causal conditions concerning types of veridical awareness—that the New Logicians, arguably motivated by problems Śrīharṣa identifies, make enormous strides. Much of what is brought out is presupposed by the earlier school, but, I would emphasize, it is merely presupposed, implicit in the early philosophy. However, from at least Vātsyāyana on, a cognition is viewed ontologically as a quality (*guṇa*), in the sense of the Vaiśeṣika category: a cognition is a quality inhering in the self or soul.[69] Cognitions are as such transitory and short-lived. That is to say, an individual has only one cognition at a time. Cognitions arise causally through certain processes, with certain instruments, e.g., the sense instruments (the eye, etc.), as key.

This ontological and causal perspective is developed in particular by Uddyotakara, and then filled out by Vācaspati and Udayana. Uddyotakara may be said to pave the way for the Nyāya-Vaiśeṣika synthesis with his theory of the "operative relation in sense perception" (*sannikarṣa* = *pratyāsatti*), in particular.[70] This is extremely important bridgework that Gaṅgeśa devotes much labor to defending. (It is crucial to his treatment of inherence: see below, pp. 241 and 243, for example, in the translation in chapter 5.) A causal story comes to be told about inferential cognitions as well, a story that Śrīharṣa tries to demolish and that is expanded by Gaṅgeśa and the New school.

Other important views concerning cognition will be elaborated in chapters 4 and 5, such as the distinction between the veridical and non-veridical. Cognitions can accurately present facts or be misleading. Furthermore, they provoke action. Cognitions leave traces preserved as memories and dispositions, *saṃskāra* (also *vāsanā*; see the glossary).

Vācaspati I, taking cues from Dharmakīrti, distinguishes between "indeterminate" and "determinate" cognitions.[71] Only the latter, he says, are conceptual and verbalizable, with the former as somehow raw data or pure sensations. The distinction comes to be a resource—and a headache sometimes—for Gaṅgeśa and the Navyas. We will review it in chapter 4 and then again in comments on translations in chapter 5.

Śrīharṣa, in turn, finds several difficulties with the entire Nyāya approach to what he calls consciousness and the intrinsic nature of the self, as we will see.

3.3. Generality

In the early literature of both the Vaiśeṣika and Nyāya schools, there was a vigorous debate with Buddhists about how to understand the respective roles of generality and particularity in various spheres: semantic, epistemological, and ontological. There was also on these topics much deepening of consideration on the part of the realists through elaboration of inherited commitments—involving some intra-camp squabbling over details. And much of this helps to fuel the fires of Śrīharṣa.[72]

Praśastapāda characterizes a universal as (in part) "what is identical among instances, the ground of the recurrent experience of itself (among its instances), subsisting wholly and equally among them."[73] That there is a recurrent experience of, e.g., cowness and that a universal is the experience's ontological ground emerges as the key argument against the Yogācāra Buddhists, who, as we saw, view experience as invariably of particulars, and concepts as imaginary constructions having, with regard to their generality, no ontological grounds. Praśastapāda seems to hold that an *anugata-pratīti*, "experience of a recurrent character," is sufficient perceptual evidence for a universal.[74] When we know two cows as both cows, a universal *accounts for* the identity of which we are aware. Moreover, argues Jayanta Bhaṭṭa, it is circular to hold with Dharmakīrti that a negative conceptualization, "not a non-cow," explains the experience of a common character running through the two objects, since negation of "non-cow" presupposes understanding what a cow is.[75] But, prodded by Buddhists,[76] Udayana and Navya-Nyāya philosophers come to realize that although all universals recur (ontologically speaking), experience of recurrence is not in itself sufficient for establishing a universal.[77] When there is a *jāti-bādhaka*, a condition blocking a universal, recurrence is not enough. Under certain circumstances, there can be an experience of recurrence without a universal as the experience's ontological ground. Udayana identifies six blocking conditions. (Śrīharṣa thoroughly exploits this retreat and the new "category" of surplus, abstract properties, *upādhi*, to which seeming or blocked universals are assigned.) We will review Udayana's list after surveying other props of the theory.

A second argument in support of universals is semantic. Universals must be introduced to understand the meaning of common nouns such as "cow," the Indian realists argue, as well as adjectives such as "blue" and verbs or action words such as "going." We use such words to refer to cows, etc., in general, that is to say, to refer to any and every cow, whether past, present, or future. The heart of the semantic argument is not to offer a reason for believing that we know the world the way it is, but to point out that unless the world exhibits general features we could not mean what we say. We do commonly presuppose that we mean what we say. Therefore, in practice we also presuppose that the world exhibits general features,[78] and the burden of proof has to be borne by those who would deny universals' reality.

Udayana presents a new causal argument, and develops the recurrent character argument in causal terms as well.[79] Causal relations—including the relations to objects of which our awarenesses are effects—are general in that they are lawful, and, though causal relations hold among particulars, they do so only in that particulars fall into kinds. Indeed, particulars are identified by the general features they exhibit. Whereas perception is a causal process invariably involving individuals—no universal can be perceived unless an individual in which it resides is perceived—universals are nevertheless epistemically prior in that only by means of lawlike causal relations—with universals responsible for the lawfulness—are we able to recognize an individual. Devadatta cannot be known except through general features he exhibits, such as being a human being, being male, etc.—features that regularly give rise to our experience of him.[80] Admittedly, we may not know the universals we experience perceptually *as* universals; even if we are able to say "cow" in the presence of Bessie, we might not recognize that we are beholding general features restricted to the natural kind to which she belongs. Recognition of universals in perception is dependent on training and breadth of experience, somewhat in the way that training is required to recognize a musical theme or a letter in an unfamiliar alphabet: universals are present in individual instances and may be recognized in a single perceptual cognition, but not everyone may be able to discern the pattern present.[81] Nevertheless, universals stand as indirect causes of bits of perceptual content through inhering, for example in the case of potness, in an individual pot in relation to a sensory faculty. In this way, the "experience of recurrent character" argument is understood in causal terms: we classify a new instance of a type X as an X presumably through the causal relation between that thing and our perception. A cow is classified as a cow because our perception of it is caused by what it is.

Thus Udayana ties together the necessary generality in our experience of a particular with the general element in all causal relations. Threads make up a cloth not as conjunctions among atoms or potential material for a bird's nest, but as threads, i.e., as instances of the universal threadness. It is as instances of this universal that the particulars stand in a causal relation to a particular piece of cloth, itself an effect of these causes insofar as they exhibit the universal clothness. Udayana gives a similar analysis of the relation of smoke and fire. In sum, universals account for the generality in causal relations among particulars.

Some scholars have claimed that Udayana offers this view of causal relations—coupled with Naiyāyika ideas about how universals are known—as a solution to the problem of how causal relations are known in their generality.[82] Universals are known through perception, at least insofar as the individuals they rest in are perceptible (atomhood is imperceptible because atoms are imperceptible). They ride piggy-back on individuals in the causal processes of knowing. So when these threads are known as the cause of this cloth, it is understood that all such effects, past, present, and future, have such causes. We do not have to have experience of future instances of smoke and fire to know the causal relation, because that relation crucially involves universals. Thus a further argument for universals would be that they are required to solve the problem of inductive generalization. The dispute among Udayana, Śrīharṣa, Maṇikaṇṭha Miśra, and Gaṅgeśa over this is presented in the translations that open chapter five.

Finally, let us review Udayana's renowned list of *jāti-bādhaka*s, conditions that "rule out (seeming) natural kinds." These, together with the definition that Praśastapāda provides[83] (on whose work Udayana is commenting), may be construed as a set of necessary and sufficient conditions for a natural kind.[84] Apparently, Udayana allows "conditional" or "accidental" (*aupādhika*) universals that fail to count as true natural kinds because of failing one of these tests, specifically, the third.[85] As will be elaborated in chapter 4, the distinction between these two types of universals (accidental and natural) becomes especially important with New Logic. Udayana, however, does not at all elaborate; his treatment is exceedingly brief; and at other places he uses the terms *jāti* (natural kind) and *sāmānya* (universal, including the accidental variety) synonymously. As presented immediately below, the conditions specified govern what it is to be a natural kind (*jāti*), and presumably all but the third condition (*jāti-saṃkara*) would rule out as well bogus "accidental universals."

(1) No natural kind (or universal) has only one instance; thus "spaceness" is not a true universal because there is only one space (as is implied by Praśastapāda's definition[86]). (2) When two apparent universals have precisely the same instances, there is only one universal with two conventional names; thus "mankind" and "humanity" are the same universal. In terms of modern set theory, this restriction says that two sets with the same members are the same set (the axiom of extensionality). (3) No intersectional, or cross-sectional, natural kinds are allowed (*jāti-saṃkara*). If two apparent natural kinds have even one instance in common without one of the two being present in every instance of the other, then neither is a true natural kind. This, the most contentious requirement, is responsible for culling out accidental universals (*aupādhika sāmānya*). It is apparently motivated by a sense that true natural kind characters—as opposed to features of things merely shared across kinds and cognitively abstracted—mark fundamental divisions in nature that cannot be bridged by any wider natural kind. A wider natural kind must entirely include the instances of one less wide. We will consider this requirement further after reviewing the remainder of the list. (4) Any apparent universal that would lead to an infinite regress is ruled out. Thus "universalhood" is not a true universal.[87] This requirement is connected to the overall realism of Udayana's position: true universals are found in nature and thus no universal should be, so to say, merely generated by the mind.[88] Then (5) there is no universal "ultimate-individualizerhood" since the work done by an ultimate individualizer is to particularize—the ultimate atoms, for example—and a universal here would block that work.[89] (6) There is no universal

"inherencehood." Inherence is the relation whereby particulars and universals are bound together. There could be no relations of this sort were there an "inherencehood," because this would require a further relation (R_2) to tie together the inherence (R_1) and "inherencehood," *ad infinitum*. (Note that this is called the "non-relation" blocker, while (4) is called the "infinite-regress" blocker.) Of course, this restriction does not constitute a solution to the problem of a relation regress, the Bradley problem. But here Udayana apparently recognizes that Nyāya realism demands that the problem be in principle resolvable. Inherence relates reals, and is itself a real. No notion can be brooked that would make inherence unable to perform its task.

Let us consider the rule that allows no "cross-section" (*jāti-saṃkara*) among true natural kinds. An example is "being an element," a property whose instances form a class some of whose members are also instances of "being corporeal" (i.e., having a material form of limited size), while others are not. Similarly, some things that are corporeal (having limited size) are elements and some are not. Thus both "elementhood" and "being corporeal" are abstract properties, or accidental universals. "Earthness," in contrast, is a true natural kind. A particular pot is (a) a pot, (b) earthen, (c) a substance, and (d) exists—all according to the kind of thing it naturally is. But its being a locus of "elementhood" may not be understood in this fashion. See figure 2.3.

Figure 2.3.

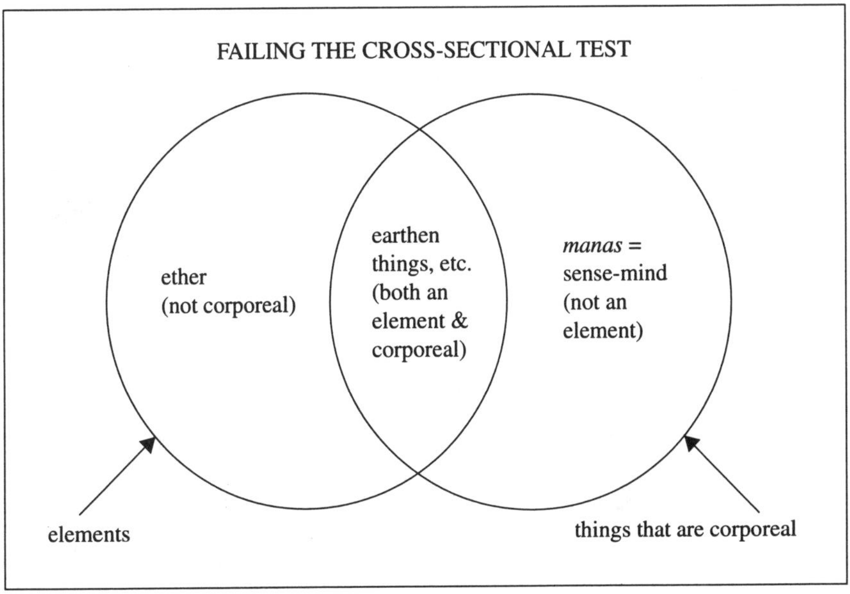

There is a hierarchy of natural-kind universals, not in the sense of disembodied reals inhering one in another, but in terms of extension. The extension of a lower natural-kind universal is included in that of a higher, or, more accurately, a wider; for example, "existence" is wider in extension than "substancehood," "substancehood" wider than "earthness," and "earthness" wider than "potness." The extension of a wider natural-kind universal includes another's extension in its extension—up to the widest natural-kind universal, "existence."

"Elementhood" cross-sects "being corporeal" since the elements earth (and things made out of earth), water, air, and fire are corporeal while another element, ether (*ākāśā*), for instance, is not corporeal. Further, *manas*, the internal organ, which channels different perceptions to the individual self's awareness (see the glossary entry), is thought to be corporeal (and of limited size), but not an element. Thus neither of the two abstractions—"elementhood" and "being corporeal"—is a true natural kind.[90]

According to this system, everything we talk about—every object of experience—can be analyzed into the natural kinds which it instances. Natural kinds are fundamental realities; they are not themselves analyzable into more basic types. For example, Devadatta's pot, as a natural kind, is a pot, earthen, a substance, and an existent. Nothing more can be said about these (except to give further examples). Thus unanalyzability is an implicit criterion: if a recurrent character is composite, it is not a natural kind. Moreover, "belonging to Devadatta" is not native to the pot *qua* the object it is; it could be sold to someone else. But it could not cease to be a pot, earthen, and so on. Qualities, by the way, do not "cross-sect" with substances. So given that Devadatta's pot is blue, the coloredness would be a true natural kind (some would say this of "blueness" as well, as found in peacock feathers, the sky, and elsewhere), although a kind with a lesser extension than "qualityhood," which is also a true natural-kind universal.

Finally, there is some confusion, or at least dissension, among our realists (and modern interpreters) about the eternality of universals, a position put forth in the *Vaiśeṣika-sūtra* and elaborated and defended by Praśastapāda (among others). That universals are eternal in a timeless sense seems to be the considered opinion. Even if all cows were to cease to exist, the universal would, in a sense, continue to subsist, and we would refer to it were we to say, "Bessie *was* a cow." Or, the eternity of universals may be interpreted as simply another way of saying that a universal is what is *constantly* the same in the particulars in which it resides.[91] Bessie and her great-grand-sire are identical in respect of being cows: "cowness" captures what is constant among all particular cows. Furthermore, universals have a different mode of existence from that of particulars, and so their eternity is distinct from what that of an everlasting individual would be (such as God), though, again, if there were never to be at least two particulars of a type, past, present, or future, there would be no universal as well. The temptation to interpret the Indian realists as proposing an other-worldly existence for universals in virtue of the constancy claim is due mainly to the influence of platonism in the West—perhaps also due to the Nyāya epistemic position that, as explained, universals are prior in the order of knowing, i.e., only by means of general features are we able to come to know particulars. Śrīharṣa has a thorough familiarity with the theory and knows well its weak spots—often he tries to exploit the "eternity" claim.[92]

3.4. Definitions in Philosophy

Vātsyāyana, in his introductory commentary on *Nyāya-sūtra* 1.1.3., says: "This science (*śāstra*) proceeds in three ways: naming (or pointing out topics), definition (or characterization, *lakṣaṇa*), and critical examination (of these)."[93] He also says, equivocally, that a definition is the characteristic (*dharma*) that distinguishes what is named or pointed out from everything that is not that.[94] Uddyotakara explains that a definition, *lakṣaṇa*, as an activity of philosophy, identifies a characteristic mark, *lakṣaṇa*, as what differentiates one type of thing from everything else.[95] Thus we would be better able to understand the types of things talked about by being able to identify what is an X and what is not. Nyāya philosophic definitions are characterizations focused on differentiating marks.

A second type of definition shows the ground for the use of a word (*vyavahāra*). Here it is the class character, a universal (*jāti*) or recurrent abstract property (*upādhi*), that does the work. For example, cowhood is the ground of the employment of the word "cow." The idea is that one must recognize the class character in order to correctly use the word.[96]

The first type of definition is real, focused on things, not words, in particular on those characteristics that differentiate one type of thing from others. For example, a cow is a distinct type (partly) in virtue of possessing a dewlap. Thus a suitable definition, *lakṣaṇa*, of a cow is that which has a dewlap, and—with the term *lakṣaṇa* used in the sense of a defining characteristic—a dewlap would be a *lakṣaṇa* of a cow.

Again, the term *lakṣaṇa* in its first sense is more "characterization" than "definition"; but "definition" has become the standard translation, and I will usually follow that practice. And it is philosophic or real definitions that will principally concern us, although at the end of this section I will say a few more words about the second, nominal type.

Udayana establishes the Nyāya tradition of a fixed form for good philosophic definitions, although he views the nature of Gautama's *NyS* definitions, as understood in particular by Uddyotakara and Vācaspati I,[97] and

Praśastapāda's Vaiśeṣika definitions as well, as conforming (usually) to his formula. A definition can be reconstructed as an inference. For example, "Everything earthen is distinct from everything non-earthen, because everything earthen is odorous," is an inference defining earthen by the characteristic of having odor. Here the term referring to what is to be defined, the definiendum (*lakṣya*), in this case "earthen," and that picking out the defining mark, "odor," in relation to the definiendum, have to be co-extensive, *samaniyata*.[98] Co-extensiveness is understood as a pervasion, and thus the inference can be constructed.

To take another example, if each and every cow has a dewlap and nothing else has one, then to characterize a cow as the possessor of a dewlap is to formulate a good definition. Thus three faults that definitions are subject to are: (1) over-extension, e.g., "horn-possessing" for cows, (2) under-extension, e.g., "being spotted," and (3) missing altogether what is to be defined, e.g., "having whole, or non-split, hooves."[99] These correspond to possible faults in the *hetu*, "reason" or "mark" of an inference, and in general the strictures on good inferences govern good definitions as well. Śrīharṣa often tries to show that a Logician definition fails on one of the three counts—as well as in other ways that presuppose the inference conversion. That a definition can be understood as an inference is, in sum, one key to his critiques.

Note that the defining mark does not have to be related to the definiendum as its class character or essence. Any feature of the definiendum that, as a matter of fact, belongs to all things of that type, and to nothing else, is suitable. This is important for distinguishing the Nyāya definitional project from the Aristotelian—as well as from the nominal definitions already mentioned as a second type within the Indian tradition (a cognition of "cowness" is the reason for use of the word "cow"). Śrīharṣa, however, sometimes bases his criticism of Logician definitions on this latter, lexical notion, where universals or essences are relevant to the formulation, as we will see.

Differentiating (philosophic) definitions are understood to be subject to further strictures than those deriving from the co-extensiveness requirement converting the definition into an inference. These are difficult to specify precisely, although Udayana lists varieties of dialectical reasoning (*tarka*)[100] and thereby seems to have suggested to Śrīharṣa additional ways to attack the definitions of Nyāya. Dialectical reasoning (*tarka*, sometimes translated "induction" or "indirect proof") is championed by Logicians as a way to help someone—or to lead an opponent—to recognize a pervasion or, in general, the truth of a Nyāya tenet, by entertaining an opposing view. Faults such as infinite regress are identified by Udayana as revealed by means of dialectical reasoning, and should lead to the relinquishment of an erroneous premise. But just how philosophic definitions are to be free of these is not as clear-cut as with formal inferential pitfalls. Śrīharṣa makes the Naiyāyikas think more deeply on this issue. In order to appreciate the *informal* fallacies, we will now review the broader context of debate and Nyāya debate theory.

3.5. Theory of Debate

Details of the rich Nyāya informal logic and theory of debate would take us far beyond what is most central in the realist/idealist controversy; we will take only an overview. With regard to commonly recognized fallacies, inadequate rejoinders, and debating errors calling for censure, New Logicians commonly treat Śrīharṣa as one of their own. They reflect on his opinions as though they were advanced by a Naiyāyika with slightly strange views.[101] Thus both Śrīharṣa and the New Logicians can be viewed as building on the debate theory and informal logic developed in early Nyāya.

However, Śrīharṣa hotly disputes the issue of pre-requisites of debate. Even if here, too, he can be seen as contributing to a common discipline, his commitment to Advaita also motivates his reasoning. We will look quickly at early Nyāya views on this score better to understand Śrīharṣa's polemic.

To complete this section, we will also look quickly at early Nyāya views of "dialectical reasoning" (*tarka*). The great Gaṅgeśa himself, as well as Maṇikaṇṭha, responds to Śrīharṣa on dialectical reasoning. Chapter 5 opens with each of the three, the Advaitin and the two Logicians, addressing the topic.

Nyāya-sūtra 4.2.48–50 implies that one should take into account considerations of personal character (including the nature of beliefs held) in deciding a strategy of debate. Debate presupposes controversy, but controversy can occur (a) among people committed to ascertaining the truth—when there are good grounds for doubt and diversity of opinion—or (b) among disputants with questionable motives. Very different strategies are to be employed in, on the one hand, debate or inquiry aimed at discovering the truth (*vāda*), and, on the other, wrangling and captious argument (*jalpa* and *vitaṇḍā*), whose purpose is to defeat a malevolent adversary and to protect right views from malicious public attack, as thorns are used to fence and protect young shoots.[102] The *Nyāya-sūtra* lays out a procedure of inquiry with a degree of sophistication extraordinary for its early date, a procedure that is extraordinarily open and undogmatic as well. The basic principle is that when there is reasonable disagreement, throwing a topic into question and arousing doubt on all sides, investigation in accordance with reliable sources of information is to be undertaken to resolve it. But over the centuries, indeed in the *sūtra*s of the *Nyāya-sūtra* itself, the results of such investigations apparently became official Nyāya doctrine. Thus, though the theory of inquiry and good-faith debate remains relatively constant, the criteria governing who was to be considered a good-faith partner in philosophic inquiry and who a target for tricky arguments came to include a person's endorsing the results of earlier inquiry, namely, planks of both Nyāya epistemology and the metaphysics of realism.

Śrīharṣa complains against the precept—the canonized procedure of critical inquiry—that a debater has to argue according to what Naiyāyikas recognize as the sources of knowledge, the "justifiers" (*pramāṇa*), in order not only to win a debate but even to be admitted as a debate contestant or fellow philosophic inquirer. As early as Vātsyāyana, suspicion is expressed concerning those purporting to demolish others' views without trying to establish their own.[103] At *Nyāya-sūtra* 4.1.37–39, there is this argument against the Mādhyamika Buddhist: if a reason is proffered in support of the thesis that all things are non-existent or empty, then the reason itself, counting as something existent and non-empty, contradicts the thesis it is supposed to establish.[104] Thus, if the Mādhyamika presents a reason, he loses because of inconsistency with the meaning of his assertion, and if he claims not to have a reason, he is to be regarded as something like a lunatic. It seems, therefore, to be understood that if one does not accept the Nyāya program of what counts as a good reason, one should not be accepted as a fellow inquirer reasoning in good faith. It is this presumption that Śrīharṣa objects to. The fact that so many New Logicians comment on and respond to his book suggests that he wins the point, although, as we will see, Śaṅkara Miśra revives the lunatic charge (below, p. 286).

Dialectical reasoning, *tarka*, is on the list of sixteen topics enumerated at *Nyāya-sūtra* 1.1.1. At 1.1.40, dialectical reasoning is defined, and at 2.1.1 it is mentioned along with "justifiers" (*pramāṇa*) as part of the method of discussion aimed at ascertaining the truth (*vāda*). In his commentary to 1.1.40, Vātsyāyana explains that though dialectical reasoning is not an independent source of knowledge, or justifier, it is used to determine just what is the source of a particular bit of information and thus can help show what justifies a particular claim. By dialectical reasoning, alternatives are eliminated through a demonstration of contradictoriness, or of another fallacy, and thus a right position can be honed in on. But no truly warranted view can be supported by dialectical reasoning alone, for dialectical reasoning is not an independent source of knowledge.

Udayana provides what appears to be the first classification of varieties of dialectical reasoning, after first roughly defining it.[105] He provides only a list; he does not elaborate any of the types (having introduced the topic in the midst of some tight argumentation concerning atoms and God). The five types are: (a) self-dependence (*ātmāśraya*), (b) mutual dependence (*itaretarāśraya*, more commonly called *anyonyāśraya*), (c) circularity (*cakraka*), (d) (vicious) infinite regress (*anavasthā*), and (e) undesired ramification (*aniṣṭa-prasaṅga*). The fifth variety appears to be a catch-all, or another characterization of dialectical reasoning in general, in that all *tarka* involves showing an undesired ramification of an alternative hypothesis. New Logicians explain, expand, and modify the list, with the fifth item tending to be replaced. Śrīharṣa replaces it with (e) contradiction (*vyāghāta*), and (f) *tu quoque* or "two wrongs make a right" (*pratibandhī*).[106] The Advaitin also suggests five additional varieties of dialectical reasoning, and specifies some common types of seeming or fallacious dialectical reasoning as well. We will look closely at his treatment—and its context—in the next chapter and then again in chapter 5. This is an important topic, since it is crucial not only to what Śrīharṣa takes himself to prove or disprove, but also to the realist response as well.

3.6. Rational Theology

Udayana and some New Logicians spend much effort on proofs of the existence of God. For the most part—or, more precisely, from the later periods of the Old school—Logicians are theists, as are Atomists, although until Jayanta and Vācaspati I, whose theism probably reflects wider cultural developments, the commitment is weak at best and problematic.

Debiprasad Chattopadhyaya argues that the *Nyāya-sūtra* is itself atheistic.[107] Clearly, theism is not prominent, for the word *īśvara*, "God," occurs only once, at *Nyāya-sūtra* 4.1.19. And the *Vaiśeṣika-sūtra* does not have even a single mention. Scholars generally agree that theism is introduced by Praśastapāda into the Atomist system. John Vattanky, on the other hand, presents a theistic reading of the *Nyāya-sūtra*, focusing on *Nyāya-sūtra* 4.1.19 and the two *sūtra*s that follow.[108] My own sense is that, with respect to the *Nyāya-sūtra*, Chattopadhyaya makes the stronger case. A system-related need for God comes to be recognized, but none is recognized in either *sūtra* text, nor by Vātsyāyana. According to Chattopadhyaya, Praśastapāda, under the pressure of Buddhist Idealists, comes to see a systemic need for God: the Buddhists argue that the antinomy of combinations of partless indivisibles shows the external world to be unreal, and Praśastapāda apparently can find no way to solve the problem except to bring in God.[109] Apart from the debate theory of Nyāya (which also does not involve theological suppositions, with one qualification, to be explained just below), both Atomism and Logic are in their earliest forms decidedly oriented toward nature and the proper understanding of nature—including human nature and our ways of cognizing—not toward God or any supernatural realm. The theistic affinities of later Nyāya-Vaiśeṣika are probably best understood as reflecting broad-based cultural movements.

A theme of a moral order in the universe is prominent in the *Nyāya-sūtra* itself, however. It is highlighted by Vātsyāyana and becomes a plank of all later Nyāya philosophy, eventually trimmed to dovetail with Nyāya theism. Moral payback is assured by the fundamental nature of things—if not in a current lifetime then in lifetimes to come will one reap the harvest of good and bad deeds. Such a belief in *karma* (see the glossary, the second sense of the term) and rebirth is pan-Indian in the ancient and early classical periods. Atheistic Buddhism and Brahminical Exegesis (Mīmāṃsā), which is also officially atheistic, endorsed such views, as did the moderately theistic metaphysic of Yoga; Nyāya surely did not stand alone with this thesis. But again, Nyāya eventually gives a theistic explanation of karmic payback—which in the context of our focus is perhaps most important with regard to the judgment concerning who may be viewed as having the character necessary for good-faith debates. Logicians come to be suspicious of those who do not believe in God, as theism, indeed monotheism, becomes increasingly prominent in the subcontinent.

Thus later Naiyāyika theists come to have much in common with Vedāntic theists who combat exegetically the Advaitic reading of the Upanishads. The two groups come to be at least loosely allied, although it is a comparatively limited deity that Udayana and most other Logicians endorse. As mentioned in the previous chapter, the most important difference between the two camps is that neither mystical experience nor the sanctity, the self-authenticating trustworthiness of scripture—the revelations of the Upanishads—are the Logicians' avowed reasons for their theistic views. Whereas theistic Vedāntins take the authority of the Upanishads as preëminent in philosophy, Naiyāyikas say that certain arguments ground their belief in God.

This is not to say that Logicians are as a group uninterested in yoga and mystical experience, although interest is decidedly more marked in the earlier period. The *Nyāya-sūtra* devotes numerous *sūtra*s to these topics. *Nyāya-sūtra* 4.2.47 explicitly endorses "yoga *śāstra* (science)," and in his commentary on the statement Vātsyāyana mentions some of the very practices spelled out in the *Yoga-sūtra*. The authority of scripture (i.e., the Veda) is said to be based, in the early period, on the authoritativeness of mystics presumed its authors. Vācaspati I and Udayana make God the author of scripture. Nevertheless, the avowed reasons for belief in God remain foremost inferences from certain presumed facts about the universe.

For example, Udayana argues cosmologically in support of a Creator: "The earth, etc., being effects, presuppose a cause that produces them."[110] As from an awareness of a pot as an effect, we can infer the existence of its instrumental cause, the potter, so from our experience of the world as an effect, we can infer the existence of God.[111] Such arguments, some of which are similar to arguments advanced in the history of Western rational theology, are not prominent with Vedāntins.

Udayana opens his *Nyāyakusumāñjali*, which is a long work devoted exclusively to the case for God, with the claim that what each and every individual faction sees as the Supreme (Brahman with Advaitins, the unattached "pure conscious being," *puruṣa*, with Yogins, the Buddha in his Bliss with Bauddhas, and so on), is nothing other than the one God whose existence Udayana is about to prove on other grounds.[112] Such inclusivism resonates with what some have called the universalism of the Veda (or its henotheism)—one God taking many forms—and is admirably defended in the modern period by such cultural giants as Ram Mohan Roy, Vivekananda, Aurobindo, and Sarvepalli Radhakrishnan. But, concerning classical Nyāya, although from Uddyotakara on there is some speculation about the nature of God,[113] nowhere that I know of does Udayana or any Naiyāyika produce a theology that synthesizes—or even seriously attempts to synthesize—the diverse classical conceptions of a supreme being or transcendent reality. My impression is that a vague theological universalism was honored culturally, and that Udayana's apparent endorsement of it is mostly hand-waving.

A final note. Nyāya objectivism and realism fit nicely with its theism. God has the perfect bird's-eye view. Everything is knowable though not everything is by human beings known. Human beings have limited cognitive capacities; many knowables remain unknown to us. But not to God. God knows everything as it is, and the objectivism implied may be taken to function eventually (perhaps as early as Vātsyāyana) as a heuristic for human knowledge.

4. Mīmāṃsā (Exegesis)

The classical school Mīmāṃsā, "Exegesis," is arguably the oldest among all the Indian schools. Its root text, the *Mīmāṃsā-sūtra*, dates to the first century BCE. This work is concerned foremost with the proper interpretation of texts viewed as revealed, namely the Veda and various appendages. As mentioned in the previous chapter, the Veda is a collection of ancient hymns and poems (c. 1200–900 BCE, prior to the Upanishads) in an archaic Sanskrit. The Exegetes looked at the Vedic literature with an eye in particular to questions of *dharma*, "duty" or "right practice," which they understood chiefly as the performance of certain rituals by a hereditary class of priests, but also as restrictions on marriage and caste interactions in general. The school may be viewed as a response to an attack on the meaningfulness of these rituals (and restrictions) and thus on the livelihood of the priests who performed them. In sum, in the earlier centuries the Exegetes are defenders of the Veda, the caste system, and certain religious rituals.

Later, Exegetes often debated Buddhists in the courts of kings and wealthy patrons, and tried to refute their arguments. The Exegetes wholeheartedly embraced realism, apparently influenced by Nyāya: objects of consciousness exist independently of it. And over time they took up almost all the philosophical topics addressed in rival schools, working out theories of their own on a wide range of issues. Such an expansion of interest parallels the development of Buddhist philosophy and of other, less conservative, Hindu schools. The key figures in this expansion are Kumārila Bhaṭṭa (c. 660) and his renegade pupil Prabhākara (c. 700). These two and their followers bring Mīmāṃsā reflection on semantics and philosophy of language in particular to great heights. And, I repeat, the Exegetes develop views on many of the issues—the self and self-awareness, the reality of the external world, justification and canons of debate and argument—that occupied Naiyāyikas, Buddhist Idealists, and philosophers generally of the eighth century and thereafter in classical India. Because of the shared realism, there are several authors in the long history of classical thought who write both as a Naiyāyika and a Mīmāṃsaka. In the areas of epistemology and philosophy of language, Mīmāṃsakas develop views at a further remove from Nyāya, especially in epistemology.

Mīmāṃsā philosophy remains vibrant through the time of Gaṅgeśa. Indeed, one of the New Logician's tasks he sets for himself is to distinguish his views from the often similar views of Exegetes and to show the latter's inadequacy. However, in the earlier periods, Buddhists are, we must bear in mind, clearly the principal rivals of Logicians—and of Exegetes as well.

Its realism notwithstanding, Mīmāṃsā stands close to Śrīharṣa's Advaita, and all Vedānta, in viewing a revealed text as the source of the most important positions: in the one case, trans-empirical views about *dharma*, "duty"; in the other, trans-empirical (or at least trans-perceptual) views about *brahman*, the Absolute and sole reality. Thus in the widest analysis, Mīmāṃsā stands as closely allied to Advaita—despite the latter's idealism—as to empiricist Nyāya. Indeed, Śrīharṣa often lifts arguments from Mīmāṃsā, in particular from Kumārila. Mīmāṃsakas develop an epistemology centered on the idea of a revealed text, an epistemology taken over by Advaita and upheld by Śrīharṣa as the mainstay of his positive philosophic program. This is the doctrine of awareness as "self-certifying," *svataḥ pramāṇa*, a view to which Logicians of all periods are adamantly opposed.

According to one version of the self-certification theory, that of the Prabhākara camp, every awareness, *qua* occurrent, is veridical and is known to be so—or, we might say, every awareness occurs pretending to be veridical. Only non-veridicality is known extrinsically, through a process whereby a later awareness reveals the composite nature of a former, as a fusion of an immediate awareness and a memory. Thus the same causal nexus that produces an awareness produces knowledge of its veridicality. On an alternative, Bhāṭṭa theory (deriving from Kumārila), veridicality is known through a process of inference: this would be the same process of inference whereby an awareness itself would be known as having occurred. An awareness produces a feature in the object it cognizes, namely, "cognizedness," and then from apprehension of this feature both the original awareness and its veridicality are known. Thus there is no difference between knowing an awareness as a fact, and knowing it as veridical. On a third view—identified by Gaṅgeśa's commentator Mathurānātha as forged by the thirteenth-century Mīmāṃsaka, Murāri Miśra—veridicality is also known by a subsequent cognition. But this is not, as with the Bhāṭṭa theory, an inference; rather, it is an "after-cognition" (or apperception, *anuvyavasāya*). This third Mīmāṃsaka view is close to the Nyāya view, an "extrinsic" view of certification. An extrinsic view is developed by Gaṅgeśa, as will be elaborated in chapter 4. But inasmuch as on the Murāri theory veridicality is intrinsic to the original awareness and nothing more is required with respect to knowledge of it than simply an "after-cognition" that takes the former cognition as its object, this view too is an "intrinsic" theory of certification. Thus, on all three Mīmāṃsaka views, every awareness is understood to be certified within its own occurrence. The differences concern how precisely the veridicality is known.[114]

Note, finally, that Śrīharṣa's position is closest to that of Kumārila. We will look closely at the Advaitin's version of self-certification in the next chapter.

5. Other Players Pre-Śrīharṣa

Contributors to the realist-idealist debate who fly banners other than what we have seen so far are Jainas and Cārvākas. Jainism is a religious movement that has much in common with Buddhism despite its realist view of the world (see the glossary entry). Several Jaina philosophers are major thinkers; Hemacandra, a great epistemologist who was roughly contemporary with Śrīharṣa (that is, c. 1150), may have been known to the dialectical Advaitin.[115] Certainly, Śrīharṣa was familiar with some Jaina texts, and lifted arguments or attacked Jaina stances on occasion, according to the overall drift of his thought. But Jainas appear to have had little influence on Logic, despite some similar positions, and should not be counted as major players by our lights.[116]

However, the same should not be said about Cārvāka, a school also known as Lokāyata, literally "those attached to the ways of the world." Cārvākas are renowned throughout the classical civilization as materialists and clever skeptics about religious matters who poke fun at superstitions. Despite the materialism and an antipathy to mysticism, Cārvāka lines up primarily on the Advaita side of our debate—at least Jayarāśi (c. 650 ?) does, a Cārvāka sympathizer if not a Cārvāka himself, who is important for his skepticism about philosophic positions, especially doctrines of epistemology.

Almost the entirety of Jayarāśi's *Tattvopaplavasiṃha* is extant. But a much more generally influential and often quoted *sūtra* text—attributed to Bṛhaspati, the school's founder—appears to have been lost, and we have no other Cārvāka works.[117] Śrīharṣa mentions Cārvāka early in his philosophic text,[118] and Gaṅgeśa near the beginning of the chapter on inference in his *Tattvacintāmaṇi* has a refutation of a skeptical argument that classical commentators identify as Cārvāka.[119] There are many criticisms voiced by Śrīharṣa that he may have learned from Jayarāśi or other Cārvākas.

Since our Advaitin has a religious motive for his anti-Nyāya stance, we may wonder why Bṛhaspati, a hedonist and materialist philosopher, would be famous for denying that inference is a source of knowledge (*pramāṇa*), and why Jayarāśi would attack understandings of several apparent sources of information about the world, including perception, inference, testimony, and "history" (*aitihya*). Concerning Bṛhaspati, the answer is close at hand—at least concerning the Bṛhaspati of late classical sources, who is presumed to accept sense perception as the only *pramāṇa*.[120] Mādhava, the fourteenth-century doxographer, makes it clear that Cārvāka skepticism about inference grows out of a fear of religious conclusions drawn by reasoning. Although Bṛhaspati is often highly reputed as a philosopher, and although Mādhava's Cārvāka stereotype is full of *joie de vivre*, the standard portrayal of a Cārvāka is of a crasser type of hedonist, not a Jeremy Bentham or John Stuart Mill. Religious inhibitions (against adultery, for example) are the prattle of fools. By attacking the principle of inference—namely, invariable concomitance, as in Mādhava's presentation—the Cārvāka armors himself against the rational clarion call—or apologetics—to lead a good life as fixed by religious criteria, i.e., to make progress towards liberation and enlightenment, or, at worst, to secure a better station in the next lifetime. The Cārvāka's main concern is to deny another world and rebirth. Mādhava expresses in a Cārvāka voice (including a number of fragments from Bṛhaspati's lost text) clever, hilarious verses of contempt for dupes of religious teachings, who perform meaningless sacrifices, speak nonsense, and mumble mantras of gibberish.[121] But Mādhava lets us see that in attacking inference, the Cārvāka resorts to the very argument patterns that he so cleverly would denounce.[122]

The case of Jayarāśi is more complex. Some scholars have questioned his textbook Cārvāka labeling.[123] With Jayarāśi there is defense neither of perception as the only knowledge source nor of a materialist view of consciousness ("awareness is a peculiar combination of material elements, like the intoxicating power of grain and yeast"), positions for which Bṛhaspati is famous. Indeed, Jayarāśi attacks definitions of perception, focusing on its putative ability to ground knowledge of anything. Jayarāśi collects—and probably in some cases pioneers—objections to the epistemological positions that had evolved by his time, around the end of the seventh century. He appears to be a philosophic skeptic of a rather contemporary, twentieth-century variety: when we look closely at the theories proposed by the august schools, we see a host of problems. The motivation and deeper allegiance of this professional critic must remain problematic, however. He finds counterexamples to various schools' proposed definitions of perception, inference, and other presumed knowledge sources (*pramāṇa*)—as well as problems with Nyāya views of universals and inherence, in the midst of his refutation of Nyāya's understanding of inference as a knowledge source—apparently to show that there is no plank of any philosophic view (*tattva*) that can withstand scrutiny. His book's title, "The Lion of Disaster for Philosophic Theories," seems to imply as much, too. Further, Jayarāśi is not a principled skeptic; he picks his counterexamples from everyday life, and thereby implicitly endorses several views commonly and pre-critically held, presumably, by any reasonable person (and post-critically in some schools). Thus it is hard to say how thoroughgoing his skepticism is, since his main occupation is to find fault with philosophic efforts, not beliefs of everyday life.[124] Moreover, Bṛhaspati's materialism is not attacked, but, again, it is also not defended; Jayarāśi's attitude appears to be that even such a straightforward position as that of the famous materialist would not survive serious questioning, "How much less the rest?"[125] In sum, the bottom line seems to be that we need not bother ourselves, according to Jayarāśi, with what philosophers have to say, and should go on with our lives. (On the other hand, Jayarāśi surely bothered himself with philosophy. His study and scholarship are apparent. Is he warning us not to further waste time?)

No one that I know of has discovered a reference to Jayarāśi in a Logician text, although Logicians fairly often refer to "Cārvāka" views (to refute them). Śrīharṣa, however, does appear to know Jayarāśi. The question of the influence of the seventh-century rebutter on our twelfth-century Advaitin has been addressed by a few scholars, most comprehensively by Ester Solomon and Phyllis Granoff.[126] Both find direct influence, but while Solomon sees the influence as significant and thoroughgoing, Granoff finds it limited and rather insignificant overall. To me, Jayarāśi seems a collector and librarian of *pūrvapakṣa*s (*prima facie* positions) and refutations of philosophic theories. By his time, the seventh century, one school's objections to the positions of its rivals had become rather polished and crystallized. Numerous objections to rival philosophies had appeared by this date—against Sāṃkhya (in the *Brahma-sūtra*), against Nyāya (in Buddhist texts), against Buddhist views (among Naiyāyikas), against both Buddhist and Naiyāyika views (among Mīmāṃsakas), and so on. Solomon is probably right with regard to the concrete instances of precursors that she cites. But Granoff's judgment appears to be correct. Jayarāśi does not press the Logician, for example, in a systematic way (Mīmāṃsā, Buddhist, Sāṃkhya, and Vedāntic views are also attacked). He has no compelling, deep insight about what is fundamentally wrong with Nyāya, but only a series of objections. He uses Buddhist-forged arguments against the Logicians' theory of universals, and he uses against Buddhist epistemology considerations that Logicians pioneered. By the twelfth century and Śrīharṣa, numerous destructive arguments must have become rather common stock among philosophic disputants. This book is not the place for a detailed tracing of argument innovation; Indian patterns of reasoning are already too various.[127] Śrīharṣa probably consulted Jayarāśi's *Tattvopaplavasiṃha* in lining up some of his refutations. Or it could be that he consulted another storehouse of philosophy's outstanding problems.[128] The Advaitin's skepticism, however, in contrast with Jayarāśi's, is principled, and Śrīharṣa apparently sees something deeply wrong with the realist outlook, underlying his specific complaints.

CHAPTER THREE

Śrīharṣa

1. A Philosopher, Poet, and Mystic

Two works by the great Śrīharṣa are extant: the philosophic masterpiece, the *Khaṇḍanakhaṇḍakhādya* (*Sweetmeats of Refutation*, henceforth *Khkh*), and the epic poem, the *Naiṣadhacarita* (*Nc*), a retelling of the *Mahābhārata* story of King Nala's romance with Princess Damayantī. Apparently other works were written by the poet and Advaitin, since some are mentioned by him or referred to by other classical authors.[1]

Except for a few probably apocryphal stories in Sanskrit commentaries, the little we know about Śrīharṣa's life comes from either the *Khkh* or *Nc*.[2] A particularly famous story concerns Udayana and Śrīharṣa's father, a story that scholar D. C. Bhattacharya is inclined to accept as true. According to Bhattacharya, the *Nc* commentator Cāṇḍū Paṇḍita (c. 1300) states that Udayana defeated Śrīharṣa's father in a public debate. The latter, Śrīhīra, then prayed to the goddess Durgā for a son to avenge him.[3] Śrīharṣa's father, Śrīhīra, and his mother as well, Māmalladevī, are named in *Nc* colophons.

Śrīharṣa states in the final sentence of the *Khkh*—before the colophon or signature verse—that he received patronage from King Kānyakubja, whom scholars believe is either Vijayacandra or his son and successor, Jayacandra. Vijayacandra reigned 1155–69 and Jayacandra 1169–94. The exact location of the kingdom is in dispute. Phyllis Granoff speculates that it was in Kashmir and that Śrīharṣa was a Kashmiri; she counters D. C. Bhattacharya's contention that our author lived instead in Bengal.[4] As with many other great names of the classical civilization, there is little clear evidence.[5]

The most interesting detail about Śrīharṣa's life we learn from the *Khkh*, in the final sentence:

> (Now ends) this work produced for the delight of the learned by the esteemed Śrīharṣa, who from Lord Kānyakubja receives a seat of honor and a pair of betel leaves, who knows immediately in highest meditations the supreme Brahman, the ocean of bliss, whose poetry is a shower of sweetness, and whose pronouncements on reasonings have brought opponents to ruin.[6]

Thus Śrīharṣa declares himself to have achieved—among other accomplishments—mystic awareness of Brahman, the Absolute. The word that I have translated "highest meditations" is *samādhi* (pluralized), which is the word used in textbooks of yoga for mystic trance, a word used as well in several distinct philosophic schools.

This personal declaration matches a summary statement Śrīharṣa makes in the middle of the *Khkh*:[7]

> Therefore, this doctrine of non-duality (*advaita*), into which you are being led by these arguments that are in accord with the definitions of cogent arguments established in your own school (i.e., Nyāya)—have faith in it, sir, even though you desire to continue to dally in the sport of (fundamental, spiritual) ignorance (*avidyā*). And after you have faith, just through that faith in the teaching of the Upanishads you will come to desire to know the supreme spiritual reality (*tattva*). Gradually, with the fluctuations of mentality silenced, you will, just by your own self, directly and immediately experience that reality, a reality that witnesses itself by its own light and surpasses (in delight) the taste of honey. And as I have related in the *Naiṣadhacarita*, in the chapter devoted to praise of the supreme person, the mind (*mānasa*), with unsteadiness rejected, plunging into the waters of the immortal nectar of self-reality, comes most easily to delight—this is the gist.[8]

Granoff discusses the difficulties of locating the exact reference within the *Nc*.[9] However, the chapter referred to is apparently the twenty-first, which contains a long hymn of praise to the "supreme person" in his special manifestations or *avatāra*s. There the only mention of such deep meditation occurs in verse 118, which immediately follows the hymn of praise. This verse reads:

> Having invoked Hari (Vishnu) in these words, Nala attained the perfection of a silent-most trance of "self-absorption with prop." Having by the force of meditation mystically experienced Vishnu, he became inclined to act in accordance with his love and devotion.[10]

Granoff finds troublesome the *Khkh* reference to this verse, apparently because of its theism (maybe also because of the *Khkh* passage's explicit endorsement of a positive program—"this doctrine of non-duality, *advaita*, into which you are being led by these arguments"—about which more below). Such theism does not fit in well with her overall *Khkh* reading. Against her, I would say that we must avoid a too easy coherence. The primary point here, however, is the mystical element with Śrīharṣa. It is key, I believe, to our overall view of his Advaita philosophy.

Later in this chapter, we will focus on the apparent tension between (a) the theism of the above and other passages and (b) the reputed atheism of Advaita. First, we will look at the arguments that the Advaitin says should lead the Naiyāyika to have faith in the teaching of the Upanishads, *non-dualistically* interpreted. For Śrīharṣa does understand the supreme mystical experience to reveal Brahman as non-dual (*advaita*).

One last remark about Śrīharṣa the person. The *Nc* is one of the finest accomplishments of world literature: an elegant poem, encyclopedic in its mythological allusions and masterful in its use of poetic figures and rhetorical devices, it brims with the wisdom and sensibility of the classical culture (at a time, moreover, that some have considered its zenith[11]). The long poem also contains many explicit, though usually playful, recountings of doctrines forged in the full array of classical schools.[12] The *Nc* may not have met with universal acclamation among scholars of an earlier generation, some of whom apparently found it distastefully erotic.[13] My sense is that within his own culture, Śrīharṣa was urbane in all the best senses of the word, and that this is reflected in his superb poem. The *Khkh* for its part is not only a central work relative to the entire span of classical Indian philosophy—about two thousand years—it is also a masterpiece of prose style, full of wit and humor, employing a vocabulary unusually rich for a philosophical text. Both the *Nc* and the *Khkh* are, moreover, very lengthy works. Śrīharṣa was a poet who was familiar with the philosophic scene of his time. The *Khkh* dismantles the Nyāya realist view detail by minute detail, and the Advaitin shows deep appreciation of Buddhist, Mīmāṃsaka, Jaina, Cārvāka, and of course Vedāntic philosophies. Even with no other works to his credit than the two extant, we have to marvel at the man's accomplishments. Then he tells us he is a yogin, a mystic knower of Brahman!

2. The Positive Program

Śrīharṣa is philosophically an Advaitin, and makes typically Advaita moves, though with great sophistication, in arguing in support of the Advaita world view. Śrīharṣa's Advaita is a monistic philosophy of awareness, an idealism in its view of what is real (only self-aware awareness itself) and also in its argumentative appeal to awareness.

Scholar and *Khkh* translator Phyllis Granoff claims, in contrast, that Śrīharṣa has no positive program. According to her reading—which has been followed by other indologists—although Śrīharṣa accepts certain (Advaita) doctrines, he does not argue in support of them, but is content to attack the positions of others, chiefly Naiyāyikas.[14] This misrepresents the thrust of the *Khkh*.[15] I repeat, Śrīharṣa is an Advaitin, proffering considerations that urge acceptance of the Advaita view. Some of his refutations—particularly in the first portion of his text—may be read as indirect proofs and thus as themselves positive argumentation bolstering planks of the Advaita stance. Later, with the refutations that follow his establishing of the Advaita view, Śrīharṣa tries to eliminate all challengers to Advaita, urging in particular that by presupposing a fundamental distinctness (*bheda*), Naiyāyikas run into a host of difficulties, as his demonstrations of contradiction and incoherence show. The argument is that the difficulties eliminate a Nyāya challenge to scripture and thus reinforce the Advaita teaching that the deep reality of non-distinctness is to be discovered mystically in meditation, in a transformed (or unperverted) self-awareness that is the true message of Advaita. Before looking at details of the refutations themselves, we will review his indirect-proof and eliminative patterns of reasoning, as well as the other, indisputably positive considerations that Śrīharṣa puts forth in support of the Advaita view.

Śrīharṣa's opening discussion in the *Khkh* centers on a question of preconditions of debate, particularly what suppositions the very act of debate constrains participants to accept. He is opposed to the Logicians' prerequisites, but admits some minimal rules. One such rule is that a winning position has to be defended by *pramāṇa*, "justifiers" or "reasons" in a broad sense. Thus he himself tells us in effect that he needs a positive program.[16] Śrīharṣa does not offer much speculation about the nature of Brahman or God. But he does present us with a full array of Advaita arguments.

2.1. The Self-Illumination, Self-Certification, and Sublation Theses

Within the context of the opening discussion of debate prerequisites, Śrīharṣa resists the argument that the epistemology and method of inquiry of the Naiyāyikas have to be accepted. He also resists the idea that any ontological position is presupposed in the act of debate.[17] And while on this topic, he introduces, and briefly defends, a very strong criterion for ontic commitment. An absolute non-sublatedness is the mark, he claims, of the truly real (or existent, *sat*): "That which is not sublated by any manner or means is to be accepted as real."[18] This claim is part of what I call the sublation thesis, or better, theme. Its full import will become clear after we review the two equally important theses, self-illumination and self-certification.

Other moves Śrīharṣa makes concerning preconditions and presuppositions of debate will be taken up by us later. Following these opening moves which span some thirty-nine paragraphs in the Sanskrit edition by N. Jha, Śrīharṣa introduces the key thesis in the Advaita understanding of awareness, namely, that awareness is "self-illumining," *svaprakāśa*. He also introduces the key principle of Advaita epistemology, the thesis that awareness is "self-certifying," *svataḥ pramāṇa*.[19]

The self-illumination thesis stands as basic to the Advaita system; it is not argued for. The self-certification principle is also essential to Śrīharṣa's Advaita polemic. But although perhaps self-certification is to be bootstrapped, Śrīharṣa at one place argues in support of it—using the self-illumination thesis and an eliminative argument form that presupposes that faults such as inconsistency eliminate views that exhibit them.

Views, or, more precisely, cognitions (*jñāna*, comprising awarenesses) are what are certified or eliminated. It is convenient to think of these cognitions as propositions or sets of interlocking propositions (such that, for example, an inconsistency shown by the Advaitin would be understood truth-functionally). But we must keep in mind not only that Śrīharṣa did not have a formal propositional calculus, but also that the question of what logical constraints he recognizes remains open to interpretation.[20]

Again, it is important to stress that the self-illumination thesis is considered basic. It blocks doubt concerning self-awareness. "The doubt never occurs, 'Am I aware or not?' "[21] Then Śrīharṣa argues that awareness is self-certifying because it is self-illumining. As he observes, "Nor does the opposite awareness, 'I am not aware,' occur. And finally, (where no awareness occurs) the veridical cognition ('I am not aware') never occurs."[22] Thus an appeal is made to what is now sometimes called pragmatic contradiction: there would be contradiction between essence and content were someone to have an awareness verbalizable as "I am not aware." (Compare a speaker saying, "I am not speaking."[23]) At certain moments at least, we simply see the truth of awareness's self-illumination. And self-illumination means that self-certification is the only epistemic principle that could possibly be applicable to questions about awareness, since only an awareness itself has, so to say, access to itself as awareness. Awareness itself is, then, Śrīharṣa sums up, the only ground relevant to any question about awareness itself, its existence or its nature. Self-certification is grounded in self-illumination.

In other words, the Advaitin is investigating not whether awareness is self-aware, but whether self-awareness is *known* to be veridically cognized, whether there is certification. His argument may be reconstructed as follows. From the perspective of an inquirer, i.e., someone wondering whether self-awareness is veridical or not (this is an epistemic perspective), there are five possibilities: (1) doubt ("Am I aware or not?"), (2) awareness of the absence of awareness (i.e., the non-veridical awareness, "I am not aware," when the person is aware), (3) non-occurrence of awareness, (4) awareness of the occurrence of awareness when there is no awareness (another non-veridical awareness), and (5) veridicality. The first four candidates are ruled out by the fact of the inquirer's awareness. Thus veridicality—here to be understood as *self*-veridicality—is the only standing possibility. It is not eliminated because it is not contradicted by something else we accept as true.[24]

Then what if, we may wonder, someone were to deny the self-illumination thesis, as indeed many have.[25] Such an opponent would not be moved by the preceding argument, hinging, as it does, on taking awareness to be self-illumining. How might an Advaitin respond to someone who claims not to see awareness as self-illumining? Now the Advaitin might not respond; he might just walk away, content in his own self-illumined awareness. But presuming a context of debate, one course would be to argue, as Śrīharṣa does, by showing faults in the alternative view. In the text immediately following the eliminative argument, Śrīharṣa imagines a Naiyāyika opponent as his adversary, and by trying to show the inadequacy of a Nyāya alternative view of awareness, he would bolster the Advaita position—this is my reading.[26]

The plank of the Nyāya realism that stands most directly in opposition to the Advaita view of awareness as self-illumining is a theory of apperception (*anuvyavasāya*). A previous awareness is known by becoming the object of an immediately subsequent awareness. Now this theory has, like the Advaita alternative, a complement concerning justification, known as *parataḥ pramāṇa*, "extrinsic certification." Thus, if the Nyāya complex of positions about awareness and knowledge could be shown to be wrong, perhaps the Logician could recognize for himself what is patently the case. In this way, Śrīharṣa would be motivated to take up and refute the Nyāya theory—or so I read the transition to the refutation in Śrīharṣa's text. In other words, Śrīharṣa seems to be claiming that there is really nothing to say in defense of self-illumination; we can just hope to remove the obstacles in the way of someone's seeing it. And self-illumination entails self-certification. Then by showing that either "extrinsic certification" or "apperception" is absurd, the Naiyāyika may be led into seeing for himself the truth of the Advaita view of awareness.

Now whatever the merits of the above interpretation, Śrīharṣa does indeed continue in his text by disputing the Nyāya position about how any veridical awareness's veridicality is known.[27] This view cannot, Śrīharṣa argues, avoid the difficulty of an infinite regress.[28] Given a context of debate or inquiry, i.e., a context where the question of justification is relevant, it is absurd to hold that another cognition is required in order to have a right to assert what is revealed in an occurrent awareness. The Nyāya view leads to an infinite regress. The context would invite further questioning.

It is significant that Śrīharṣa's primary concern is certification for self-awareness, not justification for the worldly content of an awareness, such as, say, a pot. But he argues that on the Nyāya view an object, such as a pot, could not be veridically known—if "being veridically known" is to establish a position in a debate or terminate an inquiry. "There would be no epistemologically relevant sight of objects if perception were not self-certifying."[29]

Śrīharṣa amplifies his attack with a couple of questions. But his next important move (for his positive program) is to return to the self-illumination thesis and to argue: "Since it is only what is of the nature of illumination (i.e., awareness itself) that can possibly stand as self-certifying, there is no possibility that awareness can include within its own nature any property whatsoever of a material or inconscient sort (*jaḍātmanāṃ*).''[30] Consciousness has no material attributes.

Moreover, awareness self-certifyingly illumines itself but not anything else. Why not external objects? Here Śrīharṣa has in mind (a) the well-known Advaita sublatability argument, which is part of what I call the sublation theme, and perhaps also (b) the problem of relations or Bradley problem. External objects are not in the truest sense self-certifyingly illuminated because any presentation of an external object is sublatable—possibly shown to be non-veridical experientially—whereas the self-illumination of awareness itself is non-sublatable. Thus there is an Advaita twist to the self-certification thesis: whereas all awareness may be *prima facie* self-certifying, only self-awareness is *ultima facie* self-certifying, for all content other than self-illumination is sublatable, negatable.[31] Moreover, any objective content other than self-transparent awareness would entail a duality and thus a relation between awareness and an object, a relation that is incoherent, as Śrīharṣa later shows, in that it would require a further relation (between it and its relata) *ad infinitum.*

Thus the self-certification principle is applied differently to each of the following: (1) the self (or awareness) as it is in itself and (2) cognitions with worldly content. The two tiers are differentiated according to sublatability (and defeasibility): the self as it is in itself is non-sublatable (and, as transparent to itself, not subject to the relation regress), whereas any cognition with worldly content is sublatable (and also rationally defeasible, as shown by the relation regress). This additional criterion of sublatability/defeasibility is what distinguishes Śrīharṣa's understanding of self-certification from that of the Exegetes (Mīmāṃsakas). As we saw in chapter 2, certain Mīmāṃsakas have the *svataḥ pramāṇa* principle as the centerpiece of a world-oriented epistemology. (An awareness, e.g., of a pot, is self-certifying; certification does not stem from anything outside the awareness itself, contra the Nyāya stance.)

Śrīharṣa does not, however, in the current context elaborate the non-sublatability point, nor does he bring out the problem of relations. Instead, he moves on to a question about how it is possible, on his view, to understand ''scripture,'' *śruti.* But as has been pointed out, both the non-sublatability and the relation-regress arguments were well-known, familiar within the classical context through the writings of Śaṅkara and his disciples. The two arguments stand at the heart of Śrīharṣa's Advaita polemic, and we will examine them further below. But Śrīharṣa's positive program embraces greater complexity. He puts forth other positive considerations that we must first review. His own exposition moves on to the certification of the Advaita view by scripture.

2.2. "Scripture" (śruti)

Śrīharṣa forthrightly states that scripture is a positive source of knowledge, *pramāṇa*, for the Advaita position on awareness, and further, for identification of self-awareness with Brahman, the Absolute.[32] Of course, scripture as a *pramāṇa* is not to be compared with immediate experience. In the supreme mystical awareness, as Śaṅkara points out, *pramāṇa* (perception, inference, scripture, etc.) are sublated along with all external appearances.[33] In other words, belief in the reliability of scripture is as conditioned by spiritual ignorance (*avidyā*) as is any experience, with the exception of the direct self-illumination of awareness (which is identical with Brahman). Thus in a sense, there can be only one "proof" of the Advaita view of awareness, that being the mystical experience of Brahman, the attainment of the *summum bonum*. Reinterpreting Granoff as emphasizing that there are two tiers of argumentation—with worldly *pramāṇa* viewed as conditioned by fundamental ignorance—we see the (sizable) grain of truth in her reading: no argument provides the mystical illumination.[34] However, within the conditions of spiritual ignorance, we can still come to the right intellectual view, directed thereto by scripture.

> Indeed this (awareness as self-illumining) is made known by scripture, which is a source of knowledge (*pramāṇa*) for it. (Scripture does not make it known directly, since—as I have already argued—it cannot, by its very nature, be known directly through words, but scripture) indirectly indicates it through its general purport (i.e., in considering the general purport of Upanishadic texts). Thus, although as it is it cannot be directly denoted, from the perspective of spiritual ignorance, in contrast, scripture in its general purport is to be taken as the knowledge source (*pramāṇa*) after the manner of our opponents. In reality, however, it is self-certified in the form of consciousness.[35]

Instead of immediately elaborating the import of scripture by focusing on Brahman, Śrīharṣa first considers objections to the possibility of a non-duality of action (as regards agent and object), and of experience (as regards subject and object). There is much of interest here. Like Śaṅkara, Śrīharṣa defends the possibility of superimposition (*adhyāsa*) of the world on Brahman by pointing to a similar structure in everyday experience—namely, perceptual illusion. Śrīharṣa also points to phenomena where no distinction of agent and object obtains, as, for example, "The fruit ripens on its own."[36] Then with regard to the objection that self-illumination is ruled out by the duality of the subject-object structure of everyday experience, Śrīharṣa brings out his attack on relations that underlies so many of his "refutations" of the Nyāya view. The topic of the import of scripture is thus momentarily bracketed. But what is central is that beyond proving possibility, Śrīharṣa defends the non-duality implied by the self-illumination thesis in part by attacking two types of distinctness, agential and experiential, which are considered challengers. Thus the Advaita view is again defended by the method of eliminative argument, where in this case the challengers fall to the relation regress.[37] The defense of the import of scripture continues, then, after several paragraphs of such indirectly supportive argument.[38]

Next, Śrīharṣa directs our attention to a certain content of scriptural declarations that goes beyond the self-illumination thesis. He introduces the scriptural statement of the identity of self-awareness with Brahman, the Absolute, the Blissful, and the Alone, and marshals his resources to defend the so-called identity texts (e.g., "Thou art That," *Chāndogya* 6.8.7.)

2.3. An Ontological Argument for the Absolute, Brahman

Śrīharṣa claims that the awareness of Brahman conveyed by scripture—a verbal awareness (*śābda-bodha* in Naiyāyika terms: see the glossary), with its content the one, all-inclusive Reality—is a veridical awareness that cannot be defeated, that is to say, within the conditions of spiritual ignorance, *avidyā*. Śrīharṣa's posiiton that no evidence can be brought against the Advaita view of Brahman is reminiscent of *a priori* reasoning and ontological argumentation as known in the West. Although the Advaita view of Brahman is not the same as the Judeo-Christian idea of God (used by Anselm and others), a putative uniqueness of Brahman *is* crucial to the reasoning—as, on the other side, is the uniqueness of God as perfect. Even if the "ontological" label is not warranted, a similar pattern of reasoning is central to Śrīharṣa's positive argument.

Pared of elaboration, the premises of Śrīharṣa's argument are as follows:

(1) Brahman is cognized (from scripture).

(1′) Brahman is cognized as self-conscious, all-inclusive, and non-differentiated.

(2) What is cognized is to be accepted, unless the cognizing is (challenged and) defeated. (Every cognition is innocent until proven guilty.)

(3) The logic of the content of the teaching about Brahman (or the nature of Brahman) precludes any challenge or defeat.

The conclusion is:

(4) Brahman is to be accepted.[39]

I think we may best see what this argument is up to by asking the evaluative question, Does it work? Is the argument cogent?

The first premise presents no difficulty, at least in a loose sense of "is cognized'': so long as we are not worried about the coherence of the Advaita Brahman view, we may take Śrīharṣa at his word that Brahman is cognized by him, Śrīharṣa himself. The view is also laid out in the *Khkh*, and its official source is scripture, *śruti*, i.e., certain Upanishadic texts. So Brahman is also cognized by us, let us grant. The authority of *śruti*, it is important to point out, is not relevant at this point, for with this first premise it is claimed only that Brahman is cognized, not that the cognition is correct, authoritative, valid, or actually about anything real. This first premise takes on force in connection with the other two premises (and premise 1 has to be unpacked as 1′ in connection with premise 3).

The second premise is the Mīmāṃsaka version (Kumārila's) of our familiar self-certification thesis. Its scope includes world-oriented cognitions and claims; that it to say, it is operative within spiritual ignorance. ''Concerning cognition [*dhī*, thought], self-certification is to be denied only when there is a defeater [*bhādhaka*, broadly construable as ''eliminator''].''[40] Premise 2 is, then, an epistemological thesis, which is at first blush similar to what John Pollock has called negative coherentism.[41] There is a collective and mutual obligation ''to give the benefit of the doubt'' unless there are countervailing considerations. A cognition, along with its implicit claim—here the cognition is of Brahman—is to be accepted unless challenged and eliminated. (Elimination presupposes calling a cognition into question.)

The general purport of this epistemological thesis helps to make my hermeneutical case. To briefly shift focus, the refutations Śrīharṣa directs at Nyāya views are motivated by his seeing them as potential challengers of the Brahman theory. Śrīharṣa labors to show that (a) awareness is the only reality and (b) *bheda*, distinctness, along with all appearance of diversity, is inexplicable, *anirvacanīya*. He does so out of his sense of what the Advaita Brahman view entails. Much of the Nyāya philosophy presupposes *bheda*, distinctness; it opposes premise 1′. This spurs Śrīharṣa to refute Nyāya views. ''When we look at what you Naiyāyikas see as challenging, and indeed defeating, the Advaita position, we see that your challengers cannot withstand scrutiny, that they self-destruct (and are eliminated),'' Śrīharṣa claims.

But we are getting ahead of ourselves. The ontological argument continues with the assertion that Brahman's nature, i.e., the content of the scriptural declaration, is such that that declaration cannot be defeated. An inference seems to be embedded here, and there is thus an extra step in the overall reasoning: Brahman cognition cannot be challenged, and therefore, cannot be defeated. This inference delivers premise 3, which in conjunction with premises 1 and 2 would secure the conclusion. The success of the argument depends partly on just what is to count as a successful challenge and, perhaps, defeat. If there can be no valid challenge, however, there can be no defeat.

What, then, is there about Brahman that precludes challenge and therefore defeat? After all, we could seemingly challenge Brahman cognition with this proposition:

(1N) There is no Brahman.

Proposition 1N directly denies that there is anything that fits the Brahman cognition or view; the cognition that has this proposition as its content would appear to throw "Brahman" into question. The question would be whether there is in fact anything that fits the Brahman cognition, and such a question would seemingly suffice to show that Śrīharṣa's *a priori* argument fails.

Now a counter-thesis polemically equivalent to our 1N is considered by Śrīharṣa himself in his text. I say that it is polemically equivalent because Śrīharṣa takes premise 1 to entail that all reality is the One, *without distinctions.*[42]

(1NN) Everything is distinct (from everything else).

Śrīharṣa even couples the obvious challenge to his position with the self-certificationalist epistemological thesis (premise 2) so that, apparently, the challenge would have every right to our allegiance that premise 1 has.

> Everything is distinct. This claim so long as it is not defeated is to be accepted on its own strength.[43]

The classical Western rejection of the ontological argument centers on the conceivability of a universe without God, a conceivability that parallels the objection that Śrīharṣa considers, an objection that apparently reveals why his ontological argument fails. We can conceive what should be inconceivable; presumably, we can cognize—and cognize as warranted—1NN. What, then, is there about Brahman that leads Śrīharṣa to believe that Brahman cognition precludes challenge and therefore defeat? Let us now consider premise 1′ above, isolating the part about Brahman:

(1″) Brahman is self-conscious, all-inclusive, and non-differentiated.

Śrīharṣa tries to make the most of these three predicates. Let us consider each in turn.

The first predication, self-consciousness, takes us back to the self-illumination claim. In this connection, let us take up the sublation theme again.

Brahman cognition is claimed to be non-sublatable because self-consciousness is non-sublatable. The point seems similar to that in Descartes' *cogito* argument. Now, if we could grant the Advaita supposition that I-consciousness or self is nothing but Brahman, then Śrīharṣa's ontological argument—or better, ontological *meditation* (in the spirit of Descartes')—would be a powerful piece of reasoning. But why should we grant that supposition? It is not at all evident why *Brahman* cognition (as opposed to mere self-awareness) is immune to challenge and defeat, even in light of the epistemological thesis (premise 2) that the Advaitin advances. For, to hold the very permissive thesis that every cognition (and consonant verbalized or verbalizable claim) is to be accepted by a person S unless S's own experience proves it false, entails that Śrīharṣa has no grounds for complaint against Nyāya views; the Logicians can be presumed not to experience the putative sublatings of (mystical awareness of) Brahman. Śrīharṣa does complain, however, and so we should reconsider our reading. Yet, even with a less permissive thesis—one with a wider view of "defeat" such that a somehow better founded alternative would win—the first predication still presents us with no reason to assume that Brahman cognition could not be challenged and vanquished.

Thus Śrīharṣa has no compelling argument. Let us understand the Advaitin to believe that a supreme non-dual cognition of self, *brahma-vidyā*, is a self-absorption with no worldly content. But why could not that mystical state be sublated by a fuller experience of self as *being-in-the-world*? Even if it is true that in some sense I-consciousness cannot be sublated, why could not the world-negational I-consciousness be sublated by a fuller experience of self as embodied? Why could not a fuller self-experience follow and appropriately negate an experience of self-absorption?[44]

To consider now the second predication above: the cognition of Brahman is claimed to be unchallengeable (and therefore undefeatable) because Brahman is conceived as including everything. At places, this seems to be Śrīharṣa's key contention, where he understands the non-duality of Brahman to be equivalent to Brahman's including everything. Any challenge or defeat presupposes an alternative, but there is nothing outside of Brahman.[45]

However, we have to keep in mind that Brahman is described as infinite being, awareness, and bliss. Could not a materialist with equal reason claim that her materialism thesis (say, of a strict identity of mind and body, and of a fundamentally inconscient matter) is established because on her view everything is material, because matter as she conceives it includes everything? Indeed, do not these two views, Advaita and materialism, stand opposed on the nature of what is all-inclusive, and thus don't these two challenge one another? The same could be said using Śrīharṣa's 1NN instead of materialism. So the Advaitin seems to get nowhere with this second predicate or characterization of Brahman.

Moreover, Śrīharṣa's argument is here sometimes slippery; it slides from the perspective of spiritual ignorance (*avidyā*), where justification is an issue, to (the idea of) the mystic perspective of knowing Brahman where there can be no justification nor claim, by the nature of that state. Recall that Śrīharṣa has told us that he is considering scripture as a *pramāṇa* within the condition of spiritual ignorance. The all-inclusive predication seems to hold little promise, in sum, beyond an opportunity for confusion.

However, such dismissal may miss the spirit of Śrīharṣa's reflection. What we need to hear is *how* Brahman is thought to include all actual and possible *cognitions* (assuming, for the sake of examining Śrīharṣa's argument, the idealist thesis that—though Śrīharṣa does not put it like this—a full account of cognitions would also be a full account of the world).

If Brahman is thought to include without destroying—in the psychological sense—the worldly content of all cognitions, it still seems there could be no compelling argument. Any cognition is included in the scope of the universal "all cognitions." But to say this is to say nothing whatsoever about what Brahman is as a unity. Why should we embrace the Advaita supposition that it is just Brahman (as in itself a homogeneous Bliss) that includes all cognitions? After all, my cognition seems to be other than Brahman. I am not aware of being Brahman-included.[46]

This brings us to the third predication, "non-differentiated," and to Śrīharṣa's reply to proposition 1NN above, put forth as a hypothetical objection in the *Khkh* along with (and contra Nyāya) the *svataḥ pramāṇa*, self-certification, epistemological thesis. Proposition 1NN would seem to challenge the scripturally conveyed Brahman cognition in that Brahman is thought to be everything, but in a non-differentiated, non-distinct way. In contemporary terms, there would be absurdity in holding both propositions 1″ and 1NN. One could not in epistemic good faith assert both upon reflection. Śrīharṣa seems to accept as much. Thus the question for Śrīharṣa would seem to be, how can he maintain that cognition 1NN is necessarily vanquished.[47]

In other words, Śrīharṣa would seem at this point to be forced to give up his attempt to reason *a priori*, and to realize the need to show that *śruti*, as the source of the Brahman cognition, is superior to whatever the source of the challenging cognition might be. Indeed he does at places argue explicitly this way.[48] This is one line in his strategy of refutations, and we see now one reason why he focuses on details of Nyāya epistemology. There are two other broad tactics, both of which are also tied to a defense of Brahman cognition. First, following the philosophic legacy of Śaṅkara et al., Śrīharṣa argues that propositions 1NN and 1″ could not be *about* the same thing.[49] Second—and most importantly for the bulk of the *Khkh*—the reason Brahman cognition rests unchallenged is that proposition 1NN—and similar claims—*can be shown to be incoherent.* On examination, they self-destruct. Thus no cognition having proposition 1NN as content, or any claim for that matter, can challenge Brahman cognition.

Śrīharṣa's final strategy in defense of his view that Brahman cognition is in principle undefeatable involves, therefore, three prongs: (1) the challenger's source of warrant (perceptions, etc.) is suspect; (2) to defeat another's view requires a cognition that is, let us say, "equal in scope" (*sagocara, saviṣaya*) with what it would challenge; and/or (3) the seeming challenger is incoherent. In the first case, a challenger to Brahman cognition would be put forth on the basis of what the opponent presumes to be a reliable knowledge source, such as perception, but perception, etc., can be shown to be unreliable; in the second, a challenger cognition would have to be about everything, and few cognitions have such broad scope; in the third, the challenger would not withstand scrutiny—it would be eliminated as self-contradictory, provoking a vicious infinite regress, and so on.

All three lines of strategy help to determine the direction of Śrīharṣa's attacks; they are not mutually exclusive, and indeed often overlap. That Śrīharṣa is on the attack throughout most of the *Khkh* presents therefore no difficulty for my reading emphasizing a positive program. In general, the "refutations" (*khaṇḍana*) of the *Khkh* are to be viewed within the context of the ontological argumentation reconstructed above. In particular, the Nyāya view presupposes distinctness; all its definitional projects proceed on that assumption. That everything is distinct from everything else is, however, a supposition whose ramifications are problems of many sorts (contradictions, infinite regresses, and other faults). The alternative, which is out on the table thanks to the fortunate fact of the Upanishads, is the Advaita philosophy.

Does, then, Śrīharṣa's ontological argument go through? An answer at this point would be premature: Śrīharṣa's "refutations" of distinctness may well be answerable (surely, certain New Logicians think they are). What we may say is that if Śrīharṣa's argument succeeds, it would be by the methods of eliminative argument and indirect proof. He would back into success, so to say, by showing the ineffectiveness or incoherence of what we would pre-reflectively take to be challengers to Brahman cognition.

2.4. *Refutation and Indirect Proof*

In the order of the text, the positive argumentation, sketched above, precedes the detailed refutations, *khaṇḍana*, for which the book is entitled. Specifically, the first of the four chapters of the *Khkh* has three broad divisions: (1) an introductory section on debate, (2) the Advaita program, and (3) an orderly progression of refutations. Refutations also dominate the remainder of the book. My view is that the focus of the refutations derives, most broadly, from Śrīharṣa's sense of what are the serious challengers to Advaita, and, in particular, from conflicts with the Advaita positions concerning the non-duality of awareness and the unity, or non-duality, of Brahman. Śrīharṣa's refutations support the non-duality of Brahman by showing that appearances of distinctness cannot coherently be understood.[50] This interpretive thesis—emphasizing conflicts with Advaita—is not current among scholars, and I wish to say just a few more words in its defense before going on to scrutinize the refutations.

Beginning with the third section of the *Khkh* chapter 1, the nature of Nyāya's conflicts with Advaita usually goes unstated. The refutations often seem no more than fault-finding with individual Nyāya positions (and Śrīharṣa the heir of Jayarāśi as much as of Śaṅkara). Faults, such as contradiction and infinite regress, are lodged by the Advaitin against Nyāya views—beginning with the *pramāṇa*s but including the full gamut of Nyāya positions—and against views of a few others as well—Mīmāṃsakas, Jainas—taken to be opponents. But despite the refutations' breadth of scope, the logic of eliminative argument forms deep context. Śrīharṣa tells us explicitly, in general terms, that elimination is part of his strategy, as we will see concretely in a passage I translate below.[51] With every refutation, the strategy is to back into Advaita, even when the apparent strategy is otherwise. Advaita is taken to be the deep alternative to the errors revealed. Sometimes a refutation is even said to be itself a proof of Advaita, not just an elimination of a competitor. Thus the strategy includes indirect proof, where alternatives are taken to be not only contrary competitors (both couldn't be right though both could be wrong) but true contradictories (the falsity of the one would prove the truth of the other).

There is, however, a hermeneutical problem in reconstructing Śrīharṣa's view of contradiction, which is key to the logic of indirect proof formally construed. (To prove q given premises p_1 through p_n, assume $\sim q$ and deduce a contradiction, p and $\sim p$. Since a false proposition cannot be deduced from true premises—and the premises given are assumed to be true—$\sim q$ has to be false and thus q true.) With Śrīharṣa—and with Logicians, too—indirect proof is subsumed under *tarka*, which I render as "dialectical reasoning" (see the glossary) but which usually amounts to eliminative argument. First, any fault will do to falsify a view, not just contradiction but also, for example, vicious infinite regress (*anavasthā*) and (in certain circumstances) reasoning in a circle (*cakraka*). According to Nyāya, the falsification shows that an opposed candidate view—presumed to have some independent warrant source at least marginally in its favor—is established, sometimes a contrary and sometimes a true contradictory. In this way, indirect proof is subsumed into the wider pattern of argument. And with eliminative arguments considered in general, no warrant for a position need derive from the falsification of a rival. Nevertheless, both Logicians and Śrīharṣa do employ true indirect proofs where the negation is presumed to have justificational power.

Now the hermeneutical problem. The Advaitin is particularly intent on showing fallacies that follow from the view that things are distinct, but he is also suspicious of contradiction (and thus of indirect proof), and even of the eliminative pattern of reasoning that, on my reading, is his key strategy in the

Khkh.[52] Dialectical reasoning (*tarka*) is expressly attacked by the Advaitin (see the translation in chapter 5, below, pp. 151–56). Śrīharṣa argues that contradiction is no guarantee of invariable concomitance (*vyāpti*, inference-grounding pervasion). Indeed, this latter is itself inexplicable, according to him. Is, then, the Advaitin to be looked upon as himself eschewing contradiction, indirect proof, and indeed all *tarka* and eliminative argument?

The answer is no. Naiyāyikas understand contradiction ontologically, and it is their ontological suppositions that Śrīharṣa objects to. For Śrīharṣa, the reality of Brahman entails that appearances of distinctness cannot be veridical. This, we may say, is the view from the top down. From the bottom up, the unintelligibility of distinctness, demonstrated by argument, suggests but does not strictly demonstrate the reality of non-distinctness, because cognition of non-distinctness has to have its own proper source (scripture, or better, self-experience).[53] Nevertheless, philosophy has a message; indeed, it is what has just been said. The top-down and bottom-up views of Brahman and the world converge.[54]

In sum, Śrīharṣa's use of dialectical reasoning is best understood overall as eliminative argument, where alternatives on the table need not be understood as true contradictories. He does put forth a couple of instances of true indirect proof. But his general method is to show commonly recognized faults in alternatives to Advaita; the elimination of Nyāya, for example, allows us more clearly to see the truth of the Upanishads. This is the predominant or base-line tactic.

In certain instances the plan is more complex. For example, the Nyāya view of distinctness, and its claim that perception establishes distinctness, is refuted in the *Khkh*'s first chapter. Thus perception is incapable of contradicting scripture (since perception purports to warrant incoherencies). In addition, the non-duality view is strengthened.[55] Non-distinctness is not thought to be precisely equivalent to the non-duality of Brahman. Nevertheless, the claim that distinctness is unintelligible serves to support the right view of Brahman, according to Śrīharṣa: Brahman considered in relation to the world requires an indeterminability plank. With these considerations, Śrīharṣa is concerned with more than elimination in his argument.

A straightforward example of indirect proof occurs in the fourth chapter of the *Khkh*. The Nyāya understanding of the relationship between cognition and its objects is refuted, and the refutation is said to prove that awareness is the sole reality.[56] Śrīharṣa asserts elsewhere that awareness is the only reality; this argument apparently supports that claim. In addition, in *Khkh* chapter 1, there are two passages that take an overview of the book's refutational method; they are worth reviewing at some length.

The first passage concerns the Advaita doctrine of the indeterminability of appearance.[57] The passage is important. Ganganatha Jha quotes it in his introduction,[58] and it is promoted by Granoff as establishing her reading.[59] Here Śrīharṣa seems to reject non-contradiction and the formal logic of indirect proof: although there are faults in the position that the phenomenal display of distinct things is real, these faults do not entail that distinctness is unreal. Yet Śrīharṣa uses such logic in concluding indeterminability from, so to say, the bottom up.

> By the principles of none other than our opponent is it thus concluded: because of the defeat of the effort to determine distinctions by definitions, indeterminability follows. For it is accepted that with an assertion and its denial the rejection of the one requires an embrace of the other. Thus by the method of our opponent this is to be said: the indeterminability of everything is to be embraced.[60]

Not (~) determinability, as demonstrated, is equivalent to indeterminability. This is reasoning "from the bottom up"—reasoning that is motivated, I maintain, by other reasoning "from the top down." Indeterminability, or inexplicability, is thought to follow from Upanishadic declarations about Brahman, in particular about Brahman's being everything. Thus here early in the book, the position is supported by such indirect arguments.[61]

The defense involves a promissory note: the failure of the effort to determine distinctness by definitions remains to be shown. The promissory note is paid by the refutations that follow. Inexplicability is tightly tied to non-distinctness: why there are appearances of *distinct* things (given the sole reality of non-dual Brahman) cannot be explained.

The interesting interpretive question concerning the passage above is, how seriously are we to take the "proof." One might argue, as does Granoff,[62] that the logic invoked ("the rejection of one requires an embrace of the other") is thought to constrain only those who, like the Naiyāyikas, accept it ("by the method of our opponent"). Then Śrīharṣa, speaking for himself, goes on to say:

> But in fact, we, setting down the burden firmly in the truth of Brahman, the self-proved and self-existent, the conscious soul, the alone, are satisfied and do not engage in trying to establish the reality or unreality of the whole display of diverse phenomena.[63]

My sense is that Granoff's reading is not radical enough: here Śrīharṣa invokes the mystical perspective transcendent of spiritual ignorance, *avidyā*; in the mystical perspective, no argument holds. Furthermore, Śrīharṣa does not engage in trying to show the reality or unreality of things, for Advaita takes neither position (it holds that things as distinct have, instead, an ontological status that is indeterminable, *anirvacanīya*, as real or unreal).[64] Similarly, Śrīharṣa continues:

> And it is not the case that just mention (of your views) is a cause for objection, since, as has already been pointed out, it is quite (*param*) possible to

> engage in debate and reflection, accepting that such debate can be undertaken by those indifferent to matters such as whether to accept the reality or unreality of what is mentioned within a debate.[65]

This passage is not to be understood as a denial of all positions including Advaita's, but, literally, as a denial of reality and unreality with respect to things as distinct, in an embrace of the doctrine of indeterminability. Śrīharṣa concludes:

> Then in this way it is established that the phenomenal display of diversity is indeterminable while Brahman alone is real in the supreme sense and non-dual.[66]

There is, finally, a general statement in the first chapter that is transitional between the positive program and the refutations that occupy most of the rest of the book. This follows the summary passage (*Khkh*, p. 125), quoted above (p. 76), concerning the establishment of Advaita by arguments in accordance with Nyāya canons, and on the need to have the direct experience of self-illumining awareness. Thus the subsequent verse, which I now translate, is dramatically framed: "There is no law like a king's command that blocks refutations and keeps them from being used in support of one's own views."[67] Granoff, near the end of her book, brings the overall picture into focus with respect to this verse (although she again obscures it in the very last pages):

> Although it has been said for the opponent's sake that scripture constitutes a valid means to know non-duality and that the validity of scriptures can be demonstrated by careful examination, in fact, non-duality is nothing more than self-valid consciousness, requiring no external proof and beyond the range of discursive thought marking all inquiry. For him who recognizes this fact, the proofs herein outlined have no place. As before, by means of the arguments here given, employing only those means the opponent himself has outlined as constituting legitimate reasoning, it is the opponent who is forced to accept the doctrine of non-duality. And starting from this belief, he too can come to know his own soul with the immeasurable joy that such self-realization brings. For Śrī Harṣa, then, non-duality is self-evident; for the Naiyāyika, Mīmāṃsaka and Jain it is demonstrated by the very principles they all admit.[68]

Śrīharṣa concludes the section of the first chapter on the Advaita program, prior to the refutations, by talking again, briefly, about debate.[69] We noted that according to Nyāya there are different kinds of debate; to be precise, there are *vāda*, "inquiry aiming at the truth," *jalpa*, "debating for victory (where utilizing tricky arguments is okay so long as one gets away it)," and *vitaṇḍā*, "refutational debate by captious argument with no express regard for establishing a thesis of one's own."[70] The question is, how should Śrīharṣa's refutations be taken by Naiyāyikas (and other opponents)? Fundamentally, again, the refutations are to serve to back them into the Advaita view, by means of eliminative argument and more. But Śrīharṣa anticipates that the refutations will be construed as confined in scope to the particular topics examined and the epistemological positions and ontological categories of Nyāya, et al. He anticipates as well the objection that were he, Śrīharṣa, concerned with the truth (*vāda*), he would offer an alternative, patched-up view on each of the topics. Thus Śrīharṣa has in mind someone who insists on a replacement theory for each and every individual topic in which the Logician position is shown to be untenable. His reply is that his reflection should be (provisionally) taken as being in the spirit of a radical *vitaṇḍin*, a debater who has no positive view *on that topic*. Thus he emphasizes that what principally concerns him is not any individual topic, but rather relinquishment of the entire Nyāya realist view in an embrace of the Advaita alternative.[71]

2.5. Meditation and Mysticism

Advaita, of course, faces problems of its own. There is a fundamental tension between Advaita's understanding of the content of scriptural revelation and immediate mystical experience of Brahman, on the one hand, and the non-Brahmanish content of perceptual and perception-related cognitions, on the other. Śrīharṣa is not as much of an anti-rationalist about this tension as one might think. Like Maṇḍana, Śrīharṣa regards Brahman as object, not as the *sattā*, being-ness, revealed in all cognition, but nonetheless as *the* all-inclusive and omnipresent existent, *sat*. Indications of Brahman's all-inclusiveness can be gained by reasoning and close attention. But scripture is what we mainly have to rely on, although to personally become accomplished in profound meditation (which is what scripture teaches) would be best of all. The reality of Brahman as revealed mystically and proclaimed by the Upanishads negates suffering and the display of disparate, distinct phenomena. Precisely how the negation is to be understood is admittedly problematic; we like to use perceptual illusion as an analogy. But you can begin to see the negation for yourselves by examining ramifications of the proposition that things are fundamentally distinct. We will show that the distinctness display is negated by "debate-authorized" reasons, that claims presupposing distinctness cannot withstand scrutiny. Nevertheless, we admit that the display (and the suffering) are not to be classed as fictions, like the horn of a hare. We do not want to contend the precise ontological determination: this is in part what we mean when we say that things are indeterminable, *anirvacanīya*. We do not wish to deny the appearance of distinctness altogether. What we propose is that the mystical revelation is what is to be desired. That goal is proclaimed in the Upanishads, in particular in the identity texts (Thou art That, Thou art Brahman), and we see that these proclamations are supported by realizing that their opponents are dead.

In this way might the Advaitin be expected to lash out. Of course, any two comprehensive philosophies may be expected to be at odds. Ironically, the evidence that might best resolve Advaita's disputes with Nyāya derives from mysticism. Have the Advaitins rightly understood the mystical experience that they exalt? Śrīharṣa gives us some clues about a supposed phenomenology of mystic trance, principally in the epic *Nc* but also in the *Khkh*. We will look more closely at these clues along with the question of the role of mysticism in the overall view, in the section "Advaita and Theistic Voluntarism" near the end of the chapter.

3. Realism, the Core Problems

So far our exposition concerning Advaita-Nyāya conflicts has tilted toward the Advaita perspective, how Śrīharṣa himself sees conflicts with Nyāya. We will now take a broad view of areas of Nyāya theory that come under attack, with a more even-handed approach, mindful of the Nyāya perspective as well as Śrīharṣa's. For example, where would a Naiyāyika feel particularly stung? And which Nyāya doctrines seem to need revision? Revision, we might emphasize, not relinquishment, is the overall response by New Logicians, insofar as Śrīharṣa is not judged to be simply wrong. (Of course, there may have been individual Logicians who were converted by Śrīharṣa's arguments, but there is no record of a conversion, so far as I know.) In other words, Logicians either take Śrīharṣa's attacks to be misdirected or to call for bits of mending to their theories. The best objections, then, do not lead to relinquishment of Nyāya realist positions, but to improvements therein.

We will also try to identify recurrent patterns in Śrīharṣa's "refutations," key reasonings employed in a variety of contexts. We have already reviewed the motives the Advaitin has for his overall attack: basically, he is guided by his sense of how Nyāya conflicts with the Advaita view. But often the prods used to awaken us to Advaita truths are problems identified deep within the realist perspective, and such identification often depends on a dialectical maneuver (trick?) repeatedly employed. As we will see, a primary, though not the only, weapon in Śrīharṣa's arsenal, is the problem of relations, the Bradley problem. We will have, in sum, an eye out for inadequacies revealed by the Advaitin as felt from the Naiyāyika perspective and for argument patterns in the attacks, as we review Śrīharṣa's refutations.

3.1. *Consciousness and Theory of Justification*

The nature of awareness, along with the Naiyāyika theory of veridicality and how it is known, is the area of realist reflection most transparently in conflict with Śrīharṣa's Advaita. Śrīharṣa's dialectic is, as we have seen, closely tied to his own positive program, and in this light Śrīharṣa identifies central problems with the Naiyāyika view early in the *Khkh.* The theory of awareness as not self-illumining, with one awareness requiring another for the first to be cognized, makes self-awareness impossible because of infinite regress, and leads to the faulty Naiyāyika epistemology. Furthermore, the Naiyāyika view that the success of activity based on a cognition C_1 is what proves C_1 correct is objectionable because there would be a question about the grounds for the cognition C_2 of the success of such activity, given that there is a question about the grounds for C_1.[72] Thus any answer will invite further question, *ad infinitum.* The Logicians' theory of inference as a *pramāṇa* involves a similar problem of infinite regress insofar as an inference is supposed to be known as a *pramāṇa* by another inference.[73] Everyday activity does indeed, Śrīharṣa agrees, proceed from cognition, but it is useless to suppose that there is a real world independent of consciousness and causally related to it. One who subscribes to such a view not only faces the regresses but also begs the question against the idealist. Consciousness is all that is required for life pursuits and a sense of success in action. Imaginary sweets, as in a dream, can produce the experience of flavors just as much as "real" ones. Thus the Naiyāyika begs the deep question against the idealist in talking about real causal relations in connection with his theory of justification.[74] Finally, there are the particular problems with the specific terms used in a variety of characterizations of veridical awareness and the sources of veridical awareness, where the incoherent web spun by the realist has to be patiently traced.

On the Nyāya side, the alleged regresses do not appear to call for much of a novel rejoinder. Uddyotakara and Vācaspati I work out a Logician response to similar criticism advanced by Nāgārjuna and other Buddhists, as we saw. Furthermore, the debates with the Buddhists have driven home another rebuttal: the very designation "dream" presupposes differentiation between veridical and non-veridical experience. Veridical experience has to be understood in terms of what is revealed, namely, intersubjectively accessible things that give rise to the experience. In the Nyāya view, the deep mistake that the Advaitin makes concerns the relation between cognition and object. The Advaitin fails to grasp the intentional nature of awareness and the causal nature of objects. But because of Śrīharṣa's objections against a variety of definitions of veridical awareness and the sources of veridical awareness, Logicians see the need to make further effort to come up with correct characterizations. They see that some of the objections are on target and that the errors revealed should be avoided. But they refuse to accept that the faults mean that their definitional projects cannot in principle be successfully carried out.

Now Śrīharṣa also attacks the subject-object relationship (*viṣaya-viṣayi-bhāva*) so crucial to the Logician theory. An extended attack is presented early in the *Khkh*'s fourth and final chapter; there is as well a less elaborate attack in the first chapter.[75] In both of these, an apparent paradox of relationality is key. In brief, no story can be told about the relation between awareness and its content, because that would invite the question of what ties the relation to each, *ad infinitum*. What then about self-linkage (*sambandha-svarūpāt sambandhinor*)? This proves only the identity of cognition and its content—precisely the Advaita position! The logic here is the same as with an "attribution dilemma," which is examined later in this chapter, with corresponding text from Śrīharṣa's *Khkh* translated in chapter 5 (pp. 221–22). This problem in particular taxes the Logicians, as we will see in chapters 4 and 5.

3.2. "Truth" and the "Real" (tattva)

According to Śrīharṣa, there is no world external to or independent of consciousness. In contrast, the Naiyāyika understanding of truth, or veridicality (*prāmāṇya, pramātva*), supposes such independent reality because, most generally, awareness related to it in one way constitutes truth but in another constitutes falsehood or non-veridicality. An important Naiyāyika project is to spell out these relations, and Śrīharṣa tries to show that it cannot succeed. What, he asks, is a veridical awareness (*pramā*)? "An experience of what is real, i.e., of something's being what it is, *tattva*, its *being that*," is the first Naiyāyika answer that the Advaitin examines.[76] There are two fundamental problems identified: (a) what it is to be a reality is not spelled out intelligibly, and (b) the precise cut between the illusory and the veridical is not secured.

The two are interrelated. The object of a veridical awareness is supposed to be a reality; veridical awareness captures what is fact. The object of a non-veridical awareness is in some way not a reality; non-veridical awareness does not capture fact, or presents something erroneously. Śrīharṣa argues that it is impossible to spell out what *tattva* is—what it is that a veridical awareness captures or makes known—other than by reference to the content of awareness, in which case there is no way to make the cut between the veridical and non-veridical.

Other definitions succumb to similar dilemmas. For example, the second definition examined, "Veridical awareness is experience of a thing as it is (*yathārtha*)," specifies a similarity between the awareness, or what is objectified (to use Ganganatha Jha's term[77]) in the awareness, and the supposed object in the world.[78] The problem here lies chiefly with the cut between the veridical and non-veridical. But also the Naiyāyika is incapable of spelling out an external relation of similarity (this is the same problem as provoked by the term *tattva* in the previous definition). According to the Nyāya ontology, there is always similarity between an awareness and its object or content in some respects—for example, both exist—but in other respects always dissimilarity—for example, an awareness of a pot is, *qua* awareness, a quality of the self or soul, while the pot is a substance. The color of a pot inheres, according to Nyāya, in the pot, whereas cognition has no such inherence. Furthermore, there are many respects, Śrīharṣa elaborates, in which an illusory cognition—for example, mother-of-pearl experienced as silver—has content that matches a supposedly external object: e.g., both content and object are cognized, and both are a "this" (*idaṃtā*). Even if one tries refinements specifying right and wrong respects (*prakāra*)—for example, mother-of-pearl is veridically experienced with respect to "being a this" but non-veridically experienced with respect to "silverness"—the project still fails. To the cognizer, the mother-of-pearl does in fact appear to be silver, and the person is right to say that she experienced it as silver.

Gaṅgeśa follows closely Śrīharṣa's reasoning in coming up with his Navya characterization of the veridicality of an awareness. Indeed, the New Logician appears in this instance to have the text of the *Khkh* in front of him, so closely does his reflection match, as we will see (below, chapter 5, pp. 184ff), the Advaitin's reasonings.

3.3. *Definitions and Defining Characteristics*

In the last chapter, we noted that Naiyāyikas believe that the point of definitions is to specify differentiating features (above, pp. 63–64). The activity helps us to identify something and understand what it is. Though Udayana stresses the former purpose, the latter is evident particularly in the use of definitions in the *Nyāya-sūtra* and early commentaries (pre-Udayana). As utilized in the *Nyāya-sūtra*, definition, *lakṣaṇa*, could itself be characterized as explanatory characterization, although over time there come to be special requirements.

Thus, in early Nyāya, *salient* differentiating features are focused upon, while Udayana, in contrast, insists on mere differentiation—any feature is viewed as adequate that is both (a) possessed by all tokens of type x and (b) not possessed by anything that is not an x. Nevertheless, both definitional projects center on distinctive characteristics. This presupposes that there are such characteristics (at least normally) and, more fundamentally, that things and types of things are distinct. Thus the definitional project is premised on *bheda*, distinctness, which Śrīharṣa is committed to showing unintelligible.

It is a "systematic arrangement of things," things presumed distinct from one another and related causally and otherwise, that Śrīharṣa finds objectionable.[79] Udayana, despite his disinterest in what we might call pedagogically striking features as opposed to those that formally fit his requirements, reaffirmed the tradition of explaining the Nyāya system through a series of definitions. Śrīharṣa finds it convenient to follow this procedure in dismantling it.

Udayana also, we noted, explicitly stated the requirements for good definitions (see above, p. 64). Śrīharṣa is particularly adept at taking advantage of these. But he also usually tries to reveal the spirit of a definition, the underlying view that informs it, and does not rest content with pointing out what we might call formal problems (''formal'' in the sense of Udayana). The passages from the *Khkh*, translated in chapter 5 (pp. 164–73), on the attempt to define veridical awareness, exhibit such a style.

The Logicians, for their part, seem to feel particularly stung by Śrīharṣa's attacks on what they call the *anugama* requirement of a good definition, that is, the requirement that the things defined are significantly similar (''uniform'' or exhibit a ''consecutive character''). This concern is related to the theory of universals, attacks on which we will discuss below. But it also impinges directly on the Logicians' definitional projects and indeed on Gaṅgeśa's understanding of what a good definition requires. We will see that the New Logician is willing to sacrifice *anugama* in defining veridicality.

3.4. The Attribution Dilemma

Also translated in chapter 5 is Śrīharṣa's identification of an attribution dilemma where one option is closed, he argues, because of a vicious infinite regress (below, pp. 221–22). This is the regress that results from regarding a relation as a third term, a problem, we noted, that the Buddhist Dharmakīrti pointed out and that the *Brahma-sūtra* and the Advaitin Śaṅkara applied specifically to the Nyāya-Vaiśeṣika understanding of inherence as the attributional tie. This is a refutational pattern that Śrīharṣa uses repeatedly.

Now to frame the problem as I have, as resulting from taking a relation to be a term, suggests the response credited to Bertrand Russell in addressing the Bradley problem:[80] relations are a different sort of animal; they are not terms. This response resonates with Nyāya in that inherence, *samavāya*, is regarded as an ontological primitive, neither like substances that are the bearers of qualities, motions, and universals, nor like any of these properties. It is instead just the tie. Indeed, this seems the proper and natural response to the arguments of Dharmakīrti and Śaṅkara. However, Śrīharṣa's attack is broader. In fact, with regard to attribution he presents three possibilities: (a) the property and the property-bearer are unrelated, (b) they are related by a third term, *ad infinitum*, or (c) ''it is the very nature of one of the terms to link with the other.'' The third option, he says, results in non-distinctness, a failure to keep the property and the property-bearer apart. At least, that would appear to be the problem from the Naiyāyika perspective. From his own perspective, whether this is an unwanted result is debatable. I will first address the hermeneutical question, then return to the problem as perceived from the

Naiyāyika point of view.

The passage translated below in chapter 5 concludes with a claim that perception, the supposed prover of distinctness, "proves nothing but non-duality (*advaita*)." Thus one is tempted to read Śrīharṣa as favoring the third option and even as arguing indirectly in support of a homogeneous monism. However, I am inclined to take this particular conclusion, in this particular use of the relation regress, as a joke, a pun on "non-distinctness" and "non-duality" (*advaita*), a taunt directed at Naiyāyikas. I do not believe he thinks that this is by itself a proof of the non-dual Brahman, but rather, as I have indicated, of indeterminability (*anirvacanīyatva*). The eliminative proof here is in favor of a fourth option: the seamless Advaita philosophy taught by the Upanishads. (We have to keep in mind that Upanishadic declarations are out on the table.) Śrīharṣa's view of the bridge between Brahman and the world is that it is *anirvacanīya*, indeterminable or "impossible to say." The failure of the Naiyāyika program reinforces indeterminability. Brahman's non-duality is thought to entail the unintelligibility of distinctness, but "the unintelligibility of distinctness" is not thought to be precisely equivalent to Brahman's non-duality.[81] On the other hand, at two places in *Khkh* chapter 4,[82] Śrīharṣa says explicitly that the regress shows the futility of viewing not only the qualification relation as independent of consciousness but also the subject-object relation as obtaining between externally related realities. He concludes that this proves the *idealist* thesis: "Consciousness alone should be accepted as the source of this and that everyday experience and activity, consciousness variously transformed through its capacity for self-causality."[83] He thus invokes the explanatory program of the Buddhist Idealists, but does not elaborate, nor—in these passages—differentiate the Advaita view from that of Dharmakīrti and company.

From the Naiyāyika perspective, the problem is to avoid a vicious infinite regress while maintaining a layeredness between a property, e.g., blue, and the property-bearer, e.g., a lotus; that is to say, while maintaining the asymmetry of attribution, of the qualification relation. Inherence may maintain the layeredness as an asymmetrical ontological primitive. But then what relates the inherence? If inherence is self-linking, if it relates to the lotus by its very nature, so to say, then the two seem to become non-distinct; similarly with inherence and the blue. Through inherence as self-linking, the three become one. The nature of the one includes the others; the layeredness is lost.

It is not enough to say, in the fashion of Russell, that such asymmetry of relation is just a brute fact. Śrīharṣa does not deny (nor, I believe, does F. H. Bradley[84]) that perception presents such an asymmetrical relation of properties and property-bearers. The Advaitin's claim is that the appearance is unintelligible. To avoid (a) a fundamental unrelatedness and (b) a vicious regress (that amounts to unrelatedness, since the need for a further relator undercuts the relating work that inherence is supposed to accomplish), the Logician realist is forced to embrace (c) self-linkage. This is in fact Praśastapāda's position, as we saw above (p. 49), and it comes to be the express New Logician position as well. The problem is then why self-linkage does not amount to abandonment of the layeredness between properties and property-bearers, why it is not, *unlike* what Praśastapāda says, a matter of identity (*tādātmya*). Śrīharṣa's identification of an attribution dilemma is premised on rejection of self-linkage *cum* distinctness. At several places in his text, he attacks self-linkage as amounting to a Naiyāyika capitulation precisely concerning distinctness.[85]

Śrīharṣa mounts a many-sided onslaught on the Nyāya notion of distinctness, only part of which relies on the logic in evidence here. There are also other arguments advanced. We will review the overall case after first taking up the attack on universals, which, though interspersed throughout the four chapters of the *Khkh*, may conveniently be abstracted from Śrīharṣa's own order of considered topics and denounced views.

3.5. *Universals*

Were Śrīharṣa a contemporary philosopher, he would have a career just in his criticism of the Nyāya theory of universals, *sāmānya* or *jāti*, more precisely, "natural kinds." He thoroughly exposes its weaknesses, spelling out six or seven independent lines of criticism, all of which recur, and one of which, concerning definitions and theory of meaning, is voiced throughout the *Khkh*. The most extended consideration occurs within the first half of his fourth chapter where the Nyāya-Vaiśeṣika ontology is taken up and definitions of each of the categories refuted. But almost all the lines of criticism are introduced earlier, and we will review them roughly in the order in which they appear.

Although it is not the very first difficulty raised, a problem concerning how a pot is known to be distinct from a cloth is mentioned early in the *Khkh* and is especially important for apparently provoking Gaṅgeśa to make clear how an individual is known to be an instance of a universal.[86] The problem draws on a logic similar to that of the attribution dilemma: if an individual pot can be known as a pot only through the qualifier, potness, in virtue of what is the potness known? Later, the problem is widened, and in effect we have the attribution dilemma again.[87] Just as the tie between a property and its bearer must first be accomplished by another tie tying the tie, so a property whereby a property-bearer is known must be first known by another property. Now, since every verbalization of an awareness requires mention of a qualifier through which a qualificandum is known, this, the problem of predication, is deep indeed. Though for Nyāya the problem is not on the level of language but of awareness, it remains troublesome: how can the explicit content (*prakāra*) of an awareness be known as a qualifier of a qualificandum? If the qualificandum is known to be so through a qualifier, how then is the qualifier known? (How can the qualificandum even be known as a qualificandum; qualificandum-hood would have to be mentioned or presented.) The question threatens a foundation of the Nyāya ontology, the property/property-bearer relation, as Śrīharṣa argues explicitly in the fourth chapter of the *Khkh.*[88]

In the earlier passage, i.e., in the midst of showing distinctness to be incoherent, Śrīharṣa considers the hypothesis that a pot is distinct from a cloth in virtue of having potness, which the cloth—exhibiting, in contrast, clothness—does not have.[89] The wider context is the Naiyāyika claim that it is perception that makes distinctness known. Thus, knowing perceptually the potness of a pot and the clothness of a cloth would amount to knowing the distinctness of the one from the other. Ontologically, the distinctness would be underpinned by the distinct universals or class characters. (Strictly speaking, this seems to be a misinterpretation by Śrīharṣa of the realist position: it is not the class character but the bare particular that underpins an individual's distinctness.) According to this (mis)interpretation, the class character performs, in the case of a pot and a cloth (though not with two pots), the distinguishing function. Universals particularize as well as group together.

Śrīharṣa asks how the universals are in turn known to be distinct. The distinctness of the pot from the cloth would be secured by the distinctness of the universals. But then the problem reappears one level up. What secures the distinctness of the universals? On the one hand, an infinite regress looms; on the other, a lack of distinctness at the higher level threatens to infect the distinctness of the two particulars. In other words, if some further quality or character is proposed to do the distinguishing work, that would invite further question, *ad infinitum*. Also, received Naiyāyika opinion is that no universal inheres in a universal.[90] But if, on the other hand, nothing differentiates two universals, then they cannot be distinguished and non-distinctness results, a non-distinctness infecting the particulars, which are then also non-distinct.[91]

A second difficulty identified is similar; it also involves the Nyāya tenet that particulars are never encountered unclothed. And it echoes what we called with Nāgārjuna the problem of the particularity of particulars, although Śrīharṣa's reasoning is much more complex than the Buddhist's.[92] Despite an epistemic inseparability, Logicians regard universals and their loci as distinct. But if an individual F (*qua* its particularity) is distinct from being-an-F, the distinguishing factor has to be, our Advaitin argues, in some respect its not being-an-F. Then how is this something that is not an F to be an F? By the entering into it of the universal, the being-an-F? But then how is the *universal* to have that character, the being-an-F? Again the problem would seem to duplicate itself a level up, *ad infinitum*. If, on the other hand, it is the particular in its bare particularity that is an F, then the death (*jalāñjali*) of universals would be announced. That is to say, this move is unacceptable to the Logician because according to him it is a universal that accounts for the unity of a class of individuals; what is identical in them is what grounds common experience and conception, for example, of cowhood in every cow. Śrīharṣa astutely points out that if the particularity of a particular is sufficient to ground its having a certain class character, then universals are otiose. Śaṅkara Miśra, in combating this line of attack, embraces the first horn: there is a sense in which something that is an F and its being an F are distinct. Indeed, the qualificational relation guarantees that they are distinct—this crucial rejoinder is elaborated in chapters 4 and 5.

Among other charges and problems Śrīharṣa insists upon, the exclusionary role of universals according to the Naiyāyikas is said to amount to an embrace of the Buddhist *apoha* ("exclusionary" or nominalist) theory.[93] (Śaṅkara Miśra expressly answers the taunt: see below, p. 278.) More fundamentally, the exclusion of F's from non-F's, putatively secured by the universal being-an-F, will become an exclusion of F's from things that *are* F as well, in that each particular F, in virtue of being particular, has a particular relation to being-an-F that excludes all other F's.[94]

Another line of critique—not so much *of* the theory of universals but *by* it—profits from Udayana's stricture that two true universals do not "cross-sect," i.e., have within their extension some individuals in common and some not (above, pp. 61–62). A common Naiyāyika ploy is to put forward an abstract X-hood as a definition of X, with X-hood taken to be a universal or natural kind, in order to account for why something is an X and the meaning of the term "X" (recall the discussion in chapter 2, pp. 63–64). Thus Śrīharṣa has ample call to think about universals in examining various definitions. For example, he demolishes a proposed definition of *pramā*, veridical awareness, namely, that it is "experience of reality," *tattva-anubhuti*, in part by focusing on the term *anubhūti*, "experience," and inquiring what it means. He shows that the putative universal *anubhūtitva*, "experience-hood" or "being experience," proffered to answer this question, cross-sects with "being memory" in cases of recognition, e.g., "This is that Devadatta (I saw yesterday)," and thus that it is not a true universal or natural kind.[95] This is a painful consequence for Nyāya in that a remembering is not regarded as a veridical awareness (*pramā*), while veridical awareness, being at the center of the system, has to be adequately defined. There are several other instances where features of the theory of universals are made to work against other important Naiyāyika views.[96]

Of the definitions of *sāmānya* itself that Śrīharṣa scrutinizes,[97] he is particularly astute in his criticisms of the view that a universal is the ground or cause of a recurrent experience or common conception, e.g., of two individual cows as cows. It surely is not the sole cause, he points out, since a person's senses, mind, and so on, must be factors as well. If, then, the universal is defined merely as one necessary condition for experiential recurrence—there being other necessary conditions as well—the definition fails to be sufficiently exclusive. Moreover, no satisfactory definition of recurrence is available. Then in a distinct line of critique, Śrīharṣa has a field day with the claim that universals are "eternal" (*nitya*).

Finally, our Advaitin is well aware of the embarrassingly *ad hoc* catch-all category, or non-category, of *upādhi*, variously translated as "adventitious property," "abstract property," "imposed property," and (as I sometimes say) "surplus property." This is the wastebasket of the Nyāya ontology, the miscellaneous file into which class characters that fail to pass all the tests to be true universals are stuffed.[98] The category of surplus properties is a decidedly weak plank in Nyāya. A section of the next chapter is devoted to it, as I begin to draw together the threads of Gaṅgeśa's and other New Logicians' views.

3.6. Paradoxes of Distinctness (bheda)

However much fun Śrīharṣa has with universals, they are a side show; the main attraction, or detraction, is distinctness, *bheda*. Again, the Advaitin does not deny that distinctness is commonly experienced. "Clearly it is distinctness (as of a cloth from a pot) that is being cognized—everyone bears witness to this."[99] The denial is of distinctness's intelligibility; unintelligibility, or indeterminability, is an intermediate position between a claim of reality and one of unreality, and is considered entailed by Upanishadic teachings of Brahman's all-inclusiveness and non-duality. "We do not hold that distinctness is in every way unreal, but only that it is not absolutely real. It is acceptable to us to say that this kind of thing is known through spiritual ignorance (*avidyā*), a (so to say) process that is not the truest knowing."[100] That this is not the truest knowing is shown best by mystical awareness, then by scripture, but also through paradoxes of distinctness.

I view Śrīharṣa as aiming to find paradoxes of distinctness, at least implicitly, with nearly all his refutations, since, as I have argued, he sees all the definitions he attacks as presupposing distinctness, the prime challenger to what the Upanishads say about Brahman. His fundamental objection is to any attempt to explain appearances on a supposition that distinctness is real. But he also mounts onslaughts on distinctness expressly at two places in the *Khkh*, one toward the end of the introductory portion of the first chapter, the other in the middle of the fourth chapter, which is devoted to refutation of the Nyāya-Vaiśeṣika ontology.[101]

The onslaught in the first chapter includes the attribution dilemma we have already discussed (see also the translation in chapter 5, pp. 221ff). The larger context of that dilemma is a question Śrīharṣa asks several paragraphs earlier, "And just what is that distinctness purportedly established by perception?"[102] Four candidates are proposed, and one by one demolished in the ensuing paragraphs: (a) distinctness is the very nature of an object, (b) distinctness is mutual exclusion, or mutual absence (*anyonyābhāva*), (c) distinctness is difference in properties, and (d) something else. The attribution dilemma appears within the examination of the first candidate, and Śrīharṣa makes other points with regard to such a view of distinctness, in addition to his arguments against the remaining three candidates. Phyllis Granoff has done a good job explaining the entire section.[103] I will summarize the main points, then review in somewhat greater detail the onslaught in *Khkh* chapter 4—all while trying to keep the Nyāya perspective in mind. The first three candidate views are asserted by Udayana: depending on circumstances of cognition, or what it is that is cognized (a substance, quality, etc.), distinctness appears as (a) the very nature of the object, (b) mutual exclusion, or (c) a difference in properties.[104] The fourth view, (d) something else, is filled out by Śrīharṣa as the Exegete stance that distinctness is the special attribute "separateness" (*pṛthaktva*).[105] Udayana's triple position is also the focus of the examination in *Khkh* chapter 4. In fact, Śrīharṣa quotes there a long passage from Udayana's *Ātmatattvaviveka*.[106] Overlap and repetition occur in the two treatments, but also different arguments are made.

The theme of the examination of the first candidate in *Khkh* chapter 1 is that "No cognition not revealing non-distinctness can reveal distinctness,"[107] a gauntlet thrown in the face of the Logician, who in the person of Śaṅkara Miśra (also Vācaspati II) picks it up, arguing the opposite, that all cognitions reveal distinctness, including cognitions of non-distinctness (see chapter 5, pp. 274–79 and 299–309). Śrīharṣa's principal argument plays on the logic of relations as well as the notion of something's "very nature" (*svarūpa*). Distinctness involves at a minimum two terms, the distinct entity, *x*, and that from which it is distinct, *y*.[108] But if distinctness is the very nature of *x*, then *x* must include *y*, at least in the sense that one cannot cognize *x* as in its very nature distinct without also thinking of *y*. *Qua* distinctness, *y* cannot be intellectually separated out; thus, since on this first alternative the distinctness is the very nature of *x*, *x* includes *y* in its very nature. The challenge is then to explain the logic of the relation such that *x* may remain by nature distinct, but not absorb what it is distinct from.

Śrīharṣa anticipates such a line of Naiyāyika response by examining the "adjuncthood" or "counter-correlateness" concept (*pratiyogitva*: see the glossary, the first sense of the term, *pratiyogin*). This brings us to the attribution dilemma. The adjunct of the distinctness relation is taken to be a property, and thus as little sense can be made of adjuncthood as of the property/property-bearer relation (because of *regressus ad infinitum*).

However intractable that dilemma, there remains a further special problem with distinctness, insofar as distinctness is the very nature of anything: the logic of "being the very nature" is distinct from that of distinctness. This is reflected in Sanskrit by the use of the instrumental case for the adjunct (the instrumental of separation) and the nominative for the subjunct, to express distinctness (a pot distinct *from* a cloth), while "being the very nature" would be expressed through case agreement. With this point, Śrīharṣa concludes his rejection of the first candidate, and moves on to consider (b) mutual exclusion (*anyonyābhāva*). The grammatical point is expressly resisted by New Logicians, who view the proper expression of this kind of distinctness in the form of a sentence such as "A pot is not a cloth," *ghaṭaḥ paṭo na*, where both terms are in the same case—in this instance, the nominative.

The Advaitin's first argument against the mutual exclusion view is that the attribution dilemma again applies in that mutual exclusion is a relational notion. Moreover, he continues, mutual exclusion is a kind of absence; "mutual" or "reciprocal absence" is indeed a more literal translation of the Sanskrit term. Absences, according to Nyāya, always involve a relation to an absentee, or counterpositive (*pratiyogin*: see the glossary, the second sense of the term). An absence is invariably *of* an absentee; thus absences are relations. But the problem is not just that the absenteeship relation has the same logic as that of adjuncthood.[109] That invokes, as has been pointed out, the attribution dilemma. A further problem is that identity (*tādātmya*) has to be the absentee in the case of a mutual absence, says Śrīharṣa.[110] The mutual exclusion itself (in such a relation as the mutual exclusion of a pot and a cloth) is equivalent to an absence of identity: identity has to be the absentee. The absence is an absence *of* identity between, e.g., a pot and a cloth.

Now to hold this would get the Logician in trouble, as the Advaitin makes plain. It is an established Nyāya position (*siddhānta*) that any absentee must be a real (see chapter 2: p. 51). It is sheer nonsense to say that there is an absence of a hare's horn on the floor, since there is no such thing as the horn of a hare. To deny of a hare that it has a horn makes sense, because there are horns elsewhere (on cows, etc.). And it makes sense to deny that there is a pot on the floor, since pots exist elsewhere. But it makes no sense to deny a hare's horn with regard to the floor; there would be an error concerning the negatum. (This position connects with the Nyāya empiricist theory of mind: we must have experienced what is meaningfully denied, e.g., horns, not hare's horns.) Thus, since the absentee must be a real, and presuming that identity between the pot and the cloth is what is denied—i.e., that identity is the absentee—it follows that either (a) the identity must be real (elsewhere), or (b) the notion of mutual exclusion is nonsense. Both options support the Advaita polemic, and neither is acceptable to the Naiyāyika. Gaṅgeśa along with both

Śaṅkara Miśra and Vācaspati II show where the error in this reasoning lies.

This argument is particularly important because among the three positions proposed by Udayana, the firmest commitment on the part of New Logicians appears to be to distinctness as mutual exclusion. In the next chapter, after looking at the New Logician view of absences, we will turn in particular to the Navya view of the absentee with a mutual exclusion, also the Navya view of identity.

Against the third candidate, difference in properties (*vaidharmya*), Śrīharṣa again identifies a problem with attribution, which we reviewed in discussing alleged problems with universals: if distinctness is a matter of difference of properties—e.g., potness with a pot and clothness with a cloth—then there will have to be further properties to render the putatively distinguishing properties distinct, *ad infinitum*. On the other hand, if the series ends at some point, there will be, *ex hypothesi*, no distinctness-making at the lower level, which would entail that the pot and the cloth, e.g., are non-distinct. Essentially the same argument is put against the Mīmāṃsaka view that distinctness amounts to the special property, "separateness" (*pṛthaktva*). The regress here is not the same as that with the relation between a property and property-bearer, because in that case the additional links required are between the two original terms whereas here the regress is on top of, so to say, the qualifier term. Still, the regresses are similar, and similarly vicious apparently, in that an additional link or term is required in order for a former link or term to do its work, in the one case of linking, in the other of making distinct.[111] Then Śrīharṣa invokes his theme at the end of the section ("Cognition apparently revealing distinctness reveals non-distinctness instead") by reminding us that if to avoid the untoward consequences we deny distinctness between the property (distinctness) and its locus, unity (not distinctness) results.[112] Part of the strategy of the New Logicians is to deny that the regress is vicious; another part is to invoke the logic of something's "very nature" (*svarūpa*) differently from Śrīharṣa's sense.

We turn now to the attack on distinctness in *Khkh* chapter 4, which, though occurring in the midst of an examination of Logician ontological concepts, relies heavily on epistemological points. The passage has three parts. First, Śrīharṣa presents objections to each of three views of distinctness that Udayana proposes—three of the four, namely, that were examined in *Khkh* chapter 1—without, by the way, informing us that these are Udayana's construals. Next comes the long quote from Udayana (which is not identified as Udayana's, or even as a quotation[113]). Finally, we get objections that focus on some of the counterarguments in the passage from Udayana, which itself includes objections to Nyāya views, as well as responses.[114]

Against the view that distinctness is the very nature of an object, Śrīharṣa argues that in that case it would be impossible to misperceive, e.g., silver as mother-of-pearl since that would involve perceiving something as *non-distinct* from what it is not. The Naiyāyika theory of non-veridical perception would seem to have little difficulty defusing the argument; something can be F while we fail to perceive that it is F, or even erroneously cognize that it is not-F. This objection does not provoke, so far as I can tell, any Navya response.

Against the view that distinctness is mutual exclusion, Śrīharṣa argues that perception makes positive presentations, not negative ones. Thus mutual exclusion, being negative (mutual absence), could not be known perceptually. This argument also does not much disturb our realists, since it does not much challenge the view of distinctness but only invites rehearsal of the Nyāya position on the perception of absences. Now that is a thorny topic, and it does impinge on the mutual exclusion controversy since mutual exclusion is a type of absence. Moreover, perception does seem to be positive in character, as Śrīharṣa (along with many other philosophers) claims; it is dubious whether an absence or any kind of negation could be given perceptually. The Logicians argue otherwise, as we will see. A section of the next chapter is devoted to New Logicians' views of absences, including such epistemological questions as this one of Śrīharṣa's.

Against the view that distinctness amounts to difference in properties, Śrīharṣa begins with a preëmptive strike against Udayana's view concerning the basis for the variability in how we understand distinctness. With absences, for example, distinctness has to be a matter of their "very nature" (*svarūpa*) since absences do not exhibit properties (they are never property-bearers, but only properties). Śrīharṣa (unfairly) objects that if distinctness amounts to difference in properties, an absence devoid of properties would have to be non-distinct from the entire universe, which, being then equivalent to an absence devoid of properties, would be a homogeneous negative blob! In a more serious vein, the Advaitin repeats some of his arguments of *Khkh* chapter 1, insisting, for example, that any distinctness is relational and thus there would have to be some further distinctness accounting for the distinctness between properties. Gaṅgeśa proposes immediate awareness of universals such as "cowhood" in part to avoid a regress about how a distinctive property is known. Śaṅkara Miśra fills the response out by arguing that distinctness, too, is given immediately. There remains, however, the problem of how a property is related to its bearer, a problem that, as Śrīharṣa again insists here, applies to distinctness insofar as it is regarded as a property—the problem of an infinite series of connectors required to tie it down.

We come now to the long quote from Udayana.[115] Udayana defends the "difference of properties" construal, arguing that an infinite regress is not a reason for denying a perceptual appearance; it is, rather, a reason for denying a presumption. Thus we refuse, he says, to presume further odor in an odor for the express purpose of avoiding a regress. But we do not deny that an actual odor is perceived whatever the logical fears. This argument, by the way, fits nicely with Gaṅgeśa's point that certain properties are immediately perceived. Moreover, says Udayana, without an assumption of difference in properties, we would have no notion of incompatibility and could conceive a horse as a cow and other absurdities.

Concerning distinctness as mutual exclusion, Udayana explains the Nyāya view of cognition of absences, professing that he fails to see any problem with the account. Then, concerning distinctness as something's "very nature," Udayana maintains that the odd use of words that this point gives rise to, as in the sentence "The pot is distinct," *ghaṭo bhinnaḥ*, is not to count against the Nyāya analysis. I think this cues the Navyas Śaṅkara Miśra and Vācaspati II to be ready to fight on the issue of conventional usage. In any case, a complex story comes to be told through Śrīharṣa's pressing arguments about unexpected grammatical structure in verbalizations of cognitions which the Logicians say capture distinctnesses.

Udayana also provides the lead in the delicate matter of awareness of the absentee as presupposed. About his statement, Śrīharṣa says only that it is aimed at no argument that he is aware of, at least none that he has himself advanced.[116] But a careful reading of Udayana's text shows that he has anticipated the problem and suggested to later Logicians the outline of a response (below, chapter 4, pp. 138–41). Śrīharṣa's attitude may simply be that the mess the Naiyāyika has got himself into is not his problem: let the poor Logician explain how the cognition of the absentee with one type of cognition of absence differs in such and such respects from the cognition of the absentee with another type. However, later Logicians indeed try to, and they do a pretty good job.

Finally, Udayana says that the distinctness of absences is invariably a matter of their "very nature," whereas particular substances, qualities, and motions are distinct in all three senses delineated, and universals, ultimate particularizers, and inherence are distinct in the two senses of "very nature" and "mutual exclusion." In the course of making this point, Udayana provides succinct definitions of each of the types of *bheda*, too succinct, unfortunately, to be able to withstand the onslaught from the Advaitin.

Śrīharṣa is at his dialectical best demolishing these definitions word by word. But he does not add much to the central considerations already aired. Against the contention that the need to avoid an infinite regress leads us to deny a series of distinctnesses but not a single distinctness appearing perceptually, the Advaitin alleges that the move is *ad hoc*, that he has good arguments against the intelligibility of—and thus the acceptance of the reality of—the putatively single, perceptually attested distinctness, and that the burden of proof, that is, the burden of rebuttal, is now on the other side. Moreover, he jokes, if the realist were to put forth a reason why one should presume a further odor in odor, he (objecting to the tenability of all such assumptions) would show why that reason fails too. Regarding the demolishing of Udayana's specific definitions, Śrīharṣa has little problem showing vicious circularity. The worst problem is the interlock between identity and distinctness: no effort to clear up what the one is will succeed without an unobjectionable view of the other—at least on the "mutual exclusion" construal. To try to define distinctness in the form of something's "own nature" faces insurmountable difficulties in that one would have to say what something's own nature is without referring to other things' natures or to one thing's distinctness from another (i.e., to the two's mutual exclusion). And Udayana's attempt to motivate his definition of "difference of properties" with the argument that otherwise incompatibility would be unintelligible comes to naught, because incompatibility, as Logicians think they understand it, is (indeed!) unintelligible—in that it involves pervasion, or invariable concomitance, *vyāpti* (the Logicians' putative underpinning for inference), which is itself unintelligible and unfounded.

The most interesting bit of Śrīharṣa's reflection concerns identity and distinctness, along with the question of the nature of qualification or relationality, in particular what it is for a property to share or have the same substratum as another property (*samānādhikaraṇatva*, a term that in grammar means "case agreement": the fact of sharing the same substratum would be expressed by case agreement, which is, in the verbalization of a cognition, taken as a mark of such sharing). Of all the problems to be faced by anyone who would revive Nyāya, probably the most serious concerns the relations among the various categories of reals as presented in verbalizable awareness. The problem has various dimensions, as we have seen, including—Śrīharṣa points out here—that of the "operative relation in sense perception" (*indriya-sannikarṣa*: *NyS* 1.1.4), which is the means by which the various categories and types of things perceived are causally conveyed to awareness. With a challenge to the Logician to explain the Nyāya understanding of "cause" appealed to with the "operative relation" notion, the Advaitin closes his express examination of distinctness and moves on to demolish the Logicians' view of causality.[117]

Key problems concerning identity and distinctness from a Naiyāyika point of view are: (1) the problem of how the negatum or absentee of a mutual exclusion is known (distinctness being construed as *anyonyābhava*, mutual absence), (2) what is meant by declaring distinctness (and identity) to be "the very nature" of an object, and how this construal relates to that of distinctness as mutual exclusion, (3) the grammar of conventional expression of distinctness, (4) the attribution dilemma, inherence, and self-linkage considered in general and in particular with regard to distinctness taken as an attribute, and (5) the epistemological regress concerning attributes or qualifiers, given that it is through a qualifier that a qualificandum is known. We will see that these are pretty satisfactorily resolved by Gaṅgeśa and his followers, though concerning the logic or nature of identity some difficult questions remain.

3.7. Informal Logic and Debate

Śrīharṣa's main complaint regarding the Nyāya theory of debate is against the argument that in virtue of the act of debate participation, particular epistemological and ontological positions may be presumed. At least this is his interest at the beginning of the *Khkh*, as we discussed in the last chapter. But at the end of *Khkh* chapter 1 and also at the end of chapter 4, the Advaitin examines details of Nyāya informal logic and debate theory.[118]

In both places, the larger issue is the whole Advaita/Nyāya controversy itself, whether one or the other may be said to be the acceptable position and on what grounds. In the first chapter, informal fallacies (*hetvābhāsa*s) are taken up in order to show characterizations thereof incoherent insofar as they presuppose distinctness. But also, with the weaponry of fallacies dismantled, none could be used against the Advaita stance. In the fourth and final chapter, dialectical reasoning, *tarka*—which was addressed in *Khkh* chapter 1 in connection with the issue of how an inference-grounding pervasion (*vyāpti*) is known[119]—is addressed again apparently as key to a wide range of Naiyāyika rejoinders. But as has become obvious to anyone who has toiled through Śrīharṣa's cogitations to this point, the Advaitin is a master of *tarka*. Not only is he adept at applications, he even slips in several positive contributions to Logic's *tarka* theory—here at the end of his Advaita book.[120]

One continually wonders what Śrīharṣa takes his own dialectic to show. Consistent with the reading I have already defended, I see this as indeterminability and the incapacity of any argument successfully to challenge the teaching of the Upanishads. Nevertheless, the types of dialectical reasoning that he identifies and explains are close to his heart: Śrīharṣa is fully cognizant that his refutations throughout his entire text involve identifying logical patterns that Logicians talk about as faults, whether they be informal fallacies, objectionable objections, or other censurable errors of debate (including the specific kinds of *tarka*—vicious regress, etc.—mentioned by Udayana or an anonymous Naiyāyika[121]). And all *tarka*, dialectical reasoning, involves showing a fallacy (in the broad English sense of the term) in an alternative view. But of course Śrīharṣa is opposed to any theory according to which fallacies have ontological underpinnings—he is particularly opposed to the Nyāya ontological understanding of pervasion, *vyāpti*.

Concerning whether his skepticism here is answerable, my own feeling is that Śrīharṣa tries to have his cake and to eat it too, and that Maṇikaṇṭha and Gaṅgeśa are right in their responses. But the issue is deep, and (beyond scrutinizing the text I translate in chapter 5) readers are urged to look at what Śrīharṣa says at the end of *Khkh* chapter 4 (though admittedly the Ganganatha Jha translation requires some struggle) to better make up their own minds. That passage is too long to re-translate in this book, and I will present only my sense of the challenge for the New Logicians who do in fact respond.[122] We might also note that there remains much to be mined in Śrīharṣa's treatment of debate and informal logic, and indeed in various classical treatments of these, especially in later contributions to the realist-idealist strife. Rich veins remain to be explored by future scholars and philosophers.[123]

The most important question seems to be the nature of contradiction, or opposition, *virodha*, which is, in the Nyāya view, incompatibility grounded in the nature of things and thus a type of pervasion, *vyāpti*, the underpinning of all inference. Right characterization of pervasion, reflecting right understanding, is, I dare say, the most absorbing issue throughout the entire history of New Logic, through Raghunātha and beyond. But also, it is difficult to specify precisely the nature of incompatibility itself (at least as the Logicians try to, namely, as the non-occurrence of one thing and another together, in the same manner, in the same respect), while also remaining true to the logic of the various types of negation as expressed in everyday discourse. Over time, Logicians come to distinguish truth-functional negation from several varieties of opposition among speech acts and possibilities.[124]

I cannot say in complete confidence that Śrīharṣa sparks Gaṅgeśa's use of specification techniques (*avacchedaka* techniques[125]). Vallabha (c. 1140), for one, seems to have the notion of "delimitation" (as the term *avaccheda* is commonly rendered in English) before the Navya period.[126] But the arguments that Śrīharṣa voices, I suggest, are responsible for the popularization of many of the techniques among Navya-Nyāya philosophers. A stock example that both Śrīharṣa and Gaṅgeśa cite is that of a tree as simultaneously both qualified and not qualified by a monkey-conjunction. We are to imagine a monkey in the branches, but not at the tree's roots. A monkey-conjunction (conjunction, or contact, *saṃyoga*, is a quality: see above, p. 46) and an absence of monkey-conjunction do not, however, qualify the tree at precisely the same spot; the incompatibility has to be precisely specified, delimited. Śrīharṣa profits, in his own text, by the difficulty of providing precise specification in various additional cases. The deep issue is criteria of identity. As is pretty well recognized in much contemporary philosophy, criteria of identity—and of distinctness, as well as of incompatibility—vary for *x* according to what *x* is—material object, set, number, person, event, property, et cetera.

Moreover, according to Nyāya, an absence of *x*, on the one hand, and *x*, on the other, are distinct *padārtha*s, "categories" or ontic primitives. Just how is it, then, that such distinct primitives are incompatible, the Advaitin gleefully queries, presuming that they should directly butt heads.

Finally, Śrīharṣa identifies a host of difficulties concerning the scope of negation in everyday discourse. Description of speech acts and contemplation of moral and factual possibilities is expressed with a variety of uses of negation. Śrīharṣa is especially good at playing on vagueness concerning what is negated when an expression contains a cognitive verb, such as "cognize" or "know" (and their numerous equivalents in Sanskrit). That it is false that Devadatta knows a pot as a pot does not mean that the pot is not a pot, et cetera.

Again, Advaita is supposed to be the deep alternative to the entanglements of Nyāya. (The declarations of the Upanishads are out on the table.) They are to be accepted (self-certifyingly) unless they themselves are successfully defeated, and Śrīharṣa's refutations, which may be understood as *tarka*, eliminate putative challengers.

4. Advaita and Theistic Voluntarism

An outstanding interpretive question concerns the seriousness of the apparent theism of Śrīharṣa's epic poem (the *Nc*) and the attitude toward God (*īśvara*) expressed in the *Khkh.* An exegetical tactic exploited by Śaṅkara regarding the blatantly theistic passages of the Upanishads is to applaud scripture as like a wise and compassionate guru tailoring its message to its audience's capacity for comprehension and spiritual accomplishment. The Upanishadic statements about God creating this world, etc., are not to be taken as literally true, but are aids to meditation, for in the supreme self-experience all is non-dualistically known as one: there is no God over and above, separate from the self, and no world other to the omnipresent Brahman which is strictly identical with the self.

This apparent denial of a God transcendent to *māyā* and *avidyā* (cosmic illusion and spiritual ignorance) appears all the more striking for its contrast with the reading of the Upanishads by Vedāntic theists. The appearance that Advaita is atheistic is further reinforced by the Advaita teaching of a phenomenology of meditation and mystic trance according to which a penultimate state of *samādhi* ("enstacy" or "self-absorption") "with prop" (*saṃprajñāta-samādhi*) is sublated (all further world appearance has already disappeared) by a final state of "objectless" *samādhi* (*asaṃprajñāta-samādhi*), where only the self is known—non-dualistically, "by its own light" (*svayaṃ jyotiḥ*). Śrīharṣa uses these very terms, borrowed from *yoga-śāstra.*[127] Thus the apparent theism of the epic *Nc* would be just that, apparent only. The term Śrīharṣa uses in the poem to express a meditational attainment on Nala's part is *saṃprajñāta-samādhi*, enstatic mystic trance "with prop."[128] Thus this mystic accomplishment would fall short of the truth of Advaita (though often Nala is described as a "knower of Brahman"). Nala's devotion and good works would be viewed, on this reading, as endorsed by the poet as a model for those unable to attain the ultimate state, but not as endorsed without qualification.

This is the easy way to fill the *Khkh*'s theistic aporia (in particular the vague reference, *Khkh*, p. 125, to the *Nc*'s chapter devoted to "praise of the supreme person," see above, p. 76), Alexander's way of untying the Gordian knot: cut through it with the clear, rigid logic of non-dualism borne out by the logic of sublatability. However, the extent to which Advaita jibes with a voluntarist theism—and the sincerity of Śaṅkara's and other Advaitins' theistic statements—has been underappreciated. In a passage immediately subsequent to this *Khkh* reference to the *Nc*, i.e., following the key summary statement (translated at the beginning of this chapter, above, p. 76), where Śrīharṣa urges the Naiyāyika to "have faith in the doctrine of non-duality" taught by the Upanishads and reinforced by his arguments—Śrīharṣa says that his "arguments of refutation . . . cannot be rejected (or ignored) except by accepting that the world's arrangement is by the (arbitrary) supreme command of God."[129] Ganganatha Jha translates, "[these] arguments of refutation . . . cannot be impugned by any counter-argument except by such arbitrary assumptions as that 'the arrangements of the Universe depend on the will of a personal God.' "[130] The English term "arbitrary," which both Jha and I use, does not render literally any word of Śrīhārṣa's Sanskrit. Nevertheless, it has a certain ambiguity that is convenient for bringing out the point I would like to make about Advaita and theism. Used as Jha uses it, the term has a negative connotation: acceptance of a theistic creationism and teleology would be arbitrary, unsupported by evidence, by good arguments. The arbitrariness of such an acceptance would correspond to the arbitrariness of a rejection of Śrīharṣa's arguments. From a theistic voluntarist perspective, on the other hand, "arbitrary" can have a positive connotation: God's will is more fundamental than any *logos*, any intelligibility in things; God's creation is arbitrary in the sense of being dependent on God's (humanly inexplicable) will.[131] In this sense, acceptance of theism would be arbitrary chiefly in matching the *positive* judgment that the arrangement of the world is arbitrary as dependent on God's will. Thus Śrīharṣa's refutations could be viewed as preparing a voluntarist theism, an irrationalist theism opposed to that embraced by Logicians and others—or rational in the sense of warranted only by the uneliminated proclamations of scripture. There is admittedly scant indication in the *Khkh* that Śrīharṣa favors such a theism as the cosmological side, so to say, of the Advaita taught by the Upanishads,[132] but the theism of the *Nc* is explicit.[133] Non-duality would remain the central theme, along with the inexplicability of appearance of distinctness. It would be in the inexplicability plank—the indeterminability thesis, *anirvacanīyatva*—that there would be room for voluntarist, irrationalist theism.

Finally, there is the question of the Advaita understanding of awareness of Brahman, the status of the world in that light, and the compatibility of the Advaita phenomenology of meditation and mystic trance not only with any variety of theism but also with any determinate (worldly) content whatsoever. Among classical Advaitins, we find two poles: at one extreme, the world would disappear in a supreme self-absorption, and, at the other, the world as it is in all its diversity would be Brahman. Śrīharṣa makes gestures toward both extremes, and Śaṅkara can likewise be read as favoring one position and then favoring the other. Most of his other disciples, however, more clearly tend to one or the other stance. The question hinges on the Advaita understanding of the *jīvan-mukta*, the "living enlightened," and there is much too much to take account of—both in primary Advaita texts and in modern scholarly discussions,[134] as well as in related metaphysical issues—for it to be aired here. I wish simply to repeat a summary point I made in chapter 1: the world has to be dependent on consciousness to maintain the possibility of the Advaita understanding of Brahman. Or, viewed from another angle, the Advaita understanding of mystic trance and "living enlightenment" motivates a view of the world that is thoroughly idealist. If the world is not tightly dependent on consciousness, then neither could it be sublated and disappear (on the one extreme view) nor could it be known as not separate from Brahman (on the other).

5. Śrīharṣa's Advaita Followers

Citsukha (c. 1295) is an Advaitin follower of Śrīharṣa's who voices the same Advaita positive program (i.e., the self-illumination and self-certification theses along with the sublatability argument) buttressed by similar dialectical attacks on competing views; but he also provides much greater elaboration—defensive arguments—of the Advaita understanding of illusion than occurs in Śrīharṣa's *Khkh.*[135] He also re-engages the metaphysical debate—present among earlier followers of Śaṅkara, such as Padmapāda and Vācaspati Miśra—about the locus of spiritual ignorance, *avidyā*.

Such an expanded philosophic agenda is also evident with another great dialectical Advaitin, Madhusūdana Sarasvatī (c. 1570), who masters Navya Nyāya techniques of cognitive analysis and uses them to defend the Advaita view, particularly the understanding of illusion. The positive program remains constant with Madhusūdana and still later Advaitins, who also continue to battle against all views granting distinctness reality. But there appears to be increasingly more defense of the Advaita stance on illusion and metaphysical argument about *avidyā*, while dialectical attacks seem to diminish in importance comparatively—to speak in generalities, sweeping over centuries and dozens of authors.

Arguably, then, Advaita dialectic attains its zenith with Śrīharṣa, although he stands as a teacher of scores of later Advaita reasoners. Śrīharṣa clearly gets the winner's wreath according to the judgment of Naiyāyikas; no subsequent Advaitin ever comes to command a fraction of the attention that Śrīharṣa gets from the Logicians. Madhusūdana's attacks on distinctness are answered by theistic Vedāntins, who, though they seem to learn much from the Logic school, have their own concerns, and are, generally speaking—Śaṅkara Miśra may be counted an exception—more focused on exegetical matters than are Naiyāyikas.[136]

Excepting Śrīharṣa, influence exerted by Logicians on Advaitins seems more pronounced than the other way around in the later periods. Madhusūdana, for example, takes Gaṅgeśa's characterization of veridical awareness to be a proper characterization of awareness in general. His polemic is to show that awareness has intrinsic veridicality by arguing that nothing that does not fit the formula should be counted an awareness. Thus every awareness would be intrinsically veridical.[137] Here, however, let us desist from further exposition on the Advaita side, to turn to Gaṅgeśa and Navya Nyāya.

CHAPTER FOUR

New Logic

1. Gaṅgeśa and the New School

Gaṅgeśa Upādhyāya lived in the first half of the fourteenth century.[1] He lived in Mithilā in north India, in what is now the state of Bihar. He belonged to the brahmin caste (as would be expected), but was not from a particularly distinguished family. Apparently, he had two wives, and a son—the famous Vardhamāna—with the elder, and two sons and a daughter with the younger. Though we may assume he was a prominent teacher in his hometown, we know precious few additional details about his life.[2]

We can speak confidently, however, about Gaṅgeśa's achievement in his eminent and, as far as we know, only treatise, the *Tattvacintāmaṇi* (*The Jewel of Reflection on Reality*), henceforth, *TCM*. The work is the root text of the Navya movement that came to dominate late classical philosophic thought in India. Numerous commentaries were written on the *TCM* (long treatises appeared on just small portions of it), and all later Navya-Nyāya writers presupposed acquaintance with it. It is without question a masterpiece of philosophy.

Gaṅgeśa's son Vardhamāna authored seven thick texts, commentaries, all but one of which is extant. These texts help to solidify Gaṅgeśa's achievement, because they offer Navya-trained elucidation of Udayana and the works of Old Nyāya and Vaiśeṣika. Navya Nyāya seems to have remained a Mithilā monopoly for more than a century. Both Śaṅkara Miśra and Vācaspati Miśra II (with Gaṅgeśa and Maṇikaṇṭha Miśra, these are the Navya authors translated in chapter 5) were Maithilīs of the fifteenth century, and although Vācaspati left Mithilā to serve in the court of a foreign prince, both earned reputations as brilliant scholars. Both were also, particularly Śaṅkara Miśra, esteemed teachers in their hometown.[3] But within a generation of Raghunātha Śiromaṇi (c. 1500)—who is commonly counted a philosophic genius and innovator arguably Gaṅgeśa's equal—Navya Nyāya had proliferated throughout India, as students who travelled from far to Mithilā returned and established schools in their own regions. There was, in particular, an eastward movement into Bengal and another southward to several centers of learning. New Logic also proliferated along several dimensions of culture: its logical and phenomenological techniques became utilized especially in jurisprudence and aesthetics, as well as in rival philosophic schools.

No estimation of Navya Nyāya's contribution to world philosophy is possible yet; there remains too much scholarship and investigation still to be accomplished. But its success has to be counted unparalleled in the long and rich traditions of classical Indian metaphysics. For producing the *TCM*, Gaṅgeśa, among New Logicians, is renowned above all others, with the possible exceptions of Raghunātha Śiromaṇi of the sixteenth century and the last great pre-modern Naiyāyika, Gadādhara, of the seventeenth.

Vardhamāna wrote a commentary on Śrīharṣa's *Khkh.*[4] Within a century, there appeared additional commentaries written by other Navyas as well as independent treatises of counter-refutation by Śaṅkara Miśra, c. 1430, and Vācaspati Miśra II, c. 1450, sections of which are translated in chapter 5. Although there appear further rounds of Advaita counter-response and further Naiyāyika innovations on some of the issues Śrīharṣa raises, a core of realist answers to Śrīharṣa had been worked out by the time of these two Navyas—the middle of the fifteenth century—in several instances by Gaṅgeśa himself and more comprehensively by the two later authors. In particular, Śaṅkara Miśra and Vācaspati Miśra II make clear how to respond to the Advaitin on the reality of distinctness, *bheda.*

But whereas the response to Śrīharṣa on the part of Śaṅkara Miśra and Vācaspati Miśra II is explicit, with Gaṅgeśa some digging has to be done. His normal practice in the *TCM* is to invent an interlocutor and to combat what he sees as mistaken views without attributing them to historical opponents. Most rarely does he mention a particular philosopher or school by name. On the other hand, some of the opponents within his long *pūrvapakṣa*s ("treatments of a *prima facie* position": see the glossary) are identifiable. Preëminent among these are Mīmāṃsakas. Śrīharṣa's polemics also appear to be on Gaṅgeśa's mind, as we will see. But the Advaitin's arguments figure less prominently than Mīmāṃsaka positions and reasonings.

We may readily infer, then, that the great philosopher was well read in Mīmāṃsaka texts. Mīmāṃsakas, as we have seen, champion realist positions, and are often roughly allied with Naiyāyikas in the early centuries, particularly against Buddhists. There are even some New Logicians, Vācaspati Miśra II, for example, who write commentaries on both Nyāya and Mīmāṃsā texts. As mentioned in chapter 2, in the areas of epistemology and philosophy of language Mīmāṃsakas develop views at a further remove from Nyāya, especially in epistemology. Some scholars suggest that it is because Mīmāṃsaka tenets stand close to Nyāya while at the same time significantly diverging from it that Gaṅgeśa feels especially called upon to demonstrate their inadequacy. This would be why Mīmāṃsakas are given, comparatively, so much attention in the *TCM*. Umesha Mishra says, "the Mīmāṃsakas . . . were like the claimants of common property with the Naiyāyikas. So Naiyāyikas picked up academic quarrel with them often."[5] In any case, Mīmāṃsakas are indeed the rivals whose views Gaṅgeśa most regularly attacks.[6]

But also by Gaṅgeśa's time, the fourteenth century, Buddhist philosophies, which were the prime targets of the polemics of the Old School, were in decline. Other classical systems had also seen their heyday come and go. Mīmāṃsā, on the other hand, was flourishing. The school of the Exegetes, then, could be counted the principal rival to Nyāya in the later centuries, that is, on the front of point-by-point battles.

The war with dialectical Advaita was of a different cast. The dialectical Advaita Vedānta of Śrīharṣa et al. is, from the Naiyāyika perspective, mainly an anti-theoretical stance, despite Śrīharṣa's positive program concerning Brahman. There are few positive corollaries concerning the world that could compete head-to-head with the detailed explanations of Nyāya. Mīmāṃsā, in contrast, constitutes a many-sided philosophy with a full range of positions matching and contesting Naiyāyika theories, down to apparent minutiae.

However, my own view is that Gaṅgeśa is not primarily interested in eristics, i.e., in cross-school disputes for their own sake, but in the right views on disputed topics. That the positions he rejects occasionally or even frequently turn out to be historically advanced by whomever—Mīmāṃsakas, Śrīharṣa, Naiyāyikas of the Old school (there is still much research to be done in this regard[7])—is not, it seems to me, Gaṅgeśa's apparent reason for addressing them. Rather, his use of contrary views is strategic in introducing his own considered and final positions.

Nevertheless, Gaṅgeśa is enormously learned. Either directly or indirectly through citations and rehearsals within Naiyāyika or Mīmāṃsaka texts he read, he seems to be aware of numerous authors in the more than a millennium of argument-oriented, Sanskrit-inscribed philosophy that preceded him. For example, Gaṅgeśa appears to know the pragmatist theories of Dharmakīrti, though in this case it is improbable that he had direct acquaintance with Dharmakīrti's own texts. Gaṅgeśa knows earlier Naiyāyika thought best, and Mīmāṃsā thought second best. As will become clear, he is also acquainted with Śrīharṣa's *Khkh.*

Udayana is the philosopher that Gaṅgeśa most closely follows. (Since it is Udayana who receives the brunt of Śrīharṣa's criticism, the legend that Śrīharṣa provoked the writing of the *TCM*, although strictly unwarranted, makes good folklore.) Udayana pioneered some of the techniques identified with New Logic; D. C. Bhattacharya counts Udayana as the first Navya-Nyāya philosopher,[8] and B. K. Matilal concurs in this judgment.[9] Umesha Mishra even sees Udayana as the genius who revolutionized Naiyāyika thought, inaugurating trends that Gaṅgeśa popularized, though he still counts Gaṅgeśa as the "founder" of Navya Nyāya because of the attention garnered by the *TCM* and the novelty of what he calls Gaṅgeśa's methodology.[10] Erich Frauwallner, in a "Forward" to a translation of a section of the *TCM*, talks about "Udayana's school" as though there were no question about which of the two great Naiyāyikas should be regarded as the leader of the Navya movement.[11] And Daniel Ingalls mentions the practice among some much later Naiyāyikas of referring only to Raghunātha Śiromaṇi as *navya* ("new") because of his originality, with Udayana clearly, and Gaṅgeśa implicitly, identified with an older, more tradition-bound school.[12]

Here, however, we follow the mainstream of the tradition, which sees Gaṅgeśa alone as the movement's pioneer. Udayana's works, despite their centrality to the overall development of Nyāya, do not count in the minds of post-Gaṅgeśa Naiyāyikas as part of the New school, and to this historical judgment and tradition one should adhere. Moreover—and this is of course one of my principal theses—Śrīharṣa does push, we will see, Gaṅgeśa and others to innovations. There is also the matter of the overall sterility of Udayana's definitions. Gaṅgeśa preserves some of the formal strictures of the pre-Śrīharṣa Logician, but he also re-invigorates Nyāya by formulating positions, indeed new definitions, that are pedagogically commendable, that crystallize Nyāya insight and lead to a more profound appreciation of the system—in contrast with Udayana's excessive formalism which seems blind to students' needs.

Gaṅgeśa himself, by the way, designates his own reflection as *navya*, and uses the term in reference to others of a general Naiyāyika persuasion who, apparently, by a professionalism of method had gone beyond an original Nyāya, without explicitly (so far as I am aware) including Udayana, although he does refer to Udayana respectfully as *ācāryāḥ*, "revered teacher."

Now, between Udayana and Gaṅgeśa, there stand not only Śrīharṣa but also the Logicians Śrīvallabha, Vādivāgīśvara, Śivāditya, and Maṇikaṇṭha Miśra, all philosophers with the sophistication of argument typical of Navya Nyāya who put forth a broad array of positions in many cases similar to Gaṅgeśa's.[13] Maṇikaṇṭha cites Śrīharṣa on *tarka*, "dialectical reasoning," and proffers a rejoinder (which is translated in chapter 5). At places Gaṅgeśa quotes previous or contemporary *navya*s (though without giving their names).[14] Probably we should say then that Gaṅgeśa's monumental *Tattvacintāmaṇi* solidifies but does not, strictly speaking, originate New Nyāya.

New Logicians are, in sum, philosophers who hold somewhat modified, rethought positions, supported by new and refined techniques of argument, with respect to an "Old" school which trails off in Udayana's own

Nyāya-sūtra commentary. It is important to stress that the New school does not constitute a break so much as an enormous advance with respect to the Old school's argumentation. Navya Nyāya is a reworking of centuries of Old Nyāya augmented by (in particular, Udayana's) incorporation of Vaiśeṣika speculation. Gaṅgeśa's *TCM* is the pivotal text.

The secret of the *TCM*'s success would appear to be Gaṅgeśa's uncanny ability to distill arguments, to bring out the clear thrust of a consideration, or a host of considerations and counter-considerations, and to decisively formulate a bottom line, a thesis or position established (*siddhānta*) by argument. The *TCM* is also a masterpiece of organization; its focus is epistemology, with other topics—ontology, semantics, theology, debate theory—taken up according to their relation to epistemological considerations. There are also numerous innovations, though these are more a matter of argument than of stance.

The *TCM* is comprised of four chapters, each devoted to a separate "means to veridical awareness"—the *pramāṇa* of veridical perception, cogent inference, analogical vocabulary acquisition, and reliable testimony. Within each chapter there are clearly delineated sections on various topics including reflections, mainly in the first chapter, concerning awareness and veridicality in general, considered independently of the particular instruments. Gaṅgeśa's style is lucid and precise, formal at times, but, as mentioned, not obsessed with formalism at the expense of sound pedagogy. He argues forcefully and confidently at every turn, and is ingenious in leading the reader into positions by careful examination of alternatives. Indeed, the rejections of alternative views—Gaṅgeśa's refutations—usually occupy the major portion of each section.

Thus, all in all, Gaṅgeśa's debt to previous Naiyāyikas—both those he calls New Logicians and the older philosophers—is heavy in terms of overall outlook. It is in the tight organization, lucidity, and sophistication of argument of the *TCM*—which also, despite these merits, attains a breadth comparable to the *Nyāya-sūtra*'s—that Gaṅgeśa achieves a quantum jump compared even to Udayana. There is reason for the *TCM*'s status among later generations of Naiyāyikas and its immense popularity among the learned of all specialities. On the refutational side, Gaṅgeśa seems uninterested in refutation for its own sake, but uses it to lead us into right views.

The sketch of Navya-Nyāya positions that follows is grounded principally in Gaṅgeśa's *TCM*. But there are, as mentioned, Gaṅgeśa's son Vardhamāna as well as Śaṅkara Miśra and Vācaspati Miśra II, Navyas whose contribution in particular to the Advaita debate should not be underestimated. The latter two lived in the middle of the fifteenth century. Scholars commonly count a first stage of the development of New Logic to end with Raghunātha Śiromaṇi (1475–1550), who, himself having studied many years in Mithilā, is said to have established the tradition in Navadvīpa, in Bengal.[15] Raghunātha breaks with Gaṅgeśa on several important matters, especially in ontology, and brings still more refined analytic tools into practice. Raghunātha's achievements (and failures), and those of still later Naiyāyikas, lie outside the scope of this study. Although the realist-idealist debate extends into the sixteenth and later centuries, our concern is only with the response forged by the middle of the fifteenth, before Raghunātha. Thus, especially for us, Gaṅgeśa's *TCM* holds center stage. In the sections that follow, we will keep in mind problems insisted upon by Śrīharṣa as we review the Navya Nyāya of Gaṅgeśa and the first few generations of his followers.

2. Cognition and Justification

Cognition, *jñāna*, is arguably the most important item in the whole of Gaṅgeśa's philosophy. Ontologically, cognitions are short-lived, episodic attributes or qualities of the self or soul, and, in the case of sensory cognitions, are causally continuous with physical realities as the result of sense organ-object contact. This view is essentially that held by all earlier Naiyāyikas. As explained in chapter 2, a cognition may be understood as a mental event, but it is a product or state rather than an act. Cognitions are intentional; they are invariably *of* some object or objects, or, more precisely, objective complex(es). Comprehending what someone says, doubting, inferring, remembering, perceiving, and apperceiving are important examples. Again, cognitions are not to be understood dispositionally; they are actual occurrences. Naiyāyikas talk about dispositions in terms of memory traces or habits (*saṃskāra*, subconscient valencies).

Gaṅgeśa presents, or presupposes, several important groupings of cognitions. First, awarenesses are distinct from rememberings, although a memory trace may have a causal role in an awareness's arising (as is the case with certain types of illusion discussed below). Then among awarenesses, divisions are drawn according to source: sensory, inferential, analogical, and verbal awarenesses are differentiated in this way (corresponding, that is, to the four *pramāṇa*, "sources of knowledge"). There is also a miscellaneous group identified as much by nature as by circumstance of production, for example, apperception, doubt, and dialectical reasoning (*tarka*).

Perhaps the most important distinction—for its systematic role—is that between determinate and indeterminate awareness. There is also, of course, the absolutely central division between the veridical and the non-veridical. But to understand Gaṅgeśa's definition of the veridical and other prominent distinctions as well—indeed why his is a causal theory of knowledge—we need to take a close look first at the notion of indeterminate awareness.

2.1. Indeterminate Awareness

According to Gaṅgeśa, there are sensory awarenesses below the level of what we can consciously articulate.[16] These awarenesses Gaṅgeśa calls indeterminate, *nirvikalpaka*, following Vācaspati I (in his commentary under *NyS* 1.1.4[17]).

Nirvikalpaka cognitions have often been understood by scholars writing in English as "non-conceptual." But that translational practice, while perhaps all right for Dharmakīrti's school, is misleading with regard to Gaṅgeśa's Nyāya. All sensations are "non-conceptual" according to the Buddhist school, whereas Gaṅgeśa et al. admit *savikalpaka* perceptual awarenesses, i.e., "determinate" awarenesses, as I say (following B. K. Matilal and Sibajiban Bhattacharyya[18]). In fact, the final court of appeal for claims about the world are, according to Navya Nyāya, determinate sensory awarenesses.

Now not only are indeterminate awarenesses, in contrast with the determinate, not directly expressible, they have for Gaṅgeśa an exclusively systematic role. Indeterminate awarenesses are not apperceptible (i.e., not introspectible); they are known by inference. Thus, indeterminate awarenesses are not, as with the Buddhists, somehow established phenomenologically.

However, the primary reason I find the "non-conceptual/conceptual" translation misleading is that concepts, whatever they may be, do not, according to Nyāya, intervene between a cognition and its indication, what it is about or of. It is true that every cognition is said to have constituents or factors (*ghaṭaka*), and that these factors are what are analyzed in logic and epistemology. Further, every determinate cognition is verbalizable and the verbalization analyzable according to principles of Nyāya logic, epistemology, and ontology. Moreover, all verbal expression is considered mediated by memory and training, as is our ability to recognize the content of our experience for what it is.[19] But both determinate and indeterminate awarenesses have content that is, for Nyāya, extra-mental and intersubjective; their intentionality in neither case is directed to or mediated by concepts—nor indeed by sense data or anything else dreamed up by philosophers. That is not to say that Nyāya recognizes no mental entities; cognitions are mental entities. But awarenesses are of objective realities. Even apperceptions, whose objects are prior cognitions, are of objective realities, namely, cognitions as ontological qualities or occurrences in the self or soul. Nyāya's unflinching realism insists that even with illusion the factors (*ghaṭaka*) in awareness directly indicate reals. Mother-of-pearl misperceived as silver is misperceived with respect to a universal or qualifier (silverness) which is itself a real and with which the perceiver is acquainted (having a trace thereof stored in her memory bank). It is, then, not a lack of concepts that makes indeterminate awarenesses unverbalizable and beyond the range of what we can apperceive.

Rather, such awareness is postulated because of a systematic need. A need for direct awareness of a qualifier is the sole basis for Gaṅgeśa's admitting indeterminate awarenesses into his system.

We have seen that Śrīharṣa invokes a problem of predication, or in a more literal rendering of the Sanskrit terms utilized, of qualification: to say anything about anything (as justified by perception) is to suppose a relational complex, a complex that dissolves under dialectical critique into an undifferentiated whole. For several reasons (the Nyāya view of illusion, the commitment to continuity through change, positions on individuation), Gaṅgeśa accepts the starting point of the polemic, namely, that even the simplest verbalizable awareness has an object that is ontologically complex. Such an awareness is *viśiṣṭa*, "qualified," by which he means that a qualificandum is cognized through a qualifier. Thus, in order to avoid an infinite regress of qualification (the qualifier_1 of qualificandum_1 as itself a qualificandum, qualificandum_2 to be known through another qualifier, qualifier_2, *ad infinitum*), Gaṅgeśa posits indeterminate awareness where qualifiers are directly known.

In other words, Gaṅgeśa accepts the principle that whatever is known determinately—and is thus capable of being expressed by words—presupposes acquaintance with the qualifier through which a particular presented in experience is known. To cognize Bessie as cow presupposes acquaintance with cowhood, that is, awareness of the ground for application of the term "cow." Thus there appears a danger of an infinite regress: how is the qualifier known? A qualificandum is invariably known through a qualifier; how then is the qualifier itself known? Now in cases of doubly qualificative cognition, e.g., cognition of a blue pot (where the particular known as a pot, i.e., as qualified by potness, is further known as qualified by blue), a prior determinate cognition, e.g., of a pot (or of something blue), can provide the qualificative data.[20] Also, in some cases the qualifier is furnished by a trace preserved in memory. But there are still other cases where there has to be an indeterminate prior acquaintance with the qualifier, otherwise we would be faced with an infinite regress.

Gaṅgeśa argues:

> When a person for the first time in his life has the perceptual cognition, "(A) cow," that cognition is produced by a (prior) cognition of the qualifier which is itself generated. For it is a generated, qualified cognition, like inference. And it is not the case that a remembering could be the prior cognition with this example. For he has not had in this life any prior experience of cowhood.[21]

Thus an indeterminate cognition of the qualifier cowhood has to be postulated.

Saṅkara Miśra parleys the point into a response to Śrīharṣa on distinctness: the fact that in indeterminate awareness the qualifier is not known *as* a qualifier but is nonetheless directly cognized means that in indeterminate awareness distinctness is not known *as* distinctness but is nonetheless directly cognized (distinctness comes to be the critical qualifier in the Śrīharṣa controversy). Gaṅgeśa's example is less loaded: "cowhood" is directly known—the ground for application of the term "cow"—without "cowhood-ness" being cognized. To recognize an individual cow as a cow, it is unnecessary to recognize the universal as a universal; the universal may nevertheless be directly perceived. (We will discuss the point further when we focus on distinctness.)

The epistemic precept is that anything known in an expressible awareness is known through a qualifier appearing as a factor or constituent of an awareness's content, the factor technically called predication content (*prakāra*). By embracing this precept, Gaṅgeśa appears to give the Advaita dialectic all the fuel it needs. Gaṅgeśa's brilliance is to find primitives blocking the regress to be cognized in indeterminate awareness, which stands as the immediate cause of some determinate awareness. (Śaṅkara Miśra goes on to argue that distinctness itself is such a primitive, cognized in indeterminate awareness.) That the relationship is causal is important: causality provides grounds for inferences and indeterminate awareness is inferred.

Thus, unlike his predecessors, whose discussion of non-relational, indeterminate awareness seems confused, Gaṅgeśa clearly recognizes that indeterminate awareness has to stand in a causal relation to determinate awareness so that the problem of qualification insisted upon by Śrīharṣa can be resolved. Gaṅgeśa does not mention the Advaitin in this portion of the *TCM*, but the problem of predication seems to be on his mind. Now the posit of direct acquaintance with qualifiers in indeterminate awareness does not by itself solve the problem of the relatedness—the Bradley problem—involved in the notion of determinate, verbalizable awareness indicating an objective complex, a qualificandum ontologically qualified by a qualifier. But it is an essential part of the Naiyāyika response. We will review the full-blown answer after we have more of Gaṅgeśa's theory out on the table.

In sum, here some progress is made: in indeterminate awareness, a qualifier is directly cognized, and thus an epistemological regress concerning qualification is blocked. Indeterminate awareness gives rise to determinate awareness through a natural process that has nothing to do with human desires, acts, or intentions. The relation between the two is not merely psychological, as the Dharmakīrti school insisted (confusing many Naiyāyikas of the Old school), but causal.

Gaṅgeśa does not appear to hold that an individual cow, for example, is cognized in indeterminate awareness. The individual is cognized only determinately. Sensation is a causal process spread over time, and acquaintance with an individual should be thought of as causally direct. However, verbalizable awareness of an individual is mediated by—or, better, fused with—what the individual appears as. A qualifier, and indeed a relation, are cognized in indeterminate awareness. Gaṅgeśa says explicitly that in the case of a veridical sensory awareness the relation is also so cognized and stands as the cause of the relationality of determinate sensory awareness.[22] But we have no awareness of unclothed particulars on this view; even to be aware of a mere "this" is to be aware of something clothed with "thisness." In sum, the posit of indeterminate awareness may be taken to cash out Gaṅgeśa's sense that an individual—though standing at one end of the causal process that results in a sensory determinate awareness and grounding individuation, as well as standing as what the determinate awareness is *of*, what it indicates—is known only as clothed, known only through a qualifier.

Thus, with a typical case of an awareness of a cow, there is a prior stage in the causal process that is an indeterminate perception, indeterminate in that cowness is cognized but not as related to the particular cow, the qualificandum of the ensuing determinate or qualificative awareness. Such primitives have to be directly cognized to stop an infinite regress, as we have seen, given that whatever is known determinately is known through a qualifier, e.g., a pot as a pot through its potness. Only determinate awareness is verbalizable awareness, i.e., awareness expressible in propositional form as something *a* as an F (F*a*).

This view of indeterminate perception is used to help explain non-veridical awareness, as will be elaborated below. Finally, indeterminate awareness is said itself to be neither veridical nor non-veridical (Gaṅgeśa decisively departs from Vācaspati I and Udayana here). Veridicality presupposes verbalizability and an awareness of an ontological complex, more about which below.

2.2. *The Constituents of Determinate Awareness*

All simple (as opposed to doubly, triply, etc.) qualificative or determinate cognitions have a content that exhibits a common structure: qualificandum-qualificative relation-qualifier, a-R-b.[23] Qualification is a relational abstract that obtains in the world, but it is used to talk about cognitions. The simplest veridical awareness reflects a fact or state of affairs, an individual cognized (the qualificandum) as related to a qualifier.

It depends on what types of entity are related whether each of the constituents or factors in an awareness indicates a distinct entity in the world: Gaṅgeśa periodically takes up projects of ontological reduction, an enterprise that is advanced, or rethought, by later Navya-Nyāya philosophers such as Raghunātha. (Some of this is present in the sections translated in chapter 5 on veridicality and inherence.) The essentials of Gaṅgeśa's understanding of categories of the real are reviewed later in this chapter. What is most important as background is just the schema of analysis, a-R-b, which is the bridge between Gaṅgeśa's theory of cognition and his ontology.

With the veridical awareness, "(A) pot," for example, the particular pot-inherence-potness would form the objective complex (a-R-b). The qualificandum is the bearer or possessor of properties; with the veridical awareness, "(A) pot," the particular pot is the subject of qualification (*viśeṣya*) and possesses the property of potness. The awareness "(A) pot" has "potness" as its predication content, *prakāra*.[24] This term, *prakāra*, seems to be the closest to a strictly phenomenological usage in Gaṅgeśa's system (and it, too, is to be interpreted ontologically: see chapter 5, pp. 192–94).[25] Whatever is known determinately is known through a qualifier appearing in awareness (as predication content, *prakāra*); in this case the individual pot would be known through the qualifier (appearing as predication content), potness, which happens to be one of its natural kinds. Other qualifiers appearing in cognition provoke different ontological analyses: what appears in the qualifier's place (i.e., the predication content, *prakāra*) does not have to be a natural kind character, but could be a quality (*guṇa*, e.g., blue), a motion, or indeed a property that ontologically is to be analyzed away.

The object determinately cognized is a "thick" particular, i.e., a particular as connected to its properties. The pot is potentially known under an indefinite number of qualifiers, as a substance, earthen, blue, Devadatta's property, and so on. Some of these qualifiers are, let me stress, problematic ontologically; they are called abstract or surplus properties, *upādhi*.[26] Still, the epistemological principles hold with them as with true universals or natural kinds (*jāti*), qualities, and motions. No qualifier is cognized in determinate sensory awareness separate from the thing it qualifies. And though the thing is always cognized through some qualifier or other, what it is in itself is a reality rich with multiple properties, some of which with any single awareness would not be cognized (ignoring, for simplicity's sake, the special case of God). There is an important difference for logic between the pot as cognized under one qualifier and the pot as cognized under another. Gaṅgeśa and his followers understand that in epistemic contexts substitutivity of co-referentials does not preserve truth, and arguably the most important technical apparatus they develop is that of delimitation (*avaccheda*: see the glossary) of an awareness's content. Nevertheless, ontologically a given pot cognized as blue is held to be identical with the pot cognized just as a pot, in that there is only the one (thick) particular.[27] Again, nothing like a concept (sense-datum, etc.) intervenes between an awareness and its content or indication, what it is about or of. Awareness does comprise, however, factors or constituents, which are spoken of as specifiers, or delimitors (*avacchedaka*), of the awareness's content, and their relations to the objective complex cognized. These are the factors specifying the qualificandum of the content (*viśeṣyatā-avacchedaka-avacchinna-viṣayatā*), the qualifier of the content (*viśeṣaṇatā-*

avacchedaka-avacchinna-viṣayatā), and the qualificative relation implicit in the content (*vaiśiṣṭya-avacchedaka-avacchinna-viṣayatā*).

2.3. Veridicality

Veridical awarenesses are a sub-species of each of four types of awareness differentiated by source: (1) the sensory, (2) the inferential, (3) the analogical, and (4) the verbal. These four exhaust the range of possible veridical awarenesses; non-veridical awarenesses are said, technically, to include dialectical (or hypothetical) reasoning (*tarka*) and a few other types of cognitive occurrence. As mentioned, veridical awarenesses are qualificative (i.e., relational) or determinate as opposed to indeterminate; in all cases veridicality is restricted to awarenesses as opposed to memories. Let us look at these distinctions.

Gaṅgeśa does not hold that a moment of memory (i.e., a *remembering*) can be a veridical awareness, since a remembering is not an experience or awareness, *anubhava*, although it is a cognition, *jñāna*. Experiences are the only cognitions that can be veridical awarenesses, *pramā*. The perceptual, inferential, analogical, and correct understandings based on the testimony of others that together exhaust the range of veridical awareness are thus all considered "experiences." A right remembering would be "in conformity with the object" remembered, but would not be a veridical awareness.

In English, it seems strange to speak of an inference as an experience. It must be borne in mind that Naiyāyikas are interested in bits of knowledge considered as psychological occurrences. To regard as an experience the knowledge a person has of fire on a distant hill triggered by seeing smoke is to underline that such psychological events occur and guide successful action (in this case, for example, putting out a fire before it reaches one's house). Analysis of the ontological conditions of inferential knowledge could be said to be—over the centuries—*the* principal Navya project. Although Gaṅgeśa takes occurrences of inferential knowledge to be the explananda his theory addresses, what underlies their veridicality is, according to him, a relation that holds materially—namely, *vyāpti*, "pervasion" of instances of x by instances of y—and it is thus above all this relation that is to be considered abstractly and clearly characterized. (Also, Śrīharṣa had made the need for a defensible characterization of *vyāpti* painfully clear in his assault on inference as understood by the Prācīna school, as had Cārvākas before him.[28])

To be precise, cognition of something *a* possessing a property S understood as pervaded by (or invariably concomitant with) another property F (S as invariably co-located with F) is considered by Gaṅgeśa the instrumental cause of any bit of inferential knowledge as a veridical awareness (*anumiti* as *pramā*).[29] Thus he suggests we need to be especially clear about what constitutes pervasion in general since particular pervasions are thought to ground all instances of veridical inferential awareness.

But however important (historically and otherwise) the reflection on inference may be, our focus will be chiefly on perception—as is Gaṅgeśa's in his sections on characterizing veridical awareness translated in chapter 5. These sections not only hold intrinsic interest, since an understanding of veridicality stands at the center of Gaṅgeśa's system, but they also clearly exhibit Śrīharṣa's influence. Gaṅgeśa appropriates Śrīharṣa's arguments in rejecting a variety of definitions, including earlier Naiyāyika definitions, in particular two put forth by Udayana.

The sections of the *TCM* on inference and in particular good and bad definitions of pervasion (*vyāpti*) also show the influence of the Advaitin. Śrīharṣa is especially vicious concerning how a pervasion is supposed to be known. That is to say, his attacks on specific definitions of *vyāpti* are fueled chiefly by the question of how pervasion, so defined, can be known. But he also brings out his arsenal of logical and ontological dilemmas as part of a wholesale barrage. Of six specific definitions that Śrīharṣa considers, all but one are considered by Gaṅgeśa. Moreover, at the beginning of the *TCM*'s second chapter—on inference—Gaṅgeśa voices a Śrīharṣa-like objection to the general Naiyāyika view that inference is a means of knowledge (*pramāṇa*). Admittedly, the objection most closely matches the Cārvāka position (according to which perception is a *pramāṇa* but not inference), but it clearly echoes Śrīharṣa.[30] Many of the problems the Advaitin raises seem to be on Gaṅgeśa's mind.

But on inference the Advaitin's influence is mediated, especially, it appears, by the work of Maṇikaṇṭha Miśra (c. 1300), perhaps also by Śaśadhara. These two, scholars have shown, are forerunners of Gaṅgeśa in his characterization of pervasion and his theory of inference in general.[31] Maṇikaṇṭha, like Gaṅgeśa, considers and rejects all but one of the *vyāpti* definitions taken up by Śrīharṣa. He also considers and rejects several more, as well as refinements in certain cases; Śaśadhara widens the project; and Gaṅgeśa considers and rejects a total of twenty-one.[32] Now the Advaitin's sting does penetrate the barriers of the intermediaries on the topic of how a pervasion is known, for Gaṅgeśa responds explicitly on that score, mentioning Śrīharṣa by name. But with the numerous candidate characterizations of *vyāpti*, the influence of the Advaitin has to remain hypothetical (at least a determination is beyond me by about a lifetime). Maṇikaṇṭha knows Śrīharṣa's work well and Gaṅgeśa knows Maṇikaṇṭha's, but both are rarely explicit about sources. Our concern with inference, then, will be limited to the explicit responses, which are translated—with comments—following the pertinent text from Śrīharṣa's *Khkh* in chapter 5.

Also, since this is an introductory survey of Gaṅgeśa's system, we will focus on general cognitive and ontological concepts—and on the notion of distinctness—not on details of the theory of inference.[33] Again, Gaṅgeśa's general reflections on veridical awareness lean towards sensory awarenesses as the most important examples. Indeed, sensory awareness is considered throughout Nyāya as our chief cognitive connection with the world; it is the *jyeṣṭa pramāṇa*, the eldest or fundamental source of knowledge. Any good inference must have an empirical premise, and analogical and verbal bits of knowledge also presuppose veridical sensory awareness. Inferential awarenesses that are *prima facie* considered veridical can by sensory awareness be defeated and overridden. In the opening sentence of the chapter on inference, Gaṅgeśa states that he has taken up perception first because inference depends on perception.[34]

Gaṅgeśa's is a causal theory of knowledge; veridical perceptions and all veridical awarenesses are the results of causal processes. Non-veridical awareness is due to a deficiency or deficiencies (*doṣa*) in the causal chain leading to awareness. Veridical awareness, in contrast, is due to reliability-grounding causal conditions or excellencies (*guṇa*: see the glossary, the second sense of the term). In other words, veridical and non-veridical awarenesses are not alike causally. From a first-person perspective at the time of a cognitive occurrence, whether a sensory awareness is veridical or not may not be known. We invariably act on the basis of our awareness, and if a question of veridicality arises it is normally answered by the success or failure of our acts. In some cases when a cognition proves to be non-veridical we are able to determine what caused the misperception. For example, mother-of-pearl misperceived as silver does indeed look a lot like silver. Both mother-of-pearl and silver are qualified by the color silver. The similarity lies at the bottom of the misperception. The perceiver has in her memory a trace (*saṃskāra*) of silverness (the metallic kind) from having experienced silver (through the qualifier, silverness) in the past. Furthermore, the constitution of memory is analogical and associative; that is to say, "silverness" as a trace is stored in association with traces of other qualifiers that bits of silver in the world possess. Indeterminate perception is capable of enlivening memory, and in this case the silverness trace is enlivened through a deficiency in the perceptual causal process, a deficiency attributable to the silver color shared in common by real silver and mother-of-pearl. Other cases of illusion involve different deficiencies. But the most important point is, again, just that veridical and non-veridical awarenesses result from different causal processes. With a veridical experience of silver, no story about traces would need to be told.

Some other typical cases of non-veridical sensory awareness involve the misfunctioning of a sense organ due to illness, causing, for example, something white to be perceived as yellow; heat rising in the desert causing a mirage; and so on. Possibilities for malfunction are numerous, since causal processes are complex and perceptual situations various.[35]

An oddity of Gaṅgeśa's theory is that with a non-veridical sensory awareness, the qualificandum would nevertheless be veridically known; non-veridicality would be limited to the qualifier and the relationality of the qualifier. (We will see in chapter 5 that Śrīharṣa in his own way insists on the point.) Apparently, in sensory awareness there can be no mistake about the occurrence of something or other; sensory illusions are errors concerning what the something appears as. A qualificandum, again, cannot appear alone; a qualificandum always appears in relation to a qualifier. But as Gaṅgeśa often repeats in the *TCM* section on defining veridicality (the section is translated in chapter 5), there is a veridical element in all illusory sensory awareness, and this is grounded in the qualificandum.[36]

Gaṅgeśa defines veridical awareness (*pramā*) as "experience with predication content about a ϕ-object as ϕ."[37] He also presents and defends a definition close to one formulated by Udayana, and seven or eight that employ the term *viṣayatā*, "objecthood," a term that, he points out, is surrounded by ontological controversy (controversy reviewed in comments on the translation in chapter 5). His is not, strictly speaking, a correspondence theory. In fact, correspondence theory is attacked by Gaṅgeśa following Śrīharṣa's criticisms. But what grounds veridicality, according to the great philosopher, is that a qualifier appearing in cognition as predication content (*prakāra*) be present in the thing cognized. Gaṅgeśa considers about thirty-five candidate definitions of veridicality, and in explaining his reasons for rejecting or accepting each he elaborates his overall view.

So much for a bare-bones anatomy of Gaṅgeśa's reflection on this topic; the sections of the *TCM* translated in chapter 5—including the comments provided—will flesh it out. Śrīharṣa's influence, we will see, is easily discerned with regard to Gaṅgeśa's efforts to come up with an adequate characterization. Concrete instances of influence are pointed out in the comments. To close this preliminary discussion, let me highlight one point where the Advaitin's criticism seems especially critical.

Gaṅgeśa concedes that veridicality varies significantly with the nature of what is cognized. That is, under the pressure of arguments voiced by Śrīharṣa he admits that veridicality is not a natural kind, *jāti*, but rather an "abstract" or "surplus property," *upādhi*. There is no consecutive character, *anugama*, running through instances of veridicality—a necessary condition for a true universal or natural kind. Awarenesses do not divide into the natural kinds, the veridical and the non-veridical; rather, these are convenient distinctions whose ontological basis is problematic, or, as appears to be Gaṅgeśa's view, is nothing other than the cognition itself. Is, then, the definitional project hopeless? One might suspect so, since the point is to hit upon a feature exhibited by every veridical awareness and by nothing that is not a veridical awareness.

If there is no consecutive character, how can there be a distinctive feature (*lakṣaṇa*)? Is veridicality groundless, demarcating nothing not predetermined in its outlines by our minds? This would seem a dangerous concession to idealism. On the other hand, Gaṅgeśa may be interpreted as acknowledging that ontological work needs to be done while going on with his epistemological project on the assumption that even without the consecutive character (*anugama*) necessary for a natural kind, veridical awarenesses are sufficiently uniform to be univocally defined. That is, there may be sufficient uniformity among veridical awarenesses that the variability can be accommodated with appropriate variables in the definition. My reading is that Gaṅgeśa tries to come up with a univocal definition that accommodates the variability through use of relative pronouns that function as variables, ranging over the types of things known. The admissions that there is no true consecutive character and that veridicality is not a natural kind raise problems to be resolved by further reflection, not engaged in the *TCM*. A single philosopher cannot be expected to resolve each and every issue. How truly serious the ontological problem is will be addressed in the section below entitled "Surplus Properties." In any case, on this point the arguments of Śrīharṣa seem to have scored.

2.4. Apperception

Śrīharṣa's Vedānta, along with Prābhākara Mīmāṃsā, holds both that awareness is self-aware and that it is self-certified. Gaṅgeśa's Nyāya holds, in contrast, not only (a) that the veridicality of a (non-apperceptive) awareness is inferred from the success of action, but also (b) that an awareness is cognized only in becoming the object of a subsequent awareness (*anuvyavasāya*, apperception), i.e., that no awareness is self-aware. Bhāṭṭa Mīmāṃsakas and Yogācāra Buddhists defend, respectively, positions of self-certification coupled with non-self-awareness, and other-certification coupled with self-awareness.[38] Gaṅgeśa devotes much energy to the issues involved with these views.[39] He does not, however, add much to the Naiyāyika *siddhānta* ("established position") we surveyed in chapter 2. Note that the *TCM* sections on veridicality translated in chapter 5 concern what it is for an awareness *to be* veridical, not with how we come *to know* an awareness's veridicality.[40] On the former topic Gaṅgeśa is innovative, as will be shown. Yet whatever innovations Gaṅgeśa may have achieved, his doctrine of apperception is a linchpin in his overall theory of awareness. We will survey it now to close our preliminary discussion of the cognitive dimension of his philosophy.

Apperception (*anuvyavasāya*, literally "after-cognition") is awareness whose object is a previous awareness (i.e., the "scoped awareness"[41]); it may be understood as introspection. In an apperception, constituents of the scoped awareness's content are infallibly known. An erroneous awareness of mother-of-pearl as silver (the awareness "This is silver" in the face of mother-of-pearl) would be known introspectively as an awareness whose qualificandumness would be specified by "this-ness" and whose qualifierness would be specified by "silverness." Such content would capture the objective fact (of the scoped awareness) despite the silverness failing to qualify the mother-of-pearl cognized by the scoped awareness.

No ontological ice is cut in apperception, however. For ontological analysis, Gaṅgeśa makes plain that veridicality has to be presupposed at a first level of cognition of objects that are not themselves cognitions.[42] This is another way of saying that for us sensory awareness—not introspection—is key to the nature of the world.

Furthermore, the relation between the qualificandum factor and the qualifier factor in the scoped awareness is not only not cognized as the relation obtaining (ontologically) in the objective complex, but it is not cognized directly as a relation even in apperception. It can be scoped, however, but then it appears as an abstract *term*, namely, relationality (*vaiśiṣṭya*), and the relation that binds *it* to the other terms remains implicit. The position appears to be a concession to Śrīharṣa's insistence on the relation regress. Gaṅgeśa admits the potential for a regress; it is simply that we normally have no call to make explicit in further apperception a lower-order relationality, particularly at the level of apperceptions of apperceptions. We could do so, however, for as long as one wished to play that game.[43]

Thus this part of the solution to the relation regress is structurally the same as found in the Old Nyāya's solution to the justification regress insisted upon by Nāgārjuna: we could play the game on and on; however, normally there is no call to take even the first step. Justification is called for only when a cognition is drawn into question; the epistemological default is innocence, i.e., assumed veridicality. Of course, there are occasions when we have good grounds for wondering whether an awareness is veridical or not. But ordinarily we simply act out of our awareness, not knowing—and not wondering—whether it is veridical or not. Similarly, we normally have no call to introspect. Not every fact in the world is cognized by a human being—how could it be, given the limitations of the body and senses? Similarly, not every cognition is apperceived. Everyday life does not seem to call for much apperception. As the *Nyāya-sūtra* indicates, however, some doubt does result from conflicts of theory, from the opposed positions of different schools, especially concerning the nature of cognition. Thus in philosophy we have special occasion to consult apperception to resolve higher-order doubts and disputes.

In any case, in apperception, according to Gaṅgeśa, the content of the scoped awareness is, we have seen, infallibly cognized as awareness content; that is to say, the scoped awareness is, *qua* awareness, known precisely as the phenomenon it is. Awarenesses, it must be remembered, are differentiated only by content; awareness itself is *nirākāra*, without a form of its own. On this basis, Gaṅgeśa is able to pull the rug out from under those arguing that, *qua* subjective phenomenon, an awareness is infallibly known: that is indeed the considered Naiyāyika view. The view is also key to the Naiyāyikas' being able to talk so discriminately about cognitions, despite their direct realism. It is through apperception that a determinate cognition is realized to have qualificative structure, a-R-b.

3. Ontological Grounds

Taking an overview, we see that the most important feature of the Nyāya ontology—in all periods—is just its realism in the sense of a commitment to the existence of entities independent of consciousness.[44] Everywhere we turn, we have to take account of this realism as the fundamental outlook. For example, Gaṅgeśa's definitional projects remain projects of philosophic (or systematic, interlocking) characterization, because the various definienda (veridical awareness, inference-grounding pervasion, etc.) are realities in the world. Epistemologically, realism leads Naiyāyikas to embrace fallibilism: a physical object transcends the instruments of knowledge; thus the possibility of error cannot be ruled out (except in the case of apperception). Nevertheless, realism also underpins a factual (externalist) view of knowledge. We may in fact know objects perfectly well as they are, and the mere possibility that we are wrong is not, ordinarily, enough to successfully challenge our confidence that our awareness is capturing things as they are. Naiyāyikas specify definite conditions for uncertainty or meaningful doubt (as opposed to the neurotic or philosophic doubt made familiar by Descartes). Furthermore, there are the distinct types of entity—substances, qualities, natural kinds, absences—that are viewed as reals.

Udayana makes plain an ontological ordering. In the innermost circle of being stand substances, qualities, and motions; these all exist, i.e., are loci of the universal, *sattā*, "being-ness." Next come universals, final particularizers, and inherence, which are all positive primitives, i.e., presences (*bhāva*). Absence (*abhāva*), the final category, is a negative primitive.

When we come to what Gaṅgeśa does with this inheritance, we should bear in mind that foremost the great Navya is an epistemologist and logician. His interest in questions of ontological significance is secondary and derivative. His main task, as he sees it, is to spell out the nature of veridical awareness according to its various sources and kinds. Still, Gaṅgeśa thoroughly realizes that certain ontological issues are intertwined with his epistemic theses, and many interesting and even novel ontological views are explored in the *TCM*. Gaṅgeśa's own ontological theses, however, rarely transgress parameters set by the inheritance from Udayana, and in this way he is much more conservative than many of his Navya successors. His argumentation nevertheless forms a problem space for even the most innovative of the later Logician ontologists.[45] And it is not until Raghunātha that Udayana's ontology is overhauled, although, as we will see, Śaṅkara Miśra has a novel way of utilizing the category of absence to rebut Śrīharṣa on distinctness. Here we will look only at those points of Gaṅgeśa's and his more immediate successors' ontology that are most pertinent to the Navya response to Śrīharṣa. Later developments are broached in the section, "Surplus Properties," but are by and large beyond the scope of this study.

The key bridge thesis connecting Gaṅgeśa's ontology with his epistemology is that the veridicality of veridical awarenesses is underpinned by truthmakers or objects as relational complexes. These are the thick particulars we have already discussed, i.e., particulars as connected to their properties. Ontologically considered, the relation regress insisted on by Śrīharṣa becomes a problem of attribution: how is the particular connected to its properties? Gaṅgeśa's answer comes in his reflection on inherence; the *samavāya-vāda* section of the *TCM* is translated, with comments, in chapter 5 (section 7, "Gaṅgeśa On Inherence"). Refinements are present in the texts of Śaṅkara Miśra and Vācaspati Miśra II. We will now take a preliminary view of this portion of the ontology.

3.1. Inherence and Self-linkage

Inherence, we noted in chapter 2, relates (i) substance particulars with their parts, (ii) qualities, motions, universals, and final particularizers with substance particulars, and (iii) universals with quality and motion particulars as well as with substance particulars.[46] Disregarding (i) the mereological relation, and considering inherence only in its role as (ii) and (iii), the (let us say) instantiation relation (Gaṅgeśa himself usually ignores the mereological side of inherence), we see that it accounts for a layeredness between particulars and properties: inherence separates qualificanda and qualifiers. It is, to use the terms of later Navyas, a "locus-exacting" relation (*vṛtti-niyāmika*): *x* in *y* without being absorbed by *y*.

Gaṅgeśa defends the layeredness in several ways, for example, by pointing to cases of lack of synonymity ("a cloth" versus "a white cloth") and differences in modes of experience of one and the same object (experience of a pot as colored versus experience of it as an individual substance, for instance). Without inherence, he reasons, the layeredness would collapse: "a cloth" would mean the same as "a white cloth" and experience of the blue of a pot would be the same as a blind person's experience of a pot.[47] The qualificanda and qualifiers joined by inherence as the qualificative relation fall into distinct categories, obeying distinct logics. Universals or natural kinds are identical in the particulars in which they inhere; qualities, e.g., the blue of a blue lotus, are themselves particulars, and so on. Inherence is the relation that binds certain types of qualifier with what they qualify.

Inherence, however, is not the only relation that constitutes a tie between qualifiers, or properties, and what they qualify as reflected in veridical verbalizable awareness. With, for example, the cognition "*daṇḍī*" "(A) staff-bearer," the relation is conjunction—between the staff and the person carrying it. Moreover, a relation known as self-linkage (*svarūpa-sambandha*) also, in come cases, does the binding, Gaṅgeśa says, following Udayana. Thus the qualification relation is wider, more general or inclusive, than inherence. Śaṅkara Miśra relies on this point in his response to Śrīharṣa on distinctness, as we will see.

Gaṅgeśa, for his part, sees inherence in its instantiation role as a primitive, an irreducible category, and a non-multiple real. We may be tempted to see it as a universal (in the minimal Western sense of a "repeatable"), and as identical through instances. But though it is the same everywhere (*anugata*, uniform or continuous), it seems it should not be viewed as a type with tokens.[48] Rather, it is truly singular. The relation "less than" (<), as in "2 < 3," "3 < 4," "4 < 5," and so on, does not have instances but is precisely the same identical relation; the same identical logic (which is dyadic, asymmetrical, transitive, etc.) is in evidence with each ordered pair it defines. Inherence is similarly a singular critter: it is an abstract (non-temporal, non-spatial) binder of certain types of terms according to its peculiar logic (which is asymmetrical, non-transitive, locus-exacting, etc.).

Self-linkage, on the other hand, is considered by Gaṅgeśa to be an internal aspect of a qualifier. That is to say, the link between qualificandum and qualifier is ontologically not different from the qualifier in cases of self-linking qualification. Whereas inherence is invariably distinct from its relata, which are invariably distinct from one another, self-linkage is not distinct from the qualifier. This problem space is inherited by Śaṅkara Miśra and other Navyas from Gaṅgeśa, and it presents an obvious problem in the context of forging a response to Śrīharṣa. But Śaṅkara Miśra is able to maintain the layeredness, and thus distinctness, in the case of self-linking qualification by interpreting the qualificative relation as an absence (more about this below).

Gaṅgeśa's section on inherence—translated in chapter 5—is focused as much on self-linkage as on inherence; the respective roles of each, and why, is Gaṅgeśa's concern. Insofar as we wish to speak of the relational aspect of a self-linking qualifier appearing in determinate awareness, we abstract the self-linking relationship from the complex a-R-b, namely, -R-b. Self-linkage is involved in Gaṅgeśa's response to the relation regress. He also sees it as a way to talk about relations while maintaining an ontological economy. In fact, he worries whether parsimony does not demand the elimination of inherence. To speak of self-linkage with respect to a self-linking term is to abstract the relational hook intrinsic to a qualifier without committing oneself to the existence of a relation as an additional real. (Such abstraction is also—on one interpretation, we will see—key to the problem of "surplus properties.")

A prime example of a self-linking qualifier is an absence. Absences as qualifiers do not involve a separate relation binding them to what they qualify. Absences stand as primitives for Gaṅgeśa and indeed all Navya-Nyāya philosophers, though absences do not, technically, exist. They are not a positive presence but a negative primitive. As such they appear in the qualifier place in determinate cognition. Absential relations are invariably a matter of self-linkage. For example, the content of the awareness, "There is no pot on the floor," is to be analyzed as floor(-self-linkage-absence of pot). Though the cognition has relational structure, a-R-b, and is veridical, and though Gaṅgeśa accepts the absence as a separate primitive, a negative real, the absence is a self-linking term, which relates in and of its own nature. Or, the absence may be said to be, instead of a term, a self-linking relation, negatively relating an absentee to a locus (though this is not Gaṅgeśa's preferred way of viewing the matter). In sum, while absences are considered primitive, they do not require an additional relation in that they self-link with what they qualify. Absences are self-linking.

Inherence is an additional real that (Gaṅgeśa more explicitly suggests) may be viewed as a relation or as a term. For Gaṅgeśa, as a relation it is a "peculiar reflexive relation," a relation that may be said to take itself as a term as well as the pair it joins.[49] When the question is asked, "What relates inherence to either of its terms?" inherence is treated as a term, not as a relation. The question is legitimate, since inherence can be viewed as a term. Thus seems spawned the relation regress. The solution is that inherence has a dual character. As a term, inherence stands as self-linked.

The further question is why self-linkage maintains an ontological layeredness, why qualificanda do not absorb self-linking qualifiers, and why self-linkage is locus-exacting. Śrīharṣa would insist the Naiyāyika is impaled on the other horn of the dilemma: how can something self-link while remaining itself intrinsically discrete and separate from what it is joined with? Gaṅgeśa does not address this, taking the layeredness for granted. However, Śaṅkara Miśra does come up with a response.

From the section on inherence in Gaṅgeśa's *TCM*:

> Further, it is not just as a relation that inherence is established. (If inherence were inferred as doing nothing but bringing two terms together) there would be an infinite regress. Like an awareness (and its intentionality, *viṣayitva*),

inherence must be self-linking, not only because of the threat otherwise of an infinite regress but because it grounds linguistic practices that reflect self-linkage (*sva-sambaddha-vyavahāra-kāritva*). In order that inherence indeed be without a further relation, it has to link itself by its own nature to something.[50]

Inherence is like the rope that links itself to a tree as well as to the goat around whose neck it is tied. You can look at the rope as a relator or as a term. But as a term it is a term of itself as a peculiar reflexive relation.[51]

Self-linkage is key to Navya-Nyāya philosophers' solution to the regress of relations, the Bradley problem, insisted upon by Śrīharṣa. Thus we can appreciate the urgency of the question which Gaṅgeśa wrestles with, as he reflects on how we come to know what we know through sensory awareness: if self-linkage is to be resorted to in analyzing inherence, why is inherence needed at all? The logic of self-linkage works with qualifierness (all that the relationality of an absence to its locus amounts to), which is not an additional real. Parsimony would seem to join with the relation regress in demanding the elimination of inherence. This, as we will see, is Gaṅgeśa's preoccupation in the *samavāya-vāda* section of the *TCM*.

Śaṅkara Miśra's concern, likewise that of Vācaspati II, is different. Śaṅkara is worried about fundamental layeredness, the layeredness in *any* qualification, inclusive of inherence and self-linkage. His argument is that all qualification involves distinctness. Thus distinctness is proved by every determinate awareness; it is objective content with every determinate awareness. (He has a different argument concerning indeterminate awareness.) For Śaṅkara Miśra, the logic of inherence is not the crucial concern, but rather the logic of qualification. This, he argues, invariably involves absence, i.e., mutual absence or distinctness, separating a qualifier and the qualificandum it qualifies.

In this way, the response of later Navyas to Śrīharṣa represents a broadening of focus. To appreciate the full response, we need now to review first absences, and then considerations concerning identity and distinctness. I must also say a few words about a problematic area in the overall ontology, namely, surplus properties (*upādhi*), not so much to prepare for the translations in chapter 5 and the response to Śrīharṣa, but to fill out the ontological picture and give the Advaita criticism its due.

3.2. Absences

Fortunately, concerning absences, there is a premier work of scholarship and translation of two key sections of two central texts, B. K. Matilal's book on negation.[52] Matilal provides some thirty-odd pages of annotated translation of Gaṅgeśa's *abhāva-vāda*, the *TCM* section on absence (he also translates a tract by Raghunātha on negation). Matilal provides lucid explanation of Navya views in general on the topic of absence. I will rehearse these, then explain Śaṅkara Miśra's novel utilization of absence to understand the qualification relation (in any and all qualificative or determinate cognition).

As mentioned, absences, and varieties of absence, were accepted as reals, or as objective, early in both the Nyāya and Vaiśeṣika schools. Vācaspati I introduced the distinction between, on the one hand, three types of relational absence, *saṃsargikābhāva*—(1a) prior absence (of *x* before its production), (1b) destructional absence (of *x* after its demise), and (1c) absolute absence (of *x* constantly with respect to a locus *y*)—and, on the other, (2) mutual exclusion, *anyonyābhāva* (mutual absence of *x* with respect to *y*, i.e., *x*'s distinctness from *y*).[53] Udayana accepted the schema, noting that mutual exclusion, or absence of identity, "is determined by an absentee fancying itself (*abhimāna*) the other."[54] The precise role here of identity becomes a crucial question.

Although Gaṅgeśa occupies himself mainly with the epistemology of absences, he argues that ontologically the category cannot be dispensed with, since there is no other way to account for absential awarenesses. His son, Vardhamāna, clarifies the ontology of absences, showing that types of absence may be delineated by the nature both of the absentee (or negatum or counterpositive, *pratiyogin*) and of the relation that would hold were the absentee not absent.[55] That is to say, not only is every absence *of* an absentee, the absentee is denied with respect to something according to a certain relation. For example, an absence of a particular pot on the floor has the pot as the absentee and the relation of contact as a specifier (*avacchedaka*: see the glossary) of the absentee's absenteehood, i.e., a specifier of what type of fact the absence is. An absence of a pot on the floor by contact (contact is the sort of relation that would obtain were there a pot on the floor) is not the same as the mutual absence of a pot and a floor, an absence specified by identity. The pot *present* on the floor is nevertheless mutually absent there in that the pot and the floor are not identical. Such ontological refinement is key to the Navya response to Śrīharṣa on distinctness, as Śaṅkara Miśra and Vācaspati II make plain.

Gaṅgeśa's characterizations of inference-grounding pervasion (*vyāpti*) and of other key elements in his logic and epistemology utilize the terminology of absences and absentees; he discusses problems concerning absences at several places in the *TCM*, not only in the section translated by Matilal. But he is not, so far as I can tell, as lucid as his followers, beginning with his son, Vardhamāna, concerning the criteria for delineating types of absence. However, in a notable passage in a commentary on Vallabha's *Nyāyalīlāvatī*, Vardhamāna gives his father the credit for correcting a common mistake about the nature of a mutual exclusion (the very mistake responsible for much of Śrīharṣa's confusion, according to Śaṅkara Miśra and Vācaspati II):

> With the cloth denied in relation to the pot, the specifier of the absenteehood is not a relation (such as contact or inherence) but identity, although (in a sense) a relation does specify the fact that there is an absentee. But the

practice of my father is this: the denial that depends on ascribing a relation between the absentee and the locus of the absence is (or expresses) a relational absence. On the other hand, with the cloth denied in relation to the pot there is no such relation ascribed but rather identity. This is the difference between the two (sorts of absence).[56]

Gaṅgeśa, for his part, does clearly state that the characteristic expression of a mutual exclusion has the terms for the two items in the same grammatical case, and implies that this is not so with prior, destructional, and constant absences. Thus, to deny that the cloth is a pot (*paṭo ghaṭo na*) concerns what the two things are in themselves, as on a par in what they themselves are (*samānādhikaraṇābhāva*, which Matilal translates as "nominative absence"; more literally, it is "absence to be expressed with case agreement"[57]). Gaṅgeśa (albeit in a *pūrvapakṣa*, that is, in the context of considering a Mīmāṃsaka view) says flatly that this depends on what each is in itself, its own identity and distinctness from everything else (*svarūpa-bheda*); that is, it amounts to each item's being distinct in itself.[58]

We may now look at Śrīharṣa's argument concerning conventional expression of absences. He reasons hypothetically that if distinctness (as implying negation or absence) were a matter of something's "very nature," *svarūpa* (what it is in itself), then its absentee or counterpositive, *pratiyogin*, would be expressed by terms with case agreement.[59] That is to say, distinctness as a matter of things' "very nature" (*svarūpa*) should be expressed, according to the Logicians' ontological views, by terms in the same case. But according to Śrīharṣa, distinctness is expressed conventionally by terms without case agreement (he uses the instrumental case: *x* distinct *with y*). The solution, provided by Vācaspati II (below, p. 304) and suggested by Gaṅgeśa (again, albeit in a *pūrvapakṣa*),[60] is that we do not talk very often about this sense of distinctness. When we do, however, it *is* appropriate to use the nominative case. According to the New Logicians, a mutual exclusion is distinctness as a matter of a thing's "very nature" (*svarūpa*): it involves cognizing two distinct things *x* and *y* (a pot and a cloth, the stock example) in symmetrical relation, *x* to *y* as *y* to *x*; this is appropriately expressed with both terms occurring in the nominative case ("A pot is not a cloth," *ghaṭaḥ paṭo na*). In contrast, the three kinds of relational absence are expressed, normally, with the locus of the absence in the locative case—the absentee *x* does not appear *in* a locus *y* (and it would so appear were it present)—but this does not hold with a mutual exclusion or mutual absence, *anyonyābhāva* (= *bheda*).[61]

That Gaṅgeśa has at all Śrīharṣa's attack on his mind in suggesting this point may be speculative. But there is a passage within the *pūrvapakṣa* part of the *TCM* section on absence where the Advaitin's influence is apparent. Matilal draws our attention to it; the great Logician's echoing of the *Khkh* is practically verbatim, although Gaṅgeśa (as is usually his practice) does not mention his source.[62]

The issue is how to characterize absence to account for a presumed uniformity of usage and, in particular, whether characterizations that rely on a presumed opposition of presence and absence—the incompatibility of something's absence and presence in the same locus, in the same respect, at the same time—can fly. Gaṅgeśa makes at least two points here that directly echo Śrīharṣa. First, absence cannot be defined non-circularly as opposition to presence, since no definition of opposition, i.e., incompatibility, is available that does not make mention of absence.[63] (I repeat that the terminology of absences is used to characterize inference-grounding pervasion, and incompatibility is a kind of pervasion, a negative variety: wherever *x*, there an absence of *y*, and conversely.) Second, in the same section Gaṅgeśa has an objector state that it will not do to hold the view that absence is the property of something *x* such that there is no cognition of being-ness (with respect to the absentee) in *x*, excluding the case of universals, etc., where, for systematic reasons, being-ness (*sattā*) cannot inhere. For, in this view, absence would still be a matter of circularly defined incompatibility. On these grounds, the *pūrvapakṣa* objector rejects this view in favor of a different view of incompatibility. Śrīharṣa makes very similar remarks, as Matilal points out.[64] I might add that in the same *TCM* passage, distinctness comes up, in fact that variety of distinctness called "difference in properties," *vaidharmya*, which of course is examined extensively by the Advaitin. Thus, though less marked than in the *pūrvapakṣa* portion of the *TCM* section on characterizing veridical awareness, here again Gaṅgeśa seems to have the text of the *Khkh* in front of him as he explores what is wrong with wrong views.

Gaṅgeśa's own *siddhānta* portion of the *TCM* section on absences is dominated by the delicate issue of how absences are known. Gaṅgeśa's chief insistence is that there is no cognition of an absence without prior cognition of the absentee: the necessity for awareness of an absentee is what demands acceptance of absence as a(n ontic) primitive. This position opposes an alternative view (championed by a faction of the Exegetes) that an absence is equivalent to a bare, or mere, presence of a locus, e.g., the mere ground (that has no pot on it). The question is, then, how does the awareness of the absentee figure in, and how does it do so with respect to each variety of absence. Śrīharṣa, we saw, exploits the prior-cognition precept; the challenge for later Navyas is to make clear (beyond what Gaṅgeśa says) the epistemology and ontology of each type of absence. (Gaṅgeśa himself often talks in terms that are too general.)

In historical perspective, Gaṅgeśa's insistence on prior experience of an exampled absentee is nothing new: it reflects a long-standing Nyāya empiricist theory of mind. Vātsyāyana (in his commentary on *Nyāya-sūtra* 2.2.8 through 2.2.11) says that the absentee must be something real and indeed previously known by the cognizer of the absence. Gaṅgeśa and all Navyas reaffirm this principle, with important qualifications, some brought out by Gaṅgeśa, others by Vardhamāna, et al. Let us now draw the threads of the discussion together, taking stock of the composite, pre-Raghunātha position that Śaṅkara Miśra and Vācaspati II draw on in countering the arguments of Śrīharṣa.

First, a constant absence is unlike the other two varieties of relational absence (prior and destructional) in that the absentee is not at any time cognized in the locus where it is denied. For example, air constantly lacks color. The precept that the absentee must be exampled would be mistakenly extended were it held that the absentee must at some time be present in the locus where it is denied.

Similarly, with a mutual exclusion (i.e., distinctness) the absentee is not (as Śrīharṣa had supposed) the identity of the distinct pair, which is unexampled and could not be cognized, but rather some other particular. If the locus of the distinctness cognized is a pot, the absentee would be, e.g., the cloth, or whatever particular is cognized as excluded. A mutual exclusion, we have seen, is appropriately expressed, according to Logicians, by a negative statement with case agreement between two terms ("The pot is not the cloth," *ghaṭaḥ paṭo na*). If veridical, such a cognition would capture the pot as a locus of a mutual exclusion that has the cloth as the absentee as specified by the relation of identity. Identity would be the relational specifier of the absenteehood, not the absentee itself. In other words, a pot is just in itself a mutual exclusion whose absentee or counterpositive as specified by the relation of identity is the cloth. On the rare occasion of having to apprise ourselves of a pot's distinctness, we recall a bit of cloth—with which we are familiar through its clothhood and which we remember through a clothhood trace stored in memory—and realize that the pot in front of us is distinct from, in the sense of mutually exclusive of, the bit of cloth. Thus, the fact of the absentee (being an absentee, or absentee-*hood, pratiyogi-tā*) comes to be seen as specified in two fashions: (a) as already pointed out, by the relation that would hold were the absentee present instead of absent, and (b) by the remembered character of the absentee, e.g., the cloth's clothhood, the respect in which the bit of cloth is denied.[65] The cloth is distinct from the pot not *qua* its substancehood (indeed both are substances) but *qua* its clothhood—to give an example of the latter (b).

Concerning mutual exclusion with respect to the qualification relation, Śaṅkara Miśra is interested in the problem of layeredness in all qualificative cognition. He interprets it as a matter of absence, absence of the mutual exclusion variety. Thus the qualificative relation is a negative relation: all qualificative cognition involves presentation of a qualifier as mutually exclusive of its qualificandum. In English, we would say that the "is" of predication is not the "is" of identity, because predication presupposes distinctness, which, as a type of absence, is negative. A pot known through its potness is also known as *other* than potness: to be a particular instance of potness—i.e., to be qualified by potness—is to be distinct from the qualifier, potness. This is, in Śaṅkara Miśra's estimation, a plain matter of experience of a particular. Thus would distinctness be implicit in every qualificative cognition. We will look at this conception more closely in the comments to the relevant bit of translation in chapter 5 (below, pp. 274–77).

Finally, Gaṅgeśa and his followers achieve several further refinements concerning absences. For example, since Sanskrit has no articles, there is potential ambiguity as to whether a term is being used indefinitely or definitely (*a* pot, as opposed to, *the* pot). Similarly, with expression of an absence, which is in technical discourse usually through a compound expression (*ghaṭa-abhāva*, absence-(of-)pot), there is potential ambiguity between a general denial (absence of *all* pots) and a particular denial (absence of *the* pot). The ambiguity is removed with suitable qualification: generic absence (*sāmānyābhāva*) is thus differentiated from specific absence (*viśeṣābhāva*).[66]

3.3. Surplus Properties

Whereas the reflection of Gaṅgeśa and his immediate followers (pre-Raghunātha) on the topics of self-linkage, the qualificative relation, and absences may be counted as successes on the ontological front, concerning the issue of generality the verdict is less clear. Is Gaṅgeśa's admission of the non-consecutive character of (e.g.) veridicality a crack in the floodwall? Do not Śrīharṣa's arguments reveal an arbitrariness in the Logicians' supposedly natural and empirical cubbyholes? One would think that any inadequacies exposed would eventually come to be generally recognized. Does then Raghunātha's *Padārthatattvanirūpaṇam* (*Determination of the True Nature of the Categories*), represent a full breach of the dikes?[67] There (and in other works by Raghunātha as well) the entire categorial system is rethought, with new primitives added; Raghunātha is especially unhappy with the traditional understanding of universals.[68]

According to one interpretation, Raghunātha believes the entire ontological system is thrown into a fluidity from which there could be no recovery because the pigeonholing categories are flatly indefensible.[69] That the arguments of Śrīharṣa move Raghunātha to his revisions would be the topic of another study. But clear reverberations occur;[70] and even if Raghunātha does not have the Advaitin in mind, the arguments Śrīharṣa expressed had become well known and are discernible in Raghunātha's reflections. Raghunātha's categorial innovations would not be, on this view, veritable advances, but rather stop-gap speculations, most of which, it is true, do not stick with later authors. Jagadīśa (c. 1620) and Gadādhara (c. 1660) do, to be sure, carry on the realist struggle, meticulously examining the ontological status of such crucial items as objecthood, *viṣayatā* (which Gadādhara accepts as an additional primitive[71]). But with Raghunātha one sees that the Nyāya theory of generality has been washed away at its joints—this would be the harsh assessment from a scholarly distance. The inadequacies could be summed up under the heading of *upādhi*, "accidental," "conditional," or "imposed property," the ontological garbage dump that eventually becomes so large and smelly that the realist camp tries to move, but unfortunately has limited options.

There are two other interpretations to consider. According to one, *upādhi*s are "surplus properties," ontological place-holders awaiting further reflection. According to another, *upādhi*s reflect a nominalist strand or development among late Logicians, who are able—rather successfully on this view—to dispel confusion about abstract terms and further our understanding of generalization. Thus, while a first interpretation finds *upādhi*s to reflect categorial bankruptcy, a second sees an ongoing process, and a third finds nominalist themes.

The "surplus property" interpretation has a *prima facie* plausibility: general terms that fail to demarcate true natural kinds—because they fail to fulfill one or another of Udayana's conditions (above, pp. 60–61)—nevertheless pick out, in some usages, real features of things, as attested by experience. It is no objection to the overall ontological system that there is a miscellaneous pile of something that awaits further sorting and analysis. In fact, *upādhi*s come to be divided into two groups: *sakhaṇḍa*, "composite," and *akhaṇḍa*, "simple."[72] A composite property is analyzable: black-cowhood specifies the class of cows that are black, but it is a composite of a true natural-kind universal, cowhood, and a quality, black. The property is composed of reals, but is itself no additional real over and above the natural kind and the quality. Other composite properties break down in other ways. A simple *upādhi*, in contrast, is not analyzable: for instance, etherhood (*ākāśatva*: *ākāśa* is the medium of sound) is not a universal because it does not have two or more instances (there is only one pervasive ether). Here we do want to say that etherhood is nothing other than ether; it is not truly a property, because a single ether is real. However, the point is that there is a meaningful distinction between this *upādhi* and the composite kind of *upādhi*. "Conditional properties" admit of divisions. Moreover, it becomes increasingly common, it seems, to break the category of universal into, on the one hand, true natural kinds, *jāti*, which pass all of Udayana's tests, and, on the other, "conditional universals," *aupādhika sāmānya* (the term *aupādhika* is an adjectival derivative from *upādhi*).[73] Gaṅgeśa says that an awareness of consecutive character is sufficient evidence for a natural kind unless there is a blocker or impediment, *jāti-bādhaka*.[74] Conditional or accidental universals (*aupādhika sāmānya*) are those, such as "elementhood," that fail the cross-section test (see figure 2.3, above, p. 61), and so do not reflect the deepest joints of nature, but are universals all the same.[75] Raghunātha calls these distributive (*vibhājaka*) *upādhi*s, a term that Mathurānātha also uses.[76] In sum, slowly, with patient reflection, the miscellaneous stack begins to be sorted. The mere fact that the realist ontological projects are incomplete is no reason to believe that the work so far accomplished is wrong or that the projects cannot in principle be satisfactorily brought to an end.

On the other hand, according to the "surplus property" interpretation, a reason might well emerge for scrapping the projects, particularly if, as Raghunātha seems to recognize, something in the miscellaneous pile seems to undermine the accepted categories. An open-ended view is open not only to further progress along traditional lines but also to the conclusion that no such progress can be made. The traditional ontology may present insuperable barriers. Possibly, the categories so tightly interlock or are so thoroughly mutually entailed that any tinkering with the system would do irreparable damage. The system's coherence would be destroyed. Something in the miscellaneous pile might invite division of an accepted category that demands further divisions and revisions hopelessly extensive, like falling dominoes. Thus Matilal is not entirely inconsistent when he vacillates between the two interpretations.

The third interpretation, stressing nominalist themes, is also broadly compatible with the surplus property view. Kalidas Bhattacharyya, well aware of the open-ended interpretation (and emphasizing its positive potentiality[77]), sees the ontological project as secondary to epistemology, and stresses that if a previously unrecognized real needs to be recognized to account for some presentation of experience (the objecthood of illusion, say), then the spirit of Nyāya is to admit it. This need not displace the traditional inheritance. Indeed, the success of the inherited ontology with respect to numerous cognitions means that we should be reluctant to admit an additional real, predisposed against a new candidate. But there is nothing in principle that would keep us from expanding the theory. Again, what is sacrosanct is not the particular ontological inheritance, but rather the general realist spirit.

Sibajiban Bhattacharyya sums up the epistemological mainstay of this third interpretation, "Nyāya, whether old or new, is essentially a logic and an epistemology leaving its ontology quite open."[78] But this is not all there is to the third view (if it were, the third would be only a variety of the second, the "surplus property" view). Sibajiban explains how a nominalist Logician faction is able to account for the abstraction-generating facility of natural languages (especially common Sanskrit) by expanding the early Navya analysis of qualificative cognition. Gadādhara, most notably, dispels confusion about abstract terms and the grounds for their (correct) employment with the grammatical comment that the abstract suffixes (paradigmatically, *-tva* = "-ness," though there are several ways in Sanskrit to generate abstractions) are to be understood as used to designate the meaning of non-abstract terms and lower-order abstractions. Thus the abstract term "cowhood" would designate something's being the designate of the term "cow"—something's *being a cow*—and "cowhood-ness" would designate *being-a-cow*'s being cowhood. With every abstraction the ontological question is open: "sometimes abstract terms designate real entities different from those designated by the term from which the abstract term is composed by the addition of the abstraction-suffix—i.e., the arguments of the abstraction operator. But in other cases the entities meant by the abstract terms are ontologically identical with the entities meant by their arguments."[79] Thus such grammatical or linguistic analysis would make room for nominalist moves. No Logician in any era holds that every term is a name. In deciding what there is, Nyāya realism harkens mainly to considerations concerning what determines cognitions to have the content they have: it is the way the world is that is to account for the presentations of experience.

Of course, the Logicians' reflections are not informed by modern science. On the other hand, Naiyāyikas of all periods realize that the ultimate constituents of the world cannot be simply read off of our awarenesses. Gaṅgeśa's treatment of such topics as the nature of the organ of perceptual synthesis, *manas* (in the first chapter of the *TCM*), along with that of the operative sense-object relation in perception of (a) different types of substance, (b) qualities, (c) universals, and so on, complemented by speculations about atoms and other physical phenomena, all this speaks tomes about Logic's general sense of a causally integrated world that includes cognizing human beings; it is a general sense of things not far different from science's.[80] My sense is that with little or no betrayal of the traditional spirit of Nyāya, a latter-day Naiyāyika could embrace a scientific realism (platonism) along the lines of the ontological speculation of David Armstrong among others.[81] Conversely, it is inevitable that on-going work in ontology embrace eventually the Nyāya-Vaiśeṣika tradition, i.e., when its most astute contributors, Raghunātha, Jagadīsa, and Gadādhara, have been recognized by the broad philosophic community (of the future) as the great philosophers they are. Unfortunately, this cannot happen overnight; further translations and philosophic studies must first appear.

And what about the epistemology? Is its success, or failure, tied to that of the ontology? The Naiyāyika epistemology is worked out by reflection from a first-person perspective as well as from an understanding of causal processes. Although the epistemology's final cast is a reliabilism—centered on cognition-generating processes such as perception and inference viewed externally—such externalism is fused with internalist considerations. All good epistemology has to take into account both first-person-oriented and object-oriented points of view. Doubtless, the human first-person perspective—the phenomenological perspective, we might say—is more universal, historically speaking, and has changed much less than science, the object-oriented perspective, and Gaṅgeśa and his fellow Navyas express much astute first-person epistemology. But also, because appropriate abstraction here need not be informed by, for example, sub-atomic physics, the reliabilist claims themselves reverberate with much contemporary third-person theory of knowledge. All this is remarkable especially given the limitations of the Nyāya understanding of the world. The principal task that the Nyāya ontology serves is facilitation of analyses of everyday knowledge. There it has weaknesses, but surely also great strengths. At places, it conflicts with science, despite its causal realist and empiricist temper. Conflicts with science are its most major deficiencies, not the problems with "surplus properties." However, especially with regard to cognition and its logic and place in the world, Naiyāyikas appear to have made discoveries that are independent, or largely independent, of science. This can be seen in their work on the following topics in particular: the epistemic priority of awareness of a qualifier over knowledge of a qualificandum, inductive generalization, ontological underpinnings of inferences with conclusions that are materially true, apperception, conditions of reliable testimony, and the nature of illusion. Consequently, the Naiyāyika epistemology appears to have many virtues that should be recognized, whatever one's judgment of surplus properties and other ontological flaws.

4. Identity and Distinctness

Beyond the epistemological innovations of Gaṅgeśa, the outstanding facet of the Navya response to Śrīharṣa is the clarification of an object's identity and distinctness, work which constitutes, in my judgment, an overall realist victory, despite the unfinished character of some of the reflection. Several problems in this regard, both epistemological and ontological, engage Navya authors beyond the period of our purview. Further, there are close relatives of identity and distinctness—for example, unique character (*asādhāraṇa-dharma*), synonymy (*paryāyatva*), and co-locatedness (*samānādhikaraṇatva*, "having the same substratum")—that need to be carefully distinguished from the identity (*tādātmya*) correlate to distinctness, but that are not satisfactorily delineated by Gaṅgeśa and his more immediate followers. Progress, however, clearly is made. In this final section, I will locate the trouble spots as well as present the Navya achievement of the *early* period. Again, these issues will continue to be engaged by Raghunātha and Logicians of the latest Navya period as well.

A particular object is identical just with itself; the crowning achievement of the Navyas' ontological response to Śrīharṣa is articulation of an individual's absolute identity, the qualificandum with all its qualifiers, the thick particular. However an individual is cognized, it is what it is, the property-bearer with all of its properties. The qualificandum, the thin particular, is, ontologically speaking, the same as the thick particular. Ontologically, there is no difference between the blue pot and the pot, given that the two expressions "the blue pot" and "the pot" are in a particular context of usage extensionally co-referential.[82]

Techniques of delimitation (*avaccheda*, specification) allow the Logicians to handle epistemic and logical difficulties that arise on this ontological view. A pot that is red at time t_1 and then baked black is ontologically identical with the resultant pot that is black at time t_2; the pot has a temporal spread from its production to its destruction with these color properties to be time-indexed, delimited according to the time they occur. Similarly, certain properties have to be spatially indexed, i.e., with property-bearers (physical bodies) that have spatial spread.

As we have seen, the Logicians also embrace an essentialism, at least with many things. This helps us to understand identity through change: a pot exhibits potness from its origin to its destruction even though other properties may change. A pot's potness requires no ontological delimitation, though such delimitation may serve cognition-wise as a specifier of a cognition's content. Indeed, this and related points about specifiers understood with respect to cognition, rather than the Logicians' ontological views, are what I, for one, find striking, for they are unparalleled, so far as I know, by anything Western. Puzzles of identity are not a major concern; there is nothing like the problem of Theseus's ship, questions of trans-world identity, or even reflection on the criteria of personal identity that engage the early Navyas.[83] The exception is mereology where the Logicians from the earliest period defend—against Buddhist attacks primarily—the position that the whole is more than the sum of its parts (excluding heaps, collections, and the like).[84] The worst error made is, I think, that the Logicians, even sophisticated Navyas, sometimes regard identity, like distinctness, as a property. Nevertheless, the guiding light in this entire realm is simply the rather trivial view that everything is identical only with itself, where criteria of identity vary with the different categories and types of things to be found in our rich universe.[85]

In a crucial passage translated in chapter 5 (pp. 255–57), Gaṅgeśa insists that the specifiers (*avacchedaka*) "blue" and "potness" are not only ontologically distinct (blue is a quality and potness a natural kind) but cognition-wise mutually exclusive. Specifiers are cognitively unique and atomic, the ultimate cognitive time-slices, as it were, as specifiers of episodic takes on an object or objects. It is a natural law of cognition that something appearing as F, that is, with F-ness specifying the qualifier-ness of the cognition, excludes all other possible cognitive content, even qualifiers that ontically are present and readily cognizable in the thing. Furthermore, Gaṅgeśa holds that a qualifier-ness specified by F-ness is distinct from the G-ness that specifies the qualificandum-hood in a cognition that attributes both F and G to the same object. With the cognition verbalizable as "The pot is blue," potness specifies the qualificandum-hood, and blueness qualifier-ness. Gaṅgeśa insists that though ontologically the object in question is one and the same, cognition-wise there is all the difference in the world between the specifier of the qualificandum place, so to say, of the cognition and that of the qualifier.[86] Such cognitive specification allows New Logicians to take account of subtle distinctions of presentation—and logical restrictions pertinent to cognitive context—without worrying much about ontology. (Alternatively, the point is that cognitions as entities—qualities of the soul—are distinct when there is any difference whatsoever in content, including a reversal of the specifiers of qualificandum-hood and qualifier-hood.) It is also why the Navyas' logic of cognition could be embraced by rival schools and used in various areas of learning, despite the school's distinctive realism.

R. I. Ingalalli argues that the only true identity cognition that New Logicians would accept would have its qualificandum-hood and qualifier-ness specified by identical class characters; he gives the example of *ghaṭatva* and *kalaśatva* (both terms mean "pothood"; *ghaṭa* and *kalaśa* are synonyms meaning "pot").[87] Identity, then, would be intensional identity; extensional co-reference would be insufficient. Thus Matilal, Ingalalli says, is mistaken. But Ingalalli himself mistakenly interprets Harirāma whom he says he relies on. In the passage from the V. N. Jha translation that he cites,[88] Harirāma is intent on distinguishing cognitions that are grounded ontologically by a single fact, such as a pot's being on the ground. The entire analysis presupposes the ontological identity of the ground being qualified by a pot, a reality that can be cognized in distinct ways, with the challenge being to analyze two distinct ways of cognizing it so that the (cognitive) distinctness is evident. Harirāma makes no mention of synonymy; the example of *ghaṭatva* as identical with *kalaśatva* is Ingalalli's own. Nevertheless, Ingalalli appears to have a point: no qualificative cognition of identity seems possible except insofar as the specifiers of the qualificandum-ness and qualifier-ness are identical, and expressions relying on synonymy seem the only candidates: F*a* is G*a*, where F = G, i.e., "F" and "G" are synonyms. But such a cognition would be peculiar; it is at least difficult to imagine a perceptual context other than someone explaining that two terms are synonyms with reference to a common referent. Note that Śaṅkara Miśra holds that there is no simple qualificative cognition that could be expressed as an identity, in that the qualificandum, *a* in F*a*, is in principle distinct from the qualifier, F.

Vācaspati II stresses that awareness of distinctness between *x* and *y* requires awareness of some respect, some property, in virtue of which there is no identity (below, p. 304). An outstanding problem concerning identity and distinctness—given the dual specification view explained above—is how identity as the relational specifier is known. The worry (with respect to how a mutual exclusion is known) that there is no identity of a pot and a cloth (the term is unexampled) is not entirely disarmed by the move that such identity would not be, as we discussed, the *pratiyogin*, the absential counterpositive. The Nyāya empiricist theory of mind would seem to demand that even a relational specifier be previously cognized; otherwise, it could not be a factor (*ghaṭaka*) in an awareness of distinctness. Vācaspati's solution is to hold that while the denial or negation would be cognized as obtaining with respect to the property-bearer, the property specifier and relational specifier work in tandem: there is an imaginative ascription of some property of a cloth (e.g., its clothness) as identical with some property of the pot (e.g., its potness), when a cloth is the *pratiyogin* of the mutual exclusion qualifying a pot. The term that later is used for this is *āhārya-buddhi*, a term apparently borrowed from aesthetics where it is used for the trope or metaphor of identifying *x* (e.g., the moon) with *y* (e.g., the face of the poet's beloved) while aware that in fact they are not identical. Vācaspati himself uses the term *āropa* "(imaginative) superimposition." Perceptual illusion shows that it is possible to be presented with qualifiers that do not in fact qualify the object cognized. Imaginative ascription of a property roughly parallels what occurs in illusion, except that we are fully cognizant of the imaginative, non-factual character of the awareness. Identity is in general known. Distinctness expressed through denial of identity, Vācaspati says explicitly, concerns the qualificandum or locus, but there must be an imaginative ascription of a property in order to flesh out what is being denied the relation of identity. Finally, no regress occurs because potness and clothness are known to be distinct in themselves, in virtue of what they are in themselves, *svarūpa-bheda* (see below, pp. 298–99 and 304–05).

The tendency to regard identity as a property appears to arise out of the view that identity is a relation. Relations, such as conjunction and inherence, look to be qualifiers from a certain perspective. We have to talk about identity in certain contexts, both in everyday discourse and in technical analyses. The question thus arises what sort of critter it is. The answer is that identity is a relation, a peculiar relation in that it is non-locus-exacting, relating something only to itself. (Contact, or conjunction, *saṃyoga*, is not necessarily locus-exacting, unlike inherence, but it relates different things, as does self-linkage.) As symmetrical, transitive, and reflexive, identity reflects no layeredness. But among some Navyas (e.g. Gadādhara; earlier thinkers, such as Śaṅkara Miśra, tend in this direction as well), it is treated as a real.

Vācaspati, to his credit, is inclined to view talk of identity as only "a manner of speaking," *upalakṣaṇa*, not as reflecting an underlying real; Śaṅkara Miśra is also attracted by this opinion, though in the final analysis he seems to reject it (below, pp. 284–85). Despite the problematic nature of the *upalakṣana/viśeṣaṇa* distinction ("mere designators" versus "true qualifiers"), Logicians felt there had to be a way, given weightier counter-considerations, to discount *vyavahāra*, everyday discourse, as evidence. This is a common move with Gaṅgeśa.[89] An expression that could be analyzed as indicating an *upalakṣaṇa* did not have to be taken seriously ontologically.[90] The overwhelming sense among Navyas is that a thing is identical only with itself, though we experience it through distinct qualifiers and refer to it with different words. The problem, however, is how to analyze talk about such identity, a problem that does not appear to be satisfactorily resolved.

CHAPTER FIVE

Annotated Translation of Selected Passages within Selected Texts[1]

1. Śrīharṣa on Dialectical Reasoning (*tarka*): Ascertaining Inference-Grounding Pervasion

Introduction

The context for the following passage begins on *Khkh*, p. 355, or Ganga I, par. 289, where Śrīharṣa's Logician opponent proffers "dialectical reasoning" (*tarka*) as a way to ascertain an inference-grounding pervasion (*vyāpti*). Śrīharṣa's opposition to the Logician understanding of pervasion was discussed in chapter 3, above, p. 128.

The Advaitin makes a case against the thesis that pervasion, defined as concomitance, *avinābhāva* (no *x* without *y*), can be known. Then he takes up a second definition, "pervasion is the connection of two things, *x* and *y*, such that wherever the pervaded, *y* (the probandum, *sādhya*), does not reside, there is blocking (prevention, opposition, *bādhaka*) of an occurrent probans, *x* (*hetu*)."[2] This definition he attacks by asking whether a pervasion so understood is known by a recognized source of knowledge—perception, etc.—or by "dialectical reasoning" (*pramāṇaṃ vā tarko vā syāt*).

One by one, Śrīharṣa examines candidate sources of knowledge (*pramāṇa*), arguing that each is unequal to the task at hand. He presents reasons for rejecting not only the Logicians' four sources but also an additional two (advanced by Mīmāṃsakas)—namely, presumption (*arthāpatti*) and negative perception (*abhāva*). Perception falls to the criticism that since only non-doubtful cognition satisfies Nyāya's definition of perception (*NyS* 1.1.4), a pervasion known perceptually would have to have the same non-doubtful character as, for example, a particular human being known perceptually. This, however, is not true of the Logicians' favorite example of pervasion, i.e., smoke (as probans) and fire (as probandum), since it is possible to suspect that any particular bit of smoke may have something other than fire as its cause. Inference is ruled out because that answer would involve a vicious circle and regress (inference founded cognitively in knowledge of pervasion and knowledge of pervasion founded in another inference). "Presumption" (*arthāpatti*) is a form of inference according to Nyāya, but Śrīharṣa finds separate grounds for throwing it out, too, namely, the non-generalizability of particular circumstances. The remainder of the list we need not rehearse. (See Ganga I, par. 287–88.)

The candidate *pramāṇa* for ascertaining a pervasion having been disposed of, Śrīharṣa examines dialectical reasoning, *tarka*. This is taken by Logicians not to be a separate *pramāṇa*, but rather the eliminator of an alternative to a view that has some presumption in its favor in virtue of being the product of a true *pramāṇa*. Dialectical reasoning in some cases has the structure of indirect proof: assume the negation of the proposition in question and deduce a contradiction—or show another fault such as *regressus ad infinitum*—which establishes the double negation of the proposition in question and thus the truth of the proposition in question. But *tarka* is best understood as eliminative argument, since there may be more than two alternatives and, as mentioned, the uneliminated, right view must be warranted to some extent independently. (See above, pp. 66–67.)

Śrīharṣa's arguments concerning *tarka*—which fill the next several paragraphs of his text—are admirably paraphrased by Sitansusekhar Bagchi with much elaboration.[3] The heart of the argument is all that will concern us—along with, that is, some summary text of Śrīharṣa's which I will also translate. This text is most notable in the context of our study: Gaṅgeśa himself quotes a verse from it, and directly refers to Śrīharṣa in his own treatment of dialectical reasoning. (Dialectical reasoning is also considered by the author of the *TCM* in the context of the problem of how a pervasion is ascertained: see the translation from Gaṅgeśa two sections below.)

Is dialectical reasoning, *tarka*, Śrīharṣa asks his Logician opponent, (a) founded in pervasion or (b) not founded in pervasion? The first option (a) is no good, because that leads to a vicious regress. The second (b) is no good, because if *tarka* is not founded in pervasion, then one could play fast and loose, with no *invariable* division between fallacious *tarka* and valid *tarka* (valid *tarka* would not *pervasively* exclude the fallacious).[4]

Śrīharṣa continues by examining a bit of dialectical reasoning directed against the doubt that occurrences of smoke deviate from occurrences of fire and thus that the presence of fire cannot be inferred from perception of smoke. Does the doubter, then, think that smoke has no cause? In that case, it would be eternal, and a belief to this effect would contradict, we may suppose, something else the doubter believes, namely, that smoke is produced. Thus the pervasion would be established by the method of indirect proof.

Assume: (1) Smoke has no cause. (A premise contradicting the conclusion to be established, namely, smoke is caused by fire.)

This entails: (2) Smoke is eternal. (From 1 and some suppressed premises.)

But this contradicts: (3) Smoke is a product. (Presumably, a belief firmly held by all. To resolve the contradiction, 1 is denied by way of accepting the original conclusion denied, to wit)

(4) Smoke is caused by fire.

Other options lead to other contradictions.

But, says Śrīharṣa, it is possible that a particular bit of smoke has something other than fire as its cause. Doubt based in the possibility of multiple causation cannot be pushed to contradiction through dialectical reasoning. The Logician opponent tries, however, to tease out a contradiction in several ways, and is countered in each move by our Advaitin: there is no way to be sure that any particular bit of smoke does not have something other than fire as its cause.[5]

The argument at the end comes back around to the dilemma between (a) vicious regress and (b) failure to exclude non-well-founded, fallacious *tarka*. Śrīharṣa then summarizes, rehearsing his main points.

The translation below begins with one last fresh move by the Logician opponent, concerning "immemorial foundation," then continues with Śrīharṣa's summary, Text 1.2 and following.

Text 1.1 (Khkh, p. 363) and Translation

anādi-siddha-vyāptikās te tarkā iti cen, na, tad-buddheḥ pramitatvâsiddheś, śarīreṣv ātma-pratyayasya tādṛśasya apy apramātvôpagamāt, anādi-siddheś ca ubhayatra aviśeṣāt |

Should you try the following, "(Well-grounded) dialectical reasonings rest on pervasions established immemorially," you would be wrong. It is not established that cognitions of that sort would be veridical. (A counterexample:) The cognition of self as applying to the body is of that sort (i.e., has continued from time immemorial), but we (Advaitins) see it as non-veridical. And with this example and your so-called pervasions there is no difference with respect to beginninglessness or immemoriality of their presumed establishment.

Comments

Śrīharṣa's Logician opponent apparently would try this "immemorially founded" move in order to avoid the viciousness of the circle and regress of embracing the first horn of the dilemma: to wit, that *tarka* is cognitively founded in cognition of pervasion as well as the other way around. Śrīharṣa's parry is to argue that the Logician would only fall from the one horn to the other. The dilemma has bite, to change metaphors. If you refuse to admit that *tarka* is founded in pervasion, you are going to allow the possibility of faulty *tarka*, because without pervasion, there is no touchstone whereby deviations that would vitiate inference—and *tarka* as well—could be discerned. Of course, on the pervasion option you face the infinite regress.

The example Śrīharṣa uses to counter the immemoriality move is particularly interesting in that the illusion of false identification of self with body includes behavior, according to Advaita. But it is behavior on which Gaṅgeśa hangs his response to Śrīharṣa, as we will see.

Text 1.2 (p. 363) and Translation

> na api yad yatra vyabhicāraś śaṅkyeta tadā vyāghātaḥ syād ity evaṃ-rūpāt tarkāt vyāghātâvagamaḥ vyāghāta-pratipādakasya tarkasya mūla-śaithilye tarkâbhāsatvâpātāt |

(In sum) you are not (let me repeat) able to establish pervasion as the basis of inference by arguing that when doubt should arise about a failure of x to pervade y then by dialectical reasoning (*tarka*) a contradiction would be revealed in the "deviating" option of an opposed pair that the doubt would presuppose. For "dialectical reasoning" of this sort brings about (according to you) an understanding of a contradiction (*vyāghāta*), and since this reasoning bringing about an understanding of a contradiction may not be well-founded, you still face the problem of not being able to rule out the possibility of fallacious dialectical reasoning (*tarka-ābhāsa*).

Comments

An example would be (1a) Occurrences of smoke deviate from occurrences of fire (a false original conclusion to be established). Assume (1b) Occurrences of smoke are pervaded by occurrences of fire (a premise contradicting 1a). This entails (2) Smoke is the same color as fire (by fallacious reasoning). But 2 contradicts the firmly held belief (3) Smoke is not the same color as fire. Therefore, (4) Occurrences of smoke deviate from occurrences of fire.

Text 1.3 and Translation

tādṛśasya api vyāghātôpanāyakatve vyāghātâpatteḥ sāmyam, śakyate eva tarkâbhāsād bhavato 'pi vyāghātôpanetum,

Since such reasoning can lead to what you would call a contradiction when the reasoning is fallacious, you face a problem of possible contradiction equally on each side, i.e., on both sides of the option and opposed pair, one of which the reasoning is undertaken to eliminate. Because of the possibility of fallacious dialectical reasoning, contradiction on the side that you, sir, wish to establish (as opposed to eliminate) could occur as (fallaciously) deduced. (Thus you could not in principle be free from doubt here.)

Comments

Any given bit of deducing could be fallacious: the criteria for discerning good *tarka* presupposes awareness of pervasion. In contemporary terms, Śrīharṣa may be said to have hit upon the problem of the foundations of *a priori* knowledge: there is no way to pull the canons of deductive reasoning out of the hat without putting them there to begin with. If the canons of the *a priori* have been drawn into question, there is no way to deduce them—on pain of begging the question.

Text 1.4 and Translation

atha tasya tarkasya vyāpti-mūlatā abhyupagamyate, tatra api vyabhicāra-śaṅkāyāṃ punar anavasthā eva, tatra api vyāghātôpapādane punar ittham anavasthā eva ||

Then if it is held that the "dialectical reasoning" has its foundation in pervasion, that won't help (because cognition of pervasion, you will remember, is just the problem). When there is doubt about deviation from a true pervasion, there no cognitive foundation can be upheld. In trying to prove another contradiction with respect to the unwanted option that the new doubt involves, (you presuppose another pervasion and so) again, the difficulty arises *ad infinitum*.

Comments

Infinite regress seems to be the final resting place (*avasthā*) for the Logician, which is no resting place (*anavasthā*) at all!

Text 1.5 and Translation

tasmād asmābhir apy asminn arthe na khalu duṣpaṭhā |tvad-gāthā eva anyathā-kāram akṣarāṇi kiyanty api |
vyāghāto yadi śaṅkā asti na cec chaṅkā tatastarām |
vyāghātâvadhir āśaṅkā tarkaś śaṅkâvadhiḥ kutaḥ ||

Therefore, on this topic it is not too difficult for us to read your verse (i.e., Udayana's verse) with the letters just slightly altered: "If there is contradiction, then there is doubt. If none, there is doubt all the more. Contradiction includes doubt within its borders; how then can dialectical reasoning be the limit (or end) of doubt?"

Comments

The verse from Udayana that Śrīharṣa parodies: "If there be doubt, there is inference indeed; all the more if doubt does not occur. Dialectical reasoning is regarded as the limit of doubt; anxiety does not proceed past (a demonstration of its) inconsistency."[6]

The broadest context for Udayana's verse is his project to prove (by inference) the existence of God. The more immediate context—provided by Udayana's auto-commentary—is a challenge to the *pramāṇa* status, or reliability, of inference. Specifically, Udayana construes a challenge to an $inference_1$ to be a doubt, a meaningful doubt, about possible deviation (*vyabhicāra*) of an occurrence of the probans from occurrences of the probandum (pervasion requires no deviation: wherever the probans there the probandum). But such doubt presupposes a criterion whereby deviation can be determined, namely, the pervasion between deviation and lack of grounds for inference. Thus doubt about the basis for $inference_1$ relies on a pervasion-grounding $inference_2$, the inference from deviation to well-founded doubt. Thus, "if there be doubt, there is inference." But if there is no well-founded doubt about $inference_1$, then $inference_1$ proceeds regarded as reliable (the default position).

This very reflection is an example of dialectical reasoning. It shows that doubt about the possibility of deviation cannot be generalized to undermine the reliability of inference, for it would be self-defeating, contradicting its own basis.

Śrīharṣa turns the reasoning on its head. Contradiction presupposes pervasion (in propositional logic, that p and $\sim p$ are contradictory presupposes that if the one is true, the other is false, and conversely; in a naturalistic logic of ontological opposition, if, e.g., fire and water are opposed, then wherever there is water, such as a lake, there is no fire). Thus with the burden of proof of the reliability of inference borne by the Logician, dialectical reasoning is no help at all. For dialectical reasoning presupposes the very cognitive basis of inference, namely pervasion, which is in question. To be precise, it presupposes contradiction, which, in turn, presupposes pervasion. Thus, if the Logician proffers a contradiction to solve his problem, then he simply reiterates the question—how is pervasion known? If, on the other hand, he is unable to find a contradiction in the doubt about the cognitive basis of pervasion, then by his own admission the doubt will not end.

2. Maṇikaṇṭha Miśra's Response

Introduction

Maṇikaṇṭha, who probably lived in Mithilā a generation before Gaṅgeśa, that is, around 1300, may not have been the first Logician to dispute Śrīharṣa's contentions; D. C. Bhattacharya cites Divākara (c. 1250), who wrote commentaries on at least two of Udayana's works, and is reputed to have commented on Śrīharṣa's *Khkh* as well.[7] But Divākāra's commentaries, which apparently do not survive entire, have not been published, and Bhattacharya, who consulted some manuscript fragments, does not definitely say that he contends the Advaitin's views. The works of several other Logician authors of the period between Śrīharṣa and Gaṅgeśa have been lost. Maṇikaṇṭha's *Nyāyaratna*, which is extant in its entirety and has been published, is then the first accessible Naiyāyika work where there is an attempt to counter the Advaitin's reasoning.[8]

The *Nyāyaratna* covers much the same territory as Gaṅgeśa covers in the *anumāna* (inference) portion of his *TCM*. According to classical *TCM* commentators, Gaṅgeśa cites and considers views forged by Maṇikaṇṭha.[9] However, Gaṅgeśa does not appear to have referred to Maṇikaṇṭha by name.

Maṇikaṇṭha mentions Śrīharṣa explicitly at three places in his work (pp. 18–19, 156, and 173), and refers to his work at another (p. 77) according to Nṛsiṃhayajvan. All but the first of these passages dispute the Advaitin's views on topics of informal logic as though Śrīharṣa's were rival positions of a fellow Naiyāyika. The first mention, however, meets an important refutation of Śrīharṣa's—from his own Advaita standpoint—head on. This is Śrīharṣa's refutation of Udayana's position on *tarka* as an aid in coming to grasp pervasion as the foundation of inference.

Text (p. 19) and Translation

> yat tu khaṇḍana-kṛta-uktam, vyāghāto yadi, tadā śaṅkayā bhavitavyam | anyathā kim-āśrayo vyāghātaḥ ? na ced vyāghātaḥ, tadā śaṅkayā sutarāṃ bhavitavyam, pratipakṣâbhāvād iti | tan na | tarhi na kvacid api viśeṣa-darśanāc chaṅkā-nivṛttiḥ; na vā bādhaka-pratyayād bādhya-pratyaya-nivṛttir iti | tathā ca sadhu-uktaṃ brahma-saṃvedanād anādy-avidyā-nivṛttir ity alam anena | |

But let us consider what the author of the *Khaṇḍanakhaṇḍakhādya* says (on *tarka* and the grasping of a pervasion): "If there is contradiction (*vyāghāta*, natural opposition), then there has to be doubt. Otherwise, there could be no question about the basis of contradiction (i.e., pervasion). On the other hand, if there is no contradiction (i.e., as in Udayana's view that contradiction rules out a competing position), then all the more must there be doubt, since there would be no alternative (to the doubt)." This view is wrong. (Suppose it is right.) Then never would there be cessation of doubt from an experience of particulars. Nor would a sublator (or defeater, *bhādhaka*) ever knock out a defeasible (and wrong) view. And so rightly would it be said that experience of Brahman would eliminate beginningless spiritual ignorance! Enough with this (nonsense)!

Comments

Maṇikaṇṭha hones in on an example of natural opposition in Śrīharṣa's Advaita, the opposition between mystical experience of Brahman and spiritual ignorance. Here the Advaitin clearly holds that there is a pervasion (wherever the one, there not the other). Thus, at least in this case, the Advaitin does not hold that where there is contradiction (in the sense of natural opposition) there has to be doubt. Moreover, there are the plain, everyday empirical facts of doubt ceasing through experience of particulars—for example, the doubt whether an object in the distance is a post or a person ceases with sight of hands, feet, and so on.

3. Gaṅgeśa on Dialectical Reasoning

Introduction

The passage from Gaṅgeśa translated here is taken from the second chapter of the *TCM*, on inference. The immediately preceding section, the *vyāpti-graha-upāya-prakaraṇa*, concerns the ways in which pervasion—the underpinning of inference—is grasped. One of these ways is "dialectical reasoning," *tarka*, defined loosely as "blocking the opposed view." The section devoted to *tarka*, the *tarka-prakaraṇa*, begins with a challenge to the possibility of dialectical reasoning as a way to grasp pervasion. My translation begins with the last paragraph of the previous section and continues about halfway through the *tarka-prakaraṇa* (that is, according to the standard sectioning).[10]

The previous section, the *vyāpti-graha-upāya-prakaraṇa*, has been translated by Mrinalkanti Gangopadhyay.[11] Most of it is comprised of Gaṅgeśa's refutations of alternative views. Only at the end does Gaṅgeśa present his own view about how pervasion is grasped, including the role of *tarka*. That is where my translation begins.

First, the last portion of Professor Gangopadhyay's translation (pp. 203–04), which overlap, in his last two paragraphs, the first two of mine.

> Thus, (as has been shown earlier) repeated observation cannot remove a doubt (concerning the irregularity of the *hetu* [the probans or inferential mark]) and reductio [*tarka*] is of no avail due to the fallacy of infinite regress. How,

then, is *vyāpti* [pervasion] to be ascertained?

The conclusion in this regard is now being stated. The cause of the ascertainment of *vyāpti* is the perception of the coexistence [of the *hetu*, the probans, with the *sādhya*, the probandum or term to be proved] along with the absence of cognition concerning the irregularity [of the *hetu*].

Cognition means both "ascertainment" (*niścaya*) and "doubt" (*śaṃkā*). A doubt [regarding *vyabhicāra*, deviation] results sometimes from a doubt concerning the presence of an *upādhi* [pervasion-undermining circumstance], and sometimes from the perception of common characteristics along with the non-perception of the specific characteristic.

Absence of such a doubt is sometimes caused by the reductio, which negates the opposite alternative [i.e., the possibility of *vyabhicāra*], and sometimes the absence exists by itself.

(Objection:)[12] But then the fallacy of infinite regress would ensue, for reductio [*tarka*] itself is grounded in the knowledge of *vyāpti*.

(Answer:) No, because reductio is resorted to only when there is a possibility of doubt. Thus when, due to some contradiction (*vyāghāta*) of our behavior, there cannot arise any doubt, the ascertainment of *vyāpti* follows without any reductio.

Text 3.1 and Translation

tarkasya vyāpti-graha-mūlakatvenā 'navastā iti cet, na | yāvad ā-śaṅkam tarkânusaraṇāt yatra ca vyāghātena śaṅkā eva na avatarati tatra tarkaṃ[13] vinā eva vyāpti-grahaḥ |

Objection: Since dialectical reasoning is itself grounded in the grasping of a pervasion, there would be an infinite regress (on your view).

Gaṅgeśa: No. Dialectical reasoning is appropriately pursued only so long as there is doubt. Where there would be contradiction—and, indeed, no doubt occurs—one can grasp a pervasion without resorting to dialectical reasoning.

Comments

Dialectical reasoning is called for only in special circumstances, namely, of doubt about a pervasion for which there is other evidence.

Text 3.2 and Translation

tathā hi, dhūmo yadi vahny-asamavahita-ajanyatve sati vahni-samavahita-ajanyaḥ syān na utpannaḥ syād ity atra kiṃ dhūmo 'vahner eva bhaviṣyati ? kvacid vahniṃ vinā api bhaviṣyati ? ahetuka eva vā utpatsyate ? iti śaṅkā syāt |

As an example, consider the particular doubt (against the dialectical reasoning I earlier said demolishes doubt about pervasion of occurrences of smoke by occurrences of fire). If smoke is not produced from a set of causes *ex*cluding fire, then (in conformity with the doubt about the pervasion) smoke—as not produced from a causal complex *in*cluding fire—would not be produced (a conclusion in contradiction, presumably, with the doubter's belief that smoke is produced). Now the doubt (against this dialectical reasoning): Could the smoke come to be from something that is not fire? Or just in some instances could it come to be without fire? Or could it come to be simply by chance (*ahetuka*, without a cause)?[14]

Comments

In other words, the force of the earlier bit of dialectical reasoning derives from the unreasonableness of the supposition that smoke is not produced. Given that it is produced, the alternative that it is produced from a causal complex that includes fire is more reasonable than the contrary alternative that it is produced from a causal complex excluding fire—on the grounds of wide experience. The doubt Gaṅgeśa concocts against that bit of dialectical reasoning (in its role as putatively effecting an ascertainment of a pervasion) is not premised on smoke being produced from any particular causal complex. Thus the earlier bit of dialectical reasoning does not eliminate such doubt in that there remain three possibilities, each of which would mean no pervasion: (a) it could be that smoke is produced from a non-fiery complex, (b) sometimes it could be produced from a non-fiery complex, and (c) it could come to be without a cause.

Gaṅgeśa in the preceding section uses the exact same example used by Śrīharṣa—and the same expression (*śataśo darśane 'pi*)—to argue that repeated observation ("even hundreds of times") is insufficient to *guarantee* a pervasion: not all substances made out of earth are scratchable by iron (diamonds are a counterexample).[15] Gaṅgeśa, echoing Śrīharṣa and apparently endorsing his skeptical arguments, acknowledges—indeed insists—that the possibility of a counterexample cannot be eliminated. After all, a pervasion is a truly universal and invariant concomitance. Nevertheless, we cognize pervasions, and reliably under certain circumstances, and meaningful doubt can be eliminated—this is the upshot of his view. In other words, absolute certainty is not required. We may be wrong in any particular case, but we act on the basis of the regularities in nature we take ourselves to be aware of.

Text 3.3 and Translation

yadi hi gṛhīta-anvaya-vyatirekaṃ hetuṃ vinā kārya-utpattiṃ śaṅketa tadā svayam eva dhūma-arthaṃ vahneḥ tṛpty-arthaṃ bhojanasya para-pratipatty-arthaṃ śabdasya ca upādānaṃ niyamataḥ kathaṃ kuryāt |

Were a person P, who has ascertained thoroughgoing positive correlations (x wherever y) and negative correlations (wherever no y, no x), to doubt that an effect might arise without a cause, then—to take up the example of smoke and fire—why should P, as he does, resort to fire for smoke (in the case, say, of a desire to get rid of mosquitoes)? (Similarly,) to food to allay hunger, and to speech to communicate to another person?

Comments

Thus the skeptic's behavior would give the lie to his doubt. This is the heart of Gaṅgeśa's rebuttal.

Text 3.4 and Translation

tena vinā api tat-sambhavāt | tasmāt tat-tad-upādānam eva tādṛśa-śaṅkā-pratibandhakaṃ |

For (there would be a presupposition to P's doubt, namely) that without the one the other is possible. Therefore, just the resorting to this and that (i.e., the causes of the desired effects) blocks and terminates (*pratibandhaka*) such a doubt.

Comments

Cognitive blockers, *pratibandhaka*, emerge as key to, especially, later Navyas' development of a cognitive logic. The blockers themselves are understood naturalistically: a cognition with F*a* as content is opposed, like fire to water, to a cognition with ~F*a* as content. Thus, broadly, a blocker or preventer is to be understood causally. Sibajiban Bhattacharyya puts it perfectly: "Any factor *the absence of which is necessary* for the production of an effect is a preventor [*pratibandhaka*] of the effect."[16] In the context of attacking doubt about pervasion, the question is whether there are conditions that prevent such doubt. Gaṅgeśa asserts that there are.

Let us consider: Is it possible for a person S to believe *p* and ~*p*? The Navya-Nyāya answer[17] is that, first, a disposition to believe must be distinguished from an actual cognitive occurrence. S has only one cognition at a time, generally speaking, but there is, so to say, a flow of consciousness, and one cognition gives way to another (through complex causal processes) with contiguity between cognition_1 and cognition_2, and so on. Cognition_2 displaces cognition_1 without a gap between them. There are very few general restrictions about precisely what type of cognition could follow a former. Internal factors, such as desire, as well as external factors, such as the loudness of a sound, are both potentially relevant. However, no cognition with content contradicting (opposing) that of a former can occur, with certain exceptions. A cognition with F*a* as content prevents, blocks (*pratibandhaka*), the occurrence of a cognition with ~F*a* as content. There may be a subconscious disposition to believe ~F*a*, but, again, within specified restrictions a cognition with ~F*a* as content is prevented by—and cannot follow or flow from—a cognition with F*a* as content. For more detail, in particular for explanation of the restrictions on this cognitive law, see Sibajiban's discussion (Sibajiban lists eight qualifications on the preventor-prevented relation that come to be recognized among Gaṅgeśa's followers[18]).

Text 3.5 (p. 199) and Translation

> śaṅkāyāṃ na niyata-upādānaṃ niyata-upādāne ca na śaṅkā | tad idam uktaṃ, "tad eva hy āśaṅkyate yasminn āśaṅkyamāne svakriyā-vyāghāto na bhavati" iti |

When there is doubt, there is no regular pattern of behavior. When there is (such) a regular pattern, doubt does not occur.

Thus it has been said (by Udayana): "That is doubted concerning which as doubted there occurs no contradiction with the doubter's action."

Comments

In acting (in speaking, in eating, in chasing away mosquitoes), we proceed on certain assumptions, including assumptions concerning natural pervasions. Dialectical reasoning is capable of revealing these assumptions. "Why would you speak if you believed that there were no concomitance between speaking and communicating to another?"

Text 3.6 and Translation

> na hi sambhavati svayaṃ vahny-ādikaṃ dhūma-ādi-kārya-arthaṃ niyamata upādatte tat-kāraṇaṃ tan na ity āśaṅkyate ca iti |

For it is not possible at once to resort regularly to fire and the like for smoke and the like and to doubt that fire causes it. This is how we should understand the (Udayana's) saying.

Comments

Gaṅgeśa's point is clear. He is specifying a psychological or cognitive law that comes to be more sharply formulated by his followers.

Text 3.7 and Translation

> etena vyāghāto virodhaḥ sa ca sahānavasthāna-niyama iti tatra apy anavasthā iti nirastaṃ | sva-kriyāyā eva śaṅkā-pratibandhakatvāt |

Thus we may reject the argument that contradiction—understood as natural opposition (*virodha*), governing precisely which x cannot occur along with precisely which y—cannot block an infinite regress. It is the doubter's own behavior that proves the lie to the doubt, that blocks it (*pratibandhaka*).

Comments

In fairness to Śrīharṣa and Advaita, let us consider the counterexample Śrīharṣa gave to the thesis that the foundations of good *tarka* are pervasions generally accepted (or, in his words, "immemorially founded"), namely, false identification of self with the body. This, we noted, includes behavior; one acts on the assumption of a pervasion between self and body. What is good for the body is generally presumed to be good for the self, et cetera. Śrīharṣa's view is that the presumption is false, and he believes that the teaching of the Upanishads—as well as spiritual knowledge or enlightenment (*vidyā*)—show its falsity. And whether or not he is right, the point is that even action on the basis of a presumed pervasion does not guarantee that a presumed pervasion in fact holds—no one has shown that the *summum bonum* as conceived by Advaita is impossible. The Naiyāyika, however, can readily admit this. Gaṅgeśa says explicitly (and repeatedly, in the immediately preceding section translated by Professor Gangopadhyay) that wide experience (*bhūyo-darśana*) does not guarantee that a pervasion holds in fact. A bit wider experience could show a deviation. Naiyāyikas are fallibilists. Nevertheless, experience of positive correlations (y wherever x) and negative correlations (wherever no y, no x) without experience of deviation provide sure (though not absolutely certain) grounds for acceptance of a pervasion, an acceptance to guide action. Whether some such particular acceptance is challenged by teachings of the Upanishads, or by a mystical experience, is a distinct issue, not threatening the general principle.

Text 3.8 and Translation

> ata eva "vyāghāto yadi śaṅkā asti na cec chaṅkā tatastarām |vyāghātâvadhir āśaṅkā tarkaś śaṅkā-avadhiḥ kutaḥ" |iti-khaṇḍanakāra-matam apy apāstam |
> na hi vyāghātaḥ śaṅkā-āśritaḥ, kin tu sva-kriyā eva śaṅkā-pratibandhikā iti |

Therefore, the view that the author of the *Khaṇḍanakhaṇḍakhādya* expresses with the following may be rejected: "If there is contradiction, then there is doubt. If none, there is doubt all the more. Contradiction includes doubt within its borders; how then can dialectical reasoning be the border (or end) of doubt?" For (cognition of contradiction) does not depend on (the occurrence of) doubt. Rather, behavior blocks doubt with whomever.

Comments

Thus, pointing out pragmatic contradiction—speech or other behavior operative on a presumption contradicting the negation of a thesis (about a pervasion) that is to be established—is the heart of dialectical reasoning, according to Gaṅgeśa.

Text 3.9 and Translation

na vā viśeṣa-darśanāt kvacit śaṅkā-nivṛttir evaṃ syāt |

There is the further difficulty on this (Śrīharṣa's) view that even with experience of (doubt-resolving) particulars (such as of hands and feet with respect to a doubt whether an object in the distance is a post or a person) there would never be cessation of doubt.

Comments

Maṇikaṇṭha Miśra, we saw, made this point.

Text 3.10 and Translation

na ca etādṛśa-tarka-avatāro bhūyo-darśanaṃ vinā iti bhūyo-darśanâdaraḥ |

Moreover, the dialectical reasoning such as was cited above (in text 3.2) does not come into play without wide experience of correlation between the terms of the (inference-grounding) pervasion (of the presence of smoke by the presence of fire). The dialectical reasoning depends on such wide experience.

Comments

Gaṅgeśa says this by way of endorsing the traditional view that *tarka* is not an independent *pramāṇa*.

4. Śrīharṣa on Defining Veridical Awareness

Introduction

Śrīharṣa's attacks on definitions of veridical awareness (*pramā*) are closely followed by Gaṅgeśa as the New Logician shows what is wrong with wrong views on the topic. Thus Śrīharṣa's arguments inform the problem space in which the great Naiyāyika works. Śrīharṣa's arguments are also interesting in their own right. In particular, he shows the difficulty of maintaining the right cut between veridical and illusory awareness. He also mounts a devastating critique of a correspondence theory, criticisms that force Gaṅgeśa to try a new strategy. Moreover, the Advaitin clearly shows that veridicality does not meet the Naiyāyika conditions for a natural kind, a demonstration that Gaṅgeśa not only accepts but that moves him to rethink the general project of characterization and to use, as will be explained, an appropriate variable in the most influential of the definitions of veridicality he endorses.[19]

Text (p. 130, line 3) and Translation

tattvânubhūtiḥ pramā ity apy ayuktaṃ, tattva-śabdârthasya nirvaktum aśakyatvāt | tasya bhāvo hi tattvam ucyate, prakṛtaṃ ca tac-chabdârthaḥ, na ca atra prakṛtaṃ kiñcid asti yat tac-chabdena parāmṛśyate |

The definition of veridical awareness as "experience of reality (*tattva*, thatness)" is incorrect, since it is impossible to explain the meaning of the word *tattva*. For *tattva* is said to be the "being that," and the meaning of the word "that" (*tat*) is something referred to in a context of utterance. But (with just this definition) there is nothing referred to in context that could be meant by the word "that."

Comments

This definition is given by Udayana in his *Lakṣaṇamālā*.[20] Gaṅgeśa considers and rejects it, crystalizing Śrīharṣa's objections (below, p. 185, definition D^8).

Text and Translation

atha anubhūtyā sva-saṃbandhi-viṣaya ākṣepād buddhisthaḥ kāryate, sa tac-chadbena parāmṛśyate, vaktṛ-śrotṛ-buddhi-sthāyām eva prakaraṇa-padârtha-viśrāmāt; tena yasya arthasya yo bhāvas tat tasya tattvam ucyate iti, na, arajatâder api rajatâdy-ātmanā anubhūti-viṣayatā-saṃbhavād asatyânubhūty-avyavacchedāt ||

Opponent: Then what the word "that" means is the content (*viṣaya*) presented by an experience that is by itself related to it and, we may suppose, established by the cognition (or cognitive context), since in determining meaning we do not look further than the context as established exclusively by the cognition of the speaker and hearer. Thus the meaning of *tattva* would be: for whatever object (is intended), its *being that* (reality).

Śrīharṣa: No. The definition (then) would fail to exclude non-veridical experience, since it is possible that an experience have content as, say, silver, even when it is of what is not silver.

Comments

If the "being that" is determined by cognition, then illusion will not be excluded. Both veridical and non-veridical awareness have content. There is nothing in the cognitive context alone that is capable of differentiating the veridical and non-veridical.

Text (p. 131)

> bhavitur atattva-śabdârthatva-prasaṅgena dharmy-aṃśe viśiṣṭe ca pramāyā apramātvâpātāt |

There is also the difficulty that with regard to what is (the possessor of reality, *tattva*) it should be designated by a word other than *tattva*. So a veridical awareness would be non-veridical with regard to that portion of its content that is the property-bearer, the qualified.

Comments

The possessor of reality would have to be, as the *possessor* of reality, something else as well, and the definition on the table would not capture its being in itself the property-bearer (with respect to multiple properties).

Text and Translation

> atha ucyate avayavârtha-cintayā dūṇâbhidhānam idaṃ tyajyatāṃ, yato 'yaṃ tattva-śabdaḥ sva-rūpa-mātra-vacanaḥ iti, etad apy ayuktam, svarūpatvasya jāter upādher vā svâtmani vṛtty-avṛttibhyām anupapatteḥ |svarūpa-śabdârthasya ekasya asaṃbhavena prativiṣaya-vyāvṛttyā lakṣaṇasya avyāpakatvâpātāt |

Opponent: Then please stop listing problems in the spirit of etymologizing. For this word *tattva* means simply *svarūpa*, "essential nature" or something's "own form."

Śrīharṣa: That also won't do. Whether "being an essential nature" (*svarūpatva*) is understood as a natural kind or an accidental property (*upādhi*), it cannot be nested in itself, nor can it be not nested in itself (and there is no other alternative).

Furthermore, the definition would then fail to be sufficiently inclusive, since there can be no single meaning of the word *svarūpa* as it differs with each and every object.

Comments

The first objection is Śrīharṣa's oft-utilized attribution dilemma; see section 6 below, pp. 221–22. According to Nyāya, a property, whether a natural kind character or an accidental or abstract property (*upādhi*), cannot rest in itself; it must have a distinct substratum.

The second objection—taking off from the premise that the meaning of the term *svarūpa* varies according to context—is used by Śrīharṣa in bashing the theory of universals with practically every Naiyāyika definition he examines. A definition, like a universal, has to unify its instances, or, more precisely, in the case of a definition of X, apply univocally to each and every instance of X. There must be "consecutive character," *anugama*. In particular, if the Naiyāyika insists that *tattva* amounts to *svarūpa* in the sense of the uniqueness of an individual thing known, then there can be no consecutive character in the definition of veridical awareness.

Gaṅgeśa, we will see, accepts this critique. He breaks with earlier Nyāya in admitting that his favored definition fails the consecutive character test. That is to say, he proffers what he takes to be good definitions in spite of abandoning the *anugama* requirement—an abandonment, moreover, that he explicitly defends. See below, in particular, p. 210.

Text and Translation

> kathaṃ ca tattva-iti-viparyāsâder nirāsaḥ |tathā hi, śuktau yo rajatatva-pratyayaḥ so 'pi sva-rūpa-buddhir bhavaty eva; na hi dharmī vā rajatatvaṃ vā na sva-rūpaṃ, na api pratibhāsamānaḥ saṃbandho na sva-rūpam iti yuktam |samavāyo hi tayoḥ saṃbandhaḥ pratibhāti, sa ca sva-rūpam eva ||

And how, again, is the mention of reality to exclude wrong and other non-veridical cognition? For example, an understanding of silverness with respect to mother-of-pearl is also a cognition of an essential nature, *svarūpa*. It is not the case that either the property-bearer or the silverness fails to be an essential nature. Nor does the relation that appears between the two fail to be an essential nature. For (according to your own Nyāya view) inherence (*samavāya*) is the relation manifest, and it is indeed an essential nature.

Comments

Considered objectively—and in accord with the Nyāya theory—each of the factors manifest in cognition—the property-bearer, the qualifier, and the relation—is an essential nature, though in some cases the qualifier and/or the relation may not be a separate, independent real. Even with non-veridical awareness, each is thought to exist somewhere in the world; there is no such factor that is unreal. So again there is failure to get the precise cut between an illusion and a veridical awareness.

We skip ahead now several pages to look at another definition and its refutation.

Text (p. 218) and Translation

yathârthânubhavaḥ pramā ity apy alakṣaṇam | yathârthatvaṃ hi tattva-viṣayatvaṃ vā ? artha-sadṛśatā vā syāt ? na ādyaḥ, pūrvaṃ nirastatvāt | na api dvitīyaḥ, vyabhicāriṇo 'pi prameyatvâdinā artha-sādṛśyena pramātvâpātāt | na ca prameyatvâdi-rūpasya vyabhicāriṇy api prakāśa-saṃbhavena tathā apy atiprasaṅgaḥ iti vācyam, prameyatvâdy-aṃśe prakāśamāne viṣayībhūta-dharmântarâpekṣayā vyabhicāriṇo 'pi pramātvâbhyupagamāt, iti na etad yuktam | prakāśamānena rūpâdi-samavāyitvena rūpeṇa jñānasya artha-sādṛśyânabhyupagame 'pi tatra tadīya-pramātvâṅgīkārād iti ||

"Veridical awareness is experience in conformity with the object" is also a wrong definition. For would this conformity be "content that is real (*tattva*)" or "similarity with the object?" The first alternative won't do, because that was thrown out earlier (i.e., when we examined *tattva* in connection with the definition, "Experience of reality"). Nor is the second option any better, because an erroneous awareness would have to be counted veridical in that it is similar to the object in some respects, for example, as knowable.

Opponent: The similarity intended is with the form objectified by cognition. And it is wrong to hold that there would still be unwanted inclusion in that an erroneous awareness could also appear making manifest (or objectifying) knowability, and so on. For in just such a respect's being manifest, namely, knowability, even an erroneous awareness—erroneous with respect to another characteristic objectified—is to be accepted as veridical.

Śrīharṣa: No, what you say won't do. For you accept the veridicality of an awareness that you do not view as having similarity with its object, namely, an awareness veridical with respect to color, etc., being manifest as *inherent* (i.e., objectwise, whereas on the other hand, cognition-wise, color, etc., do *not* inhere).

Comments

Color as a quality inheres in colored substances, e.g., blue in a pot, but color manifest in an awareness does not inhere in the awareness.

Text (p. 219) and Translation

prakāśamānena rūpeṇa viśeṣaṇa-bhāvād artha-sādṛśyam anubhavasya vivakṣitam, arthasya ca yathā samavāyād rūpaṃ viśeṣaṇībhavati tathā viṣaya-bhāvād jñānasya api tad viśeṣaṇaṃ bhavaty eva ? iti cen na; evaṃ hi purovartitvâdinā rūpeṇa tathā-bhāva-sambhavāt purovartinīṃ śuktiṃ rajatatayā avagāhamānaṃ jñānaṃ pramā syāt |

Opponent: The similarity between the object and awareness we intend derives from the qualifier as the manifest form. So in the case of the form objectified deriving from inherence on the side of the object, there would likewise be, on the side of the awareness as well, something (a qualifier, namely, inherence) derived from the awareness's content. That we call the qualifier (both cognition-wise, as informing the content of the awareness, and object-wise, as an objective real).

Śrīharṣa: Wrong. For in that case an awareness fathoming mother-of-pearl as silver would have to be counted veridical: mother-of-pearl that is right in front, and thus in this respect, being right in front, would be just as you have specified, namely, with such (manifest) form.

Comments

Here Śrīharṣa's opponent provides the germ of the sophisticated response of Navya Nyāya. Śrīharṣa's counter-response is accepted by Gaṅgeśa; that is to say, Gaṅgeśa endorses the view that an erroneous awareness can be veridical in part, e.g., with respect to the "being in front." Moreover, the next move the opponent makes is criticized by the Logician with Śrīharṣa's exact argument.

Text and Translation

> na ca vācyam iṣyata eva sā pramā api iti na vyabhicāra-codanā iyaṃ yuktimatī iti, yathārthatā-viśeṣaṇa-vaiyartha-prasaṅgāt | anubhūtiḥ pramā ity ukte eva hi tāvan, na asty atiprasaṅgaḥ, sarvasya vyabhicāry-anubhavasya antato 'nyathā-khyāti-vādi-naye dharmiṇy api pramātva-sambhavena pramāyām eva anubhavatvasya sthairyāt ||

Opponent: That is just the consequence we want! Such an awareness would be veridical, too. Your urging a deviation is no argument.

Śrīharṣa: No, this should not be said, because you invite the objection that the term in the definition *yathārthatā*, "conformity with the object," would be meaningless. For experience would be equivalent to veridical awareness according to this statement of yours, so that there would indeed be no incongruity (in there being no illusory awareness at all). All deviant awareness, according to the (Nyāya) "misplacement" theory (*anyathā-khyāti-vāda*), as being about a property-bearer, too (i.e., no less than a non-deviant awareness), would, in the final analysis, show veridicality. With respect to (defining) veridical awareness, "being experience" would indeed be the firm conclusion.

Comments

Gaṅgeśa is forced by these considerations to view every illusory awareness as veridical in part, that is, as veridical with respect to making manifest a "being a this."

We skip ahead now several pages to a definition attributed to Dharmakīrti.

Text (p. 231) and Translation

avisaṃvādy-anubhavaḥ pramā ity api na yuktam |avisaṃvāditvaṃ hi jñānântareṇa tathā eva ullikhyamānârthatvaṃ vā ? jñānântareṇa viparītatayā 'pratīyamānârthatvaṃ vā ? pratīyamāna-vyāpya-viṣayatvaṃ vā ? anyad eva vā kiṃcit ? na prathamaḥ, dhārā-vāhino bhramasya pramātva-prasaṅgāt |na ca pramā-bhūtaṃ jñānântaraṃ vivakṣitam iti vācyam, pramāyā eva lakṣyamānatvāt |

"Veridical awareness is experience not failing to conform (or agree) with others." This too is wrong. For is lack of failure of conformity to be (1) with another awareness only insofar as its object is explicitly mentioned (or manifest), or (2) with another awareness whose object is not cognized as opposed, or (3) whose content is pervaded by (the content) being currently cognized, or (4) is it something else? The first option is no good, because an error that continues in a series (e.g., a sequence of misperceptions of silver as mother-of-pearl) would have to be counted veridical. And it should not be said that the other awareness specified has to be veridical, since it is just veridical awareness that is being defined.

Comments

This passage seems closely followed by Gaṅgeśa: see below, p. 184. He even repeats the phrase, *tathā ullikhyamāna*, "insofar as it is made explicit." Probably Gaṅgeśa had the text of the *Khkh* in front of him while he composed the *TCM* section on defining veridical awareness. Converting the double negation, he focuses, however, on "awareness in conformity with others," in other words, on Śrīharṣa's third alternative, not on the other three.

Śrīharṣa himself, in a rare mention of a historical figure, identifies the definition as Dharmakīrti's (*Khkh*, p. 236). Phyllis Granoff finds it endorsed by several other authors.[21]

Text and Translation

na api dvitīyaḥ, anupajāta-bādha-bhrama-vyāpanāt; svastha-daśôtpannasya śukla-śaṅkhâdi-jnānâder duṣṭêndriya-daśôtpanna-tat-pītim ajñānâdy-ullikhita-viṣaya-vaiparītyasya apramātva-prasaṅgāc ca |

Nor will the second alternative do. This would include errors that have not yet been proved wrong. Moreover, this would involve counting as non-veridical an awareness occurring when one is healthy, an awareness of, say, a white shell, which is opposed to another whose explicit content is, say, yellow, occurring when the sense organ is not properly functioning.

Comments

Thus the later veridical experience of white would have to be counted as non-veridical, since it fails to conform. Coherence as the sole criterion of veridicality does not cut the ice between fiction and fact, as is often remarked by contemporary epistemologists.

We are now near the end of Śrīharṣa's treatment of definitions of veridical awareness. I will summarize the Advaitin's next few paragraphs, and then translate one last section.

The definition targeting coherence as the mark of the veridical cannot be saved by stipulating that the agreement has to be with other *right* cognitions, for what is meant by "right" is in question. The third alternative (from p. 231) fails because of the unavailability of a viable sense for "pervasion." Moreover, an entire life with a series of cognitions having the same content would be required to make a cognition veridical, and a break at the end would undermine the whole chain.

Next, Śrīharṣa fills out the fourth option, "something else," with a sympathetic presentation of Dharmakīrti's pragmatism (*Khkh*, p. 235; Ganga I, par. 286). The phrase "not failing to conform" in the coherentist definition is interpreted pragmatically, that is, as cashed out in successful action, action satisfying desire. Śrīharṣa objects that it is possible that we have a wrong view of "successful action." Moreover, the intentions or desires of a cognizer can change over time, vitiating the pragmatic touchstone. The Advaitin closes with a summary statement that on no interpretation will the coherentist view fly, and also with this concession, "This approach of Dharmakīrti's is pretty difficult to rule out, and one has to be careful with it" (*Khkh*, p. 236, lines 1–2).

Śrīharṣa continues with the observation that the time problem faced by Dharmakīrti's theory also wreaks havoc with the understanding of veridical awareness as "undefeated experience," *abādhita-anubhūti*. Every awareness is undefeated at the time it occurs, and if one wants the deeper undefeatedness that would take into account the cognitions of everyone, that is unavailable. Now since Śrīharṣa has gone to great lengths to defend a similar epistemology earlier in his work, we might worry that these remarks—albeit occurring in a single sentence in the midst of a long examination of faulty definitions—draw into question the seriousness of his earlier espousal of a positive epistemological program whereby he would defend the Advaita world view. However, there is indeed a crucial difference in context: here undefeatedness is taken as a proposal of a mark of absolutely veridical awareness, whereas earlier undefeatedness is championed as the mark of what we have a right to assert and believe (i.e., the content of undefeated awarenesses). Śrīharṣa wants to reserve veridicality exclusively for the mystical awareness of Brahman, as he wants to reserve reality (*sattā*) exclusively for Brahman, the One.

Text (p. 236, line 5) and Translation

tarka-saṃśaya-viparyaya-smṛti-vyatiriktā pratītiḥ pramā ity api na, smṛti-vyatiriktatva-khaṇḍana-nyāyena nirastatvād iti, jāti-saṃkaram icchataś ca pramātva-lakṣaṇa-jāty-abhisaṃbandhāt pramā ity api durlakṣaṇam, asya ajñātasya tad-vyavahāra-janakatve pramāyām apramā-bhrama-saṃśayau na syātām |

"Veridical awareness is awareness other than dialectical reasoning (*tarka*), doubt, erroneous awareness, and memory," also is no good (as a definition), for it is thrown out by the same reasoning that refutes (the definition of veridicality as an awareness's) being other than memory (*Khkh*, p. 171: that is, with regard to the phenomenon of recognition, Śrīharṣa has argued, (a) awareness and (b) memory cannot be distinguished).

Therefore, to try to define veridical awareness according to the relation to a natural kind characterizing a class—namely, veridicality—is a bad idea, unless one wants a confusion or cross-section of kinds. (Moreover,) there could be no error or doubt about a non-veridical awareness's being veridical if it (veridicality), without itself being cognized, were to be responsible for everyday usages of the term (*pramā*, veridical awareness).

Comments

Here Śrīharṣa again shows his command of the Nyāya theory of generality, exploiting it for his own purposes. As the natural kind character cowhood is responsible for identification of an individual as a cow, so veridicality, according to the current proposal, would be responsible for identification of an awareness as veridical. One problem is then that just as being-a-cow would be given in perception such that it would not normally be subject to (meaningful) doubt, so veridicality would have to be perceptually given and likewise not subject to doubt. This, we will see, is the consideration with which Gaṅgeśa opens his discussion of the veridicality characterization project. He also repeats the "cross-section" objection, agreeing with the Advaitin that, for that reason, too, veridicality is not a natural kind.

Śrīharṣa goes on to anticipate Gaṅgeśa's own view that veridicality varies with the types of things that there is veridical awareness of. First he argues (*Khkh*, p. 237, bottom) that if veridicality is known not perceptually but by way of an inferential mark, then supposing veridicality to be a natural kind would be otiose. All that we would need is a clear statement concerning the inferential mark, or marks. And just what might these be? You owe us an answer, the Advaitin avers. Whatever you might suggest, we will be able to show it to be in error. Then Śrīharṣa promises further details in a later section where he says that the "extrinsic justification" view is refuted. Finally (*Khkh*, p. 239), Śrīharṣa proffers a general objection against all definitions—not just purported definitions of veridical awareness—that they are either (if analytic) otiose (we already know that) or (if synthetic) too wide (that's not what we mean).[22]

5. Gaṅgeśa on Defining Veridical Awareness

Introduction

The following is an annoted translation of the *pramā-lakṣaṇa-vāda* and the *pramā-lakṣaṇa-siddhānta* portions of the *TCM*, where Gaṅgeśa scrutinizes definitions of veridical awareness, rejecting about twenty-five proposals and defending seven or eight. See note 80, pp. 359–60, for the place of the passage within the *TCM* as a whole.[23] See note 34, p. 363, on the division of the passage into two sections, a *pūrvapakṣa* and a *siddhānta*.

Text (p. 409) and Translation

atha kim tat prāmāṇyam | na tāvaj jātiḥ | yogya-vyakti-vṛttitvena pratyakṣatve pramātva-saṃśayânupapatteḥ, pramātvasya anumeyatvāc ca |

Now what is that veridicality (previously mentioned)? First of all, it is not a natural kind, *jāti*. (If it were a natural kind, then it would be perceptible in veridical perceptions; and) if it were perceptible insofar as its individual instances were perceptible, then it would be impossible to doubt the veridicality (of perceptual awarenesses). (However, such doubt commonly occurs.) Moreover, veridicality is known by inference.

Comments

The question is whether veridicality is a natural kind, *jāti*. Natural kinds are known perceptually riding piggy-back on the individuals in which they inhere insofar as those individuals are themselves known perceptually. But, Gaṅgeśa points out, we cannot merely read off the veridicality or non-veridicality of particular awarenesses. We can tell directly from a perceptual awareness of, e.g., an individual cow that she is a cow; in other words, we are directly aware of "cowness," a natural kind to which the individual belongs: universals are presented in perception insofar as their instances are presented in perception. And what is presented in perception is not normally subject to (meaningful) doubt, according to Nyāya. Thus doubt about veridicality with respect to perceptual awarenesses shows that veridicality is not a natural kind, *jāti*.

Moreover, Gaṅgeśa says, the veridicality of an awareness is known by inference—from pragmatic effects, we may add. The veridicality of an awareness is inferred from the success of action based on the awareness.

Text (p. 410) and Translation

sākṣāttvâdinā saṃkarâpatteś ca |

Also (veridicality is not a natural kind) because that would involve a cross classification with (other characteristics of awarenesses such as) "immediacy," for example.

Comments

Although veridical perceptual awareness is both immediate and veridical, cogent inference (*anumāna*) is not immediate but is veridical, and perceptual illusion is immediate but not veridical. That there would thus be cross classification (*jāti-saṃkara*, cross-sectioning) rules out veridicality as a natural kind—just as Śrīharṣa argues, as we saw.

Text and Translation

bīja-sāmyena gune 'pi tasya doṣatvāt | tāratvâder utkarṣa-rūpatayā jātitva-niyame ca ananya-gatikatayā ca nānātvāt | pramātva-nānātve tv ananugamaḥ |

Although veridicality concerns a quality (as opposed to a substance such that the criticism of "cross classification" does not hold, according to some), the reason (*bīja*) this is to be avoided obtains here just as it does there (with substances). For example, if the shrillness of a sound (a quality) as loud (as opposed to soft) were to be accepted as a natural kind, then to retain a fixed rule for what it is to be a natural kind, *jāti*, we would have to embrace a manifold of *jāti*s here (one for each individual sound: the sound "ka," the sound "kha," etc., would each exemplify a distinct universal of shrillness when uttered in a shrill voice). But if veridicality were to be viewed (similarly) as various or manifold (varying with each veridical awareness), then there would be no recurrent, unifying character, *anugama* (another criterion that any true *jāti* must meet).

Comments

One might think that threat of cross classification would eliminate only putative natural kinds of substance, whereas natural kinds of qualities, such as shrillness, can obtain with overlap. Shrillness would obtain in the sound "ka" when that sound is shrill, but the abstract property "ka-ness" would also obtain there. This latter property is found in instances of shrillness and of non-shrillness alike, in that the "ka" sound is sometimes uttered in a low voice, sometimes in a shrill voice. Similarly, a "kha" sound can also be uttered in both a low and a shrill voice. But "ka-ness" obviously does not inhere in a "kha" sound, and so there would be "confusion of class." Gaṅgeśa cites a contemporary Naiyāyika opinion that there is no special difficulty with such examples because they concern classification of qualities, and qualities, as opposed to substances, do not fall into neat, non-overlapping classes. But this move will not work for the defender of veridicality as a natural kind. Unlike shrill "kha"s where the abstract property shrillness pulls all the instances together under a common character, veridicality once admitted to be multiple would fail to do any unifying. There is no point in talking about a natural kind (or any universal for that matter) that does not bring at least two particulars into the unity of a class.

Text (p. 414) and Translation

kiṃ ca evam apramāyā aṃśe pramātvaṃ na syāt, jāter vyāpya-vṛttitā-niyamāt |

Moreover, (if veridicality were a natural kind) then there could be no veridicality in part of a non-veridical awareness. Natural kinds are invariably "locus-pervading" (*vyāpya-vṛtti*).

Comments

Cowhood is present throughout each cow; it is not the case that some parts of a cow exhibit the natural kind while others do not. An awareness, however, can exhibit partial veridicality. For example, the awareness "This is silver" in the face of mother-of-pearl would be veridical in the "this-ness" part. One would indeed be confronted with "this." Mathurānātha uses the example of a group awareness (*samūha-ālambana-jñāna*) of two pieces of silver when in reality the two things are a piece of silver and a piece of tin.

Text and Translation

na ca iṣṭâpattiḥ | aṃśe saṃvādini visaṃvādini ca samūhâlambane pramātvâpramātvayor anubhūyamānatvena eka-śeṣasya kartum aśakyatvāt |

Do not say that the above criticism is the fallacy of "maligning what is desired" (*iṣṭa-āpatti*), i.e., that it would be all right to rule out the possibility of partial veridical awareness. Consider an awareness of a group of two things, one of which is veridically perceived, the other not (e.g., a piece of tin and a piece of silver seen as two pieces of silver). Since here we experience both veridicality and non-veridicality, we cannot make a single determination.

Comments

Experience shows that a single awareness can be both veridical and non-veridical.

Text and Translation

> atha viparyayasya aṃśe na pramātvam, kiṃ tu smṛtivad yathârthatvam eva iti cet, tarhi yathârthânubhavatvam eva prāmāṇyam, āvaśyakatvāt | na ca tad api iti vakṣyate |

Objection: Then it is wrong to hold that in a portion of an erroneous awareness there can be veridicality. Rather, let us say, like memory, there is "conformity with the object" (in the right part of the erroneous awareness, but not veridicality).

Answer: Then to be veridical would be simply "to be experience in conformity with the object," as would be the necessary consequence of your suggestion. But even that is not correct, as will be explained.

Comments

As we remarked in chapter 4, Logicians hold that a moment of memory, a remembering, cannot be a veridical awareness, since a remembering is not an experience or awareness, *anubhava*, although it is a cognition, *jñāna*. All experiences, *anubhava*, are, like rememberings, cognitions, *jñāna*, but only experiences can be veridical awarenesses, *pramā*. Thus a right remembering would be "in conformity with the object" remembered but would not be a veridical *awareness*. Gaṅgeśa draws out the consequence of the opponent's suggestion: to be veridical would be to be experience in conformity with the object. The "to be experience" requirement would rule out moments of memory. Gaṅgeśa will explain his objections to this view below, in examining the putative characterization I have labelled D^3.

Text (p. 415, line 3) and Translation

> atha yathā bhāvo 'bhāvo vā na avyāpya-vṛttir iti niyamaṃ tiraskṛtya abādhitânubhava-balāt saṃyoga-tad-abhāvayor avyāpya-vṛttitvaṃ, tathā jātir vyāpya-vṛttir eva iti vyāptim abhibhūya anubhava-balād eva pramātva-tad-abhāvayor avyāpya-vṛttitvam astu | na ca yad avyāpya-vṛtti tan na vyāpya-vṛtti, yac ca vyāpya-vṛtti na tad avyāpya-vṛtti iti vyāpteḥ pramātvasya na ubhaya-rūpatvam iti vācyam | saṃyogâtyantâbhāve vyabhicārāt | na ca tasya abhāva-

dvayaṃ mānâbhāvāt | guṇa-doṣayor ekatra sattve avyāpya-vṛttitvam, guṇa-mātra-sattve vyāpya-vṛttitvam ity anyathôpapatteś ca | anyathā pramātvasya upādher apy atyantâbhāva-sāmānâdhikaraṇyaṃ[24] na syāt sāmānyatvāt na syāc ca ubhaya-rūpatvam iti |

Objection: Rejecting the rule that a presence or absence (need exclude the other, i.e.,) is locus-pervading, one must accept through uncontroverted experience that conjunction, for example, is non-locus-pervading, as is an absence of conjunction. (A conjunction can be present and absent at the same time with respect to a single thing; for example, with "A monkey is in the tree," we have an awareness of a conjunction between a monkey and a tree—specifically, in its branches—a tree that is devoid of the conjunction at its roots.) Similarly, let us accept on the force of uncontroverted experience—overcoming the false assumption of concomitance—that a natural kind need not be locus-pervading, so that neither veridicality nor absence of veridicality would be expected to be locus-pervading. It should not be said that there is a concomitance, namely, that what is non-locus-pervading is not locus-pervading and conversely, such that veridicality could not have both forms, since a clear exception is absolute absence of conjunction. (This absence is non-locus-pervading in some cases, e.g., a floor with a pot on it is not *pervaded* by an absence of conjunction with a pot—in contrast with an absence of a conjunction in a sound which, as a quality, categorially guarantees that there be a locus-pervading absence of conjunction, in that no sound could be conjoined with anything.) And there are not two types of absence (of conjunction), since there is no reason (to postulate two; there is only one, sometimes locus-pervading and sometimes not). Furthermore (if we try to save the concomitance by restricting it to presences such that for any existent, as opposed to an absence, if it is locus-pervading it would not be non-locus-pervading and conversely, then) what is in fact the case would be impossible, namely, that when with regard to a single *existent* (awareness) correct causal conditions and defective conditions co-exist, veridicality is not locus-pervading, but when only correct causal factors are present, veridicality is locus-pervading. (Thus veridicality with regard to a veridical awareness, e.g., "This is silver," when it is indeed silver in one's hand, would be locus-pervading, but in the erroneous awareness, "This is silver," when it is mother-of-pearl, the veridicality would be non-locus-pervading, being confined to the "this" portion.) Otherwise (if the concomitance holds as restricted to presences), veridicality, although considered an accidental property, *upādhi* (not a *jāti*, natural kind), will not be present in the same locus (an awareness) along with its absolute absence (that is to say, non-veridicality) because the same considerations hold, nor (even as an accidental property) could it have both forms (the locus-pervading and the non-locus-pervading).

Comments

Some things pervade the loci that they qualify; others do not. The locus of veridicality is awareness. Some awarenesses are veridical, some not. But an awareness is complex, and may be veridical only in part. We saw Śrīharṣa in his own way make this point. When an awareness is veridical only in part, the veridicality is non-locus-pervading. But when an awareness is entirely veridical, the veridicality is locus-pervading—such is the suggestion here.

Generally I follow Mathurānātha in filling in ellipsis. Mathurānātha tells indeed a more elaborate story focusing on the example of an absence of conjunction and the phrase "since there is no reason." Without two types of absence of conjunction—one applicable to (a) substances, things that sometimes exhibit conjunction (*saṃyoga*, contact), the other to (b) qualities, etc., things that never exhibit conjunction, since they categorially exclude the possibility—we have to give up the idea that what is locus-pervading is never non-locus-pervading.

In this way, Gaṅgeśa sets up a *prima facie* position and argument, which he will refute in text to follow.

Text and Translation

mā evam | avacchedaka-bhedaṃ vinā viruddhayor ekatra asamāveśāt apratīteś ca |

Answer: This is wrong. Without a difference of specification (or delimitor, *avacchedaka*), two opposed (properties) cannot be present in the same thing, nor are they ever so experienced (*apratīti*).

Comments

Here Gaṅgeśa uses the important *avacchedaka* concept, which proves valuable in a variety of contexts. Specifiers, *avacchedaka*s, make abstractions precise. Thus they prove crucial in eliminating ambiguity and vagueness. For example, the apparent contradiction of a tree possessing both a monkey-conjunction and an absence of monkey-conjunction is eliminated through specifying precisely where in the tree the monkey-conjuction is occurrent and where it is not. Similarly, veridicality is absolutely opposed to non-veridicality—the two cannot occur together—although through specification, *avaccheda*, we can differentiate precisely what in an awareness is veridical and what is not.

Text and Translation

na ca viṣaya eva aṃśa-rūpaḥ pramātva-vṛttāv avacchedakaḥ | tad-viṣayatvasya bhrame 'pi sattvāt |

Moreover, it should not be said that the relevant specification of where or how veridicality is present takes the form of a part only with respect to the object (indicated by an awareness). "Having that as object" is also present in cognitive error (and so it would have to be counted veridical).

Comments

The question is how to delimit or specify veridicality in the cognitive context. Gaṅgeśa, mindful of the difficulties (stressed by Śrīharṣa) of securing the precise cut between the veridical and the non-veridical, will focus on factors or constituents of awareness, as we discussed in chapter 4.

Text (p. 416) and Translation

> nanu viśeṣyâvṛtty-aprakāratvaṃ viśeṣyâvṛtti-prakāratvaṃ ca pramātva-tad-abhāvayor vṛttāv avacchedakam asti iti cet,

Objection: Veridicality is to be understood as (D^1) "lack of predication content, *prakāra*, that does not exist in the qualificandum"; non-veridicality is (D^{1e}) "presence of a predication content not existing in the qualificandum." Thus the occurrence is delimited (or specified) in the relevant way.

Comments

The qualificandum is the bearer or possessor of properties; with the veridical awareness, "(A) pot," the particular pot is the subject of qualification (*viśeṣya*) and possesses the property of potness. The awareness "(A) pot" has "potness" as its predication content, *prakāra*. Gaṅgeśa's rejection of D^1, which is voiced in the immediately following text, has to be understood in the full context of the characterizations that he endorses: D^1 is not far from what he himself proposes. (See below: D^{26} and D^{27}.) The awareness "(A) pot" in the presence of a pot would not have any predication content that did not exist in the individual pot, which would be the qualificandum. Similarly, the awareness "Silver" in the presence of mother-of-pearl would have predication content not existing in the mother-of-pearl, which would be the qualificandum.

Text and Translation

> tarhi tayor eva pramâpramā-vyavahāra-janakatvam astu, āvaśyakatvāt prathamôpasthitatvāc ca, kiṃ jātyā | na ca tad api iti vakṣyate |

Answer: Well, if this is your view, then you should say that these two (the lack of or presence of such content as the appropriate specifiers, *avacchedaka*) are by themselves responsible for our everyday linguistic practices regarding the veridical and non-veridical. Let them be so conceived. Then since this would be the necessary consequence of your proposal and since one of the two (as the specifier) would be what is first established in awareness, what would be the point of (viewing veridicality as) a natural kind? Also, we do not accept the definitions, as will be explained.

Comments

Gaṅgeśa puts the final nails into the coffin of taking veridicality to be a natural kind by rejecting the move, voiced above, to couple a natural-kind account with qualification theory—spelled out in terms of specifiers—to get the right cut between veridical and erroneous awarenesses. As Mathurānātha makes plain, the rule is that the specifier makes known the specified, as in general, according to Nyāya, the general makes known the particular (see above, p. 59). Since a specifier—here in effect D^1 or D^{1e}—would guide identification of an awareness as veridical or not, there would be no point, Gaṅgeśa argues, in viewing veridicality as a natural kind, *jāti*.

Gaṅgeśa also has qualms about the definitions uncoupled from the natural-kind account. He indicates he will inform us about that later.

Text and Translation

na api yathârthâgṛhīta-grāhitvaṃ loka-siddha-pramātvam, dhārā-vāhika-buddhy-avyāpteḥ | na ca pratyakṣasya vartamānârtha-grāhitvena svâśraya-kṣaṇa-viśiṣṭa-stambhâdi-grāhakatvena agṛhīta-grāhitvaṃ loka-siddham, anyathā eka-samaye jñāna-yaugapadya-prasaṅga iti vācyam |

Nor is it correct to hold (with the Bhāṭṭa Mīmāṃsakas) that veridicality as it is known in everyday speech belongs to (D^2) "the awareness that is the grasper of what has not been grasped (previously) concerning an object as it is." This putative characterization is no good because it would exclude veridical awarenesses that form a continual stream of awareness of one and the same thing (e.g., "This is a pot" cognized at time t_1 and "This is a pot" cognized immediately subsequently at time t_2).

And you should not try to defend the definition by claiming that a perceptual awareness as the grasper of a current object—as the grasper, say, of a post in its role as the possessor of a distinct time qualification—is commonly accepted as veridical, arguing that otherwise we would face the difficulty that awarenesses (as independent of time qualification) would occur at a single instant. (Each new awareness in the chain of awarenesses would cognize something not previously grasped in cognizing the post *as* qualified by a particular time instant, *kṣaṇa*.)

Comments

The reason awarenesses would occur simultaneously is that awarenesses are themselves real things in the world, and if things in the world are not differentiated through time qualification then awarenesses are not differentiated through time qualification. If awarenesses are not differentiated through time qualification, then it could be said that all of a person's awarenesses occur on one single occasion (*samaya*). A person's awarenesses obtaining at a single instant is opposed to the phenomenological fact of an awareness series (*krama*). Gaṅgeśa now goes on to say what is wrong with this defense.

Rucidattamiśra attributes D^2 to the Bhāṭṭa Mīmāṃsaka, i.e., Kumārila and his followers.

Text (p. 417) and Translation

kṣaṇānām atīndriyatvāt sthūlôpādhim ādāya vartamānatva-grahāt sva-rūpa-sat-kramika-kṣaṇôtpattikatvena jñānâyaugapadyāt |

Instants of time are not graspable in sense perception (and so your qualification fails to save your definition. Concerning your argument that such qualification is required to rule out simultaneity of awarenesses:) the point is that present time is grasped only with reference to "thick" or "gross" accidental properties (*upādhi*). The non-simultaneity of awareness is due to its nature as produced serially.

Comments

Gaṅgeśa apparently accepts Udayana's understanding of time as a single, unitary container. Temporal divisions are "accidental" or "imposed properties" (*upādhi*). The smallest is the point instant (*kṣaṇa*). But nothing enduring only for an instant is perceptible. Relative to our awareness considered from a first-person perspective, it is only with reference to properties that are "gross" or "thick," i.e., that endure for more than an instant, that we are aware of the present.[25]

Naiyāyika views on time and temporal relations become increasingly complex in the history of, in particular, the Navya movement.[26]

Text (p. 418) and Translation

na ca stambhâdiṣu pratikṣaṇaṃ guṇa-karmâdy-utpattir asti, yena tad ādāya agṛhīta-grāhitvaṃ syāt | vedāt kramôtpanna-vedârtha-gocara-dhārā-vāhika-buddhy-avyāpteś ca |

You cannot say that there is "grasping of what has not been grasped previously'' (the Bhāṭṭa definition of veridical awareness still under scrutiny, D^2) on the grounds that in a post, etc., qualities, motions, etc., arise every instant. (For there is no such production.)

Furthermore, because the definition does not cover veridical awareness due to scripture, the definition is no good; that is to say, D^2 is no good because it fails to include the serial awareness whose content is the meaning of a scriptural statement and whose cause is the scriptural statement. (The same scriptural text may be read by person S at time t_1 and at time t_2. According to the definition proposed, the later awareness would not be veridical.)

Comments

With these two additional arguments, Gaṅgeśa concludes his refutation of D^2. The clincher argument is that the object cognized does not change with every point instant of time. But let us not confine ourselves to consideration of perception, Gaṅgeśa says. According to the Mīmāṃsaka, the premier *pramāṇa* is scripture. Scripture clearly does not change from moment to moment. But according to D^2, whenever a person read or heard a scriptural passage for a second time, that could not count as a veridical cognition.

Text (p. 419) and Translation

> na api yathârthânubhavatvam, jñāne ghaṭatvâdinā yathā-śabdârtha-sādṛśyâbhāvāt | sādṛśya-mātrasya bhrame 'pi gatatvāt |

Nor is the abstraction (D^3) ''experience matching the object'' (or, alternatively, ''as is the object, so is the experience'') the right abstract with which to characterize veridicality. The word *yathā* (''matching'' or ''as'') means similarity, and there is not similarity between, for example, potness and an awareness of a pot. (Potness exists in pots, and awareness is a quality of the self or soul.) Further, if it is similarity in general that is proposed (or, just any similarity), that would also obtain with non-veridical awareness.

Comments

Both an awareness, as a quality of the soul, and an object of awareness, e.g., a pot, *exist*. There would invariably be this much similarity. But a non-veridical awareness would also be a quality of the soul and thus would also exist, as would the object erroneously cognized, e.g., mother-of-pearl cognized as silver. Thus such similarity is not relevant to characterizing veridicality. Śrīharṣa presents, we saw, this argument, and apparently it has forced Gaṅgeśa to renounce an easy correspondence view, which is close to the spirit of Nyāya.

In the translation here, I render an abstract suffix affixed to the Sanskrit definition as "the abstraction." In many of the definitions proposed, there is an abstract suffix employed, and in those cases veridical*ity*—and not veridical awareness—is what is being defined. However, henceforth I normally ignore the abstract suffix in the interests of readability. Note that this is not an important point for Gaṅgeśa, for with definitions D^{12} through D^{15} he himself drops the suffix and explicitly defines not veridicality, *pramātva*, but veridical awareness, *pramā*.

Text and Translation

na ca guṇa-janyânubhavatvam, doṣâbhāva-janyânubhavatvaṃ vā | tayor ananugatatvāt pramâpramā-nirūpyatvāc ca |

Nor is (D^4) "experience produced by reliability-grounding causal conditions" (i.e., "by excellencies," *guṇa*) any better, or (its equivalent, D^{4a}) "experience produced not by any reliability-undercutting condition" (i.e., "not by a faulty causal condition," *doṣa*). Neither of these terms (i.e., "produced by excellencies" and "produced not by a faulty condition") applies unequivocally to all instances of veridical awareness. Also, (there is circularity in that) "produced by excellencies" and "produced not by a faulty condition" are determined by whether it is a veridical awareness or not that has been produced.

Comments

"Produced by excellencies" means one thing with (a) veridical perceptions, another with (b) veridical inferential awarenesses, still something else with (c) analogical acquisitions of vocabulary, and with (d) bits of knowledge based on testimony—the four Naiyāyika types of *pramā* matching four "sources of veridical awareness," *pramāṇa*—whereas the reigning assumption, for the moment at least, is that a definition of veridicality must be unequivocal. Later, in explicating his own definitions, Gaṅgeśa will qualify this requirement, trying to best preserve the spirit of this causal view of veridicality, which, as with the previous definition, does come close to capturing the spirit of Nyāya.

Text and Translation

na apy abādhitânubhavatvam | bādhasya viparīta-pramātvāt |

Nor (D^5) "experience whose content is undefeated (or unsublated)." (This definition exhibits the fault of "self-dependence" in that) the defeating (or sublating) awareness would possess veridicality with respect to an opposed awareness.

Comments

Since veridicality is what we are endeavoring to define, it will not help to talk in terms of defeated or sublated awarenesses, since an awareness is determined to count as defeated only through the occurrence of a veridical awareness. Thus, D^5 is culpably circular.

Text and Translation

na api saṃvādy-anubhavatvam | jñānântareṇa tathôllikhyamānatvasya saṃvāditvasya bhrama-sādhāraṇatvāt |

Nor (D^6) "experience whose content agrees with another cognition." Agreement or conformity with another cognition insofar as it is made explicit is (potentially) common to error.

Comments

Śrīharṣa presents this argument (above, p. 170) in refutation of what we called the coherentist definition. To elaborate, two people can both see mother-of-pearl erroneously as silver and say in agreement erroneously, "This is silver." Or, the conformity could be with another of one's own awarenesses. D^6 is thus too wide.

Text and Translation

na api samartha-pravṛtti-janakânubhavatvam | upekṣā-pramāyām avyāpteḥ | tad-yogyatāyāḥ pramā-nirūpyatvāt |

Nor (D^7) "experience that leads to successful activity." This would not include those veridical awarenesses to which we are indifferent (that are not acted upon). Furthermore (this characterization exhibits the fault of "self-dependence" in that) the potentiality here (for successful activity) presupposes veridical awareness.

Comments

D^7 is commonly considered the contribution of Yogācāra Buddhist philosophers, especially Dharmakīrti (c. 640). But note that the oldest commentary on the *Nyāya-sūtra*, Vātsyāyana's (c. 410), stresses the idea that successful activity depends on veridical awareness—in the very first sentence. See Vātsyāyana's introductory commentary to *Nyāya-sūtra* 1.1.1.[27]

Text and Translation

na api tattvânubhavatvam, avastuno 'bhānāt |bhāne vā bhrama-sādhāraṇyāt |

Nor (D^8) "experience of reality." What is not a real object does not appear. Or if it does appear, then D^8 would apply also to erroneous awareness.

Comments

Udayana puts forth this definition (*tattvânubhūti pramā*) in his *Lakṣaṇamālā*.[28] It is explicitly attacked by Śrīharṣa (see above, pp. 165–66). Gaṅgeśa crystalizes Śrīharṣa's objections in his own rejection of D^8.

Text (p. 420, line 5) and Translation

na api viśeṣya-niṣṭhâtyantâbhāvâpratiyogi-dharma-prakārakânubhavatvam |

Nor (D^9) "experience having as a predication content a property that is not the counterpositive (*pratiyogin*) of an absolute absence resident in the cognized thing."

Comments

For example, the awareness "(A) pot" would be veridical when the thing cognized is a pot since its predication content, potness, would not be (properly speaking, the specifier of) the *pratiyogin*(-ness) of an absolute absence resident in the pot. (Gaṅgeśa introduces the "specification" refinement with the next definition considered, D^{10}.) An example of such an absolute absence would be an absence of cloth, where cloth would be the *pratiyogin* (and clothness the property specifier of the *pratiyogin*-ness). On the other hand, the awareness "Silver" when one is looking at mother-of-pearl would be non-veridical according to D^9, because there would be an absolute absence of silverness in the thing cognized, so that silverness would be both a predication content and the ruled-out (specifier of) *pratiyogin*(-ness).

An absolute absence is a constant non-occurrence of x in y, with, again, x as the counterpositive or absentee, *pratiyogin*, of the absence.

Text and Translation

saṃyogâdi-pramâvyāpteḥ |abhāve vyāpya-vṛttitva-viśeṣaṇe saṃyoga-bhrame 'tivyāptiḥ |tad-atyantâbhāvasya ekatvāt |

D^9 fails to include veridical awareness of conjunction and the like (qualities that are non-locus-pervading; for example, "The tree has a monkey in it," is an awareness of something, a tree, where there is an absolute absence of what is predicated, namely, conjunction with a monkey; that is, such an absence obtains at the tree's roots). If you would qualify the term "absence" in the definition to require that it be locus-pervading, then too much would be let in. Errors about conjunctions would have to be counted veridical in that there is just one kind of absolute absence of conjunction.

Comments

Gaṅgeśa is unwilling to admit that there are two kinds of absolute absence of conjunction, one that is invariably non-locus-pervading (with regard to substances, which are things that sometimes exhibit a conjunction) and one that is invariably locus-pervading (with regard to qualities and other things that could not possibly exhibit a conjunction). In order to be able to count as veridical an awareness of a monkey in a tree when a monkey is there, the advocate of D^9 proposes that the absolute absence specified in the definition has to be locus-pervading. Now absolute absences are constant, ever present in what they qualify, and an absolute absence of a conjunction in a substance is, like a conjunction, non-locus-pervading. So the only possible non-veridical awareness about a conjunction would be, e.g., "The quality exhibits a conjunction" (because, in fact, no quality ever exhibits a conjunction: conjunctions are categorially excluded from qualifying qualities—this absence is locus-pervading). By setting the standard for the pertinent absence so high, we would make the requirement for veridicality too weak. An error about any possible conjunction whatsoever (i.e., with regard to any substance) would have to be counted veridical since there would *not* be a constant, locus-pervading absence of a monkey, say, anywhere such a conjunction might be.

Thus no definition that employs in this way the notion of a counterpositive to an absolute absence will be able to get around the difficulty Gaṅgeśa cites regarding awareness of a conjunction, unless we have reason to suppose that there is not only one kind of absolute absence of conjunction. The rule there is that a difference concerning type of locus is not enough to secure a difference of absence.[29] (And despite the credit that Vardhamāna gives his father with regard to making plain the logic of different types of absence—see above, p. 138—and despite the explanations of the *TCM* commentators, one has to suspect from this and some other passages that Gaṅgeśa had not gotten clear about them.)

Text (p. 421, line 1) and Translation

na api viśeṣya-vṛtty-anyonyâbhāva-pratiyogitâvacchedaka-
dharmâprakārakânubhavatvam, avyāpya-vṛtti-pramânupagrahāt |

Nor (D^{10}) "experience that does not have as its predication content a property that specifies the counterpositive-ness (*pratiyogi-tā*) of a mutual exclusion resident in the thing cognized." This also fails to include veridical awarenesses about properties that are not locus-pervading.

Comments

As discussed in chapter 4, a *pratiyogitā-avacchedaka* property is a property that specifies, ties down, or delimits the counterpositive-ness that is appertinent to a distinctness or mutual exclusion (*anyonyābhāva*, mutual absence). For example, a pot is distinct from a cloth, with the cloth as the counterpositive of the distinctness resident in the pot. Thus clothness is the property that delimits the relevant counterpositive-ness. With the veridical awareness "(A) pot," this property is not predication content. However, there remains the problem concerning awarenesses of conjunctions, which are properties that are not locus-pervading, as Gaṅgeśa elaborates in the text below.

Text and Translation

> mūle vṛkṣaḥ kapi-saṃyogavān na āgre ity abādhitânubhavāt saṃyogavad-anyonyâbhāvasya avyāpya-vṛttitvāt | bhedâbheda evaṃ syāt iti cet, anubhavam upālambhasva, yad-balād avaccheda-bhedena atyantâbhāvavad anyonyâbhāvasya apy avyāpya-vṛttitvam upeyam | ata eva pakve idānīṃ na śyāma iti dhīḥ samaya-bhedād aviruddhā tatra eva tad-anyonyâbhāvam avalambate |

A tree, for example, does not have a conjunction with a monkey at its roots while it does in its branches. (The tree would be the locus of a quality, a monkey-conjunction, that would be the counterpositive of an exclusion, an exclusion of monkey conjunction, of which it would also be the locus.) This is a common, uncontroverted experience. Exhibiting a conjunction and not exhibiting a conjunction, though mutually exclusive, are not locus-pervading.

"So in this way there would be both distinctness and non-distinctness." If you are prone to think this, then we say, "Pay attention to experience." Experience shows that a mutual exclusion should also be accepted as non-locus-pervading—that is, so long as there is distinct specification, *avaccheda*—just as in the case of an absolute absence. In this way, the judgment, "Having been baked, the pot is not now black," is not self-contradictory, because of the distinctness of occasion (black before baking, red afterwards). There is experience that both sides of a mutual exclusion can be present in this way in just a single thing.

Comments

Thus D^{10} falls to the same argument that felled D^{9}, since the logic of mutual exclusion is not significantly different from that of absolute absence, i.e., in the context of trying to characterize veridicality. The general difference between the two is—as explained in chapter 4—that of *x*'s not being *y* (mutual exclusion) as opposed to *x*'s never being in *y* (absolute or constant absence). But in the present context, both would require *ad hoc* specification according to particular circumstances, e.g., awareness of a conjunction. Thus both definitions fail to be sufficiently general.

Text (p. 422) and Translation

> na api viśeṣyâvṛtty-aprakārakânubhavatvam | ekaika-viśeṣyâvṛtti-nānā-prakāraka-samūhâlambanâvyāpteḥ | na ca prakārasya eka-viśeṣya-vṛttitayā na viśeṣyâvṛttitvam iti vācyam | pramâpramā-rūpa-samūhâlambanâtivyāpteḥ |

Nor (D[11]) "experience without predication content that does not exist in the thing cognized, *viśeṣya*." This putative characterization is no good because it fails to apply to a veridical awareness of a group of things (pot, cloth) conceived under various predicates (potness, clothness) that do not apply to each and every individual in the group.

"But 'non-existence in the cognized' is not to be taken unqualified; it is to be understood with respect to the predication content residing in each individual item singly." No, this response is patchwork that should not be tried. The definition would still fail because then it would include too much; it would include, namely, the non-veridical awareness of a group of things where some of the items are veridically cognized and some not.

Comments

D[11] would allow an awareness of a group to be veridical when any single item is veridically cognized although other items are erroneously cognized with the result that—according to common usage and supposition—the group awareness is non-veridical. An example would be an awareness of a piece of tin and a piece of silver as both silver. Both D[11] and the variation suggested patently suffer from ambiguity: the one lets in too little and the other too much. We see here, however, Gaṅgeśa honing in on the right way to characterize veridicality.

Text and Translation

> na ca yāvad-viśeṣyâvṛttitvaṃ vivakṣitam | ekaika-viśeṣya-vṛtter yāvad-viśeṣyâvṛttitvena samūhâlambanâvyāpteḥ | eka-viśeṣyake yāvad-arthâbhāvāc ca |

"With respect to however many items are cognized" (as a qualification or elaboration of D[11]) also should not be tried. That patchwork would fail to include veridical awareness of a group in that each item could exhibit something that does not exist in the cognized "with respect to however many items are cognized." Moreover, a veridical awareness of a single thing does not include any notion of "however many."

Comments

Gaṅgeśa's objection is clear. He is insisting on precision.

Text (p. 422, line 6) and Translation

atha viṣayatāyā āśrayo viśeṣyaḥ, jñānaṃ tat-pratiyogi | bhrame ca śukti-vṛttir viṣayatā vyadhikaraṇena rajatatvena avacchidyate | rajata-vṛttis tu samānâdhikaraṇena rajatatvena | viṣayatā ca viṣaye na jñānâhitā jñātatā-rūpā vivakṣitā | apasiddhāntād asiddheḥ, atītânāgata-pramāyāṃ tad-abhāvāc ca |

The locus of objecthood (*viṣayatā*) is the thing cognized; awareness is the determining correlate (*pratiyogin*) of that. And with erroneous awareness, objecthood exists in, for example, the mother-of-pearl—objecthood, that is, as specified by silverness, which is something not present in that same locus. (In veridical awareness) silverness is present in the same locus with the objecthood that exists in (some bit of) silver (when it is cognized).

And objecthood should not be taken as a "cognizedness" produced in the object by cognition. Not only would such an unproved view depart from Naiyāyika theory, but also with veridical awareness of things that are past or future, "cognizedness" could not arise.

Comments

Gaṅgeśa has assumed a Naiyāyika perspective—and the discussion has been intra-camp—beginning with Udayana's definition, D^8 (and possibly as early as D^7). By making precise certain technical usages with a Naiyāyika voice but within a *pūrvapakṣa* ("oppositional") section of the text, Gaṅgeśa gives himself room to work.

The term *pratiyogin* in the text here means *nirūpaka*, "determining correlate." Objecthood exists only in an epistemic context; it exists in the object cognized only so long and insofar as it is cognized. So *viṣayatā-pratiyogitā*, "counter-correlateness to objecthood," is an abstract pertaining to awarenesses correlate to objects whose objecthoods they determine. The object cognized, the *viśeṣya* (or *dharmin*), is the *anuyogin* of objecthood, i.e., its locus. These are the key terms for Gaṅgeśa'a characterization project. (Consult the definitions given in the glossary.)

To repeat, objecthood exists only in an epistemic context. To be an object, *viṣaya*, is always to be an object of a particular awareness. The relation between the awareness and its object can be considered from the side of the object or from the side of consciousness. In the former case, it is called objecthood, which is, again, said to reside in the object. The relation is a (tertiary) property or attribution about whose ontological status there is much debate among Navya-Nyāya philosophers, some of which Gaṅgeśa is about to acknowledge both in immediately subsequent text and at the end of the passage.

In the text above, Gaṅgeśa is, in part, disputing a position belonging to Bhāṭṭa Mīmāṃsakas (to which, presumably, some of Gaṅgeśa's Naiyāyika contemporaries were attracted), namely, that cognition creates a property in a cognized object, "cognizedness." According to Kumārila's school, this property becomes the basis for an inference to the occurrence of our own cognition. Gaṅgeśa has combatted this view earlier in the *TCM*.[30] He will combat it further in a subsequent section devoted to "apperception," *anuvyavasāya*: according to the Navya-Nyāya philosopher, a cognition is known, not inferentially from perception of cognizedness in an object, but in apperception, i.e., with the previous cognition as the object of a following apperceiving. Gaṅgeśa may be construed in this passage as pointing out against the Bhāṭṭa view that awareness cannot change objects that are past, nor, just by itself (presumably), things to come.

But the main point here is not to get clear on how we know our own awareness—or to dispute a Mīmāṃsaka position—but rather to get clear about ontological concepts crucial to the current project of characterizing veridical awareness, in particular, objecthood. Gaṅgeśa is warning us not to confuse objecthood either with a property of awareness or with "cognizedness" as understood by the Bhāṭṭas.

Text and Translation

> kiṃ tu jñānasya viṣaye viśeṣaṇatā-viśeṣaḥ kaścit | para-jñānaṃ jñānatvena tad-viṣayaṃ ca ghaṭatvena jñānato ghaṭam ayaṃ jānāti na vā iti saṃśayād viṣaya-jñāna-sva-rūpâtiriktasya svâśraya-svâbhāvâdi-viśeṣaṇatā-viśeṣasya āvaśyaṃ svīkārāt |

(For the reasons mentioned, we Naiyāyikas understand objecthood differently:) objecthood is a particular type of attribution, or qualifier (*viśeṣaṇatā*), that resides in the object of an awareness. Another person's awareness—cognized as awareness—and its object, a pot, can become the content of a doubt, "Is he aware of the pot or not?" The fact that such a doubt can occur shows that (according to some Naiyāyikas) objecthood is something ontologically over and above both the object cognized and the cognizing awareness. Objecthood is a particular type of attribution, or qualifier, *viśeṣaṇatā*, that is distinct from such qualifiers as (a) the awareness whose locus is the person and (b) absence of that awareness (whose locus is also the person).

Comments

According to the reasoning and example here, the *viṣayatā*, objecthood, rests in the other's awareness—let us say, in S's awareness—since S's awareness is the object of the doubt. But it is not just the occurrence of awareness that is doubted, since S may be presumed to have awareness of something or other. The doubt is whether S is aware of a particular pot. That is, at least in part, its object or content. Also, it is not just the pot that is doubted. Thus the doubt's object must be something over and above both S's awareness and the pot—that is, according to certain Naiyāyikas whom Gaṅgeśa will answer (in the text following D^{36e} below). The awareness is known and the pot can be ruled out, so the object of the doubt has to be something else. The proposal here is that it is objecthood as a separate and distinct category of the real.

Gaṅgeśa does not himself subscribe to the theory that objecthood is an additional real, and, as I say, he eventually counters this argument. But it seems that he has no terribly strong feelings on the point, because often in the *TCM* he takes into consideration this rival Naiyāyika view. Even in the following *siddhānta* section (where Gaṅgeśa presents his own views), he formulates several characterizations of veridical awareness in which he follows the contours of the rival Naiyāyika ontological position, as we will see. And in this *pūrvapakṣa* section (where Gaṅgeśa is occupied principally with disputing opponents' views), the notion of objecthood as an additional real is not among the faults that Gaṅgeśa targets in the definitions he rejects.[31]

According to the rival ontological view, cognition is only indirectly related to an object cognized and to its properties; that is, it is related by way of the objecthood that it determines. Thus the predication content, *prakāra*, would belong to the peculiar objecthood that occurs in a thing cognized when it is cognized—at one remove from the cognition itself. The predication content would occur within, so to say, the objecthood that an awareness determines. Objecthood (or "contenthood," *viṣayatā*) has predication content, although an objecthood correlate to an experience and impregnated with a certain content can fail to reside in the same locus as its predication content (as in error). Moreover, the object cognized would be directly related to the objecthood, which then would stand between—would stand ontologically between—an awareness and the qualificandum. This understanding of predication content and objecthood is present in many of the definitions still to be considered.

Again, while the ontologically conservative Gaṅgeśa does not himself subscribe to this view, he is willing to think about what veridicality looks like from the perspective of one who sees objecthood as such an additional real.

Doubt (*saṃśaya*) figures crucially in the argument of the rival ontological camp. Epistemologically, no Navya-Nyāya philosopher (so far as I am aware) sees doubt as other than a species of non-veridical awareness. But the ontological status of a doubt's content is much disputed and discussed. Gaṅgeśa shows below (see the text following D^{36e}) something of how he understands the ontological underpinnings that make doubt possible. Here we get Gaṅgeśa's Nyāya mixed in with a rival camp's views.

Text and Translation

anyathā ghaṭatvena jñāto 'rtha iti tṛtīyârthâsaṃbhavaḥ |

Otherwise (if objecthood were not a particular type of qualifier ontologically something over and above both a given awareness and its object), it would not be possible to use the instrumental case to convey that an object is cognized *as* (e.g.,) a pot.

Comments

The argument hinges on an exotic use of the instrumental case in Sanskrit, the "predicative instrumental." The example is of the instrumental case used to express the notion "as a pot." If objecthood as an additional real were not a qualifier of the object, then the object, the thing cognized, could not be predicated of in this way.

Mathurānātha glosses the designated sense of the instrumental as expressing "being predication content" (*prakāratva*) through a "nominal primary affix" (*kṛd-arthe*), i.e., a qualificandum identified through "any manner or state of being" whatsover (Pāṇini 2.3.21). The term *prakāra* is used in the Pāṇinian commentarial literature (e.g., *Kāśikā* 2.3.21) to capture this sense of the instrumental. (An early example: "An ascetic by the matted hair," *jaṭābhis tāpasaḥ*.) The idea seems to be that if objecthood were not an independent qualifier qualifying the object, the thing cognized, then the object could not be predicated of by means of a noun in the instrumental case. The instrumental case used predicatively requires an objecthood that links together the qualificandum and the qualifier. Gaṅgeśa's example is that we could not know an object (a pot) by its potness, i.e., as a pot.

Text and Translation

prakāratvam api viṣayasya jñāne viśeṣaṇatā-viśeṣa eva, na tu viṣayatvam atiprasaṅgāt |

Being a predication content (or predication-content-hood, *prakāratva*) is also a specific type of qualifier (*viśeṣaṇatā*), one that (in contrast with objecthood) is of the object but is in awareness. It is that only. It is not equivalent to objecthood (which resides directly in the object). To suppose it is equivalent would be to suppose too much.

Comments

Here Gaṅgeśa contrasts "being a predication content," *prakāratā*, with objecthood. Specifying the predication content of an awareness vis-à-vis the objecthood an awareness determines is crucial to several of Gaṅgeśa's own characterizations of veridicality.

The ontological status of an awareness's predication content is tricky business because of illusion. Ontologically, an epistemic context is to be analyzed solely in terms of (1) awareness, an episodic quality of the self or soul, and (2) objects of awareness. But a qualifier presented in awareness does not necessarily belong to the object cognized; otherwise erroneous awareness would be impossible. "Being a predication content" is a notion that cuts across the veridical/non-veridical distinction. Ontologically, where does predication content reside? According to the current passage—within a *pūrvapakṣa* exploration of faulty definitions including ones proposed by good Naiyāyikas—*being* a predication content (*prakāratā*) is an abstraction from an awareness-of-an-object (as a quality of the soul), an abstraction most directly related to—or residing in—awareness, as opposed to the awareness's object. This presents a problem in that any particular bit of predication content Gaṅgeśa consistently treats as ontologically a qualifier obtaining somewhere in the world. The view expressed is not that of the Naiyāyika camp that (according to Mathurānātha's elaboration) sees predication content as belonging to the objecthood that an awareness determines. The text says that "being a predication content" belongs to, or rests in, awareness. But any given bit of predication content is simply a (world-residing) qualifier appearing in awareness. It is in virtue of appearing in awareness that a qualifier is called a predication content.

The way, then, I read the current statement as consistent with Gaṅgeśa's view that ontologically a predication content belongs to an object concerns a point about qualifiers taken in abstraction (*viśeṣaṇa-tā*). There are two ways to abstract from qualifiers to capture the relation between awareness and its objects, objectwise and awarenesswise. Objecthood is a relational abstraction in the former direction; predication-content-hood goes in the latter direction. Thus to say that predication-content-hood is *in* awareness does not mean that particular bits of predication content rest ontologically in awareness. All particular bits of predication content are qualifiers of objects in the world—in illusion, they are misperceived regarding where they actually obtain. A qualifier appearing in awareness is the predication content of the awareness, and predication-content-*hood* is a relational abstraction in the direction of awareness. Rāmakṛṣṇādhvarin, in his subcommentary on Rucidatta's *Prakāśa*, says that predication-content-hood contrasts with objecthood in that objecthood is a qualifier resting directly in the object cognized whereas predication-content-hood rests directly in the (distinct) qualifier appearing in awareness (*Nyāyaśikhāmaṇi*, p. 424).

Note that for Gaṅgeśa neither of the abstracts is an independent real. But in the present context, both of these key relational notions are presumably taken to be independent reals, and—this seems to be the main point—predication-content-hood is not to be viewed as equivalent to objecthood: one is an independent real preëminently bound up with the object (although "determined," *nirūpaka*, by awareness) and the other a real preëminently bound up with awareness (wherever the loci of the particular bits of predication content may be). Or, the point is that we need the distinction in order to do our epistemology and logic and will later worry about how precisely to view these ontologically: we are now ready to review some veritable contenders for an adequate characterization of veridical awareness.

Text (p. 424, line 4) and Translation

evaṃ ca viṣayatā-samānâdhikaraṇa-prakārakânubhavaḥ, prakāra-samānâdhikaraṇa-viṣayatā-pratiyogy-anubhavo vā sva-samānâdhikaraṇa-dharma-prakāraka-viṣayatā-pratiyogy-anubhavo vā sva-samānâdhikaraṇa-dharmâvacchinna-viṣayatā-pratiyogy-anubhavo vā pramā iti cet, na |

And in this way the following characterizations of veridical awareness are arrived at: (D^{12}) "experience whose predication content has the same locus as the objecthood," (D^{13}) "experience correlate to an objecthood that has the same locus as the predication content," (D^{14}) "experience correlate to an objecthood with a predication content in the form of a property that has the same locus as the objecthood," and (D^{15}) "experience correlate to an objecthood that is specified by (*avacchinna*) a property that has the same locus as the objecthood."

(Gaṅgeśa:) No, these are wrong.

Comments

Armed with a technical apparatus, Gaṅgeśa presents a series of rival Naiyāyika definitions. We come back fully to Gaṅgeśa's own voice with his rejection of these. Note the increasing complexity of the definitions. Also, D^{14} and D^{15} in particular may be read as formulated in accordance with the views of the rival ontological camp that, as mentioned, is addressed in the following *siddhānta* section. But these definitions are not, according to Gaṅgeśa, the best definitions that that camp might propose. Later, with definitions D^{28} through D^{36e}, Gaṅgeśa puts forth what he sees as, in contrast, acceptable definitions according to the view that objecthood is an additional real.[32]

Text (p. 425) and Translation

> nirvikalpakâvyāpteḥ, viṣayatā-samānâdhikaraṇêdantva-prakāraka-bhramasya api pramātva-prasaṅgāc ca |

To name two reasons these candidate characterizations are all wrong: (a) they fail to include indeterminate awareness (*nirvikalpaka jñāna*), and (b) an erroneous awareness can have as predication content a "this-ness" having the same locus as the objecthood correlate to the experience, and so would have to be counted veridical.

Comments

"Indeterminate awareness," *nirvikalpaka jñāna* (see the glossary), has no *predication* content (*prakāratva*); it has bits of content, but they are unrelated in the qualificandum-relation-qualifier structure (a-R-b) that all determinate awareness has. Note also that here Gaṅgeśa presumes that his opponent believes *nirvikalpaka* awareness can be veridical. Later, he will himself argue that indeterminate awareness is neither veridical nor non-veridical.

"This silver" cognized in the presence of mother-of-pearl includes "this-ness" as predication content, a "this-ness" that does indeed reside in the object cognized, the mother-of-pearl.

Text and Translation

> bhramas tatra aṃśe pramā eva iti cet, tarhi anubhavatvam eva pramātvam, vyartham adhikam | anubhava eva kvacid aṃśe pramâpramā ca iti cet, na | ukta-lakṣaṇe tādṛśâlābhāt |

If it is objected that erroneous cognition *is* in that portion veridical, then (having equated the veridical and the non-veridical) one would say simply that "to be an experience" is "to be veridical." To say more would be pointless.

If it be contended that experience in some part is veridical and in some part not, we respond that the definitions on the table do not yield that view.

Comments

The first argument is made by Śrīharṣa (see above, p. 169). Gaṅgeśa has heeded the Advaitin and acknowledged that the erroneous awareness, "This is silver," when the object cognized is mother-of-pearl, is veridical in the "thisness" bit of its predication content. The problem, then, with the definitions is that they do not differentiate bits of predication content perspicaciously. A successful characterization must both capture the overall non-veridicality of an erronenous awareness and the veridicality of whatever bit of predication content is correctly cognized. Note that the "this-ness" of Gaṅgeśa's example is content that will always be veridical: "this-ness" pertains to the qualificandum only as the object cognized, and there can be no error concerning the mere fact of something being cognized, according to the great Naiyāyika.

Text (p. 426) and Translation

> atha sva-vyadhikaraṇa-prakārânavacchinna-viṣayatā-pratiyogy-anubhavaḥ pramā | samūhâlambane ca prati-viśeṣyaṃ viṣayatā-bhedād eka-vṛttir viṣayatā na apara-vṛttinā avacchidyate | ato na avyāptir iti cet, na |

Objection: Then veridical awareness is (D^{16}) "experience correlate to an objecthood that is *not* specified by a predication content not present in the same locus as that of the objecthood." (This characterization does not fall to the criticism previously made, against D^{11}, namely, that it fails to include veridical awareness of a group of things.) In veridical awareness of a group, the criterion applies to each cognized thing, since there is in the case of each item a distinct objecthood. So objecthood resides in each thing separately, not (as in the previous faulty characterization) in the other (*apara*) things, too.

Gaṅgeśa: No, you are wrong again.

Comments

Thus in my veridical awareness, "This is a book," the objecthood correlate to the experience is specified by the predication content "bookness," which as a property does indeed reside in the book of which I am aware. The locus of the bookness, namely, the book, is the locus of the objecthood correlate to the experience. In the terms of D^{16}, the awareness is correlate to an objecthood that is not specified by a predication content, e.g., potness, that does not have the same locus as the objecthood; potness is indeed located not in the book of which I am aware but in pots. With the veridical awareness of a group of things, for example, "A book and a pot," the definition is said to fit since each object is known under the separate specification that is true of it. Two distinct objecthoods correlate to the experience are specified by two distinct bits of predication content.

Text and Translation

bhramâṃśa-pramāyām avyāpteḥ | na hi yā viṣayatā vyadhikaraṇa-dharmeṇa avacchidyate sā tad-anavacchinnā, virodhāt |

The current candidate fails because it does not apply to what is veridical, the awareness being erroneous in part. For an objecthood (correlate to the experience, e.g., tin) that is specified by a property (e.g., silverness) that does not have the same locus as the objecthood is not equivalent to an objecthood that is not specified like that, because of contradiction.

Comments

An example would be a partially veridical awareness of silver when confronted with silver and tin, "This and that are silver." Silverness would be an example of "predication content not present in the same locus as that of the objecthood" that would be present in the tin. The problem is that "silver" would be correct with respect to the piece of silver but would not be counted so. According to D^{16}, then, an awareness that was erroneous with regard to any objecthood correlate to the experience would have to be counted as entirely erroneous, even though one thing, for example, the silver of the pair silver and tin, would be veridically cognized.

Text and Translation

na api prakāra-vyadhikaraṇa-viṣayatvâpratiyogy-anubhavaḥ pramā | prakāra-vyadhikaraṇa-viṣayatā-pratiyogini tad-apratiyogitvasya abhāvena bhramâṃśa-pramâvyāpteḥ |

Nor is it correct to characterize veridical awareness as (D^{17}) "experience not correlate to an objecthood not present in the same locus as the predication content." This fails to handle the veridical in a partially erroneous awareness (e.g., silver and tin cognized as only silver) in the right way, since in that case there is a correlate to an objecthood (namely, the tin's objecthood) not present in the same locus as the predication content, but (with regard to the veridically cognized object) the non-correlation with that (objecthood not present in the same locus with the predication content) does not occur.

Comments

The "silver" of an awareness of silver and tin as only silver is predication content that both resides in and does not reside in a locus that is the same as that of an objecthood not correlate to the experience. The problem is that D^{17} fails to differentiate what is and what is not veridically cognized here.

Text and Translation

na api sva-vyadhikaraṇa-dharmâvacchinna-viṣayatvâpratiyogy-anubhavaḥ, svâdhikaraṇâvṛtty-aprakāraka-viṣayatā-pratiyogy-anubhavo vā pramā, tata eva | bhrame viṣayatāyāḥ sva-vyadhikaraṇa-prakārâvacchinnatvāt svâdhikaraṇâvṛtti-prakārakatvāc ca |

Nor, for the same reason, should veridical awareness be characterized as (D^{18}) "experience not correlate to an objecthood specified by a property present in a locus not the same as that of the objecthood," nor as (D^{19}) "experience correlate to an objecthood without predication content that does not reside in the same locus with the objecthood." With erroneous awareness there is (such) objecthood that is specified by a predication content residing in a locus not the same as that of the objecthood, while there is also such predication content (in the veridical portion of an erroneous awareness), not residing, that is, in the same locus with an objecthood (not correlate to the experience).

Comments

I follow Mathurānātha in filling in the ellipsis here. He takes the *tata eva*, "for the same reason," to refer to the problem of the veridical in a partially erroneous awareness—the tin and silver example. But also, he says, Gaṅgeśa points out that D^{18} and D^{19} fail to be sensitive to the veridical portion—the "this-ness"—of an erroneous awareness, e.g., "This is silver" when the object cognized is mother-of-pearl.

Text and Translation

na api sva-samānâdhikaraṇânyonyâbhāva-pratiyogitâvacchedaka-dharmânavacchinna-viṣayatā-pratiyogy-anubhavaḥ pramā |

Nor should veridical awareness be characterized as (D^{20}) "experience correlate to an objecthood not specified by (*anavacchinna*) a property that specifies the counterpositive-ness of a distinctness (or mutual exclusion, *anyonyābhāva*) resident in the same locus with the objecthood."

Comments

For example, the veridical awareness "A pot" on the part of person P would be P's experience as correlate to an objecthood resident in the pot not qualified by a property—such as clothness—that is excluded—as is clothness—by a distinctness that resides in the cognized pot, namely, the distinctness of the pot from a cloth. Again, technically the property excluded by the distinctness resident in something is called the specifier of the distinctness's counterpositive-*ness* (*pratiyogitā*, an abstract from *pratiyogin*:

see the glossary, the second sense of *pratiyogin*).

Text and Translation

bhramâṃśa-pramâvyāpteḥ | anyonyâbhāvasya avyāpya-vṛttitvena avyāpya-vṛtti-pramāyām avyāpteś ca |

This too fails to cover correctly the veridical in a partially erroneous awareness. Furthermore, since the relation of mutual exclusion (or distinctness) is not locus-pervading, the definition fails to cover veridical awareness of the non-locus-pervading.

Comments

Gaṅgeśa's second objection runs as follows. D^{20}, as tied to the logic of distinctness, i.e., mutual exclusion, is incapable of capturing correctly veridical awareness of facts that do not exhibit that logic. For example, a "conjunction with a monkey" can be veridically cognized as qualifying a tree. But since the logic of mutual exclusion is not sensitive to the fact that the conjunction does not reside in the roots of a tree (being limited to the branches), such an awareness would be counted by D^{20} as non-veridical. That is to say, the tree would be the locus (a) of an objecthood correlate to the experience, an objecthood specified by a property—absence of the conjunction (i.e., at the roots)—that specifies the counterpositiveness of a distinctness—i.e., a property that is excluded by a distinctness—that (b) resides in that same locus, the tree (i.e., the distinctness from non-monkey-conjunction that resides in the tree's branches).

Text (p. 427, line 5) and Translation

yat tu pramātvâpramātvayor virodha eva bhramo na pramā iti, tat tuccham | aṃśa-bhedam ādāya ubhayasya anubhavāt | anyathā bhramasya ubhaya-bahir-bhāvâpatteḥ | etena sva-vyadhikaraṇa-prakārakaṃ jñānaṃ bhramas tad-anyo 'nubhavaḥ pramā, bhramo dharmy-aṃśe na pramā iti nirastam |

"Then given that veridicality and non-veridicality are mutually opposed, an erroneous awareness is not (contrary to your assumption) veridical (in any portion)."

No, that is an empty proposal. It is a common experience to realize that what one was aware of as a "this" was and remains veridical while what one was aware of as "silver" is known as non-veridical. If it were otherwise, an erroneous awareness would be neither veridical nor non-veridical. Therefore, according to the definition of erroneous awareness as (D^{21e}) "cognition whose predication content does not reside in the same locus as that of the objecthood," and the definition of veridical awareness (D^{21}) "experience that is not like that (namely, having predication content not residing in the same locus as that of the objecthood)," the thesis that erroneous awareness cannot be veridical, even in the portion concerning the object as a possessor of properties (*dharmin*), should be thrown out.

Comments

Here Gaṅgeśa tips his hand and gives a definition that is almost identical to one he accepts, with qualification, in the subsequent section, D^{28}. D^{21} matches our intuition that there is something veridical in an erroneous awareness, e.g., the "thisness" of "This is silver" when faced with mother-of-pearl. The appearance of D^{21} at this point in the text—in a *pūrvapakṣa*—intimates that the definition is to be taken only provisionally as correct. Below we will see precisely why Gaṅgeśa's acceptance of the similar definition, D^{28}, is indeed qualified.

Text and Translation

> na api prakārâdhikaraṇâvṛtty-aprakāraka-viṣayatā-pratiyogy-anubhavaḥ, prakārânadhikaraṇâvṛtti-viṣayatā-pratiyogy-anubhavo vā pramā | prameyam idam iti jñāne prakārânadhikaraṇasya aprasiddheḥ |

Nor (D^{22}) "experience correlate to an objecthood not resident in the same locus with a predication content that it does not have"; nor (D^{23}) "experience correlate to an objecthood that does not reside in the same locus with the predication content." Both these definitions fail because with the awareness, "This thing is knowable," there is no instance (*aprasiddhi*) where the predication content does not have a locus.

Comments

Everything is knowable, *prameya*. Therefore, both definitions rely on a potentially empty expression: if "being knowable" is the predication content, then there is no locus where it does not reside. The Naiyāyika commitment to a realism of reference demands that such expressions as "a non-locus of knowability" be counted as meaningless.[33]

Text (p. 428) and Translation

> kiṃ ca rajatatva-prakāraka-viṣayatāyā rajata-vṛttitva-niyamāt rajatatvâvacchinnā eva rajata-bhrame rajata-vṛtti-viṣayatā | ato rajata-bhramo 'pi rajate pramā syāt |

Moreover, the definitions fail because in an erroneous awareness of silver the objecthood that exists in silver is indeed specified by silverness. The rule is that an objecthood having silverness as predication content exists in silver. Therefore on these definitions an erroneous awareness of silver would have to be counted veridical (not only in the "thisness" portion but) also concerning the silver (since there are real pieces of silver in the world).

Comments

Gaṅgeśa uses *rajata-vṛtti* to mean silver as considered in general. The problem is that the "silverness" in the erroneous awareness is tied to real pieces of silver in the world not by way of the objecthood that arises with the (erroneous) awareness, but only with respect to silver in general.

Text and Translation

atha rajata-purovartinor ekā eva viṣayatā | sā ca prakārânadhikaraṇa-vṛtti-dharmâvacchinnā eva iti cet, tarhi dharmy-aṃśe 'pi taj-jñānaṃ pramā na syāt, vyadhikaraṇa-prakārakatvasya tulyatvāt | dharmy-aṃśe tu pramātve rajate 'pi pramā syāt |

Objection: Then silver and "being in front" (or "thisness") have only a single objecthood. And that objecthood is indeed specified by a property that does not have the same locus as the predication content. (So an awareness of silver in the face of mother-of-pearl would be erroneous and the definitions may stand.)

Gaṅgeśa: (No.) Then even with the object as simply a bearer of properties (*dharmin*), the awareness would not be veridical, since there would still be (*tulyatvāt*) a having of predication content not residing in the same locus. But if the portion concerning the object as simply a bearer of properties is to be considered veridical, then the silver portion as well would have to be veridical (since there is only a single objecthood according to the current proposal).

Comments

This passage is clear. Gaṅgeśa is firmly committed to the rule that no awareness is non-veridical in all respects: in particular, every awareness is veridical with regard to an object cognized as a mere "bearer of properties" (*dharmin*). Thus an erroneous awareness must be correlate to more than one objecthood.

Text (p. 430) and Translation

atha rajatâṃśe dharmy-aṃśe ca taj-jñānaṃ pramā eva | vaiśiṣṭyâṃśe na pramā iti cet, na | vaiśiṣṭyasya pūrva-jñānâviṣayatvena aprakāratvāt | vaiśiṣṭya-vṛtti-viṣayatāyāṃ rajatatva-purovartinoḥ prakāratvena bhramasya vaiśiṣṭyâṃśe pramātvâpramātvâpātāt |

Objection: Then in both the portion concerning silverness and that concerning the bearer of properties, awareness is only veridical. (That is to say, silverness exists in the real silver in the world, and "silverness" picks it out; thisness exists in the object in front, and "thisness" picks it out.) But in the portion that relates the two the awareness is not veridical. (The problem is in putting the two veridical awarenesses together; wrongly related (sub-)awarenesses result in an erroneous awareness.)

Gaṅgeśa: No. The relationality—the relating of the two—not being an object in the preceding (indeterminate, *nirvikalpaka*) awareness—is not a predication content. Moreover, if the objecthood that resides in the relationality is determined by both "silverness" and "being in front" (i.e., "thisness") as predication content, then there would be both veridicality and non-veridicality in the relational portion of the erroneous awareness.

Comments

A *savikalpaka* awareness, a relational or determinate awareness, is preceded and caused by a non-relational, indeterminate cognition where a qualifier of an object is directly presented though not as related to the thing cognized—as we discussed in chapter 4. Erroneous awareness involves putting together a qualifier with a qualificandum to which it does not belong—a position that Gaṅgeśa elaborates in a subsequent section of the *TCM*. The presentation of the qualifier that gets misplaced arises, it may seem, in the non-relational cognitive moment, for where else could the data, so to say, that is put together in relational awareness come from? But whereas even relations, such as conjunction and inherence, are cognized in the non-relational stage, the relationality—the actual togetherness—is not. Thus relationality is not a candidate for the status of a misplaced qualifier. Furthermore, it is impossible, Gaṅgeśa says, for a single relationality to be both veridical and non-veridical.

Text (p. 431) and Translation

> na api sva-vyadhikaraṇa-prakārânavacchinna-viṣayatā-pratiyogy-anubhavaḥ pramā | prameyam idam iti jñāne prameyatva-prakāraka-viṣayatânāśrayasya aprasiddhyā avyāpteḥ |

Nor is veridical awareness to be characterized as (D^{24}) "experience correlate to an objecthood that is not specified by a predication content present in a locus that is not the same as that of the objecthood." This definition fails to cover the awareness, "This thing can be known." There does not occur (*aprasiddhi*) anything with a different locus than that of the objecthood with the predication content "knowability."

Comments

And so, again, the definition fails because one of its terms fails to refer when the particular bit of veridical awareness, "This thing is knowable," is plugged in. There is nothing that is "a locus that is not the same as that of the objecthood" if the objecthood is that having the predication content "knowability."

Text (p. 432) and Translation

> na ca saṃyogitvâdinā prameyatva-prakāraka-viṣayatā-vyatireko ghaṭâdau prasiddha iti vācyam | pratiyogitâvacchedaka-rūpavattvena pratiyogi-jñānasya abhāva-dhī-hetutvāt |

Objection: There does occur such a locus: for example, "being in the relation of conjunction" (which is not a *self-linking* relation as opposed to *viṣayatā-vṛtti*, "being a locus of objecthood," which is self-linking). This is appertinent to pots, etc., and is a counter-instance (*vyatireka*) to the objecthood with "knowability" as predication content. (The relation conjunction is related to its relata by inherence; so the alleged fault would be disarmed.)

Gaṅgeśa: No, this should not be said. What causes an awareness of an absence is (in part) awareness of the counterpositive or absentee, *pratiyogin* (so that there cannot be awareness of an absence if the *pratiyogin* term fails to refer; moreover, "being in a different locus" cannot count as the *pratiyogin* with an absence). (Technically,) this awareness of the counterpositive (of an absence) is to be understood as making counterpositive-ness concrete, *pratiyogitā-avacchedaka*, specifying it.

Comments

The claim is that there is a counter-instance to the objecthood determined by "knowability," but where could this counter-instance be? What could be its locus? The objector says that "being in the relation of conjunction" is an example of the requisite counter-instance in that this contrasts with "being a locus of objecthood": the former is not a self-linking relation—a conjunction between x and y *inheres* in both x and y with the inherence as an ontically real relator—whereas the latter is self-linking, i.e., involves no relator over and above the relata. But this does not fulfill the requirement for a counterpositive.

Gaṅgeśa elaborates the requirement in the *anumāna-khaṇḍa* of the *TCM*, in the *vyadhikaraṇa* section, *TCM*, vol. 2, pp. 49 and 63 (with commentary filling the intervening pages). There he repeats his view that the property of "being in a different locus" cannot be the specifier of counterpositive-ness because awareness of an absence's counterpositive is in part responsible for awareness of the absence. He goes on to add that otherwise the statement, "There is no rabbit's horn on the cow," would make sense.

Text and Translation

> kiṃ ca yat kiṃcid-vyadhikaraṇa-prakārânavacchinnatvaṃ bhrama-sādhāraṇam, prakṛta-jñāna-vyadhikaraṇa-prakārânavacchinnatvaṃ nirvikalpakâvyāptam, tasya niṣprakārakatvād iti |

Moreover, whatever would meet the stipulation "not specified by predication content present in a locus that is not the same as . . ." would include erroneous awareness. Further, D^{24} fails to cover indeterminate awareness, since indeterminate awareness does not have predication content. Your definition states that the objecthood has to be not specified by predication content present in a locus that is not the same as (that of the objecthood correlate to) the awareness in question. (But that is impossible in the case of *nirvikalpaka* awareness.)

Comments

An erronenous awareness would fulfill the terms of D^{24} in its veridical portion.

Again, Gaṅgeśa will later rule that indeterminate awareness falls outside the veridical/non-veridical distinction. (Indeterminate awareness does not have predication content—there no qualifier appears as a qualifier qualifying a qualificandum—and both veridical and non-veridical awareness presuppose predication content.) Here he again prepares that move by showing that D^{24} fails to cover indeterminate awareness.

Text (p. 434) and Translation

> ucyate[34] | yatra yad asti tatra tasya anubhavaḥ pramā |

Gaṅgeśa: The right way to characterize veridical awareness is as follows: veridical awareness is (D^{25}) "experience of S^s as S^p with S^s's being S^p."

Comments

Thus experience of a pot as a pot with the pot's being a pot would be a veridical awareness. "S^s" may be taken to represent any subject of predication, the qualificandum or *viśeṣya* (i.e., bearer of properties, *dharmin*), and "S^p" any predication content that might belong to a cognized object. Note that in Sanskrit, first, only correlative pronouns are used and, second, the use of the locative case suggests the presence or absence of properties at a location:

"experience of something there where it is" renders the text preserving the Sanskrit construction. But the "there" and "where" represent a *dharmin*, "bearer of properties" (an *adhikaraṇa* in the sense of an *ādhāra*: see *Kāśikā* 1.4.45), and thus in translation the language of attribution is appropriately used. Another translation: veridical awareness is "an experience that ϕx only if ϕx," in other words, an experience that something is ϕ only if that something is indeed ϕ.

D^{25} is close to one of the definitions Udayana gives in the *Kusumañjali* (4.5). Since it is and since the next definition, D^{26}, is that focused on by later Navyas and generally identified as Gaṅgeśa's considered view, discussion of a key interpretive question—that of the variables I use to render Gaṅgeśa's correlative pronouns—will be taken up by us after D^{26} is out on the table. Moreover, a few sentences later Gaṅgeśa himself addresses the question of the meaning of the pronouns. We will enjoin the interpretive issue at that point.

Another issue is of course whether this, or any of Gaṅgeśa's definitions, is really any good. Someone familiar with Western philosophic literature on the definition of knowledge might think that here a crucial condition has been left out, namely, the justification condition. All Gaṅgeśa spells out is the truth condition. A long-standing definition of knowledge as "justified true belief" has been shown inadequate, but not because any of the three conditions is not necessary for knowledge. Those three conditions are (a) that a proposition *p* be true, (b) that *p* be believed by the knower S, and (c) that S be justified in believing *p*. The problem is not that any of these is not necessary for knowledge but that together they are not sufficient. Edmund Gettier shows this with his famous counterexamples.[35] Or, the justification condition has to be strengthened relative to the traditional views so that justification involves a tie to *p*'s truth. In any case, Gaṅgeśa's definition, which does not include a justification condition, does not appear to be in the ballpark of what knowledge has been taken to be—that is, by philosophers familiar with Socrates's arguments in Plato's *Meno* (98) and *Theaetetus* (210). If belief is not tied down by justification, then a true belief will be only a lucky guess. We require more of knowledge than just happening to hit the truth.

Gaṅgeśa's definition of course is not of propositional knowledge, i.e., knowledge understood as having a belief component. Gaṅgeśa's concern is rather with veridical awareness which is an experience. Nevertheless, since all veridical awarenesses are relational awarenesses—non-relational awarenesses are neither veridical nor non-veridical, we will learn just a few sentences below—and since any relational awareness is verbalizable, i.e., expressible propositionally, the difference is not so great as it might at first seem. Furthermore, claims of veridical awareness figure in classical Indian discussions—both intra-Nyāya and across schools—in much the same way that knowledge claims do in Western debates. Then what about the justification condition? I see it as implicitly present in the notion of "experience" or "awareness," *anubhava.* Remember that the entire *TCM* is organized around the concept of *pramāṇa,* "sources of veridical awareness," with four distinct sources, or means, identified and at great length discussed: right perception, cogent inference, analogical acquisitions of vocabulary, and reliable testimony. These means are thought of as having *causal* roles in the production of veridical awarenesses; any awareness is thought of as an effect of certain causes, both the veridical and the non-veridical. The causal presupposition takes the place of, I believe, the justification condition. In the section of the *TCM* preceding the translation here Gaṅgeśa has gone to great lengths to defend a tie between veridical awareness and causal "excellences" (*guṇa*) or "reliability-grounding causal conditions." He develops his causal theory of veridical awareness in many later sections of the *TCM* as well.

Veridical awareness so characterized—including the causal presupposition—still would not be knowledge. An awareness of a pot in a subject S's hand caused by electrodes fastened to S's brain when there is indeed a pot in S's hand would count as a veridical awareness according to D^{25}, but I dare say few would count it as knowledge. The causal presupposition needs to be flushed out and filled out in order to complete the project, it seems.

Text (p. 436) and Translation

tadvati tat-prakārakânubhavo vā |yatra yan na asti tatra tasya jñānaṃ, tad-abhāvavati tat-prakāraka-jñānaṃ vā apramā |

Or, (D^{26}) "experience with predication content about a ϕ-object as ϕ."

Non-veridical awareness (conversely) is (D^{25e}) "experience of S^s as S^p with S^s's *not* being S^p." Or, (D^{26e}) "awareness with predication content about a *non*-ϕ object as ϕ."

Comments

According to D^{26}, experience with predication content about a pot as a pot would be a veridical awareness. According to D^{25e}, experience of mother-of-pearl as silver with the mother-of-pearl's not being silver would be a non-veridical awareness. Or, according to D^{26e}, awareness with predication content about something—mother-of-pearl—that is not silver as silver would be a non-veridical awareness.

Again, in Sanskrit the locative case is used to express attribution: "experience with predication content there where it is." And, I repeat, it is the usage of "there where" to express a *dharmin,* "bearer of properties," that grounds the renderings I make.

D^{26} and D^{26e} are elaborations of D^{25} in the direction of the distinction, worked out in the previous section, between predication content and objecthood. (Gaṅgeśa will say more about what predication content is immediately below.)

Now, since the new characterizations are also proposed under the causal presupposition, it would not seem that they stand up any better to the objection presented above—considering the Western discussion—that an awareness that fulfilled D^{25} need not be knowledge. But perhaps that objection is off the mark in that an electrode-induced pot-experience of S's (having all the right predication content, i.e., predication content indistinguishable, from the first-person perspective, from predication content when there is a veritable case of knowledge) would not be *about* the pot in S's hand. Gaṅgeśa's characterization does clearly state that the predication content has to be *about* the object that has that predication content as a qualifier. Awareness has intentionality,[36] and implicit in Gaṅgeśa's characterizations is that with veridical awareness the intentionality must be successfully grounded in the real. With my counterexample to taking D^{25} as a definition of knowledge, it is dubious that the electrode-induced awareness would be about the pot that is actually in S's hand. If the causal relation is not what it needs to be to constitute knowledge, then a defender of Gaṅgeśa could claim that the predication content in the example is not about the ϕ-object, the real pot.

Gaṅgeśa does not pellucidly spell out, all told, the causal presupposition vis-à-vis his characterizations of veridical awareness. He will say a few things just below, however, and, as mentioned, he does talk a lot about perception as a causal process throughout the entire first chapter of the *TCM*. Nevertheless, there would have to be much more filling out on the part of a sympathetic Navya-Nyāya philosopher—more than I am capable of—to make Gaṅgeśa's characterizations really fly in the context of contemporary attempts to define knowledge.[37]

Text (p. 438) and Translation

> tad-anyatve sati anubhavatvam eva vā pramātvam | tat-prakārakatvaṃ ca tad-vaiśiṣṭya-viṣayakatvaṃ tad-viśeṣaṇa-jñāna-janyatvaṃ vā |

(Are the veridical and the non-veridical mutually exclusive? Yes,) veridicality may also be defined simply as the class of experiences different from the non-veridical. (What is it to have "predication content," *prakāra*?) Having ϕ as predication content is to have "being qualified by ϕ" as content. Or, it is to be capable of being generated by an awareness of ϕ as a qualifier.

Comments

Predication content is produced by a preceding "indeterminate" (*nirvikalpaka*) awareness, i.e., a non-relational awareness, of a qualifier ϕ of a thing, as we have had several occasions to remark. Gaṅgeśa provides some explanation of the causal role of *nirvikalpaka* awareness in the immediately following text; a whole section is devoted to indeterminate awareness later, near the end of this the first chapter of the *TCM*.

Text (p. 441) and Translation

īśvarasya tad-viśiṣṭa-viṣayaṃ jñānaṃ na tu tat-prakārakam | pramâpramā-bahir-bhūtam eva, vyavahārânaṅgatvāt | avyapadeśya-padena tad-upagrahasya nāma-jāty-ādi-yojanā-rahitam api pratyakṣam asti iti atra tātparyam | idaṃ rajatam iti jñānam idantvavati tad-anubhavatvāt pramā, rajatatvâbhāvavati tat-prakāraka-jñānatvād apramā | aṃśe samūhâlambanaṃ ca na apramā | eka-prakārâbhāvavaty api tad-apratīteḥ |

"Having content qualified by ϕ" applies to God's awareness, but not "having ϕ as predication content" (insofar as this is understood as being generated by a preceding indeterminate awareness, since God's awareness is not generated).

Non-relational awareness (i.e., indeterminate awareness) is outside the scope of the veridical/non-veridical distinction; these terms do not apply. (Veridicality and non-veridicality fall within the province of linguistic practice, and) non-relational awareness is not linguistic. The word *avyapadeśya* (in the *Nyāya-sūtra*'s characterization of perception, *NyS* 1.1.4), "inexpressible," is used to include non-relational awareness as a type of perception, according to the *Tātparya* commentary (of Vācaspati Miśra): (unlike relational awareness) it is devoid of the binding (to a cognized object) of name, natural kind, etc. (which binding makes a relational awareness have predication content).

The awareness "This is silver" (when faced with mother-of-pearl) is veridical concerning the "thisness," since the cognized object is a "this," and "this" is presented in the experience. The "silver" portion is not veridical since the cognized object is not silver (or, possesses the absence of silverness) while the experience has that as predication content.

An awareness of a group of things need not be non-veridical concerning each item (even when the whole is wrongly cognized). Although some bit of predication content may be lacking (with regard to the group or to a particular individual item while some other individual item has it), that (right bit) need not appear (to qualify the whole or the items that lack it).

Comments

In this passage, Gaṅgeśa makes several disconnected clarificational remarks. Only the first of the two explanations in the immediately preceding text of what it is to have predication content applies to God's awareness; "being generated by an awareness of ϕ" does not apply, since God's awareness is considered ungenerated.

Next we have the explicit statement that non-relational awareness falls outside the veridical/non-veridical distinction, and Gaṅgeśa goes on to say a few words about how he understands non-relational (i.e., indeterminate) awareness. The *Nyāya-sūtra* defines "perception" (*pratyakṣa*) as "cognition produced through an operative relation, or contact, between an object and a perceptual organ, a cognition that is non-linguistic, (or) undeviating, and determinate."[38] Vācaspati Miśra I in his *Tātparyaṭīkā* commentary argues that *nirvikalpaka* (indeterminate) perception is meant by the term *avyapadeśyam*, "non-linguistic" or "inexpressible." Gaṅgeśa here uses the point to elaborate his understanding of a non-relational (i.e., indeterminate) awareness as non-verbalizable because it lacks the binding to a name, natural kind, etc., which is characteristic of determinate awareness.

Finally, Gaṅgeśa takes up the topic of dual or multiple content in cognition, asserting, again, the doctrine of partial veridicality. This applies to an awareness of a group of things, "A pot and a cloth," for example. If one were to have this awareness when there is instead a pot and a piece of paper, the awareness would be veridical only in the "pot" portion.

Text (p. 442) and Translation

> nanu evam avyāpya-vṛtti-bhāvâbhāvayor ekatra pramâpramā ca syāt tad-abhāvavati tat-prakāraka-jñānatvād iti cet, na |bhinna-bhinnâvacchedena hi vṛkṣe saṃyoga-tad-abhāvau, na vṛkṣa-mātre, virodhād ananubhavāc ca |tathā ca yatra vṛkṣe saṃyogo na tatra tad-abhāvaḥ |yad-avacchedena yatra yad asti iti vā vivakṣitam |

Objection: According to your definitions, an awareness of a single object (e.g., a tree) both as having a property (e.g., monkey-conjunction) that is non-locus-pervading and at the same time lacking it would be both veridical and non-veridical. The object in fact exhibits an absence of the property, but the awareness has the property as predication content.

Gaṅgeśa: No; for only according to distinct specification (*avaccheda*) is there both the presence and absence of a conjunction in a tree (for example). The two do not exist merely in the tree (taken as a whole); that is contradictory and never experienced.

For example, (D^{25} holds with regard to monkey-conjunction and a tree in this way:) the conjunction (that is cognized) in S^s, the tree, (secures a veridical awareness). It is not cognized where it is not. Or we should say (veridical awareness is D^{27}), "(experience of) S^s as S^p according to the relevant specification of S^s (with S^s's being S^p according to that specification)."

Comments

Next, Gaṅgeśa considers the case of an awareness of a qualifier that is non-locus-pervading with respect to its qualificandum, using the stock example of a monkey-conjunction qualifying a tree. Such cases, it will be recalled, were the straits through which several of the definitions considered earlier could not sail. Gaṅgeśa is exceedingly casual here, given how serious the problem was taken to be earlier. He dismisses the objection by saying, in effect, that the difficulty is a pseudo-problem. A property ϕ and its opposite not-ϕ do not qualify the same qualificandum except through ignoring a difference of specification. If one wants to insist that the characterizations of veridical awareness be sensitive to this type of possibility, then, Gaṅgeśa says, what is needed is a modification of D^{25}, to wit, D^{27}. Presumably, a similar modification could be constructed for D^{26}. The deep problem here is to keep the definitions suitably abstract and variable so that they fit the wide range of cases of veridical awareness, and at the same time remain sufficiently specific to handle such cases as awareness of qualifiers that do not pervade what they qualify. The general notion of (relevant) specification is suitably variable and seems to do the trick. Specification, as we have noted, becomes throughout Navya Nyāya a principal clarificational tool.

Text (p. 451) and Translation

> gotvâder api sāsnâdy-avacchedena vṛtteḥ | pāka-rakte śyāmo 'yam iti dhīḥ pramā eva | kadācit tatra tat-sattvāt | idānīṃ śyāma iti tv apramā eva | na ca yat-tadbhyāṃ lakṣaṇânanugamaḥ, na hi pramā sarvatra pramā, kiṃ tu kvacit | tathā ca kiṃ jñānaṃ kutra pramā iti tat-tad-viśeṣasya lakṣyatvena yat-tadbhyām eva lakṣaṇaṃ yuktam |

(But with certain things and predicates, a cow, for example, no specification is needed, since "cowhood" is locus-pervading. Thus D^{27} cannot be right. No,) even with cowhood, etc., there is relevant specification with respect to a dewlap, etc. The cognition (*dhī*), "This (was) black," with regard to a pot now red from baking, would be veridical. At one time, it was like that. But "Now it is black" would indeed be non-veridical.

Moreover, the correlative pronouns used in the definitions do not make the definitions equivocal (although there is much variation in the objects to which they may refer), since veridical awarenesses are not alike with regard to every possible object of awareness (*sarvatra*) but only in restricted instances. For example, the question "Which awareness is veridical about what?" is relevant to the sense in which the pronouns are to be taken in an appropriate characterization (*lakṣaṇa*) with regard to this and that particular (veridical awareness) to be characterized (*lakṣya*).

Comments

Gaṅgeśa shows that he is aware of the Scylla as well as the Charybdis of characterization of such varied phenomena as veridical awarenesses: the particularization move made with D^{27}—he now suggests in the voice of an objector—is irrelevant to awarenesses of locus-pervading properties such as cowhood. But specification is always potentially relevant, Gaṅgeśa answers. For example, a cow is not to be defined just by the locus-pervading property, cowhood, but also by the characteristic mark, having-a-dewlap, which is non-locus-pervading.

Veridical awarenesses vary considerably according to what they are about. Thus correlative pronouns have to be used whose meaning varies with substitution. D^{27} is thus doubly sensitive to differences reflected in cognition according to the nature of the object cognized. Cognition has no form of its own; it is *nirākāra*. Thus one cannot say so much that is significant about veridical awareness in abstraction from what there is veridical awareness *of*. Śrīharṣa, as we noted, appears to have pushed Gaṅgeśa to this avowal.

Specifically, the pronouns *yat* and *tat*, "which *x*" and "that *x*," univocally refer to one and the same object as cognized; the pronouns are true correlatives and function logically like a single variable. That is to say, whatever substitution instance the one admits the other must take also. But the objects to be substituted according to the various instances of veridicality are not uniform. Thus, in a sense, these pronouns used in the definitions are not univocal in that the nature of the objects over which they range—or about which there can be veridical awareness—varies significantly. Gaṅgeśa, we may say, sees each of the good definitions as an open sentence, where the variables occur free, i.e., unquantified. In other words, Gaṅgeśa is saying that there is no definition of veridicality applicable to every instance of veridical awareness, but if one substitutes one object known at a time—under the predication content it is known as—the definitions are okay. Thus Gaṅgeśa's definitions are good *although* they lack universal applicability under any univocal interpretation since the correlative pronouns (along with the specification clause in D^{27}) vary with the variations. Here, in sum, the lack of universal applicability under any univocal interpretation (*ananugama*) is not a fault.

Later Navyas are unhappy with this abandonment of universality, of consecutive character (*anugama*) in what is defined.[39] They develop techniques to eliminate the pronouns concerning this and other key definienda in the system through relational abstraction, securing equivalents of universally quantified statements. The techniques developed are quite complex, and provoke ontological controversy about their interpretation.[40] Thus Śrīharṣa's pushing Gaṅgeśa to admit the variability of veridical awareness may be said to provoke developments within Navya Nyāya well past Gaṅgeśa. Most of these developments are beyond our purview. But we will soon see further definitions of Gaṅgeśa's that inform the *anugama* and ontological preoccupations of Raghunātha, Jagadīśa, Gadādhara, and others.

For Gaṅgeśa himself, the variability is a primary reason why he holds that veridicality is not—as he stated at the beginning of the section—a natural kind, *jāti*.

Text (p. 452) and Translation

anye tu, anubhavatvam eva prāmāṇyam, bhrame 'py aṃśam ādāya pramā-vyavahārāt | rajatâdi-pramâpramā ca viśiṣya lakṣaṇīyā, rajatatvavati tad-anubhavaḥ tad-abhāvavati tad-anubhavo vā ity-ādinā |

Some say, on the other hand, that to be veridical is simply to be experience, for, they say, one speaks of veridical awareness even with respect to erroneous awareness, focusing on the (veridical) part. And while (this is wrong in that) veridical and non-veridical awareness of silver and so on are to be distinguished, the two are indeed to be characterized together: e.g., (as has been done here) "experience of x as silver, with x's being silver," and "experience of it as that, without its being that."

Comments

Gaṅgeśa here hurries to point out that there is, in spite of what he has just said, important commonality, too. For example, every instance of veridicality presupposes experience. Experience is hardly the whole story, however, since veridical and non-veridical awarenesses are not to be confused. Nevertheless, even across that divide there is commonality: non-veridicality is to be understood invariably in opposition to veridicality.

Text (p. 453) and Translation

nanv anubhavatvasya pramâpramā-sādhāraṇyena taj-jñānasya na niṣkampa-pravṛtty-aṅgatvam iti cet, satyam | viśeṣa-viṣaya-pramāyā eva pravartakatvāt |

Objection: Experience as what is common between veridical and non-veridical awareness is not the cause of unwavering action (with regard to x) when there is awareness of x.

Gaṅgeśa: That is true. It is veridical awareness (not *qua* awareness nor even *qua* veridical, but rather) with a particular as its content that is the impeller.

Comments

The cash value of much awareness is paid out in human action. This is where the variability of veridicality is most evident, though even here a common story can be told (at the proper level of abstraction), namely, that the various objects of awareness, in their peculiar natures, are what we work to acquire or avoid.

Text (p. 454) and Translation

atirikta-viṣayatā-pakṣe viṣayatâśrayâvṛtty-aprakārakânubhavaḥ pramā |
kevalânvayini viṣayatâśrayâvṛttir avṛttir eva prasiddhaḥ |

According to the view (held by some Navya Naiyāyikas) that objecthood (*viṣayatā*) is something ontologically over and above (the cognized object as well as awareness), veridical awareness would be (D^{28}) "experience that does not have a predication content not located in the substratum of the objecthood." With regard to a claim that has no counter-instance (*kevala-anvayin*, e.g., "This is knowable") the non-existence (required by the definition) of something not located in the substratum of the objecthood is well-known.

Comments

First note that by use of the relational abstract, "objecthood," correlative pronouns prove unnecessary, and, presumably, *anugama* (universality or consecutive character) would be preserved, though Gaṅgeśa himself does not say so. This gain, however, would be outweighed, apparently, by a corresponding ontological cost, namely, objecthood as an additional, irreducible real.

Moreover, Gaṅgeśa rejected D^{22} and D^{23} because each contained a term that was potentially empty; that is to say, each contained a term that would be empty with respect to the veridical awareness, "This is knowable" (occurring in the presence of anything whatsoever). Such a determinate awareness has no counter-instance (*kevala-anvayin*, more literally, "is exclusively positive"). The problem pointed out with the two rejected definitions—and, it would seem, with D^{28} as well—is that they are formulated negatively and thus cannot capture the exclusively positive claim.

But here, Gaṅgeśa, lessening the worries of the camp that finds objecthood to be an independent real, suggests that there is something—according to Rucidatta, *gagana*, the sky or space—which is an example of such a counter-instance. To take up Rucidatta's example, the sky can be only a container, not contained. It itself has no substratum. Thus all the terms of the definition would be exampled even with the awareness, "This is knowable."

Gaṅgeśa does not immediately try to refute the rival Naiyāyika theory. He goes on to give other definitions in accord with the views of this camp. Only near the very end of the section does he try to knock down what he apparently sees as the principal prop for the position that objecthood is a separate real—the argument, namely, from the content of doubt, which was introduced earlier.

Text and Translation

yad vā yat-prakārikā yā viṣayatā tat-prakāra-samānâdhikaraṇa-viṣayatākaḥ, sva-prakāra-samānâdhikaraṇa-viṣayatāko vā anubhavaḥ pramā | yat-prakārikā yā viṣayatā tat-prakāra-vyadhikaraṇa-viṣayatākaṃ sva-prakāra-vyadhikaraṇa-viṣayatākaṃ vā jñānaṃ bhramaḥ | prakāra-bhedena ekatra viṣayatā-bheda iti lakṣaṇa-dvaya-samāveśāt pramā-bhrama-saṃkaraḥ |

Or, veridical awareness is (D^{29}) "experience with a corresponding objecthood that has the same locus with that predication content which is the predication content had by the objecthood." Or, (D^{30}) "experience with a corresponding objecthood that has the same locus as the experience's predication content."

Erroneous awareness is (D^{29e}) "cognition (*jñāna*) with a corresponding objecthood that does not have the same locus as that of the predication content, which predication content is that had by the objecthood." Or, (D^{30e}) "cognition with a corresponding objecthood that does not have the same locus as that of its predication content." The mixture of veridical and erroneous awareness (that occurs, e.g., with "This is silver" when the cognized object is mother-of-pearl) is explained through the co-operation here of two characterizations (one of the error, one of the right awareness), since there will be distinct objecthoods (one determined by "silverness," the other by "thisness") in the case of the awareness, along with distinct predication content.

Comments

Bracketing the ontological question, Gaṅgeśa gives other characterizations utilizing the relational abstract, objecthood.

Text and Translation

yad vā viśeṣya-niṣṭhâtyantâbhāvâpratiyogi-prakāraka-viṣayatā-pratiyogī, viśeṣya-niṣṭhâtyantâbhāva-pratiyogi-prakārânavacchinna-viṣayatva-pratiyogī vā, viṣayatā-samānâdhikaraṇâtyantâbhāva-pratiyogi-prakāraka-viṣayatvâpratiyogī vā, viṣayatā-samānâdhikaraṇâtyantâbhāva-pratiyogi-prakārânavacchinna-viṣayatâpratiyogī vā anubhavaḥ pramā |

Or, veridical awareness is (D^{31}) "experience correlate to an objecthood with predication content that is not the counterpositive of an absolute absence resident in the thing cognized." Or, (D^{32}) "experience correlate to an objecthood not specified by a predication content that is the counterpositive of an absolute absence resident in the thing cognized.'' Or, (D^{33}) ''experience that is not correlate to an objecthood with a predication content that is the counterpositive of an absolute absence that shares the same locus with the objecthood.'' Or, (D^{34}) ''experience correlate to an objecthood not specified by a predication content that is the counterpositive of an absolute absence sharing the same locus with the objecthood.''

Comments

These characterizations are all equivalent, given that we ignore the difficulties about the ontic status of objecthood, as well as that of potentially empty terms. Note that Gaṅgeśa relies here on a duality of objecthoods correlate to an experience—a point he has already explicity made and will continue to emphasize.

Text (p. 456) and Translation

> sva-samānâdhikaraṇa-prakārânavacchinna-viṣayatā-pratiyogi jñānaṃ, sva-vyadhikaraṇa-prakārâvacchinna-viṣayatā-pratiyogi jñānaṃ vā bhramaḥ | idaṃ rajatam iti bhrame ca viṣayatā-dvaye vyadhikaraṇa-prakārâvacchinnatva-tad-anavacchinnatvayoḥ viṣayatva-pratiyogitva-tad-apratiyogitvayor avirodhāt | samūhâlambane ca viṣayatā-bhedān na pramâpramā-lakṣaṇe 'vyāpty-ativyāptī |

Erroneous awareness is (D^{35e}) ''awareness correlate to an objecthood not specified by a predication content sharing the same locus with the objecthood.'' Or, (D^{36e}) ''awareness correlate to an objecthood specified by a predication content that does not have the same locus as that of the objecthood.'' The erroneous awareness ''This is silver'' determines two objecthoods. There is no essential opposition (*avirodha*) between (a) a correlation to an objecthood that is specified by predication content that does not have the same locus—or to one not specified like that—and (b) a non-correlation to an objecthood so specified or not so specified (in one and the same awareness). Moreover, since there can be distinct objecthoods, there is no problem (for our definitions) presented by the example of an awareness of a group of things: our characterizations of veridical and non-veridical awareness cover neither too much nor too little.

Comments

''A pot and a cloth'' is an awareness determining two objecthoods, one in the pot and another in the cloth. The analysis of such an awareness of a group of things is parallel to that of an erroneous awareness veridical in its ''thisness'' part, since the erroneous awareness also determines two objecthoods.

Text and Translation

vastutas tu viśeṣaṇatā-viśeṣo na asti eva, mānâbhāvāt |

But in fact, objecthood is not a special qualifierhood, *viśeṣaṇatā* (ontologically over and above awareness and the object of awareness), for there is no argument.

Comments

There appears to be an argument, which was earlier rehearsed, p. 190, above. Gaṅgeśa is saying that the argument is indecisive. The argument is that if I doubt whether person S is aware of a particular pot or not, the content—or object—of my doubt must be something over and above both S's awareness and the particular pot. Thus objecthood would have to be a distinct and irreducible real. If objecthood were not ontologically something over and above both awareness and the recognized categories of objects of awareness, such doubt could not occur. Gaṅgeśa proceeds to refute this reasoning.

Text and Translation

sāmānyato jñāne jñāte tasya kvacid-viśeṣaṇatā iti sāmānyato viśeṣaṇatā-jñāne 'pi ghaṭam ayaṃ jānāti na vā iti saṃdeha-tādavasthyāt |

A cognition can be cognized in general simply as a cognition. In other words, a cognition can be cognized in general with its qualificative content (unspecified, i.e., as simply) about something in some regard. Through cognition of it (just) as having some kind or other, i.e., general, qualificative content, there can be doubt (for example) whether a particular person is aware or not of a particular pot.

Comments

Gaṅgeśa makes a phemomenological appeal in resisting the ontological posit of the rival camp. He apparently presumes that the rival Naiyāyikas see the content of the doubt as something definite, which cannot, however, be pinned down to precisely one of the accepted categories. Thus they are motivated to make the posit of objecthood as an additional real. Gaṅgeśa denies that the content of the doubt is definite. To be sure, in the example it is about an awareness, but what the awareness is about is undetermined. As about an awareness with undetermined content, the content of the doubt does not need to be further specified as this type of thing or that. Indeed, the very point of the doubt, we might elaborate in this vein, is to wonder what it is that S is aware of. Doubt has content, but the content in some instances may not be specifiable other than very generally as "something in some regard."

Text (p. 457) and Translation

> tasmāt ghaṭa-taj-jñānayoḥ sva-rūpa-grahe 'pi tadīyatvaṃ na gṛhītam iti tad-viṣayatve saṃdehaḥ | tadīyatvaṃ ca sambandhaṃ vinā tat-sambandha-svabhāvatvam | tad uktam, "prakāśasya satas tadīyatā-mātra-nibandhanaḥ sva-bhāva-viśeṣaḥ tad-viṣayatvam" iti |

Therefore, even when the very nature (*svarūpa*) of a pot and of a cognition of it have been grasped, the state of "belonging to that" (*tadīyatva*, or, "relating to that")—i.e., whether it is *that object's* objecthood (as determined by a particular awareness)—need not be grasped. So the doubt could occur whether the objecthood belongs to a particular thing (as determined by a particular awareness).

And the state of "belonging to that" is to be understood as the very nature (*svabhāva*) of a relation to that (i.e., as a self-linking relation), without a (further) relation. Thus it has been said, "A thing's objecthood is a self-linking relation (*svabhāva-viśeṣa*) that ties the awareness (*prakāśa*) (determining the objecthood) to a state of belonging to that (thing)."

Comments

Here we have some of Gaṅgeśa's reflection about self-linkage, which is developed in a later section of the first chapter of the *TCM*, on *samavāya*, "inherence," translated below. Recall from the discussion in chapter 4 that self-linkage is viewed by Gaṅgeśa as accomplished by the second term in a relational complex a-R-b, namely, -R-b. In cases of self-linkage, -R-b is to be taken ontologically as a single thing, a single qualifier-cum-relational-tie with respect to a qualificandum, *viśeṣya*, although we may speak of each of the three separately. Here with objecthood, the qualifier is just awareness itself, which by nature is relational, having an intrinsic, though open-ended, coupler, so to say. Objecthood (*viṣayatā*) is the name of the abstracted relationality, abstracted objectwise; its first term is the object, the second, awareness. It is matched by another abstracted relationality, subjecthood (*viṣayitā*), which resides in awareness and has the object cognized as its second term. There is in the cognitive episode, abstractly considered, nothing real in addition to awareness and its object. Thus, objecthood, which is, I repeat, one way of talking about the relationship, has to be self-linking, in Gaṅgeśa's view. Later Navya-Nyāya philosophers, for example, Gadādhara, depart from him on this point, agreeing apparently with the rival Naiyāyika camp that Gaṅgeśa has referred to.

It is not hard to appreciate the other side, for ontologically Gaṅgeśa seems here to try to have his cake and eat it too. He identifies the relationality of objecthood to be what the doubt is about. In this way, he would keep the cake. But he would eat it too in that ontologically this relationality disappears; a self-linking relation is no additional real. As pointed out, Gaṅgeśa is ontologically a conservative, and is loathe to depart from the view that he inherited from Udayana.

The quotation, which is slightly altered from the original, is from Udayana's *Ātmatattvaviveka.*[41]

Text (p. 458) and Translation

> saṃbandhaṃ vinā kathaṃ tadīyatvam, saṃbandhasya eva svabhāvatvāt, yathā tava eva viśeṣaṇatāyām |anyathā anavasthānāt |anyatra api sva-rūpa-saṃbandhe eṣā eva gatiḥ |anyathā sāmānyena abhāva-samavāyayor jñāne 'dhikaraṇe jñāte tayoḥ saṃśayo na syāt, adhikaraṇa-tad-ubhaya-sva-rūpāṇāṃ jñātatvāt |

If it is asked (by you who advocate the view that objecthood is something ontologically over and above awareness and the recognized categories of objects of awareness) how without a (further) relation there can be the state of "belonging to that," we say that it is the self-linking nature of the relation itself, as you yourself accept with "qualifierhood" (*viśeṣaṇatā*). Otherwise, there would be an infinite regress. There are other cases as well where, without understanding the relations involved to be self-linking, an impasse would ensue. If this move were ruled out, there could be no doubt concerning absences in general nor about inherence in general when there is awareness of a locus, since the locus and the general nature of either (the absence or the inherence) would be known.

Comments

Though Navya-Nyāya philosophers disagree about precisely which relations are self-linking, many hold, with Gaṅgeśa, that awareness and its object, an absence and its locus, and inherence in relation to those things related by it are related through self-linkage. Gaṅgeśa's view is that self-linkage varies with each particular instance, so that an individual awareness provides no general knowledge about the relation or relata. Thus this is unlike the knowledge of cowhood implicit in the veridical awareness, "A cow." In other words, the self-linkage conception is crucial to understanding how it is possible to have doubts about particular awarenesses, relationships, and absences, since were all relationships cases of inherence, which is a single and uniform (*anugama*) relator, there would be no room for doubt once that single relator was known. Similar considerations apply with awarenesses and absences.

There is further advantage to the self-linkage notion invoked by Gaṅgeśa here, as we have remarked. Self-linkage is a way to talk about relations while avoiding an infinite regress. To speak of self-linkage with respect to a self-linking term is to abstract the (open-ended) relational hook that is considered intrinsic to a qualifier without committing oneself to the existence of a relation as an additional real. Thus the relation regress is solved. I have more to say on this in comments on the *TCM* section on inherence, translated below.

Gaṅgeśa's point in the passage here is that we have to invoke self-linkage to solve another problem; so there is no harm in invoking it with respect to objecthood. Furthermore, he says, all Naiyāyikas think of absential qualifierhood as self-linking. We are able to abstract without ontological commitment; doing so in the case of objecthood (qualifierhood, etc.) allows us to talk about awarenesses in general and thus to do our logic and epistemology.

Text and Translation

> tatra apy abhāva-samavāyayor viśeṣaṇatā-viśeṣo na gṛhīta iti cet, na | sāmānyatas tad-grahe 'pi saṃśayāt |

Objection: In that case, the particular instance of a qualifier in the case of an absence or an inherence would also not be grasped.

Gaṅgeśa: No. Even though that (particular qualifier) is grasped, there can be doubt about what is generalizable.

Comments

Gaṅgeśa repeats the point that doubt rules out inherence, which is single and uniform (*anugama*), as the relator. Self-linkage, in contrast, is unique in all its occurrences. We can generalize about cows from the example of Bessie, but we cannot generalize from the qualification relation, which is self-linking.

Text (p. 459) and Translation

> yat tu samūhâlambana-viśiṣṭa-jñānayor viśeṣânubhavād viśiṣṭa-jñāne viśeṣaṇatām ādāya api samūhâlambana-saṃbhavāt | tatra api viśeṣaṇatântara-svīkāre 'navasthā |

Objection: Since a difference is experienced between an awareness of a group of things and a relational awareness (of just one thing), in the case of the relational awareness the awareness's object has to be considered a different type of qualifier (from those involved in awareness of a group).

Gaṅgeśa: No. Even considering the qualifierhood (to be no more than what pertains to individuals), awareness of a group of things would be possible. Furthermore, if another type of qualifierhood (*viśeṣaṇatā*) is postulated, there would be an infinite regress.

Comments

The question is whether an awareness of a group of things, e.g., of a pot and a cloth, can be analyzed in the same way as a relational awareness of a single thing, i.e., invoking the schema a-R-b. Gaṅgeśa avers that it can be, that there is no essential difference. Indeed, if one required an additional tool of analysis to handle an awareness of a group of two things, then there would be no end to the additional tools needed for analyzing awareness of three things, four, *ad infinitum*. We have to accept more than one objecthood determined by an awareness of a group of things—and thus qualifying the awareness—but we do not have to suppose any difference of kind.

Text and Translation

> samūhâlambanāt tu viśiṣṭa-jñānasya viśeṣaḥ kāraṇa-kṛtaḥ kārya-kṛtaḥ prakāra-kṛto vā |

The difference between awareness of a group of things and relational awareness (of just one thing) is attributable to different causes, to different effects, or to different predication content (not to an ontologically distinct type of qualifier).

Comments

Awarenesses do vary enormously, but the differences do not force us to accept fundamentally distinct types of qualification.

Text (p. 461) and Translation

> prakāro 'pi viśeṣaṇatā-viśeṣaḥ sa ca dharmiṇy eva astv iti cet, na |tam ādāya api samūhâlambana-saṃbhavāt |

Objection: Predication content (*prakāra*) is also a distinct type of qualifier. And it exists just in the thing cognized (*dharmin*, the bearer of properties). (So you need not worry about accepting an ontologically distinct type of qualifier, which is, again, what you need to explain awareness of a group of things.)

Gaṅgeśa: No. Awareness of a group of things is possible although we take that (*prakāra*) as we have explained it.

Comments

Predication content is a distinct type of qualifier; it is a qualifier that appears as content of awareness. Not all qualifiers so appear, since everything is not cognized in its full array of properties (except by God). We have no problem analyzing an awareness of a group of things using the notion of predication content as we have explained it.

6. Śrīharṣa on Distinctness and the Relation Regress

Introduction

No further introduction of this portion of Śrīharṣa's text is needed: see above, pp. 98–100.[42]

Text (107, line 6) and Translation

> kiṃ ca, dharmasya tasya dharmiṇā samam asaṃbandhe 'tiprasaṅgaḥ, saṃbandhânantye 'navasthā, prathamato 'ntato gatvā vā sva-bhāva-saṃbandhâbhyupagame saṃbandhy-antarasya api tat-sva-bhāva-praveśâd abhede eva paryavasānaṃ syād iti ||

Moreover, if the property is unrelated to the property-bearer, there is an obvious problem; (if, on the other hand, it is related) there will be an endless number of relations and thus infinite regress. Or if at the beginning or the end the relation is admitted to be of the very nature of one of the terms (property or property-bearer), then since even the other term of the relation would enter into the very nature of that (the combined relatee-relator), nothing but non-distinctness would result.

Comments

Here Śrīharṣa identifies what we have called the attribution dilemma and the relation regress. Three options are sketched: (1) a property, such as blue, is unrelated to the property-bearer, such as a pot; (2) if there is a relation that relates them, such as inherence, then there has to be further relations to relate the inherence to each of the terms, the blue and the pot, *ad infinitum* (aRb, aR'R, aR''R', *ad infinitum*, likewise with the second term); unless, (3) it is the very nature of one of the terms to link with the other: such linkage would amount to non-distinctness. Gaṅgeśa and his followers embrace the third option: it is, at some point, the very nature of one of the terms to self-link. Of course, Naiyāyikas do not, however, embrace non-distinctness.

Text (p. 108) and Translation

evam anyasminn api dharma-vikalpe iti | tasmāt sva-rūpa-bhede pramāṇaṃ bhavat-pratyakṣam advaite eva pramāṇaṃ bhavati |

Any other view of properties is to be addressed in this way. Therefore, your "prover," *pramāṇa*, of perception, sir, which was supposed to show an essential distinctness among things, proves nothing but non-duality (*advaita*).

Comments

Thus it seems that Śrīharṣa would back into the Advaita view, that is, on the assumption that only the third option is viable. However, my interpretation is, again, that this is a taunt, that what Śrīharṣa seriously takes himself to show is the incoherence of the realist position. Thus it cannot be a challenger to the idealism taught by the Upanishads.

The context of this passage is the Logician claim that perception establishes distinctness. But since perception is thought to reveal layered facts—properties, property-bearers, and relations tying them together, with distinctness understood as a property—it seems perception establishes non-distinctness instead. Note that the argument does not depend on taking distinctness to be the property in question; any property would do.

7. Gaṅgeśa on Inherence (*samavāya*)

Introduction

As is usually his practice, Gaṅgeśa begins his treatment of inherence by outlining, and defending, a *pūrvapakṣa* (*prima facie*) position, to be answered later in text traditionally labelled *siddhānta* (concerning the "right view"). The *pūrvapakṣin* is referred to here as the "original objector" since he voices a position that Gaṅgeśa eventually answers in presenting the right view (*siddhānta*). Gaṅgeśa proceeds in this opening reflection by putting forth several (secondary) objections (not necessarily reflecting his own views) to the original objector's position. This original objector may be supposed to be a Naiyāyika developing certain plausible theses on the difficult topic of inherence.

In the immediately preceding section of the *TCM*, Gaṅgeśa explains six distinct operative relations, *sannikarṣa*, in sense perception—namely, the six that were first proposed by Uddyotakara. For the list of these, see note 70, p. 340. Note that only in the sixth case—perception of absence—does Gaṅgeśa *not* consider the operative relation to be an independent real. He has much to say about this near the end of the *siddhānta* section translated below.[43]

For the place of the *samavāya-vāda* within the entirety of the *TCM*, see note 80, pp. 359–60.[44] See note 52, p. 364, on the division of the passage into two sections, a *pūrvapakṣa* and a *siddhānta*.

Text (p. 645) and Translation

> nanu samavāyâsiddheḥ na sā pratyāsattiḥ | vipratipattiś ca śuklaḥ paṭa iti pratītiḥ viśeṣaṇa-viśeṣya-saṃbandha[45]-viṣayā na vā iti |

Original objector (in particular to the previously explained position that "inherence" is one of six "operative relations" in sense perception and in general to accepting inherence as an additional primitive): Since inherence is not established, it is not an immediate sensory relation. (Clearly it is not established, for) there is dissension whether the relation along with the qualifier (e.g., white) and what it qualifies (e.g., a piece of cloth) in the cognition, e.g., "The cloth is white," is an object or not.

Comments

If the relation is an object, then inherence should be accepted; but if it is not, inherence need not be supposed. The very debate shows that the relation is not established as objective. Śaṅkara, the Advaitin, denies it. Kumārila and his Bhāṭṭa branch of Exegesis, though embracing a realist ontology, do not grant inherence the status of a distinct primitive, but reduce it to its terms.[46] The Prābhākara wing of Exegesis sees it as independent, but not, contra Udayana, as eternal. Praśastapāda views inherence as inferred;[47] early Logicians, in contrast, take it to be perceptible. Clearly there is no consensus.

Text and Translation

> atha jāti-guṇa-kriyā-tadvantau mithaḥ saṃbaddhāv anubhūyate | na hi asaṃbaddha-sva-rūpa-dvaye viśiṣṭa-dhī-vyapadeśāv iti cet, na |

Objection (to the original objector): It is together, as relata, that these are experienced: (i) a natural kind (*jāti*) and what possesses it, (ii) a motion and what possesses it, and (iii) a quality and what possesses it. For it is not the case that if the pair did not appear as essentially related there could be relational cognition and its expression.

Answer (by the original objector): No.

Comments

An example of an awareness of a natural kind had—or exhibited—by a particular is the awareness "(A) pot," which is to be analyzed as "*a* has potness"; "*a* is moving up" illustrates an awareness of a motion and its possessor in relation, and "*a* is blue," of a quality and its possessor.

Text (p. 646) and Translation

> saṃbaddhânubhavena hi saṃbandho na viśeṣaṇam bhāsate, tasya prathamam ajñānāt, saṃyogināv imāv iti-vat samavāyināv ity ananubhavāc ca |

In the experience of (these) relata, the relation does not appear as a qualifier. There are two considerations in support of this: (i) there is no awareness of the relation in what is epistemically prior, and (ii) there is no experience of a pair as related by inherence as there is of a pair conjoined.

Comments

As noted, Praśastapāda regards inherence as inferred, while others—for example, Advaitins and the Bhāṭṭa Mīmāṃsakas—deny its separate reality altogether. Gaṅgeśa's view will be elaborated in the following *siddhānta* section. In brief, he believes that inherence is perceived when the relata it relates are perceived. The main point now in this *pūrvapakṣa* section is that it is at least not commonly admitted that a relation other than contact is known perceptually.

Text and Translation

> na api viśeṣyaḥ, anayoḥ samavāya ity ananubhavāt | na api sva-rūpeṇa bhāsate | samavāyaṃ jānāmi iti viṣayatânanubhavāt |

Moreover, inherence is not experienced as a qualificandum (i.e., as the bearer of properties, *dharmin* or *viśeṣya*), since there is no direct awareness of the form, "Inherence between the two" (with the inherence expressed linguistically in the nominative case, reflecting its status as the qualificandum-factor in the awareness and the qualificandum in nature). Nor does inherence appear just in itself (rather than implicitly through the relata appearing). There is no experience that has as its content, "I am aware of an *inherence*."

Comments

On the face of it, this surely seems right. Gaṅgeśa is not shy about the difficulties facing the traditional Naiyāyika view.

Text and Translation

> nanu nīlo ghaṭa ity-ādy-anubhavo viśeṣaṇa-viśeṣya-saṃbandha-viṣayaḥ viśiṣṭa-

pratītitvāt daṇḍi-jñāna-vad iti cet,

Objection (to the original objector): The following argument (A[1]) establishes that an awareness such as "The pot is blue" has the relation along with (the relata, namely) the qualifier and the qualificandum as objective content. The reason: it is a qualified cognition (*pratīti*), like awareness of a staff-bearer.

Comments

The analogy to an awareness of a staff-bearer is made because there the relation tying together the qualificandum (the person bearing the staff) and the qualifier (the staff) is conjunction, *saṃyoga*, which is commonly admitted to be both a real piece of furniture in the world and known perceptually.

Text and Translation

na | aghaṭaṃ bhūtalaṃ jñātam iṣṭaṃ kṛtaṃ ca ity atra vyabhicārāt |

Answer (by the original objector): No. There are awarenesses that are qualified cognitions where there is (according to accepted Nyāya theory) no relation as objective content: for example, "The floor has no pot," "Something is known," "Something is desired," and "Something has been done."

Comments

According to inherited Nyāya theory, in some instances of qualified cognition, the relation is to be analyzed away as no additional ontological reality. For example, "The floor has no pot" (i.e., "There is no pot on the floor") is to be analyzed as floor-self-linkage-absence of pot. The absence is a "self-linking" term; similarly *mutatis mutandi* with the other examples.

Thus the original objector is pointing out that there has to be a special story told to justify positing inherence as an additional real; just to point to the fact of qualified cognitions having relational structure is insufficient.

Text and Translation

saṃbandha-viṣayatve bādhakaṃ vinā iti viśeṣaṇam iti cet,

Objection (to the original objector): My argument (A[1]) needs to be modified by adding a qualification to the reason given, to wit, "without a counter-consideration ruling out the possibility of objective content." (In the case of each of your counter-examples, "The floor has no pot," etc., there is such a counter-consideration, but not with "The pot is blue" and other qualified cognitions) where the relation should be considered objective content.

Comments

The counter-consideration is not spelled out, but presumably Gaṅgeśa could refer to places in his book (for instance, the end of the section on absences[48]) where a reason is given against relational reification. However, to Gaṅgeśa this formulation apparently seems sloppy, as the original objector dismisses it almost with a sneer.

Text and Translation

> na | bādhakâbhāvasya eva samarthatve śeṣa-vaiyarthyāt sādhakâbhāvena sat-pratipakṣāc ca | bādhakâbhāvasya sādhakatva-vat sādhakâbhāvasya bādhakatvāt | tasmād ubhayâbhāve saṃśayaḥ syāt |

Answer (by the original objector): No. If the efficacy of "lack of a counter-consideration" were accepted, the rest of the argument would be pointless. (There would be no need to put forth as the reason, "it is a qualified cognition"; saying "lack of a counter-consideration" would be sufficient.) Moreover, by the same token the opposite position would be established, with the reason being "absence of a positive consideration." Lack of a counter-consideration is like having a positive consideration; lack of a positive consideration is itself a counter-consideration. Therefore, when we have neither, doubt cannot be resolved.

Comments

If there were no counter-consideration in a strong sense, then there would be a cogent consideration in favor of the conclusion, the original objector seems to say. But, so far, no *cogent* consideration has been put forth on either side. Thus doubt cannot be resolved.

Text and Translation

> na ca pratītir eva samavāya-sādhikā, tasyās tad-viṣayatvâsiddheḥ | anyathā anyonyâśrayāt |

Furthermore, the cognition (*pratīti*) by itself ("The pot is blue," for example) does not establish the objective reality of inherence. That inherence is at all objective content with it is not established. If another route (than what has already been tried and rejected, namely, inference) be ventured to establish the reality of inherence, there would be "begging the question" (*anyonyāśraya*).

Comments

In Sanskrit, there is no predicative copula with the expression translated, "The pot is blue"; that no term designating inherence occurs in the linguistic usage expressing the cognition seems to motivate the original objector's position.

The commentator Rucidatta Miśra suggests an interpretation of how there would be "begging the question," assuming that we take the "other route" to inherence to be inference. Let the reason for inferring the reality of inherence be: "Cognitions, such as 'The pot is blue,' are relational cognitions." But with this premise, we presuppose that relations such as inherence are real; otherwise we not would presume that they are *relational* cognitions, at least not in the "thick" sense (i.e., as not simply reflecting the self-linkage of self-linking terms)—from which it would follow that there must be relations, such as inherence, that are real.

Text (p. 647) and Translation

atha aghaṭaṃ bhūtalaṃ jñātam ity-ādy api viśiṣṭa-dhīḥ saṃbandha-viṣayā, kiṃ tu bhrāntā, bādhaka-sattvād iti cet,

Objection (to the original objector): Then let us say that qualified cognitions, such as "The floor has no pot," are cognitions with the relation as objective content. But (the difference—between these where the relation is self-linkage and those with inherence as the relator, in the cognized objective complex, aRb—is that here but not there) error occurs, since there are counter-considerations ruling out the veridical reality of the relation.

Comments

The original objector's response to the argument A^1 that relational awarenesses establish the reality of inherence was that there are relational awarenesses without an ontologically distinct relation over and above the relata. Here his opponent—the proponent of A^1—is arguing that that response does not cut the ice, since the counterexamples can be ruled out as errors.

Text and Translation

tarhi bhūtale 'ghaṭatvasya jñātatvâdeś ca abhāvaḥ syāt | tathā ca vyavahāra-vilopaḥ | saṃbandhaś ca na saṃyogaḥ samavāyo vā anyataro vā bādhād asiddher vā | na api saṃbandha-mātram, jñāpakatvâdinā siddha-sādhanāt |

Answer (by the original objector): Then (since the awarenesses would be non-veridical) there would be no fact of the floor's not having a pot on it (even when there is), and nothing known, etc. (the other examples of self-linkage). And thus theory would break with linguistic practice.

The relation (with any of these types of awareness) is not conjunction (or contact, *saṃyoga*), nor is it inherence, nor is it conjunction in some cases while in others it is inherence. Counter-considerations rule out the possibility of conjunction, while inherence is not established as a possibility. Nor should it be held that we have here "relation in general" (*saṃbandha-mātra*), for if this amounts to a making known (*jñāpakatva*), etc., you would commit the fallacy of establishing what is already established.

Comments

All awarenesses presuppose some kind of relation between the qualifier and the qualificandum but not necessarily a distinct relation; for example, the qualifier invariably makes the qualificandum known. With the awareness, "(A) pot," the qualifier "potness" makes the particular pot known. So if this is all the proponent of the reality of inherence is claiming, then he would commit the fallacy of trying to prove what is already granted.

Text and Translation

na apy aviśiṣṭa-vyāvṛtta-viśiṣṭa-jñāna-niyāmakaḥ | abhāva-jñānâdāv iva sva-rūpa-saṃbandhena arthântaratvāt | na ca saṃbandhi-bhinnatvaṃ sādhye viśeṣaṇam | abhāva-jñānâdinā vyabhicārāt | bādhakâbhāvasya ca viśeṣaṇatvaṃ hetau nirastam eva | vinā api bhinna-saṃbandham abhāva-jñānâdāv iva viśiṣṭa-dhī-saṃbhavena aprayojakatvāc ca |

Nor should it be held that inherence is a relation that secures relational awareness as invariably distinct from non-relational awareness. Concerning awareness of an absence, etc., there would be the fallacy of the argument establishing just what you do not want (namely, self-linkage), because in these cases the relation is that of a self-linking term.

Nor should you add the qualification concerning what you want to prove, the qualification, namely, that the relation be distinct from the relata. (Again) the examples of awareness of an absence, etc., would be counterexamples.

Any attempt to patch up the reason in the argument that would add the qualification "without counter-considerations" has already been rejected. Also, the argument in this case would suffer from the fallacy of *aprayojakatva*, a "misleading reason," since indeed concerning awareness of an absence, etc., there is the possibility of relational cognition even without a distinct relation.

Comments

The *aprayojaka* fallacy is defined as the occurrence of the *hetu* term—the "reason" or "prover"—somewhere that the *sādhya* term—"that which is to be proved"—does not appear.

Text and Translation

viśeṣaṇatā-viśeṣa-rūpaḥ prakārâdi-kṛto vā viśeṣaḥ saṃbandhâviṣayatve 'pi tulyaḥ |

Or let us say you try to differentiate (between relational awarenesses with self-linkage and those without) by proposing either that the distinction takes the form of a distinct qualifierness or that it is secured by the predication content, etc. Then, note that the same distinction would hold on the view that relations are not objective content.

Comments

The predication content "blue," for example, is distinct from that of "absence of a pot." But the issue of precisely how these are distinct is independent of the question of the reality of the relation cognized by a relational cognition, the original objector avers.

Text and Translation

> syād etat |avaya-guṇa-kriyā-jāti-tadvatāṃ iha tantuṣu paṭaḥ,[49] iha paṭe śauklyaṃ, iha calanaṃ paṭatvaṃ ca iti iha-pratyayaḥ ādhārâdheya-saṃbandha-nimittakaḥ yathârthêha-pratyayatvād iha kuṇḍe badaram iti pratyaya-vad iti cet,

Objection (to the original objector): That may be. But there is the following argument that establishes the reality of inherence. The cognition of "being here" that applies to the relation of the whole to its parts, a quality to what has it, a motion to what exhibits it, and a universal or natural kind to its instances—for example, "the cloth is here in the threads," "the color white is here in the cloth," "the movement is here (in this thing)," and "clothness (is here in this cloth)"—secures (as ontologically distinct) the relation as that between the containing and the contained (*ādhāra-ādheya*). The reason: it is both a cognition that matches reality and a cognition of "being here." The confirming example: it is like the cognition (that establishes the reality of the relation, contact), "The jujube fruit is in the bowl."

Comments

Praśastapāda presents this argument.[50]

Text and Translation

> na |iha bhūtale ghaṭâbhāvo jñānaṃ ca ity-ādau vyabhicārāt, bādhakaṃ vinā ity asya nirastatvāt, tathā eva ādhārâdheya-bhāvād eva upapatteś ca |utpattaye sthitaye jñaptaye ca apekṣaṇīyasya ādhāratvāt |

Answer (by the original objector): No. There are clear counterexamples to your reason, namely, the cognition, e.g., "*Here* on the floor there is an absence of a pot." And again, do not try the patchwork qualification, "without counter-considerations," for that move has already been ruled out. In sum, your argument is no good because the relations you cite are possible without a "containing/contained" relation that is ontologically something over and above the relata. All we need say about "containing" in the case of production (as a cloth from threads), of maintenance (as a cloth in the threads that make it up after it has been produced), and in making known (as a pot causing an awareness of itself) is that there is a necessary dependence (a self-linking relation): that's what it is to "contain" (in this sense).

Comments

The original objector relies on the assumption, presumed acceptable to all parties, that in the case of an awareness of an absence the relation in the complex a-R-b is not distinct. The factor -R-b—namely, the absence—is taken to be self-linking. The argument is that the factor, -(necessary-dependence)-contained, need not be supposed to be otherwise.

Text (p. 649, line 10) and Translation

> anye tu, śabda-jāti-rūpâdir indriya-saṃbaddhaḥ pratyakṣatvād ghaṭa-vad ity-anumānāt saṃyoga-bādhe indriya-saṃbandha-ghaṭakatayā samavāya-siddhiḥ, indriyasya saṃbaddha-grāhakatvāt | ata eva samavāyo na pratyakṣaḥ indriyeṇa asaṃbandhāt | na ca saṃbandhatvena tat-siddhiḥ | anavasthānāt, sva-bhāvād eva jñāna-vat sva-saṃbaddha-vyavahāra-kāritvāc ca | samavāyo hi saṃbandhaṃ vinā eva sva-bhāvād eva kasyacit |

(Objection to the original objector:) Some others offer the following inference in favor of positing inherence. There is a relation to a sense organ in the case of an awareness of sound, of a universal, of color, etc., because they are perceived, like a pot. According to this reasoning, it is supposed that when contact is not the element (*ghaṭaka*) accomplishing the relation to the sense organ, inherence is established (by inference).

The sense organ grasps what is related to it. Thus, inherence is not directly perceptible because (as the relation or relator) it is not what is *in* relation to the sense organ.

Further, it is not just as a relation that it is established. (If inherence were inferred as doing nothing but bringing two terms together) there would be an infinite regress. Like an awareness (and its intentionality, *viṣayitva*), inherence must be self-linking, not only because of the threat otherwise of an infinite regress, but because it grounds linguistic practices that reflect self-linkage (*sva-saṃbaddha-vyavahāra-kāritva*). In order that inherence indeed be without a further relation, it has to link itself by its own nature to something.

Comments

Here Gaṅgeśa expresses the "Bradley problem" insisted upon by Śaṅkara and Śrīharṣa. An infinite regress of relations can be avoided only by supposing self-linkage at some step. Simply to suppose inherence to be the relator would not avoid the problem, since there would have to be inferred another relation to relate inherence itself to each of the terms, another relation to relate that new relation, *ad infinitum*. In other words, the Advaita argument narrows the problem space for Gaṅgeśa's consideration of relations. Self-linkage is the only viable option. The key question is then why inherence should be admitted at all, since, as the objector says, it seems unnecessary to explain the ontological underpinnings of some qualificative cognitions and it itself has to be viewed as self-linking with its terms. Considerations of ontological parsimony would appear to demand that it be pruned away.

Indeed, here in this *pūrvapakṣa* section, the advocate of inherence (the objector to the original objector) seems to present every traditional reason for the posit. Gaṅgeśa is setting himself a difficult task by having the original objector rebut all these arguments.

Text and Translation

> na ca jāty-āder api sva-bhāvād eva sva-saṃbaddha-vyavahāra-kāritve samavāya-vilopaḥ | jāty-ādeḥ indriyâsaṃbandhe samavāya-vad apratyakṣatvâpātād iti |

(The objector to the original objector continues:) The same reasoning does not hold with respect to natural kind characters (*jāti*, universals) and so on, such that they themselves would be what ground the linguistic practices of self-linkage (when they are involved) without a role for inherence. If natural kind characters and so on did not stand (as non-self-linking terms) in relation to a sense organ, then like inherence they would be imperceptible—an implication that is contrary to fact.

Comments

It is supposed that we can perceive universals when their instances are perceptible, e.g., cowhood in a cow.

Text (p. 650, line 6) and Translation

> tan na | samavāya-svīkāre 'pi sva-rūpa-saṃbandhasya āvaśyakatvāt | ghaṭa-jñānayoḥ bhūtalâbhāvayor iva vā dravyeṇa guṇa-jāty-ādibhiḥ sva-rūpam eva saṃbandho 'stu | tathā ca śabdasya indriya-viśeṣaṇatayā, śabdatvasya viśeṣaṇa-viśeṣaṇatayā, rūpâdi-jāty-āder indriya-saṃbaddha-viśeṣaṇatayā, rūpatvâder indriya-saṃbaddha-viśeṣaṇa-viśeṣaṇatayā sva-bhāva-saṃbandha-rūpayā grahaṇa-saṃbhave kiṃ samavāyena |

Original objector: But this is the wrong approach. Even were we to accept inherence as a real, the notion of self-linkage would have to be used. (So why bother postulating inherence?) So let us say that a substance (*dravya*) is related to a quality (*guṇa*) or to a natural-kind universal (*jāti*) and so on by, in each case, the latter's own nature as a self-linking term (*svarūpam eva saṃbandha = svarūpa-saṃbandha*), like (the clear examples of) the relation between a cognition of a pot and the pot or between the ground and an absence (when there is no pot there). And so sound (which is a quality) would be related to the auditory sense organ by the (self-linking) relation "qualifierness" (or "being a qualifier"). (Other examples of self-linking relations in the processes of perception by means of the sense organs include) the universal "sound-hood" (being related to the sense organ) by the relation of a "second-order qualifierness" (another self-linking relation); color, etc., and (some) universals, etc., by the relation of "qualifying what is related to the sense organ"; abstracts or the natural kinds of color, etc., by the relation of a "second-order qualifying of what is related to the sense organ." Since perceptual cognition (*grahana*) is possible (i.e., can be explained) in each of these cases taking the relation to be self-linking, what's the point of positing inherence?

Comments

Again, ontologically speaking, the proposal is not self-linkage of a relation but of a term. To talk of self-linking relations is to focus on the coupling aspect of the self-linking term, to abstract the hook, so to say. And in specifying that the relation is self-linking, one does not reify the abstraction. In each of these cases, the linkage would occur through the second term's being simply a qualifier. Thus a variety of the self-linking relation "qualifierness," not inherence, would be the relation in each case.

Now it is supposed on both sides that there has to be a relation of some sort (though not necessarily a relation that is a distinct real) between each sense medium and the object perceived, since we do perceive things. Thus we try to explain what the natures of the various "operative relations" are, concerning the various types of things perceived. The view that is rejected by the original objector is that inherence must be ontologically distinct in order for sound to be perceptible, and so on. This original objector, who, I repeat, has the voice of a Nyāya sympathizer exploring the ontological inheritance, proposes a replacement for each of the operative relations that, according to Gaṅgeśa, as we will see, involve inherence in some way. (Again see note 70, p. 340, concerning the six types proposed by Uddyotakara and endorsed by Gaṅgeśa in the immediately preceding section of the *TCM*; recall in particular that, according to the Nyāya theory, the visual organ travels like a ray out of the eye and comes into contact with substances having color and shape.) For example, the operative relation in the perception of color would be a *qualifying* of what is related to the sense organ by contact, i.e., there would be contact between (a) the substance perceived and *qualified* by color and (b) the sense organ. Thus these operative relations—and not that of an *inhering* in what is related to the sense organ by contact, etc.—would perform the required theoretical role, and we would, it seems suggested, maintain an ontological economy (hence the statement, "what's the point of positing inherence").

In the *siddhānta* section just a few pages below, Gaṅgeśa refutes each of these counter-proposals.

Text and Translation

> dravye sva-bhāva-saṃbandhād na indriyeṇa grahaṇam iti kathaṃ guṇâdes tena graha iti cet, samavāyena api na dravya-grahaṇam iti tulyam |

Objection (to the original objector): on this view, since the operative perceptual relation would be self-linking, perception (even) in the case of a substance would not be mediated by (a particular relation with) a sense organ, and so how could qualities etc. be grasped by one?

Answer (by the original objector): even in postulating inherence there would be equally the problem that perception of a substance (as distinct from perception of other sorts of things) would not occur by means of inherence (but rather by a different relation, contact).

Comments

The self-linkage view would seem to be insensitive to the distinct ways objects are known. If the relation between an individual substance and all its properties is self-linking, the various ways the sense organs operate with respect to distinct objects, substances, colors, sounds, etc., would be irrelevant. The original objector responds that even accepting inherence, the problem remains how to explain, in the case of perception of a substance, that the relation is distinct.

Text (p. 650, line 13) and Translation

> apare tu, ekatra ghaṭe āma-pāka-daśāyāṃ krameṇa śyāma-rakta-rūpôpalambho 'sti | sa ca na tad-ubhaya-nibandhanaḥ, rūpasya nityatvena ekadā upalambhâpatteḥ | nityatvād eva ca na tayor utpāda-vināśau | tasmāt tayoḥ saṃbandhasya tau syātām, sa eva samavāya iti |

(Objection to the original objector:) But others argue: in one and the same pot, which has the color of raw earth at the time of its baking, we experience a gradual change from black to red. And this experience (according to your view) could not be based on its *being* both colors, since a color is an unchanging entity (with the relation between the substance and its color as self-linking and the color as a self-linking term). Thus your view is faced with the difficulty that an experience of color at one time would forever fix that quality. And because of the unchangingness, there could be no arising nor destruction of either of the two colors. Therefore, in order that there be such a possibility, the arising and destruction must be *of a relation* with the two. That relation is inherence.

Comments

Rucidatta identifies the argument as belonging to Prabhākara (who is commonly referred to, as here, as *guru*). Color and all class characters (*jāti*) are eternal, according to this view. With change or the appearance or destruction of a particular instantiating one of these eternal things, a new relation appears or disappears.[51]

Text (p. 651) and Translation

> tan na |śyāmaṃ naṣṭam, raktam utpannam, ity-ādy-abādhitânubhavāt samavāyasya utpāda-vināśânullekhāc ca |tvan-mate tasya atīndriyatvāt |anyathā avayavi-jñāna-gandha-rasâder api nityatvaṃ samavāyasya utpāda-vināśāv iti kiṃ na rocayet |na hy utpāda-vināśa-pratītir aprāmāṇikībādhakaṃ vinā iti ||

(Answer by the original objector:) This also is wrong. "The black is destroyed; the red is produced," such is an uncontroverted experience. But here (to express the predication content) there need be no mention of either an arising or destruction of inherence. On your view, inherence would have to be imperceptible. So on other matters as well—with a whole having parts, cognition, smell, taste, etc.—why shouldn't a view of unchangingness find favor with you, with the arising and destruction confined to the inherence? For it is no option to hold that an appearance of arising or destruction is not veridical, unless you can put forth definite counter-considerations.

Comments

The rebuttal Gaṅgeśa puts in the mouth of his *pūrvapakṣin* (the original objector) is forceful and clear. Our experience is not of the destruction of *inherence* but rather of *colors*. Thus an imperceptible inherence would have to arise and disappear. Similarly with other types of change. To claim that all these are illusory is no option, unless you have an independent argument. An assumption of veridicality is the cognitive default.

Text (p. 651, line 5) and Translation

ucyate[52] | guṇa-kriyā-jāti-viśiṣṭa-buddhayo viśeṣaṇa-saṃbandha-viṣayāḥ viśiṣṭa-buddhitvāt, daṇḍī iti buddhi-vat |

Gaṅgeśa: We answer. Relational awarenesses of qualities, motions, and universals (*jāti*) have both the qualifier and the relation as objective content. The reason: they are relational awarenesses. The confirming example: the awareness, "The staff-bearer."

Comments

A staff-bearer is a person holding a staff. The person and the staff are in conjunction or contact, *saṃyoga*. According to the Nyāya-Vaiśeṣika Gaṅgeśa inherits, contact is a quality that inheres in two substances simultaneously, here the person and the staff. Like other qualities that inhere in perceptible things, it itself is perceptible; it is perceived riding piggy-back on the substances in which it inheres. Thus the objective complex, person-contact-staff, gives rise to the perceptual awareness, "Staff-bearer," where the person is the qualificandum, the staff is the qualifier, and contact the relation between them. In this relational cognition, the relation is patently objective content. Gaṅgeśa's argument is that awarenesses of qualities, motions, and universals or natural kinds are pertinently the same type of awareness, and that, like contact in the confirming example, inherence is an objective real (though of course not a quality).

Text (p. 653) and Translation

na ca vyabhicāraḥ | abhāvâdi-viśiṣṭa-buddher api sva-rūpa-saṃbandha-viṣayatvāt |

The reason in this argument does not admit of counterexamples (unlike the arguments put forth previously). Relational awarenesses of absences and so on also have the relation as objective content, the relation, namely, of self-linkage.

Comments

Gaṅgeśa's point is that the self-linking aspect of a self-linking term is objective. He is not saying that the self-linkage is an *independent* real. The argument so far is thus only a first step; a second follows. Here he establishes that relational awarenesses have the relation as objective content. This shows that as the fundamental tie in relational cognitions, both inherence and self-linking terms are realities in the world.[53] Although self-linkage is not an independent real, self-linking things are reals, and self-linkage, as an abstraction based in their nature, shares in their reality, so to say. Now Gaṅgeśa is ready for a second step, to distinguish inherence from self-linkage.

Text and Translation

> na ca evam atra api tena eva arthântaram, yato guṇa-kriyā-jāti-viśiṣṭa-buddhīnāṃ pakṣa-dharmatā-balena viṣayaḥ saṃbandhaḥ sidhyan lāghavād eka eva sidhyati |sa eva samavāyaḥ, na tu sva-rūpa-saṃbandhaḥ, tat-tat-sva-rūpāṇām anantatvāt saṃbandhatvena akḷptatvāc ca

And do not object that in this way we would be reasoning to counter purposes, establishing just what we do not want (committing the fallacy of *arthāntara*). In our argument, the reason (namely, being a relational awareness) is found in all those things to which the first term of the argument (i.e., the *pakṣa* or subject term) refers, namely, relational awarenesses of qualities, of motions, and of natural kinds. The argument establishes an objective relation. Then that the relation is single, uniform, is established on the basis of parsimony. So the relation is indeed inherence, not self-linkage. The self-linkage of self-linking terms is infinitely varied according to the particular natures of the infinitely many things that are related by self-linkage. Furthermore, self-linkage as a relation is not a (separate) existing thing.

Comments

Gaṅgeśa's response centers on the economy of the inherence posit. Parsimony is what secures inherence over self-linkage—an irony in that inherence is the additional primitive.

Let us consider Gaṅgeśa's claim that the reason in the argument is *pakṣa-dharmatā*, "found in all those things to which the first term of the argument refers." According to standard Nyāya theory, all cogent arguments hinge, first of all, on an invariable occurrence of the term to be proved, *sādhya*, wherever the reason, *hetu*, occurs; that is to say, they hinge on *vyāpti*, as in "Wherever smoke, there fire." But they also hinge on the co-occurrence of the reason with the first term of the argument. That is to say, the reason, the smoke in the stock example, must occur on, or above, the mountain, the subject or *pakṣa* term of the stock argument whose conclusion is "There is fire on the mountain." Gaṅgeśa is claiming that his argument meets this requirement in that awarenesses of qualities, motions, and universals or natural kinds are indeed relational awarenesses.

Since Gaṅgeśa admits that the self-linkage of self-linking terms also falls within the domain of the argument which constitutes step one of his two-step strategy to establish inherence, there is also no fallacy of "deviation," i.e., the reason admitting of counterexamples. This is how he undercuts the main line of objection expressed earlier. Self-linkage is objective but is not a distinct real, according to Gaṅgeśa. To secure inherence as truly a distinct real, there is now further argument, namely, parsimony (*lāghava*) as step two. The relation in the case of awarenesses of qualities, etc., must be regarded as inherence because that is the economical view, in that self-linkage varies according to the infinitely many things that are so related. Self-linkage is as particular as all the instances of qualification in which it is the relation linking a qualifier with a qualificandum.

Text (p. 654) and Translation

athavā viśeṣaṇa-saṃbandha-nimittikā iti sādhyam |

Or, there is another argument. That which is to be proved is the having of a relation with a qualifier as a cause (which is predicated of relational awarenesses of qualities, etc.: that is to say, relational awarenesses of qualities, etc., have a relation with a qualifier as a cause).

Comments

Relational awarenesses are thought to have the relation in the objective complex as a causal factor in their arising.

Text and Translation

hetau tu satyatvaṃ viśeṣaṇam | viśeṣaṇa-saṃbandhaś ca kāraṇatvena eka eva sidhyati | lāghavād anugata-kāryasya anugata-kāraṇa-niyamyatvāc ca | na tu svarūpa-saṃbandhaḥ, teṣām ananugatatvād anantatvāc ca |

Concerning the reason in this (second) argument, the following qualification has to be made: (relational awarenesses of qualities, etc., have a relation with a qualifier as a cause, insofar as) they are (not just relational awarenesses but) *veridical* relational awarenesses. Moreover, the relation with a qualifier is proved to be—as a cause—single or uniform, on the basis of parsimony and the rule to be maintained, "Effects of the same type, causes of the same type." These requirements exclude self-linkage, because self-linking terms are not identical through multiple instances but are infinitely various.

Comments

The relation with a qualifier perceived in non-relational awareness stands as a cause of the relationality of relational awareness, that is, Gaṅgeśa hurriedly points out, in the case of veridical awarenesses, not with the non-veridical. Non-veridical awarenesses involve misperceiving the qualifier and relational tie vis-à-vis a qualificandum. But with veridical awarenesses, the relation—which is grasped in non-relational awareness (though not *as* doing its relational job, i.e., it is grasped merely as an independent factor)—stands as a causal factor for relational awareness. There is then a second step as with the previous argument, namely, parsimony and the causal rule, "Like effects, like causes." Self-linkage is excluded on both grounds in that self-linkage is infinitely various.

Text and Translation

> na ca ubhayam apy aprayojakam | viśiṣṭa-sākṣātkārasya sambandhâviṣayatve tad-ajanyatve vā gavâśvâdāv api viśiṣṭa-buddhi-prasaṅgāt |

Furthermore, with neither of these two arguments is the fallacy "misleading reason" committed (*aprayojaka*, the fallacy defined as the occurrence of the *hetu* term—"smoke"—somewhere that the *sādhya* term—"fire"—does not appear). If relational experience were to occur either without having the relation as objective content or without having been caused (in part) through the relation with the qualifier, then it would be possible to be aware of a cow as a horse and other absurdities.

Comments

Gaṅgeśa supplements the arguments on the table with a bit of counterfactual reasoning. He says that if relational experience were to occur without having been caused (in part) by the relation with the qualifier, then it would be possible to be aware of a cow as a horse and other absurdities. In other words, the relation with the qualificandum (e.g., Bessie) must be so tight that it causes its reflection in awareness; otherwise we might see her as a horse.

However, I must say that, considered independently of the nature of the relata, the inherence tie would seem to be in principle no tighter than the original objector's self-linkage. Thus Gaṅgeśa's counterfactual reasoning does not help to secure the self-linkage distinction. Nor, indeed, does he claim that it does. The point is, rather, that, again, the relation in the objective complex has to be real. Parsimony, then, supplemented by the economical principle concerning causality, appears to be the mainstay of Gaṅgeśa's defense of inherence over self-linkage.

Text (p. 660) and Translation

> navyās tu, guṇa-kriyā-jāti-viśiṣṭa-buddhiḥ sambandi-bhinna-viśeṣaṇa-sambandha-viṣayā nirviṣayaka-bhāva-viśeṣaṇaka-viśiṣṭa-buddhitvāt |

There are, however, Navya Nyāya philosophers who reason differently. (With respect to our first argument establishing inherence, they add qualifications:) relational awarenesses of qualities, of motions, and of natural kinds have the relation with the qualifier as objective content *insofar as* the relation is to be considered distinct from the relata (thus excluding self-linkage). The reason: because they are relational awarenesses with a qualifier (i) that is a presence (not an absence) and (ii) that itself does not have content.

Comments

The cases excluded in the reason are awarenesses of absences and awarenesses of awarenesses. An absence is not a "presence." It also is invariably *of* something, e.g., of a pot; thus, awarenesses of absences are excluded on both counts.

An awareness is the content of awareness in apperception, *anuvyavasāya*. Every awareness is intentional, i.e., has content, sometimes a previous awareness that itself has content. Awareness is a presence and an existent in that it is a quality (*guṇa*) of the soul. Thus apperception is excluded only on the second count.

Relational awarenesses that are apperceptions, along with awarenesses of absences, need to be excluded from the extension of the *hetu* term of the argument—that is, from the extension of the "reason"—because self-linking terms are excluded from the *sādhya*, "that which is to be proved." An absence self-links with what it qualifies, and an apperception scopes a prior cognition whose content qualifies it by self-linkage.

The commentators Rucidatta and Mathurānātha do not say to whom Gaṅgeśa is referring as *navya*. Rāmakṛṣṇādhvarin, in his subcommentary on Rucidatta's commentary, says that it is Jayadeva. However, no Jayadeva is known prior to or contemporary with Gaṅgeśa. Thus this may be an opinion expressed by Maṇikaṇṭha in a lost work—or by another contemporary of Gaṅgeśa's.

Text (p. 663) and Translation

itara-nirūpaṇânirūpya-viśeṣaṇaka-viśiṣṭa- buddhitvād vā | ato 'bhāvâdi-viśiṣṭa-buddhau na vyabhicāraḥ |

Or (the reason may be formulated still differently:) because they are relational awarenesses not having a qualifier that is determined by another's determining. Thus, there is no deviation with regard to relational cognitions of absences, et cetera.

Comments

As explained in chapter 4, an absence of *x* has *x* as its *pratiyogin*, counterpositive or absentee. The *pratiyogin* is said to determine the absence as a qualifier. With an awareness of a lack of a pot on the floor, the absence is the qualifier and it is determined by the pot, i.e., what the absence is *of*. Thus, since an absence is determined by the absentee, awareness of absence is excluded.

Further, according to Nyāya, awareness has no intrinsic shape or content of its own; it is *nirākāra*, "formless." It is only the object, *viṣaya*, that shapes awareness and provides content and form, on the Nyāya view. So here *nirūpaṇa*, "determining," is also used to exclude apperception, which cognizes a previous awareness determined by its content. In other words, the qualifier factor of an apperception is the content of the scoped awareness as qualifying the scoped awareness. Thus an apperception's qualifier is determined by a determining, and apperception is thus excluded from what counts as the *hetu*, the proving "reason" in the argument.

Text and Translation

> na ca aprayojakam, nirupādhi-saṃbandha-śālitvāt | saṃbandhaś ca aviśiṣṭa-vyāvṛtta-viśiṣṭa-dhī-niyāmakaḥ |

Moreover, the fault of "misleading reason" (*aprayojaka*) cannot be alleged, because this is an inference that admits no exceptions in the relating of the two (that is to say, there is concomitance, *vyāpti*). And the relation unfailingly secures a distinction between relational and non-relational awarenesses.

Comments

All relational awareness presupposes a relation as objective content. But in non-relational, indeterminate awareness, no relation is cognized as doing relational work.

It is difficult to wrap one's mind all the way around the argument that Gaṅgeśa attributes to Navyas who find, apparently, the mark of self-linkage to be a qualifier's "being determined by another's determining." The position seems to be that only qualifiers that are subjective—(1) an awareness's content as qualifying an awareness (as known in apperception) and (2) an absentee's absence as qualifying a locus—are self-linking. Memory provides the absentee of an absence, while a scoped awareness's content, viewed as qualifying the scoped awareness by a scoping apperception, is provided by the scoped awareness. Such qualifiers are indeed viewed throughout Navya Nyāya as self-linking. (Awareness has to be able to roam freely, so to say, has to be capable of an infinite variability.) The problem is that this leaves out (at the least) the self-linkage of inherence to its terms. Inherence has to be self-linking. (There are also hints that Gaṅgeśa regards qualifiers such as "known," "desired," and "made," as self-linking as well. Many later Navyas see temporal and spatial relations as self-linking, among other relational items.[54])

Text (p. 664) and Translation

> yad vā indriya-pratyāsattitvena samavāya-siddhiḥ | tathā hi guṇa-kriyā-jāti-sākṣātkāraḥ indriya-saṃbandha-sādhyaḥ janya-pratyakṣatvāt daṇḍi-jñāna-vad ity ataḥ sākṣāt-saṃbandha-bādha-kāraṇatvena indriya-saṃyukte saṃbandhaḥ sidhyan pakṣa-dharmatā-balāl lāghavena anugataḥ samavāya eka eva sidhyati, anugata-kāryasya anugata-kāraṇa-janyatvāt |

Or, there is another argument. Inherence is established because it is a variety of the operative relation of connection with the sense organ. That is to say, any awareness (*sākṣātkāra*) of a quality, motion, or natural kind is brought about by a relation with the sense organ, because such awareness is generated perception, like cognition of a staff-bearer. According to this argument, a relation other than direct contact (*sākṣāt-saṃbandha* = *saṃyoga*, between a substance and a sense organ) that is operative through the contact is established since we are talking about (*pakṣa-dharmatā*) awarenesses of qualities, motions, and natural kinds (none of which is ever in direct contact with a sense organ). Then that this relation is continuous (*anugata*), single (and thus) inherence is established on the basis of parsimony. Again, we have the rule that effects of the same type are to be considered as produced by causes of the same type.

Comments

This fourth formally formulated argument, which is given by far the greatest elaboration, focuses on sensory presentation: inherence is "an operative relation in sensory awareness." Following Uddyotakara and others, Gaṅgeśa endorses six different relations operative in sense experience, four of which involve inherence; thus inherence would be directly or indirectly responsible for certain sense perceptions—not of substances, but of qualities, etc. Contact is a relation restricted to substances; the sense organs do not come into contact with qualities, motions, or universals. The weight of the pot is known *through* the tactile contact with the pot as a substance. The sense organ is in contact with the pot, and the weight is known by its inherence in the pot.

A problem would then seem to be just as Gaṅgeśa's own objector has stated: in some cases of operative relation, self-linkage is the relator. Thus, it is parsimony and the economy governing causal suppositions that here, as before, demands inherence rather than self-linkage. Gaṅgeśa elaborates the point in subsequent text.

The qualification "generated" excludes God's awareness from counting as an instance of the *hetu* in the argument. God's awareness is not generated.

Text and Translation

na tu saṃyukta-viśeṣaṇatā-rūpa-sva-rūpa-saṃbandhaḥ, tasya ca tat-tad-rūpâdi-rūpatvena ananugatatvāt |

The relation cannot be (as postulated by the original objector earlier, the *pūrvapakṣin*) the self-linking relation "qualifying that which stands in a relation of contact" (*saṃyukta-viśeṣaṇatā*), because that relation (as an example of self-linkage) takes this, that, and the other form; it is not continuous or uniform.

Comments

Again, each instance of self-linkage is particular to the particulars self-linked.

Text (p. 665, line 3) and Translation

evaṃ rūpatva-rasatva-sākṣātkāre 'pi kāraṇatvena indriya-saṃbandhaḥ samavāya eva anugataḥ sidhyati lāghavāt | na tu indriya-saṃbaddha-viśeṣaṇa-viśeṣaṇatā[55], tasyā rūpatvâdi-svarūpatvena ananugatatvāt |

In this way, in the case of awareness of colorness (a universal of a quality), or tastehood as well, the (operative) relation to the sense organ is just inherence, because it stands as a cause.

Inherence, which is uniform and continuous (*anugata*), is established on the basis of parsimony. The relation is not (as the *pūrvapakṣin* proposed earlier, that of) "qualifying a qualifier of what is in relation with a sense organ." This would be to link colorness etc. by a self-linking relation, which, as such, would not be uniform and continuous.

Comments

The argument is that although viewing inherence as an additional real means including it on the list of ontological primitives, better that for maintaining an economy with the relationality of universals and so on than there to admit the infinitely various relations of self-linkage. Analogously, to accept cowhood as a universal commits one to an additional real over and above all cows. But this is the parsimonious position—literally "lighter" (*lāghava*)—in the sense of "more orderly," in that the unity of the kind reduces complexity. Indeed, the same term, *anugata*, "continuous, uniform," is used here by Gaṅgeśa with respect to inherence—differentiating it from self-linking relations—as is used to express the epistemic reason for admitting universals.

Text and Translation

ata eva saṃyogo viśeṣaṇatā ca pratyāsattir astu, na tu samavāyâdi-catuṣṭayam iti nirastam |tasyās tat-tat-svarūpatvena ananugatatvāt |

Hence let us accept that contact and "qualifierness" are types of operative relation in sense awareness. But this move does not exclude the view that there are four others that in one way or another involve inherence. (If we followed the *pūrvapakṣin* in his proposal of four alternative relations—all variations on "qualifierness" and all self-linking—then) the operative relation in each of these cases would be, as self-linking, not uniform and continuous.

Comments

Therefore, what would follow from the *pūrvapakṣin*'s position would not be the parsimonious position.

Recall once more the six types of operative relation in sense perception: (1) contact (for example, in perception of a pot as a substance); (2) inherence-in-the-conjoined (for example, in perception of blue which inheres in a pot in conjunction with the sense organ); (3) inherence-in-the-inherent-in-the-conjoined (for example, in perception of blueness); (4) inherence (in the case of sound); (5) inherence-in-the-inherent (in perception of soundness); and (6) qualifierhood (in perception of an absence). Gaṅgeśa does accept that absences self-link with the loci they qualify and thus that the operative relation in this one type of case is the self-linking "qualifierhood." His objections to viewing this last relation as a single, uniform "relationality" are explained a few sentences below.

Text and Translation

pratyāsattitvena abhyupagate ca samavāye pratyakṣatā saṃbandhi-dvaya-pratyakṣatvāt |

Further, since inherence is to be accepted as sometimes itself the operative sensory relation (that is, when we have a case of sound or soundness), inherence must be perceptible in certain cases, namely, in those cases where both relata are perceptible.

Comments

Thus Gaṅgeśa lines himself up with the early Naiyāyika position as opposed to the Vaiśeṣika: see above, p. 49. Gaṅgeśa takes a similar stance with respect to universals or natural kinds: they are perceptible when their instances are perceptible.

Text (p. 666) and Translation

nanv evam abhāva-viśiṣṭa-pratyakṣe 'pi viśiṣṭa-buddhitvāt saṃyoga-samavāya-bādhe 'nugataṃ vaiśiṣṭyaṃ sambandho viṣayaḥ nimittaṃ ca bhaved iti cet,

Objection: In this way, with regard to a relational perception that is of an absence, the relation called relationality, *vaiśiṣṭya*, would be established for the (same) reason that it is a qualified cognition. Contact and inherence can in this case be ruled out. Thus we would have left this "relationality." It is uniform and continuous. It is objective, and it is a cause (of perceptions of absences).

Comments

By the same reasoning that Gaṅgeśa would establish inherence, an objector now urges that another relation, namely, the relationality obtaining between absences and their loci, should be viewed as a separate real.

Text and Translation

na | tasya hi samavāya-vad ekatve ghaṭâbhāvavati paṭavati paṭâbhāva-dhī-prasaṅgaḥ | ghaṭâbhāva-vaiśiṣṭyam eva hi paṭâbhāva-vaiśiṣṭyam | paṭâbhāva-vaiśiṣṭya-sattve 'pi paṭâbhāvo na asti tataḥ tasya bhinnatvād iti cet, na | paṭâbhāvâbhāvasya abhāvatve so 'pi vaiśiṣṭyena sambandhena tatra asti, vaiśiṣṭyasya ekatvāt | paṭâbhāvâbhāvasya bhāvatve ca paṭa eva pratibandhako vācyaḥ | evaṃ paṭâbhāvaḥ paṭâbhāva-dhī-hetuḥ syāt | paṭâbhāvasya vaiśiṣṭyena sambandhena tatra asty eva |

Answer: No, for were this "relationality" single like inherence, then when one locus exhibits both an absence of a pot and the presence of a cloth, we would have to say the cloth was also absent. This is the difficulty. The relationality of a *pot's* absence would be equivalent to the relationality of a *cloth's* absence. It would not work to say that given the reality of the relationality of a cloth's absence, it is not necessarily so that an absence of the pot has to be there, too, since the two (the relationality and the absence) are distinct. First, since relationality would be identical everywhere (*ekatvāt*), the absence of an absence of a cloth, as itself an absence, would have to be there, too, by the relation, relationality. (So we would have both an absence of a cloth and an absence of an absence of a cloth in one and the same place.) And it has to be held that (with regard to an awareness of a cloth's absence) the cloth itself (when perceived) is the "preventer," *pratibandhaka* (blocking the possibility of awareness of the absence). In this way, an absence of a cloth is what grounds the cognition of a cloth's absence. An absence of a cloth is related to its locus by the relation of relationality (but relationality is not like inherence but varies with each occurrence).

Comments

Gaṅgeśa's case against a single "relationality" is a knock-down argument. Cued by Raghunātha (who rejects the singularity of inherence), we sense that the deep question is, similarly, how inherence can be a single, identical relation, everywhere the same. Below, Gaṅgeśa will address some of the problems the view raises.

Note the use of the term *pratibandhaka*, "preventer." As we saw in the section on *tarka* (pp. 161–62), this term is used by Gaṅgeśa to express what he takes to be a natural opposition in cognitive logic.

Text (p. 667) and Translation

> vaiśiṣṭyasya pratyabhāva-vyakti nānātve ca abhāva-viśiṣṭa-buddhau na ekaḥ saṃbandhaḥ kāraṇaṃ viṣayo vā iti tad-abhāva-pratyakṣe 'nanugatam eva vaiśiṣṭyaṃ viṣayaḥ kāraṇaṃ ca vācyam | tathā ca 'nanugata-tat-tat-sva-rūpa-rūpā viśeṣaṇatā eva astu kḷptatvāt kiṃ ananta-vaiśiṣṭyena | samavāyasya vaiśiṣṭyasya ca pratyakṣatve tvayā api indriya-saṃbaddha-viśeṣaṇatā-svīkārāt |

Relationality is distinct according to each particular absence (that it relates to a locus). Moreover, with regard to relational awarenesses of absences, relationality is not single and uniform as a relation or as a cause of the awareness or as its content. Thus, we hold that relationality is non-continuous and non-uniform (*ananugata*) as both content of an awareness and as a ground. And so let us say that it is just a type of qualifier and self-linking with each of its diverse and discontinuous instances. Since "being a type of qualifier" (*viśeṣaṇatā*) is a notion we are already working with, what's the point of postulating an (additional) infinitely varied "relationality?" Therefore, with regard to (the whole range of) perception, you have to accept both inherence and relationality as types of qualifiers qualifying what is in relation with a sense organ.

Comments

Again, the unique character of any absence is what urges that the relationality that binds it to its locus is neither inherence nor another separate real. Absences are non-repeating particulars. (After all, each absence is cognitively determined by a unique cognitive act, in that the cognizer's memory provides the absentee.)

"Being a type of qualifier" includes both inherence and self-linking relationality. There is no point in introducing additional conceptual tools when those we are already using perform just fine. Economy is to be maintained along every dimension so long as our system is capable of explaining our experiences and linguistic practices.

Text (p. 672) and Translation

> nanu samavāyasya ekatve kathaṃ rūpi-nīrūpa-vyavasthā | ghaṭena saha rūpa-saṃbandha-rūpatvaṃ samavāyasya na vāyunā iti cet, na | rūpa-saṃbandha-rūpatvaṃ hi samavāyasya sva-rūpam eva yadi, tadā rasa-saṃbandha-rūpatvaṃ na syāt tayor virodhāt, anyac ca durvacam iti cet,

Objection: If inherence is single and uniform, how can there be the natural order of colored things as distinct from the non-colored? If you were to respond that in the case of a pot, but not in the case of air, inherence would constitute the relation tying down the color, we can rebut that view. For if inherence performing its function of tying down color would do so (in a single and uniform way) as part of its intrinsic nature (*svarūpa*), then it could not constitute the relation that ties down taste to what has it, since (a) the two qualities are in some instances (naturally) opposed to one another and (b) no other explanation is available (for how inherence could be operative in such cases).

Comments

The quality of touch perceived in air is thought of as tied down by inherence. But if inherence is single and uniform and is what ties down color to colored things as well as touch to air, air would have to be colored. Similarly, the relation tying down taste cannot be the same as what ties down color, particularly since there is in some cases a natural opposition (or natural correlation) here, for example, between green, in the case of a mango, and a bitter taste. Inherence as invariable thus cannot do the work it is purported to do.

Text (p. 673, line 3) and Translation

> ucyate | vāyau rūpa-samavāya-sattve 'pi rūpâtyantâbhāvo 'sti na ghaṭe | katham

evam, adhikaraṇa-sva-bhāvād abādhita-rūpi-nīrūpa-pratīteś ca |

Gaṅgeśa: In the case of air, there is, we admit, inherence to be understood as (by its intrinsic nature) tying down color. Nevertheless, there is also present in air an *absolute* absence of color; this is not the case with a pot (which is invariably colored). You ask, how can this be? It is due to the intrinsic nature of the particular locus. Furthermore, this view is in accordance with uncontroverted experience concerning the colored and the non-colored.

Comments

Gaṅgeśa answers the objection (focused on the variable natures of the items linked by inherence) that indeed these natures are variable: air simply is by nature never colored. Thus we can happily say that the inherence that ties touch to air is the same inherence that ties down color (e.g., to a pot). But air by its intrinsic nature blocks the color-tying function of inherence. The natural absolute absence of color in air overpowers, so to say, the natural color-tying function of inherence.

Text and Translation

nanv evaṃ jñāto ghaṭa iti pratīteḥ jñātatā api syāt vartamāne bādhakâbhāvāt |
atītânāgatayoś ca tad-dhīḥ bhrāntā iti cet,

Objection: In this way (i.e., on the grounds whereby you support inherence), "having been cognized" would stand as a real and distinct property (inhering in things cognized). The reason to accept it would be the occurrence of, for example, the awareness, "The pot is cognized." Further, there is no counter-consideration that would rule it out in the present. Concerning something now past (i.e., destroyed) or something in the future (i.e., not yet produced), the thought that it possesses the property would be an error.

Comments

Bhāṭṭa Mīmāṃsakas insist on this view; Naiyāyikas generally deny it, as does Gaṅgeśa. In fact, Gaṅgeśa has battled this notion in several preceding sections of the *TCM*, in particular those concerned with the definition of veridicality (*pramātva*)—see above, p. 190—and the nature of apperception (*anuvyavasāya*). In that larger context, it is as though Gaṅgeśa is facing a relentless advocate of the Mīmāṃsaka position; the topic in the narrower context seems a digression.

The objector here tries to skirt the problem that although we cognize past objects in memory, it seems unreasonable to say that our present memory cognition creates a property inhering in an object that is no longer. The same can be said with cognitions, or plans, about objects we intend to create, as a potter a pot in the future. Gaṅgeśa's objector tries to avoid the difficulty by claiming the attribution concerning objects past or future would be erroneous. Otherwise, the opponent implies, the qualificative form of the cognition, "The pot is cognized," is parallel to that which Gaṅgeśa uses to establish the objective reality of qualities and the inherence that binds them to their loci.

Text and Translation

> na | atītânāgatayoḥ jñātatāyā abhāve vyavahārâbhāvâpatteḥ, tasya jñātatā-sādhyatvāt | na ca jñātatā-jñānam eva vyavahāra-hetuḥ | gauravāt | atītâdau jñāna-tad-viṣayāv eva jñātatā-dhī-gocarāv iti cet, tarhi vartamāne tāv eva tad-viṣayau | na hy atīta-vartamānayoḥ jñātatā-pratītyoḥ viṣaya-vailakṣaṇyam īkṣāmahe |

Gaṅgeśa: No. Given the non-existence of the property "apprehendedness" with things that are no longer or are still to come, there should be no practice of speaking of past things as having been cognized or of cognizing things yet to be produced. But this is a common practice. Furthermore, it is on the basis of such linguistic practice that we impute such properties in the first place.

Moreover, the ground for the linguistic practice is not simply awareness of "apprehendedness." That would be too cumbersome an explanation (*gaurava*). If you were to expand your view to say that concerning a past object, etc., it is both awareness and its content that are what the idea of "apprehendedness" is about, then concerning something in the present the same two should be what it is about, too. (But in the present, what apprehendedness is about is, you yourself say, the thing.) For we do not see an essential difference of content between something past and something present when both are conceived as apprehended.

Comments

In rebuttal, Gaṅgeśa points out, first, that with a thing that is non-existent, the property could hardly be said to exist since it must exist *in* that thing. Thus, there is an insuperable difficulty concerning cognitions of past and future objects.

With cognitions such as "I am thinking about Julius Caesar" and "I am thinking about the picnic we will have tomorrow," the cognizedness that arises seems to belong to the instance of cognition as much as to an extra-subjective object. But then we should take the same view with regard to cognizedness and currently existing things. This the Bhāṭṭa does not do.

Text (p. 675) and Translation

nanu rūpa-ghaṭayor na samavāyaḥ, kiṃ tu abhedaḥ | daṇḍī puruṣa ity atra daṇḍi-puruṣayor iva nīlo ghaṭa ity atra api nīla-ghaṭayor abādhitâbhedânubhavāt | nīlo ghātaḥ daṇḍī puruṣa iti buddhyoḥ viśeṣaṇa-saṃbandha-mātra-gocaratve nīlo ghaṭa iti-vat daṇḍa puruṣaḥ, daṇḍī puruṣa iti-vat nīlī ghaṭa ity api syāt | tasmād ekatra abhedo viṣayaḥ aparatra viśeṣaṇa-saṃbandaḥ, viṣayeṇa eva dhiyāṃ viśeṣāt |

Objection: The relation between the blue and the pot, for example, is not inherence but "non-distinctness." As with the awareness, "The man is a staff-bearer," so also with the awareness, "The pot is blue": there is uncontroverted experience of non-distinctness between the staff-bearer and the man, on the one hand, and the blue and the pot, on the other. If, to consider the two cognitions, "The pot is blue" and "The man is a staff-bearer," the mere relation with the qualifier were objective content (*gocara*), then, like "The pot is blue," we would say, "The man is a staff"; alternatively, like "The man is a staff-bearer," we would say, "The pot is a blue-bearer." Therefore, in the one case (i.e., "The pot is blue"), the content is non-distinctness; in the other (i.e., "A staff-bearer"), there is a relation with a qualifier (namely, contact, *saṃyoga*, between the man and the staff). We make this distinction on the basis of the content of the respective awarenesses.

Comments

This view is also maintained by Bhāṭṭa Mīmāṃsakas,[56] and Śrīharṣa echoes the perspective in attacking the Naiyāyika notion of qualification (*viśiṣṭa-viśeṣaṇa*) so crucial to the Navya ontology.[57] The Bhāṭṭa position constitutes a tough challenge to Gaṅgeśa's view, and with this objection Gaṅgeśa launches an extended treatment, first exploring and then defeating the notion that "non-distinctness" is the relational tie.

In Sanskrit, the word for "blue" is an adjective in the nominative case agreeing with "pot"; thus with an awareness of a blue pot verbalized as "The pot is blue," the word for "blue" is, just as in English, a predicate adjective. The word for "staff-bearer," in contrast, is a nominal derivative, a noun, "staff," transformed into an adjective by a possessive suffix, "-bearer," or, to better reflect the Sanskrit, "-bearing." Gaṅgeśa's objector is taking the use of the possessive suffix to indicate the real relation, contact, which is evident perceptually in the man's holding the staff. The lack of a term or suffix indicating a relation with "The pot is blue" (the predicative copula is, I repeat, understood in Sanskrit), the objector interprets as reflecting an ontological identity. Thus the subject term (the qualificandum) would absorb the predicate term (the qualifier), so to say. There is only a single reality, expressed by different terms, "pot" and "blue."

This section is a good example of Gaṅgeśa's style, that is, of his honing in on what he sees as the right position by considering increasingly close alternatives. He is about to present the Bhāṭṭa view with a sophistication typical of his own final position. As discussed in chapter 4, Gaṅgeśa holds that ontologically a blue pot is indeed non-distinct from the pot not cognized as blue. The difference is epistemic only.

Text and Translation

athavā viśeṣaṇatā-viśeṣyatâvacchedakayor nīlatva-ghaṭatvayoḥ eka-vṛttitvaṃ jñāyate, daṇḍitva-puruṣatvayor iva puruṣe |evaṃ nīla-ghaṭa-padayoḥ śābdam api sāmānâdhikaraṇyaṃ yujyate |nīlatva-ghaṭatvābhyāṃ bhinna-pravṛtti-nimittābhyāṃ tayor eka-pravṛtteḥ |na ca matupo lopāt abhedôpacārād vā nīla-padaṃ nīlavat-param iti vācyam |na hi prayogaṃ sādhakaṃ brūmaḥ, kiṃ tu nīla-ghaṭayor abheda-pratītim |pade 'pi na upacārâdi-kalpanā, gauravāt mukhye bādhakâbhāvāc ca iti |

In other words, (with the cognition, "The pot is blue") a single entity is cognized by way of specifiers (delimitants, *avacchedaka*), namely, (1) a qualifier, specified by blueness, and (2) a qualificandum, specified by pothood. It is one entity that is cognized (nevertheless), just as it is a single man that is cognized (with the cognition "The man is a staff-bearer"), with "staff-bearingness" and "man-ness" (as the specifiers). In this way, the cognition is expressed verbally with the words *nīla*, "blue," and *ghaṭa*, "pot," used in the same case (the nominative case), appositively. Although the abstracts, blueness and pothood, give rise to distinct verbal expressions, they are invoked for a single meaning, a single intention (*eka-pravṛtti*).

Nor should it be said that here there is ellipsis, with a dropping of an implicit possessive suffix, or that the non-distinctness is figurative, such that the word "blue" would mean "having blue." We do not say that the verbal usage is what establishes the non-distinctness. It is, rather, the appearance of the blue and the pot as non-distinct. Nevertheless, concerning the words used (our case is re-inforced:) it should not be imagined that there is any figurative meaning, etc. Not only would that be a cumbersome explanation (*gaurava*), there is no consideration against taking the expression in its primary, denotative sense.

Comments

With the terms "pot" and "blue" having a single meaning, namely, the single reality of the blue pot, there would be no need to postulate inherence as what relates them. If there were some such relator doing real work, we would say that the pot *has* blue instead of that the pot is blue; in Sanskrit, the possessive suffix would be used. To suppose that such usage, or any metaphorical sense, is implicit is unreasonable when a usage can be straightforwardly interpreted in its primary, denotative sense. Thus it is non-distinctness, and not inherence, that plays the relational role—with awarenesses such as "The pot is blue."

Text (p. 676, line 5) and Translation

ucyate | śukla-paṭa-śabdayoḥ ekârthatve ghaṭaḥ kumbha iti-vat śuklaḥ paṭa iti saha-prayogo na syāt | andhasya paṭa-graha-vat rūpa-grahaḥ, rūpâgraha-vat paṭâgraho 'pi vā syat | mahārajata-rakte paṭa-graha-vat śukla-grahaḥ, śuklâgraha-vat paṭâgraho 'pi bhavet | paṭam ānaya ity ukte yaṃ kaṃcit śuklam ānayet | apaṭaḥ paṭa iti-vad aśuklaḥ paṭa iti virudhyeta, paṭa-śuklayor abhedāt | agni-saṃyogād ekatra śyāma-raktayoḥ vināśôtpāde ghaṭasya tau syātām, ghaṭa-sattve vā tayor api na syātām |

Gaṅgeśa: We answer. If (with the verbalized cognition, "The cloth is white") the word "white" and the word "cloth" meant one and the same thing, then like *ghaṭa* (pot) and *kumbha* (pot) (which are synonyms), the two would not be used together. Further, a blind person in apprehending a cloth (in his hand by the sense of touch) would apprehend its color; or in not apprehending its color would not apprehend the cloth. And after a white cloth has been dyed with tumeric, white still would be apprehended when the cloth is apprehended; or with the white not grasped, the cloth would not be grasped. When "Bring the cloth" is said, anything white would be brought. Further, like "The cloth is not a cloth," to say "The cloth is not white" would be self-contradictory, since there would be no distinctness between the cloth and the white. Once a pot has been baked in fire, the arising and destruction of the black color and of the red color—both colors (simultaneously)—would belong to the pot. Or, we would have to say that neither (the arising nor the destruction) of the two concerns what the pot is.

Comments

Gaṅgeśa's objections are clear, and appear cogent. The non-distinctness view has other advantages, however, and Gaṅgeśa's upholding inherence faces further difficulties, as we will see.

Gaṅgeśa is defending an ontological hierarchy and layeredness: the pot can be both red and black, with temporal delimitation. Moreover, there is the distinction between the thin and the thick particular. As a mere qualificandum (the thin particular), the pot is thought of apart from all its determinations or specifications, as a locus capable of bearing properties.

Śrīharṣa, by the way, astutely questions whether qualificandumness is a property.[58] Gaṅgeśa, however, does not address that question, but he does continue to worry about the fundamental ontic tie.

Text and Translation

atha śuklatvâdīnāṃ dravya-bhedāt tad-bodhârthaṃ saha prayogaḥ | andhâdinā śuklâdi-grahe śuklatvâdīnām agraha upapadyate | śuklatvâdi-jāteś ca dravyeṇa abhedo na samavāyaḥ, kiṃ tu sva-rūpa-saṃbandha iti cet,

Objection: Universals such as whiteness do differ from substances (but qualities such as white do not differ from substances). In the examples you gave, the usage of terms together (that you showed were not synonyms) is to make such difference known. Non-apprehension of whiteness, etc., by a blind person, etc., is possible though there is apprehension of white, etc. Moreover, there is a sense in which there is non-distinctness (even) between the substance and universals such as whiteness. It is not (as you say) inherence; rather, it is self-linkage.

Comments

The objector is claiming that the white thing would be grasped by the blind person by the organ of touch, for example, but the thing *as white* would not be grasped because the universal whiteness would not be grasped. Apparently, it would be grasping the universal that would bring the color into consciousness. The objector seems to want to collapse the distinction between (a) bare or thin particulars and (b) particular qualities (though what the text says is substances and qualities) but not that between universals and their instances. Moreover, the objector says that even with an admission of that distinction, no relation as an additional real need be supposed in that the two terms are self-linking.

Text (p. 677, line 1) and Translation

na | śuklatva-madhuratva-surabhitvôṣṇatvâdīnāṃ dravya-vṛttitve dravya-grāhaka-tvag-ādibhiḥ grahaṇa-prasaṅgāt | rūpatvâdīnāṃ dravya-vṛttitve pratiniyatêndriya-grāhyatā eva na syāt, yogya-vṛttitvena jāter grahaṇa-yogyatvāt | tat-taj-jātitvena yogyatve 'nanugamāt |

Gaṅgeśa: No. If whiteness, sweetness, fragrance, hotness, etc., were modes (*vṛtti*) of substance, then when a substance is apprehended by any sense organ—the organ of touch, for example—there would be apprehension (of all of these). This is the difficulty. If colorness, etc., were only modes of substance, then there would not be cognizability according to the specific sense organ. A universal is capable of being apprehended according to the fittingness to be apprehended of that in which it exists (i.e., colorness, for example, is not a mode of substance directly but rather of color and will be apprehended only in color being apprehended). The fittingness of this and that universal to be apprehended is not uniform.

Comments

According to Gaṅgeśa's Nyāya, the universal colorness is cognizable only by the sense organ capable of apprehending color, the visual organ. In more general terms, the cognizability of a universal depends on the cognizability of that in which the universal most immediately exists, as colorness in color.

Text and Translation

> tasmād rūpatvâdīnāṃ pratiniyatêndriya-grāhyatā api guṇa-guṇi-bhede mānam | abhede ca kathaṃ paṭasya śuklaṃ rūpam iti bheda-buddhiḥ | paṭo nīlimā iti buddhi-prasaṅgaś ca |

Therefore, the fact that colorness and other universals are cognizable only by specific sense organs is further proof of the distinction between quality and quality-possessor. And if they were non-distinct, how could the cognition of distinctness in "The cloth *has* a white color" be explained? Moreover, there would be the difficulty that (in the case of a blue cloth) we would cognize "The cloth is blueness" (as opposed to "The cloth is blue").

Comments

Gaṅgeśa implies that it is perfectly good usage to say "The cloth *has* a white color," making verbally explicit the relational tie. The view that there is an ontological layeredness, a firm distinction between the property-bearer and its properties, has, in sum, several advantages, not the least of which is its ability to explain differences of sense presentation, an ability not shared by the non-distinctness view.

Text (p. 677, line 7) and Translation

> nanv ekântâbhede sarvam idaṃ dūṣaṇam | vayaṃ tu bhedâbheda-vādinaḥ | tathā ca bhedam ādāya apaunarukty-ādi | bhedâbhede ca uktam eva pramāṇaṃ pratyakṣam | atha vā ubhaya-siddha-bhede sāmānâdhikaraṇya-dhīr abhede pramāṇam | yad vā atyantam abhede bhede ca na sāmānâdhikaraṇyam iti tata eva bhedâbheda-siddhiḥ | na ca bhedâbhedayoḥ paraspara-viraha-rūpatayā viruddhayoḥ katham ekatra samāveśa iti vācyam | saṃyoga-tad-abhāvayor iva avirodhāt | pākânantaraṃ rakto 'yaṃ na śyāma ity abādhitânubhava-balāt tatra eva tad-anyonyâbhāva-siddheḥ tvayā api bhedâbheda-svīkārāt |

Objection: If we held strictly to a position of non-distinctness, you would be right: all this we have said would fail. But we (Bhāṭṭa Mīmāṃsakas) hold the position of distinctness within non-distinctness (between properties and property-possessors). And so by accepting the distinctness, use of terms non-synonymously, etc., can be explained. Just as we claimed, moreover, the proof of our position of distinctness within non-distinctness is perception. Or, given that both of us accept the distinctness plank, let us present an argument only for non-distinctness: it is that the use of terms appositively in the same case to express certain cognitions (for example, with "The blue pot," "blue" and "pot" are both nominatives in apposition) demands it. Alternatively, note that in the case of an absolute non-distinctness (as with the synonyms *ghaṭa* and *kumbha*, both of which mean "pot") and in the case of an absolute distinctness (as with the meanings of "horse" and "cow"), use of appositives does not occur. Therefore, just for this reason, our position of distinctness within non-distinctness is proved.

Nor should it be asked how it is possible for distinctness and non-distinctness—understood as mutually opposed, each entailing the absence of the other—to occur together in one thing. The possibility is shown by the fact that a contact (*saṃyoga*) and its absence can so occur. (For example, a monkey can be in contact with a tree while in the same tree there is also absence of the contact.) You (Naiyāyikas) also accept this our (Mīmāṃsaka) "distinctness within non-distinctness" position: it is an uncontroverted experience that after baking a pot is red and no longer black, and you accept that a red thing and a black thing are mutually exclusive (*anyonyābhāva*).

Comments

That it is one and the same pot, at one time black and later red, would secure the non-distinctness; the change from black to red would secure the distinctness. The position is indeed not far from Gaṅgeśa's own view, but he rejects the argument about appositional usage.

Text and Translation

> anyonyâbhāvatvam avyāpya-vṛtti-vṛtti[59] nityâbhāva-vṛtty-abhāvatva-sākṣād-vyāpya-dharmatvāt[60] atyantâbhāvatva-vat | nitya iti vā na viśeṣaṇam avyāpya-vṛtti-pratiyogika-prāg-abhāva-pradhvaṃsayor avyāpya-vṛttitvāt ity ato 'pi bhedâbheda-siddhiḥ |

Consider another argument. Mutual exclusion is not locus-pervading. The reason: it is a property that is thoroughly (*sākṣāt*) pervaded by the type of absence that is constant, *nityābhāva* (and a constant absence is not locus-pervading). The confirming example: an absolute absence. Alternatively, the qualification in the reason that mutual exclusion is a *constant* absence is unnecessary. (Thus the reason would be that mutual exclusion is a type of absence, with all absences as non-locus-pervading.) The absence of x before its production (*prāgabhāva*) and the absence of x after its destruction (*dhvaṃsābhāva*) involve absentees that are not locus-pervading; hence, they too are not locus-pervading (and thus need not be excluded by the qualification, "constant," in the reason given). Therefore, because of this argument as well, our view of distinctness within non-distinctness is established.

Comments

The argument is premised on the supposition that distinctness, understood as mutual exclusion, is not locus-pervading. Thus it would not rule out non-distinctness. That is, distinctness and non-distinctness would be compatible as the qualificational tie. Apparently, distinctness as a qualifier would be non-distinct from its qualificandum but also distinct in that it would not exhaust what the qualificandum is. This would be possible because the qualifier would not thoroughly pervade the qualificandum. Absences are non-locus-pervading, and distinctness is a type of absence, mutual absence or mutual exclusion, *anyonyābhāva*.

Text (p. 679) and Translation

ucyate | tasya eva tatra abhāvo 'vaccheda-bhedena vartate jñāyate ca yathā saṃyogâdy-abhāvaḥ | śyāmâvacchinnasya tasya eva anyonyâbhāvas tatra eva raktâvacchinne | tad-anyonyâbhāvâbhāvaś ca śyāmâvacchedena | tad iha api nīlasya anyonyâbhāvo ghaṭatvâvacchedena iti nīlāt ghaṭasya bhedo 'stu | abhedas tu nīlânyonyâbhāvâbhāva-rūpo na ghaṭe ghaṭatvâvacchedena eva, virodhāt | ekâvacchedena bhāvâbhāvayoḥ ekatra avṛtter ajñānāc ca |

Gaṅgeśa: We answer. When there is an absence of something x in something y, the absence both exists and is known by way of a distinctness of specification (e.g., of exact location), as, for example, an absence of a conjunction (at a spot, e.g., in a tree conjoined with a monkey elsewhere). A mutual exclusion (concerning the color of a pot) delimited by black (as what is excluded) obtains precisely in the case of a pot as delimited in color as red. Further, the absence of mutual exclusion has to be precisely specified as well, as, e.g., with regard to the black (at an earlier time). So (to consider your distinctness within non-distinctness view), we will accept that there is distinctness between a pot and its blue, a distinctness understood as a mutual exclusion of blue delimited or precisely specified by potness. However, we take a different attitude toward the non-distinctness you claim. There is no non-distinctness, understood as an absence of mutual exclusion of blue in a pot specified indeed by potness, since that would be contradictory. There does not occur at a single locus both a presence and an absence with one and the same (precise) delimitation, *avaccheda*. Nor is such ever cognized.

Comments

This is a particularly revealing passage, showing how Gaṅgeśa thinks about specifiers, *avacchedaka*s, as well as the predicative tie. Indeed, he intimates the argument of Śaṅkara Miśra that the qualificative relation is to be understood as a mutual exclusion obtaining between the qualifier and qualificandum terms ("a distinctness understood as a mutual exclusion of blue delimited or precisely specified by potness").

The main point, however, is to counter the appositional argument. Gaṅgeśa takes it up along with the example of an awareness verbalized as "(A) blue pot" (or, "The pot is blue"), where "potness" specifies the qualificandum-hood and "blueness" the qualifier-hood in the awareness. Unlike the cases of a monkey in a tree at a precise location and of a pot at one time black and another red, the distinctness within non-distinctness view would require that the counterpositive of the mutual exclusion, here the qualifier blue, be present in the qualificandum specified in the same way as it is specified when the qualifier is viewed as excluded or absent. This is contradictory, Gaṅgeśa maintains.

Now Gaṅgeśa has already shown that the thing cognized, the qualificandum, has to be distinct from a qualifier such as blue. It could be another color, a blind person could know it by touch without knowing its color, et cetera. But even cognized as only a pot, with potness as the qualifier (or as specifying the qualifierhood), the qualificandum would remain distinct. Though Gaṅgeśa does not do as good a job as Śaṅkara Miśra in articulating a general position and argument (see below), he intimates an epistemological reason for the stance: the pot could be cognized as something else, as earthen, for example, and cognition-wise (with respect to inferences, etc.) there is all the difference in the world between being aware of something as a pot and being aware of it as earthen, although the thing cognized is one and the same.

Text (p. 679, line 6) and Translation

na apy avacchedakântareṇa | ghaṭatvâvacchinne ghaṭe tad-abhāvāt tad-ajñāne 'pi nīlo ghaṭa ity anubhavāc ca |

Nor is there a presence and an absence at a single locus secured by another specifier. First, in a pot specified (as the qualificandum in awareness) by potness, there is no other specifier. Second, though there may be a possibility for another that is not currently cognized, the point is that the current awareness is just "The pot is blue."

Comments

With this particular awareness, there is no content over and above potness, nothing that could be identical with the pot cognized as a qualificandum just precisely as a pot. In principle, there could be another qualificandum factor, e.g., substance-hood (the thing cognized is a substance and it is possible that one have a veridical awareness, "The *substance* is blue"), but that is not the specifier of qualificandumhood with the particular awareness that is to be verbalized as "The pot is blue." Moreover, we might add, the qualificandum and qualifier factors would have to be the same to maintain non-distinctness, as in "The blue thing is blue." Now not only would this verbalization be objectionable as needlessly repetitive, but it would express a complex cognition having as a component the simple qualificative cognition, "Something blue." This simple cognition is to be analyzed, in turn, as manifesting a distinctness between the thing cognized and its qualifier blue.

Text (p. 679, line 7) and Translation

na ca anyonyâbhāva-rūpo bhedo 'stu, abhedas tu na bhedâbhāvaḥ kiṃ tv anya eva iti vācyam |abheda-vyavahāre tasya ahetutvāt |tasmāt nīlo ghaṭa ity atra nīla-saṃbandha eva bhāsate |

Nor should it be said that in accepting distinctness as mutual exclusion, we should see non-distinctness not as the absence of distinctness but as something else. In that case, there would be no reason for employing the term "*non*-distinctness."

Therefore, here with the awareness, "The pot is blue," a relation with the blue is indeed manifest.

Comments

Gaṅgeśa's "Therefore" (*tasmāt*) seems to signal the conclusion of his overall argument. The preceding two sentences make only a semantic point concerning negation.

Text (p. 680, line 2) and Translation

tathā sati nīlī ghaṭa dhīḥ syād ity uktam iti cet, nīlī ghaṭa ity atra buddhau yadi saṃbandha-viṣayatvam āpādyate, tad iṣyata eva |atha nīlo ghaṭa iti prayoge saṃbandha-vācaka-padavattvaṃ tad api iṣyate eva |matupo lopāt abhedôpacārād vā nīla-padam eva nīlavat-param iti |

Objection: Then this being the case, the expression should be "The pot *has* blue" (not "The pot *is* blue").

Gaṅgeśa: If the cognition, "The pot has blue," were to occur (or be expressed) showing the relation to be objective content, that certainly would be okay.

Objection: So you admit that with the usage, "The pot is blue," that there be a word expressing the relation is also desired by you. (But there is none.)

Gaṅgeśa: Well, either there is a dropping of the possessive suffix or the (use of apposition suggesting) non-distinctness is figurative. The word "blue" in this usage means "having blue."

Comments

Again, Sanskrit uses no word for the "is" in the English translation, "The pot is blue": the expression is more literally "Blue (is the) pot." With the expression that I have translated, "The pot has blue"—more literally, "Blue-possessing (is the) pot"—a suffix conveys the meaning of "has." Thus in the latter expression, there is an explicit expression of relation.

Here ends Gaṅgeśa's discussion of the non-distinctness/distinctness alternative. He does not explicitly counter the point made earlier that a construal of a term in its primary meaning is, *ceteris paribus*, to be preferred over a secondary or metaphorical reading. But the implication is that all things are *not* equal, that there is good reason for supposing ellipsis or metaphorical usage.

Text (p. 680, line 7) and Translation

> nanu śabda-rūpâdiṣu viśeṣaṇatā indriya-saṃbaddha-viśeṣaṇatā vā grāhikās tu kiṃ samavāyâdinā | atha viśeṣaṇatāyāṃ samavāyaḥ indriya-saṃbaddha-viśeṣaṇatāyāṃ ca saṃyukta-samavāyâdir upajīvyaḥ, tair vinā tayor abhāvād iti cet, viśeṣaṇatā-sva-rūpe teṣām upajīvyatvam, na tu tasyāḥ pratyāsattitve 'pi | tair vinā api samavāyâbhāvayor viśeṣaṇatā-sattvāt |

Objection: The relation "qualifierness" (or "being a qualifier") with regard to sounds, colors, and so on, or (not simply this but) "being a qualifier related to the sense organ" is what brings about sense perception. So why postulate inherence and the others (the types of so-called "operative relation," *sannikarṣa*, in sense perception)? Say you offer this objection, "With regard to the relation of 'being a qualifier,' inherence is required—and with regard to 'being a qualifier related to the sense organ' the required relation is 'inherence in what is in contact with the sense organ'—on the grounds that without these there could not be the relations (necessary for sense perception)." Then our reply is that what is required is the view that they are simply by nature "qualifierness," i.e., types of qualifier (*viśeṣaṇatā-svarupe teṣām*). But "qualifierness" need not also be understood as what you call an "operative relation in sense perception" (although the relation is crucial to bringing sense perception about). Without going so far as to admit all the types of so-called operative relation that you propose, we say that both (your) inherence and absence are types of qualifier.

Comments

Both would, then, be subsumed into the ontic status of qualifierhood, which is, as Gaṅgeśa has made explicit with regard to the relationality of absences, no additional real. Thus, according to the objector, qualifierhood is the key relation in the causal process resulting in perceptual awareness. If Gaṅgeśa insists that inherence is necessary, too, sometimes, in order to explain how sense perception comes about, the objector says his camp can agree in that "qualifierness" or "being a qualifier" on his view includes inherence and its function. The point is, again, that this new inherence would not be an independently real relator, but would be absorbed into the class of qualifiers, all of which are related through self-linkage.

Text (p. 681) and Translation

> saṃyukta-samavāyâdir api tatra asti iti cet, āstām, na tu pratyāsattiḥ, kiṃ tu viśeṣaṇatā eva, kḷptatvāt | saṃyukta-samavāyâdikaṃ vinā viśeṣaṇatā rūpâdau na jñāyata cet, mā jñāyi | na hi sā pratyāsattir jñātā, api tu sva-rūpa-satī |

(Moreover,) if you object, "But there are also other relations that have to be accepted, 'inherence in what is in contact with the sense organ,' and so on." Then we say, let them be. But they are not to be considered the "operative relation in sense perception" (as you understand it). Rather, simply "being a qualifier" fills that role; this is an accepted notion (and none other is needed).

If you say, "But 'being a qualifier' without the further relations of 'inherence in what is in contact with the sense organ' and so on is not cognized with regard to colors, etc." Then we say, you stop cognizing (in that faulty way). There is no "operative relation in sense perception" that is ever cognized. Rather, "being a qualifier" is self-linking.

Comments

Gaṅgeśa's objector is arguing that "being a qualifier" is the parsimonious position. This subsumes the theorizing about the *sannikarṣa*, "operative relation in sense perception," that takes into account the nature of objects cognized, their relations to the sense organs, et cetera.

Text and Translation

> mā evaṃ | śabdâdīnāṃ sākṣātkāra-viṣayatvena indriya-saṃbaddhânumitau śabdâdau samavāyâdikaṃ jñātvā eva viśeṣaṇatā-graha ity avaśyaṃ | prathamôpasthitatvāt samavāyâdir eva viṣayo na viśeṣaṇatā, caramôpasthitatvāt |

Gaṅgeśa: You are all wrong. Sounds, etc., are inferred to be in relation to the sense organs since sounds, etc., are the objects of immediate experience. Only after cognizing the relations of inherence, etc., with regard to sounds, etc., is there apprehension of the abstract, "being a qualifier." Therefore, because relations such as inherence are epistemically prior (*prathama-upasthita*), it is just they that are objective content (in the immediate experience), not "being a qualifier," which is epistemically posterior.

Comments

The Nyāya thesis of epistemic priority was discussed above, both in chapter 2 (p. 59) and in comments on the *TCM* section on characterizing veridical awareness (p. 228). Bracketing the question of the cogency of Gaṅgeśa's argument here, we see that his point is not to deny that each of the operative sensory relations can be viewed as a type of qualifier—each, when explicitly focused on, appears as qualifying the object cognized—but that their being viewed like this is an abstraction from their givenness in the simplest—i.e., epistemically prior—sensory awareness. There they appear as conjunction, inherence in the conjoined, and so on. The problem with Gaṅgeśa's argument is that it seems arbitrary to claim an epistemic priority here when the separate reality of what is supposed to be epistemically prior has been drawn into question.

Text (p. 684) and Translation

> nanu abhāva-grahe na indriya-saṃbaddha-viśeṣaṇatā pratyāsattiḥ, cakṣuṣā saṃyukte paramâṇvâdau yogyasya jalatvâder abhāva-graha-prasaṅgāt | kiṃ tu sva-grāhya-saṃbaddha-viśeṣaṇatā |

Objection: In apprehension of an absence, it is not the case that the operative relation is "being a qualifier of what is related to the sense organ." Since the visual organ is in contact with the ultimate atoms (e.g., of earth) and the like, then, if you were right, there should be apprehension of the absence of wateriness and the like which are capable of being perceived. Instead, the position should be (that an absence is perceived through the relation of) "being a qualifier of what is related to the sense organ insofar as that is capable of being perceived by the particular sense organ."

Comments

Śrīharṣa presents this argument.[61] While his main concern is the Nyāya attempt to understand cognition causally and, in particular, so to understand self-cognition, he is pecking away by drawing out this and other seemingly absurd consequences of various Nyāya positions. Śrīharṣa even anticipates, and attacks, the qualification, also expressed here, that perceptibility should obtain only "insofar as that (qualifier] is capable of being perceived by the particular sense organ."

In other words, wateriness as absent from the atoms of earth could, Gaṅgeśa's objector says, stand as "being a qualifier of what is related to the sense organ." Thus, absence of wateriness in the atoms of earth should be perceived when the sense organ is in contact with earth-composed things. But obviously this does not occur. No sense perception of atoms occurs, though a sense organ is in contact with them. Given that this is an insuperable difficulty for Gaṅgeśa's position, the objector offers his qualification as a replacement for Gaṅgeśa's view about the operative relation in the perception of an absence.

Text and Translation

mahati vāyau udbhūta-rūpâbhāvasya, kusume saurabhâbhāvasya, guḍe tikta-tvâbhāvasya vā na cakṣur-ādinā grahaḥ, api tu yogyânupalabdhyā so 'numīyate |

Concerning air as a gross element (and not the atoms), there is an absence of manifest color, but that is not grasped by the visual organ. Rather, we know this through inference based on the fact that color is in no way perceived (*anupalabdhyā*) and that we would perceive it if it were present in air (*yogya*). Similarly concerning an absence of fragrance in a flower and the absence of bitter taste in sugar.[62]

Comments

The organ of smell, unlike the visual and tactile organs, is considered incapable of apprehending a substance; it grasps qualities only. Similarly with the organ of taste. Absences are not qualities but rather qualifiers that self-link with substances. So in the case of an absence of smell or of taste, the organ would be incapable of perceiving the substance to which the qualifier is related. Thus such an absence must be known by an inference that has as a premise: were a smell or taste present, it would be perceived. Gaṅgeśa's objector is maintaining that the same type of inference is responsible for the apprehension of an absence of color.

Text (p. 684, line 5) and Translation

indriya-viśeṣaṇatā api na pratyāsattiḥ | cakṣur-ādinā sva-viśeṣaṇa-jalatvâdy-abhāva-graha-prasaṅgāt |

Nor is "being a qualifier of the sense organ" the operative relation. If that were right, absence of wateriness, etc., should be grasped by the visual organ, etc., since it would stand as the organ's own qualifier.

Comments

The visual organ is thought to be made out of fiery atoms. Thus, it is itself qualified by an absence of wateriness.

Text and Translation

yadi śabdâbhāvaḥ pratyakṣaḥ tadā pratyāsatty-antaraṃ kalpyam | tad-abhāve pratyakṣa eva na bhavati iti cet,

If an absence of sound were directly perceptible (and not just inferable, as is our counter-proposal), then still some other operative relation would have to be dreamed up. Given that you have not come up with one, you might as well admit that these absences are not directly perceptible.

Comments

Neither "being a qualifier of what is related to the sense organ" nor "being a qualifier of the sense organ" is an adequate view, the objector is supposing, considering his previous arguments against these to be conclusive. Thus the simplest view would be that absences are inferred.

Text (p. 685, line 3) and Translation

mā evam | lāghavād indriya-saṃbaddha-viśeṣaṇatā eva pratyāsattiḥ | na ca evaṃ paramâṇau jalatvâdy-abhāva-graha-prasaṅgaḥ | yatra hi yat sattvam anupalabdhi-virodhi tatra tasya abhāva indriya-saṇṇikarṣeṇa gṛhyate |

Gaṅgeśa: It is not so. Because of parsimony, it is just "being a qualifier of what is related to the sense organ" that is to be viewed as the operative relation in perception of an absence. And you are wrong to allege that this view entails that such an absence as that of wateriness in ultimate atoms should be perceived. (There is the following concomitance:) Where the existence of something stands opposed to its non-perception, there only is its absence to be perceived through the operative relation in sense perception.

Comments

Looking back at the text (at *TCM*, p. 684), we see that Gaṅgeśa's principle departs only ever so slightly from the qualification suggested by the objector (and Śrīharṣa): whereas the objector proposes that the qualifier has to be perceptible, Gaṅgeśa says precisely concerning absences that an absence of x is perceptible only if its presence is opposed to its non-perception (other conditions—looking in the right direction, etc.—presumably being fulfilled).

Text (p. 691) and Translation

na ca paramânv-ādau jalatvâdi-sattvam anupalabdhi-virodhi |yogya-saṃyukta-samavāyâbhāvena pṛthivītva-vad-anupalabdhi-saṃbhavāt |mahati vāyv-ādau udbhūta-rūpâdy-abhāvaś cakṣur-ādi-grāhya eva |tatra udbhūta-rūpâdi-sattve 'nupalabdhy-anupapatteḥ |ata eva stambhe piśāca-tādātmyâbhāvaḥ pratyakṣaḥ stambha-tādātmye ca tasya stambhasya iva anupalambhâsaṃbhavāt |evaṃ śabdasya apy abhāvaḥ pratyakṣaḥ tadā tatra śabda-sattvasya anupalabdhi-virodhitvād iti tatra indriya-viśeṣaṇatā eva pratyāsattiḥ |cakṣuṣi jalatvâdi-sattvaṃ ca na anupalabdhi-virodhi iti cakṣuṣā na tad-grahaḥ |

This condition is not fulfilled with respect to such an absence as that of wateriness in the likes of ultimate atoms. The existence of wateriness there does not stand opposed to its non-perception; similarly with other cases. Non-perception in such cases is possible (even though the wateriness exists) because, like earthenness (which is present in the ultimate atoms of earth where wateriness is absent), there is no inherence in something capable of being perceived when it is in contact with the sense organ (in that no ultimate atom can be perceived).

Concerning air, etc., as a gross element, absence of manifest color, etc., is indeed perceptible by the visual organ, etc. In such a case, there would not be an impossibility of perception if, for example, the manifest color existed. (Air, by nature, simply has no color.) Therefore, the absence of identity between a stump and a demon is perceptible in the stump, since if there were identity with the stump it would not be impossible, as it were, that it be perceived.

In this way, absence of sound is also perceptible. The existence of sound does not stand in opposition to its perception. So it is indeed "being a qualifier with regard to the sense organ" that is the operative relation when there is perception of no sound. And again, it is not the case that the existence of the likes of wateriness would not stand in opposition to its perception by the visual organ. Therefore, its absence is not grasped by the visual organ.

Comments

As we will see with Vācaspati II, the issue of the perceptibility of the absentee is important to the Navya response to Śrīharṣa on distinctness. In fact, Vācaspati echoes Gaṅgeśa's example of a demon and a stump. Gaṅgeśa's point is that certain absences are directly perceived, not inferred. Vācaspati's point is similar: an absence of identity can be perceived although one of the terms—the demon—is not perceived, or even, he seems to say (contra Gaṅgeśa), perceptible.

Like other perceptible absences, an absence of sound is perceived through its standing as a qualifier in relation to the sense organ, here the *ākāśa* or ether—which is thought to be the medium of sound propagation—in the ear.

Text (p. 692, line 4) and Translation

nanv abhāve na viśeṣaṇatā pratyāsattiḥ | kiṃ tu samavāya eva samavāya-sādhaka-viśiṣṭa-pratīter aviśeṣāt | na ca samavetatve tasya bhāvatvâpattiḥ | bhāvasya tattve 'bhāvatvâpattir iti vaiparītya-saṃbhavāt | rūpâdau pratyāsattitvena samavāya-kalpanam abhāve 'pi tulyam | viśeṣaṇatā api tulyā |

Objection: Okay then, with perception of an absence, (your view) "being a qualifier" is not the operative relation. It is instead nothing but inherence, because the reason given for accepting inherence applies here just as much as it does elsewhere, the reason, namely, that a cognition of an absence is a relational awareness. Nor does this view—namely, that an absence is related to its locus by inherence—entail the absurdity that the absence would have to be regarded as a presence. For there would equally be the possibility of the opposite: when it is a presence that stands in that relation, it would have to be regarded as an absence. That inherence is the operative relation with perception of color and the like holds true equally with perception of an absence (in that there, too, the relation is indirect). Also, both equally involve "being a qualifier."

Comments

According to Gaṅgeśa's Nyāya-Vaiśeṣika tradition, perception of color does not involve direct contact with the sense organ but an indirect relation: the color inheres in a substance that both has color and is in contact with the sense organ. Thus, to hold that the operative relation in the case of perception of an absence is inherence would be to claim no more than what is claimed with regard to perception of color, namely, a mediated relation of the sense organ to the absence. The opponent's chief argument is that absential awareness is relational awareness, but his point is shored up by the parallel he draws with color.

The opponent's strategy is to argue that by the same considerations Gaṅgeśa would use to establish the objective reality of inherence, the relationality of absences would also be established as objectively real, and so we might as well call it inherence.

Text and Translation

prag-abhāva-pradhvaṃsau pratiyogyâśraye samavetau | pratiyogy-āśraya-nāśa-janya-dhvaṃso deśe samaye vā samavaiti, tatra eva nirūpaṇāt |

Prior absences and destructional absences inhere in the substrata of the absentees. The destructional absence of *x* generated by the destruction of the substratum of *x*—with *x* as the absence's absentee—inheres in a particular location or occasion, because it is experienced there only.

Comments

According to Gaṅgeśa's objector, the prior absence of a cloth—with the cloth as the absence's absentee (*pratiyogin*)—inheres in the threads that make it up; the destructional absence of a pot inheres in the pieces into which the pot is broken. Concerning destructional absence: a piece of cloth's "inherent cause" consists of the threads that make it up; with their destruction, it is destroyed. The destruction occurs at a particular place. So Gaṅgeśa's opponent says the absence inheres there.

Text and Translation

> na ca samvāyi-nāśe dhvaṃsa-nāśaḥ, ghaṭônmajjana-prasaṅgāt bhāvatvasya upādhitvāc ca | anyathā tava api tasya janyatvena nāśâpattiḥ |

And it is not the case that when the inherent cause is destroyed (e.g., when the halves of a pot are destroyed), there is destruction of the destructional absence (e.g., destruction of the destruction of a pot and so therefore the preservation of the pot), because that idea is mired in the presence of the pot and it entails treating a destruction as a presence, as a positive real (*bhāva*). If somehow this move were disallowed, you too would face the difficulty of regarding a destruction as a positive real, because insofar as something is regarded as a cause of a destruction it would be regarded as a destroyer (and thus an existent).

Comments

Gaṅgeśa focuses on this purported conflict between his reflections on inherence and his view of absences in order to lead us to better appreciate their coherence.

Text (p. 693, line 5) and Translation

> atha evam anyonyâtyantâbhāvayor nityatve 'neka-samavetatve ca jātitva-prasaṅgaḥ |

Objection to the objector: Then in this way, mutual exclusion and absolute absence would have to be counted (against accepted theory) as natural-kind universals (in that both would fulfill the key conditions of the traditional definition): (1) they are eternal and (2) inhere in more than one thing.

Comments

As noted in chapter 2, Praśāstapāda defines a universal or natural kind as something eternal that inheres in more than one thing. If mutual exclusion and absolute absence are to be counted as universals, absence would not be a seventh category or primitive, against the inherited theory. The objector to the original objector now elaborates.

Text and Translation

> na ca tatra bhāvatvaṃ tantram |gauravāt |na ca abhāvānāṃ viśiṣṭa-pratītau viśeṣaḥ, yena atra samavāya-parityāga iti cet,

(And if they are accepted as universals) one is not also forced to view them as positive reals, because that would be more cumbersome. Nor is there (we agree) any relevant difference in the relational cognition of absences (as opposed to relational cognitions of positive reals), such that one need reject the notion of inherence with regard to the one and not the other.

Comments

Thus the objector to the objector would apparently shore up the latter's original attack: there is no reason to separate out the relationality of absences from what inherence is supposed to accomplish. But this wrinkle is rejected by the original objector.

Text and Translation

> na |ghaṭatvâbhāvâder jātitve sattva-dravyatva-pṛthivītvâdinā parâpara-bhāvânupapatteḥ |teṣāṃ vyāpyatve ghaṭe tad-abhāva-prasaṅgaḥ |vyāpakatve sāmānyâdau ghaṭatvâbhāvo na syād iti |

Answer (by the original objector): No. If there were such a universal as "absence of potness," then it would be impossible to maintain the ordering of kinds among "existence," "substancehood," and "earthenness," for example (which all inhere in a pot). With regard to the requirement that universals are pervaded by one another successively (up to the widest, "existence"), if these (existence, substancehood, and earthenness) pervade an absence of potness, then they would not be there in a pot. (Clearly, existence and the others are there in a pot.) With regard to the requirement that a succession of universals be pervaders, an absence of potness could not figure in the succession (for fear of cross-section).

Comments

As explained in chapter 2 (pp. 61–62), Nyāya finds a hierarchy of universals or natural kinds, *jāti*, based on breadth of extension, with each successive universal including the extension of an immediately narrower universal within its extension: for example, every instance of "earthenness" is also an instance of "substancehood." The problem with counting absences as such universals is that there would be a "confusion of class," *jāti-sāṃkarya*, that would break down the natural ordering based on the entire inclusion of the extension of a lower *jāti* in that of a higher. According to Udayana and Navya-Nyāya philosophers generally, this is, as we have several times remarked, one of the conditions that must not be violated by a true natural kind. No natural-kind universal "cross-sects" with another.

Text (p. 694) and Translation

> ucyate | samavetatve dhvaṃsasya samavāyi-kāraṇa-nāśāt nāśaḥ syāt | na ca nāśyatve bhāvatvaṃ tantram, gauravāt prāg-abhāve 'bhāvāc ca |

Gaṅgeśa: We answer. If a destructional absence is to be taken as *inhering* in its locus, then upon the destruction of its inherent cause (the locus) it would be destroyed (resulting in a presence). And it is not the case that only positive reals can cease to exist (and so you cannot avoid the difficulty on these grounds). Not only would that be an overly cumbersome view, but there could be no ceasing of a prior absence.

Comments

Prior absence, of a pot, say, is a relevant causal factor in the pot's production, according to standard Nyāya theory. Its ceasing is equivalent to the pot's production. Gaṅgeśa makes this point by way of challenging the assumption that a causal factor has to have an inherent cause. An absence may well be a causal factor, but no absence inheres in what it qualifies. It is, instead, self-linking.

Text (p. 697) and Translation

> asamavetatve tad-dhvaṃsasya janyatve 'pi na nāśaḥ āśraya-nāśâder abhāvāt | ghaṭônmajjanâpatteḥ na naśyati iti cet,

Objection: But if the destructional absence of something does not inhere somewhere, then once something has arisen—and even though it has arisen (so that we expect it should perish in time)—destruction would not occur:

there would be no destruction, etc., with regard to a substratum (since the destruction would not have a substratum). To avoid the difficulty of again having the pot, we would have to say that it does not perish (to begin with).

Comments

The opponent claims that it is Gaṅgeśa's view that would entail the impossibility of destruction, not his own. Only that which has a substratum can be a causal factor; thus a destructional absence must have a substratum.

Text and Translation

> na |na hi prayojana-kṣati-bhayena sāmagrī na kāryam arjayati |tasmād unmajjanâbhāva-nirvāhakaṃ dhvaṃsasya asamavetatvaṃ kalpyatām | sva-samavāyi-nāśāt dhvaṃsa-paramparā-kalpane ca ghaṭa-kapālâdeḥ ā-paramâṇu nāśe ghaṭâdi-tad-dhvaṃsa-virodhī caramo dhvaṃsaḥ paramâṇu-vṛttiḥ syāt tathā ca na pratyakṣaḥ |ghaṭa-dhvaṃsasya kapāla-samavetatve ca na bhūtale nirūpaṇaṃ syāt |ubhaya-vṛttitve ca vyāsajya-vṛttitvena kapālaṃ vinā na nirūpyeta |

Gaṅgeśa: That's wrong. For we do not, out of fear of loss of a causal factor, say that a causal nexus sufficient to bring about an effect (*sāmagrī*) does not bring it about. Therefore, a destructional absence has to be considered not to inhere in order to avoid becoming mired (in the re-appearance of the destroyed pot). Let us imagine a series of destructions occurring through the ceasing to exist of something's inherent cause so that we would have the destruction of a pot through the destruction of its halves down to its ultimate atoms or minutest parts. The problem is that this last destruction, which would stand opposed both to the pot along with the series of smaller parts and to their destructions, would obtain in the ultimate atoms (which are imperceptible). And so, therefore, it could not be perceived. Furthermore, if the destruction of a pot inhered in the halves into which it is broken, the destruction would be experienced (there in the halves), not on the floor (where it is in fact experienced). And if you were to say that it exists in both, then, because they would be so closely bound up together, the halves would be necessarily an element of all the experience.

Comments

Thus, neither does a destructional absence nor any absence inhere anywhere. The relationality of absences is particular to each absence. A destructional absence of a pot could not occur in its ultimate atoms; perceiving on the floor a pot smashed to smithereens, we would not perceive its atoms but its destruction there where it occurs—on the floor.

8. Śaṅkara Miśra on Relationality and Distinctness

Introduction

See chapter 4, above, p. 150, for a few details about Śaṅkara Miśra's life.[63] The *Bhedaratna, The Jewel of Distinctness*, the work from which the following passages are drawn, is one of ten philosophic texts attributed to the fifteenth-century Naiyāyika.[64] Most notable among the others is a lucid commentary on Śrīharṣa's *Khkh*, where Śaṅkara Miśra explicates the Advaitin's reasonings, not, as here in the *Bhedaratna*, answering them. Śaṅkara Miśra has also to his credit a commentary on the *Vaiśeṣika-sūtra*.[65] According to D. C. Bhattacharya, Śaṅkara wrote poetry and drama and commented on *dharma-śāstra* in addition to his work as a Naiyāyika.

Text and Translation

māyâvidyā-prakṛtir iti yad gīyate dṛṣṭam etat
sāhityena tri-bhuvanamayīṃ sṛṣṭim etāṃ vitanvan |
ānando 'haṃ citir aham idaṃ manmayaṃ sarvam ittham
yaḥ svaṃ stauti śrutimaya-girā taṃ numo bhinnam īśam ||1 ||

mokṣāya spṛhayālavaḥ śruti-girāṃ śraddhālavo 'rthe ṛjau
tarkôdarka-vibhāvanāsu sutarāṃ vyājena nidrālavaḥ |
bhede dṛk-patham āgate 'pi sahasā tandrālavaś chāndasāḥ
kaivalyāt patayālavaḥ śṛṇuta sad-yuktiṃ dayālor mama ||2 ||

bheda-ratna-paritrāṇe tārkikā eva yāmikāḥ
ato vedāntinaḥ stenān nirasaty eṣa śaṅkaraḥ ||3 ||

dehâdes tāttvikād bhedam satyam ātmany ajānatām |
mumukṣūṇāṃ na mokṣo[66] 'sti ity ato bhedo nirūpyate ||4 ||

na sā dhīḥ kvacid apy asti yatra bhedo na bhāsate |
ata eva na tan-mānaṃ yan na bheda-pramāṇakam ||5 ||

(1) What is celebrated as Māyā, Avidyā, Prakṛti ("Magical Appearance," "Spiritual Ignorance," "Nature"), that is known in poetry as creation comprised of three worlds, O Omnipresent. "Bliss am I, awareness am I, all this, such as is, is made out of me"—who sings a song of himself in praise, with words of revelation, him we honor, the distinct Lord.

(2) Those desirous of liberation, with faith in the words of revelation, become exceedingly sleepy and lose good faith when it comes to presentations of arguments and consequences on topics painstakingly considered. Revealed verses are indeed a path showing the reality of distinctness, but some are lazy and liable of a sudden to fall away from enlightenment. So listen to my good reasoning—I am compassionate.

(3) For protection of the jewels of distinctness, logicians alone are diligent. Therefore this Śaṅkara is refuting those Vedāntin thieves.

(4) There is no liberation for seekers who do not know, concerning the self, the reality of its distinctness from the body and such. Therefore distinctness is here determined and defined.

(5) There is no cognition whatsoever where distinctness does not shine forth. Just for this reason there is no proof for anything that is not a proof of distinctness.

Comments

The last verse mocks Śrīharṣa's declaration that, as shown by his dialectic, there is "no cognition revealing distinctness that does not reveal non-distinctness as well."[67]

Throughout these verses of traditional opening (*maṅgala-vācana*, auspicious benedictory verses at the beginning of a text), Śaṅkara Miśra's aggressive tone is be noted. The expression "this Śaṅkara" in the third verse recalls Śaṅkara, the great Advaitin, in a disrespectful manner. There are also the explicit denouncements, in particular, the inflammatory "thieves."

Text and Translation

> tathā hi, "sa ha uvāca etad vai tad akṣaraṃ gārgi brāhmanā abhivadanty asthūlam anaṇv ahrasvam adīrgham alohitam asneham acchāyam atamo avāyv anākāśam asaṅgam asparśam agandham arasam acakṣuṣkam aśrotram avāg amano 'tejaskam aprāṇam asukham anāmā agotram ajaram amaram amṛtam arajo 'śabdam avivṛtam asaṃvṛtam apūrvam aparam anantam abāhyam na tad aśnoti kañcana na tad aśnoti kaścana" iti śrutyā 'nyonyâbhāvâtmaka-bhedasya eva naṅ-arthatvāt | tathā ca sthūlaṃ yac charīrâdi tad bhinnaṃ brahma ity arthaḥ | evam aṇu yan manas tad bhinnaṃ brahma ity arthaḥ | praśna-prakramāt |

For instance, consider the following scriptural passage (*Bṛhadāraṇyaka* 3.8.8):

> Then he (the *ṛṣi* Yājñavalkya) said, "O Gārgī, this indeed is that Imperishable. Sages say that it is not stout, not tiny, not short, not long, has no blood, does not stick to anything, is without shadow, is not dark, has not air, nor sky, is not attached, is beyond touch, beyond smell, beyond taste, beyond sight, beyond hearing, beyond speech, beyond the sense mind (*manas*), is not fiery, does not have breath nor a mouth, is beyond measure, without caste, does not age, is not dying, has no fear, is immortal, beyond passion, does not speak, is neither open nor closed, is neither before nor after, neither inside nor outside, does not reach anything nor does anything reach it."

Here the negative particle is used in the sense of mutual exclusion, which is the same idea as distinctness. And so it is to be understood that Brahman is distinct from what is stout, namely, the body and so on. It is also to be understood that Brahman is distinct from what is tiny (or atomic), such as the *manas* (sense-mind). This is the way to proceed on the issue.

Comments

In the original Sanskrit, most words in the Upanishadic passage are negative in meaning in virtue of the negative prefix *a-* ("un-"). There are a few phrases where the negative particle *nañ* ("not") is used instead.

Text and Translation

> asthūlam iti sthūlâtyantâbhāvavad ity artha iti cet, tathā api vaidharmya-bhedasya nañ-arthatvam | tathā ca anyonyâbhāva eva tad-arthaḥ | bheda-pratipatty-artham eva hi vaidharmyâbhidhānam | anyathā vaidharmyâbhidhānânarthakya-prasaṅgāt |

Even if "not stout" is to be understood in the sense of an absolute absence (as opposed to a mutual exclusion) of the stout, still the negative particle would express distinctness in the sense of qualitative distinctness, and so the meaning would still involve mutual exclusion. For it is just to communicate a distinctness that there is this mentioning of differences (or qualitative difference, *vaidharmya*); otherwise, the mentioning of differences would be meaningless—this is the difficulty.

Comments

Śaṅkara Miśra accepts Udayana's three types of distinctness: (a) distinctness by nature (*svarūpa*), (b) mutual exclusion (*anyonyābhāva*), and (c) difference in properties (*vaidharmya*). See above, pp. 104ff. However, he is not clear about just how the three differ and overlap. A difference in properties entails, he seems to say here, a mutual exclusion. As we saw, just what precisely is Udayana's position is also unclear; he seems to admit overlap but also explains the logic of each of the three differently. Vācaspati II, we will see, presents a more exact view.

Text and Translation

> na tad aśnoti kaścana iti | tad brahma kañcana ātmānaṃ na aśnoti na vyāpnoti | na vā kaścid ātmā tad brahma vyāpnoti | kena apy ātmanā kṣetrajñena na etat sambadhyate | vibhunoḥ saṃyoga-kāraṇânyatara-karmôbhaya-karmâvaya-saṃyogânupapattau saṃyogâbhāvād iti sva-rūpa-varṇanam |

"It does not reach anything" is to be understood as saying that Brahman does not coincide with (*vyāpnoti*) anything; nor does anything, any self, coincide with That, with Brahman. Brahman is not joined with any soul, any "knower of its field," since there is no action on the part of Brahman or a soul, both of which are pervasive, that could join them—nor an action by them both nor by their parts nor by a conjunction of their parts. This has to do with what each is in itself.

Comments

According to Nyāya, although there are indefinitely many individual souls, each is pervasive or of ubiquitous magnitude (*vibhu*), as is God (= Brahman). In the debate with Advaita, this view is plainly exploitable, although Śrīharṣa leaves it alone. My feeling is that Logicians generally were not very confident about the position, and it is not a primary interest. Some Logicians even have Advaita leanings on the score,[68] though not, we can see, Śaṅkara Miśra.

Text and Translation

evaṃ "mṛtyoḥ sa mṛtyum āpnoti ya iha nānā iva paśyati" iti śruti-bhede māṇam | sa puruṣo mṛtyoḥ saṃsārān[69] mṛtyum saṃsāram āpnoti punaḥ punaḥ saṃsarati, ya iha nānā iva paśyati, na tu vastu-gatyā eva nānā paśyati ity arthaḥ | iva-pada-sambandhāt | anythā nānā paśyaty eva syāt |

"He who sees here diversity, as it is apparently, goes from death to death" (*Bṛhadāraṇyaka* 4.4.19; *Kaṭha* 4.11), is also a scriptural passage that (despite what it has sometimes been taken to mean) proves distinctness. "Death" in this passage means rebirth, the round of birth and rebirth. So he, the individual conscious being (*puruṣa*), who sees here variously, as it is apparently, is reborn again and again. Note that the passage does not say that seeing diversity as it is in fact leads to rebirth; otherwise the word *iva*, "as it is apparently," would have been omitted. This is how the word ties in with the meaning of the statement. Otherwise (on the commonly supposed Advaita reading), the statement should have been, "He who indeed (*eva* instead of *iva*) sees diversity."

Comments

The Advaitin Śaṅkara of course reads the verse differently: "Apart from the superimposition of spiritual ignorance (*avidyā*), there is no duality (*dvaita*) concerning what is truly real—this is the meaning."[70]

Text and Translation

"sa kila eko draṣṭā advaito bhavati" iti śrutir api bheda-parā |anye tu draṣṭāraḥ kṣetrajñā bhedavantaḥ ity arthasya sa kila ity anena dhvananāt |"tat tvam asi" iti śrutir api bheda-parā |yuṣmac-chabdasya gamyamāna-bhinna-sambodhya-viṣayatvāt |"na tu tad-dvitīyam asti" iti śrutir api bheda-tātparyârthikā |tad brahma dvitīyaṃ na asti iti dharmy-uparāgeṇa niṣedhāt |anyathā hi dvaitaṃ na asti iti dharmôparāga-mātreṇa eva niṣedhaḥ syāt |

Also the scriptural passage, "He indeed comes to be a single seer, non-dual" (*Bṛhadāraṇyaka* 4.3.32), conveys distinctness. Other seers, the knowers of their fields, are distinct: this meaning is suggested through the use of *kila*, "indeed." "Thou art That" (*Chāndogya* 6.8.7 and elsewhere) is still another scriptural passage intending distinctness. The use of a form of the second-person pronoun is intended by implication as an address to someone distinct (from the speaker). The scriptural passage, "But it is not a second to that (that he may see)" (*Bṛhadāraṇyaka* 4.3.23), also conveys distinctness. The denial is focused on *that which possesses qualities* (the *dharmin*), and so the sense is that there is no second Brahman. For, otherwise, if the denial had concerned qualities, the text would have said, "There is no duality."

Comments

These passages are quoted by Śaṅkara and other Advaitins in support of their views. Śaṅkara Miśra's use of the word *yuṣmat*, the "second person pronoun," is particularly biting. It echoes sarcastically the opening sentence of the *Brahmasūtrabhāṣya* by the Advaitin Śaṅkara, where a distinction is drawn between the self (the real) and the non-self (the unreal) with this term used as shorthand for the latter.

Text and Translation

evaṃ "ekam eva advitīyaṃ brahma" iti śrutir api |brahmâtirikta-padârtha-nānātva-svīkāra eva brahmaṇi brahma-pratiyogitāka-bhedasya eva niṣedhāt |dharmi[71]-viśeṣa-samabhivyāhāra-balena eva tathā eva vyutpatteḥ |yathā iha bhū-maṇḍale eka eva nara-patir iti vākyād rāja-gata-nānātva-vyatirekaḥ pratīyate, na tu hasty-aśva-padātīnām api |yathā iha kānane kiṃśuka-tarur eka eva na tu nānā ity abhidhāne kiṃśuka-gatam eva nānātvaṃ niṣidhyate, na tu sāla-tamāla-hintālâdi-gatam api |

And in this way also the scriptural passage, "Brahman is one alone, without a second" (*Chāndogya* 6.2.1), is to be understood. It is definitely to be accepted that there is a diversity of things in addition to Brahman, because what is denied is that there is distinctness with respect to Brahman, i.e., the denial is of a distinctness (with respect to Brahman) whose counterpositive (*pratiyogin*) is Brahman (that is, that there is a second Brahman is denied).

This is based on etymological analysis precisely in accordance with the correlative force (*samabhivyāhāra-balena*) of mentioning a particular subject.

If we say that there is only one king on earth, then with the statement we are rejecting multipleness with respect to kings, not with respect to elephants, horses, and foot-soldiers, too. And if we say that there is in this forest only one Kiṃśuka tree, we are denying multiplicity with respect to the Kiṃśuka tree, not with respect to the Śāla, Tamāla, Hintāla, and other trees, too.

Comments

Śaṅkara Miśra uses *samabhivyāhāra* in the technical sense of a grammatical correlative requiring a complement, as with the correlative pronouns *yat* and *tat* (compare in English: *either . . . or*).[72]

The tendentious interpreting of Upanishadic passages continues for a dozen or so sentences. Śaṅkara Miśra's principal argument is that the texts presuppose distinctness, that without understanding one kind of distinctness or another we could not understand these passages of revelation. We skip ahead now to a summary statement, which is followed by an argument concerning relational awareness and an ingenious response to a crucial objection.

Text (p. 3, line 21) and Translation

> . . . tathā ca na sā śrutiḥ yatra śabda-balād artha-balād vā bhedo na bhāsata iti |

And so scriptural revelation is such that nowhere either by force of words literally or by force of intention does distinctness not shine forth.

Comments

Like the last of the opening verses, this summary statement—concluding Śaṅkara Miśra's Upanishadic exegesis—mocks Śrīharṣa's contention that there is no cognition that does not, upon analysis, establish non-distinctness. In his next statement, the Naiyāyika directly contradicts the Advaitin again.

Text and Translation

> kiṃ ca na sā dhīr yatra bhedo na viṣayaḥ | tathā hi, viśiṣṭa-jñānānāṃ vaiśiṣṭya-viṣayatayā eva bheda-viṣayatā | vaiśiṣṭyasya padârthântaratvânupapattau pariganita-bhāva-padârthânantarbhāve atad-vyāvṛtti-rūpânyonyâbhāvâkhya-bheda-rūpatayā eva vācyā | tathā ca vaiśiṣṭya-viṣayaka-jñānānāṃ siddhā bheda-viṣayatā | tad āhur kiraṇāvalyām | "atad-vyāvṛttir vaiśiṣṭyam"[73] iti |

Moreover, cognition (*dhī*) is such that in no case is distinctness not its content. For so it is that qualificative (or relational) cognitions, just in having the qualificative relation as objective content, have distinctness as objective content. That is, this objective content is to be described as consisting simply of distinctness (*bheda*), distinctness also known as mutual exclusion (which is a type of absence or negative real, the seventh category) in the form of an exclusion: there is no reason to suppose that the qualificative relation is an entirely new category, but also it is not included in those categories of positive things that are admitted in the system (*pariganita*). And thus it is established that distinctness is cognized in cognitions whose content is qualificative (or relational). So he (our revered teacher Udayana) has said in his *Kiraṇāvalī*, "The qualificative relation involves exclusion."

Comments

The quotation is indeed from Udayana's *Kiraṇāvalī*.[74]

Now we face an interpretive problem. Relationality involves exclusion in two distinct ways: (a) exclusion of the qualifier from what is not that (for example, blue from the non-blue[75]), and (b) non-identity (= mutual exclusion) of the qualifier and the particular it qualifies (for example, the blue and the lotus). Udayana's focus is on the former exclusion, concerning the nature of a qualifier. But he may be read as understanding a qualified cognition as involving exclusion in both ways.

Udayana's context is the nature of number as a qualifier caused by an enumerative cogntion, that is to say, by an act of counting. Numbers are real qualifiers, existing in objects, but are short-lived (except for the number one) as brought about by an enumerative cognition. An especially important point made in passing is that without a qualificandum as distinct from its qualifiers, counting would be impossible. The qualificandum—as bare particular—would secure the necessary individuation. Udayana says explicitly that there is "no identity between the property and the property-bearer,"[76] and then rehearses the point about preconditions of counting. Thus his view that being single (*eka*) is an enduring property independent of cognition (whereas the numbers two, three, and so on are dependent on the act of counting) suggests he is thinking of the qualificandum as the fundamental individuator. But, admittedly, in the paragraph as a whole his chief interest is the exclusion accomplished by the qualifier with regard to other qualifiers (the blue from the non-blue).

Nevertheless, my inclination is to read Śaṅkara Miśra as meaning (b) lack of identity between qualifier and qualificandum entailed by the qualificative relation. Thus Śaṅkara would expand on Udayana's reflections to understand the relationality of qualified cognition to involve, in all cases, distinctness between qualifier and qualificandum. This interpretation makes Śaṅkara Miśra's insistence that all cognition reveals distinctness more than mere hand-waving: all relational cognition is shown to do so by the present argument; all non-relational (indeterminate) cognition is shown to do so by an immediately subsequent argument. Reading the term *vaiśiṣṭyam*, then, as relation, the point is that the relation separating the qualificandum from the qualifier is to be understood, most generally, as distinctness (or, perhaps, as presupposing distinctness). Thus analytic truths would be ruled out;[77] all relational cognitions would be—in their verbal expression—synthetic, proving distinctness by way of the difference between the meanings of the subject and predicate terms, so to say. Even the simplest qualified cognition, "(A) pot," for example, would reflect a distinctness between a qualifier, potness, and a particular as qualificandum.

This reading does not imply that Śaṅkara Miśra is abandoning the traditional view that inherence (*samavāya*) is, at least often, the relation underpinning a relational cognition. Inherence is, to be sure, "included in those categories of positive things that are admitted in the system (*pariganita*)," and it is unlikely that Śaṅkara Miśra would overlook this or fail to flag a departure from the traditional ontology. Inherence is included in the much wider (albeit ontologically problematic) relation that involves qualifiers and qualificanda. In many instances of qualification—for example, of an absence and its locus—no inherence is involved. Thus relationality in general, though including inherence, falls outside the six categories of positive reals.

Finally, this reading fits well with an upcoming objection that Śaṅkara Miśra puts to himself that his view is indistinguishable from the Buddhist *apoha*, "exclusion," theory of meaningfulness.

On the other hand, in text that follows, Śaṅkara Miśra seems to take "relationality" to involve both types of exclusion: the exclusion that the qualifier accomplishes and the distinctness presupposed in the relation between the qualifier and the qualificandum. Here I am tempted to say that even great thinkers commit small errors of equivocation, but, as we saw with Gaṅgeśa on inherence, a crucial argument for the distinctness between qualifier and qualificandum is that the latter can be cognized in distinct ways. Thus the exclusion at the level of qualifiers informs the exclusion between qualifier and qualificandum.

Śaṅkara Miśra's manner of framing his argument is unimpressive; he follows the tradition of Udayana in giving a (too!) succinct formulation. The reason he gives for saying that the relationality of relational cognitions amounts to, most generally, a distinctness between the qualificandum and qualifier terms is that it cannot be included among the six positive categories and that there are no grounds to suppose that it is an additional primitive. This way of putting the point disguises its forcefulness. We can explain at length why relationality is not a substance, quality, motion, and so on; again, it does not amount to inherence, although it includes it, because, for instance, the relationality of absential cognitions does not involve inherence. Then, before we grant it the status of an additional primitive, we look first at the seventh category and see if it can be plugged in there. And it can. The bare particular transcends qualificative determinations. Śaṅkara Miśra's point could be elaborated and shored up in a number of ways (in the manner of Gaṅgeśa: see above, pp. 251–52). Unfortunately, he does not elaborate here.

Now, not every cognition is a relational or determinate cognition. There are also indeterminate cognitions. Thus, to show that every cognition has distinctness as content, Śaṅkara Miśra has to take up the indeterminate variety. This he proceeds to do after first countering an objection that supposes that relationality (entailing distinctness of qualifier and qualificandum) is not objective content in indeterminate cognition and thus could not be so in determinate cognition.

Text and Translation

> nanu nirvikalpakânantarbhāvino ghaṭo 'yam iti savikalpaḥ syāt |tad-vyāvṛttir ajñātā pūrvaṃ kathaṃ viṣaya iti cen na |vaiśiṣṭya-viṣayatvânyathânupapattyā saṃjñā-smaraṇasya iva nirvikalpaka-samanantara-kālīnasya pratyayasya atad-vyāvṛtti-viṣayatva-kalpanāt |sarvathā hy anyathânupapattir balīyasī |

Objection: In that case, a determinate cognition such as "This is a pot" would not derive from a (preceding) indeterminate cognition (contrary to common Nyāya theory). The exclusion is not cognized in the preceding (indeterminate cognition). How, then, can it be objective content (in the succeeding determinate cognition)?

Answer: Wrong. There is a cognitive act that immediately follows the indeterminate cognition—somewhat like a remembering of terms—which is to be considered (*kalpanāt*) as having the exclusion as objective content—otherwise it would be impossible that there be qualificative objective content. For (as Kumārila says) in all cases the reasoning that otherwise some fact would be impossible is overwhelming.

Comments

The process of the change from indeterminate to determinate awareness is an area of Nyāya theory that is not well worked out. Śaṅkara Miśra may be taken to contribute to the project by insisting that in the process relationality (i.e., qualificative distinctness) does become determinate content, as is the case with the other factors in relational cognition. The terms of a relational cognition are not cognized playing their roles of qualificandum and qualifier in indeterminate awareness; the relation has to be in place, so to say, for them to be so cognized. In the process of the change from indeterminate to determinate, qualificative cognition, the relation assumes its role as relational content. Of course, this view entails that distinctness has to be cognized as a factor in indeterminate awareness. But since, as Gaṅgeśa argues, indeterminate awareness is itself a theoretical demand, Śaṅkara Miśra assumes that the same consideration shows that the relation must be somehow cognized in indeterminate cognition. Later, he will elaborate a little.

The quote from Kumārila mocks Śrīharṣa in that the Advaitin also cites this tenet of the Mīmāṃsaka concerning the demands of theoretical supposition (*arthāpatti*, see the glossary).[78]

Text and Translation

> evaṃ saty anyâpohaḥ syāt |tathā ca jitaṃ bauddhair iti cen na |gotvâdīnāṃ padânupasthitau vaiśiṣṭyam api kasya bhāsate, yena anyâpohatā syāt |tathā ca bauddha-pakṣād ayam eva bhedo yat tair anyâpoha eva padârthatvâvacchedako dharmo aṅgīkriyate |asmābhis tu gotvâdir iti nirvikalpaka-dhiyāṃ yady api vaiśiṣṭyaṃ na viṣaya iti anyonyâbhāvo bhedo na bhāsate, tathā 'pi sva-rūpa-bhedo ghaṭâdi-vaidharmyaṃ ca ghaṭatvâdir bhāsate tena eva bheda-viṣayatā |tad api bhedatvena na bhāsata iti[79] yat kiñcid etat |

Objection: If this is right, then "excluding the other" would be what it amounts to. And so you would give the victory to the Buddhists (who embrace such a view of qualification and determinate cognition).

Answer: No. According to them, there is no verbal memory of (the universals) cowness and the like. So with what would there be a qualificative relation made manifest, whereby there would be an "exclusion of the other?"

And so our view is distinct from that of the Buddhists in this way: what by them is accepted as a characteristic specifying a meaning, namely, just an "excluding of the other," according to us amounts to (real universals) cowhood and the like.

Although (of course) the qualificative relation is not objective content with respect to indeterminate cognition—and so distinctness as mutual exclusion is not manifest—still the essential distinctness and the having of different qualities by a pot and so on, which amounts to the presence of (the universals) potness and so on, does appear. Therefore, the objectivity of distinctness. Even if it does not appear *as* distinctness, what does it matter?

Comments

In indeterminate cognition, a pot does not appear as a pot. That a pot appear as a pot requires that the individual be cognized through the qualifier potness. Potness is cognized in indeterminate cognition but not as qualifying the qualificandum. Similarly, distinctness is cognized in indeterminate cognition, but not *as* distinctness (*bhedatvena*). Of course, the qualificative nature of qualificative cognitions is not manifest in indeterminate awareness: if it were, there would be no indeterminate awareness. Distinctness is present in indeterminate awareness in the same way as the universals potness and so on are, i.e., as cognized in indeterminate awareness but not as manifest. Distinctness is a ground of qualificative cognition, as are universals.

The key consideration ruling out the Buddhist *apoha* view (see chapter 1, pp. 23–24, for elaboration) is that no account of memory is available. Without direct acquaintance with real universals, there would be no basis for the subsumption of perceptual information under one heading rather than another. Qualifiers do differentiate; to this extent the Buddhists are correct. But on the Buddhist view, there is nothing to be differentiated from. Assimilation to previous experience of tokens of the same type cannot be accounted for without admitting the objective reality of universals and other qualifiers.

Śaṅkara Miśra also argues that the relationality of determinate cognitions would be essentially incomplete without the reality of the likes of universals. There would be nothing for the qualificandum to relate to.

Text and Translation

tad evaṃ sarva-dhiyāṃ bheda-viṣayatve siddhe sarva-pramāṇānāṃ bheda-pramā-ekatvam ayatna-siddham |

So since it is in this way established that every cognition has distinctness as objective content, unanimity is easily shown with all the sources of knowledge (perception, inference, etc.) with regard to knowledge of distinctness.

Comments

Thus Śaṅkara Miśra's argument has had two steps: first, showing that determinate or qualificative cognition has distinctness as objective content, and second, showing that indeterminate cognition has distinctness as objective content, albeit not as manifest content, in accordance with the indeterminate nature of the cognition.

Next, Śaṅkara Miśra goes on to put in a few good words about the enterprises of philosophy (*anvīkṣā*) for those seeking liberation (*mumukṣūṇām*), arguing that reasoning is necessary just for the interpretation of scripture. We skip ahead one paragraph (five sentences) to an epistemological argument, which is followed by Śaṅkara Miśra's statement of and response to a key dialectical argument of Śrīharṣa's.

Text and Translation

nanu bhedaś ced yuktiṃ na sahate, tadā śruti-vākyānām api bheda-paratvena tvayā upadarśitānāṃ tātparyântaram eva unnetum arhati iti cet |yuktiṃ na sahata iti ko 'rthaḥ ? kiṃ bhedânubhava eva na asti, sann api vā na yathârthaḥ |na tāvad ādyaḥ |ghaṭāt paṭau bhinna ity-ādi-bhedânubhavasya laukika-parīkṣakasya apalāpânarhatvāt |na api dvitīyaḥ |ayathārthatā hi viṣaya-bādha-gamyā, bādhakaṃ ca viparīta-pramā, sā ca na prakṛte[80] prātyakṣakī tāvan na asti, ghaṭaḥ paṭo na bhavati iti pratyakṣânantaraṃ ghataḥ paṭa eva iti viparīta-pratyakṣasya abhāvāt |

Objection: But if distinctness does not bear up under argumentative scrutiny, then another sense of the sentences of scripture than that—namely, distinctness—represented by you should be brought forward.

Answer: What do you mean by "distinctness does not bear up under argumentative scrutiny?" Do you mean that there is no experience of distinctness, or that, though experienced, distinctness is not in conformity with the way things are?

First, the former option is ruled out. There is no point in denying the common experience of distinctness had by ordinary people and philosophers alike, for example, "The cloth is distinct from the pot." Nor is the latter option any good. For non-conformity with the way things are is to be known from the negation (or sublation, *bādha*) of a content, and this negation would be a true cognition of something opposed (to the former content). And this, in the case under consideration (*prakṛte*), simply does not occur perceptually: there is no contrary perception, "The pot is just a cloth," that ever follows the perception, "The pot is not a cloth."

Comments

Śaṅkara Miśra uses the Advaita term (*bādha*, "sublation") for understanding illusion, apparently to make his argument all the more forceful from an Advaita perspective.

However, his point is not denied. That people commonly experience distinctness is expressly admitted by Śrīharṣa, who is echoed here.[81] Śaṅkara Miśra adds that there never occurs a perceptual, sublational cognition expressible as "The pot is a cloth." It seems to me that Śrīharṣa could accept this as well. On the other hand, the Advaitin would want to assert that an unverbalizable sublation (revealing Brahman) does occur.

Text and Translation

nanu nīlaṃ tama iti pratyakṣânantaraṃ na idaṃ nīla-tama iti prātyakṣika-bādhâbhāve 'pi yathā tava mate tad-bādhyatvam eva, ahaṃ sthūlo gauro vā ity-ādi-pratyayânantaraṃ na ahaṃ sthūlo gaura ity-ādi prātyakṣika-bādhâbhāve 'pi bhrāntatvaṃ, tathā prkṛte 'pi syāt |yaukika-bādhasya ubhayatra api tulyatvād iti cet |mā evam |bheda-bodhaka-yukty-abhāvāt |

Objection: But how about "Darkness is blue?" Here, even if there is no perceptual sublation, "Darkness is not blue," as you would require, still the cognition is to be rejected (since it is in error). In this way, with such cognitions as "I am stout" or "I am light-complexioned," though there is no perceptual sublation, "I am not stout" or "I am not light-complexioned," that follows upon the idea of an "I," still they are in error. So, too, would be the case under consideration (namely, cognition of distinctness). The rational rejection (*yaukiki-bādha*) is the same in both cases.

Answer: No, there is no rational consideration urging rejection of distinctness.

Comments

Advaitins from as early as Padmapāda distinguish two types of perceptual illusion: (a) the rationally corrigible (*sopādhika*, "conditional"), such as the sight of a double moon by an astigmatic, the red appearance of a crystal because of the proximity of a red flower, and the reflection of an object in a mirror, and (b) the rationally incorrigible (*nirupādhika*, "unconditional"), such as a silver/mother-of-pearl illusion and a rope taken to be a snake. The former are presentations that remain misleading, Padmapāda points out, even after one understands that they do not present a true reality, unlike the case of the snake and the rope.[82] "Darkness is blue" is another example that is known to be an illusion not through experiential sublation, but through non-phenomenological considerations, that is to say, through rational rejection (*yaukika-bādha*). A story can be told in each instance why what appears, and continues to appear, one way is not like that. What considerations, what arguments, are there as to why the distinctness of distinct things should be considered a perceptual error? In this way, Śaṅkara Miśra lays the burden of proof at the feet of the Advaitin.

In other words, the objector holds that the "I" is nothing but Brahman, the Absolute, and thus that any physical attribution such as being stout would be an error, although there are perceptual presentations with such content. The objector presumes that the error can be demonstated rationally—without the mystical sublation that shows the "I" to be Brahman. What, then, is the argument undermining distinctness?

Text and Translation

nanv asti sā | tathā hi, bhedavattayā ghaṭâdayo bhinnā ity abhidhīyate | tatra[83] bhedo 'bhinne vartate bhinne vā | tatra na abhinne, virodhāt | na hy abhinnaṃ bhinnaṃ bhavati | dvitīye tu tad-bheda-vṛttau kathaṃ na ātmâśrayaḥ | sva-viśiṣṭe vṛttāv aṃśataḥ sva-vṛtteḥ | bhedântareṇa bhinne 'dhikaraṇe bheda-vṛtty-abhyupagame tatra api evam abhyupagamena[84] kathaṃ na anavasthā | ekena bhedena bhinne dvitīyas tena bhinne prathamo[85] bhedo vartata ity ātmâśrayânavasthayoḥ parihāre 'py anyonyâśrayaḥ |bahavo bhedā yugapad eva jñāyamānam[86] vastu parirambhante ity abhyupagame kiṃ-bheda-viśiṣṭe ko bhedo vartata[87] iti teṣām anyonya-kalaho dussamādhaḥ |prathamena eva bhedena bhinne vastuni dvitīyâdi-bhedâbhyupagame vaiyarthyam |uttarôttara-bhedâṅgīkāre ca kṛtakatvena pūrva-pūrva-bheda-vilopa iti cet |

Objection: No, there is an argument for the rejection. Consider. Pots and the like are distinct in that they "have distinctness," on your view. Now when you say this, is the distinctness in something non-distinct or distinct? Of the two alternatives, it is not the non-distinct, because that would be contradictory. For the non-distinct does not come to be distinct. But then concerning the second option—where the distinctness is in something distinct from itself, in the locus or occurrence (*vṛtti*) of that distinctness—how is this not the fault (according to your own view) of "self-dependence?" Its occurrence would be qualified by itself because it would have to occur in itself, at least partially. If it is held that the distinctness occurs in a substratum (*adhikaraṇa*)—with that (substratum) as distinct from some other distinctness—then with this view too there is a problem: how is there not an infinite regress (one distinctness existing in something distinct from another distinctness)? In something distinct from a first distinctness, there is a second, and the first distinctness occurs in something distinct from that. So even if you avoid self-dependence and infinite regress, you have the problem of "mutual dependence." Many distinctnesses simultaneously embrace the thing being cognized. Even if you can swallow this, we must ask: which distinctness exists in that qualified by which distinctness? Among these (distinctnesses) you have a mutual quarrel and a situation impossible to reconcile. It is useless to postulate a second distinctness and so on in a thing distinct from a first distinctness. And if you go on accepting one distinctness after another—or, artificially constructing one after another, we should say—there will be, with one in front of the other, a break in the distinctness relation.

Comments

"Self-dependence" (*ātmāśraya*) is listed by Udayana as a type of "dialectical reasoning" (*tarka*); that is, it is an undesired consequence that would eliminate a position entailing it. According to the *Nyāyakośa*, it is a matter of something presupposing itself with respect to production, continued existence, or knowledge.[88] For example, if the production of something required that it already be produced, it could not occur because the presupposition could not be fulfilled. What is needed is a prior production P_2, but that would presuppose P_3, *ad infinitum*. Similar remarks hold for "mutual dependence" (*anyonyāśraya*) except that an additional factor is involved: x presupposing y

and vice-versa with respect to production, etc.

These problems are voiced by Śrīharṣa, though not all at once as we have them here.[89]

Text and Translation

> mā evam | vartata iti saṃyoga-lakṣaṇāṃ samavāya-lakṣaṇāṃ vā vṛttim adhikṛtya yadi praśnas tadā anyonyâbhāvâtmako bhedo na vartata ity eva uttaram | abhāvasya saṃyoga-samavāyayor anaṅgīkārāt |

Don't think like that. Listen. Taking "occurs" (or "exists in," *vartate*) as an abstract (*vṛtti*) to be indicated by conjunction or by inherence with a question (about what distinctness in this regard amounts to), then the response should be that in that sense distinctness—mutual exclusion—does not *occur in* anything, it does not *exist in* in that sense. We do not accept either conjunction or inherence of an absence.

Comments

Mutual exclusion or distinctness is a type of absence. The logic of the relationality of absences is different from that of conjunction and inherence.

Text and Translation

> atha sva-rūpa-lakṣaṇāṃ vṛttim adhikṛtya praśnaḥ tadā ghaṭaḥ sva-bhāva-niyamān nityena anyonyâbhavena uparakto bhāsata ity eva uttaram |

But, on the other hard, if the question is framed taking the abstract "occurrence" or "existence in" to introduce a self-linking term, then the response should be just that a pot (for example) presents itself by force of what it is by nature under the mode of (or, colored by, *uparakta*) a constant mutual exclusion (or absence).

Comments

Thus, Śaṅkara Miśra hangs his hat on self-linkage. The problem is, as we have discussed, how this is able to avoid a charge of identity (*tādātmya*) between the terms related (here *distinctness* as qualifier of a qualificandum), and, in particular, loss of layeredness between qualifier and qualificandum, notwithstanding the previous argument that the relationality of relational cognitions is a matter of distinctness between qualifier and qualificandum. That argument would fall to infinite regress without self-linkage.

The pot's ontological identity just with itself underpins the notion of "what it (a pot) is by nature." Identity is a non-occurrence-exacting relation;

similarly distinctness; neither occurs *in* a locus or substratum. I take it that this is the reason why Śaṅkara Miśra uses the term *uparakta*, "tinged" or "colored by," invoking the semantic polemics of the "mere designating expression" (*upalakṣaṇa*): this self-linkage is not, strictly speaking, a matter of "occurrence." Thus the question of how there can be distinctness as a self-linking *attribution* seems all the more pressing.

But however urgent that question, Śaṅkara Miśra addresses himself next to objections to the constancy or eternity of the relation—in a paragraph omitted here. Distinctness is "eternal" in the sense that a pot never was, is, nor could be a cloth. A similar story is told with universals: cowhood and a cow become inseparably related as soon as the individual is born. Thus, to the question, how can distinctness be an eternal relation when the distinct individual (e.g., a pot as distinct from a cloth) is non-eternal, the answer is that the eternity is like that of universals whose instances are non-eternal. (No universal exists apart from its instances, but given that there are cows, for example, what it is to be a cow is forever fixed.)

Within the same paragraph, Śaṅkara Miśra addresses a different charge, "self-dependence" (*ātmāśraya*). Undercutting the objection, he says, "We do not hold that there is any further distinctness in a distinctness." What backs up this reply is the view that "The occurrence (or existence, *vṛtti*) of the qualificandum is not the same as that of the qualifier. For when someone says, 'There is color in the pot,' neither the color nor the thing's being present exists in the universal potness as well as in the particular pot; nor is there an appearance to this effect." In other words, one has to be sensitive to subtle differences of relation and mode of existence or occurrence. The way distinctness qualifies a qualificandum is distinct.

Śaṅkara Miśra has begun to hone in on the qualificandum-qualifier relationship with respect to distinctness. The next issue raised is the distinction between the mode of relatedness of a true qualifier, *viśeṣaṇa*, and that of a mere designating attribute, *upalakṣaṇa*. This is potentially crucial in that certain ontological problems could be skirted by arguing that talk of identity and distinctness is not to be taken as reflecting true qualifiers. Rather such talk would be mere designating devices. Later, however, Śaṅkara Miśra rejects this view. (Vācaspati II, on the other hand, seems prone to accept it, as we will see below.) For a few sentences, Śaṅkara seems to get sidetracked with the problem of the eternity of distinctness (again). Then returning to the *upalakṣaṇa* issue, he argues that whereas distinctness could be viewed as a mere designating attribution (such as "perching crows," said of Devadatta's house just to pick it out, not to say what it is), it is better or more properly viewed as a true qualifier. After all, the point seems to be, designating attributions, although external and extrinsic to what a thing is, may nonetheless be true of it.[90] We return to the text now with this answer by Śaṅkara Miśra.

Text (top of p. 6) and Translation

> vastutas tu viśeṣaṇatve 'pi na doṣaḥ | pratyāyya-vyāvṛtty-adhikaraṇatâvacchedakatvaṃ sva-kāla-niyata-vyāvṛtti-bodha-janakatvaṃ vā viśeṣaṇatvam | tac ca viśeṣya-vṛtti-dharmânadhikaraṇatāyām api sambhavaty eva | tathā ca tad-bhedânāśrito 'pi sa bhedas tad-bhedavad āśrito bhaviṣyati iti na virodhaḥ |

But as a matter of fact, there is no fault in understanding this (i.e., distinctness) too to be a case of qualifiers. To be a qualifier is to specify a locus whereby the thing to be known becomes a differentiator, or it is to make known an exclusion fixed at the time of the cognition of the thing cognized. And that indeed is possible even with qualities that exist in the same qualified thing but not at precisely the same place (or time). And similarly, a distinctness, although it is not the locus of that distinctness, will be supported by something that has the distinctness: there is no contradiction here.

Comments

There are many respects in which a thing is distinct from other things, infinitely many, we may say, assuming something's properties and relations to other things are infinite. What is expressly excluded depends on what properties are cognized; in this sense, distinctnesses are fixed at the time of cognition. Distinctness occurs along with any qualification whatsoever. But a qualifier is also distinct as qualifying something distinct from itself. The ground for calling the qualifier distinct in this way is not, however, an entity existing in the qualifier. The higher distinctness is identical with the qualifier.

What is a qualifier? A qualifier makes known a difference of its locus from other loci. But qualifiers admit delimitations; similarly, distinctness. Thus, there is no contradiction between distinctness in one direction—toward the qualificandum—and distinctness in another direction—toward loci the qualificandum is different from. This response appears to be Śaṅkara Miśra's outstanding contribution to the realist cause.

Śaṅkara now goes on to defend the sense in which distinctness—i.e., mutual exclusion—is an eternal relation. The point is, again, that the eternality is like that of universals: what it is to be a cow is eternally fixed by the cowhood inhering in just two cows. It would not matter were all cows to disappear. Similarly, mutual exclusions are eternally fixed by the nature of the things that do the excluding.

In the following paragraph, Śaṅkara Miśra attacks the trickiness in Śrīharṣa's questions as indicating bad character. We skip ahead to ten lines from the bottom of the page (p. 6).

Text and Translation

paṭa-pratiyogiko bhedaḥ paṭâbhinne[91] ghaṭe vartate paṭa-bhinne vā iti viśiṣya praśne kṛte sāmānyena uttaraṃ na ghaṭata iti cet |na |anunmattasya etādṛśa-praśnânupapatteḥ |virodhitâvacchedaka-prakāreṇa upasthitasya dharmiṇo viruddha-prakāratvâvacchedena praśnasya adṛṣṭa-caratvāt |na hi bhavati mṛnmayo 'yaṃ ghaṭas tejomayo, na vā brāhmaṇo 'yaṃ caitraḥ śūdro[92] na vā |anyathā vijñānâtmakaṃ brahma jaḍaṃ na vā, sukhâtmakaṃ brahma duḥkhâtmakaṃ na vā iti pṛcchato yukti-śatena tvayā sādhyamāne 'pi vijñāna-sukhâtmakatve pṛcchā-nivṛttir na syāt |yadi vā ahṛdayasya[93] kadācid evaṃ-vidha-praśna-sambhavas tadā uttaraṃ dattam eva anveṣṭavyam |

Objection: The distinctness that has as its counterpositive a cloth, does it exist in a pot as non-distinct from the cloth or as distinct from the cloth? Once this question has been put concerning particulars, it is impossible to come up with an answer in general.

Answer: No, because no person who was not mad[94] would pose such a question. Once something's nature has been established by way of a determination of what it is opposed to, we do not see arising (at least on the part of sane persons, or those of good faith) questions challenging whether there really is the opposition. For there is no question whether a pot made out of clay is made out of a fiery substance or not; nor whether the brahmin Caitra is a śūdra or not. Otherwise (to consider your Advaita view), there might be a question whether Brahman, the Absolute, which is by nature consciousness, is inconscient or not, or whether Brahman, which is by nature blissful, is full of pain or not. For someone questioning like this, there would be no end to it—about the consciousness or bliss of Brahman—though the matter be established by you by a hundred arguments. And if someone with no heart (in bad faith) happens to put forth this sort of question, then just the sort of answer that has been given is to be searched out.

Comments

The objection is a paraphrase of Śrīharṣa.[95]

In his reply, Śaṅkara Miśra echoes misgivings of the *Nyāya-sūtra* commentators about those who try to pick holes in a position without being motivated out of a sense of the demands of their views, as we discussed in chapter 2 (above, pp. 65–66).[96]

Text and Translation

bheda kutra vartate ity atra praśne, yatra pratīyate ity uttaram |kutra pratīyata ity atra praśne yatra vartata ity-ādy apy uttara-vaicitryaṃ vārtikânusāreṇa draṣṭavyam |

To the question, "Where does distinctness exist," the answer is, "Where it appears."

"Where does it appear?"

"Here where it exists." This sort of strange answer is to be given in conformity with our realism as articulated, for example, (by Uddyotakara) in the *Nyāyasūtra-vārttika.*

Comments

Uddyotakara is referred to, it seems to me, because he is the first Logician to respond in depth to Buddhists whose attacks are similarly oblique. I have been unable to find a specific passage in his *NyS-V,* however, that matches this reply of Śaṅkara's.

Śaṅkara continues by advising his compatriots who happen to find themselves in debates with Advaitins ("who are difficult to deal with"), to stick to their guns, foremost, but also to try to turn the tables of the slippery arguments of the adversary by questioning him about Brahman in relation to its non-distinctness. Then, for several sentences, much of Śrīharṣa's barrage concerning distinctness is reversed, mirrored in questions about Brahman and its non-distinctness, for example, "Is Brahman non-distinct from just that non-distinctness or with another?" We will skip this section—it is mostly mere *tu quoque* (*pratibandhī*) and does not advance the essentials of the argument—and pick up the text with the very last line of page 7.

Text (p. 7, last line) and Translation

nanu ghaṭâdi-sva-rūpaṃ ced bhedaḥ, tadā yato yato bhedas taṃ tam atha apy antarbhāvayet |na hi niśpratiyogika-ghaṭâdi-sva-rūpa-bhedaḥ |tathā ca sati bheda eva tan na syāt |niṣpratiyogikasya bhedasya tvayā anabhyupagamāt |abhyupagame vā paribhāṣâpatteḥ |tathā ca ghaṭa-pratiyogikaṃ ghaṭa-sva-rūpaṃ bheda ity arthâvasāne ghaṭo 'pi paṭa-sva-rūpaṃ syāt |ato bhedâvatārāya so 'bheda-sādhana-paryavasāyī iti mahā-tārkikatvam |evaṃ ca ghaṭa-sva-rūpasya bhedasya pratiyogi-paṭasya sva-rūpam ity anayā rītyā ghaṭo 'pi paṭa-sva-rūpa-magna ity abheda eva iti cet |

Objection: If distinctness is just what a pot, etc., are, their "very nature" (*svarūpa*), then from whatever there is distinctness that also would be included in it. For there is no distinctness—(albeit understood) as the very nature of a pot and so on—without a counterpositive (something that the pot, etc., would be distinct from). And this being the case, distinctness indeed! It would not be, since you yourself do not accept a distinctness devoid of a counterpositive. Or if you do accept it, then you are still in a fix because you have abandoned your definition. And similarly, a pot too would be of the very nature of a cloth given this view of distinctness, namely, that it is the very nature of a pot possessing the (necessarily correlate) counterpositive of the pot, as was concluded. Therefore, your troubling yourself to make distinctness appear winds up establishing non-distinctness. Oh you clever reasoners! And in this way, through the manner of reasoning that the very nature of a distinctness in the form of a pot has a cloth as its counterpositive, the pot becomes absorbed into the very nature of a cloth: therefore non-distinctness.

Comments

Śaṅkara Miśra is setting up his position concerning what a counterpositive is by having a *pūrvapakṣin* opponent rehearse this argument of Śrīharṣa's. Recall that the Nyāya position concerning the counterpositive of an absence—the absentee—is not only a matter of logical analysis but also reflects the Nyāya empiricist theory of mind: *x* must have been previously cognized by a person for the person to have an awareness of the absence of *x*.

Text and Translation

> mā evam, paṭa-pratiyogikaṃ ghaṭa-sva-rūpaṃ bheda ity ucyamāne paṭaḥ pratiyogī yasya iti bahuvrīhi-samāsâśrayaṇād eva samasyamāna-padârthībhūtāt paṭāt tad-anya-padârtho ghaṭo bhinnatve tvayā eva upadarśita iti, tvayā eva abhedâpādanasya apahastitatvāt | samasyamāna-padârthād anyasya eva bahuvrīhy-arthatvāt | na hi citra-gur devadatta ity ukte citrayā gavā api devadattasya abhedaḥ pratīyate, kiṃ tarhi go-viśeṣaṇa-mātram | prakṛte 'pi ghaṭa-bhedatvena paṭa-sva-rūpe nirūpya-māṇe ghaṭasya viśeṣaṇatva-mātram abhyupetaṃ na abhedo 'pi iti[97] |

Answer: You are wrong. It is indeed our view that distinctness is the very nature of (e.g.) a pot having a counterpositive that is (e.g.) a cloth. But in saying that the pot is something other than the cloth, the cloth has become something referred to through being compounded in this fashion: "The cloth is the counterpositive *of* something (the pot referred to)." The reason for this is just that the dependence is like that (in grammar) of a *bahuvrīhi* compound (where a phrase that does not *directly* refer to a referent, e.g., "much rice," is to be analyzed as related to a referent by a relation, e.g., possession, typical of this type of compound, e.g., *he who has* much rice). The something, the pot, would have to be explained even by you as distinct, since even for you non-distinctness has to be taken in a grammatical construction where it would stand as that *from* which there would be something apart (i.e., the meaning of the ablative case in Sanskrit), because, again, according to the meaning of *bahuvrīhi* compounds, there has to be something (not mentioned directly by the words in the compound, that is) quite other from what is being compounded. For when it is said, "Devadatta is a *brindled-cow(-owner)*," it is not to be thought that Devadatta is not distinct even from the brindled cow but that the cow is just a qualifier. Although the subject under discussion is the very nature of a cloth as distinct from a pot—inasmuch as the cloth as distinct is being determined with respect to a pot—nevertheless, the qualifier status of the pot is what it comes to, not at all non-distinctness.

Comments

Almost anything can play the role of a property, *dharma*, with respect to a property-bearer, *dharmin*; the relation is the same as that between a qualifier and a qualificandum. For example, the floor with a pot on it may be said to have the pot as a property; the pot would be a qualifier of the floor. Technically, the relation would be said to be delimited by the more immediate relation of conjunction, since it is by means of conjunction that the pot is a property of the floor and qualifies it. Still, disparate substances, such as Devadatta and a cow, or a pot and a cloth, may in certain contexts be said to stand in the qualifier-qualificandum relation.

Śaṅkara Miśra's argument is to point to a grammatical phenomenon, which, he claims, exhibits the same logical structure as cognition of the "very nature" type of distinctness. The grammatical phenomenon proves the structure to be possible since it is actual. The grammatical compound means something other than what would be picked out by the words uncompounded; similarly, the counterpositive status of a pot is evoked by the expression of a cloth as in its very nature distinct. Moreover, in the Sanskrit, "brindled-cow(-owner)" agrees in case with "Devadatta" just as "pot-counterpositive-possessor" agrees with "cloth" in the expression of an awareness of a distinctness. The cognitive verbalizations, "Devadatta is a brindled-cow(-owner)" and "The cloth is distinct (as-a-pot-counterpositive-possessor)," are thus grammatically parallel. Śaṅkara Miśra's point is that there is also an ontic parallelism: the brindled cow with respect to Devadatta is a qualifier (qualifying through a certain relation, in this case, ownership), and the pot with respect to the cloth is also a qualifier (qualifying through the counterpositive relation set up by a distinctness).

Text and Translation

evaṃ ghaṭa-sva-rūpa-bheda-pratiyogī paṭa ity ukte kathaṃ paṭasya ghaṭa-sva-rūpâtmakatvaṃ | pūrva-yukteḥ sattvāt | tathā ca yad yad vākyam uccārya tvayā paṭa-sva-rūpe ghaṭo ghaṭa-sva-rūpe paṭo niveśanīyaḥ, tena tena tvad-vacanena bhedo vyavasthāpanīya iti yathā yathā tava bheda-nirāsāya yatnas tathā atidhṛṣṭa-bālaka iva purovartī bheda iti |

In this way, when it is said that a cloth is the counterpositive of the distinctness that is of the very nature of a pot, how is the pot one with the cloth, given the previous argument? And similarly, with whatever statement you make to the effect that a pot is included in the very nature of a cloth—and a cloth in the very nature of a pot—that very utterance of yours establishes the distinctness (of the two). So the more you work to reject distinctness, the more distinctness comes forward obtrusively, like an impudent boy.

Comments

Śaṅkara Miśra's point appears to be that any claim of non-distinctness would involve a counterpositive whose relationality, on analysis, would turn out to involve distinctness. But since non-distinctness would seem to be just something's identity, it is difficult to take his point as other than a taunt. On the other hand, were there a qualificandum qualified by both potness and clothhood, such that a cognition "The pot is a cloth" would be veridical, the specifiers, clothhood and potness, would nevertheless, on the Naiyāyika analysis, be distinct realities.

Text and Translation

> anya-sākāṇkṣâpatti-bibhiṣikā api nirastā eva | kiñ ca kā iyam anya-sākāṅkṣatā nāma | ghaṭâdayo niṣpratiyogikā | ta eva ced bhedāḥ syus tadā sapratiyogikāḥ syur abhāvavat samavāyavac ca iti cet | bhavantu nāma sapratiyogikāḥ na naḥ kiñcid bādhyate | na hi svābhāvābhāvatvena nirūpyamāṇān ghaṭâdīn api sapratiyogikān na aṅgīkurmaḥ |

Also refuted is another attempt to find intimidating difficulties manifest through expressions that set up a syntactic (and, by extension, logical) expectancy of something else. What is this difficulty involving such expectancy of another? If things such as a pot and so on are considered apart from all (correlative) counterpositives, they would be distinct entities. But then (conceived as distinct entities) they would also have to have (correlative) counterpositives, like an absence and like inherence. If this is the worry, then let them be indeed "with (correlative) counterpositives." Here there is nothing that runs counter to our view. For it is not the case that we do not accept that such things as pots—when being characterized with regard to their natural exclusions (of other things)—also have (correlative) counterpositives.

Comments

I put the term "correlative" in parentheses since Śaṅkara Miśra appears to appeal to the wider sense of the Sanskrit term *pratiyogin* that is correlative to *anuyogin* as the terms of any dyadic relation (see the glossary)—as opposed to the narrower sense that means "absentee," i.e., "counterpositive of an absence." He is concerned most with the Nyāya empiricist theory of mind, and will direct the discussion of counter-correlateness to allay epistemic worries.

Śaṅkara Miśra stresses that although an object such as a pot is a reality rich in properties and relations with other objects in the world, cognition is selective. Thus, there is no antinomy between cognitions of a pot as having and not having a (correlative) counterpositive. Considered alone, a pot evokes no notion of a (correlative) counterpositive. But considered as distinct from something else, a pot is considered in relation to something else, technically called the *pratiyogin*. Moreover, the relations are real; thus both a (correlative) counterpositive and a relation of having a (correlative) counterpositive are realities.

In grammar, *sākāṅkṣā*, expectancy, is the phenomenon of a word or words being required to complete the sense of a sentence. In Nyāya philosophy of language, the term also means "syntactic expectancy," and it is generalized to one of three or four commonly specified requirements for a sentence to have meaning. All the words have to interlock syntactically in the ways that constitute a proper sentence (for instance, a transitive verb requires a direct object, and provokes such "expectancy").[98]

Text and Translation

> tarhi abhāvavad eva itara-nirūpaṇâdhīna-nirūpaṇāḥ syuḥ, savikalpaka-jñāna-viṣayāś ca iti cet | tat kiṃ sapratiyogika-padârthasya ayaṃ niyamo yad itara-nirūpaṇena eva nirūpyate | tathā sati prameyatvâbhidheyatvâdinā api prakāreṇa nirūpyamānā abhāva-samavāyâdaya itara-nirūpaṇam apekṣeran |

Objection: But then, like an absence, their determination is dependent on the determining of other things. And thus they would be objects (only) with determinate cognition (not, as was previously argued, with indeterminate cognition as well).

Answer: If this is the objection, we ask: Is there a rule about something that has a (correlate) counterpositive, the rule, namely, that it can be determined or characterized only through the characterization of something else? If this were the case, then absence, inherence, and the like would depend on determinings of other things when they were being described as knowable, nameable, and so on.

Comments

Something may have a counterpositive—or, let us say, a counter-correlate—with respect to a certain trait, whereas with respect to other traits (e.g., knowability, nameability) there is no such indication. Absences and inherences are relations; they require terms to fill out their logic. But with respect to sheer knowability or nameability, for example, understanding them does not require the relation to a counter-correlate to be explicit.

Śaṅkara Miśra has now definitely slid from the narrower sense of *pratiyogin* (*abhāvīya*, the absential) to (a sense at least closer to) the broader sense (i.e., as the second term of any dyadic relation), a usage that he will define with an eye to epistemic concerns.

Text and Translation

> ātmānam eva upālabhasva, yena evaṃ niyamam aṅgīkuruṣe iti cet | na | abhiprāya-niyamam[99] aviduṣas tava eva upālabhyatvāt |[100]

We consider a possible objection: perceive only the self, since, as explained, you are accepting the rule. We reply: Wrong. It is just you who are ignorant of rules of meaning, and you are the one to be blamed.

Comments

According to one reading, the retort would be that it is the opponent who is wrong about the self, the field of merit and demerit, etc. Or the words could be interpreted as saying that only the objector is ignorant about what scripture says. In any case, the two sentences could be omitted without hurting Śaṅkara Miśra's overall argument.

Text and Translation

> na vayaṃ sapratiyogikatvaṃ niṣpratiyogikatvaṃ vā vastunaḥ svābhāvikam eva aṅgīkurmaḥ, kiṃ tarhi yat-prakārâvacchedena yatra jñānaṃ niyamato yad viśiṣṭa-jñānam apekṣate tat-prakārâvacchedena tad-vastu tat-pratiyogikam iti brūmaḥ |

We do not accept that the essential nature of a thing is exclusively with or without a counter-correlate. What, then, you may ask. We say that when a cognition of x (*yatra*) as specified by the predication content ϕ invariably presupposes a qualificative cognition of y, then that thing x as specified by that predication content ϕ has that other, y, as counter-correlate.

Comments

This epistemic understanding of counter-correlateness is another linchpin in Śaṅkara Miśra's overall response to Śrīharṣa. It is framed as a definition, which is to be taken in the spirit of Gaṅgeśa's use of relative pronouns (see above, p. 210). A determination of counter-correlateness (including the absential variety but not limited to it) is relative to cognition; on the other hand, whatever aspect of a particular appears in cognition is not all that the particular is in reality. In this sense, all predication content is relative to cognition:

any particular cognition is limited with respect to what properties of which particular or particulars there is awareness. That in no way entails that what a bit of predication content reflects is less than fully real.

Śaṅkara Miśra continues with the example of a pot cognized simply as a pot, that is to say, with potness as the qualifier appearing as predication content. In this case, the cognition invokes no awareness of a counter-correlate. With an awareness of an absence, in contrast, there is dependence on awareness of a counter-correlate (= a counterpositive).

Determination of counter-correlateness depends on cognition. Śaṅkara Miśra cites inferential cognition of fire depending on perceptual awareness of smoke. There are special considerations to be taken into account depending on what and how something is cognized, and Śaṅkara Miśra does not shy away from difficult questions concerning cognition of universals and epistemic priority.

In particular, we have at this point the observation that the reason the directly perceptual cognition of, e.g., fire does not have a counter-correlate even though it depends on an indeterminate (*nirvikalpaka*) perception of the universal fireness is that the dependence is not on another relational cognition. Thus the definition of counter-correlateness can stand. The dependence of determinate perception on indeterminate perception is a contact with the world that is not itself cognitively relational.

I will now summarize the arguments and themes for several paragraphs before focusing on, and translating, one further section.

Summary of Text (pp. 9–11)

An objector questions the basis for the distinction between having a counter-correlate and not having one, in particular with respect to natural oppositions (such as cowhood and horsehood) and contact (*saṃyoga*). Śaṅkara Miśra reiterates his view that the criterion is whether or not there is dependence on relational cognition. Cognition of contact does not exhibit such dependence in that each of the terms of the relation, and the relation itself, are expressly cognized all at once.

Next, the discussion turns to the expression "distinctness by nature" (*svarūpa-bheda*) (new paragraph, p. 9). This does not involve a counter-correlate in Śaṅkara's sense because the expression would be about a particular in itself. Śaṅkara Miśra gives a technical definition of "own-nature-hood" (*svarūpatva*): the abstract property that does not share a locus with an absolute absence of any of the properties that an object has (*svaniṣṭha*). Thus, the "own nature" of a pot is not a cloth since a cloth is the locus of an absolute absence of at least one of the properties of a pot, its potness, for instance. "Nor is one pot the own nature of another since we can be sure that, there as well, one or another property of a different type will not be present in the other."

After some wrangling over the definition, and over some of the terms—especially "absolute absence"—that are used, Śaṅkara Miśra explains the point of talking about something's own nature: "we are trying to distinguish this or that particular thing *qua* particular, with all of its properties; that is to say, we are trying to make known in speech a particular pot, a particular cloth." Moreover, understanding distinctness only as mutual exclusion is insufficient with respect to absences. Since absences do not have properties (i.e., never appear as qualificanda), distinctness with regard to them has to be understood as a matter of their "own nature." (Udayana, it will be recalled, makes this point.)

But then, an opponent objects, how is it possible that when the "own nature" of, e.g., mother-of-pearl is grasped it still can be cognized as non-distinct from silver (p. 10, par. 1)? Śaṅkara Miśra replies with an analysis of perceptual illusion that entails the reality of distinctness: without the distinctness of (e.g.) silverness and mother-of-pearl-hood, there would be no possibility of illusion. He makes other straightforward, hard-headed replies about something's being blue, without presupposing yellowness (thus answering Śrīharṣa at *Khkh*, p. 105). And he sounds his counter-theme again by claiming that far from every cognition presupposing non-distinctness, every cognition of non-distinctness presupposes distinctness. The argument is that that type of cognition does involve a counter-correlate; it is dependent on another relational cognition, namely, on cognition of each of the qualifiers as distinct. This argument, insofar as it is not a mere mocking of Śrīharṣa's reasoning, evokes a distinction between (a) numerical or absolute identity, as opposed to (b) epistemic identity, cognitions with identical content. The Morning Star and the Evening Star are the same object, but the properties under which the object is known are distinct (respectively, that is, "appearing in the morning" and "appearing in the evening")—as was discussed at the end of chapter 4.

The Advaitin opponent tries to salvage a different understanding of non-distinctness (p. 11, par. 1). But, of course, whatever he tries reinforces the Naiyāyika stand. Śaṅkara Miśra indulges a bit more *tu quoque*, echoing some of Śrīharṣa's questions about distinctness with respect to the "non-duality" (*advaita*) putatively taught by scripture. On all construals, distinctness is presupposed.

Text (p. 11, par. 3, line 23) and Translation

nanu sva-rūpa-bhedas tadā syād yadi nānā sva-rūpaṃ syāt | nānātvaṃ ca anyonyâbhāvâdhīnaṃ tvayā vācyam | anyonyâbhāvas tu bhedaḥ sarvathā apy anupapannaḥ | tathā hi anyonyâbhāvas tādātmyâbhāvaḥ | tasya ca tādātmyaṃ ghaṭa-paṭayoḥ pratiyogi vācyam | tathā ca tat-siddhau siddham advaitam |

Objection: There could be an "own nature" type of distinctness only if "own nature" were manifold. And manifoldness depends on mutual exclusions, according to what you yourself say. But mutual exclusion in no way arises. To be explicit, the relation of mutual exclusion is the absence of identity. And its (the absence's) counterpositive is the identity of, for example, a pot and a cloth. And if this is the case, then non-duality (*advaita*) is established.

Comments

With this passage, the topic of identity is introduced as what distinctness opposes. We will close our dip into Śaṅkara Miśra's *Bhedaratna* by examining now the Logician's views on identity and distinctness, building on our reflections of chapter 4.

The opponent continues his argument with the claim that if his analysis of identity and distinctness is incorrect, then the only alternative would be that the "absolutely unreal" (*atyanta-asat*) would be the counterpositive. But according to Nyāya theory of mind, the absolutely unreal cannot be a qualifier or even a "mere designating attribution" (*upalakṣaṇa*) and so cannot be an absential counterpositive. Moreover, there are other problems with the Nyāya division of "relational" (*saṃsargika*) absences on the one hand and mutual exclusion on the other. "The fourfold classification of absences that you have put forward is childish." Furthermore, the objector continues, rehearsing much of Śrīharṣa's anti-absence weaponry, a pot cognized as a pot is, according to the Nyāya analysis, a pot specified by its potness; similarly, a cloth and its clothness. But since there is no specifying property in potness and none in clothness, the presence of the one in the other cannot, on Nyāya realist assumptions, be rejected. There is no mutual exclusion. And since there is none, the properties of each are present in the other. "Thus, the non-distinctness of a pot and a cloth is the conclusion." We pick up the text again with Śaṅkara Miśra's answer.

Text (p. 12, line 6) and Translation

mā evam | abhiprāyânavagamāt | na hi[101] anyonya-tādātmyaṃ pratiyogi brūmaḥ | anyonyâbhāve yena pratiyogy-aprasiddhy-anibandhana-tad-viśiṣṭa upalakṣita-pratīty-anudaya-prasaṅgaḥ | na vā ghaṭatva-paṭatvayor eva pratiyogitvam ācakṣmahe, yena saṃsargâbhāvâviśeṣa-prasaṅgaḥ | na vā ghaṭatva-paṭa-tvâvacinnayor ghaṭa-paṭayor anyonyasmin niṣedhāt tādātmyâbhāvaṃ vyavaharāmo yena ghaṭatva-paṭatvayoḥ sva-gatâvacchedaka-dharmâviraha-nibandhanas tayor anyonyâbhāva-viraha syaṭ, kiṃ nāma ghaṭam[102] eva pratiyoginaṃ brūmaḥ | sa ca yadi saṃsargâvacinno niṣidhyate tadā saṃsargâbhāva-pratītiḥ | tādātmyâvacinnaś cen niṣidhyate, tadā tādātmyâbhāva-pratītir iti viśeṣaḥ |

Answer: Your thinking is all wrong. You have not comprehended our positions. For we do not hold that an identity (e.g., between a pot and a cloth) is the counterpositive of a mutual exclusion. If we did, we would face the difficulty with regard to mutual exclusion (generally) that, whether taking cognition of it to be a matter of an essential qualifier or of a designating qualifier, no such cognition could arise, in that there would be no well-known (epistemic) foundation for the counterpositive. But we do not (hold identity to be the counterpositive). Nor do we say that, e.g., potness and clothhood are counterpositives such that there would be nothing distinctive about relational absences (as you complained). Nor do we talk about an absence of identity as entailed by a denial concerning each of two mutually exclusive things, e.g., a pot and a cloth, as specified by the one's potness and the other's clothhood, such that potness and clothhood's not excluding one another would amount to their being tied to (and undermining) their individuating character. Rather, we say that it is just the pot that is the counterpositive. And if there is a denial of something as specified relationally, then there would be cognition of a relational absence. If there is denial of it as specified by identity, then there would be cognition of an absence of identity. This is the difference.

Comments

Here Śaṅkara Miśra articulates the criterion for distinguishing a relational absence from a mutual exclusion: relational specification of counterpositivehood (*pratiyogitā-avaccheda* as conjunction, inherence, etc.) versus identity as the relational specifier. As discussed in chapter 4, Navyas come to realize that this type of specification is one, but only one, dimension of what it is to be an absential counter-correlate, i.e., a counterpositive or absentee. Simply the pot is the *pratiyogin* of the mutual exclusion that qualifies the cloth, an absence whose *pratiyogin*-hood is specified relationally by identity and property-wise by potness. Thus the epistemic principle may be upheld: the *pratiyogin* (the pot, not a mysterious identity) presumably has been previously cognized.

Śaṅkara Miśra continues by insisting that "identity is never a counterpositive." The objector then puts forward the following loaded example of a cognition where identity does seem to assume a counterpositive role, "There is no identity with a cloth in a pot." But Śaṅkara Miśra makes clear that there are counter-considerations that undermine this evidence, that the expression is only a manner of speaking, with a grammar that does not directly reflect reality. Identity is simply not relational on a par with contact, inherence, and so on.

Śaṅkara Miśra continues by citing pragmatic concerns: we could not mean what we say—in a variety of contexts and on whatever construals—did we not presuppose the reality of distinctness, nor could we get along very well in our everyday activity—a cloth might be brought when a pot is asked for, for example. His Advaitin adversary retorts that all the examples cited belong to the world of spiritual ignorance that is sublated with awareness of the truly real, Brahman. Several pages are then devoted to the metaphysics of Brahman and enlightenment, with the Advaitin on the defensive. Against the position that all except Brahman is sublatable, Śaṅkara Miśra astutely inquires why Brahman should be unsublatable. He does not attack the possibility of liberation, or the reality of Brahman, but only the Advaita understanding of these. Later, he develops the Nyāya empiricist theory of mind in discussing dream: dream objects are not unreal; rather, in dreams objects appear unreal. They have been previously cognized. Then several further untoward consequences of the Advaita view are drawn out, without much development of Nyāya positions.

Thus Advaita is routed, with, as we have seen, answers supplied to Śrīharṣa's questions supplemented by attacks on the coherence of the Advaita stance. Some of the more interesting topics interspersed in the remaining discussion are the nature of causal relations, the meaning of injunctions, and expressibility. These and other concerns hold forth much general philosophic allure; the mainstays of the response to Śrīharṣa we have, however, surveyed.[103]

9. Vācaspati Miśra II on Distinctness

Introduction

See chapter 4 (above, p. 150) for a few details about Vācaspati's life.[104] Vācaspati wrote as a Mīmāṃsaka as well as a Naiyāyika; indeed it is under the former banner that he is best known to modern scholars. But he is also a great Navya author. According to D. C. Bhattacharya, a commentary by Vācaspati on the *Nyāya-sūtra* is first-class. He has a total of six or seven Nyāya works to his credit, including a commentary on Maṇikaṇṭha's *Nyāyaratna*.

The selection translated here is from Vācaspati's *Khaṇḍanoddhāra*, where the Logician "uproots" (*uddhāra*) the refutations of Śrīharṣa.[105] The selection is a Naiyāyika *siddhānta*, or accepted position, on distinctness. It is preceded by a long *pūrvapakṣa* where Vācaspati rehearses arguments of Śrīharṣa. The *pūrvapakṣa* section begins with this objection: "When it is said that cognition of distinctness counters scripture, how is that distinctness to be understood? Four views have been presented." And Vācaspati lists the four views along with Śrīharṣa's refutations of each.[106] In comments below, I fill in whatever background argument is necessary to understand Vācaspati's response.

Text (p. 194) and Translation

atra ucyate | yathāyatham̱ tāvat trayo bhedāḥ | tathā hi sva-rūpam̱ tāvad bhedaḥ bhidyate vyāvarttyate abheda-dhī-virodhi-viṣayī-kriyate 'nena iti vyutpatteḥ | svâtmanā ca paṭas tathā-kriyata eva ato na sva-rūpasya bhedatvam̱ pāribhāṣikam̱ vaidharmyânyonyâbhāva-vat sva-rūpe 'pi vyutpannatvāt | ata eva ātmatattvaviveke | trīn api bhedān ācāryā āhuḥ |

In response to this, we give the following answer. First of all, there are, in due order, three kinds of distinctness. One of these is the "natural," or distinctness by nature. There is an etymological reason in support of this distinctness: distinctness distinguishes, excludes. It is the content of the cognition (*dhī*) that opposes a cognition of non-distinctness. And a cloth, for example, does this by itself. Therefore "natural distinctness" is not a technical usage like "qualitative difference" and "mutual exclusion." Although it is the natural one (what something is in itself), it is (on analysis) derivative.

And so our revered teacher (Udayana) has also said in his *Ātmatattvaviveka* that there are three kinds of distinctness.

Comments

The *Ātmatattvaviveka* classification was discussed above in chapters 3 and 4 (pp. 106–09 and 138ff).[107] Natural distinctness, *svarūpa*, qualitative distinctness, *vaidharmya*, and mutual exclusion, *anyonyābhāva*, are reaffirmed here by Vācaspati as meant (according to circumstances of usage) by the term "distinctness," *bheda*. But, Vācaspati says, natural distinctness is reducible to the other two.

Text and Translation

nanu sva-rūpa-bhedavattā sva-rūpasya na sambhavaty abhedāt | na hi sa eva tadvām̱s tena eva bhavati iti cet | mā bhūt | na hi sva-rūpa-bhedavatas tena bhedavattām̱ brūmaḥ | kim̱ tu pratiyogy-apekṣa-vilakṣaṇa-dhī-viṣayatā-mātram | pratiyogitvâbhimatâbhedâropa-virodhi-dhī-paryālocana-nibandhanas tatra ghaṭād bhinnaḥ paṭa ity-ādiḥ pratibhāsaḥ |

Objection: Something in itself cannot possess natural distinctness because it is non-distinct (from itself). For it is not the case that something comes to possess itself by means of just itself.

Answer: That is wrong. For we do not hold that something possessing a natural distinctness is *by that* distinct (from itself). Rather, we hold that it is just its having become the object of a differentiating cognition (*dhī*), differentiating with respect to something else, (technically called) the *pratiyogin* (counterpositive). When it appears to someone, "The cloth is distinct from the pot," or any similar cognition, the appearance is based on a considering (of the cloth) from a perspective cognizant of the object's opposition to ascribing to it a non-distinctness imagined with respect to a counterpositive.

Comments

The relation to the particular mentioned, i.e., the counterpositive, runs through awareness: we commonly do not think of something as distinct in itself; we come to see that it is distinct in itself when we regard it in relation to something else. *We* pick out the something else. However, the distinctness is natural, "in itself" (*svarūpa*), not dependent on the particular we pick out.

Here the term *āropa*, "ascription" or "superimposition," is used in connection with an imaginative non-distinctness. Vācaspati is about to expand on this, in explaining the cognitive logic of distinctness and non-distinctness or identity. A particular, a thick particular (a particular with all of its properties), is identical with itself and distinct from everything else. Such identity and distinctness are analyzable in the terms of Nyāya cognitive logic avoiding the difficulties Śrīharṣa alleges—such is Vācaspati's thesis.

Text (p. 196) and Translation

> tathā ca sva-rūpa-bheda-sthale abhedaṃ na ullikhantī dhīr ity-ādi yad uktam | tad ayuktam | na hi tatra bhedo vā bhinnatā vā cakāsti | kiṃ tu bhedântaram antareṇa eva vilakṣaṇa-dhī-mātraṃ tatra udeti | tad uktam |

And so what has been said (by Śrīharṣa) in a passage concerning natural distinctness, namely, that there is no cognition (*dhī*) that does not presuppose non-distinctness, etc., that is dead wrong. For it is not the case that either distinctness or "being distinct" shines forth directly with every cognition; rather, cognition arises having as content difference in things—without requiring another distinctness (leading to an infinite regress)—as we have said.

Comments

There is a rich world out there. It seems rarely are we aware of distinctness explicitly, as the express content of our cognition. However, cognitive content presupposes distinctness. Thus distinctness is established. Moreover, there is no infinite regress, as alleged, in awareness of distinctness. Distinctness amounts to what something is in itself (*svarūpa*). The relationality is contributed by awareness focusing on something in particular that a distinct thing is distinct from.

Vācaspati cites the passage from the *Khkh* that Śaṅkara Miśra also found so objectionable. Vācaspati at the end of this section constructs his own parody.

Text and Translation

kiṅ ca vastu svata eva vilakṣaṇam iti | yad vā ghaṭâdi-vyakteḥ paṭâdi-sākāṅkṣatvam eva tad-bhedatvam | yady api ghaṭâdi-vyaktir na sva-rūpeṇa paṭâdi-sākāṅkṣā | tathā api tat-pratiyogiko bhedo bhavati iti tat-sākāṅkṣā eva |

Moreover, a thing by itself distinguishes (itself from other things). Or, we may say that the distinctness of an individual pot, etc., just amounts to an expectation that there is a cloth, etc. (that it is distinct from). Although by itself an individual pot, etc., as (an awareness's) content does not involve expectation that there is something like a cloth (that it is distinct from), still distinctness (as an awareness's content), having such a counterpositive, does involve such expectation.

Comments

Distinctness is not explicit predication content with every awareness of an individual. We may know the pot simply as a pot, without its distinctness (from a cloth, say) coming into awareness. But cognition of an individual as distinct, on the other hand, does involve awareness of a counterpositive, something the individual is distinct from. Cognition of distinctness gives rise to an expectation (*sākāṅkṣā*, a grammatical term) about a counterpositive—like a grammatically incomplete sentence giving rise to an expectation about the element that would complete it.

Text and Translation

pratiyogitvaṃ ca ghaṭâdeḥ bhedatva-prakāraka-paṭâdi-dhī-kāraṇībhūta-dhī-viśeṣa-viṣayatvam |

Being a counterpositive amounts to being the content of a cognition *x* (that is partly responsible for) giving rise to a cognition *y* that has a cloth or the like as predication content cashing out the distinctness (cognized) of a pot or the like (as that from which the pot is distinct).

Comments

Gaṅgeśa, in line with Vātsyāyana and the Old School, insists that there is no awareness of an absence without prior awareness of the absence's absentee.[108] Likewise, Vācaspati views awareness of a counterpositive as part of the causal process giving rise to an awareness of an absence. So he defines what it is to be a counterpositive with respect to this process (as does Śaṅkara Miśra, who takes *pratiyogin* in a wider sense, as we saw). Gaṅgeśa makes just about the same point, when he says that an awareness qualified by a counterpositive (or absentee)—i.e., having content qualified by a counterpositive—is a cause of a cognition of an absence.[109] In the same passage, Gaṅgeśa says also that this cause is not an indeterminate awareness, suggesting that an enlivened memory trace supplies the counterpositive.

Text and Translation

anyonyâbhāvas tu yady api tadātmī-bhavator ghaṭa-paṭayor na abhāvau, na api tayos tādātmyasya abhāvo 'sau yena atyantâsat-pratiyogikaḥ syāt |na apy atādātmī-bhavatoḥ |yena stambhaḥ piśāco na bhavati ity atra tasya ekasya ekam eva jñānaṃ stambhe pratyakṣaṃ piśāce ca apratyakṣam āpadyeta |

Mutual exclusion (to take up the second of Udayana's three construals so wrongly attacked by you), however, does not amount to two absences with regard to a pot and a cloth as though they could come to be identical. Nor is the absence to be understood as *of the identity* of the two. This (the basis of your misinterpretation and lame attacks) would mean that something absolutely non-existent would be the counterpositive (and nothing absolutely non-existent can be a counterpositive). Nor are there two absences with regard to the two as though they could come to be non-identical, such that with regard to the cognition, "It is a stump, not a demon," which is a single cognition of a single thing, we would have to say that the cognition is perceptual concerning the stump (and its distinctness from a demon) but non-perceptual concerning the demon (and its distinctness from the stump).

Comments

The demon-stump example occurs within counterfactual reasoning that draws out a ramification of Śrīharṣa's misunderstanding of distinctness. Such context makes interpretation of an obscure example daunting. Fortunately, however, Gaṅgeśa uses the example (in his discourse on inherence, above, p. 263), as does Udayana, too.[110] Gaṅgeśa's point is that the absence is perceptible because were the demon somehow identical with the stump it would be perceived. Vācaspati's point is similar: the absence is perceptible because its substratum is perceptible even though (he may be interpreted, contra Gaṅgeśa) the demon is not only not perceived but imperceptible.

Udayana, just after having distinguished relational absences from *anyonyābhāva* (mutual exclusion, mutual absence, absence of identity), uses the example of an awareness that an object is a stump and not a demon (*piśāca*) to show that there is no relation, such as contact or inherence, between the two. Then he also says: "There is no identity of a demon with a stump as its (common) substratum, (no identity) established by any source of knowledge whatsoever whereby it (the identity) would be a candidate for denial. Rather, this denial ("It's a stump, not a demon") is of a demon brought into connection (*prasañjita*) with the nature of the stump."[111] Udayana's last statement is mysterious, and, unfortunately, he does not say anything more about mutual absence except at the end of the passage to point out that mutual absences, like universals, are eternal or constant (*nitya*). But according to the seventeenth-century Naiyāyika, Viśvanātha, with relational absences (prior absence, destructional absence, and constant absence), the absentee must be perceptible if the absence is to be perceived; whereas with mutual exclusion (mutual absence), all that is required is that the substratum of the absence, e.g., the stump, be perceived.[112]

Surendranath Dasgupta quotes a use of the stump-demon figure by Vyāsatīrtha II (c. 1535), a follower of the Dualist Vedāntin, Madhva, in his work (strikingly entitled) *Bhedojjīvana* (*Reviving Distinctness*).[113] In a footnote, Dasgupta provides a sentence of Vyāsatīrtha's Sanskrit, which indicates that the Madhvite does not accept that the counterpositive of an absence has to be previously cognized, or, to be precise, that it has to be perceptually cognized (*pratiyogi-pratyakṣaṃ*). Similarly, the distinctness between the world and God (Brahman) is known, although God is not perceptually cognized, Vyāsatīrtha (as reported by Dasgupta) says.

Now I provide my best guess, informed by these sources, about what Vācaspati means.

You are walking along in the dark and assure yourself at one point that the object you see is a stump, not a demon. The stump is immediately perceived; so is the exclusion or absence. Whether demons can or cannot be perceived is not the point (contra Dasgupta and Vyāsatīrtha). The point is that the *exclusion* is perceptual. (Gaṅgeśa says explicitly in his context that the absence is perceptual as opposed to being inferred.) If there were another exclusion residing in the demon, then it would have to be non-perceptual (since the demon is not perceived). Śrīharṣa's misunderstanding implies that there be two absences with two absentees when distinctness is cognized. This suggests that two should be cognized, an absence in the stump and an absence in the demon. The one would be perceptual and the other somehow non-perceptual. However, there is both phenomenologically and in fact a single perception of a single thing or locus and a single absence and a single absentee.[114]

Vācaspati is arguing from the Navya perspective according to which a mutual exclusion does not have an identity as absentee. Identity is the relation specifying what type of absenteeship is involved with a mutual exclusion. As discussed in chapter 4, identity is the relational specifier of the absenteeship, not the term specifier. Above all, identity is not itself the absentee.

B. K. Matilal extrapolates the Nyāya understanding of perceptual illusion—as *anyathā-khyāti* (see the glossary)—to give an account of fictional entities, gold mountains, Hamlet, and so forth.[115] Imaginary entities are mental constructs, constructs out of perceptual information. That is to say, the primary data of a construct—for example, a gold mountain—are perceptual: (a) what it is to be gold and (b) mountainhood. These are combined (by the internal organ, *manas*, presumably) into the complex cognition (somewhat like the imaginative cognition called by later Navyas *āhārya-buddhi*[116]). If to interpret the stump-demon figure we become worried about how a subliminal impression of a demon could be drawn on, we should approach the problem broadly along these lines (a *saṃskāra* informed by memory of gold and of mountains, or the components of a demon, as the case may be). However, I repeat that I do not think the question of how a demon is known is relevant to understanding Vācaspati here.

Text and Translation

> na api ghaṭe paṭa-tādātmyasya abhāvo yena saṃsargâbhāvaḥ syāt | kiṃ tu ghaṭaḥ paṭe ity-āropa-rūpa-śarīram | eṣa ca ghaṭe paṭatvâropaḥ tathā eva anubhavāt |

Nor is there with respect to the pot an absence of identity with the cloth that should be understood as a relational absence. The fact of the matter is that a cognition of the pot in the cloth would embody an imaginative ascription (or superimposition, *āropa*). And that this would be an imaginative ascription of clothness in the pot is precisely in conformity with experience.

Comments

It is important not to confuse mutual exclusion with relational absence. These are fundamentally distinct realities. We may call identity a relation and non-identity—or mutual exclusion, *bheda*—an absence, but identity and distinctness have a different logic from relational absences (*saṃsargābhāva*), specifically, constant absence, prior absence, and destructional absence. One important difference emphasized by later Navyas such as Raghunātha is that identity and distinctness are not locus-exacting, whereas relational absences are: neither identity nor distinctness rest *in* a substratum, whereas any relational absence does. Here Vācaspati seems to make the point without using the technical term, "locus-exacting," *vṛtti-niyāmika*.

Thus to say that there is no pot in a cloth (as Śrīharṣa tries to push the Logician into construing distinctness) is only to make an imaginative ascription or superimposition with respect to a counterpositive. In other words, such is not a matter of experience.

The point about such imaginative ascription is that one knows all the while that the counterpositive cognition is non-veridical.[117]

Text and Translation

> niṣedhas tu paṭasya eva tasya eva sāmānâdhikaraṇyena anvayāt | vaiyadhikaraṇyena tu tad-anvaye ghaṭe paṭo na ghaṭe paṭatvaṃ na iti bādha-dhīḥ syāt | tasmād abhāvâdhikaraṇe pratiyogitâvacchedakam dharmam āropya yo niṣedhaḥ pratīyate so 'nyonyâbhāva iti vijñeyam |

But negation (in the case of a pot's distinctness from a cloth) is just of the cloth because the logical connection is a matter of the same locus or substratum (as expressed by the case agreement between the terms of the verbalization of the cognition, "A pot is not a cloth," here "pot" and "cloth" in the nominative case). But were the logical connection a matter of a different locus or substratum (as expressed by terms without case agreement), the negational cognition would be (expressed as) "The cloth is not *in* the pot," or "Clothness is not *in* the pot." (And this is not what people mean in everyday discourse in talking about distinctnesses experienced.) Therefore, with respect to the locus of a (mutual) absence, the property specifying the absenteehood is imaginatively superimposed. With this going on, the negation that is cognized is a mutual exclusion—this is what is to be understood.

Comments

As explained in chapter 4, Gaṅgeśa rejects as nonsense the view that there is a type of absenteehood specified by a property that the absentee does not have. That would seem to be the right analysis of "The pot as qualified by clothness is not here." The spirit of his rejection accords with his refusal to admit absences of "unexampled terms"; that is, to say that on the floor there is no horned hare is also nonsense.

Recall that absences are distinguished by their absentees, which are in turn specified by what determines the absenteehood, namely, (a) the relational specifier (= identity, in the case of a mutual absence) and (b) the property specifier (= the respect in which the absentee is cognized). Vācaspati understands the property specifying the absenteehood of the mutual exclusion verbalized as "The pot is not the cloth" as clothhood. The feature of the situation exploited by the Advaitin is that the cloth is denied with respect to the pot, with respect to that single locus. Vācaspati's point is that understanding the absenteehood as specified by the property clothhood requires an imaginative ascription of clothhood where it in fact does not occur, namely, in the pot. This is an *imaginative* ascription, one that is defined by awareness of a non-actualized combination of elements (like a gold mountain). Such is what is involved in awareness of mutual exclusion, distinctness.

Text and Translation

nanu dharma āropyate dharmī niṣidhyata iti durghaṭam | āropitasya aniṣedhān niṣedhyasya ca anāropād iti cen na | ārope niṣedha-buddhyā ca ghaṭa-paṭayor bhānam ity anubhava-siddham kiṃ tv anubhava-vaicitryād āropo dharma-prādhānyena | niṣedhas tu dharmi-prādhānyena tathā eva anubhavād iti dik vaidharmyeṣu vaidharmyôpagame 'navasthā na doṣāya prāmāṇikatvāt | tatra sva-rūpa-bhedena bhinna-dhī-sambhavād vā iti ||

Objection: This view—namely, that a property is superimposed (imaginatively ascribed) and thus the property-bearer denied—is difficult to maintain. For there is no negation of the superimposed, nor is there superimposition of what is to be denied.

Answer: No. It is established by experience that with the negational cognition the pot and the cloth look to be in superimposition. But since (here) the experience is diverse (a denial of identity involves potentially any of the respects in which a pot and a cloth, say, are distinct), (we should stress) the imaginative ascription concerns properties (not loci or property-bearers). The negation, on the other hand, concerns the property-bearer. (It is the particular pot that is not the cloth.) Such is experience. This is the gist of our view.

With regard to the dissimilarities (between, say, a pot and a cloth, implied by their mutual exclusion), that we accept the possibility of an endless process of (comprehending) dissimilarity does not mar our view, for this possibility is well-founded. Or, in this case (there is no fault) because of a possibility of cognizing distinct things through a "natural distinctness" (*svarūpa-bheda*).

Comments

The superimposition, or imaginative ascription, is not of two things, but rather of the properties of something, e.g., a cloth, on something else, a pot, at hand. Awareness of the distinctness involves awareness of some respect in which there is no identity, Vācaspati suggests. But, of course, properties are manifold, and the specifier of the absenteehood can be a natural kind character—e.g., clothness—of the negatum, but also some other property. Vācaspati thus stresses that there is no superimposition, contra Śrīharṣa, concerning property-bearers. The pot as identical with the cloth is not imagined counterpositively. Rather, some property of the cloth is entertained with respect to the pot counterpositively. The ways in which a pot differs from a cloth are potentially infinite. The possibility of an infinite series is, however, no mar to our view, in that the series would be well-founded (*prāmāṇika*).

Text (p. 199, last line) and Translation

yat tu bhedo bhinne niviśata ity-ādi | tat tuccham | tasya nitya-samāprapañcatvāt | na hi tad-bheda-viśiṣṭe tad-bheda-vṛttiṃ na apy abhinne bheda-vṛttiṃ brūmaḥ | kiṃ tu bhedôpalakṣite bheda-vṛtter mayā upagamāt |

But (the view that Śrīharṣa ascribes to us, namely) that a distinctness enters into something distinct, that is a misconception, since it exhibits the fallacy *nitya-samā* (composition, a category mistake or level shift as with certain false reasoning concerning sound as eternal: though in a sense any sound would be *eternally* non-eternal, particular sounds are non-eternal). For we do not hold that there is an occurrence of a distinctness in something qualified by that distinctness, nor an occurrence of a distinctness in something (previously, or somehow in itself) non-distinct. Rather, it is accepted by us that any "occurrence" of distinctness would be a (mere) designating expression (that is, a manner of speaking, not a matter of what a thing essentially is).

Comments

Gautama at *Nyāya-sūtra* 5.1.34 explains the "futile rejoinder" (*jāti*: see the glossary, the second sense of the term) *nitya-samā* as false reasoning deriving from a confusion of qualifier and qualified. Naiyāyikas hold that sound is non-eternal. A Mīmāṃsaka opponent retorts with a question whether sound is eternally or non-eternally non-eternal. The Nyāya view is that sound, considered in general, is eternally non-eternal. But this does not somehow imply that sound is eternal, because of the level distinction: this would be the qualifier_2 of a qualifier_1, on the one hand, and a qualifier_1 of the qualified, on the other.

As discussed above, Gaṅgeśa tries to explain the difference between designating attributions (*upalakṣaṇa*) and true qualifiers (*viśeṣaṇa*) near the end of the first chapter of the *TCM*: whereas an expression such as "where the crows are circling" appears to pick out a qualifier of Devadatta's house, "below the circling crows" is an attribution useful only for identifying the house, not for characterizing what it is.[118] Vācaspati's point is that there is no *occurrence* of distinctness *in* a locus; we might, however, he admits, talk as though there were. But the talk should be understood as a designating attribution, like pointing out Devadatta's house by referring to circling crows. In other words, epistemological and ontological considerations undercut (semantic) considerations about usage, and we have a way to explain away the apparent force of the semantic consideration, too.

Text and Translation

kiṃ ca yadā yatra bhedo vartate tat tadā tad-bhedavad eva tat-pūrvaṃ tu na asty eva | na hi gaur gotvâdi-śūnyaḥ kṣaṇam api jāter jāta-sambandhatvāt anyonyâbhāvasya [ca] sva-rūpa-bhedasya ca tat-samatvāt sva-rūpa-bhedasya piṇḍe niveśânupagamād vā | etena prāg-lopêty-ādi khaṇḍitam aprasaktatvāt |

When and where there is a distinctness, then and there indeed there is something (in a manner of speaking) having that distinctness, but it is simply not true that there is any (ontic) priority. For a cow does not exist even for the smallest increment of time bereft of cowhood. This is the case because of the relation of a natural kind to its instances (it is there the instant they are born). Mutual exclusion and natural distinctness are the same way, or, we should say, we do not accept an entering into an indistinct individual (*piṇḍa*) of a natural distinctness. In this way (too) is refuted the accusation that there is "loss of the preceding members," because that objection has no applicability here.

Comments

Vācaspati introduces the "loss of preceding members" argument of Śrīharṣa's in the long *pūrvapakṣa* that precedes these translated paragraphs (p. 188). Śrīharṣa argues that the view of distinctness as a property faces an infinite regress, an infinite series of distinctnesses, for a property has to be related to a property-bearer by a distinct relation. Otherwise, there would be no distinct relation, and the property and property-bearer would collapse into an undifferentiated whole. Now in case someone might think an infinite series of distinctnesses is not an unhappy ramification, Śrīharṣa argues that if each distinctness is thought to attach itself to the property-bearer in succession, then, since the regress results from the need for a distinct attacher, a connector, there would be "loss of the preceding members." That is to say, embrace of an infinite series is no real option.[119] Vācaspati points out here that the Naiyāyika view of distinctness does not embrace an infinite series, and thus there is no context (*prasakta*), or applicability, for this objection. Cowhood and a cow cannot be pried apart. Similarly, something's distinctness is inalienable, a matter of what it in itself is.

Text and Translation

> nūnaṃ kiṃ gavi gotvam uta agavi iti vadatā dharma-dharmi-vairiṇā bauddhena śikṣito 'si yad īdṛśāny asārāṇi pralapasi |dharma-dharmi-bhāva eva mahyaṃ na rocata iti cet |nūnam ajño 'si yad abhinnaṃ pratijānīṣe dharma-dharmi-bhāvâbhāvaṃ tv apajānīṣe iti |abheda-dharmā hi dharmī abhinna iti dharma-dharmi-bhāvâbhāve kva apy abhinnam iti |

Now someone asking whether cowhood occurs in a cow or in a non-cow proves himself a Buddhist, i.e., an enemy of "property-bearers having properties"—by him are you taught when you prattle such superficialities! If you say that the property/property-bearer relation does not find favor with you, then you are ignorant, since you assert (a property and its bearer) to be non-distinct and you deny the property/property-bearer relation. For with your view that the property-bearer having the property of non-distinctness is (thus) non-distinct, given that there is no relation of property and property-bearer (i.e., according to you), with regard to what indeed would this be non-distinct?

Comments

Śrīharṣa might admit that he has indeed been taught by Buddhists. A perjorative connotation has apparently become established across schools by Vācaspati's time.

The argument is that a denial of distinctness as equivalent to an assertion of non-distinctness—non-distinctness understood in turn as a property of something that is non-distinct—is self-contradictory: it presupposes the property/property-bearer relation. The Buddhist is similarly barred by the logic of his view from telling a story about what it is that universals exclude. (Cf. Śaṅkara Miśra's discussion: above, p. 278.)

With this passage, Vācaspati begins a dialectical reversal, using Śrīharṣa-like arguments against the Advaitin's polemic. (Śaṅkara Miśra does this as well, we noted.) The argument relies on a rhetorical question at the end, and it is not altogether fair, since non-distinctness or identity need not be understood as a true property (it could be a mere "designating attribution," *upalakṣaṇa*). Let us look at just a few more sentences.

Text and Translation

> kiṃ ca bhedâbhāve katham abhinna iti | na hi dharmi-mātram na apy abheda-mātram abhinna iti | kiṃ tv abhedavān abhinna iti evaṅ ca abhinnatā api bhinnam upajīvya eva pravartate abheda-dharmiṇor bheda-dhiyam antareṇa abhinnatā-dhiyo 'sambhavād iti |

Moreover, if there is no distinctness, how can anything be said to be non-distinct? For there is no mere property-bearer, nor no mere non-distinctness, with regard to something cognized as non-distinct. Rather, something non-distinct has non-distinctness. And thus even something as non-distinct indeed presupposes something distinct. Without cognition of distinctness, a cognition to the effect that non-distinctness and its bearer were non-distinct would be impossible.

Comments

In part, Vācaspati is mocking Śrīharṣa, turning his reasoning on its head. Vācaspati may also be read as disingenuous—it is not that non-distinctness is *had* by the x that is non-distinct (a possessive suffix is used in the Sanskrit, a usage that would be metaphoric given what something's identity is, namely, itself, complete with all its properties). On yet another interpretation (and perhaps here I stretch it a bit), Vācaspati could also be asserting that qualification presupposes distinctness. However, with regard to this last interpretation, unlike Śaṅkara Miśra, Vācaspati presents no argument. He simply moves on to construct a verse parodying the famous conclusion of the Advaitin (that is, a verse similar to the last of Śaṅkara Miśra's opening verses in the *Bhedaratna*).

Text (p. 203, last line) and Translation

> tasmāt, anullikhantī bhedaṃ dhīr na abhedôllekhana-kṣamā |tathā ca ādye pramā sā syād antye svâpekṣya-vaiśasāt ||iti ||

Therefore, (there is the following verse:) No cognition that does not indicate (or make explicit) distinctness is capable of indicating non-distinctness. And thus in the former instance (only) is it a veridical awareness, since in the latter it would destroy that which it depends upon.

Comments

The verse reverses Śrīharṣa's: "No cognition not expressing non-distinctness is capable of expressing distinctness. And thus cognition must be valid for the former, not the latter, because in that case it would destroy what it depended upon."[120]

APPENDIX A

Guide to Sanskrit Pronunciation

Vowels (omitting two that rarely occur):

a	like 'u' in 'mum': *manas* (both vowels: ma-nas)
ā	like 'a' in 'father': Nāgārjuna (naa-gaar-ju-na)
i	like 'i' in 'sit': *jina*
ī	like 'ee' in 'feed': Śrīharṣa (shree-har-sha)
u	like 'u' in 'pull': *mukti*
ū	like 'oo' in 'moon': *svarūpa* (sva-roo-pa)
ṛ	(You won't pronounce this correctly; try:) 'rea' in 'really' (while turning the tip of the tongue up to touch the palate): *Ṛg Veda*
e	like 'a' in 'maze': *prameya* (pra-may-ya)
ai	like 'i' in 'mine': Vaiśeṣika
o	like 'o' in 'go': *yoga*
au	like 'ow' in 'cow': *aupādika* (ow-paa-di-ka)

Consonants and semivowels (which are best understood as a particular class of consonants) are pronounced roughly as in English. A few special cases are worth noting:

kh	exactly like 'k' in Sanskrit—that is, like the 'k' in 'kite'—except aspirated, that is, breath out, as with 'keel': Sāṃkhya All other aspirated consonants follow the same principle: 'gh' like 'g' except aspirated, 'th' like 't', and so on.
c	like 'ch' in 'churn': *avacchedaka* (a-vach-chay-da-ka)
ch	another aspirate, same principle: *avacchedaka*
ṭ	There is no English equivalent: a 't' sound (as in 'tough') but with the tip of the tongue touching the roof of the mouth:
ṭh	aspirated 'ṭ'
ḍ	like 'd' in 'deer' but "lingualized" as with 'ṭ'
ḍh	aspirated 'ḍ'
ṇ	lingualized 'n' sound

There are three sibilants:

ś	like 'sh' in 'shove': Śrīharṣa (shree-har-sha)
ṣ	lingualized 'sh' sound: Śrīharṣa
s	like 's' in 'sun': Sāṃkhya

Special sounds:

ḥ	calls for breath following a vowel. For example, *duḥkha* (''pain'') is pronounced as follows, 'du', and then breath (very short) and then 'kha'.
ṃ	This is shorthand for all nasals, the particular type determined by the class of the following consonant: 'ṅ' is guttural, 'ṇ' lingual, and 'n' dental. For example, the 'ṃ' in 'Sāṃkhya' is equivalent to 'ṅ', since 'kh' belongs to the guttural class. (Do not try to remember this rule; just nasalize.)

APPENDIX B

Sanskrit Glossary

1. Proper Names

(of philosophic schools and religious movements, including designations of proponents)

Advaita Vedānta: a prominent school of classical philosophy subscribing to an Upanishadic monism ("All is Brahman," including—and especially—the seemingly individual consciousness or self).

Brahmin: priest; member of the highest Hindu caste.

Brahminism: the strand of Indian religion centered on rituals and liturgies performed by priests called Brahmins, who are the highest of four principal Hindu castes.

Buddhism: a world religion founded by Siddhārtha Gautama (the Buddha, or the "Awakened One") who taught that a supreme felicity and end to suffering occur in a special experience termed *nirvāṇa*, and who laid out a way or ways to attain it.

Cārvāka: a materialist and skeptical school also known as Lokāyata, "those who follow the way of the world."

Dvaita Vedānta: "Dualistic Vedānta"; see Theistic Vedānta.

Hīnayāna: "the abandoned vehicle"; a term used in Mahāyāna (q.v.) to refer to those fellow Buddhists who do not subscribe to the Mahāyāna ideal of becoming a *bodhisattva* (q.v.); see also Theravāda.

Jainism: an ancient Indian religion founded by Mahāvīra, c. 500 BCE, who, like the Buddha, taught a philosophy of a "supreme personal good"; in later periods, Jaina philosophers addressed a broad range of issues.

Lokāyata: see Cārvāka.

Mādhyamika: the Buddhist school of skeptical philosophy founded by Nāgārjuna; sometimes called Buddhist Mysticism or Buddhist Absolutism.

Mahāyāna: Northern Buddhism; the "Great Vehicle."

Mīmāṃsā: "Exegesis"; a long-running school of classical philosophy devoted to defending what is taken to be a scriptural revelation in the Vedas; the classical school most closely tied to Brahminism (q.v.).; though realist in overall outlook, the philosophers of this school are opposed by Logicians especially in matters of epistemology; the *Mīmāṃsā-sūtra* (c. 100 BCE) is the root text, and Kumārila Bhaṭṭa (c. 650) and Prabhākara (c. 700) the chief proponents.

Mīmāṃsaka: an advocate of Mīmāṃsā (q.v.).

Naiyāyika: an advocate of Nyāya (q.v.).

Navya Nyāya: "New Logic"; the revolutionary Nyāya (q.v.) of, preëminently, Gaṅgeśa (c. 1325) and his followers, pioneered in part by Udayana (c. 1000), who unified Nyāya epistemology and logic with the ontology of Vaiśeṣika (q.v.).

Nyāya: "Logic"; a school of realism and common sense prominent throughout the classical period, from the *Nyāya-sūtra* (c. 200) on, developing out of canons of debate and informal logic; explicitly combined with Vaiśeṣika in the later centuries beginning with Udayana (c. 1000); focused on issues in epistemology but taking positions on a wide range of metaphysical issues.

Prācīna Nyāya: "Old Logic"; the philosophy of the *Nyāya-sūtra* and its commentaries, including that of Udayana (c. 1000), and of a few independent treatises; see Nyāya.

Pūrva Mīmāṃsā: "Former Exegesis" or "Exegesis" proper, contrasting with Uttara ("Later") Mīmāṃsā also known as Vedānta (q.v.); see Mīmāṃsā.

Sāṃkhya: "Analysis"; an early school of Indian philosophy concerned with achieving a "supreme personal good" through psychological disidentification.

Theistic Vedānta: any of several subschools of classical Vedānta (q.v.) espousing a view of (a) a creative God (*īśvara*), (b) God's reality and distinctness from the individual soul (also from the world, which is real), and (c) the *Bhagavad-Gītā* as well as various Upanishads as sacred revelation.

Theravāda: "the Doctrine of the (Buddhist) Elders"; an early school of philosophic Buddhism, appearing in the Southern Buddhist Canon.

Upanishad: "secret doctrine"; various prose and verse texts (appended to the Vedas, q.v.) with mystic themes centered on an understanding of the self and its relation to the Absolute or God, called Brahman; the primary sources for classical Vedānta philosophy.

Uttara Mīmāṃsā: "Later Exegesis" or Vedānta, contrasting with Pūrva ("Former") Mīmāṃsā, i.e., Mīmāṃsā proper.

Vaiśeṣika: "Atomism"; a classical philosophy focusing on ontological issues ("What kinds of things are there?") and defending a realist view of material things as composed of atoms; explicitly combined by Udayana (c. 1000) with Nyāya with no separate literature during the Navya-Nyāya period (1325+).

Veda: "revealed Knowledge"; the four Vedas, comprised principally of hymns to various indo-european gods, are the oldest texts composed in Sanskrit (possibly as early as 1500 BCE), .

Vedānta: originally an epithet for the Upanishads; in the classical period, the philosophy of the *Brahma-sūtra* and of several subschools defending Upanishadic views, in particular, Advaita (q.v.) and Theistic Vedānta (q.v.).

Yoga: a classical philosophy of a "supreme personal good" much like Sāṃkhya (q.v.) but proposing various exercises of "self-discipline" (i.e., *yoga*) as the means thereto.

Yogācāra: Buddhist Idealism, conveniently divided into (A) Early and (B) Late, sometimes referred to as Buddhist Logic: Late Buddhist Idealists (Dignāga, Dharmakīrti, and their followers) propose a much more advanced epistemology concerning worldly knowledge—and are less concerned with the concept of a "storehouse consciousness" (*ālaya-vijñāna*)—than are their Yogācāra predecessors; this school is the principal rival of Prācīna ("Old") Nyāya.

2. Terms

abhāva: (1) absence; negative fact; (2) negative perception (a source of knowledge, *pramāṇa*, according to Mīmāṃsā).

abhidhā: name, designation; primary meaning (i.e. a word's reference) as opposed to the suggestive or connative, *lakṣaṇā* (q.v.).

abhidheya: referent of a name, what is to be designated; nameable.

ādhāra: support, container, location.

ādheya: what is to be supported, contained, or attributed.

adhikaraṇa: (1) locus; location; (2) grammatical relation, esp. agreement.

adhikārin: qualified, entitled; fit (by yogic practice, scriptural study, etc.) for mystical experience, according to Advaita and some other classical schools.

adhyāsa: superimposition (or perceptual illusion, in some, chiefly Vedāntic, usages).

aitihya: traditional instruction, legendary account (regarded as a *pramāṇa* by some classical philosophers).

ākāśa: ether (the medium of sound), one of five material elements, according to Nyāya-Vaiśeṣika and other classical views.

akhaṇḍa upādhi: unanalyzable inessential or imposed property (see also *upādhi*), contrasting with *sakhaṇḍa upādhi* (q.v).

ālayavijñāna: "storehouse consciousness"; a principal concept in early Yogācāra.

ānanda: bliss; spiritual ecstasy; the nature of Brahman considered affectively, according to much Vedānta.

anātman: "no self," or "no soul"; an important Buddhist doctrine.

anavasthā: infinite regress.

aniṣṭa-prasaṅga: unwanted consequence of a thesis.

anirvacanīya: "impossible to say"; the Advaita view of both (1) the ontological status of the everyday world in relation to Brahman and (2) the status of the object of perceptual error in regard to the "real" objects revealed in veridical perception.

anubhava (anubhūti): experience, awareness (perceptual, inferential, and other veridical awarenesses—*pramā*—are all experiences; a remembering is a "cognition," *jñāna*, but not an "experience," *anubhava*, according to Navya Nyāya).

anugama (anugata): uniformity, consecutive character; one of the criteria of a true universal or natural kind, *jāti* (q.v.); experience of a consecutive character is taken by Naiyāyikas to be evidence for a universal or natural kind.

anumāna: cogent inference; one of four *pramāṇa* (q.v.) according to Nyāya.

anumiti: the cognitive act of inferring.

anuvṛtti-pratyaya: experience of a common character; see *anugama*.

anuvyavasāya: apperception, "after-cognition," introspection.

anuyogin: relational correlate to a counter-correlate, *pratiyogin* (q.v.).

anvaya: positive correlations (wherever *x* there *y*) entailed by a natural pervasion, *vyāpti* (q.v), constituting evidence for a pervasion; see also *vyatireka*.

anyathā-khyāti: the view of perceptual error (championed by Naiyāyikas) that stresses the reality of the thing misperceived and the reality of the thing which the presented object is misperceived *as*; usually some doctrine of the role of memory in the process of misperception is also put forth by proponents within an overall story emphasizing departure from a normal causal process.

anyonyābhāva: mutual exclusion, mutual absence (= *bheda*, distinctness).

anyonyāśraya: mutual dependence as a logical fault and eliminator (as in *a* required for the production of *b* and *b* required for the production of *a*).

āpta: expert; a person whose testimony is reliable.

arhat: the "saint" who, according to Theravāda Buddhism, has realized *nirvāṇa*.

arthāpatti: presumption; circumstantial implication (deemed an independent *pramāṇa* by Mīmāṃsakas and some other classical philosophers).

asādhāraṇa-dharma: "uncommon property"; a property, such as "having a dewlap," that defines individuals belonging to the same class, such as cows; the understanding of identity (*tādātmya*) advanced by the late Navya Naiyāyika, Gadādhara.

asaṃprajñāta-samādhi: mystic trance "without prop," utter mystic self-absorption; equivalent to enlightenment and *brahma-vidyā* according to some Vedāntins.

āsana: various stretching exercises and meditational postures taught as part of some disciplines of *yoga*.

asiddha: "unestablished"; the logical fallacy of an unwarranted premise.

ātman: Self or soul; the Upanishadic term for an individual's true or most basic consciousness.

ātmāśraya: "self-dependence"; the confuter or defeater of any thesis that proposes an impossible self-causation or self-qualification.

atyantābhāva: absolute absence, constant absence of *x* in *y*.

aupādhika sāmānya: conditional universal, a universal that is not a natural kind (*jāti*) because of failing the cross-sectional test, *jāti-saṃkara* (q.v.).

avaccheda: specification, delimitation, "paring down to"; techniques used by Navya Naiyāyikas to remove vagueness.

avacchedaka: specifier, delimitor.

avatāra: divine incarnation.

avidyā: spiritual ignorance; in much Vedānta, lack of direct awareness of *brahman* (q.v.) or God.

avinābhāva: invariable concomitance (no *x* without *y*), equivalent to "pervasion," *vyāpti* (q.v.).

ayutasiddha: inseparable connection; a characterization of inherence (*samavāya*) according to much Nyāya-Vaiśeṣika.

bādha: experiential "sublation," as a verdical perception of a rope correcting an illusory perception of a snake; contradiction; epistemic or justificational defeating.

bādhaka: (1) sublator, epistemic defeater; (2) blocking, opposition.

bhāṣya: commentary.

bhāva: presence (as opposed to absence, *abhāva*).

bhāva-cakra: the wheel of birth, death, and rebirth, according to Buddhism.

bheda: distinctness; see *aṇyonyābhāva*.

bhrama *(bhrānti)*: erroneous awareness; opposed to veridical awareness, *pramā*.

bhuyo-darśana: "wide experience"; the key condition leading to knowledge of a natural pervasion (*vyāpti*, q.v.) of *x* by *y*, according to Nyāya.

bodhisattva: the religious ideal of Mahāyāna Buddhists; the saint who has progressed to the brink of *nirvāṇa* but who refuses a personal salvation out of compassion for all sentience, intent on world teaching and good works.

brahman (Brahman, *brahma*): the Absolute; the key concept of the Upanishads and all Vedānta (q.v.) philosophy.

brahma-sākṣātkāra: immediate awareness of the Absolute; *brahma-vidyā*.

brahmavid: knower of Brahman.

brahma-vidyā: mystical knowledge of Brahman, the Absolute (or God); the *summum bonum*, according to Vedānta.

buddha: the Awakened; an epithet of Siddhārtha Gautama, the founder of Buddhism, after his enlightenment.

cakraka: "circularity," the epistemic defeater of any thesis that proposes an impossible circular chain of causation or qualification.

citta-vṛtti-nirodha: cessation of the fluctuations of mentality; the definition of *yoga* given by the *Yoga-sūtra*.

darśana: a world view or philosophy, a "viewing."

dharma: (1) duty; right (religious) practice; (2) quality or state of awareness (in Buddhism); (3) property.

dharmin: property-bearer (= *viśeṣya*, q.v.).

doṣa: "fault," a reliability-undercutting causal condition with respect to a non-veridical awareness, according to Gaṅgeśa and Navya Nyāya.

dravya : substance, one of seven ontic primitives or categories of Nyāya-Vaiśeṣika.

gaurava : (theoretic) "heaviness," the fault of being cumbersome relative to a competing view, contrasting with parsimony, *lāghava* (q.v.).

ghaṭaka : factor, constituent, element; specifier (= *avacchedaka*).

guṇa : (1) "causal excellence," a reliability-grounding causal condition with respect to awareness, according to Gaṅgeśa and Navya Nyāya. (2) quality; one of the seven fundamental categories (*padārtha*, q.v.) in traditional Nyāya-Vaiśeṣika ontology. (3) strand of nature; there are three of these according to Sāṃkhya, (a) light and intelligence, (b) activity and passion, and (c) inertia and darkness.

hetu : the inferential mark, the *probans* or "prover" term of a cogent inference (in the stock example of inference of fire on a mountain from sight of smoke—see above, p. 55—smoke or possessing-smoke).

hetvābhāsa : false inferential mark (cf. *hetu*).

idaṃtā : "this-ness," being-in-front, said of an object of perception.

indriya-sannikarṣa : contact or relation between sense organ and object perceived (= *pratyāsatti*); see note 70, p. 340.

īśvara : God.

itaretarāśraya : see *anyonyāśraya*.

jalpa : debating for victory where (in contrast with *vāda*, q.v.) using tricky arguments is all right so long as one gets away with it.

jāti : natural kind, true universal.

jāti-saṃkara : cross classification; one of the criteria that, according to Udayana, Gaṅgeśa, and some of their followers, rules out certain seeming universals; see figure 2.3, p. 61.

jīvan-mukti : "living liberation"; a person's knowledge of the Absolute or God, and "liberation" from all entanglement in the world while alive, according to some schools of Vedānta.

jñāna : cognition; awareness (properly, only "cognition" since a remembering is a *jñāna* but not an "experience" or "awareness," *anubhava*, but in certain contexts the term may be rendered "awareness"); an episodic quality of the self or soul, according to Nyāya-Vaiśeṣika.

jñeya : knowable; object of cognition.

jyeṣṭa pramāṇa : perception as the fundamental ("eldest") *pramāṇa* (q.v.), according to Nyāya: non-perceptual *pramāṇa* are each said to depend in some way on perception.

karma : (1) "action"; (2) psychological dispositions to act in a certain manner accrued through previous actions; habit.

khaṇḍana : "refutation."

khyāti : a moment of perception or consciousness: whereas *pratyakṣa* is defined by

Nyāya and other schools so as to exclude non-veridical perceptual events (*jñāna*s), a *khyāti* is a neutral term—both veridical and non-veridical perceptual moments are *khyāti*s.

kriyā : motion, action, one of seven ontic primitives or categories of much Nyāya-Vaiśeṣika.

kūṭastha : transcendent (said of Brahman by Vedāntins and of the individual conscious being, *puruṣa*, by Yogins).

lāghava : (theoretic) "lightness," parsimony, contrasting with (theoretic) "cumbersomeness," *gaurava* (q.v.).

lakṣaṇa : characterization, (putatively right) definition.

lakṣaṇā : metaphoric or secondary meaning, as opposed to primary meaning, *abhidhā* (q.v.).

lakṣya : the definiendum, that which is to be defined or characterized.

manas : the internal organ or sense-mind, the conduit of sensory information to the perceiving self, soul, or consciousness, according to several classical schools.

maṅgala-vāda : auspicious speech; the traditional opening of a philosophic, literary, or scientific text, comprised of verses usually addressed to a god.

māyā : illusion, cosmic illusion.

mleccha : foreigner.

mukti : liberation, salvation.

nāma-rūpa : "name and form"; the Upanishadic term for individuation.

neti neti : "not thus, not thus"; a famous Upanishadic proclamation about *brahman*.

nigrahasthāna : "grounds for rebuke" in a debate; informal fallacy (several are identified in the *Nyāya-sūtra*).

niḥsvabhāva : "without intrinsic being," an important ontological thesis within certain Buddhist schools.

nirākāra : "without form," said of cognition by Naiyāyikas, who see cognitions as distinguished only by their content.

nirvāṇa : extinction (of suffering); enlightenment.

nirvikalpaka jñāna : indeterminate awareness, relationless awareness, "concept-free" awareness, non-propositional awareness; according to Gaṅgeśa, in indeterminate awareness all the factors of determinate awareness (*savikalpaka jñāna*, q.v.) are cognized but not as linked together in the (propositional) structure, a-R-b, characteristic of determinate awareness; for this reason indeterminate awareness is considered not directly verbalizable.

niścaya : definite ascertainment; certainty.

niṣedha : prohibition; propositional denial.

nitya : constant; eternal.

padārtha : category, primitive, "type of thing to which words refer"; there are seven fundamental categories according to Nyāya-Vaiśeṣika, (1) substance, (2) quality, (3) motion, (4) natural kind, (5) final particularizer, (6) inherence, and (7) absence.

pakṣa : locus, the "subject" term in a cogent inference, that in which the *hetu* (q.v.) is known to reside (e.g., the mountain in the stock example: see above, p. 55).

parama-puruṣārtha : "supreme personal good."

pāramitā : perfection; there are six moral and spiritual perfections exhibited by a *bodhisattva* (q.v.), according to Mahāyāna Buddhism.

parataḥ pramāṇa : "extrinsic justification," certification by another; an epistemological thesis opposed to self-certification (*svataḥ pramāṇa*).

parināma : change, transformation.

paryāyatva : synonymy.

prajñā : wisdom; spiritual insight; one of the "perfections," *paramitā* (q.v.) or marks of a *bodhisattva* (q.v.), according to much Mahāyāna Buddhism.

prajñā-pāramitā : the "perfection" of wisdom; see *prajñā*.

prakāra : predication content (of a determinate awareness, *savikalpaka jñāna*, q.v.), in Gaṅgeśa's usage; literally "way."

prakaraṇa : topic; section of a text.

prakṛti : Nature; a principal Sāṃkhya concept.

pralāya : cosmic dissolution; the re-absorption of the world into the One, according to much popular Hinduism.

pramā : veridical awareness; determinate awareness (*savikalpaka jñāna*, q.v.) with predication content (*prakāra*, q.v.) that is a property of the object cognized (*viśeṣya*, q.v.), according to Gaṅgeśa.

pramāṇa : justifier; source of knowledge; means to veridical awareness; according to Nyāya, there are four *pramāṇa*, veridical perception, cogent inference, analogical vocabulary acquisition, and authoritative testimony.

prāmāṇya (*pramātva*) : veridicality.

prameya : object of veridical awareness; the knowable.

pramiti : act of veridical awareness; veridical awareness (= *pramā*).

prasaṅga : dialectical difficulty; Nāgārjuna's refutational method.

pratibandhī : the fallacy *tu quoque* or "two wrongs make a right."

pratibandhaka : preventor, blocker.

pratiyogin : (1) the Navya-Nyāya term for the counter-correlate or relatum of a dyadic relation, i.e., the second term of a relation, where the *anuyogin* is the first term (e.g., the *pratiyogin* of objecthood, *viṣayatā*, is awareness; the *pratiyogin* of subjecthood, *viṣayitā*, is the object of awareness); (2) counterpositive of an absence (e.g., with an absence of a pot on the floor, the pot is the *pratiyogin*), absentee.

pratyāsatti : "operative relation in sense experience"; see note 70, p. 340.

pratyakṣa : perception; one of four *pramāṇa* (q.v.) according to Nyāya.

pṛthaktva: "separateness"; a quality (*guṇa*), according to Nyāya; the Mīmāṃsaka understanding of distinctness, *bheda*.

puruṣa: "individual conscious being" according to both Sāṃkhya and Yoga.

pūrvapakṣa: the *prima facie* position, the opponent's position; a portion of a text devoted to exploring views not accepted by the author.

śābda-bodha: the mental event of understanding a speaker's sentence.

saccidānanda: (Absolute) Existence-Consciousness-Bliss, a popular Vedāntic characterization of *brahman*.

sādhya: the term which is to be proved in a cogent inference (e.g., fire or possessing-fire, in the stock example: see above, p. 55).

sākāṅkṣā: expectation; syntactic expectancy (a condition on the intelligibility of a statement, according to Naiyāyikas and others).

śākhā: branch of Vedic recension.

sakhaṇḍa upādhi: an accidental property, *upādhi*, that is ontologically composite and analyzable, e.g., "blue-cow-hood," which is a composite of the quality, blue, and the natural kind, cowhood.

samādhi: mystic or yogic trance.

samānādhikaraṇābhāva: "nominative absence," absence with respect to the same substratum or locus.

samānādhikaraṇatva: (1) the state of having the same locus or substratum; (2) grammatical agreement.

samaniyata: co-regulated, similarly restricted, co-pervasive.

sāmānya: universal (cf. *jāti*).

sāmānyābhāva: generic absence, e.g., absence of all pots, contrasting with an absence of a particular thing, *viśeṣābhāva*, e.g., an absence of a particular pot.

samavāya: "inherence"; the ontic glue, according to Nyāya, relating certain types of things to their loci, such as true universals, *jāti*; e.g., cowness inheres in cows.

sambandha: relation.

saṃkara: see *jāti-saṃkara*.

saṃketa: sign, signal; agreement.

saṃprajñāta-samādhi: mystic trance "with prop"; the penultimate stage of mystic accomplishment according to yoga texts; see *asaṃprajñāta-samādhi*.

saṃsargikābhāva: relational absence, including prior absence (*prāgabhāva*), destructional absence (*dhvaṃsābhāva*), and absolute absence (*atyantābhāva*), according to Nyāya.

saṃśaya: doubt, uncertainty.

saṃskāra:subliminal impression, disposition.

samūha-alambana-jñāna: awareness of a group of things.

saṃyoga: contact, conjunction.

sannikarṣa: see *indriya-sannikarṣa.*

śāstra: an individual science or craft; a scientific textbook.

satkāryavāda: a view of causality appearing in Sāṃkhya as well as in Advaita Vedānta: the effect in some sense pre-exists in the cause.

sattā: being-ness.

savikalpaka jñāna: determinate awareness, relational awareness, propositional awareness, verbalizable awareness; according to Gaṅgeśa and Navya Nyāya, awareness of a qualificandum (*viśeṣya,* q.v.) in relation to a particular qualifier (*viśeṣaṇa,* q.v.) or property, thus having (or reflecting) the structure a-R-b; opposed to *nirvikalpaka jñāna* (q.v.).

siddhānta: the right view; an author's own position or that of his school; a portion of a text devoted to elaborating an author's own views.

skanda: a grouping of qualities (*dharma*), according to some Buddhist philosophies.

sphoṭa: the quality of "bursting open"; according to some classical philosophers, an intrinsic quality of words mysteriously carrying their sense.

śruti: "hearing"; scripture; the Veda, including the Upanishads, according to Vedānta and other schools.

sūtra: "thread"; a philosophic aphorism.

svaprakāśa: see *svayamprakāśamāna.*

svaprakāśamāna: see *svayamprakāśamāna.*

svarūpa: "own nature," "own form."

svarūpa-bheda: distinctness in itself, intrinsic distinctness.

svarūpa-sambandha: self-linking relation.

svasamvedana: self-awareness (a Yogācāra Buddhist term).

svataḥ pramāṇa: self-certification, self-warrant.

svātma-vṛtti: resting in itself, occurring in itself.

svayamprakāśamāna: "irreflexively self-illuminating": an Upanishadic doctrine of the nature of self-consciousness.

tādātmya: identity.

tarka: dialectical reasoning; according to Nyāya and other classical schools, a hypothetical argument that shows a fallacy in maintaining a position ~*p* opposed to another position *p* that is thus shown to be right—so long as *p* has some additional evidence in its favor.

tarkābhāsa: an apparant or fallacious instance of dialectical reasoning, *tarka* (q.v.).

tattva: reality, "that-ness"; principle of being or reality.

upādhi: in Nyāya, (1) an "imposed property" ontologically identical with its locus and contrasting with a *jāti* (q.v.); (2) a special condition that vitiates an inference, an exception to a rule or pervasion (*vyāpti*), a pervasion-undermining circumstance.

upalakṣaṇa : mere designating expression; a feature of *x* that has little or nothing to do with what *x* is but referred to in order to point *x* out, e.g. "where the crows are roosting" said of Devadatta's house.

upamāna : "analogy"; analogical acquisition of vocabulary, a *pramāṇa* (q.v.) according to Nyāya.

vācana : a public speech; statement.

vāda : debate or inquiry aiming at the truth.

vaidharmya : difference in properties.

vaiśiṣṭya : relatedness, relation, qualifiedness; predicative tie; relational awareness.

vāsanā : generalized subliminal impression and valency; *karma* (q.v., the second sense of the term).

vidhi : injunction; propositional assertion.

vidyā : spiritual knowledge.

vijñapti-mātra : "consciousness only"; a central doctrine of Yogācāra Buddhism.

virodha : opposition; contradiction.

viṣaya : object; content (of awareness).

viṣaya-viṣayi-bhāva : the relation between subject and object.

viṣayatā : objecthood, one side of the relation between an awareness and its object, with the other as *viṣayitā* (q.v.), according to Navya Nyāya.

viṣayitā : subjecthood, one side of the relation between an awareness and its object, with the other as *viṣayatā* (q.v.).

viśeṣa : individualizer, particularizer, or numeralizer; the Vaiśeṣika concept of that which differentiates atoms of the same type (e.g., water), as well as individual souls; one of seven ontic primitives or categories according to much Nyāya-Vaiśeṣika.

viśeṣābhāva : absence of a particular thing, contrasting with *sāmānyābhāva*, general absence.

viśeṣaṇa : qualifier; qualities (e.g., blue), universals (e.g., cowhood), motions, and other unclassified qualifiers appear qualifying a qualificandum, *viśeṣya*, according to Nyāya.

viśeṣya : the thing cognized, the bearer of qualifiers, the qualificandum (= *dharmin*).

viśiṣṭa : qualified; a thing with its qualifiers; a cognition reflecting such a thing.

vitaṇḍā : refutational debate by captious argument with no express concern to establish a thesis of one's own.

vivarta : "transmogrification"; the Advaita doctrine that Brahman does not lose its native state—i.e., does not really change but only "transmogrifies"—as it becomes the individuated objects of the world.

vṛtti : occurrence; existence; locus.

vṛtti-niyāmika : "locus-exacting"; the relation of *samavāya*, inherence, for example, is *vṛtti-niyāmika* in that it secures a layeredness between the inherent and what it inheres in, according to Navya Nyāya.

vyabhicāra : deviation of the occurrence of *x* from the occurrence of *y* such that there is no pervasion (*vyāpti*, q.v.) of *x* by *y*.

vyākaraṇa-śāstra : the science of grammar.

vyāpya-vṛtti : locus-pervading; all true universals, e.g., cowhood, are locus-pervading, but some qualities, e.g., contact (*samyoga*), are not (the universal "cowhood" pervades every part of every cow, whereas the quality "contact" occurs within a delimited locus of one or both of the two things so related, as a monkey in contact with a tree), according to Navya Nyāya.

vyatireka : negative correlations (wherever no *y* there no *x*) entailed by a natural pervasion, *vyāpti* (q.v), constituting evidence for a pervasion; see also *anvaya*.

vyāpti : pervasion (of *x* by *y*), invariable concomitance; a factual relation that grounds inference according to Nyāya.

vyavahāra : conventional discourse; everyday speech (taken by Naiyāyikas and other classical philosophers as *prima facie* ontological evidence that by counter-considerations, however, can be overriden).

yadṛcchā : chance; accident.

yāna : religious career, vehicle for salvation.

yathārtha : matching or corresponding to an object, "as something is (or was)."

yoga : self-discipline.

yogyatā : semantic fittingness, a condition of the intelligibility of a statement according to Naiyāyikas and others.

APPENDIX C

A Chronology of Ancient and Classical[1] Works and Authors[2]

Ṛg Veda	1200–900 BCE (excluding the 10th bk.)
Early Upanishads	800–300 BCE
Middle and late Upanishads	c. 300 BCE–1000 CE
The Buddha (Siddhārtha Gautama)	c. 500 BCE
Mahāvīra (founder of Jainism)	c. 500 BCE
Pāṇini (grammarian)	c. 400 BCE
Southern Buddhist Canon	c. 300–200 BCE
Mahābhārata (*Great Indian Epic*):	
earliest portion	c. 500 BCE
latest portion	400+ CE
Bhagavad-Gītā	
earliest portion	200 BCE
latest portion	400 CE

1. The term "classical" is used here, and throughout this book, to distinguish an earlier period or culture from the modern. Classical Indian philosophy contrasts with modern philosophy in India in several respects. A convenient but not infallible mark is Sanskrit: almost all classical Indian literature—philosophical and otherwise—is expressed in Sanskrit, whereas very little of the modern is expressed in the language. However, the classical culture has several periods and variations according to region and, let us say, discipline. Classical Indian mythology, for example, begins several centuries earlier than classical Indian metaphysics. Moreover, the Vedic and Upanishadic periods are not usually counted as classical although their literature is expressed in Sanskrit. Too little continuity obtains between (a) the ancient, and (b) the long phase of previous Indian civilization that most saliently contrasts with the modern, to group these together: thus, the ancient Vedic and Upanishadic period (roughly, 1500–500 BCE), the classical period (roughly, 500 BCE–1700), and the modern (roughly, 1700 on). Classical Indian philosophy may be considered to commence with Nāgārjuna and to tail off in the nineteenth century.

2. Most of these datings follow Karl Potter's listings in his *Bibliography*, which is vol. 1 of his *Encyclopedia of Indian Philosophies*, and are supplemented by the numbers given in his *Nyāya-Vaiśeṣika*, vol. 2 of the *Encyclopedia*; sometimes I have rounded off for easier memory. Classical chronologies are inexact; any individual listing is relative to a host of considerations and datings for other authors and texts.

Mīmāṃsā-sūtra	200 BCE–200 CE
Brahma-sūtra	200 BCE–200 CE
Patañjali (grammarian)	c. 150 BCE
Vaiśeṣika-sūtra	c. 100 CE
Mahāyāna scriptures	100 BCE–800 CE
Nāgārjuna (Mādhyamika)	150 CE
Āryadeva (Mādhyamika)	fl. 180
Nyāya-sūtra (Gautama)	c. 200
Yoga-sūtra	300–400 (final redaction)
Vasubandhu (early Buddist Idealism)	fl. 360
Sāṃkhya-kārikā	c. 375
Vātsyāyana (Nyāya)	fl. 410
Bhartṛhari (grammarian)	c. 450
Dignāga (Buddhist Idealism)	c. 500
Gauḍapāda (Advaita)	fl. 525
Candramati (Vaiśeṣika)	c. 550
Praśastapāda (Vaiśeṣika)	c. 575
Uddyotakara (Nyāya)	c. 600
Dharmakīrti (Buddhist Idealism)	fl. 625
Kumārila (Mīmāṃsā)	fl. 660
Prabhākara (Mīmāṃsā)	fl. 700
Maṇḍana Miśra (Mīmāṃsā and Advaita)	c. 680–750
Śaṅkara (Advaita)	c. 700–750
Padmapāda (Advaita)	c. 750
Jayarāśi (Cārvāka)	c. 750
Sureśvara (Advaita)	fl. 750
Bhāskara (theistic Vedānta)	fl. 750
Dharmottara (Buddhist Idealism)	fl. 770
Jayanta Bhaṭṭa (Nyāya)	c. 875
Jñānaghana (Advaita)	c. 900
Bhāsarvajña (Nyāya)	c. 950
Vyomaśiva (Vaiśeṣika)	c. 950
Vimuktāman (Advaita)	c. 950
Vācaspati Miśra I (chiefly Advaita and Nyāya)	fl. 960.
Śrīdhara (Vaiśeṣika)	fl. 990
Udayana (Nyāya-Vaiśeṣika)	975–1050
Sarvajñātman (Advaita)	fl. 1027
Śaṅkhapāṇi (Advaita)	c. 1070
Rāmānuja (theistic Vedānta)	fl. 1120
Śrīvallabha (or Vallabha, Nyāya-Vaiśeṣika)	fl. 1140
Śrīharṣa (Advaita)	c. 1150
Keśava Miśra (Nyāya-Vaiśeṣika)	1225–1275
Madhva (theistic Vedānta)	c. 1280
Citsukha (Advaita)	fl. 1295

Maṇikaṇṭha Miśra (Navya Nyāya)	c. 1300
Gaṅgeśa (Navya Nyāya)	fl. 1325
Vardhamāna (Navya Nyāya)	fl. 1360
Śaṅkara Miśra (Navya Nyāya)	c. 1425
Vācaspati Miśra II (Navya Nyāya)	c. 1450
Raghunātha Śiromaṇi (Navya Nyāya)	c. 1500
Rucidatta Miśra (Navya Nyāya)	fl. 1510
Mādhava (intellectual historian, Advaita)	fl. 1515
Vallabha (theistic Vedānta)	fl. 1525
Vyāsatīrtha II (theistic Vedānta)	fl. 1535
Madhusūdana Sarasvatī (Advaita)	c. 1570
Bālabhadra (Advaita)	c. 1610
Jagadīśa (Navya Nyāya)	c. 1620
Viśvanātha (Navya Nyāya)	fl. 1640
Mathurānātha (Navya Nyāya)	c. 1650
Rāmakṛṣṇādhvarin (Navya Nyāya)	fl. 1650
Gadādhara (Navya Nyāya)	c. 1660
Gauḍa Brahmānanda (Advaita)	c. 1680

NOTES

Introduction: The Realist-Idealist Debate

1. Appendix A is a pronunciation guide.

2. Surendranath Dasgupta, B. K. Matilal, and others have proposed it. See, for example, Surendranath Dasgupta, *A History of Indian Philosophy*, vol. 2 (1932), p. 124, and B. K. Matilal, *Nyāya-Vaiśeṣika* (1977), p. 101: "It may be added that Śrīharṣa also contributed indirectly to the development of Navya Nyāya. He attacked Udayana and refuted each definition of Nyāya categories by developing very intricate and technical arguments. In this way, I think, the philosophic activity in India took a distinct turn."

3. Typical is the statement by the Japanese scholar Toshihiro Wada, "It is said that Śrīharṣa's criticism fired Gaṅgeśa's enthusiasm for writing the *Tattvacintāmaṇi*." See Wada, *Invariable Concomitance in Navya Nyāya* (1990), p. 15. (Gaṅgeśa is commonly counted the first New Logician.) Note the impersonal, indirect construction in Dr. Wada's statement, which occurs without any elaboration whatsoever.

4. B. K. Matilal, for example, states erroneously that Śrīharṣa "enters debate simply to refute others and it is not his responsibility to state his position much less to defend it." See Matilal, *Perception* (1986), p. 65.

Chapter 1: Early Indian Idealism and Mysticism

1. Appendix C, which is a chronology, discusses use of the term "classical" in the Indian context.

2. Numerous Upanishadic passages exhibit this and the other themes to be identified. With each theme, I list only a few especially noteworthy proof-texts. Later, in elaborating the Advaita reading, I provide other, rather lengthy quotations.

The best English translation of early Upanishads remains Robert E. Hume's *The Thirteen Principal Upanishads*, 2d ed. (1971 reprint). But the Upanishadic translations here are my own. The Sanskrit text is taken from *Upaniṣat-Saṃgrahaḥ*, ed. J. L. Shastri (1970).

Important passages supporting this first theme are *Bṛhadāraṇyaka* (*Bṛ*) 2.4.12 ("This great being, infinite, without bounds, is just a mass of consciousness"), *Bṛ* 2.5.19, *Chāndogya* (*Chā*) 6.8.7 ("Thou art That"), *Aitareya* 3.5.1, and *Māṇḍūkya* 3.

3. For example, *Bṛ* 3.6 and 4.5.11 ("From this great being has been breathed forth . . ."), *Kaṭha* 6.1, and *Muṇḍaka* 2.1.3ff.

4. For example, *Chā* 8.14, *Muṇḍaka* 3.2.8, and *Praśna* 6.5.

5. For example, *Īśā* 4-7, in particular, verse 5: "That moves; That moves not. That is far; That is near. That is on the inside of all this; That is on the outside as

well."

6. For example, *Bṛ* 4.5.15 and *Taittirīya* 2.6.

7. For example, *Chā* 6.8.7ff.

8. For example, *Bṛ* 4.3.32–33, *Taittirīya* 2.9, and *Kaṭha* 1.2.10–23, in particular, verse 22:"Knowing the comprehensive, pervasive Self, a person is wise and sorrows no longer."

9. For example, *Bṛ* 4.5.6 ("The Self is to be seen, heard, reflected on, and discovered in meditation"), *Muṇḍaka* 3.1.5ff, and *Śvetāśvatara* 1.14.

10. For example, *Bṛ* 4.4.21, *Taittirīya* 2.9.1, and *Kena* 1.3ff.

11. Among the most significant theistic passages is *Bṛ* 3.7.1–23, in particular, verse 3: "He who dwelling in the earth is other than the earth, whom the earth does not know, whose body the earth is, who controls the earth from within—is the Self, the Inner Controller, the Immortal." (This refrain repeats substituting "waters" etc. for "earth.") The word *īśvara* and cognates (such as *īś*) appear in early Upanishads dozens of times.

12. The earliest realist texts make scant and problematic mention of God: see this book, p. 67.

13. Some of Śaṅkara Miśra's interpretations are funny. See chapter 5, pp. 273–74.

14. *Bṛ* 1.4.7: *taṃ na paśyanty akṛtsno hi | sa prāṇann eva prāṇo nāma bhavati vadan vāk paśyan cakṣuḥ śṛnvañ śrotraṃ manvāno manas | tāny asya etāni karma-nāmāny eva | sa yo 'ta ekaikam upāste na sa veda akṛtsno hy eṣo 'ta ekaikena bhavati | ātmā ity eva upāsīta atra hy ete sarve ekaṃ bhavanti.*

15. The reasoning is particularly well exhibited at *Bṛ* 4.5.15: Given non-duality, "whereby and whom would one see?"

16. *Bṛ* 4.3.9–32.

17. *Bṛ* 4.4.19. Repeated at *Kaṭha* 4.11 and echoed in other Upanishads.

18. *Bṛ* 4.2.4 and 4.4.22.

19. *asya lokasya sarvāvato mātrām apādāya svayaṃ vihatya svayaṃ nirmāya . . . , sa viśvakṛt sa hi sarvasya kartā* |*Bṛ* 4.3.9–10.

20. *salila eko draṣṭā advaito bhavaty eṣa brahma-lokaḥ samrāḍ iti ha enam anuśaśāsa yājñavalkya | eṣā asya paramā gatir eṣā asya paramā sampad eṣo 'sya paramo loka eṣo 'sya paramo ānandaḥ | etasya eva ānandasya anyāni bhūtāni mātrām upajīvanti* | |*Bṛ* 4.3.32.

21. Several scholars have argued that the *Māṇḍūkya Upaniṣad*—along with Gaudapāda's *kārikā*s (c. 525 CE ?)—is the Upanishad with the greatest influence on Advaita Vedānta. A dream analogy, and a theory of states of the soul, both echoing this *Bṛhadāraṇyaka* passage, dominate the *Māṇḍūkya*.

22. See chapter 3, p. 76.

23. Moreover, there are many Upanishadic passages that, without using the word *yoga*, say that practices of meditation and austerity are crucial. Some of the explicit mentionings are found at *Kaṭha* 6.11, *Muṇḍaka* 3.2.6, and *Śvetāśvatara* 2.10ff.

24. Mircea Eliade, *Yoga: Immortality and Freedom*, trans. Willard R. Trask, 2nd ed. (1969); and J. W. Hauer, *Der Yoga* (1958), contain classic treatments. Georg Feuerstein's numerous works, including *The Encyclopedic Dictionary of Yoga* (1990) contain much about yoga and Vedānta.

25. One important discovery is a so-called proto-Shiva clay figure found at the archeological site of Mahenjadaro, a city pre-dating the invasion of Sanskrit-speaking tribes by more than a thousand years. The figure apparently illustrates a yogic meditational pose. See Eliade (1969), pp. 354–56.

26. *Nyāya-sūtra* 1.1.3, 1.1.22, 4.1.58ff and commentaries, for example. (For editions of this work, see the bibliography entries under *Nyāya-sūtra*. Translations are by Ganganatha Jha, 1984, and Mrinalkanti Gangopadhyaya, 1982.)

27. *Khaṇḍanakhaṇḍakhādya*, p. 7.

28. See, for example, Buddhaghoṣa's lists in *The Path of Purification*, trans. Bhikku Nyanamol, vol. 2 (1976).

29. *Majjhima-Nikāya*, Sutta 13, trans. Henry Clarke Warren, in *Buddhism in Translation* (1896), pp. 117–28. The statements in quotes are paraphrases.

30. For example, *The Book of Kindred Sayings*, trans. C. A. F. Rhys Davids, vol. 3, pp. 3–4.

31. See, for example, *The Book of Kindred Sayings*, vol. 2, pp. 1–2.

32. Christian Lindtner, among others, has made a strong case for this reading in *Nagarjuniana* (1986). But there seems to be, at least in some of Nāgārjuna's works, denial that any intellectual statement makes sense, even such meta-theses. On this reading, the "understanding" of "without a reality of its own" would have to be a non-intellectual discernment rather than something statable, for *all* intellectual understanding is revealed, on analysis, to be absurd.

33. *Vigrahavyāvartanī*, *kārikā*s 24, 28, 38, and 42, for example. See also Kamaleswar Bhattacharya (1978), pp. 240–41.

34. Nāgārjuna's mention of "the Owl's system" occurs in his *Ratnāvalī* at 1.61 (*ulūkya*). The disciple, Āryadeva, makes his attack in his *Catuḥśataka*, chap. 14.

35. *yadi ca pramāṇatas te teṣāṃ teṣāṃ prasiddhir arthānām* | *teṣāṃ punaḥ prasiddhiṃ brūhi kathaṃ te pramāṇānām* || *anyair yadi pramāṇaiḥ pramāṇa-siddhir bhavet tad-anavasthā* | *Vigrahavyāvartanī* 31–32a. See also Kamaleswar Bhattacharya's translation, *The Dialectical Method of Nāgārjuna* (1986), p. 115.

36. John Pollock credits the expression to John Rawls. See Pollock's *Contemporary Theories of Knowledge* (1986), pp. 5ff.

37. Several first-class modern Western metaphysicians—such as Franz Brentano in the late nineteenth century, Bertrand Russell, Ludwig Wittgenstein, Gustav Bergmann, W. V. O. Quine, many others—have worried about this. An interesting contemporary treatment is found in Edward N. Zalta, *Intensional Logic and the Metaphysics of Intentionality* (1988).

38. *Vv* 42–64.

39. See Lindtner's discussion, *Nagarjuniana*, pp. 10–11.

40. These paradoxes and the revealing of them came to be known as *prasaṅga*, dialectical refutation. Nāgārjuna's dialectical criticism is commonly referred to in English as the *prasaṅga* method. The term is sometimes also used for the objections we have already surveyed in the *Vv*. But the dialectical method of the *MMK* is typically to reveal paradoxes of relation.

In the *MMK*, unlike the *Vv*, there is apparently no thesis of Nāgārjuna's at stake (though one might argue that there is at least a meta-thesis insinuated in various ways).

41. In the last few decades, Nāgārjuna studies have come to be a sort of hermeneuticist carnival. Recently, Claus Oetke has helped clear some of the air by identifying tensions in Nāgārjuna's thought, many of which stem from ambiguously expressed theses. See Oetke's "Remarks on the Interpretation of Nāgārjuna's Philosophy" (1991).

42. *gamyamānasya gamanaṃ kathaṃ nāma upapatsyate* | *gamyamānaṃ hy agamanaṃ yadā na eva upapadyate* ||

43. Another possible translation of the verse is: "How indeed could it occur that there be a being-cognized of what is currently being cognized? And that something

that is currently being cognized not be a being-cognized is never possible." This reading takes the sense of the verb *gam*, not in its most common meaning of "to go" or "to move," but in a second sense—which is frequently found—of "to know, cognize, or understand." Though I have no argument ready, I am inclined to think that the verse should be read in both ways.

44. It is not clear to me whether or not in the *MMK* Nāgārjuna comes up with the Bradley problem, that is to say, the relation regress (aRb, aR_1R, aR_2R_1, *ad infinitum*, with a similar regress vitiating the link between R and b) that stands at the center of many of Śrīharṣa's polemics and exercises Gaṅgeśa and other top Naiyāyika minds. I await a Buddhist scholar's judgment on this. Again, Nāgārjuna does not flag the logical patterns that underlie his polemics. However, the Yogācāra Buddhist logician Dharmakīrti clearly does state the Bradley problem, and was likely prompted in this by Nāgārjuna or one of his followers. (See the next section of this chapter.) Or, less probably, Dharmakīrti learned it from the grammarian Bhartṛhari (450 ?), whose "paradox of signification" is reviewed in this chapter's last section, on Vedānta—or, he learned it from the *Brahma-sūtra* (see note 69 below).

45. See, e.g., the *Suraṅgama-sūtra* in *A Buddhist Bible*, ed. and trans. Dwight Goddard (1938).

46. See David Seyfort Ruegg's discussion in "La luminosité de la Pensée," which is part 4 of his *La théorie du Tathāgatagarbha et du Gotra* (1969), especially chapters 3 and 4.

47. Alternatively, we could say that the Buddhist school echoes Upanishadic thought. Buddhism's relation to the Upanishads is in fact complex. For comparable teachings concerning self-awareness, see Sanjay Govind Deodikar, *Upaniṣads and Early Buddhism* (1992), pp. 157 and 173. That awareness is "self-illumined" (*svayaṃ-jyoti*) is said at *Bṛhadāraṇyaka* 4.3.9.

Dignāga, a later Yogācārin, defends the doctrine that self-awareness is intrinsic to cognition (*svasamvedana*), by arguing that otherwise there would be an infinite regress: see *Pramāṇasamuccaya*, the first chapter translated and annotated by Masaaki Hattori as *Dignāga, On Perception* (1968), p. 30. This is an important argument and doctrine for Śrīharṣa.

48. In his *chef d'oeuvre*, the *Pramāṇasamuccaya*, whose first chapter is translated by Masaaki Hattori (1968).

49. Naiyāyikas as early as Jayanta and Vācaspati accept indeterminate perception: see chapter 2, p. 57. Gaṅgeśa makes crucial use of the notion: see chapter 4: pp. 122–25.

50. This view has an affinity with early Buddhist Idealism in that the earlier Yogācārins hold that awareness is in its true nature the Supreme Reality such as was discovered by the Buddha in *nirvāṇa* experience. The perversions of thought (misinterpretation) and desire (systemized as the workings of the *vāsanā*, "subliminal impressions") are what prevent us from realizing this.

51. "Perception is (right) cognition so long as it is not affected by such illusion (causing circumstances) as cataracts, rapid motion, joltings on board a ship, etc." *Nyāyabindu* 1.6, Kashi Sanskrit Series edition, p. 12: *timirāśu-bhramaṇa-nauyāna-saṃkṣobha-ādy-anāhita-vibhramaṃ jñānam pratyakṣam*. Compare the translation by F. T. Stcherbatsky, *Buddhist Logic*, vol. 2 (1962), p. 24.

52. *Pramāṇaviniścaya*, the *pratyakṣa* chapter translated from Tibetan into German by Tilmann Vetter (1966), pp. 77–79; see also *Nyāyabinduṭīkā* (Kashi Sanskrit Series), p. 2, and Dharmakīrti's *chef d'oeuvre*, the *Pramāṇavārttika*, III.206.

53. Vātsyāyana (c. 410), the earliest commentator on the *Nyāya-sūtra*, Nyāya's

root text, says in his introduction that successful activity depends on right cognition and that right cognition arises from specific causes or sources. Moreover, that some inferences are grounded in causal relations is also a Nyāya doctrine.

54. *dvayor eka-abhisambandhāt sambandho yadi tad-dvayoḥ | kaḥ sambandho 'navasthā ca na sambandha-matis tathā ||* *Sambandhaparīkṣā* (*SP*), verse 4. Also interesting is verse 3: "if two entities are different, how can they be related? and if they are not different, what is the point of talking about a relation?"

The *SP*, *Examination of Relation*, translated by Erich Frauwallner into German (1934), has recently been translated into English by V. N. Jha (1990). (Jha provides in this book a Sanskrit edition of the *SP*, which I have used, but the *SP* translations here are my own.)

Though Dharmakīrti clearly expresses the problem of relations, a Vedāntin text earlier than Dharmakīrti, the *Brahma-sūtra*, identifies it, too: see note 69 below.

55. Most of the *SP* in fact concerns the impossibility of causality.

56. See also Tilmann Vetter's translation (from Tibetan into German) of Dharmakīrti's *Pramāṇaviniscaya* (1966), pp. 41 and 43, where Dharmakīrti explains that though color and taste have absolutely nothing to do with one another, we in some instances take them to stand as sign and signified. That we can touch what we see is an important argument used by Naiyāyikas of the early period to combat Buddhist Idealism. See in this text, chapter 2, pp. 45 and 47.

57. *ity amiśrāḥ svayaṃ bhāvāstān miśrayati kalpanā.* *SP*, verse 5b.

58. Two excellent presentations of the Old Nyāya school's debate with the Buddhists are D. N. Shastri, *Critique of Indian Realism: A Study of the Conflict between the Nyāya-Vaiśeṣika and Buddhist Dignāga School* (1964), and B. K. Matilal, *Perception: An Essay on Classical Indian Theories of Knowledge* (1986).

59. See *Nyāyabindu* 3.74ff, pp. 73ff, and *Pramānavārttikasvavṛtti* (Dharmakīrti wrote a prose commentary, or *svavṛtti*, on one chapter), ed. R. Gnole (1960), p. 144. See also F. T. Stcherbatsky, *Buddhist Logic*, vol. 1 (1962), pp. 400–13, Tilmann Vetter, *Erkenntnisprobleme bei Dharmakīrti* (1964), p. 15, and J. L. Shaw, "Negation and the Buddhist Theory of Meaning" (1978).

60. This law would seem to hold also on the meta-level, where Dharmakīrti abandons the epistemology based on causal relations: the precise contradictory of the (meta-)concept of the generality of concepts is the particularity of the object of sensation. Thus, by the particularity of the real Dharmakīrti can be taken to mean the contrast with the most general feature of concepts, namely, their generality (*sāmānyalakṣaṇatva*).

61. See my discussion in "Dharmakīrti on Sensation and Causal Efficiency" (1987).

62. One camp, stemming from Padmapāda (c. 740), insisted on a *vivarta* view: Brahman "transmogrifies" but does not somehow change (*parināma*) in becoming the world. Another camp, stemming from Vācaspati (c. 960), agreeing that Brahman does not change, found *avidyā*, "spiritual ignorance," to be rather substantial, almost a veritable objective Nature that is re-absorbed into Brahman only in a universal dissolution (*mahā-pralāya*).

63. See Śaṅkara's, Rāmānuja's, and other commentaries on *Brahma-sūtra* 1.3.34ff, for example, where the lowest castes are excluded from study of sacred texts.

64. See the *Encyclopedia of Indian Philosophies*, ed. Karl Potter, vol. 4, *Sāṃkhya*, ed. Gerald Larson and Ram Shankar Bhattacharya (1987), in particular the second part of the introduction, pp. 43–103.

65. The cosmology of Vācaspati, for example, has a close affinity to Sāṃkhya.

66. *Vākyapadīya* 3.3.1ff (1991), pp. 235ff. An available translation is K. A. Subramania Iyer's *The Vākyapadīya of Bhartṛhari*, chap. 3, pt. 1 (1971), pp. 76ff. Pāṇini's convention is to use a word to mean itself as a word as well as its referent, and this appears to be what worries the much later grammarian. See K. Kunjunni Raja's discussion in *The Philosophy of Indian Grammarians*, ed. Howard G. Coward and K. Kunjunni Raja, which is vol. 5 of *Encyclopedia of Indian Philosophies*, ed. Karl Potter (1990), p. 113.

H. Herzberger and R. Herzberger, "Bhartṛhari's Paradox" (1981), pp. 3–32, discuss at length the paradox, trying to motivate it through use of tools of modern logic. B. K. Matilal translates Bhartṛhari's statement of the argument, using it to launch insightful discourse on J. Derrida's deconstructionism: see Matilal's *The Word and the World* (1990), pp. 128–32.

67. There are, by the way, distinct echoes of Nāgārjuna in Bhartṛhari's work: e.g., *Vākyapadīya* 3.3.44.

68. For example, the so-called Sannyāsa Upanishads, "Upanishads on Renunciation," probably pre-date Śaṅkara. Some of them express a decidedly Advaita outlook. See, e.g., A. A. Ramanathan's translations, *The Saṃnyāsa Upaniṣads* (1978), pp. 27, 93–94, 107–08, 113–24, and so on.

69. The *Brahma-sūtra* is the earliest extant attempt to systematize ideas of the early Upanishads. But it is so aphoristic and elliptical in style that both Advaitic and theistic interpreters can agree that it presents the teachings of scripture. (The Sanskrit word *sūtra* means "thread" and *sūtra* literature was in general composed to be memorized; thus the aphoristic quality of the *Brahma-sūtra*, *Nyāya-sūtra*, and so on.) Georg Thibaut argues in an introduction to his translation of Śaṅkara's *Brahma-sūtra* commentary (1962 reprint), pp. xvi–xxxi, that Śaṅkara and his followers are wrong to read the *Brahma-sūtra* as expounding an Advaitin as opposed to a theistic world view, though right to find their Advaita expressed in several early Upanishads. Śaṅkara's commentary on the *Brahma-sūtra* is the earliest commentary extant.

The founders of the prominent Vedāntic subschools—the theists Bhāskara, Rāmānuja, Nimbārka, Madhva, and Vallabha as well as the Advaitin Śaṅkara—all write commentaries on the *Brahma-sūtra*. But the Upanishads themselves, and not the *Brahma-sūtra*, are the foundational Vedāntic texts. This is unlike the situation with, for example, Nyāya, where the *Nyāya-sūtra* is veritably the foundational text, as will be explained in chapter 2.

Nevertheless, *Brahma-sūtra* 2.2.12, *samavāya-abhyupagamāc ca sāmyād anavasthiteḥ* ("Because of [the Atomists'] acceptance of inherence, [their view suffers from] infinite regress due to sameness [in the logic of the relation]") may be the earliest expression of the relation regress in Indian philosophy. (Later in this chapter, I translate a portion of Śaṅkara's commentary on this *sūtra*: see p. 30.) However, there is much dispute about the *Brahma-sūtra*'s date, and several scholars place it after Nāgārjuna.

70. *Khaṇḍanakhaṇḍakhādya*, p. 7.

71. *BSB*, introduction to 1.1.1.

72. *BSB* 1.1.1: *na na aham asmi iti*.

73. *BSB*, introduction to 1.1.1: "perception and the other sources of knowledge (including scripture)—and the sciences as well—determine objects invariably presupposing spiritual ignorance." *avidyāvad-viṣayāṇy eva pratyakṣa-ādīni pramāṇāni śāstrāṇi ca* |

74. For example, *BSB*, introduction to 1.1.1. Georg Thibaut (1962 reprint) translates the term this way. (His is, by the way, in general an admirable effort, a

highly readable English rendering of the great Advaitin's prose—and Śaṅkara himself is a master prose stylist.)

75. At places, Śaṅkara does say that Brahman is the world's material cause. But it is difficult to know how seriously to take that claim—at least with him as opposed to later Advaitins. At other places in Śaṅkara's large corpus, the claim seems, as indicated, assimilated to a psychological model drawn on analogy to perceptual illusion. The characterization of *adhyāsa* that Śaṅkara gives at the very beginning of his *BSB* (*smṛti-rūpaḥ paratra pūrva-dṛṣṭa-avabhāsaḥ*, "superimposition is the appearance, in the form of a memory, of something previously experienced in something else") is interpreted by some to imply that Brahman is only psychologically a locus; other followers dispute this reading.

76. For example, *Upadeśasāhasrī* 2.16.23–57.

77. *api ca kārya-kāraṇayor dravya-guṇa-ādīnāṃ ca aśva-mahiṣa-vad-bheda-buddhy-abhāvāt tādātmyam abhyupagantavyam* | *sama-vāya-kalpanāyām api samavāyasya samavāyibhiḥ sambandhe 'bhyupagamyamāne tasya tasya anyonyaḥ sambandhaḥ kalpayitavya ity anavasthā-prasaṅgaḥ, anabhyupagamyamāne ca viccheda-prasaṅgaḥ* |*BSB* 2.1.18; see also 2.2.13 and 2.2.17.

78. *BSB* 2.1.18.

79. *Brahmasūtrabhāṣya* (*BSB*), introduction to 1.1.1; concerning Śrīharṣa, see chapter 3, p. 95. Śaṅkara's is not the earliest presentation of the rebuttal; Jayarāśi is one earlier philosopher who articulates it (see chapter two, pp. 72–74). Arguments and counter-arguments seem to have floated freely across schools. (There is no indication that Śaṅkara was familiar with Jayarāśi's work.)

80. *BSB* 2.1.1. Cf. Śaṅkara's *Bṛhadāraṇyaka-bhāṣya* 2.1.20. For Śrīharṣa's endorsement of the point, see chapter three, p. 87.

81. *BSB* 2.1.11.

82. *samudrād udaka-ātmano 'nanyatve 'pi tad-vikārāṇāṃ phena-vīcī-taraṅga-budbudādīnām itaretara-vibhāga itaretara-saṃśleṣa-ādi-lakṣaṇaś ca vyavahāra upalabhyate* | *na ca samudrād udaka-ātmano 'nanyatve 'pi phena-taraṅga-ādīnām itaretara-bhāva-āpattir bhavati* | *na ca teṣām itaretara-bhāva-anāpattāv api samudra-ātmano 'nanyatvaṃ bhavati* | *evam iha api bhoktṛ-bhogyayor itaretara-bhāva-āpattiḥ, na ca parasmād brahmano 'nyatvaṃ bhaviṣyati* | *yady api bhoktā na brahmaṇo vikāraḥ . . . tathā api kāryam anupraviṣṭasya asty upādhi-nimitto vibhāga ākāśasya iva ghaṭa-ādi-upādhi-nimitta ity ataḥ parama-kāraṇād brahmaṇo 'nanyatve 'py upapadyate bhoktṛ-bhogya-lakṣaṇo vibhāgaḥ samudra-taraṅga-ādi-nyāyena ity uktam* |

83. This was one of the first classical philosophic texts translated into English—by E. B. Cowell and A. E. Gough, *Compendium of All Philosophies* (1892).

84. The arguments against the objectivity of *bheda* occur particularly in the second chapter of the *Brahmasiddhi*, entitled "On Dialectical Reasoning" (*tarka-kāṇḍa*), where Maṇḍana is occupied with responding to various objections to the Advaita view he has put forth in his first chapter. Allen Thrasher has summarized the entire book in *Advaita Vedānta*, vol. 3 of *The Encyclopedia of Indian Philosophies*, ed. Karl Potter (1981). The arguments against the reality of distinctness are summarized on pp. 376–87; also, Potter discusses them in his general introduction, pp. 71–72. Incidentally, the first chapter of the *Brahmasiddhi* was translated into German and French in publications appearing the same year (1969): by Tilmann Vetter, and by Madeleine Biardeau in her *La philosophie de Maṇḍana Miśra*, pp. 139–343. Biardeau also has a section on the arguments against distinctness: pp. 39–55. The Sanskrit edition referred to is edited by S. Kuppuswami Sastri.

85. Biardeau (1969), p. 40.

86. Allen Thrasher, "Maṇḍana Miśra's Theory of Vikalpa" (1978).

87. *Brahmasiddhi*, pp. 48–49. We may note also that Maṇḍana attacks inherence as the relation—according to the Atomists and Logicians—that ties together a universal and a particular: pp. 60–61.

88. See Karl Potter's discussion in *The Encyclopedia of Indian Philosophies*, vol. 3 (1981), pp. 346–47 and 420.

89. *Bṛhadāraṇyaka-bhāṣya-vārtikka*, introduction to bk. 1, ed. and trans. T. M. P. Mahadevan (1958), pp. 484ff.

90. Karl Potter presents a very readable summary of Padmapāda's philosophic oeuvre in his *Encyclopedia*, vol. 3 (1981), pp. 563–97. See also my paper, "Padmapāda's Illusion Argument" (1987).

91. In contending Buddhist positions, Śaṅkara even sounds like a Logician realist, arguing in support of *external* objects and providing criteria that distinguish dreaming and waking experiences: *BSB* 2.2.28–30.

92. *Nyāya-sūtra* 4.2.31–37 concerns the possibility that no worldly objects are really revealed by the sources of knowledge, as with objects in a dream. Uddyotakara, a commentator prior to Vācaspati, takes the passage to address a dispute with Buddhist Idealists. Vācaspati follows this precedent. But in his subcommentary under *sūtra*s 4.2.33 and 34, with a central plank of idealism under attack—viz., that awareness itself takes on the form of objects (as in a dream)—Vācaspati retorts that in all non-veridical awareness—and here the words of his list include the Advaitin term *māyā* (Taranatha and Amarendramohan edition, p. 1045)—what is experienced has been veridically experienced previously, otherwise no account could be given of its non-veridical appearance. Non-veridicality presupposes veridicality, and veridicality requires that the world is real. This and other arguments are barbs from an Advaitin perspective. The clincher, however, concerns views of perceptual illusion. Vācaspati both names and attacks the Advaita theory of "indeterminability" (*anirvacanīya-khyāti*), in endorsing the Logician theory (as I will explain in chapter 2); see the Taranatha and Amarendramohan edition, pp. 72–75. Then from the Advaita perspective, Vācaspati argues—at the beginning of his famous *Bhāmatī* subcommentary on Śaṅkara's *BSB*—that the Logician view of illusion is wrong, in endorsing the Advaita "indeterminability" view; see the S. S. Suryanarayana Sastri and C. Kunhan Raja edition and translation, pp. 28ff. Note, finally, that Vācaspati in this Advaita work devotes not just a few paragraphs to the Nyāya view, but labors with it and every other view of perceptual illusion he knows of in an extended reflection. (It seems he is pushed by Naiyāyika arguments to admit an infinite series of psychological impressions—to account for the content of illusory, i.e., unliberated, experiences—impressions that lie latent even in *pralāya*, the period of absorption of the world in Brahman.) Vācaspati is, in sum, a complex philosopher; given his philosophic acumen and the extraordinary voluminousness and diversity of his corpus, he seems (I would hope to someone other than myself) a particularly inviting target for further research.

93. Karl Potter, ed., *Encyclopedia*, vol. 2 (1977), p. 15.

94. Dasgupta, vol. 2 (1932).

Chapter 2: Early Systematic Realism

1. By the time of Patañjali (150 BCE), there may have been an early form of Vaiśeṣika, although Karl Potter dates the *Vaiśeṣika-sūtra* at approximately the time of Nagārjuna, that is, 150 CE.

2. In particular, there are literary critics in the late classical age enamored of a mystical *sphoṭa*, or bursting, creative-word theory of (especially) poetic communication. See, e.g., Daniel Ingalls' introduction to *The Dhvanyāloka of Ānandavardhana* (1990). Or see S. N. Ghoshal Sastri's discussion in the introduction to his translation of the *Kāvya-Prakāśa* by Mammaṭa Bhaṭṭa (1973), pp. 12–14. (Ānandavardhana and Mammaṭa are premier literary critics.)

3. Harsh Narain, *Evolution of the Nyāya-Vaiśeṣika Categoriology* (1976), makes the case that the contribution of grammarians was crucial: pp. 113–88.

4. The discussion appears in the vast *Mahābhāṣya* of Patañjali (c. 150 BCE), and is advanced by Bhartṛhari, among others. For an overview, see Louis Renou, *Terminologie grammaticale du sanskrit* (1957), the entry on *jāti*, "universal," pp. 148–49, and Coward and Raja, eds., *The Philosophy of Indian Grammarians*, pp. 116–17. See also Harsh Narain (1976), pp. 114–17.

5. Harsh Narain (1976), p. 116, draws our attention to a passage in Patañjali's *Mahābhāṣya* where the early grammarian "classifies parts of speech into words signifying substance or individual (*dravya* or *yadṛcchā*), attribute (*guṇa*), motion (*kriyā*), and class (*jāti*)."

6. See Harsh Narain (1976), pp. 188–92. See also Coward and Raja, eds., *The Philosophy of Indian Grammarians*, pp. 116–17, 124–26, and 194, in particular.

7. The phrase is George Cardona's. See his *Pāṇini: A Survey of Research* (1976), p. 328. Cf. B. K. Matilal's discussion of definition, *Logic, Language and Reality* (1985), pp. 164ff.

8. Sanskrit has no grammatical feature that cannot be rendered in English translation, and so when a philosopher makes a point about syntactical connections within a sentence or about the meaning of a certain affix, the point can be made in English (though this sometimes requires rather lengthy explication). It would be, however, almost impossible to read the Indian grammatical literature in translation without a knowledge of Sanskrit, since one would not have intuitions about what is being talked about.

9. See chapter one, pp. 10–11.

10. The first three chapters of vol. 1 of Ester Solomon's pioneering two-volume work, *Indian Dialectics* (1976), traces in painstaking detail these occurrences and treatments in the pre-classical literature (i.e., before Nāgārjuna).

11. *Mahābhārata* 12.320.78ff (Bombay edition). I follow Solomon's discussion (1974), pp. 26-28.

12. Ganganatha Jha, in an introduction to his translation, *Padārtha-dharmasaṃgraha of Praśastapāda* (1982 reprint), quotes the Navya author Vardhamāna (c. 1350) propounding a new, wider definition of "commentary" (*bhāṣya*) with the evident purpose of justifying the practice of referring to Praśastapāda's work by this term: "The *Bhāṣya*, according to this, is that which gathers the topics dealt with in the *Sūtras* and explains them, without taking into account the order of the *Sūtras*" (p. iv).

13. Even the earliest *Nyāya-sūtra* commentator, Vātsyāyana, makes explicit mention of the Vaiśeṣika categories: *Nyāyasūtra-bhāṣya* 1.1.9 and 2.1.34. At 2.1.34, his argument hinges on them.

14. B. K. Matilal rehearses the evidence in *Nyāya-Vaiśeṣika* (1977), pp. 59–62.

15. Muni Sri Jambuvijayaji, ed., *Vaiśeṣikasūtra of Kaṇāda with the commentary of Candrānanda* (1961). Anantalal Thakur states in the introduction, p. 23, "We find no mention of him [Candrānanda] in later Vaiśeṣika literature." Candrānanda's date is uncertain.

16. H. Ui translated the Chinese text into English: *Vaiśeshika Philosophy* (1962).

17. Erich Frauwallner, *History of Indian Philosophy*, vol. 2 (1974), p. 134.

18. D. C. Bhattacharya, *History of Navya-Nyāya in Mithilā* (1958), pp. 8–11, lists eight instances where Udayana is clearly responding to Śrīdhara.

19. *Nyāya-sūtra* (*NyS*) 2.1.12–20 and 4.2.33–37.

20. *NyS-bhāṣya* (*NyS-Bh*) 1.1.9. There is the passage at 2.1.34 where Vātsyāyana's argument hinges on acceptance of the Vaiśeṣika categories. Otherwise, however, Vaiśeṣika does not seem so influential on him, especially as compared with his successors.

21. For example, *NyS-Vārttika* (*NyS-V*) 2.2.61.

22. Karl Potter, *Encyclopedia*, vol. 2, *Nyāya-Vaiśeṣika up to Gaṅgeśa*, pp. 341–42 and 399.

23. Namely, the *Ātmatattvaviveka*, which is directed principally against Buddhist positions, and the *Nyāyakusumañjali*, where Udayana purports to establish rationally the existence of God.

24. Wilhelm Halbfass (1983), pp. 87–88, chides Sarvepalli Radhakrishnan for reading Udayana as a religious and philosophic universalist who finds an essential harmony among major positions. Halbfass goes on himself, however, to read Udayana as a compatibilist and inclusivist (p. 90), citing a passage from each of two of Udayana's works, the *Nyāyakusumāñjali* and the *Ātmatattvaviveka*. But in the latter, I would point out, Udayana clearly does not, as Halbfass says (p. 90), "arrang[e] the other systems of thought, including Advaita Vedānta, as preliminary stages of the Nyāya *system*, which he calls the 'ultimate Vedānta' " (italics mine). Rather, Udayana says that the Nyāya view of the "supreme personal good," liberation (*mukti*), is achieved through a meditational discipline and process that includes as stages the disciplines—and meditational goals—advocated by other philosophies such as Advaita Vedānta. Udayana says this Nyāya position is the "ultimate Vedānta" because he is well aware that Nyāya teachings about liberation grow out of Upanishads. As will be explained, in this same work, the *Ātmatattvaviveka*, Udayana launches a diatribe against Advaita. In the *Nyāyakusumāñjali*, Udayana does say that what Naiyāyikas see as God (*īśvara*) others see differently; e.g., Advaitins see God as Brahman. Here, Udayana does propose that there is somehow a harmony of view on the topic of God's existence and nature. However, as I explain in a later section, he does not try to pay up this promissory note, and one is left with the impression that the passage is introductory hoopla (the passage opens the *Nyāyakusumāñjali*), and that Udayana does not see very much that is compatible between Advaita and Nyāya.

25. See chapter 3, pp. 106–09, and chapter 4, pp. 138–41.

26. If texts were typed into a machine-readable data base, computer vocabulary searches could help the construction of a fuller intellectual history, for often a new idea will lie undeveloped in an earlier author's works (thus detection is difficult), and then be emphasized by a later author who fails to credit his source. Gaṅgeśa's relationship to Udayana presents several such examples that I am aware of, and doubtless there are more.

27. The *Vaiśeṣika-sūtra* has several *sūtra*s spelling out the ideas I will highlight; the *Padārthadharmasaṃgraha* has a separate *prakaraṇa* or section on each of the categories. These are my principal sources. Ganganatha Jha's translation of the latter (1982 reprint) sorts the *prakaraṇa* of an early Sanskrit edition into English chapters and sections—in rough correspondence with the section division in the *Padārthadharmasaṃgraha* Sanskrit edition I use—by Durgadhara Jha (1977, henceforth *PDS*).

28. *NyS* 3.1.1: "There is grasping of a single object through sight and touch. Therefore (the self is distinct from perceptions, and has distinct sense organs)" (*darśana-sparśanābhyām eka-artha-grahaṇāt*). Thus in Nyāya, a substantial self distinct from and enduring through different sense experiences is thought to match the substantiality of external objects. Arindam Chakrabarti has carefully reconstructed the argument in "I Touch What I Saw" (1992).

29. Bhāsarvajña denies that motion is a distinct category, viewing motions as qualities. But he stands alone in the opinion among pre-Navya authors. (See B. K. Matilal's summary in *Nyāya-Vaiśeṣika*, vol. 2 [1977] of *Encyclopedia of Indian Philosophies*, ed. Karl Potter, pp. 414–15. See also L. V. Joshi's discussion in *A Critical Study of the Pratyakṣa Pariccheda of Bhāsarvajña's Nyāyabhūṣaṇa* [1986], pp. 508–11.) For a good overall treatment of the relatively few divergences in Vaiśeṣika pre-Udayana, see B. K. Matilal, *Nyāya-Vaiśeṣika* (1977).

30. *NyS* 2.2.66.

31. *NyS-V* 2.2.4 (p. 667).

32. *Vaiśeṣika-sūtra* (*VS*) 1.2.12, e.g., implies this; the use of the term *sāmānya-viśeṣa*, "particular genus" or "inclusive particularity," is indeed rather frequently employed implying the particularizing as well as the unifying function of universals.

33. *PDS*, the *viśeṣa-nirūpaṇa* section, pp. 765–72; *Padārthadharmasaṃgraha of Praśastapāda*, trans. Ganganatha Jha, pp. 671–75. The non-atomic substances are traditionally five (both in Nyāya and Vaiśeṣika): ether (*ākāśa*, the medium of sound), time, space, the individual soul, and the peculiar mind-body bridge, the mental organ (*manas*: see the glossary).

34. The difficult problem of how the Vaiśeṣikas think of atoms in relation to time and space is involved in this question of interpretation: see Wilhelm Halbfass, "The Vaiśeṣika Concept of Time," chap. 9 in *On Being and What There Is* (1992), pp. 205–28. Praśastapāda says that a yogin is able to identify an individual atom over stretches of space and time by means of direct perception of its ultimate particularizer, though it has no other marks to distinguish it from other atoms of its type: *PDS*, the *viśeṣa-nirūpaṇa* section, pp. 767–70.

35. Śrīharṣa does, however, specifically target it, in the fourth and final chapter of his *Khaṇḍanakhaṇḍakhādya*, where he intends to be rather comprehensive in his demolition of the realist ontology.

36. *NyS* 2.1.34–36 and 4.2.4–17, along with the commentaries.

37. *NyS-V* 1.1.14.

38. Thus, here English would appear to have the advantage over ordinary Sanskrit, where the predicative copula is usually elliptically understood.

39. Praśastapāda defines inherence as the relation between the containing and the contained insofar as these are *ayutasiddha*, inseparably connected or dependent, adding that inherence is the ground of the notion of "being here": *ayuta-siddhānām ādhārya-ādhāra-bhūtānāṃ yaḥ sambandha iha-pratyaya-hetuḥ sa samavāyaḥ* (*PDS*, the *samavāya-nirūpaṇa* section, p. 773).

40. *PDS*, p. 779; Ganganatha Jha's translation, p. 679. The container (*ādhāra*) and the contained (*ādheya*) vary in nature; thus there is no possibility of a confusion (*saṃkara*) of the categories. The inherence is one and the same relation; the relata, however, vary according to categorial status and in other ways. (I paraphrase *PDS*, pp. 778–79.)

41. B. K. Matilal provides this gloss in *Epistemology, Logic, and Grammar in Indian Philosophical Analysis* (1971), pp. 57–58.

42. Contact belongs to the category of quality. As noted, it is a peculiar quality in that a single contact is considered to rest in two substance particulars simultaneously, specifically, in two conjoined. But despite its peculiarity, epistemically contact is unproblematic: depending on the perceptibility of the things in contact, the contact is directly known in perception. Concerning how contact gets related to each of its terms, the view is that, as with all qualities, inherence is the relator. A contact inheres in each of two substances conjoined. Thus the thorny issue of the fundamental binder is pushed back and borne by inherence.

43. *kayā punar vṛttyā dravya-ādiṣu samavāyo vartate ? na saṃyogaḥ sambhavati, tasya guṇatvena dravya-āśritatvāt | na api samavāyaḥ, tasya ekatvāt | na ca anyā vṛttr asti iti ? na, tādātmyāt | yathā dravya-guṇa-karmaṇāṃ sad-ātmakasya bhāvasya na anyaḥ sattā-yogo 'sti | evam avibhāgino vṛtty-ātmakasya samavāyasya na anyā vṛttir asti, tasmāt sva-ātma-vṛttiḥ | ata eva atīndriyaḥ sattā-ādīnām iva pratyakṣeṣu vṛtty-abhāvāt, sva-ātma-gata-saṃvedana-abhāvāc ca | tasmād iha buddhy-anumeyaḥ samavāya iti* | | *PDS*, pp. 783–85.

44. Udayana's extant commentary on Praśastapāda's *PDS* does not extend as far as the section on inherence.

45. *Lakṣaṇāvalī*, verses 1 and 2, in *The Structure of the World in Udayana's Realism*, ed. and trans. Musashi Tachikawa (1981), p. 57. Although the *Vaiśeṣika-sūtra* itself discusses types of non-existence, the recognition of a separate category, apparently first proposed by Candramati, occurs gradually. Śrīdhara and Udayana both accept absences, discussing at length how they are known and their logic. But Praśastapāda is himself ambiguous on the question of the categorial status, although both Śrīdhara and Udayana find a way of reading him such that absence is on his list: see *Nyāyakandalī* on *PDS*, ed. Durgadhara Jha, p. 18; Ganganatha Jha's translation, chap. 1, sec. 2, p. 15; *Kiraṇāvalī*, ed, J. Jetly (1971), pp. 4–5. The *NyS* commentaries, which show surprising sophistication on this score as early as Vātsyāyana, discuss absences under *NyS* 2.2.7–11. See B. K. Matilal's translation and discussion, *The Navya-Nyāya Doctrine of Negation* (1968), pp. 104–08.

46. The *Vaiśeṣika-sūtra* discusses the four as varieties of the non-existent (*asat*), *VS* 9.1.1–11. Vācaspati Miśra I, according to Matilal (1968), p. 108, deserves the credit for the bifurcation, which is accepted by the New school.

47. Arindam Chakrabarti (see the bibliography) deserves the credit for hitting upon "absentee" and for championing it at the expense of the "counterpositive" used by Ingalls, Matilal, Potter, et al.

48. Gaṅgeśa takes care to distinguish a generic absence from a specific absence (e.g., an absence of all pots at a spot as distinct from an absence of a specific pot), but often the Sanskrit expression, *ghaṭābhāva*, "pot-absence," is ambiguous.

49. This seems to be Vātsyāyana's view: *NyS-Bh* 2.2.8. Under *NyS* 2.2.9 and 2.2.11, he discusses the requirement of prior knowledge of the absentee.

50. Both epistemology and the category theory are concerns of both early Vaiśeṣikas and early Naiyāyikas. Uddyotakara, in particular among Naiyāyikas, makes important ontological innovations (see, e.g., note 70 below on "operative relations," p. 340). And Praśastapāda engages in lengthy epistemological discussions. However, with Udayana's synthesis, prior Nyāya views have to be taken as epistemologically mainstream, not the Vaiśeṣika. Furthermore, early Nyāya epistemology is more elaborated than the Vaiśeṣika. In the following discussion, Nyāya sources are mainly relied on.

51. *prameyā ca tulā-prāmāṇyavat*

52. *NyS* 1.1.23 lists five circumstances for meaningful doubt. *NyS* 2.1.1 through

2.1.6 elaborates these circumstances. The commentators, of course, bring in much detail.

53. *NyS* 4.2.30 through 4.2.33, as interpreted by Vātsyāyana, is a powerful presentation of this argument.

54. Vātsyāyana opens his *NyS-Bh* by tying successful action to right cognition (*pramiti*).

As we will learn in chapter 4, Gaṅgeśa finds an exception to the general fallibilism—concerning apperception, where a preceding cognition is infallibly known.

55. This division—knowables on the one hand, sources of knowledge on the other—becomes organizational with the popular textbook, the *Tarkabhāṣā* by Keśava Miśra. This book seems to be post-Śrīharṣa by about a century (Potter's dating). However, it does not present a Navya perspective.

Umesha Mishra (among others) has argued for an earlier date. Professor Mishra places Keśava in the twelfth century. The *Tarkabhāṣā* opens by proclaiming itself a textbook, meant to introduce students (*bālo 'pi*) into the system: see *Tarkabhāṣā* (Iyer edition), p. 3. Gaṅgeśa is apparently unaware of the book, though some scholars have wondered whether its organizational structure influenced him. Umesha Mishra's comments about this are amusing: "the *Tarkabhāṣā* is so petty a work that it does not deserve any mention in the *Tattacintāmaṇi* [Gaṅgeśa's masterpiece of New Logic]." Umesha Mishra, *History of Indian Philosophy*, vol. 2, p. 229.

56. Witness the introductory portions of the commentaries, prefatory to *NyS* 1.1.1, where relations among successful activity, right awareness, and the sources of right awareness are expounded.

57. Westerners may find it striking that the word for perception, *pratyakṣa*, does not include non-veridical perceptions. But the point of the *Nyāya-sūtra* characterization is not to provide criteria whereby veridical and non-veridical awarenesses are distinguished. The question of such criteria for discerning illusions is a separate concern. The *Nyāya-sūtra* tries to characterize perception, *pratyakṣa*, just insofar as it is a *pramāṇa*, an instrument of veridical awareness.

58. I am not the first to voice this complaint. Fritz Staal (1973), for one, says the same thing in "The Concept of Pakṣa in Indian Logic," pp. 56–57. Matters have improved, though early errors of interpretation persist, having assumed in English a life of their own and been perpetuated by textbook accounts. Sibajiban Bhattacharyya's papers in *Doubt, Belief and Knowledge* (1987) are probably the best presentation of the Navya theory to date by a professional philosopher drawing on contemporary logic.

59. For a fuller treatment, see Karl Potter's "Logical Theory" in his *Encyclopedia of Indian Philosophies*, vol. 2, *Nyāya-Vaiśeṣika*, pp. 179–206.

60. It is fallacious to reason from an unwarranted premise: this would be a variety of the fallacy *asiddha*, the "unestablished."

61. The early Nyāya position is, to be sure, somewhat less sophisticated than the expression "a rule of inference" might suggest: a *single* rule of inference is developed as key, as will be explained.

62. Indeed, much reflection is devoted to how to rule out *upādhi*s, "pervasion-destroying conditions," that would vitiate inference. For example, we cannot infer that a mountain possessing fire also possesses smoke because of the *upādhi*, wet fuel, which is concomitant with all smoke but not all fire (it is thought that all smoky fires have fuel that is at least slightly wet).

63. Udayana, in particular, stresses fallibilism concerning pervasions. Dharmakīrti is, in contrast, an infallibilist about inference. Against Dharmakīrti's view that

pervasions, which are either causal relations or class inclusions, are, in both instances, known infallibly, Udayana points out that in inferring tomorrow's sunrise from today's sunrise, the pervasion relied on appears to be neither causal nor a class inclusion: *Kiraṇāvalī*, ed. J. Jetly, p. 200. Wide experience, *bhuyo-darśana*, with respect to the question of positive correlations (*anvaya*) and negative correlations (*vyatireka*), is the general answer Naiyāyikas give about how to avoid error with regard to (inference-grounding) pervasions: see *Nyāyakusumāñjali*, autocommentary under 2.7, Mithila Institute Series, p. 379.

64. *PDS*, chap. 6, sec. 10; in Ganganatha Jha's translation, pp. 448ff.

65. *NyS* 2.2.2 and commentaries.

66. *NyS-Bh* 1.1.7. Vātsyāyana says so long as one knows the truth and is motivated to represent it as it is, then even a *mleccha*, a foreigner or barbarian, can be an *āpta*.

67. Thus the stock example: you are told that a *gavaya* (a kind of buffalo) is like a cow though different in certain respects that are specified. You have never seen one at the time you receive this information. Then walking along, you see an animal that fits the description and exclaim, "O, a *gavaya*." See, e.g., *NyS* 1.1.6 and commentaries.

68. See Shiv Kumar's discussion in *Upamāna in Indian Philosophy* (1980), pp. 13–62.

69. See, for example, *NyS-Bh* 1.1.14–15 and 3.2.18ff.

70. Advanced under *NyS* 1.1.4 (Thakur edition, p. 199). The six are (filling out a bit, in accordance with later theory): (1) in the case of perception of some substances, contact of a sense organ and the substance, e.g., a pot as a substance in contact with a sensory organ; (2) in the case of certain qualities, motions, and universals, inherence-in-the-conjoined, e.g., blue inhering in a pot in conjunction with the visual sense organ (in that the visual organ travels like a ray out of the eye and comes into contact with substances having color and shape); (3) in the case of other universals, inherence-in-the-inherent-in-the-conjoined, e.g., colorness inhering in the blue, etc.; (4) in the case of the perception of sound (a quality of ether), inherence (the auditory organ is conceived as the ether in the ear such that the sounds that come to inhere in that area of ether delimited by the auditory organ would be heard); (5) in the case of sound-ness (the universal or natural kind comprising particular sounds), inherence-in-the-inherent; (6) and in the case of perception of an absence, qualifierhood (an absence, e.g., of a pot on the floor, is a qualifier, *viśeṣaṇa*, of the floor).

71. Under *NyS* 1.1.4 (Thakur edition, p. 220). Jayanta Bhaṭṭa also discusses the distinction: *Nyāyamañjarī*, pp. 88ff; in the translation by J. V. Bhattacharyya, pp. 198ff.

72. It has also fueled some excellent modern scholarship. Dharmendra Nath Shastri's *Critique of Indian Realism* (1964), Raja Ram Dravid's *The Problem of Universals in Indian Philosophy* (1972), and Pradyot Kumar Mukhopadhyay's *Indian Realism* (1984), contain rich and detailed analyses, making the footing in this area of Nyāya study much more sure.

73. *PDS*, pp. 741–42: *sāmānyaṃ sva-viṣaya-sarva-gatam abhinna-ātmakam aneka-vṛtti eka-dvi-bahuṣv ātma-sva-rūpa-anugama-pratyaya-kāri sva-rūpa-abhedena ādhāreṣu prabandhena vartamānam anuvṛtti-pratyaya-kāraṇam.* Unabbreviated, this important passage translates: "A universal is present pervasively in all its instances; it is identical in all its instances, of whatever number, and is the basis of the comprehension (or idea, *pratyaya*) of itself recurrently; it is the basis of comprehension of inclusion inasmuch as it subsists wholly in each (*prabandhena*) of its substrates."

74. See P. K. Mukhopadhyay's discussion (1984), pp. 61ff.

75. *Nyāyamañjarī*, p. 278; the translation by J. V. Bhattacharyya (1978), pp. 635–36.

76. D. N. Shastri (1964), pp. 327–31, shows this clearly with reference to texts by the Buddhists Aśoka Paṇḍita and Śāntarakṣita.

77. As Shastri points out, even Uddyotakara seems to admit this, at *NyS-V* 2.2.64, p. 668: *na punaḥ sarvo 'nuvṛtti-pratyayaḥ sāmānyād eva bhavati*, "But not every experience of a recurrent character results just from a universal" (my translation).

78. Just about every word or term can be used to designate generalities, but whether or not a usage is meant explicitly to point to a general feature of things seems to depend on context: this is what *NyS* 2.2.59ff is about. The same common noun, for example, can be used in at least three different ways, Gautama himself states, only one of which explicitly designates a universal: (a) "the cow is grazing" where "cow" is used chiefly to refer to the particular cow that is grazing; (b) "Bessie is a cow" where "cow" refers to the universal; and (c) "Give Devadatta a clay cow" where "cow" refers to the shape cows typically have. The *NyS* commentators make a case for the thesis that the universal designation of the term is implicit in every usage. However, they also stress, with Gautama, that there are variations of meaning determined by context.

79. R. R. Dravid (1972), pp. 22–25, reconstructs Udayana's reasoning, with references to Udayana's *Nyāyakusumañjali*, the first chapter. See also *Kiraṇāvalī*, pp. 155–60 (Sarvvabhouma edition), and *Nyāyakusumañjali*, autocommentary under 1.44, pp. 159–60 (Goswami edition).

80. Jayanta Bhaṭṭa observes that a particular never appears unclothed in our experience, but invariably appears as something general. (Dravid, p. 22, referring to *Nyāyamañjarī*, p. 286 [Medical Hall edition]).

81. See P. K. Mukhopadhyay's discussion (1984), pp. 61–81.

82. Dravid, p. 24. Kisor Chakrabarti, "The Nyāya Theory of Universals," (1975), pp. 364–65, classifies this as an additional argument.

83. See the quote from Praśastapāda at the beginning of the section, p. 58.

84. *Kiraṇāvalī* (Sarvvabhouma edition), pp. 161ff; Dravid, pp. 26–33.

85. The expression "accidental universal" (*aupādhika sāmānya*) appears a few sentences after the list: *Kiraṇāvalī* (Sarvvabhouma edition), p. 169.

86. Thus Vardhamāna comments, p. 161: *anyathā jāti-lakṣaṇa-vyāghātāt* ("Otherwise, the definition of a natural kind (universal) would be contradicted").

87. Here we may note that earlier Naiyāyikas preceded Udayana on some of these points. For example, Uddyotakara cites *VS* 8.1.5 and defends the view expressed there that no natural kind inheres in a natural kind. And he himself imagines an opponent asking what it means to say that "humanity" and "cowhood" are *natural kinds*. See *NyS-V* 2.2.64, p. 668. (This passage anticipates a criticism of Śrīharṣa's; that Uddyotakara's response seems forced probably best indicates the dangers native to these theoretic straits.)

88. In modern set theory, there is a similar restriction: the "set of all sets" is an impossibility because the set would have to include itself thereby generating another set, *ad infinitum*.

89. This is a doctrine peculiar to the Vaiśeṣika notion of an ultimate "individualizer" or "numeralizer," *viśeṣa* (recall our discussion under section 3.1 in this chapter).

90. *Kiraṇāvalī* (Sarvvabhouma edition), pp. 169–70. See also Sibajiban Bhattacharyya's discussion in *Gadādhara's Theory of Objectivity*, vol. 1, (1990): pp. 60–63.

91. The Sanskrit term *nitya* can mean either "eternal" or "constant."

92. A widely held religious belief in the classical period was that God, or Brahman, periodically re-absorbs the universe in a universal *pralāya*, "cosmic destruction." How then could universals be truly eternal? Some Logicians take the problem seriously and talk about latencies or the like.

93. *tri-vidhā ca asya śāstrasya pravṛttiḥ, uddeśo lakṣaṇaṃ parīkṣā ca* | *NyS-Bh*, preface to 1.1.3 (Taranatha and Amarendramohan edition), p. 83.

94. ibid., p. 84.

95. *NyS-V* 1.1.3 (Taranatha and Amarendramohan edition), p. 86.

96. However, one need not recognize the class character *as* a class character or universal. See P. K. Mukhopadhyaya (1984), p. 296, note 11.

97. See, for example, Uddyotakara's opening comments under *NyS* 1.1.4 (Thakur edition), p. 199.

98. Not all Naiyāyikas accept this stricture; Bhāsarvajña, for example, does not. See B. K. Matilal, *Logic, Language and Reality* (1985), pp. 185–88, for illuminating discussion of Udayana's criticism of Bhāsarvajña on the point.

99. *Nyāyakośa*, under *lakṣaṇābhāsa*, p. 701.

100. *Ātmatattvaviveka* (Asiatic Society edition), p. 863.

101. Maṇikaṇṭha Miśra, for example, treats Śrīharṣa this way. Although Maṇikaṇṭha's response to the Advaitin on "dialectical reasoning" (translated in chapter 5) is abrupt and dismissive, later in Maṇikaṇṭha's *Nyāyaratna*, Śrīharṣa's views are, though still refuted, taken seriously: see *Nyāyaratna*, pp. 155ff and 173.

Moreover, the Buddhists and the Naiyāyikas, in the earlier period, learn much informal logic from one another. Indeed, concerning inference as formalized syllogistically, Indian science marched on, largely unheeding metaphysical divisions—although theory of concepts, or universals, and the idealist/realist partition, did make a difference in how the underpinnings of inference were viewed and in how logic was viewed in relation to knowledge of the world.

102. The names of these strategies of argument are in fact mentioned in the very first *sūtra* of the *Nyāya-sūtra*, where sixteen principal topics are listed. The predominance of these and other topics of epistemology and debate theory in the list of sixteen (doubt, the steps of inference, informal fallacies, etc.) reveals the original heart of the school as decidely a-metaphysical, or much less metaphysical than the *Nyāya-sūtra* as a whole.

The entire first chapter is devoted to elaborations of the sixteen. Vātsyāyana in his commentary on *NyS* 1.2.2, where a type of debate is elaborated, refers ahead to *NyS* 4.2.50, where the thorn metaphor is evoked. Vācaspati I, in his subcommentary on *NyS* 1.2.1, explains that even a person of good character may put forth tricky arguments, with unfounded premises, when an opponent (revealing bad character) first uses tricky arguments: see his commentary under *NyS* 1.2.1 (Taranatha and Amarendramohan edition), p. 339. Uddyotakara says that if the debater intent on demolishing an opponent's position is not motivated through a sense of contradiction with a position of his own, he is like a lunatic (*unmatta-vat*): see *NyS-V* 1.1.1 (Taranatha and Amarendramohan edition), p. 45.

103. *NyS-Bh* 1.1.1 (Taranatha and Amarendramohan edition), p. 44.

104. Nāgārjuna himself expresses this argument, *Vv*, verse 17, and answers it, *Vv*, verse 68.

105. *Ātmatattvaviveka*, pp. 863–64.

106. *Khaṇḍanakhaṇḍakhādya*, p. 722. Sitansusekhar Bagchi writes: "This is not an original formulation of Śrīharṣa, but only a restatement of the position of an

adherent of the Nyāya school who must remain anonymous for want of data available to us." *Inductive Reasoning* (1952), p. 152.

107. *Indian Atheism* (1969), pp. 262–85.

108. *Gaṅgeśa's Philosophy of God* (1984), pp. 4–11.

109. *PDS*, pp. 121ff; Ganganatha Jha's translation, pp. 108ff. Uddyotakara seems to make the same move, but he also offers several lines of defense that emphasize the distinct nature of atoms in contrast with material things of larger size: *NyS-V* 4.1.21, p. 945) and 4.2.25 (p. 1065ff). Chattopadhyaya identifies the Buddhist attack in Vasubandhu (1969), p. 255. Dignāga also voices the argument; see his *Ālambanaparīkṣā*, trans. N. Aiyaswami Sastri (1942), part of which is anthologized in D. Bonevac and S. Phillips (eds.), *Understanding Non-Western Philosophy* (1993), pp. 160–62.

110. *Nyāyakusumāñjali*, Mithila Institute Series, p. 547. See the beginning of the fifth "cluster": *kṣity-ādi kartṛ-pūrvakaṃ, kāryatvāt.*

111. Probably the best treatment of the plethora of theistic arguments Udayana puts forth is George Chemparathy's *An Indian Rational Theology* (1972), though Karl Potter's brief reconstructions are clearer, *Encyclopedia of Indian Philosophies*, vol. 2, pp. 102–10. See also John Vattanky (1984), pp. 87–119.

112. *Nyāyakusumāñjali*, Mithila Institute Series, p. 13.

113. Uddyotakara has in fact quite a lot to say at *NyS-V* 4.1.21, pp. 943ff.

114. See J. N. Mohanty's discussion, *Gaṅgeśa's Theory of Truth* (1989), pp. 5–11.

115. Phyllis Granoff (1976), p. 226, makes this suggestion. She also identifies other Jaina influences.

116. In *Nyāya-Vaiśeṣika*, vol. 2 of his *Encyclopedia*, p. 16, Karl Potter says summarily: "References to Jain views in classical Nyāya-Vaiśeṣika texts are very rare."

117. A single manuscript of the *Tattvopaplavasiṃha* was discovered in 1926, and was edited by Sukhlalju Sanghavi and R. C. Parikh (1940). The first half of the text was re-edited and translated into English by Eli Franco: *Perception, Knowledge and Disbelief* (1987). A portion of the second half—against inference as a knowledge source—was translated by S. N. Shastri and S. K. Saksena, with revisions by S. C. Chatterjee, and included in *A Source Book in Indian Philosophy*, ed. Sarvepalli Radhakrishnan and Charles Moore (1957), pp. 236–46. Debiprasad Chattopadhyay has collected, in English translation, classical references to Cārvāka, including fragments attributed to Bṛhaspati, along with reconstructions of Cārvāka views according to several modern scholars: see his *Cārvāka/Lokāyata* (1990).

118. *Khaṇḍanakhaṇḍakhādya*, p. 7. As explained at the beginning of the next chapter, Śrīharṣa also wrote an epic poem. In the seventeenth canto, a Cārvāka belts out a long anti-religious speech (including the anti-philosophical argument, echoing Śaṅkara, that reasoning is not be trusted because philosophers with mutually opposed positions are able to come up with what appear to be good arguments). He is answered by the gods Indra, Yama, Agni, and Varuṇa.

119. *Tattvacintāmaṇi*, vol. 2, pp. 38–42. Rucidatta Miśra, e.g., identifies the skeptical argument as Cārvāka: see *TCM*, vol. 2, p. 38.

120. Gaṅgeśa, for example, has this position in mind in his argument defending inference mentioned just above.

121. Radhakrishnan and Moore's *Source Book* (1957), pp. 228–34, reprints the Cowell and Gough translation of Mādhava's Cārvāka section.

122. This is also part of Gaṅgeśa's response.

123. See the discussions by Walter Ruben and K. K. Dixit in Chattopadhyay's collection (1990).

124. On the other hand, at the end of the work Jayarāśi seems to express a sweeping skepticism that would include everyday beliefs: "So with philosophic theories in this way incurring disaster, conventional views may be delighted in only so long as they are not examined." *tad evam upapluteṣv eva tattveṣu avicārita-ramaṇīyāḥ sarve vyavahārā ghaṭanta* | *Tattvopaplavasiṃha*, p. 125.

125. The text is corrupt at the end of the opening passage where this translated phrase occurs. See Franco (1987), p. 69.

126. Ester Solomon, *Indian Dialectics*, vol. 2 (1978), pp. 526–627 passim; Phyllis Granoff (1978), esp. p. 53.

127. With regard to the concrete instances of Jayarāśi's influence on Śrīharṣa that Solomon cites, see especially vol. 2 (1978), pp. 549 and 553 (concerning Buddhist definitions of veridical awareness). See also pp. 610 and 625, note 55 (which purports to show an interesting parallelism concerning conventional versus philosophic statement). Herein lies the heart of her reading of a deep agreement in skepticism between the two (a reading with which I disagree).

128. We may note that Jayarāśi does not identify the Bradley problem; also, infinite regress is not one of his stock complaints.

Chapter 3: Śrīharṣa

1. Navikanta Jha, in a Hindi introduction to the Sanskrit edition of the *Khkh* that is cited here (1970), lists eight other works that could belong to Śrīharṣa: p. 26. Anand Svarup Misra in a study in Hindi, *Mahākavi Śrīharṣa*, finds references to all but one of these in the *Nc*: p. 19. The *Khkh* is also referred to in the *Nc* (in the sixth chapter), as is the *Nc* and several of the other works in the *Khkh*.

Apparently the *Nc* and *Khkh* were written, or revised, simultaneously.

2. In particular, a conventional author's colophon, or signature verse, at the end of the *Khkh*, and one at the end of each canto of the *Nc*, contain small bits of biographical information. Though it is possible that these were not written by Śrīharṣa himself, it seems more likely that they were.

3. D. C. Bhattacharya (1958), pp. 50–51,

4. Granoff (1978), p. 60, note 5.

5. Anand Svarup Misra (1988), p. 12, dismisses the various opinions as all unfounded.

6. *tāmbūla-dvayam āsanaṃ ca labhate yaḥ kānyakubja-īśvarād yaḥ sākṣāt kurute samādhiṣu para-brahma pramoda-arṇavam, yat-kāvyaṃ madhu-varṣi dharṣita-parās tarkeṣu yasya uktayaḥ, śrī-śrīharṣa-kaveḥ kṛtiḥ kṛti-mude tasya abhyudīyād iyam* || *Khkh*, p. 754.

7. It also can be read in the *Khkh*'s opening verse (albeit that follows a conventional formula for openings): "I salute the Lord *(īśvara)* . . . who was and is not only understood by (the Goddess) Umā but later by me too." *Khkh*, p. 1.

8. *tad idam etābhir ātma-mata-siddha-sad-yukti-lakṣaṇa-upapannābhir yuktibhir upanīyamānam advaitam avidyā-vilāsa-lālaso 'pi śraddhātu tāvad bhavān, tad-anucānayā eva upaniṣad-artha-śraddhayā adhyātmaṃ jijñāsamānaḥ parama-artha-tattvaṃ kramād vṛtti-vyāvṛtta-cetāḥ sva-prakāśa-sākṣikaṃ mākṣika-rasa-atiśāyi sva-ātmanā eva sākṣat-kariṣyati* | *yathā ca parihṛta-cāpalam tattva-amṛta-sarasi nimajya rajyati nirāyāsam eva mānasaṃ tathā aham akathayaṃ naiṣadhacaritasya parama-puruṣa-stutau sarge, ity eṣā dik* || *Khkh*, p. 125.

9. Granoff (1978), pp. 252–54, note 170.

10. *ity udīrya sa harim prati samprajñāta-vāsitatamaḥ samapādi |
bhāvanā-bala-vilokita-viṣṇau prīti-bhakti-sadṛśāni cariṣṇuḥ ||
ity udīrya sa harim prati samprajñāta-vāsitatamaḥ samapādi |
bhāvanā-bala-vilokita-viṣṇau prīti-bhakti-sadṛśāni cariṣṇuḥ ||*

11. Granoff (1978), pp. 1-2, forcefully presents the case.

12. K. K. Handiqui has translated the *Nc* in what is itself an elegant work (though much of the charm of any poetry, it bears reminding ourselves, is dependent on peculiar features of a particular language, and Śrīharṣa is a master of Sanskrit). In a long appendix, Professor Handiqui discusses all the philosophic allusions in the text: (1965), pp. 509–36.

13. S. K. De writes: "Śrīharṣa is careful . . . to show that his learned preoccupations in no way rendered him unfit for dealing with the refinements of the erotic art. One whole canto, for instance, of more than a hundred stanzas, impedes the progress of the narrative by a minute and frankly sensuous inventory of Damayantī's beauty of limbs commencing from the hair of the head and ending with the toe-nails of her feet; but what is indicative of a singular lack of taste is that the description comes from Nala himself who views her from an invisible distance! . . . the poet does not hesitate to introduce vulgar innuendoes in what is supposed to be witty repartee of a more or less cultured society. It is no wonder, therefore, that, judging from modern standards, an impatient Western critic should stigmatize the work as a perfect masterpiece of bad taste and bad style!" *A History of Sanskrit Literature*, ed. S. N. Dasgupta, vol. 1 (1st ed., 1946), p. 328. Later, Professor De identifies "his impatient Western critic": "[Moriz] Winternitz, in commenting on it, says: 'What a difference between the delicate chastity with which the love between Nala and Damayantī is depicted in the *Mahābhārata* and the sultry erotics bordering on obscenity in Cantos XVIII–XX of the *Naiśadhacarita*' " (p. 624). In case, dear reader, you are now in a hurry to look up these cantos in the English translation, note that the translator, K. K. Handiqui, refuses to render a few verses, flagging them with footnotes saying, "indelicate": e.g., p. 277.

14. Her contention is pervasive: e.g., pp. 54 ("Śrī Harṣa . . . never independently proves anything at all"), 111, 203, and 226, note 64. (Maybe he indeed fails to *prove* anything, but he does *argue for* something.)

Others scholars have made this error. For example, Aghehananda Bharati, a modern deconstructionist for whom Śrīharṣa stood as something of an idol, practically takes it for granted that the Advaitin's arguments are solely attacks. See, for instance, his *Ochre Robe* (1980), p. 237. V. A. Sharma (1974), summarizing the Śrīharṣa scholarship, writes (in a book on Citsukha, one of Śrīharṣa's followers): "As a *vaitaṇḍika* [a debater intent on refutation by any means] he [Śrīharṣa] has no position of his own to maintain, . . . he has only to disprove the opponent's viewpoint" (p. 22). And B. K. Matilal, a dean of philosophic studies of the classical systems during most of the last thirty years, says: "The sceptic may claim, as Śrīharṣa explicitly did, that he enters debate simply to refute others and it is not his responsibility to state his position much less to defend it." (*Perception* [1986], p. 65). This is simply wrong; Śrīharṣa both states his position and defends it. As I indicated in the introduction, probably Matilal was misled by Granoff's book.

15. Granoff is, however, a capable translator, and often an insightful commentator. Above all, her scholarship is thorough, and my debts to her are many.

16. *Khkh*, p. 15; cf. Granoff's translation, p. 79, and her elaborate discussion, pp. 78–81, that somehow misses Śrīharṣa's admission that a winning position must be supported by *pramāṇa* (in a broad sense).

17. About this, Granoff is entirely correct: see in particular *Khkh*, p. 9, and

Granoff, p. 76.

18. *yatra sarva-prakārair bādhitvaṃ na asti tat sad ity abhyupagantavyam* || *Khkh*, p. 21.

19. The section introducing these theses commences *Khkh* (N. Jha edition), p. 44; in the translation by Ganganatha Jha, par. 66 of vol. 1 (henceforth, Ganga I: the first volume is comprised of the entirety of Śrīharṣa's first chapter, the second volume of the remaining three chapters, henceforth referred to as Ganga II, III, and IV, in accordance with Jha's own numeralization); and in the translation by Phyllis Granoff on p. 110. (Granoff, as pointed out in the introduction, has translated approximately the first sixth of Śrīharṣa's text—ironically the portion where the positive argumentation is best in evidence.)

20. Śrīharṣa appears to acknowledge a principle of non-contradiction ($\sim(p \cdot \sim p)$) at various places early in his first chapter. Later, he attacks the Nyāya understanding of a contradiction's ontological underpinnings. But although in the course of that discussion he sometimes plays fast and loose (taking advantage of an intuitive sense of various types of negation), he seems to hold on to an ontologically unexplicated principle of (roughly) truth-functional negation in propositional logic ($\sim\sim p \equiv p$). See the end of *Khkh*, chapter three, p. 560—Ganga III, par. 5—where Śrīharṣa explicitly endorses such a principle. See also *Khkh*, pp. 70 and 71; Ganga I, par. 92 and 93; Granoff, pp. 140 and 141. (I say "roughly" because while Śrīharṣa is expert in employing various valid argument forms, he has, I repeat, no formal calculus.)

21. *Khkh*, p. 44, within the opening sentence of the paragraph; Ganga I, par. 66, and Granoff, p. 110.

This statement of Śrīharṣa's echoes a famous passage within Śaṅkara's *Brahmasūtrabhāṣya*, *BSB* 1.1.1: *sarvo hy ātma-astitvaṃ pratyeti, na 'na aham asmi' iti*: "Everyone cognizes the existence of self; no one thinks, 'I am not.' "

22. *Khkh*, p. 44.

23. In the linguistic terms of John Lyons, the *phrastic* component of an utterance is the propositional content, e.g, "S is not speaking," which would stand in tension with the *tropic*, the component of the utterance that is S's making a declarative statement (as opposed to issuing a command, requesting information, etc.): Lyons, *Semantics* (1977), vol. 2, p. 749.

24. A more literal rendering of part of the argument: "This (dual) group of absences—(a) of an awareness of what is not real (including the doubt, 'Am I aware or not' as well as the non-veridical awareness, 'I am not aware') and (b) (absence) of an arising of veridical awareness of awareness's non-existence—implies that S's own self-awareness—with S as the person who is inquiring—is self-pervasively (self-reflexively) veridically known." *tena jijñāsitasya atattva-jñāna-vyatireka-pramāṇām abhāva-samudayaḥ sva-vyāpakaṃ jijñāsitasya pramitatvam ānayati* | *Khkh*, p. 44.

Granoff, p. 111, gets this just about right in her commentary, but she goes wrong in the end in declaring, "At first reading it would appear that Śrī Harṣa is introducing the inference as an independent proof for the fact that knowledge [i.e., self-awareness] is validly known, . . . In reality, he does nothing of the kind."

25. It is not evident that any and all awareness is self-aware. Can I not be absorbed in what I am aware *of*, *un*self-consciously, unmindful of my own awareness?

26. The method is recognizably what Logicians call *tarka*, hypothetical or dialectical reasoning aimed at eliminating alternative views.

27. *Khkh*, p. 45.

28. *Khkh*, p. 47.

29. *Khkh*, pp. 45–48, ending with, *sā iyam apratyakṣa-upalambhasya na artha-*

dṛṣṭih prasiddhyati, which translates more literally, "Perception of objects would not be established as valid (i.e., as epistemologically relevant) for one whose perception is not perceptually given." The statement apparently belongs to Dharmakīrti, though its locus is unknown. Granoff, p. 224, note 60, cites several classical authors' quotation of it.

30. *prakāśa-ātmatā-mātrasya eva svataḥ-siddhi-sambhave jaḍa-ātmanāṃ dharmāṇāṃ keṣām api tad-antarbhāva-anupapattiḥ* || *Khkh*, p. 53; Ganga I, par. 75; and Granoff, p. 122.

31. The Sanskrit term is *bādha*, translated by Granoff consistently as "contradiction," and by Ganganatha Jha usually as "sublation," sometimes as "rejection." Jha's rendering is decidedly superior—the negation concerns awarenesses, not statements or propositions—but Granoff's rendering has the merit of capturing the logical side of Śrīharṣa's usage. According to Nyāya, verbalizable cognitions have propositional content, and we talk about them by way of that content. Cognitions as expressed in everyday discourse, *vyavahāra*, are taken to form a common stock of examples for Naiyāyikas and Advaitins such as Śrīharṣa—and for other players on the scene as well. *Prima facie*, they count as evidence on a broad range of issues. But for both Advaita and Nyāya, cognitions themselves are the fundamental evidence, not the verbal expressions. For Advaita, sublation, as experiential negation, is the premier way an alternative content is ruled out. (The temporal order seems significant, as in an illusion of a rope sublated by a later veridical appearance of a snake.) But for the purposes of debate, there are other ways the content of a cognition is defeated, such as inconsistency and infinite regress—here we encounter an extended meaning of *bādha*, Jha's "(rational) rejection." Later, to render this wider sense I say "defeat" or "defeating," with *bādhaka* (*aka* in Sanskrit is an agentival suffix) as "defeater."

32. For example, *Khkh*, pp. 55 and 125; Ganga I, par. 77 and 164; Granoff, pp. 124 and 201.

33. See this text, pp. 28–29.

34. See in particular Granoff, p. 202, quoted in this text, p. 92, where she brings this into focus.

35. *tad etat tu śrutyā pramāṇena upalakṣaṇa-nyāyāt tātparyataḥ prakāśyate; tena parama-arthato abhidhāna-abhidheya-bhāva-virahe tātparyataḥ śrutis tasmin avidyā-daśāyāṃ para-abhyupagama-rītyā pramāṇam iti ucyate | vastutas tu sva-ātma-siddham eva cid-rūpam* || *Khkh*, p. 55; Ganga I, par. 77; and Granoff, p. 124.

Indirect verbal indication, *upalakṣaṇa*, is discussed by Naiyāyikas with such examples as "Devadatta's house is the one with the crows on it." The attribution is for the purpose of pointing out Devadatta's house in a particular context, and is not intended as a salient characterization of the house itself. Apparently, what Śrīharṣa has in mind is what is sometimes called ostensive definition, e.g., "Red is the color of ripe apples." One is told where to look to know directly what "red" means. Thus scripture would indicate where to look—in oneself—for the self-illumination of awareness.

36. *Khkh*, p. 61; Ganga I, par. 80; and Granoff, p. 130.

37. *Khkh*, pp. 62–67; Ganga I, par. 81–87; Granoff, pp. 131–36.

38. That is, it is recommenced at *Khkh*, p. 81; Ganga I, par. 102; Granoff, pp. 147–48.

39. *Khkh*, pp. 80–95; Ganga I, par. 102–20; Granoff, pp. 147–60.

40. *dhiyāṃ svataḥ-prāmāṇyasya bādhaka-eka-apodyatvāt*, *Khkh*, p. 80.

41. John Pollock, *Contemporary Theories of Knowledge* (1986), p. 72.

42. For example, *Khkh*, p. 122; Ganga I, par. 159; and Granoff, p. 198.

Upanishadic verses are quoted that, as Śrīharṣa understands them, stress Brahman's identity with the world and the reality of unity and non-distinctness: e.g., "Brahman alone is this, is everything" (*Muṇḍaka* 2.2.11). Śrīharṣa goes on to make perfectly plain that he accepts the traditional Advaita view of Brahman as an all-pervading, homogeneous, all-blissful unity. He concludes the passage by reminding us of the Advaita analysis of illusion: the locus of the error—the mother of pearl wrongly perceived as silver—is all the time real. Similarly, Brahman is everything.

43. *etena sarvaṃ bhinnam iti vākyena vinā bādhaṃ svataḥ pramāṇena* . . . . *Khkh*, p. 93.

44. Śrīharṣa does say, curiously, that an erroneous awareness cannot sublate a veridical one: *Khkh*, p. 119. He does not say why, however.

The relation of sublation requires that two awarenesses be opposed in content such that both cannot be veridical. But I have found no Advaitin who has cogently explained why even an actually non-veridical experience could not sublate a veridical experience—or, if that is ruled out by how the term "sublation" is used, why a non-veridical experience could not at least appear to sublate a veridical experience, from a first-person perspective. Eliot Deutsch, however, in *Advaita Vedānta: A Philosophical Reconstruction* (1969), sees sublational Brahman-awareness as a matter of something axiologically superior being revealed: pp. 16ff.

45. *Khkh*, pp. 120–22.

46. If Śrīharṣa holds that the non-sublatable cognition of Brahman includes everything worldly, then he also faces the immense problem of how a psychological state accessible to a human being could so include everything.

47. Again, I think we have to interpret Śrīharṣa's "cognitions" (*jñāna*) generally as propositions in order not to become enmired in psychologism. The Advaitin patently does not simply mean that it is psychologically impossible to read the identity statements of scripture and think 1NN at the same time. Cognitions are abstractions serving the purposes of debate; they are roughly equivalent to "claim," "assertion," and "belief" in informal talk in English.

48. *Khkh*, p. 97; Ganga I, par. 122; Granoff, p. 163. He thus echoes Śaṅkara (e.g., *BSB* 2.1.11) and many previous Advaitins.

49. Compare Śaṅkara's statement that *śruti* is authoritative about Brahman in the way that the sun is authoritative concerning things that have color, *BSB* 2.1.1.

Note that Śrīharṣa's final word on the *authority* of *śruti* is that *śruti* carries the ultimate weight just because of what it is *about*, namely self-conscious, all-inclusive, non-differentiated Brahman.

50. Ganganatha Jha, in his two volumes of translation, presents a running synopsis of the *Khkh*'s chapters and sections that stresses an apparent disarming of attacks on Advaita through disarming the weaponry of the attacks, namely (in particular, Nyāya) views of *pramāṇa* and points of censure in a debate. Thus Jha stresses what I have identified as only a first line of strategy (out of three). The sources of potential challengers of Brahman cognition—perception, inference, etc.—are indeed the focus of the refutations of the latter half of the first chapter. But this is not the only direction of Śrīharṣa's efforts; in particular, the long fourth and final chapter as well as many of the details of the first chapter are directed against the Nyāya ontology of distinct things.

51. It is also voiced at *Khkh*, p. 125, quoted in this chapter, p. 76: "this doctrine of non-duality (*advaita*), into which you are being led by these arguments that are in accord with the definitions of cogent arguments established in your own school."

52. In *Khkh* chapter 2, the entire (albeit comparatively short) discussion is devoted

to the question of what counts as self-contradiction in the context of a debate, and what self-contradiction in that context shows. There the Advaitin is at his dialectical best in bringing out subtle distinctions of what are sometimes called performative and propositional negations (compare the truth conditions of, for example, "The door is not open" and "I do not assert that the door is open").

53. *Khkh*, pp. 122-25; Ganga I, par. 159–66; Granoff, pp. 198–202.

54. *Khkh*, p. 124.

55. See *Khkh*, p. 125; Ganga I, par. 164; Granoff, p. 201.

56. *Khkh*, p. 613; Ganga IV, par. 67. A similar argument occurs in *Khkh* chap. 1, pp. 62–67.

57. *Khkh*, p. 71.

58. Ganga I, pp. x–xi.

59. Granoff, pp. 141–42.

60. *Khkh*, p. 71: *parasya eva vyavastayā evaṃ paryavasyati, nirvacana-pratikṣepād anirvacanīyatvaṃ, vidhi-niṣedhayor ekatara-nirāsasya itara-paryavasāyitāyās tena abhyupagamāt* | *tataḥ parakīyā-rītyā idam ucyate, anirvacanīyatvaṃ viśvasya paryavasyati* |

61. The terms Śrīharṣa uses to express contradictoriness between an assertion and its denial, viz., *vidhi* and *niṣedha*, are employed broadly in this sense. More narrowly, Mīmāṃsakas in particular use the terms for injunctions and prohibitions. Note that in the logic of mands (commands, requests, etc.) negation need not be understood propositionally such that $(\sim\sim p) \equiv p$. However, I do not in this instance believe Śrīharṣa is trying to be ironic. That would be to suppose a more sophisticated, more formal understanding of negation than he gives evidence of; Śrīharṣa is thoroughly informal in his reasoning.

62. Granoff, p. 142, for example.

63. *Khkh*, p. 72: *vastutas tu, vayaṃ sarva-prapanca-sattva-asattva-vyavasthāpana-vinivṛttāḥ svataḥ siddhe cid-ātmani brahma-tattve kevale bharam avalambya* [text reads: *avalabhvya*] *carita-arthāḥ sukham āsmahe* |

64. Cognitions with worldly content are sublated in Brahman-awareness and thus worldly things are not absolutely real. They are also not absolutely unreal since they appear. (Something absolutely unreal—e.g., the son of a barren woman—does not appear.)

65. *Khkh*, p. 73: *na ca upanyāsa eva nirbandha-kāraṇam, vicāra-upanyāsasya sad-asattā-upagama-ādy-udāsīnair vicāryam ity upetya eva paraṃ vicāra-pravartanāyāḥ śakyatvam ity āveditatvāt* |

66. *Khkh*, p. 75: *tad evaṃ bheda-prapañco 'nirvacanīyaḥ, brahma eva tu parama-artha-sad advitīyam iti sthitam* ||

67. *Khkh*, p. 126: *abhīṣṭa-siddhāv api khaṇḍanānām akhaṇḍi-rājñām iva na evam ājñā* |

68. Granoff, p. 202.

69. *Khkh*, pp. 127–29.

70. *NyS* 1.2.1–3 and commentaries. Concerning *vitaṇḍā*, see Ester Solomon, who makes clear that Naiyāyikas came to regard debate of this type as *motivated* by a positive position, not skepticism for its own sake: *Indian Dialectics*, vol. 1, p. 116.

71. See *Khkh*, p. 525, in particular the term *prakṛte*, "on the current topic"; Ganga II, par. 11.

72. *Khkh*, p. 48; Ganga I, par. 69; Granoff, p. 115.

73. *Khkh*, p. 352; Ganga I, par. 424.

74. *Khkh*, p. 40; Ganga I, par. 62; Granoff, p. 107.

75. *Khkh*, pp. 608ff; the earlier attack occurs on p. 62.

76. *Khkh*, pp. 130ff; see chapter 5 of this text, pp. 165ff; Ganga I, par. 174ff. (Granoff's translation ends just prior to this point, but in her preface she discusses Śrīharṣa's argument, pp. 4–11.) The definition (*tattva-anubhutiḥ pramā*) belongs to Udayana, *Lakṣaṇamālā*, p. 1.

77. Ganga I, par. 261.

78. *Khkh*, pp. 218–23; in this text, see pp. 168ff. Cf. Ganga I, par. 261–66, and Granoff's discussion in her preface, pp. 31–32.

79. *lakṣya-vyavasthitir*, *Khkh*, p. 130; cf. Ganga I, par. 173.

80. Bertrand Russell, *Our Knowledge of the External World* (1926), pp. 16–18 and 54–61.

81. At *Khkh*, p. 78 (Ganga I, par. 101; Granoff, p. 146), Śrīharṣa does say that just as a person can have a right cognition that there is fire on the mountain from mistaking fog for smoke—when there is indeed fire there—so a Naiyāyika can be led to a cognition of *advaita* that is correct but that is not produced by a *pramāṇa*. This point would seem to suggest that though a dialectical "establishing" of *advaita* would not be a true *pramāṇa*, the cognition of *advaita* arrived at would be correct. However, I remain unconvinced that this is Śrīharṣa's position.

82. *Khkh*, pp. 572ff (Ganga IV, par. 13ff), and *Khkh*, pp. 608ff (Ganga IV, par. 63ff).

83. *buddhir eva sva-kāraṇa-sāmārthyāt tathā-utthitā tat-tad-vyavahāra-prasavitrī svīkriyatāṃ*, *Khkh*, p. 578 (cf. Ganga IV, par. 20).

84. This reading is maintained by Sushil Saxena, *Studies in the Metaphysics of Bradley* (1967), pp. 121–26.

85. *Khkh*, p. 62 (Ganga I, par. 82; Granoff, p. 131); *Khkh*, pp. 107–8 (Ganga I, par. 134; Granoff, pp. 107–8; in this text, see pp. 221–22); *Khkh*, p. 611 (Ganga IV, par. 88); *Khkh*, pp. 631–32 (Ganga IV, par. 88).

86. *Khkh*, pp. 112ff; Ganga I, par. 139ff; and Granoff, pp. 182ff. Gaṅgeśa's response is outlined here in chapter 4, pp. 123–25.

87. *Khkh*, pp. 572ff; Ganga IV, par. 13ff.

88. *Khkh*, pp. 576–77; Ganga IV, par. 17. There is also another statement later, within the final diatribe against distinctness, *Khkh* 623: *viśiṣṭa-pratītyā viśeṣaṇasya avaśya-ullekhyatvāt viśiṣṭasya viśeṣaṇa-ghaṭita-mūrtitvāt* | "Cognition of a qualificandum necessarily entails explicit awareness of a qualifier, since the very form of something as a qualificandum is made possible by a qualifier." (Cf. Ganga IV, par. 85.)

89. *Khkh*, p. 113; Ganga I, par. 140; and Granoff, p. 184.

90. This is one of Udayana's six "blockers," *jāti-bhādhaka*s: see my text, p. 60.

91. The converse side of the problem, much discussed in modern treatments, is the apparent similarity of universals: the universal *redness* seems a lot more like *orangeness* than does *cowhood*. If universals account for the similarities among particulars, what accounts for the similarity among universals?

92. *Khkh*, pp. 29–31; Ganga I, par. 44–47; Granoff, p. 94. Cf. the discussion above in chapter 1, pp. 18–19.

93. For example, *Khkh*, p. 315; Ganga I, par. 396.

94. *Khkh*, p. 174; Ganga I, par. 226. (The problem is framed in terms of a particular universal, but, I take it, it is generalizable.)

95. *Khkh* pp. 136–70. Cf. Granoff's discussion, pp. 11ff.

96. The criticism of the role of universals in the Nyāya theory of inference is significant. Nyāya holds that universals are known through sense perception—that is,

insofar as their instances are perceptible—and thus would explain how an inference-underpinning pervasion is known. But with universals such as "knowability" and "diversity," the implication would be that one is omniscient, knowing all knowables and every diverse thing past, present, and future. (That these are not true universals—they fail the cross-secting test—does not alter the basic point.) Moreover, if universals are known through perception, how could one ever be wrong? It was thought that all substances made out of earth could be cut by iron before the discovery of diamonds. (This is Śrīharṣa's counterexample.) See *Khkh*, pp. 345ff; Ganga I, par. 417ff.

97. *Khkh*, pp. 586–90; Ganga IV, par. 30–36.

98. A good example occurs at *Khkh*, p. 583 (Ganga IV, par. 27), where a proposed definition of *guṇa*, "quality," is examined, one that invokes the notion that qualities are resided in by universals. This notion is vitiated by the fact that the adventitious properties, nameability, knowability, and the like, must also reside, according to Nyāya premises, in qualities.

99. *Khkh*, p. 109: *bheda eva . . . sphuṭaṃ sarva-loka-sākṣikaḥ pratīyamāno.* Cf. Ganga I, par. 136; Granoff, p. 179.

100. *Khkh*, p. 118: *na vayaṃ bhedasya sarvathā eva asattvam abhyupagacchāmaḥ, kiṃ nāma, pārama-arthikaṃ sattvam | avidyā-vidyāmānatvaṃ tu tadīyam iṣyate eva.* Cf. Ganga I, par. 153; Granoff, p. 193.

101. *Khkh*, pp. 103–18 and 623–58.

102. *Khkh*, p. 103; Ganga I, par. 128; Granoff 171.

103. Granoff, pp. 171–92.

104. *Ātmatattvaviveka*, Asiatic Society, p. 569.

105. Granoff makes this identification: p. 171.

106. *Khkh*, pp. 641–45; Ganga IV, par. 99–105. *Ātmatattvaviveka*, Asiatic Society, pp. 563–69.

107. *Khkh*, p. 104 (bottom).

108. Śrīharṣa uses the terms *anuyogin*, subjunct, and *pratiyogin*, adjunct, in the Navya Nyāya technical sense of the terms of an ordered pair or of an asymmetrical dyadic relation. Karl Potter says that Bhāsarvajña (c. 900) was the first Naiyāyika to use the terms in this way: *Encyclopedia of Indian Philosophies*, vol. 2, p. 50.

109. In Sanskrit, the same term, *pratiyogitva*, is used, unfortunately. Even if the absenteeship relation is an application of the more general relation of adjuncthood, the possibility for confusion and conflation is rife.

110. *Khkh*, p. 110; Ganga I, par. 138; Granoff, p. 180.

111. Śrīharṣa in fact identifies this and two further untoward consequences of the regress: *Khkh*, p. 114 (a verse). Granoff explains pretty well the other two: pp. 184–87.

112. *Khkh*, p. 117. Granoff, p. 191, translates, skipping a step in the argument: Śrīharṣa says "if we deny distinctness between a distinctness and its locus," not (as she says) "if the identity of a difference and its locus is admitted" (*bheda-bheda-āśrayor bhedasya asvīkāre*).

113. Śaṅkara Miśra in his commentary—published in the Navikanta Jha edition I have been citing—identifies Udayana as the author (p. 641), and presumably Śrīharṣa took it for granted that his (contemporary) audience knew whose views these were. Classical authors in general rarely identify sources.

114. *Khkh*, pp. 623–40 (first section), pp. 641–45 (the Udayana quotation), and 646–58 (the final section); Ganga IV, par. 99–105 (the entire passage); and *Ātmatattvaviveka*, Asiatic Society, pp. 563–69.

115. *Khkh*, pp. 641ff; Ganga IV, par. 99ff.

116. *Khkh*, p. 649; Ganga IV, par. 110.

117. Since there is much of interest in *Khkh* chapter 4 that I cannot discuss here, I lay out, for the benefit of those who wish to consult Ganganatha Jha's translation, the overall order of the refutations.

In *Khkh* chapter 3, which is short, Śrīharṣa examines possible meanings of interrogative pronouns, taking as an example the question, "*What* is the proof (*pramāṇa*) of God's existence?" He plays with ideas about the presuppositions of the question, without clearly indicating what he himself believes. At the beginning of chapter 4, his interlocutor, assuming (erroneously?) that he accepts the existence of God, insists that since God is an entity (*bhāva*) there has to be *pramāṇa* in support of acceptance of God's existence. Śrīharṣa asks in response, "What is an entity?" The interlocutor's answer launches an examination of the Nyāya-Vaiśeṣika ontology: (a) entity, (b) non-entity or absence (including the notion of "being qualified," since absences are said to qualify their loci), (c) definitions of substance, quality, motion, universal, and ultimate particularizer, (d) relations (including inherence as a relation, along with contact and others), (e) substratum or container (as key to the Naiyāyika understanding of inherence) along with self-linkage as a contrasting relation, (f) the subject-object relation as an example of self-linkage (where the attribution dilemma is taken to prove the idealist thesis of dependence of everything on consciousness), (g) definitions of subject and of object, (h) distinctness (the long passage we have just reviewed), (i) causality, (j) time (since notions of before and after are crucial to the Naiyāyika understanding of causality), (k) doubt (to counter the Naiyāyika retort that whereas explaining in precise detail the divisions of time may be problematic, or doubtful, the divisions are nonetheless real as commonly accepted), (l) Nyāya views of opposition or contradiction, *virodha* (key to the occurrence of doubt according to Nyāya, with doubt, according to Śrīharṣa, found to be indistinguishable from "definite ascertainment," *niścaya*), (m) dialectical reasoning, *tarka*, (n) varieties of dialectical reasoning, and (o) concluding remarks. Śrīharṣa's masterpiece, especially the fourth chapter, deserves more detailed attention than we can pay it here.

118. *Khkh*, pp. 418–509 and 710–51.

119. It is concerning knowledge of *vyāpti* where Gaṅgeśa replies directly to the Advaitin's attack.

120. An important example is explanatory simplicity or parsimony, *lāghava*, "lightness," along with its correlate, *gaurava*, "heaviness" or explanatory cumbersomeness, lack of parsimony: *Khkh*, p. 742; Ganga IV, par. 198. Many of Gaṅgeśa's arguments hinge on this criterion; see, for example, chapter 5 of this text, pp. 242ff.

121. Recall the discussion above in chapter 2, esp. note 106, p. 342.

122. An excellent secondary treatment is Sitansusekhar Bagchi, *Inductive Reasoning* (1953), pp. 215–29. Nandita Bandyopadhyay's "The Concept of Contradiction in Indian Logic and Epistemology" (1988), is also helpful (though it is less accessible to non-sanskritists than Bagchi's work).

123. Scholarship on Indian logic has been much too much influenced by modern mathematical logic, i.e., formal logic, which is not concerned with material truth and warranted premises, as opposed to informal logic, which is so concerned. Fallacies in Indian logic are informal in the sense that they break one or another condition for cogent reasoning (which requires warranted premises and good faith as well as valid argument forms or proper inductive procedure). See Nandita Bandyopadhyay's *The Concept of Logical Fallacies* (1977) for a typical example of secondary literature that tries to assimilate fallacies to formal requirements. In other words, what is needed is

research from the perspective of pragmatics and the canons of reasoning in everyday life. It is *informal* logic, I stress, that is so rich in the Indian context.

124. Nandita Bandyopadhyay (1988), "The Concept of Contradiction in Indian Logic and Epistemology," pp. 232–34.

125. Dinesh Chandra Guha, *Navya Nyāya Theory of Logic* (1979), identifies and explains about twenty of these, many of which are innovated after Gaṅgeśa.

126. Karl Potter makes the identification in *Encyclopedia of Indian Philosophies*, vol. 2, pp. 50. See also, in the same source, J. N. Mohanty's summary of Śrīvallabha's *Nyāyalīlāvatī*, p. 614.

127. For example, *Yoga-sūtra* 1.17 and Vyāsa's introduction to and commentary on 1.18.

128. *Nc*, chap. 21, verse 118; see this text, p. 76.

129. *Khkh*, p. 126: *khaṇḍana-yuktayaḥ . . . yāsām īśvara-para-vaśāṃ viśva-vyavasthām anāsthāya nirasanam aśakyaṃ*. Cf. Granoff, p. 202, and Ganga I, par. 167.

130. ibid.

131. Wilhelm Windelband, *A History of Philosophy*, vol. 1, pp. 328ff, presents succinctly the medieval Western debate concerning the primacy of God's intellect (intellectualism) or will (voluntarism).

132. Śrīharṣa in several places in the *Khkh* mentions a lost work, the *Īśvarābhisaṃdhi, The Intention (or Scheme) of God*—at least a suggestive title.

133. There is, to mention a single striking example, the passage where Indra and other gods answer a Cārvāka with popular theistic teachings: *Nc*, the seventeenth canto. The passage is ironical in that it is *gods* standing right in front of the Cārvāka who answer his atheism.

134. See, for example, A. G. Krishna Warrior (1961), and Andrew Fort (1991). An accessible classical text is the *Jīvanmuktiviveka* of Vidyāraṇya, trans. S. Subrahmanya Sasti and T. R. Srinivasa Ayyangar (1978).

135. Citsukha wrote a commentary on Śrīharṣa's *Khkh*, published in the Chowkhamba Sanskrit Series, ed. Surya Narayana Sukla (1936, 1948). His most major work, however, is not a commentary: the *Tattvadīpikā* (also known as the *Citsukhī*), ed. Udasina P. Svamiyogindrananda (1974). Surendranath Dasgupta summarizes the text in volume 2 of his *History of Indian Philosophy* (1932), pp. 148–63. An extensive study has been done by V. A. Sarma, *Citsukha's Contribution to Advaita* (1974).

136. Surendranath Dasgupta's *History of Indian Philosophy*, vol. 4 (1951), contains extensive discussion of the debate between the followers of the theistic Vedāntin Madhva (c. 1280), who draw on Navya Nyāya, and Advaitins, in particular Madhusūdana Sarasvatī and commentators on his *Advaitasiddhi*.

137. See J. N. Mohanty's discussion (1989), pp. 14 and 16–17.

Chapter 4: New Logic

1. D. C. Bhattacharya, *History of Navya-Nyāya in Mithilā* (1958), pp. 99–104, makes a thoroughly researched case for this dating. The few biographical details presented in the main text are also taken, principally, from Bhattacharya's work. Umesha Mishra, *History of Indian Philosophy*, vol. 2 (1966), pp. 239–45, presents a comparable summary story about the life of Gaṅgeśa, and, in addition, the material history of Navya Nyāya to the nineteenth century.

2. According to D. C. Bhattacharya (1958), pp. 97–98, Gaṅgeśa is mentioned in

genealogical records of Mithilā families of the era, records discovered by R. Jha. I quote Bhattacharya's summary of this evidence:

> Gaṅgeśa thus belonged to a family of which the Mūlagrāma [home village] was Chādana, a village which remains yet to be identified in Mithilā. The family which was inferior in social status is now extinct in Mithilā. According to the *Gotrapañjī* [the genealogical record] it belonged to the Kāśyapa gotra [a subcaste of the brahmin priestly caste]. . . . The [Gaṅgeśa's] daughter's son Ratnākāra, on the other hand, belonged to one of the best families in Mithilā. The *Pañjīs* [genealogical record] give elaborate accounts of the latter family, recording Ratnākāra's alliances in great details. Gaṅgeśa's family is completely ignored and we are not expected to know even his father's name (p. 98).

3. D. C. Bhattacharya (1958), pp. 134–57.

4. This is the *Khaṇḍanaprakāśa*, which is unedited and unpublished but of which there is a microfilmed manuscript in the library of the Asiatic Society, Calcutta. Scholar Anukul Bhattacharya of the Sanskrit Sahitya Parishat, Calcutta, transcribed this for me from the Bengali script (with which I am unfamiliar) to the more common script, Devanagari.

5. Umesha Mishra, vol. 2 (1966), p. 240.

6. In the very first line of the verse with which Gaṅgeśa begins the *TCM*, he in fact makes an allusion to Prabhākara.

7. The identification of historical sources has been done so far principally by classical commentators.

8. D. C. Bhattacharya (1958), p. 1.

9. B. K. Matilal, *Nyāya-Vaiśeṣika* (1977), p. 101.

10. Mishra, vol. 2 (1966), pp. 238 and 269–70.

11. Erich Frauwallner, *Die Lehre von der Zusätzlichen Bestimmung in Gaṅgeśa's Tattvacintāmaṇi* (1970), p. 5.

12. Daniel H. H. Ingalls, *Materials for the Study of Navya-Nyāya Logic* (1951), p. 5.

13. Summaries of the works of these authors appear in Karl Potter's *Encyclopedia of Indian Philosophies*, vol. 2, *Nyāya-Vaiśeṣika up to Gaṅgeśa*.

14. For example, *TCM*, vol. 1, pp. 403 and 522. Such mentions are particularly significant in that no previous author gets more than three explicit mentions in the long first chapter of the *TCM*. (See Dr. Tatacharya's appendix to *TCM*, vol. 1, p. 894.)

15. Satis Chandra Vidyabhusana, whose work on the history of Indian logic is—though now dated—a watershed, recounts the development of the "University of Nadia" and the material history of Navya-Nyāya studies in Bengal, especially within the town of Navadvīpa before the British conquest in 1757. See Vidyabhusana's *The History of Indian Logic* (1921), pp. 523–27. He tells the story of Raghunātha Śiromaṇi, who, with some question about the propriety of his action, first established the tradition in Navadvīpa. (Some scholars now believe that Navya Nyāya was established there a generation earlier.) Daniel H. H. Ingalls, whose *Materials for the Study of Navya-Nyāya Logic* (1951) is a second watershed, gives a more elaborate (but still largely apocryphal) version of Raghunātha's life (pp. 9–17).

16. Here Gaṅgeśa works from a line of thought introduced relatively late into the Old school, apparently under the pressure of Buddhist analyses.

17. *TCM*, vol. 1, esp. p. 641 (where Vācaspati's commentary is mentioned).

18. Sibajiban Bhattacharyya has recently published a translation of the *nirvikalpaka-vāda* section of the first chapter of Gaṅgeśa's *TCM*: *Gaṅgeśa's Theory of*

Indeterminate Perception (1993). Sibajiban has used the "determinate/indeterminate" translation in other works as well. A *locus classicus* for the English terminology to render the technical terms of the system is B. K. Matilal's *The Navya-Nyāya Doctrine of Negation* (1968), although often Matilal follows Ingalls (1951). Of course, many scholars have contributed to terminological innovation in English translation; another outstanding work just along this dimension, which I have often relied on, is Gopinath Bhattacharya's translation, *Tarkasaṃgraha by Annaṃbhaṭṭa* (1976). A recent work in Sanskrit that is practically indispensible for anyone concerned with terminological clarity is the *Nyāya-kośa, Dictionary of Technical Terms of Indian Philosophy*, compiled by Bhimacarya Jhalakikar and revised and edited by Vasudev Shastri Abhyankar (1978). This book collects pertinent quotations and definitions throughout the entire history of Nyāya, from the *NyS* through Gadhādhara and even later Sanskrit authors.

19. This is an extremely important point in the Advaita debate, about which Śaṅkara Miśra, as we will see, has telling insight. In the secondary literature, P. K. Mukhopadhyay (1984), pp. 61ff., draws special attention to it.

20. *TCM*, vol. 1, p. 860.

21. *prāthamikaṃ gaur iti pratyakṣaṃ jñānaṃ janya-viśeṣaṇa-jñāna-janyaṃ janya-viśiṣṭa-jñānatvāt anumitivat | na ca smaraṇaṃ tatra saṃbhavati | taj-janmani tena gotvasya ananubhavāt* | *TCM*, vol. 1, p. 863. Cf. Sibajiban Bhattacharyya (1993), p. 54.

22. *TCM*, vol. 1, p. 654; see the translation in chapter 5: pp. 237–38. For example, with the cognition *ghaṭaḥ*, "A pot," potness would be cognized as related to the particular by inherence; with *daṇḍī*, "A staff-holder," a staff would be cognized as related to a person by contact or conjunction, *saṃyoga*; and with *bhūtale ghaṭo na asti*, "There is no pot on the ground," an absence of pots would be cognized as related to the ground by self-linkage. (Self-linkage is explained in this chapter in the section on ontology.)

23. B. K. Matilal, e.g., *The Navya-Nyāya Doctrine of Negation* (1968), p. 15, and Sibajiban Bhattacharyya, e.g., *Doubt, Belief and Knowledge* (1987), pp. 215–17, have popularized the notation. (Sibajiban stresses that "R"—in addition to "a" and "b"—is to be understood as a variable that takes as substitution instances inherence, conjunction, etc. [p. 217].)

Matilal, by the way, in the book just cited, tries to interpret the corresponding Sanskrit terms (*viśeṣya*, *vaiśiṣṭya*, and *viśeṣaṇa*) as consistently logical/phenomenological, as terms of analysis of cognitions unencumbered by ontological import: see Matilal (1968), p. 18 (and throughout the book). This interpretation is an error. These may be the most important bridge terms between the realms of the objective and subjective, but they too are considered with respect to worldly objects: for example, to analyze cognition of a pot ("A pot"), the pot (in the world, not in the head) is the qualificandum, potness the qualifier, and inherence the qualificative relation. In later works, Matilal seems to have abandoned the too strictly logical interpretation.

24. In Sanskrit, although it appears that the content of a simple determinate cognition can be expressed as briefly as by a single word, the case termination is thought of as added to the stem so that the two together carry propositional force: for instance, to take Gaṅgeśa's favorite example, *ghaṭaḥ* is to be analyzed *ghaṭa* + *sup* (the case ending) = "(A) pot." This may be said to be the content of the assertion, "It is a pot," *Fa* (where "F" stands for the predicate, "is a pot").

25. The term *prakāra* means literally "way," and although it is not the word for "adverb," the adverbial view of perceptual presentations of R. M. Chisholm (1977), p. 30, resonates with Gaṅgeśa's conception.

26. Matilal (1968) champions the view that the label serves as an ontological place-holder; the properties it classes await proper ontological analysis and further development of the system. I discuss this interpretation in the section "Surplus Properties." I also discuss the more subjectivist interpretation that Matilal puts forward in *Perception* (1986), as well as the interpretations offered by Kalidas Bhattacharyya and Sibajiban Bhattacharyya.

27. The notions of thick and thin particulars—the particular considered with all of its properties (thick) and without them (thin)—are used lucidly by D. M. Armstrong, e.g., in his *Universals and Scientific Realism*, vol. 1 (1978), pp. 114–15.

The position on identity (e.g., "A blue pot = a pot") is elaborated in the final section of this chapter.

28. *Khkh*, pp. 337–83; Ganga I, par. 411–63. Some of Śrīharṣa's attack on inference is translated at the beginning of chapter 5 of this text.

29. *TCM*, vol. 2, p. 5: *vyāpti-viśiṣṭa-pakṣa-dharmatā-jñāna-janyaṃ jñānam anumiti*: "Inferential knowledge is cognition generated by cognition of a property-belonging-to-a-locus-and-qualified-by-a-pervasion." (I use hyphens in the translation to indicate that the cognition has to have all this as content.) Gaṅgeśa's position is innovative, at least somewhat innovative; throughout Prācīna Nyāya awareness of pervasion is accorded a causal role in inferential knowledge.

30. *TCM*, vol. 2, pp. 38–39. Cf. *Khkh*, p. 345; Ganga, par. 417. Gaṅgeśa's objector concludes that only perception counts as *pramāṇa*, and Śrīharṣa of course denies that too (with qualifications concerning what we mean by "deny").

31. Matilal (1977), p. 103, and Wada (1990), pp. 106–13.

32. See Wada's discussion, ibid.

33. D. H. H. Ingalls, C. Goekoop, B. K. Matilal, Sibajiban Bhattacharyya, Kamaleshwar Bhattacarya, Mrnalkanti Gangopadhyay, V. N. Jha, and Toshihiro Wada have translated the inference sections of Gaṅgeśa's text and have analyzed and laid bare in great detail (in English, except for Kamaleshwar Bhattacarya who writes in French) this portion of the great philosopher's reflection. (See the bibliography.) Although they rarely mention Śrīharṣa, I do not wish to rehash this scholarship, at least not in detail. (This book is long enough.) There is, of course, more work to be done, especially concerning the interpretations by later Navyas as well as better bridging to contemporary logic. But it seems to me better to break new ground with translations—and corresponding concerns in an introduction—than to rehearse the work of others, albeit *there is a project* in tracing the full impact of Śrīharṣa's attack on inference.

34. *TCM*, vol. 2, p. 1: *pratyakṣa-upajīvakatvāt pratyakṣa-anantaraṃ . . . anumānaṃ nirūpyate.*

35. Not all illusions involve enlivening of memory traces, as Vācaspati I and Udayana make plain according to B. K. Matilal, *Perception* (1986), p. 209. In this study of Naiyāyika epistemology, Matilal provides careful analyses of several typical illusions.

36. We might well wonder about dream. A dream counts as a non-veridical awareness, but no qualificandum is veridically cognized by the dreamer. But neither is a dream a sensory awareness. How could that be known from the perspective of the dreamer? Probably it cannot be, but Gaṅgeśa's project is not to say how an awareness is known to be sensory, etc., but to analyze the nature of sensory awarenesses, etc.

37. *tadvati tat-prakāra-anubhavaḥ*, *TCM*, vol. 1, p. 436.

38. The controversy shows even greater diversity in that some Mīmāṃsakas hold that while veridicality is known intrinsically, non-veridicality is known extrinsically.

39. In particular, *TCM*, vol. 1, pp. 114–305 passim, and 841–56.

40. A chief Mīmāṃsaka argument in favor of self-certification is that we act with a sense of certitude, guided by our cognitions. Gaṅgeśa and other Naiyāyikas defuse the argument by readily admitting that a non-veridical awareness often carries with it a sense of certitude, *niścaya*. (See J. N. Mohanty's discussion, *Gaṅgeśa's Theory of Truth*, 1989, passim.) Since we are not able to differentiate the veridical and the non-veridical at the time of the awareness itself, it is, so goes the Logician counter-argument, only through the success or failure of action based on an awareness that we are able later to do so. The grain of truth in the Mīmāṃsaka position is that often we do act confidently on the basis of an awareness that we later realize is non-veridical.

41. B. K. Matilal uses the term "telescopes" in *Epistemology, Logic, and Grammar in Indian Philosophical Analysis* (1971), p. 82.

42. For example, *TCM*, vol. 1, p. 654ff; see this text, chapter 5, p. 237ff.

43. About the requirement that without apperception the relationality of a relational awareness—and the distinctness implicit there as well—must remain implicit, Śaṅkara Miśra says, "What does it matter?!" See chapter 5, p. 278.

44. The only dependence on consciousness there is concerns God: the world has been created by God (though, as discussed, hardly *ex nihilo*). Such theism is devoutly maintained by Gaṅgeśa, following Udayana.

John Vattanky, *Gaṅgeśa's Philosophy of God* (1984), presents an extended account of Gaṅgeśa's place in the development of Nyāya theism, as well as a translation of the portion of the *TCM* devoted to arguments for God's existence.

45. A prime example concerns Gaṅgeśa's ontological reflection on *viṣayatā*, "objecthood" or "contenthood," an abstract that figures prominently in several definitions of veridical awareness that Gaṅgeśa considers: see chapter 5, esp. pp. 190–91. Gaṅgeśa does not view objecthood as an independent real; many later Naiyāyikas, however, do. The point is that though Gadādhara (c. 1660) and others oppose Gaṅgeśa on this (and other concerns), it is he who identifies the issue and his reflection is not ignored.

46. Inherence should be called inherence-converse, because of the direction of the tie in Gaṅgeśa's view. Sibajiban Bhattacharyya makes this point in *Gadhādara's Theory of Objectivity*, vol. 1 (1990), p. 30. The particular pot as property-bearer is the first term of the relation between it and potness; potness is the second term. So, strictly speaking, we would have pot-inherence=converse-potness as the relational complex meant by the expression of a veridical cognition of a pot. But it is less cumbersome to speak of inherence than inherence-converse, and so I will say inherence here.

47. *TCM*, p. 676; translated in this text, p. 251.

48. This interpretation, which was impressed upon me (resisting it) by conversations with Kisor Chakrabarti and Arindam Chakrabarti, runs counter to B. K. Matilal's in his *Navya-Nyāya Doctrine of Negation*, pp. 34, 43, and 125. Of course, inherence is not a universal in the Nyāya sense. Gaṅgeśa stresses that it is single (*eka*), but he also says repeatedly that it is *anugata*, "uniform" or "continuous" (which lends support to Matilal's taking it to be a type with tokens).

49. For the notion of a "peculiar reflexive relation that takes itself as a term," I am indebted to Sibajiban Bhattacharyya, *Gadhādara's Theory of Objectivity*, vol. 1, "General Introduction to Navya-Nyāya Concepts" (1990), p. 12.

50. *na ca saṃbandhatvena tat-siddhiḥ* | *anavasthānāt, sva-bhāvād eva jñāna-vat sva-saṃbaddha-vyavahāra-kāritvāc ca* | *samavāyo hi saṃbandhaṃ vinā eva sva-bhāvād eva kasyacit* | *TCM*, vol. 1, p. 649: see also the comments on the translation in chapter 5, pp. 230–31. Though this passage appears in a *pūrvapakṣa*, it may be

taken to reflect Gaṅgeśa's own views.

51. Karl Potter uses an analogy to glue in "Ontology of Concrete Connectors" (1961), p. 62. About this B. K. Matilal writes in *The Navya-Nyāya Doctrine of Negation*, p. 41: "The glue example, however, should not be pressed too far. It only serves to illustrate the point we are trying to make. Nyāya, of course, will relate glue to the paper by *saṃyoga* (conjunction), since both the relata here are, according to them, substances."

52. *The Navya-Nyāya Doctrine of Negation* (1968), already referred to several times.

53. See Matilal (1968), p. 108.

54. *Kiraṇāvalī* (Jetly edition), p. 220: *tadātmatva-abhimāna-pratiyogi-nirūpyaḥ*

55. This clarification may have been inspired by Śrīharṣa, whose *Khkh*, we noted, Vardhamāna wrote a commentary on.

56. *ghaṭa-saṃsargaḥ paṭo na ity atra tu saṃsarga-avacchinna-pratiyogikatve 'pi tādātmyaṃ pratiyogitā-avacchedakaṃ na tu saṃsargaḥ | asmat-pitṛ-caraṇās tu pratiyogy-adhikaraṇayoḥ saṃsargam āropya yo niṣedhaḥ sa saṃsarga-abhāvaḥ, ghata-saṃsargaḥ paṭo na ity atra tu saṃsargo na āropyate, kin tu tādātmyam ity anayor bhedaḥ | Nyāyalīlāvatīprakāśa*, ed. Dhundhiraj Sastri (November 1931), pp. 573–74.

57. The term is ambiguous: it may also mean (and sometimes does) "absence with respect to the same locus." This would hold with a mutual exclusion (a mutual absence) whose locus is a pot in that the cloth, the absentee, is denied with respect to its identity *with that same locus.*

58. *TCM*, vol. 1., pp. 736–37; Matilal (1968), pp. 116.

59. *Khkh*, p. 105; in this book, see p. 105, above.

60. *TCM*, vol. 1, pp. 736–37; Matilal (1968), p. 116. Udayana, it may be recalled, himself suggests this response: above, p. 108.

61. Śrīharṣa's point profits from the grammar of the past passive participle in Sanskrit: this form of the verb *bhid* is used as an adjective meaning "distinct," with the instrumental case used in virtue of the verbal form for what the distinct x is said to be distinct from (x distinct, *bhinna*, with y). The (implicit) Nyāya response is that here the grammar of the expression is misleading about the logic of the relation in nature. Cf. the similar point Gaṅgeśa makes in a passage translated in chapter 5, pp. 257–58.

62. Matilal (1968), pp. 122–24.

63. Matilal (1968), p. 122; *Khkh*, p. 569; Ganga IV, par. 8.

64. Matilal (1968), pp. 122, 124; *Khkh*, p. 563; Ganga IV, par. 2.

65. Śaṅkara Miśra and Vācaspati II both express the schema. It is uncertain who originated it.

66. For other refinements, consult B. K. Matilal's book (1968).

67. Karl Potter has translated this important work, providing extensive commentary, in *The Padārthatattvanirūpaṇam of Raghunātha Śiromaṇi* (1957).

68. See, e.g., Potter's commentary (1957), p. 66.

69. One who suggests this is Daniel Ingalls: (1951) pp. 2, 38, 54, and 76. In *The Navya-Nyāya Doctrine of Negation* (1968), B. K. Matilal vacillates between this and a "place-holder" interpretation (to be discussed): "Although some Naiyāyikas such as Raghunātha wanted to reshuffle the categories, since the rigid system presented almost insuperable difficulties, the new school worked on the whole within the framework of the traditional categories, and consequently kept trying [unsuccessfully!] to adjust its logical theories to the traditional scheme" (pp. 68–69).

70. For example, see the argument concerning "being-ness," *sattā*, in Potter's

translation, p. 61. There also exists a commentary on Śrīharṣa's *Khkh* attributed to Raghunātha. This work exists only in manuscript, however, and no one to my knowledge has made a definitive case that its author is indeed the famous Naiyāyika.

71. See Sibajiban Bhattacharyya's annotated translation, *Gadādhara's Theory of Objectivity*, vol. 2 (1990). See also V. N. Jha's annotated translation of a text by Harirāma (c. 1640) on the same topic: *Viṣayatāvāda of Harirāma Tarkālaṅkara* (1987).

72. Karl Potter writes in the *Nyāya-Vaiśeṣika* volume of his *Encyclopedia* (1977), p. 136: "Śrīdhara [c. 990] notes that *universalhood* is not a proper universal, and likewise for *inherenceness*, and explicitly identifies the former as an imposed property. This is the earliest use of *upādhi* in the sense of imposed property that I have been able to locate" (italics in the original).

Vardhamāna in his commentary on that portion of Udayana's *Kiraṇāvalī* where Udayana lists his six "blockers" (*jāti-bādhaka*), uses the terms *sakhaṇḍa-upādhi* and *akhaṇḍa-upādhi*: see *Kiraṇāvalīprakāśa* (Sarvvabhouma edition) p. 163. The terms probably came into currency somewhat earlier, but Udayana does not use them in the *Kiraṇāvalī* passage. Nor have I found this refinement in Gaṅgeśa's *TCM*.

73. As we noted in chapter 2 (p. 60), Udayana himself makes this move, though he does not elaborate: see *Kiraṇāvalī* (Sarvvabhouma edition), p. 169. Gaṅgeśa does not seem sensitive to the distinction.

74. For example, *TCM*, vol. 1, p. 623: *bādhakaṃ vinā anugata-buddher jāti-viṣayatvāt.*

75. Ingalls (1951) points out that most later Navyas (he mentions Viśvanātha and Mathurānātha in particular) eschew altogether the cross-sectional test (p. 42).

76. That is, according to the *Nyāyakośa*, p. 771, where Mathurānātha is cited. There Mathurānātha is said to give a notable example, veridicality! (However, I have been unable to find the usage in Mathurānātha's commentary on the *pramā-lakṣaṇa-vāda* portion of the *TCM* where the issue of whether veridicality is a *jāti* is broached by Gaṅgeśa.)

For Raghunātha's usage, see Potter's translation (1957), p. 66.

77. He writes: "Some Nyāya-Vaiśeṣika thinkers hold that even if objects and forms of objectivity cannot be reduced to the catalogued *padārthas* there is nothing to be ashamed of. They believe that the sevenfold classification of *padārthas* is not final, but only a prescription. They hold if *per force* other types of *padārthas* have to be admitted this would not go against the Nyāya-Vaiśeṣika spirit. Nyāya-Vaiśeṣika, in their opinion, is *aniyatapadārthavāda* [a system without a fixed view of categories]." Kalidas Bhattacharya, "The Indian Concepts of Knowledge and Self" (1955), p. 32.

78. *Gadādhara's Theory of Objectivity*, vol. 1 (1990), p. 88.

79. Sibajiban Bhattacharyya, *Gadādhara's Theory of Objectivity*, vol. 1 (1990), p. 88.

80. The best way for me to show here that Gaṅgeśa's understanding is holistic and causal, incorporating the science of his age, is to list the sections of the *TCM*'s first chapter, on perception. (I will refer back to this listing in chapter 5, to locate my *TCM* translations.) The book opens with (sections a and b, chapter one) *maṅgala-vāda*, comprised of benedictory verses along with two sections of discussion of the convention of opening a work in such a way. Then there appear two groups of two sections each, whose topics are, first, (sections c and d) the issue of how a veridical awareness is known to be veridical, in particular whether a judgment of veridicality is intrinsic or extrinsic to an occurrent awareness—Gaṅgeśa advocates the extrinsic view—and, second, (sections e and f) the question, given the context of Gaṅgeśa's

extrinsic theory, of how an awareness, as veridical or as non-veridical, is produced. Following these, two sections (sections g and h, translated in chapter 5) serve to characterize veridical awareness. They are followed by sections (i and j) on perceptual illusion; (section k) on the operative sensory relation in various types of perceptual awareness differentiated according to content (i.e., awarenesses of individual substances through touch or sight, of qualities such as colors that inhere in individual substances, of universals or natural kinds, of absences, and so on); (sections l and m, also translated in chapter 5) on inherence as the ontic glue binding qualities to individual substances and natural kinds to their instances, etc.; (section n) on the question whether non-apprehension is a special means of knowledge; (sections o and p) on the nature of absences; (section q) on further issues concerning perception and the range of things perceptually cognized, including atoms and air; (sections r and s) on the internal organ or faculty of perceptual synthesis; (sections t and u) on apperception; (section v) on indeterminate awareness; (section w) on the distinction between expressions of true qualifiers and mere designating devices; and (section x) on determinate awareness. Then we have the chapter on inference, whose central topic is naturally occurring concomitances or pervasions (*vyāpti*). The weight of the book cannot be said to be naturalistic—as though Gaṅgeśa entirely abandoned first-person epistemology for an "epistemology naturalized." But he does try to account for cognitive processes within a holistic understanding of the world.

81. Armstrong, *Universals and Scientific Realism*, 2 vols. (1978).

82. The example has elicited some heated controversy in the secondary literature. Ingalls (1951) writes, "Navya-naiyāyikas are forced to keep constant guard against contradictions arising from (1) ['A blue pot is essentially identical with a pot']. Only the most uncompromising realism could force a school of logic to accept such a theorem" (p. 71). Matilal in *The Navya-Nyāya Doctrine of Negation* (1968) devotes an entire section of his introduction to "Identity and the Puzzle 'a pot = a blue pot' " (pp. 45-51). He notes the diverse reactions of Karl Potter and J. F. Staal, in separate reviews of Ingalls' book (ibid., p. 48), to the statement I quote from Ingalls. He goes on to articulate the interpretation of absolute identity that, approximately, I will present here. Sibajiban Bhattacharyya in *Doubt, Belief and Knowledge* (1987: English version of a lecture given in 1973) quotes the same statement from Ingalls and says, "Now this is a complete misunderstanding of the problem. . . . The Navya-Nyāya answer to this is that by knowing something through certain modes of presentation we are not knowing something different because, ontologically, the thing, as qualified by the characters known, remains identical with the object *itself*" (italics in the original), p. 225. As I will elaborate, this brings out an epistemological dimension of the position beyond what Matilal makes plain; nevertheless, Sibajiban's and Matilal's interpretations are in accord. R. I. Ingalalli, however, disputes this understanding of Navya Nyāya's view of identity. In a recent publication, *Tādātmya-Sambandha* (1990), he draws on (incorrectly, I will argue) the translation by V. N. Jha of Harirāma's *Viṣayatāvāda* (1987) and brings out a sense of identity that is indeed distinct from the ontological variety that Matilal and Sibajiban focus upon. Still another type of identity (specifically, unique character, *asādhāraṇa-dharma*) is brought out by Dinesh Chandra Guha (1968), pp. 58–60, who draws on the works of Gadādhara. Though we cannot provide the appropriate examination here, an error of treating identity as a property seems to be committed.

83. An individual human being exhibits humanity, the natural kind, from birth, her origin, to death, her end, with other properties spatially and temporally delimited. Sibajiban Bhattacharyya reports the practice among some very late Navyas to regard

an individual human being as exhibiting a distinct universal as well, "that-personness," a universal whose instances are the time slices of the individual's life.

84. For example, *Ny-S* 4.2.4ff and the commentaries.

We might also mention an interesting idealist thesis in the Naiyāyika position on counting, a stance that is also taken very early: cognition has first to determine the boundaries, so to say, of what is to be counted. Since, e.g., Bessie is an animal, a substance, a knowable, etc., as well as a cow, counting depends on a prior determination of the qualifier through which she is known. Moreover, numbers larger than one are cognition-dependent in a strong sense in that they are created and last only by the act of counting. (Thus their status as qualifiers is much the same as that of "objecthood," which is also created by cognition but, according to some Navyas, exists in the object cognized and is to be understood as a distinct primitive.) The theses about number are advanced by Praśastapāda, and no later Logician, so far as I know, disagrees that numbers, except for the number one, exist in any way independent of the act of counting. See Udayana's *Kiraṇāvalī* (Jetly edition), pp. 124ff.

85. Among the many Westerners who have put forth a view of ontological identity that reverberates with that of the Naiyāyikas' is Baruch Brody, whose *Identity and Essence* (1980) expresses a theory centered on what Brody (following Leibniz and a long tradition) calls the identity of indiscernibles. The Logicians hold that any two things that are distinct will not have all their properties in common: see my translation, text from Śaṅkara Miśra, pp. 293–94. Brody also subscribes to an essentialism. See p. 134 for his list of conditions for an essential property, conditions that, it is easy to see, are all accepted by Logicians concerning natural kind characters.

86. We review this reasoning on pp. 256–57, in the comments on the *TCM* section on inherence. The context is Gaṅgeśa's battling against identity as championed by an opponent as the fundamental ontic tie.

87. Ingalalli (1990), pp. 55–57.

88. Ingalalli (1990), pp. 51–53.

89. See, e.g., this text, p. 258.

90. On the other hand, Gaṅgeśa flags the *upalakṣaṇa/viśeṣaṇa* distinction as problematic by presenting several unequivalent glosses: *TCM*, vol. 1, pp. 869–79.

Chapter Five: Annotated Translations

1. Concerning my translational style, the need of an editor to fill out or in, so that the translated material can be read by non-specialists, is the origin of the parenthetic expressions included in each of the following nine sections of translation. Bits of background theory are often elliptically supposed or referred to by means of propositional anaphora. I use parentheses to supply what, in my judgment, seems essential to comprehension of the texts in English. More extensive elaboration of background theories, either presupposed or alluded to, are provided in the comments. In the comments, the author's cogitations are also often restated in terms that draw on Western and current philosophy, or I say a few words to try to make the author's reasoning come alive in the context of contemporary issues.

I believe that each of the authors rendered has meant everything that I have provided in English under the headings "Text and Translation," even the long expressions in parentheses. But in some cases the line between the truly implicit and necessary background is hard to draw. In general, I have tried to be as faithful to canons of comprehensibility and good English style as to the author's Sanskrit. The two criteria need not compete, and greater elegance in English could by some better writer be achieved, I firmly believe.

2. *yatra vipakṣe vṛttau hetau bādhakam asti tayor anvayo vyāpti* | *Khkh*, p. 352.

3. Sitansusekhar Bagchi, *Inductive Reasoning: A Study of Tarka and Its Role in Indian Logic* (1953), pp. 278–302.

4. *Khkh*, p. 355; Ganga I, par. 289.

5. *Khkh*, pp. 357–63; Ganga, par. 289–95; and, again, Sitansusekhar Bagchi (1953) elaborates the details of the reasoning: pp. 279–302.

6. *Nyāyakusumañjalī*, third chapter, seventh *kārikā*, Mithila Institute, p. 379:
śaṅkā ced anumā 'sti eva na cec chaṅkā tatastarām |
vyāghātā-avadhir āśaṅkā tarkaś śaṅkā-avadhiḥ mataḥ ||

7. D. C. Bhattacharya, *The History of Navya-Nyāya in Mithilā* (1953), pp. 68–74.

8. The *Nyāyaratna* is published in the Madras Government Oriental Series, ed. V. Subrahmanya Sastri and V. Krishanmacharya (1953), with a Sanskrit commentary by Nṛsiṃhayajvan (c. 1540) and two long introductions by the editors, one in English and one in Sanskrit. The work has been summarized by V. Varadachari in Karl Potter's *Encyclopedia of Indian Philosophies*, vol. 2, *Nyāya-Vaiśeṣika up to Gaṅgeśa*, pp. 669–82.

9. D. C. Bhattacharya (1953), pp. 83–85.

10. The Sanskrit text is taken from Gaṅgeśa's *TCM*, edited by N. S. Ramanuja Tatacharya, vol. 1, pt. 1, anumāna-khaṇḍa (1973), pp. 192–201. The Asiatic Society edition, by K. N. Tarkavagisa, has also been consulted (pp. 219–34). (There is a slight difference between the two editions concerning where the section breaks—by a few sentences.)

11. Mrinalkanti Gangopadhyay, "Gaṅgeśa on Vyāptigraha: The Means for the Ascertainment of Invariable Concomitance" (1975).

12. Gaṅgeśa's text is retranslated from this point.

13. Reading, with the Asiatic Society edition, "tarkaṃ" instead of "tarka."

14. The Asiatic Society edition adds here: *sarvatra svakriyā-vyāghātaḥ syāt*: Should there be this doubt, it would be opposed in all instances by a person's behavior.

15. *TCM*, vol. 2, p. 171, and this text, note 96, pp. 350–51. See also Gangopadhyay (1975), p. 171.

16. Sibajiban Bhattacharyya (1987), p. 209 (italics in the original).

17. For the following, I rely on—beyond what Gaṅgeśa says—later Navyas, in particular Raghunātha, who, along with several others, is quoted by the *Nyāyakośa* under the entry *pratibandhakatvam* (pp. 532–33), as well as lucid exposition by Sibajiban (1987), pp. 208–13.

18. Sibajiban Bhattacharyya (1987), p. 211.

19. The Sanskrit text is taken from *Khkh*, pp. 130–239, passim; cf. Ganga I, par. 174–293, passim.

20. Sasinath Jha, ed. (1963), p. 1.

21. Granoff (1976), p. 35.

22. This particular puzzle seems to have been successfully resolved by Udayana with the notion of an exclusively negative inference. See B. K. Matilal's discussion, *Logic, Language and Reality*, pp. 187–93.

23. The Sanskrit text is taken from the Kendriya Sanskrit Vidyapeetha edition, vol. 1, the *pratyakṣa-khaṇḍa*, with the *Prakāśa* commentary by Rucidatta Miśra and a subcommentary by Rāmakṛṣṇādhvarin, ed. N. S. Ramanuja Tatacharya, (1972), pp.

409–62. The page numbers placed in parentheses refer to this edition. Also used has been vol. 1 of the Asiatic Society edition (1884–1901), with a commentary by Mathurānātha, edited by Kamakhyanath Tarkavagish, pp. 372–429.

24. Reading with the Asiatic Society edition "atyantâbhāva-sāmānâdhikaraṇyaṃ" for "antâbhāva-sāmānâdhikaraṇyaṃ."

25. I am indebted to J. N. Mohanty for this reading; in correspondence, Mohanty suggests a similarity here to Immanuel Kant's "Second Analogy," to wit, that "since empty time is not perceived we need a perceptible substance, or causal series, to ascribe a temporal series."

26. See Ingalls (1951), pp. 78–79, for an introductory discussion. See also Guha (1979), pp. 48–50.

27. In M. Gangopadhyay's translation (1982), p. 1.

28. *Lakṣaṇamālā* (1963), p. 1.

29. See Kamakhyanath Tarkavagish's notes to Mathurānātha's commentary, p. 385.

30. See Mohanty (1989), pp. 7–8 and elsewhere, for details.

31. Mohanty (1989), pp. 171–73, elaborates the rival theory following a statement of Mathurānātha's (in the *Māthurī* commentary, vol. 1, Asiatic Society edition of the *TCM*, p. 261, which translates): "When Gaṅgeśa says, 'On the theory that objecthood is something additional ontologically,' what he refers to is the view that objecthood, which belongs to the object cognized, *viśeṣya*, is an additional category of the real (*padārtha*). And this objecthood is viewed as what has both a predication content and a qualificandum. Cognition, *jñāna*, (on this view) is not (directly) in relation to either a thing cognized nor a predication content." (*atirikta-viṣayatā-pakṣa iti viṣayatā viśeṣya-vṛttir atiriktaḥ padārthaḥ sā eva ca saprakārikā saviśeṣyikā ca na tu jñānam saviśeṣyakaṃ saprakārakaṃ vā iti mata ity arthaḥ.*) Mathurānātha makes practically an identical statement in glossing Gaṅgeśa's statement here that objecthood "is something ontologically over and above both the object cognized and the cognizing awareness" (ibid., p. 361).

32. Both Rucidatta and Mathurānātha gloss *sva* consistently as *viṣayatā*—that is, until D^{30}.

33. See Matilal (1968), p. 93, on unexampled terms.

34. In the Vidyapeetha edition of the *TCM*, Dr. Tatacharya as editor has not entitled the previous section a *pūrvapakṣa* ("prima facie position") in contrast with a *siddhānta* ("right view"). The Asiatic Society edition does, however, and the voice beginning here with *ucyate*, "We answer," clearly is that of Gaṅgeśa asserting and defending his own characterizations. (The discrepancy is easily accounted for: chapter and especially section titles of classical works—which were recopied over the generations—are often due to the copiests.) Further, the word *ucyate* is Gaṅgeśa's usual signal for introducing a *siddhānta* following a *pūrvapakṣa* section. But the previous section contains, as we have seen, not only refutations on Gaṅgeśa's part of wrong views—the practice typical of a *pūrvapakṣa*—but also several long expatiations crucial to understanding the right characterizations of veridical awareness Gaṅgeśa is about to put forth. In any case, the word *ucyate* does signal us to be ready for Gaṅgeśa's final words on this topic of characterizing veridical awareness.

35. Edmund Gettier, "Is Justified True Belief Knowledge?" (1963).

36. Cf. Mohanty (1989), p. 29.

37. See, e.g., Alvin Goldman (1986), for an approach similar to Gaṅgeśa's.

38. *NyS* 1.1.4: *indriya-artha-sannikarṣa-utpannaṃ jñānam avyapadeśyam avyabhicāri vyavasāya-ātmakaṃ pratyakṣam.*

39. Here I follow Sibajiban Bhattacharyya's discussion in *Gadādhara's Theory of Objectivity*, vol. 1 (1990), pp. 104–10.

40. Sibajiban in vol. 1 of *Gadādhara's Theory of Objectivity*, p. 110, interprets one technique used in achieving universality as the functional abstraction pioneered by Gottlob Frege and Alonzo Church, utilizing Church's lambda operator. See, e.g., W. V. O. Quine, *Mathematical Logic* (1940), pp. 225–29.

41. The Dvivedin and Dravida edition, p. 508: *sa (viṣaya-viṣayi-bhāva) ca prakāśasya satas tadīyatā-mātra-rūpaḥ sva-bhāva-viśeṣaḥ.*

42. The Sanskrit is taken from *Khkh*, pp. 107–08; cf. Ganga I, par. 134, and Granoff, p. 176.

43. Also at *TCM*, vol. 1, p. 613.

44. The Sanskrit text is again taken from the edition by Dr. Tatacharya, *TCM*, vol. 1, pp. 645–97.

45. Reading "saṃbandha" for "sabandha."

46. For example, *Slokavārttika* 4.146–50.

47. *PDS*, pp. 774ff. See the discussion in chapter 2 of this text, p. 49.

48. *TCM*, pp. 764–65; cf. Matilal (1968), p. 142.

49. Reading "paṭaḥ" for "ghaṭaḥ."

50. *PDS*, pp. 774–75; Ganganatha Jha's translation, pp. 675–76.

51. See Ganganatha Jha's discussion in *The Prābhākara School of Pūrva Mīmāṃsā* (1978 reprint), p. 100.

52. As remarked with respect to the veridicality section (see note 34 above, p. 363), in the Vidyapeetha edition of the *TCM*, Dr. Tatacharya has not entitled the previous section a *pūrvapakṣa* ("prima facie position") in contrast with this following section as a *siddhānta* ("right view"). Here the Asiatic Society edition also does not divide the treatment of *samavāya*. But the voice with *ucyate*, "We answer," clearly is that of Gaṅgeśa asserting and defending his own views, whereas the previous section was dominated by an opposed voice—if only, in some cases, one converging with Gaṅgeśa's own in rejection of views of third parties. And again, the word *ucyate* is Gaṅgeśa's usual signal for introducing a *siddhānta* following a *pūrvapakṣa* section. Admittedly, there do appear several objections below which are followed by an answer also beginning with *ucyate*. Nevertheless, this does appear to be Gaṅgeśa's first expression of his own views on inherence. The argument here is the first taken by Gaṅgeśa to be successful in establishing the independent reality of inherence.

53. Cf. Guha (1976), p. 42, who cites Jagadīśa's definition of relation as the contentness other than the qualificandumness and the qualifierness of a qualified cognition.

54. *Nyāyakośa*, p. 1057. Cf. Matilal (1968), pp. 42–44.

55. Reading with Dr. Tatacharya (in taped comments) "indriya-saṃbaddha-viśeṣaṇa-viśeṣaṇatā" for "indriya-saṃbaddha-viśeṣaṇatā." While both the Vidyapeetha and Asiatic Society editions have the latter reading, presumably Gaṅgeśa would formulate his adversary's alternative proposal accurately.

56. See, for example, Ganganatha Jha's translation, *Ślokavārtika* (1983 reprint), section 13 (on *ākṛti*), pp. 283ff and 291ff.

57. *Khkh*, pp. 572ff; Ganga IV, par. 13ff.

58. *Khkh*, p. 620; Ganga IV, par. 77.

59. Reading with the Asiatic Society edition "avyāpya-vṛtti-vṛtti" for "avyāpya-vṛtti."

60. Reading with the Asiatic Society edition "nityâbhāva-vṛtty-abhāvatva-sākṣād-vyāpya-dharmatvāt" for "nityâbhāvavad-vṛtty-abhāvatva-sākṣād-vyāpya-dharmatvāt."

61. *Khkh*, p. 152; Ganga I, par. 199.

62. For clarity's sake, my translation departs from the syntax of the original more than is my usual practice. The translation is nonetheless literal and not a paraphrase.

63. D. C. Bhattacharya (1958), pp. 134–43, provides a fairly extensive account of Śaṅkara Miśra's life and works.

64. Two editions of the *Bhedaratna* have been published: Mangesh Ramkrishna Telang's (1927) and Surya Narayana Sukla's (1933). The "corrections page" (*śuddhi-patram*) of the latter runs thirty-four pages, with alternative readings from a second manuscript as well as a long list of misprints and no differentiation between the two types of entry. I follow, generally, the Telang edition (whose corrections page is confined to misprints and runs less than a page in length). Occasionally, I have preferred Sukla's text, as indicated in notes. Though in this way I combine the two editions, I have not consulted manuscripts nor "critically edited" the portions of the text translated here—except to have preferred the Sukla reading whenever the Telang reading seems to make decidedly less sense.

65. Translated by Nandalal Sinha (1974 reprint).

66. Reading "mokṣo" for "bhedo" with the Sukla edition.

67. *Khkh*, p. 104.

68. See Karl Potter's discussion in *Encyclopedia of Indian Philosophies*, vol. 2 (1977), pp. 98–100.

69. Reading "saṃsārān" for "saṃyogān" with the Sukla edition.

70. *Bṛhadāraṇyaka-bhāṣya* 4.4.19.

71. Reading "dharmi" for "sadharmi" with the Sukla edition.

72. *Nyāyakośa*, p. 957.

73. Reading "atad-vyāvṛttir vaiśiṣṭyam" for "atad-vyāvṛtti-vaiśiṣṭyam" with the Sukla edition.

74. *Kiraṇāvalī* (Jetly edition), p. 130. There is a minor variation: Udayana says *viśiṣṭatvam*, whereas Śaṅkara Miśra's says *vaiśiṣṭyam* (both terms are abstract derivatives from *viśiṣṭa*, "qualified").

75. Udayana's example is a qualified cognition, "A blue lotus," with the qualifier "blue" excluding, within the class of lotuses, the non-blue.

76. *Kiraṇāvalī* (Jetly edition), p. 130: *na hi dharma-dharmiṇos tādātmyam.*

77. A verbal indication of a strict identity, $a \equiv a$, would not be viewed as expressing a qualified cognition; the perceptual and the other causal processes that result in qualified cognition invariably present more than an identity, minimally *a* qualified by "being that name *a*," alternatively, "this-ness."

78. Śrīharṣa's citation occurs in *Khkh*, p. 67: *anyathā-anupapattir . . . sarva-bala-adhikā*. Cf. Ganga I, par. 86; Granoff, pp. 135–36.

79. Reading "iti" (and without a daṇḍa or full stop) for "iti cet" with the Sukla edition.

80. Reading "prakṛte" for "phale" with the Sukla edition.

81. *Khkh*, p. 109; see in this text, p. 103.

82. *Ppk*, pp. 98–113.

83. Reading "tatra" (without a daṇḍa) for "tan na" with the Sukla edition.

84. Reading "abhyupagamena" for "anuyoge" with the Sukla edition.

85. Reading "prathamo" for "prathame" with the Sukla edition.

86. Reading "jñāyamānaṃ" for "jāyamānaṃ" with the Sukla edition.

87. Reading "vartata" for "vartatām" with the Sukla edition.

88. *Nyāyakośa*, p. 122, where Viśvanātha Pañcānana is cited.

89. *Khkh*, p. 116, Ganga I, par. 150, Granoff, p. 191; *Khkh*, p. 637, Ganga IV, p. 94; *Khkh*, p. 113, Ganga I, par. 142, Granoff, p. 184; and this text, pp. 221–22.

90. Gaṅgeśa, we noted, takes up the distinction in a passage that occurs between the *nirvikalpakavāda* and *savikalpakavāda* sections of the *TCM*'s first chapter (pp. 869–79). His son Vardhamāna, by the way, throws up his hands with it, saying that there is no hard and fast way to secure it. (See his commentary on Udayana's *Kiraṇāvalī*, p. 73: *na tu yad viśeṣaṇaṃ na tad upalakṣaṇaṃ yad upalakṣaṇaṃ na tad viśeṣaṇam iti.*) As mentioned, Vācaspati II takes a different view.

91. Reading "paṭâbhinne" for "paṭa-bhinne" with the Sukla edition.

92. Reading "śūdro" for "śuddho" with the Sukla edition.

93. Reading "ahṛdayasya" for "sahṛdayasya" with the Sukla edition.

94. Or, with the Sukla edition, "of good character," reading "anuttama-tulyasya" for "anunmattasya."

95. *Khkh*, p. 105; Ganga I, par. 133; Granoff, pp. 174–75.

96. Uddyotakara makes the charge of madness (*unmattavat*) in *NyS-V*, p. 45.

97. Reading "na abhedo 'pi iti" for "tattva-bhedo 'pi iti" with the Sukla edition.

98. Other requirements are proper contiguity (there must not be too much of a pause between the utterance of one word in a sentence and another) and plausibility (we would not presume to understand "I saw him bathing with fire"): see, e.g., Swami Madhavananda (trans.), *Bhāṣā-pariccheda of Viśvanātha* (1977), pp. 166–72, or Purushottama Bilimoria (1988), chaps. 5 and 6.

99. Reading "abhiprāya-niyamam" for "āśayam" with the Sukla edition.

100. According to the corrections page of the Sukla edition, this passage does not appear in one of the manuscripts the editor consulted.

101. Reading "na hi" for "tarhy" with the Sukla edition (p. 27, three lines from the bottom).

102. Reading "ghaṭam" for "ghaṭatvam" with the Sukla edition.

103. For a detailed summary of the remainder of the text, see the forthcoming Navya-Nyāya volume (unpublished at the time of this writing but most likely out by the time this is read) in Karl Potter's *Encyclopedia of Indian Philosophies*, edited by Potter and Sibajiban Bhattacharyya.

104. D. C. Bhattacharya (1958), pp. 143–58, provides a fairly extensive account of Vācaspati's life and works.

105. The text is taken from the only edition I have been able to find—by Ramananda Pithadhisa, who is also the author of an extensive Hindi commentary (1973). There are so many misprints that I will not flag the corrections I have made in the transliteration. Except for the obvious misprints, I have not, however, re-edited the selection.

106. That is, he follows *Khkh*, pp. 103–18 (cf. Granoff, pp. 170–92, and Ganga I, par. 128–92). A portion of this material has been translated in this text: pp. 221–22. The *pūrvapakṣa* runs from p. 181 through p. 193 of Pithadhisa's edition.

107. Vācaspati's reference is to *Ātmatattvaviveka*, the Asiatic Society edition, p. 569.

108. *TCM*, vol. 1, pp. 751ff; Matilal (1968), p. 128; cf. this text, pp. 140–41.

109. *tad-viśiṣṭa-jñānasya abhāva-dhī-hetutvāt* | *TCM*, Vol. II, p. 49.

110. *Kiraṇāvalī* (Jetly edition), p. 220.

111. *na vai stambha-piśācayos tādātmyaṃ pramāṇa-siddhaṃ kiñcid asti yat pratiṣedhanīyam; kin tu stambhâtmatayā prasañjitasya piśācasya ayaṃ pratiṣedha iti* |

112. See Swami Madhavananda's translation, *Bhāṣā-pariccheda with Siddhāntamuktāvalī* (1977), p. 99.

113. Dasgupta, *A History of Indian Philosophy*, vol. 4 (1951), p. 178.

114. The *Nyāyakośa*, p. 44, quotes the *Siddhāntamuktāvalī* passage cited

immediately above, to show that a mutual absence is perceptible when its substratum is perceptible.

115. Matilal (1986), pp. 208–20.

116. *Nyāyakośa*, pp. 135–36.

117. This does seem to be a clear example of what later Navyas call *āhārya-buddhi*. See *Nyāyakośa*, pp. 135–36.

118. *TCM*, vol. 1, pp. 869–79.

119. *Khkh*, p. 114; cf. Granoff, p. 184.

120. *Khkh*, p. 104; cf. Ganga I, par. 131, and Granoff, p. 172.

BIBLIOGRAPHY

1. Classical Sanskrit Texts (with Abbreviations)

Āryadeva: see Karen Lang.

Ātmatattvaviveka of Udayana. Ed. Vindhyesvariprasada Dvivedin and Lakshmana Sastri Dravida. Bibliotheca Indica 170. Reprint, the Asiatic Society, Calcutta, 1986.

Bhartṛhari: see *Vākyapadīya*.

Bhedaratna of Śaṅkara Miśra. Ed. Ramkrishna Telang. Bombay: Manilal Itcharam Desai, 1927.

Bhedaratna of Śaṅkara Miśra. Ed. Surya Narayana Sukla. Benares: Princess of Wales Saraswati Bhavana Texts, 1933.

Bhāmatī of Vācaspati I: see *Brahmasūtrabhāṣya* of Śaṅkara.

Brahmasiddhi of Maṇḍana Miśra. Ed. S. Kuppuswami Sastri. Madras Government Oriental Series, 1937. Reprint, Delhi: Sri Satguru, 1984.

(*BSB*) *Brahmasūtrabhāṣya* of Śaṅkara. With the *Bhāmatī* commentary by Vācaspati Misra. Ed. J. L. Shastri. Delhi: Motilal Banarsidass, 1980.

Bṛhadāraṇyaka-bhāṣya of Śaṅkara. Ed. E. Roer, Calcutta, 1849–56. Reprint, Osnabruck: Biblio Verlag, 1980.

Bṛhadāraṇyaka-bhāṣya-vārtikka of Sureśvara: see T. M. P. Mahadevan.

Candrānanda: see *Vaiśeṣikasūtra*

Catuḥśataka of Āryadeva: see Karen Lang.

Citsukha: see *Tattvadīpikā*.

Dharmakīrti: see *Nyāyabindu*, *Pramāṇavārtika*, *Pramāṇaviniścaya*, and *Sambandhaparīkṣā*.

Dignāga: see N. Aiyaswami Sastri.

Gaṅgeśa: see *Tattvacintāmaṇi*.

Jayanta Bhaṭṭa: see *Nyāyamañjarī*.

Jayarāśi: see *Tattvopaplavasiṃha*.

Jīvanmuktiviveka of Mādhava: see S. Subrahmanya Sastri.

Kāśikā of Vāmana and Jayāditya. Ed. S. N. Misra. Kashi Sanskrit Series 37. Varanasi: Chowkhamba, 1969.

Keśava Miśra: see *Tarkabhāṣā*.

(*Khkh*) *Khaṇḍanakhaṇḍakhādya* of Śrīharṣa. Ed. Navikanta Jha, Kashi Sanskrit Series 197. Varanasi: Chowkhamba, 1970.

Khaṇḍanoddhāra of Vācaspati II. Ed. Ramananda Pithadhisa. Jaipur: 1973.

Kiraṇāvalī of Udayana. Ed. Jitendra S. Jetly. Gaekwad Oriental Series 154. Baroda: Oriental Institute, 1971.

Kiraṇāvalī of Udayana. With the commentary of Vardhamāna. Ed. Siva Chandra Sarvvabhouma, 1911. Reprint, Calcutta: Asiatic Society, 1989.

Kumārila: see *Ślokavārttika.*

Kusumāñjali: see *Nyāyakusumāñjali* (of Udayana).

Lakṣaṇamālā of Udayana. Ed. Sasinatha Jha. Mithila Institute Series 13. Darbhanga, 1963.

Lakṣaṇāvalī of Udayana: see Musashi Tachikawa.

Mādhava: see S. Subrahmanya Sastri.

Mahābhārata. Ed. Ramchandrashastri Kinjawadekar. 6 vols. Reprint of the "Bombay edition," New Delhi: Oriental Books, 1979.

Maṇḍana Miśra: see *Brahmasiddhi.*

Maṇikaṇṭha Miśra: see *Nyāyaratna.*

Mathurānātha: see *Tattvacintāmaṇi.*

(*MMK*) *Mūlamadhyamakakārikā* of Nāgārjuna. Ed. J. W. de Jong. Madras: Adyar, 1977.

Nāgārjuna: see *Mūlamadhyamakakārikā, Ratnāvalī,* and *Vigrahavyāvartanī.*

(*Nc*) *Naiṣadhacarita* of Śrīharṣa. Ed. Narayan Ram Acharya. New Delhi: 1986.

Nyāyabindu of Dharmakīrti. With the *Nyāyabinduṭīkā* commentary of Dharmottara. Ed. A. C. Sastri. Kashi Sanskrit Series 22. Banaras: Chowkhamba, 1954.

Nyāyadarśana of Gautama (chap. 1). With the Bhāṣya of Vātsyāyana, the Vārttika of Uddyotakara, the Tātparyaṭīkā of Vācaspati, and the Pariśuddhi of Udayana. Ed. Anantalal Thakur. Mithila Institute Series, Ancient Texts 20. Darbhanga, 1967. (This text is sometimes referred to as the Thakur edition of the *Nyāya-sūtra.*)

Nyāyakandalī (commentary on *PDS*) of Śrīdhara: see *Padārthadharmasaṃgraha,* ed. Durgadhara Jha.

Nyāya-kośa: see Bhimacarya Jhalakikar.

Nyāyakusumāñjali of Udayana. Ed. Mahaprabhulal Goswami. Mithila Institite Ancient Texts Series 23. Darbhanga, 1972.

Nyāyalīlāvatī of Vallabha. With the *Nyāyalīlāvatīprakāśa* commentary of Vardhamāna. Ed. Dhundhiraj Sastri, Chowkhamba Sanskrit Series 407. Benares: 1927–34.

Nyāyamañjarī of Jayanta Bhaṭṭa. Ed. Surya Narayana Sukla. Kashi Sanksrit Series 106. Varanasi: Chowkhamba Sanskrit Series Office, 1971.

Nyāyaratna of Maṇikaṇṭha Miśra. Ed. V. Subrahmanya Sastri and V. Krishnamacharya. Madras: Madras Government Oriental Series, 1953.

(*NyS*) *Nyāyasūtra* (Nyāyadarśanam). With four commentaries, the *Nyāyasūtra-bhāṣya* of Vātsyāyana, the *Nyāyasūtra-vārttika* of Uddyotakara, the *Nyāyasūtravārttika-tātpāryaṭīkā* of Vācaspati Miśra, and the *Vṛtti* of Viśvanātha. Ed. A. M. Tarkatirtha, Taranatha Nyayatarkatirtha, and H. K. Tarkatirtha. Calcutta Sanskrit Series 18. 1936–44. Reprint, New Delhi, Munshiram Manoharlal, 1985.

Nyāyasūtra: see also *Nyāyadarśana of Gautama.*

(*NyS-Bh*) *Nyāyasūtra-bhāṣya* of Vātsyāyana: see *Nyāyasūtra.*

(*NyS-V*) *Nyāyasūtra-vārttika* of Uddyotaka: see *Nyāyasūtra*.

Padmapāda: see *Pañcapādikā*.

(*PDS*) *Padārthadharmasaṃgraha* of Praśastapāda (*Praśastapādabhāṣyam*). With the *Nyāyakandalī* commentary of Śrīdhara. Ed. with a Hindi translation by Durgadhara Jha. Varanasi: Sampurnanand Sanskrit Vishvavidyalaya, 1977.

(*Ppk*) *Pañcapādikā* of Padmapāda. Ed. S. Srirama Sastri and S. R. Krishnamurti Sastri. Madras Government Oriental Series 155. Madras: 1958.

Pramāṇavārttika of Dharmakīrti. With the commentary of Manorathanandin. Ed. Dvarikadas Sastri. Varanasi: Bauddha Bharati, 1968.

Pramānavārttikasvavṛtti of Dharmakīrti. Ed. R. Gnole, *Serie Orientale Roma* 23. Rome, 1960.

Pramāṇaviniścaya of Dharmakīrti: see Tilmann Vetter.

Ratnāvalī of Nāgārjuna: see H. Chatterjee Sastri.

Rucidatta Miśra: see *Tattvacintāmaṇi*.

(*SP*) *Sambandhaparīkṣā* of Dharmakīrti: see V. N. Jha.

Śaṅkara: see *Brahmasūtrabhāṣya*, *Bṛhadāraṇyaka-bhāṣya*, and *Upadeśasāhasrī*.

Śaṅkara Miśra: see *Bhedaratna*.

Slokavārttika of Kumārila. Ed. Dvarikadas Sastri. Varanasi: Tara Publications, 1978.

Śrīdhara: see *Padārthadharmasaṃgraha*.

Śrīharṣa: see *Khaṇḍanakhaṇḍakhādya* and *Naiṣadhacarita*.

Sureśvara: see *Bṛhadāraṇyaka-bhāṣya-vārtikka*.

Tarkabhāṣā of Keśava Miśra. Ed. Devadatta Ramkrishna Bhandarkar and Pandit Kedarnath. Bombay Sanskrit and Prakrit Series 84. Bombay, 1937.

(*TCM*, vol. 1) *Tattvacintāmaṇi* of Gaṅgeśa, vol. 1, *pratyakṣa-khaṇḍa*. With the *Prakāśa* commentary by Rucidatta Miśra and a subcommentary by Rāmakṛṣṇādhvarin. Ed. N. S. Ramanuja Tatacharya. Kendriya Sanskrit Vidypeetha Series 20. Tirupati, 1972.

(*TCM*, vol. 2) *Tattvacintāmaṇi* of Gaṅgeśa, vol. 2, *anumāna-khaṇḍa*. With the *Prakāśa* commentary by Rucidatta Miśra and a subcommentary by Dharmarājādhvarin. Ed. N. S. Ramanuja Tatacharya. Kendriya Sanskrit Vidypeetha Series 33. Tirupati: 1982.

Tattvacintāmaṇi of Gaṅgeśa, vol. 1, *pratyakṣa-khaṇḍa*. With the *Māthurī* commentary of Mathurānātha. Ed. Kamakhyanath Tarkavagish. Asiatic Society. Calcutta, 1884–1901. Reprint, 1991.

Tattvacintāmaṇi of Gaṅgeśa, vol. 2, pt. 1, *anumāṇa-khaṇḍa*. With the commentary of Mathurānātha. Ed. Kamakhyanath Tarkavagish. Asiatic Society. Calcutta, 1884–1901. Reprint, 1991.

Tattvadīpikā of Citsukha. Ed. Udasina P. Svamiyogindrananda. Varanasi, 1974.

Tattvopaplavasiṃha of Jayarāśi. Ed. Sukhlalju Sanghavi and R. C. Parikh. Gaekwad Oriental Series 40. Baroda, 1940.

Udayana: see *Ātmatattvaviveka*, *Kiraṇāvalī*, *Lakṣaṇamālā*, *Lakṣaṇāvalī*, *Nyāyadarśana of Gautama*, and *Nyāyakusumañjalī*.

Uddyotaka: see *Nyāyasūtra-vārttika*.

Upadeśasāhasrī of Śaṅkara: see Sengaku Mayeda.

Upaniṣat-Saṃgrahaḥ. Ed. J. L. Shastri. Delhi: Motilal Banarsidass, 1970.

Vācaspati Miśra I: see *Brahmasūtrabhāṣya* of Śaṅkara, *Nyāyasūtravārttika-tātparyaṭīkā* (under *Nyāyasūtra*), and *Yogasūtra*.

Vācaspati Miśra II: see *Khaṇḍanoddhāra*.

Vaiśeṣikasūtra of Kaṇāda. With the commentary of Candrānanda. Ed. Muni Sri Jambuvijayaji. Gaekwad Oriental Series 136. Baroda: Oriental Institute, 1961.

(*VS*) *Vaiśeṣika-sūtra* of Kaṇāda. Ed. Jayanarayana Tarka Panshanana. Biblioteca Indica 34. Reprint, Osnabrück: Biblio Verlag, 1981.

Vākyapadīya of Bhartṛhari, pt. 3. Ed. Raghunatha Sarma. Varanasi: Sampurnanand Sanskrit Univerity, 1991.

Vallabha: see *Nyāyalīlāvatī*.

Vardhamāna: see *Kiraṇāvalī* and *Nyāyalīlāvatī*.

Vātsyāyana: see *Nyāyasūtra-bhāṣya*.

(*Vv*) *Vigrahavyāvartanī* of Nāgārjuna: see Kamaleshwar Bhattacharya.

Yogasūtra. With the commentaries of Vyāsa and Vācaspati Miśra. 3rd. ed. Ed. Jibananda Vidyasagara. Calcutta, 1940.

2. Other Works

Armstrong, D. M. *Universals and Scientific Realism*. 2 vols. Cambridge: Cambridge University Press, 1978.

Bagchi, Sitansusekhar. *Inductive Reasoning*. Calcutta: Munishchandra Sinha, 1953.

Bandopadhyay, Nandita. *The Concept of Logical Fallacies*. Calcutta: Sanskrit Pustak Bhandar, 1977.

———. "The Concept of Contradiction in Indian Logic and Epistemology," *Journal of Indian Philosophy* 16 (1988), pp. 225–46.

Bharati, Aghehananda Bharati. *Ochre Robe*. Santa Barbara: Ross-Erikson, 1988.

Bhattacharya, Dinesh Chandra. *History of Navya-nyāya in Mithilā*. Darbhanga: Mithila Institute, 1958.

Bhattacharya, Gopinath. *Tarkasaṃgraha-dīpikā on Tarkasaṃgraha by Annaṃbhaṭṭa*. Calcutta: Progressive Publishers, 1976.

Bhattacharya, Kamaleshwar. "Le *Siddhāntalakṣaṇaprakaraṇa* du *Tattvacintāmaṇi* de Gaṅgeśa avec la *Dīdhiti* de Raghunātha Śiromaṇi et la ṭīkā de Jagadīśa Tarkālaṃkāra." *Journal Asiatique* (1977): pp. 97–139; (1978): pp. 97–124; (1980): pp. 275–322; (1982): pp. 401–13; (1984): pp. 47–82.

———. "Some Notes on the *Vigrahavyāvartanī*." *Journal of Indian Philosophy* 5 (1978), pp. 240–41.

———. *The Dialectical Method of Nāgārjuna*. Delhi: Motilal Banarsidass, 1986.

Bhattacharyya, J. V., trans. *Jayanta Bhaṭṭa's Nyāyamañjarī*. Delhi: Motilal Banarsidass, 1978.

Bhattacharyya, Kalidas. "The Indian Concepts of Knowledge and Self" (second installment). *Our Heritage* 3 (1955).

Bhattacharyya, Sibajiban. *Doubt, Belief and Knowledge*. New Delhi: Indian Council of Philosophical Research and Allied Publishers, 1987.

———. Introduction, pt. 1 of *Gadādhara's Theory of Objectivity*. New Delhi: Indian

Council of Philosophical Research, 1990.

———. Gadhādara's *Viṣayatāvāda*, pt. 2 of *Gadādhara's Theory of Objectivity*. New Delhi: Indian Council of Philosophical Research, 1990.

———. "Some Features of the Technical Language of Navya-Nyāya." *Philosophy East and West* 40, no. 2 (April 1990): pp. 129–49.

———. *Gaṅgeśa's Theory of Indeterminate Perception*. New Delhi: Indian Council of Philosophical Research, 1993.

Biardeau, Madeleine. *La philosophie de Maṇḍana Miśra*. Paris: École Française d'Etrême-Orient, 1969.

Bilimoria, Purushottama. *Śabdapramāṇa: Word and Knowledge*. Dordrecht: Kluwer, 1988.

Bonevac, Daniel, and Stephen Phillips, eds. *Understanding Non-Western Philosophy*. Mountain View, California: Mayfield, 1993.

Brody, Baruch. *Identity and Essence*. Princeton: Princeton University Press, 1980.

Cardona, George. *Pāṇini: A Survey of Research*. The Hague: Mouton, 1976.

Chakrabarti, Arindam. "Plato's Indian Barbers." In *Analytical Philosophy in Comparative Perspective*, ed. B. K. Matilal, pp. 299–326, Dordrecht: D. Reidel, 1985.

———. "I Touch What I Saw." *Philosophy and Phenomenological Research* 52, no. 1 (March 1992): pp. 103–16.

Chakrabarti, Kisor. "The Nyāya Theory of Universals." *Journal of Indian Philosophy* 3 (1975).

Chattopadhyaya, Debiprasad. *Indian Atheism*. Calcutta: Manisha, 1969.

———. *Cārvāka/Lokāyata*. New Delhi: Indian Council of Philosophical Research, 1990.

Chemparathy, George. *An Indian Rational Theology*. Vienna: De Nobili, 1972.

Chisholm, Roderick M. *Theory of Knowledge*. 2nd ed. Englewood Cliffs, New Jersey: Prentice-Hall, 1977.

Coward, Howard G., and K. Kunjunni Raja, eds. *The Philosophy of Indian Grammarians*. Vol. 5 of *Encyclopedia of Indian Philosophies*, ed. Karl Potter. Delhi: Motilal Banarsidass, 1990.

Cowell, E. B., and A. E. Gough, trans. *Compendium of All Philosophies* (Mādhava's *Sarvadarśanasaṃgraha*). London: Kegan Paul, 1892.

Dasgupta, Surendranath. *A History of Indian Philosophy*. Vol. 1. 1922. Reprint, Cambridge: Cambridge University Press, 1969.

———. *A History of Indian Philosophy*. Vol. 2. 1932. Reprint, Cambridge: Cambridge University Press, 1973.

———. *History of Indian Philosophy*. Vol. 4. 1951. Reprint, Cambridge: Cambridge University Press.

Dasgupta, Surendranath, and S. K. De. *A History of Sanskrit Literature*. 1st ed. vol. 1. Calcutta: University of Calcutta, 1946.

Davids, Caroline A. F. Rhys, trans. *The Book of Kindred Sayings*. 5 vols. Pali Text Society. 1917–30.

De, S. K.: see Surendranath Dasgupta.

Deodikar, Sanjay Govind. *Upaniṣads and Early Buddhism*. Delhi: Eastern Book Linkers, 1992.

Deutsch, Eliot. *Advaita Vedānta: A Philosophical Reconstruction.* Honolulu: University of Hawaii Press, 1969.

Dravid, Raja Ram. *The Problem of Universals in Indian Philosophy.* Delhi: Motilal Banarsidass, 1972.

Eliade, Mircea. *Yoga: Immortality and Freedom.* Trans. Willard R. Trask. 2nd ed. Princeton: Princeton University Press, 1969.

Feuerstein, Georg. *The Encyclopedic Dictionary of Yoga.* New York: Paragon House, 1990.

Fort, Andrew. "Śaṅkara on Jīvanmukti." *Journal of Indian Philosophy* 19, no. 4 (December 1991): pp. 365–89.

Franco, Eli. *Perception, Knowledge and Disbelief.* Stuttgart: Franz Steiner, 1987.

Frauwallner, Erich, trans. "*Sambandhaparīkṣā* (of Dharmakīrti)." *Wiener Zeitscrift für des Kundes Morganlandes* 41 (1934): pp. 261–300.

———. *Die Lehre von der Zusätzlichen Bestimmung in Gaṅgeśa's Tattvcintāmaṇi.* Vienna: Österreichische Akademie der Wissenschaften, Philosophisch-historische Klasse, Sitzungsberichte, 266. Band 2. Abhandlung, 1970.

———. *History of Indian Philosophy,* trans. V. M. Bedekar. 2 vols. New York: Humanities Press, 1974.

Gangopadhyay, Mrinalkanti. "Gaṅgeśa on Vyāptigraha: The Means for the Ascertainment of Invariable Concomitance." *Journal of Indian Philosophy* 3 (1975), pp. 167–208.

Gangopadhyay, Mrinalkanti, trans. *Nyāya-Sūtra with Vātsyāyana's Commentary.* Calcutta: Indian Studies, 1982.

Gettier, Edmund. "Is Justified True Belief Knowledge." *Analysis* 23 (1963), pp. 121–23.

Goddard, Dwight, ed. and trans. *A Buddhist Bible.* Boston: Beacon Press, 1938.

Goekoop, C. *The Logic of Invariable Concomitance in the Tattvacintāmaṇi.* Dordrecht: D. Reidel, 1967.

Goldman, Alvin. *Epistemology and Cognition.* Cambridge: Harvard University Press, 1986.

Granoff, Phyllis. *Philosophy and Argument in Late Vedānta* (containing a translation of part of Śrīharṣa's *Khaṇḍanakhaṇḍakhādya*). Dordrecht: D. Reidel, 1978.

Guha, Dinesh Chandra. *The Navya-Nyāya System of Logic.* 2nd ed. Delhi: Motilal Banarsidass, 1979.

Halbfass, Wilhelm. *Studies in Kumārila and Śaṅkara.* Reinbek: Inge Wezler, 1983.

———. *On Being and What There Is.* Albany: State University of New York Press, 1992.

Handiqui, K. K., trans. *Śrīharṣa's Naiṣadhacaraita.* Poona: Deccan College, 1965.

Hattori, Masaaki. *Dignāga, On Perception,* an annotated translation of the first chapter of the *Pramāṇasamuccaya.* Cambridge: Harvard University Press, 1968.

Hauer, J. W. *Der Yoga.* Stuttgart: W. Kohlhammer, 1958.

Hayes, Richard P. *Dignāga on the Interpretation of Signs.* Dordrecht: Kluwar, 1987.

Herzberger, H. and R. Herzberger. "Bhartṛhari's Paradox," *Journal of Indian Philosophy* 9 (1981): pp. 3–32.

Herzberger, Radhika. *Bhartṛhari and the Buddhists.* Dordrecht: D. Reidel, 1986.

Hume, Robert E., trans. *The Thirteen Principal Upanishads*. 2nd ed. London: Oxford University Press, 1931.

Ingalalli:, R. I. *Tādātmya-Sambandha*. Delhi: Sri Satguru, 1990.

Ingalls, Daniel H. H. *Materials for the Study of Navya-Nyāya Logic*. Cambridge: Harvard University Press, 1951.

Ingalls, Daniel H. H., J. Masson, and M. Patwardhan, trans. *The Dhvanyāloka of Ānandavardhana*. Cambridge: Harvard University Press, 1990.

Iyer, K. A. Subramania. *The Vākyapadīya of Bhartṛhari*. Poona: Deccan College, 1971.

Jha, Ganganatha. *The Prābhākara School of Pūrva Mīmāṃsā*. Reprint, Delhi: Motilal Banarsidass, 1978.

Jha, Ganganatha, trans. *Padārthadharmasaṃgraha of Praśastapāda*. Reprint, Varanasi: Chaukhambha Orientalia, 1982.

———. *Ślokavārtika*. Reprint, Delhi: Sri Satguru, 1983.

———. *The Nyāya-sūtra of Gautama* (with the commentaries of Vātsyāyana and Uddyotakara). 4 vols. 1912–19. Reprint, Delhi: Motilal Banarsidass, 1984.

———. *The Khaṇḍanakhaṇḍakhādya of Śrīharṣa*. Reprint, Delhi: Sri Satguru, 1986.

Jha, V. N., trans. *Viṣayatāvāda of Harirāma Tarkālaṅkara*. Pune: University of Poona, 1987.

———. *The Philosophy of Relations*, an edition and translation of Dharmakīrti's *Sambandhaparīkṣā*. Delhi: Sri Satguru, 1990.

Jhalakikar, Bhimacarya, compiler. *Nyāya-kośa (Dictionary of Technical Terms of Indian Philosophy)*. Ed. and rev. Vasudev Shastri Abhyankar. Poona: Bhandarkar Oriental Research Institute, 1978.

Joshi, L. V. *A Critical Study of the Pratyakṣa Pariccheda of Bhāsarvajña's Nyāyabhūṣaṇa*. Ahmedabad: Gujarat University, 1986.

Kaviraj, Gopinath. *The History and Bibliography of Nyāya-Vaiśeṣika Literature*. Ed. Gaurinath Sastri. Reprint, Varanasi: Saraswati Bhavana Studies, 1982.

Kumar, Shiv. *Upamāna in Indian Philosophy*. Delhi: Eastern Book, 1980.

Lang, Karen, ed. and trans. *Āryadeva's Catuḥśataka*. Copenhagen: Akademisk Forlag, 1986.

Larson, Gerald, and Ram Shankar Bhattacharya, eds. *Sāṃkhya*. Vol 4. of *Encyclopedia of Indian Philosophies*, ed. Karl Potter. Delhi: Motilal Banarsidass, 1987.

Lindtner, Christian. *Nagarjuniana*. Delhi: Motilal Banarsidass, 1986.

Lyons, John. *Semantics*. 2 vols. Cambridge: Cambridge University Press, 1977.

Madhavananda, Swami, trans. *Bhāṣā-pariccheda of Viśvanātha*. Calcutta: Advaita Ashrama, 1977.

Mahadevan, T. M. P., ed. and trans. Introduction to Bk. 1 of Sureśvara's *Bṛhadāraṇyaka-bhāṣya-vārtikka*. Madras: University of Madras, 1958.

Matilal, B. K. *The Navya-Nyāya Doctrine of Negation*. Cambridge: Harvard University Press, 1968.

———. *Epistemology, Logic, and Grammar in Indian Philosophical Analysis*. The Hague: Mouton, 1971.

———. *Nyāya-Vaiśeṣika*. Wiesbaden: Otto Harrassowitz, 1977.

———. *Logic, Language and Reality*. Delhi: Motilal Banarsidass, 1985.

———. *Perception*. Oxford: Oxford University Press, 1986.

———. *The Word and the World*. Delhi: Oxford University Press, 1990.

Matilal, B. K., and J. L. Shaw, eds. *Analytical Philosophy in Comparative Perspective*. Dordrecht: D. Reidel, 1985.

Mayeda, Sengaku. *A Thousand Teachings* (an annotated translation of Śaṅkara's *Upadeśasāhasrī*). Tokyo: University of Tokyo, 1979.

Mishra, Umesha. *History of Indian Philosophy*. 2 vols. Allahabad: Tirabhukti, 1966.

Misra, Anand Svarup. *Mahākavi Śrīharṣa*. Lucknow: Sulabh Prakashan, 1988.

Mohanty, J. N. *Gaṅgeśa's Theory of Truth*. Reprint, Delhi: Motilal Banarsidass, 1989.

Mukhopadhyay, P. K. *Indian Realism*. Calcutta: K. P. Bagchi, 1984.

Narain, Harsh. *Evolution of the Nyāya-Vaiśeṣika Categoriology*. Varanasi: Bharati Prakashan, 1976.

Nyanamol, Bhikku, trans. *The Path of Purification*. Vol. 2. Boulder: Shambala, 1976.

Oetke, Claus. "Remarks on the Interpretation of Nāgārjuna's Philosophy." *Journal of Indian Philosophy* 19 (1991): pp. 315–23.

Phillips, Stephen H. "Padmapāda's Illusion Argument." *Philosophy East and West* 37, no.1 (January 1987): pp. 3–23.

———. "Dharmakīrti on Sensation and Causal Efficiency." *Journal of Indian Philosophy* 15 (1987): pp. 231–59.

Pollock, John. *Contemporary Theories of Knowledge*. Towota, New Jersey: Rowman & Littlefield, 1976.

Potter, Karl H. "Ontology of Concrete Connectors." *Journal of Philosophy* 58, no. 3 (February 1961).

Potter, Karl H., ed. *Encyclopedia of Indian Philosophies*. Vol. 2. *Nyāya-Vaiśeṣika*. Delhi: Motilal Banarsidass, 1977.

———. *The Encyclopedia of Indian Philosophies*. Vol. 3 *Advaita Vedānta*. Delhi: Motilal Banarsidass, 1981.

———. *Encyclopedia of Indian Philosophies*. Vol. 1. 2nd ed. *Bibliography*. Delhi: Motilal Banarsidass, 1983.

———. *Encyclopedia of Indian Philosophies*. Vol 4. *Sāṃkhya*. Ed. Gerald Larson and Ram Shankar Bhattacharya. Delhi: Motilal Banarsidass, 1987.

———. *Encyclopedia of Indian Philosophies*. Vol. 5. *The Philosophy of Indian Grammarians*. Ed. Howard G. Coward and K. Kunjunni Raja. Delhi: Motilal Banarsidass, 1990.

Potter, Karl H., trans. *The Padārthatattvanirūpaṇam of Raghunātha Śiromaṇi*. Cambridge: Harvard-Yenching Institute, 1957.

Quine, W. V. O. *Mathematical Logic*. Cambridge: Harvard University Press, 1940.

Radhakrishnan, Sarvepalli, and Charles Moore, eds. *A Source Book in Indian Philosophy*. Princeton: Princeton University Press, 1957.

Ramanathan, A. A., trans. *The Saṃnyāsa Upaniṣads*. Madras: Adyar, 1978.

Rao, S. K. Ramachandra. *Jīvanmukti in Advaita*. Bangalore: IBH Prakashana, 1979.

Renou, Louis. *Terminologie Grammaticale du Sanskrit*. Paris: Librarie Ancienne, 1957.

Ruegg, David Seyfort. *La théorie du Tathāgatagarbha et du Gotra*. Paris: École Française d'Etrême-Orient, 1969.

Russell, Bertrand. *Our Knowledge of the External World*. London: George Allen & Unwin, 1926.

Sarma, V. A. *Citsukha's Contribution of Advaita*. Mysore: Kavyalaya Publishers, 1974.

Sastri, Guarninath. *Maṅgalavāda*. Calcutta: Asiatic Society, 1979.

Sastri, H. Chatterjee. *The Philosophy of Nāgārjuna as contained in the Ratnāvalī* (including the Sanskrit text). Calcutta: Saraswat Library, 1977.

Sastri, N. Aiyaswami, ed. and trans. *Ālambanaparīkṣā*, by Dignāga. Madras: Adyar, 1942.

Sastri, S. N. Ghoshal, trans. *Kāvya-Prakāśa*, by Mammaṭa Bhaṭṭa. Varanasi: Chowkhamba Sanskrit Office, 1973.

Sastri, S. Subrahmanya and T. R. Srinivasa Ayyangar, eds. and trans. *Jīvanmuktiviveka of Vidyāraṇya*. Madras: Adyar, 1976.

Saxena, Sushil. *Studies in the Metaphysics of Bradley*. London: George Allen & Unwin, 1967.

Shastri, Dharmedra Nath. *Critique of Indian Realism*. Agra: Agra Univerity, 1964.

Shaw, J. L. "Negation and the Buddhist Theory of Meaning." *Journal of Indian Philosophy* 6 (1978): pp. 59–77.

Solomon, Ester. *Indian Dialectics*. 2 vols. Ahmedabad: Gujarat Vidya Sabha, 1976.

Staal, J. F. "The Theory of Definition in Indian Logic." *Journal of the American Oriental Society* 81 (1961): pp. 122–26.

———. "The Concept of Pakṣa in Indian Logic." *Journal of Indian Philosophy* 2, no. 2 (August 1973).

Stcherbatsky, F. T. *Buddhist Logic*. 2 vols. Reprint, New York: Dover, 1962.

Tachikawa, Musashi. *The Structure of the World in Udayana's Realism*, including editions and translations of Udayana's *Lakṣaṇāvalī* and a portion of his *Kiraṇāvalī*. Dordrecht: D. Reidel, 1981.

Thibaut, Georg, trans. *The Vedānta Sūtras of Bādarāyana*, a translation of Śaṅkara's *Brahma-sūtra* commentary. 2 vols. Sacred Books of the East, 1890. Reprint, New York: Dover, 1962.

Thrasher, Allen. "Maṇḍana Miśra's Theory of Vikalpa." *Wiener Zeitscrift für die Kunde Südasiens and Archiv für Indische Philosophie* 22 (1978): pp. 133–57.

Ui, H. *Vaiśeshika Philosophy*. Chowkhamba Sanskrit Series 22. Reprint, Varanasi, 1962.

Valiaveetil, Chacko. *Liberated Life*. Madurai: Dialogue Series, 1980.

Vasu, S. C. *Aṣṭādhyāyī of Pāṇini*. 2 vols. 1891. Reprint, Delhi: Motilal Banarsidass.

Vattanky, John. *Gaṅgeśa's Philosophy of God*. Madras: Adyar, 1984.

Vetter, Tilmann. *Erkenntnisprobleme bei Dharmakīrti*. Sitzungsberichte der Österreichische Akadamie der Wissenschaften 245, Band 2, Abhandlung 2. Vienna: Böhlaus, 1964.

Vetter, Tilmann, trans. Dharmakīrti's *Pramāṇaviniścaya*, *pratyakṣa* chapter translated from the Tibetan. Sitzungsberichte der Österreichische Akademie der Wissenschaften 250, Band 3. Vienna: Böhlaus, 1966.

———. Maṇḍana's *Brahmasiddhi*. Sitzungsberichte der Österreichische Akademie der Wissenschaften 262, Band 2. Vienna: Böhlaus, 1969.

Vidyabhusana, Satis Chandra. *The History of Indian Logic*. 1921. Reprint, Delhi: Motilal Banarsidass, 1971.

Wada, Toshihiro. *Invariable Concomitance in Navya Nyāya*. Delhi: Sri Satguru, 1990.

Warren, Henry Clarke. *Buddhism in Translation*, including selections from the *Majjhima-Nikāya*. Reprint, Cambridge: Harvard University Press, 1986.

Warrier, A. G. Krishna. *The Concept of Mukti in Advaita Vedānta*. Madras: University of Madras, 1961.

Windelband, Wilhelm. *A History of Philosophy*. Trans. James H. Tufts. Vol. 1. 1901. New York: Harper & Row, 1958.

Zalta, Edward N. *Intensional Logic and the Metaphysics of Intentionality*. Cambridge, Massachusetts: MIT Press, 1988.

INDEX

2277